DAILY, DAILY, SING TO MARY

Daily, Daily, Sing to Mary

Celebrating with Our Lady
Every Day of the Year

Paul Haffner

GRACEWING

First published in England in 2017
by
Gracewing
2 Southern Avenue
Leominster
Herefordshire HR6 0QF
United Kingdom
www.gracewing.co.uk

The publishers have no responsibility for the persistence
or accuracy of URLs for websites referred to in
this publication, and do not guarantee that any content
on such websites is, or will remain, accurate or appropriate.

ISBN 978 085244 896 0

Typeset by Gracewing

Cover design by Bernardita Peña Hurtado
featuring seventeenth-century icon
of the *Theotokos of the Apocalypse* from Mount Athos

Daily, daily, sing to Mary,
sing my soul, her praises due;
all her feasts, her actions honour,
with the heart's devotion true.
Lost in wond'ring contemplation
be her majesty confessed:
call her Mother, call her Virgin,
happy Mother, Virgin blest.

CONTENTS

Daily, Daily, Sing to Mary

ABBREVIATIONS

AAS =   *Acta Apostolicae Sedis. Commentarium officiale.*
           Rome: Vatican Polyglot Press, 1909– .

CCC =   *Catechism of the Catholic Church.* Dublin: Veritas,
           1994.

CCL =   *Corpus Christianorum series latina.* Tournai:
           Brepols, 1954– .

CSEL =   *Corpus Scriptorum Ecclesiasticorum Latinorum.*
           Wien: 1866– .

DS =   H. Denzinger. *Enchiridion Symbolorum,*
           Definitionum et Declarationum de rebus fidei et
           morum. Bilingual edition edited by P. Hünermann.
           Bologna: EDB, 1995.

OR =   *L'Osservatore Romano,* daily Italian edition.

ORE =   *L'Osservatore Romano,* weekly English edition.

PG =   J. P. Migne. *Patrologiae cursus completus, series*
           graeca. 161 vols. Paris: 1857–1866.

PL =   J. P. Migne. *Patrologiae cursus completus, series*
           latina. 221 vols. Paris: 1844–1864.

SC=   *Sources Chrétiennes.* Paris: Cerf, 1942– .

The Scriptural quotations and abbreviations in this work are generally
taken from the New Jerusalem Bible.

PREFACE

VERY DAY OF THE YEAR is a day for the Lord, but also for His Blessed Mother, Mary. *Daily, Daily Sing to Mary* lies in the tradition of the Marian Calendar, a collection of feasts honouring the Blessed Virgin Mary.[1] Each day brings to mind the actions the Mother of God has undertaken on behalf of Christians of all nations and kingdoms throughout the ages. The story for each day of the year also brings its own lesson for us.

The original Marian Calendar was first published when King Louis XIV of France was still a boy, and it is in reality a collection of famous sites of pilgrimage to the Blessed Virgin throughout all of Christendom. It is unnecessary to remind the reader that things have changed a great deal since the time the Marian Calendar was first published. At that time Christendom was still flourishing, and there were a great many religious buildings consecrated to the Mother of God. Owing to various upheavals and revolutions, some of these sites are now nothing more than a pile of ruins.

In our time there are very few people who even remember the Marian Calendar, and those who do usually have nothing more than a list of devotions, with no explanation of the actual historical event they attempt to recall. This work is offered to the Christian world for the hundredth anniversary of the apparitions of Our Lady at Fatima, where Pope Francis exclaimed: "We have a Mother! Clinging to her like children, we live in the hope that rests on Jesus."[2] The daily accounts in this book provide abundant proof that Mary, the Mother of God, has indeed claimed the hearts of Christians from the earliest centuries down to the present day. They are also evidence of the value of the Blessed Mother's influence and mediation on the behalf of her children before the throne of God.

In these pages, for each day of the year, we have endeavoured to list a particular liturgical celebration, miracle, apparition, conversion, or healing which took place on that day through the maternal hands of Our Lady. On occasions we also recall events in which Our Lady saved people from all kinds of danger, at sea or on land. We have also documented simple events, like the finding of a Marian image which may not seem in themselves to be miraculous, but point to a deep care which the Mother of God has for her Son's people. We have taken episodes from all parts of the world in a truly Catholic way, showing that Our Lady has influenced so many people's lives and often in non-Catholic and even non-Christian lands. It may well be as these events are so numerous that we will have left out some important manifestation of Our Lady. This has not been done deliberately, but there are only 365 days in the year and so we ask pardon of any of our readers if their favourite devotion has been omitted.

Among the marvels which the Lord has worked through His Mother as recorded in the pages, some have been been approved by the highest Church authorities, others by local bishops, others again are awaiting reception and recognition. Some may be of ambiguous status, but as far as possible we have tried to keep to those apparitions, revelations and miracles which would in no way counter Scripture and Tradition as interpreted by the living Magisterium of the Church.

We have tried to adhere as close as possible to the actual date of the celebrations, but sometimes this has not been possible owing to the simultaneous celebration of various festivals in different places on the one date. We have separated the celebrations so as to offer the reader a Marian feast every day of the year. In this way not only are peoples consecrated to the Immaculate Heart of Mary, but also time, in the sense that the whole year is now dedicated to her honour and therefore to her Son. Each day, each month, each season will become a hymn of praise to Our Lady in the spirit in which St Cyril of Alexandria preached these words about the Mother of God:

Hail, O Mary, Mother of God, Virgin and Mother! Morning Star, perfect vessel. We salute you, Mother of God. Hail, O Mary, Mother of God! holy temple in which God Himself was conceived. We salute you, Mother of God. Hail, O Mary, Mother of God! chaste and pure dove. We salute you, Mother of God. Hail, O Mary, Mother of God! ever-effulgent light; from you proceeds the Sun of Justice. We salute you, Mother of God. Hail, O Mary, Mother of God ! You enclosed in your sacred womb the One Who cannot be encompassed. We salute you, Mother of God. Hail, O Mary, Mother of God! With the shepherds we sing the praise of God, and with the angels the song of thanksgiving: Glory to God in the highest and peace on earth to people of good will. We salute you, Mother of God. Hail, O Mary, Mother of God! Through you came to us the Conqueror and the triumphant Vanquisher of hell. We salute you, Mother of God. Hail, O Mary, Mother of God! Through you blossoms the splendour of the resurrection. We salute you, Mother of God. Hail, O Mary, Mother of God! You saved every faithful Christian. Hail, O Mary, Mother of God! Who can praise you worthily, O glorious Virgin Mary! We salute you, Mother of God.[3]

Rome, 13 May 2017
Feast of Our Lady of Fatima

Notes

[1] The hymn *Daily, Daily Sing to Mary* was written by Bernard of Cluny, a twelfth-century French Benedictine monk, and a copy of it was found beneath the right temple of St Casimir's incorrupt body when his grave was opened.

[2] Pope Francis, *Homily at Mass for Canonization of Francesco Marto e Giacinta Marto* (13 May 2017).

[3] St Cyril of Alexandria, *Sermon at the Council of Ephesus* (431).

JANUARY

1 January: Mary, Mother of God

ODAY THE CHURCH celebrates the Solemnity of Mary, Mother of God, our Lady's greatest title. This feast is the octave of Christmas. In the modern Roman Calendar, only Christmas and Easter enjoy the privilege of an octave. Before the Calendar was reformed after the Second Vatican Council, the old liturgy celebrated three feasts on this day. The first "the octave day of the Nativity of the Lord", and the greater part of the Mass was of the octave of Christmas with many extracts from the Masses of Christmas. However, various parts of the Mass and Office celebrated the divine maternity of Mary. The third feast was that of the Circumcision of Our Lord which has been celebrated since the sixth century. On New Year's Day, the octave day of Christmas, the Church now celebrates the Solemnity of the Holy Mother of God. The title of "Mother of God" was implied by St Elizabeth at the Visitation. At that moment, Elizabeth said, "Why should I be honoured with a visit from the mother of my Lord?" (Lk 1:43). The first Marian Dogma that Mary is the Mother of God was declared by the Church at the Council of Ephesus in the year 431. The Council of Ephesus with more than 200 bishops, presided over by St Cyril of Alexandria representing Pope Celestine l, defined the true personal unity of Christ, declared Mary the Mother of God (*Theotokos*) against Nestorius, Bishop of Constantinople. New Year greetings also include an expression of hope for a peaceful New Year. This has profound biblical and Christological origins. Since 1967, the Holy See has also designated the first of January as the World Day for Peace.

The human mind can never fully comprehend all that is contained in the title "Mother of God". It is the way in which the faithful love to address Mary. The Church has sanctioned it by her infallible authority. All the beauties of nature, all the riches of grace, all the splendours of glory pale before the majestic grandeur of such a title as this. For, by the very fact of having conceived the Word made Flesh, Mary has been united to God by the same ties which unite a mother to her true son.

The dignity of Mary belongs to a superior order, on account of her position as Mother of God. This title is precisely the source and the measure of all those gifts of nature, grace and glory wherewith the Lord was pleased to enrich her. This title is not only the source of incomparable greatness in her, it is also a potent means to ground us firmly in the true faith, and to bring us to a more perfect knowledge of the divine attributes. What glory accrues to the Goodness of God from the Divine Maternity of Mary! For, in predestining Mary to be the Mother of the Word, God also decreed to give her to us as our Mother. He willed that she should accomplish in union with her Son the work of our Redemption, and that by regenerating us to the life of grace, she should become our Mother in the spiritual order. The Divine Maternity is the starting point of the work of our salvation. In believing Mary to be the Mother of God, we also believe that the Word was made Flesh. St John Damascene writes about this mystery in these terms:

> We proclaim the holy Virgin to be in strict truth the Mother of God. For inasmuch as He who was born of her was true God, she who bore the true God incarnate is the true Mother of God. For we hold that God was born of her, not implying that the divinity of the Word received from her the beginning of its being, but meaning that God the Word Himself, Who was begotten of the Father timelessly before the ages, and was with the Father and the Spirit without beginning through eternity, took up His abode in these last days for the sake of our salvation in the Virgin's womb, and was without change made flesh and born of her. For the holy Virgin did not give birth to mere man but to true God: and not only God but God incarnate, Who did not bring down His body from Heaven, nor simply

passed through the Virgin as a channel, but received flesh from her, of like essence to our own and subsisting in Himself ... Mary is justly and truly called the Mother of God, and that this name encapsulates the whole economy of salvation.[1]

2 January: Virgin Most Faithful

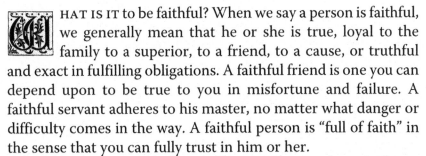 HAT IS IT to be faithful? When we say a person is faithful, we generally mean that he or she is true, loyal to the family to a superior, to a friend, to a cause, or truthful and exact in fulfilling obligations. A faithful friend is one you can depend upon to be true to you in misfortune and failure. A faithful servant adheres to his master, no matter what danger or difficulty comes in the way. A faithful person is "full of faith" in the sense that you can fully trust in him or her.

Never was there a heart so faithful as Mary's. First of all, in her own life on earth, how true she always was to Our Lord in every need or sorrow or trial of His Life, from the sufferings and privations of his Infancy, the terrors of the Flight into Egypt, all through His Passion and Death on the Cross, she was always with Him, always ministering to Him, and even at the last, when she could do nothing more for Him, She stood by the Cross to the very end, fearing no danger to herself, all her thoughts fixed on Him. "Near the cross of Jesus stood His Mother" (Jn 19:25). These words are a history, a picture, of Our Lady's fidelity, its crown and consummation.

However, there remained what was perhaps a still more searching test of her fidelity to Jesus. He left her bereft of His visible presence. He left to her the care of His Church, His Mystical Body, then in its infancy as it were, just born, and needing a mother's care. Her whole Heart was with Jesus; earth was to her without Jesus nothing but a blank wilderness, and yet she carried out this last hard task for her Son's sake, just as she had done so many others. For many long, weary years she lived patiently on without Him, fulfilling the charge He had left to her, ministering to His Church, as she had done to Him in His Infancy, watching over His Apostles and disciples, sympathizing with them in their difficulties, advising them in their doubts, encouraging them in their trials, assisting by every way in her power, saving souls by her example and her mighty intercession.

She was ever most faithful to Jesus, She was all for Him, all His; Jesus filled in her the place that self holds in us. When we say with St Gabriel, "the Lord is with you", one meaning of the prayer is that Our Lord is with her inseparably and in a sovereign manner, even as self is dominant in us. She is ever holding Him up to us, even in her statues and icons, saying: "Do whatever He tells you" (Jn 2:5).

3 January: Our Lady of Sichem

HE SHRINE IN BRABANT in the duchy of Louvain, is a replica of the one below Mount Garizim, Israel. Hadrian restored the temple on Mount Garizim and dedicated it to Jupiter. A small Christian community settled there; and on several occasions they suffered greatly at the hands of the Samaritans. In 474 the emperor, to avenge an unjust attack on the sect, gave Mount Garizim to the Christians, who built on it a church dedicated to the Blessed Virgin.

After the Muslim conquest, Christianity practically disappeared from the district. The French made amends by erecting a shrine to Mary in the duchy of Louvain. The ancient statue of Our Lady of Sichem, or as Our Lady of Montaigu, which is the title more commonly used today, has been venerated in Belgium from very early times. The Mother of God rewarded the faithful magnanimously for their pious attention.

According to legend, a shepherd boy originally found the statue of Our Lady after it had apparently fallen from a niche cut in an old oak tree. The statue was mysteriously too heavy for him to lift alone, so he ran to find his master, and have him return to help him replace the statue in its place in the old oak.

It is said that in 1306 the Blessed Virgin Mary moved the hearts of the people by causing four drops of blood to flow from the eyes of the statue dedicated to her. This revived the faith of the people and increased their fervour. A small chapel was built beneath the tree, which was rebuilt in 1602, and the dedication of Our Lady of Sichem took place in the year 1604 by the Archbishop of Malines, Mathias Hovius.[2]

From that time forward there were many miracles as Our Lady seemed to demonstrate her appreciation by granting many favours. The statue was soon venerated as miraculous, and there have been many pilgrimages to the site during the centuries, continuing even until this day.

4 January: Our Lady of Treves

S T JEROME EMILIANI, founder of the Congregation of Semasca, when still a layman, experienced in a marvellous way the mercy of Our Blessed Lady. A capable soldier, he was once entrusted with the defence of Castelnuevo, in Fruili, Italy, when this was stormed by the Venetians, who were commanded by Maximilian I. Jerome was captured and confined in a dark prison, where he was loaded with chains.

Being a man of many vices, he began to feel remorse for his past life, almost to the point of despair. Then, he thought of Mary, the Mother of God, as the Mother of Divine Mercy. To her he turned, promising to lead a better life in the future, if this loving Mother would deliver him from his miserable condition. In an instant, Jerome beheld his prison filled with light, and the Virgin Mary descending from Heaven to loose with her own hands, the chains with which he was bound. Moreover, she handed him a key with which to open the door of the prison and escape. Eluding his captors, he directed his steps toward Treves, to the shrine of the Mother of God.

When he arrived in Treves, he prostrated himself before the image of Our Lady and laid on her altar the instruments of his torture. He then retired to a life of penance until God sent him companions to start his order, also known as the Company of the Servants of the Poor. He was especially concerned with the souls of homeless orphans, and so he established orphanages to care for them. He always exhorted not only these, but all with whom he came in contact, to reverence the powerful Queen of Heaven by often reciting the "Hail Holy Queen" and other Marian hymns. St Jerome Emilani died a holy death in 1537 while caring for the victims of plague. Pope Benedict XIV proclaimed him a saint in the year 1767.

The cathedral of Treves is also famous as the location where the "Holy Coat" is exposed for veneration. This is the same that is piously believed to have been worn by Our Lord Jesus Christ, and is the seamless garment for which the soldiers cast lots on Calvary during His passion and death.[3]

5 January: Our Lady of Abundance

HE BLESSED VIRGIN under this title is venerated at Cursi, Italy. The story begins in the first half of the seventeenth century. At that time the Puglia region of Italy was suffering from a severe drought, and for almost three years not a drop of rain had fallen. By the spring of 1641, matters had become desperate. April had arrived and the heat was like in mid-summer. Thus prospects for relief and a good harvest that year appeared dim.

Then the people of Cursi and vicinity prayed fervently to the Blessed Mother, begging her to come to their aid and save them from the famine that drew ever nearer. The Blessed Virgin heard their plea. She appeared to a shepherd, Baglio Orlando Natali. Thoroughly frightened by the appearance of the lovely lady, he ran away. The Mother of God called him back, reassured him gently, and told him who she was. The Queen of Heaven said that she felt compassion toward Baglio and the people of that region for the misfortune that had befallen them.

The Blessed Virgin told Baglio to go to the pastor of the parish, and tell him in her name to assemble all the people of Cursi and come back with them to that very place where she wished a Church to be erected. When it was completed she would take Cursi and the surrounding section under her protection. As a token of her deep regard, she promised Baglio that at the end of that same year there would be a harvest of such abundance as none had ever seen before. Finally, she told Baglio that he was to change his way of life, for she had selected him to be her true follower, and that he was to serve in the new church when it would be completed. So saying she vanished as suddenly as she had appeared.

Baglio lost no time in telling the pastor of this strange happening. The good Father gathered together the people, and led by Baglio, they all marched to the spot where the Virgin had appeared. There they fell to their knees and with one voice raised their hearts in prayers of praise and love to the Most Holy Virgin. After some little time they reassembled and started on the return march to town. They had gone but a short distance, when a little cloud drifted into sight—then another, until the entire sky was overcast. Rain fell and drenched the whole crowd; but not one minded—in fact, all were so happy, that they laughed and shouted and played around in the downpour. It rained for three days.

The news of this happening quickly spread and great crowds hurried to the place of the apparition to offer their thanks to the Madonna. When the time of the harvest arrived, the crops in that area were so abundant that every barn was filled to overflowing. Soon the grateful people erected a church in honour of Holy Mary of Abundance or of Prosperity. Baglio, his old life behind him, donned the garb of a hermit and vowed to spend the rest of his life in prayer and in looking after the new shrine.

Some years later this church was destroyed by fire resulting from a lightning stroke; but the people, recalling the goodness of the Virgin, immediately set to work and built the Present beautiful sanctuary. On the high altar there is a Greco-Byzantine fresco of the Madonna of Abundance or Prosperity—it depicts the Virgin with the Divine Infant. In their hands both hold sprigs of olives and ears of corn.[4]

6 January: Our Lady of Cana

ACRED SCRIPTURE RECOUNTS what happened at Cana when Jesus and our lady performed their first miracle:

> On the third day there was a wedding at Cana in Galilee. The mother of Jesus was there, and Jesus and His disciples had also been invited. And they ran out of wine, since the wine provided for the feast had all been used, and the mother of Jesus said to Him, "They have no wine." Jesus said, "Woman, what do you want from me? My hour has not come yet." His mother said to the servants, "Do whatever he tells you." There were six stone water jars standing there, meant for the ablutions that are customary among the Jews: each could hold twenty or thirty gallons. Jesus said to the servants, "Fill the jars with water", and they filled them to the brim. Then He said to them, "Draw some out now and take it to the president of the feast." They did this; the president tasted the water, and it had turned into wine. Having no idea where it came from—though the servants who had drawn the water knew—the president of the feast called the bridegroom and said, "Everyone serves good wine first and the worse wine when the guests are well wined; but you have kept the best wine till now." This was the first of Jesus' signs: it was at Cana in Galilee. He revealed His glory, and his disciples believed in Him (Jn 2:1–12).

Mary was interested in this couple because she is merciful, and the Mother of Mercy, and willingly assists all the poor and afflicted who fear God. From this incident, St Bonaventure judges of the many graces which we can hope for through Mary, now that she reigns in heaven; "For," says he, "if Mary while yet on earth was so compassionate, how much more so is she now, reigning in heaven!" He gives the reason by adding: "Mary now that she sees the face of God, knows our necessities far better than when she was on earth, and in proportion to the increase of her compassion, her power to aid us has been augmented." Why do we not take refuge in all our necessities to this merciful mother, who although unasked assists the needy?

Mary of Cana is not only a figure of biblical tradition; her words to the servant are not merely yesterday's news. As Vatican II reminds us: "Taken up to Heaven she did not lay aside her salvific duty ... By her maternal love she cares for the brothers and sisters of her Son who still journey on earth."[5] Our Lady of Cana bears a promise which points beyond the very human features of her face, and the fragile gesture of her hands. Speaking for her Son, and her Son only, her message to us is simple. It holds in two words: invitation and direction. Mary of Cana is a gatherer and a sender. With her right hand she extends an invitation to all people of good will. She gathers the friends of her Son in community and communion; she brings them together and prepares them for the eternal wedding feast of the Lamb. With her left hand she sends and directs, a gesture accompanied by the well known words: 'Do whatever he tells you!' She points to the jar, but the jar is no longer filled with water. The time of Cana is no longer in the past. The jar is now filled with wine: the wine of God's presence in this world. In the words of Pope Benedict XVI:

> Christ gives a sign, in which he proclaims his hour, the hour of the wedding-feast, the hour of union between God and man. He does not merely "make" wine, but transforms the human wedding-feast into an image of the divine wedding-feast, to which the Father invites us through the Son and in which he gives us every good thing, represented by the abundance of wine. The wedding-feast becomes an image of that moment when Jesus pushed love to the utmost, let his body be rent and thus gave himself to us for ever, having become completely one with us—a marriage between God and man.[6]

Prayer to Our Lady of Cana

Lady of Cana, at the wedding feast you saw they had no more wine, and you took this concern you saw to your beloved Son. Please pray with me as I bring to Jesus the concerns I have for the neighbours who are in need. I place before your Son the hungry, the sick, the homeless, the lonely old, and the lonely young, those who are out of work, suffering abuse, or dying. May Jesus, who changed the water into wine, touch them and change their sadness into joy. May the love of your Son help them to always know that they are dearly loved by God. Amen

7 January: Our Lady of Egypt

NLY ONE CHILD escaped the cruel sword of Herod, Mary's Son, safe in the arms of His Mother fleeing with Him into Egypt. How much Our Lady suffered during that long journey across the desert: anxiety, fatigue, hunger, thirst, lack of shelter! While in Egypt, Mary's interest in the Gentiles must have greatly increased. It was not in vain that Mary and her Son were sent into Egypt; God had his reasons.

Jesus' flight into Egypt is a true prefiguration of the Blessed Sacrament, hidden away in so many Tabernacles, surrounded by so many people who do not suspect His presence; He is hidden to so many that pass by. But what is it to those who know? What was Jesus to Mary and Joseph in the land of Egypt? He was their All—with Him exile did not exist; with Him, God's will was easy, God's arrangements, the best; with Him, it was impossible to complain, impossible to have any regrets about the past or impatient concern about the future. Mary was absorbed in the present, because she had Jesus with Her: He had to be cared for, fed, taught, thought about, worked for, lived for—Egypt!

It was in Egypt that the Child grew, and it was there that Mary heard His first words, watched His first tottering steps, and taught Him His first (vocal) prayers. And as the Child grew, Mary grew, too, in grace and virtue; imbibing more and more of the spirit of her Son from the services she rendered Him; Making great progress in her new school, the school of the Cross; getting daily more food for meditation and prayer, enlarging her heart and preparing herself to become a second Eve—the Mother of all the living. What a blessing and joy to the people of Egypt to have the Holy Family living amongst them! How this must have stirred up their zeal and courage!

Joseph knew least about it all, and yet had apparently to take the chief part and bear all the anxiety. He received the warning message from the Angel; he had to break the news to Mary that the Child's life was in danger and that they must flee immediately—even in the middle of the night. Joseph had to take the Child and His Mother into Egypt; to anyone else but Joseph this would have seemed an unreasonable command. Those who live close to Jesus and Mary do not criticize God's dealings; they have only one thing to do—obey. Peace and joy will result.[7]

8 January: Our Lady of Prompt Succour

OR ALMOST TWO hundred years the Ursuline nuns of New Orleans, Louisiana, have owned and venerated a golden, miraculous statue of Our Lady under the title, Our Lady of Prompt Succour. This lovely statue, which today stands above the high altar of the Votive Shrine or chapel, was brought from France by a humble and holy Ursuline Sister in fulfilment of a vow. Today, Our Lady of Prompt Succour is one of the few miraculous statues in North America. The favours granted by Our Lady of Prompt Succour are so numerous and wonderful, that whole books could be written about them.

At the outbreak of the French Revolution, an Ursuline nun, Madame St Michel Gensoul (Frances Agatha Gensoul), was obliged to leave her convent in France, return to the world and wait the time when convents would be reopened. Meanwhile she received a letter from a relative in the Ursuline Convent in New Orleans (Mother St Andre Madier), saying that sixteen other

Ursulines, to excape the government of France, had come to Havana, Cuba, to open a community there. Mother St Michel decided to devote herself to spiritual labours in Louisiana, but her Bishop refused consent, since he hoped the convents of France would soon resume activity, and he told the religious that only the Pope could give her permission, and since he, the Pope was a prisoner of Napoleon, the entire project was out of the question.

Following an impulse, Mother St Michel wrote to the Pope and then turning for aid to Our Blessed Mother, she prayed:

> O most Holy Virgin Mary, if you obtain for me a prompt and favourable answer to this letter, I promise to have you honoured at New Orleans under the title of Our Lady of Prompt Succour.

The letter was sent from Montpellier to Rome on 19 March 1809, and despite all things to the contrary, Pope Pius replied on 29 April 1809. The request had been obtained thru the prompt aid of Our Lady. In thanksgiving, Mother St Michel ordered sculptured a beautiful statue of Our Lady holding the Infant Jesus in her arms, Our Lady of Prompt Succour. In this statue, Jesus holds in His Hands a globe, representing the world. Bishop Fournier, recognizing in all this the acts of Divine Providence, asked permission to bless the statue.

Mother St Michel and several postulants with the precious statue of Our Lady of Prompt Succour, arrived in New Orleans 31 December 1810. The statue was set up in the chapel of the Sisters on Ursuline St and Mother St Michel who taught there, lost no time in spreading devotion to Our Lady, which soon became popular.

Two special favours showed Our Lady's pleasure at the devotion: in 1812 a great fire broke out near the convent, which was doomed for destruction. An old lay sister placed a small statue of Our Lady of Prompt Succour on a window ledge facing the approaching flames; at the same time Mother St Michel fell on her knees and prayed: "Our Lady of Prompt Succour, we are lost if you do not come to our aid." The wind veered, the fire died down and the convent was saved.

Another great favour was bestowed during the Battle of New Orleans, 8 January 1814. Never before was the city in hopelessly greater danger. Very Rev William Doubourg urged the people to pray to Our Lady. Early Sunday morning while the raging battle could be heard in the city, the convent chapel of Our Lady of Prompt Succour was crowded with petitioners, begging Mary for prompt aid. The statue was placed upon the altar and Mother Superior in the name of the community vowed if the American forces were victorious and God spared the city, the Ursulines would see that each year a Mass of Thanksgiving be offered in honour of Our Lady of Prompt Succour. The battle lasted 25 minutes; the routed British lost 2,600 of their 20,000 men, while Jackson lost 13 of his 2,000. Jackson declared only the aid of the Almighty could have brought about such results. He went himself to the convent afterwards to thank the Ursulines for their prayers and for their nursing of the American wounded. Many favours continue to be obtained through Mary's intercession, as records testify.

On 21 June 1894, Pope Leo XIII issued a decree of privilege to crown the famous statue, which was carried out 14 November 1894. The two crowns:,one for the infant, the other for Mary were made of "exquisite artistry"—gold, silver, precious stones, donated by hundreds of faithful devotees of Our Lady. This was the first of many like ceremonies conducted in the United States.[8]

9 *January: Our Lady of Clemency*

 HE SHRINE IS probably the only one in the world where Our Lady's shrine is enclosed in glass. It dates from the late eighteenth century. On a dark snowy day in 1797, Rosina Bucher, a young girl of the village of Absam near Innsbruck, was sitting by the window sewing. It was between three and four in the afternoon and the light was just beginning to fade.

Rosina looked up and saw a face in the window pane. She looked closely, not sure that she saw right, and finally called her mother.

Others, including the parish priest, were called in to observe the strange happening. All agreed that it was a face, the face of the Mother of Sorrows. It was turned slightly and there was a strange expression on it. The window was made up of several small panes of glass quite dark in colour. They removed the pane of glass with the picture on it, which was on the inside of the double window. After they had examined the glass, it was sent to experts in painting and glasswork. Here it was discovered that the face disappeared when water was put on the glass, but came back as soon as the glass was dry. They analysed it chemically, and could not discover by what process the picture had been placed there.

Rosina's mother thought it was an omen of trouble. The parish priest, on the contrary, felt that Our Lady's blessing must rest on the house. He asked her to let him have the picture for the Church. Here it soon became a popular shrine. Our Lady of Clemency of Absam has since become a place of pilgrimage. Many miracles have been recorded from the pilgrims who prayed there. The picture is quite small, the size of a small pane of glass. It is not especially pretty, and is popularly known as Our Lady of Mercy and Clemency of Absam—clemency, because Mary's heart is filled with love and kindness to those who pray at this shrine and implore her help.[9]

10 January: Our Lady of Guides

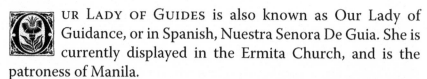 UR LADY OF GUIDES is also known as Our Lady of Guidance, or in Spanish, Nuestra Senora De Guia. She is currently displayed in the Ermita Church, and is the patroness of Manila.

One of the sailors to land on the island of Luzon in 1570, while walking in the woods near the native settlement of Manila, came upon a religious ceremony held by the Natives. They were honouring an image of the Mother of God, a statue on a rough pedestal. The natives told the Spanish that the statue had the power to make their petitions come true, and indeed, miracles were performed. Regarding the mysterious nature of the statue's unknown origin, some think the statue floated in from a wrecked ship, and was thus seized by the natives. Since nothing of the origin could be learned, the sailors determined to name the statue by some title of Our Lady; the lot fell upon "Our Lady of Guidance" for everyone agreed she had guided them on their dangerous journey.

When the cathedral at Manila was built the statue was enshrined there. A hundred years later, this cathedral having been destroyed, a new church was built, and it is visible from the sea. In its high tower a light was set as a beacon to incoming ships, a fit place for Our Lady of Guides. Later the statue was placed within the walls of the restored cathedral.

The statue of Our Lady of Guidance was canonically crowned in the year 1955 by the Papal Nuncio to the Philippine Islands. The shrine is visited by labourers seeking employment in many countries, and when they return they leave gifts of thanks for the Queen of Heaven before her statue. Today the devotion to Our Lady of Guides still flourishes. For all of us who travel this wide lonely world, she is the patroness, the Queenly Lighthouse, the Star of the Sea.[10]

11 January: Our Lady of Bessières

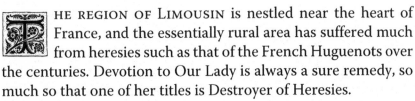 HE REGION OF LIMOUSIN is nestled near the heart of France, and the essentially rural area has suffered much from heresies such as that of the French Huguenots over the centuries. Devotion to Our Lady is always a sure remedy, so much so that one of her titles is Destroyer of Heresies.

Among the many miracles said to have taken place at the shrine of Our Lady of Bessières, near Trignac in Limousin, France, is one told of a certain heretic named Jean Cellerion who had derided the devotion paid to Our Lady. He would hide in the woods and waylay pilgrims on their way to the shrine. Fearing neither God nor his Holy Mother, he would block their way, mock them for undertaking such a journey, sneer at their Christian beliefs, and taunt them with sarcastic reproaches and foul ridicule.

The unhappy man was soon to regret his folly. He was severely punished one day, as upon returning home, he saw his house go up in flames before his very eyes. Even with the assistance of his neighbours, all attempts to put out the flames were fruitless. In a matter of minutes his house was fully engulfed in flames.

As the fire was at its height, Our Lady appeared in the flames in all her majesty and was seen to frown upon the heretic. This vision was witnessed by all present, who immediately fell upon their knees, urging the heretic to do the same. A broken man, frightened and frustrated, he prostrated himself, calling upon the Mother of God to be merciful to him. His pleas were not in vain, but it was not his house that she saved, but his soul. In that moment he experienced a true and lasting conversion. He went on to live a very penitential life, and died a true believer.[11]

12 January: Our Lady of Conquest

N THE NORTH CHAPEL of the beautiful cathedral of Santa Fe, New Mexico, stands a little statue (scarcely a metre tall) of Our Lady holding the Child Jesus. It was skilfully carved by loving hands in Spain. Mary is clad in a richly embroidered dress, topped by a jewelled crown. Her regal countenance wears a serene, detached expression that is strangely impressive. This is Our Lady of Conquest, or *La Conquistadora*.

The statue of Our Lady of Conquest came to the new world in the care of the Franciscan missionary Fray Alonso da Venevides. She was installed with great ceremony in a church in Santa Fe. Over the ensuing decades, as often happens, the men living in the region did not practice their religion as they should. Mary appeared in a vision to a young girl, warning her that the colony would be overrun due to the loss of reverence for priests and the Faith.

In the year 1680 the local Indians rose up and attacked the Spanish. Twenty-one priests were killed, and the colonists completely driven out of the region. The statue was rescued from the burning church and taken back to Mexico with the colonists who escaped the wrath of the Indians.

It was not until the year 1691 that Don Diego de Vargas was sent by the King of Spain to attempt the resettlement of the city of Santa Fe. Like so many Spanish heroes who had accomplished seemingly impossible deeds during their lifetimes, he was as fervent a Catholic as he was a capable knight. Don Diego de Vargas carried with him the statue of Our Lady as he reentered New Mexico. Although he had only a small force, he was able to peacefully negotiate a peace with the various Indian nations. He attributed his success to "the Sovereign Queen, Most Blessed Mary". He is said to have vowed to build a chapel for her and hold a yearly procession if she would grant him a speedy and blood-less victory over the Indian, which she did.

Upon reaching his goal, however, the Indians refused to allow the Spanish colonists to return to Santa Fe. The Spanish under Don Diego were few in number, and they were forced to fight a numerically superior force. The colonists prayed the rosary before the statue of the Blessed Virgin as the men engaged the Indians in battle. The fighting lasted all day, and it was not until evening when they reclaimed the city. Once again, Mary was credited for the victory, and to show her sovereignty, Don Diego placed an officer's baton in her hand.

The shrine symbolizes a spirit of deep-rooted Faith and devotion which characterized the *Conquistadores* of this land. There is still a great deal of devotion shown to Mary at the Cathedral of St Francis that includes processions, fiestas and other celebrations. The statue was formally crowned by Cardinal Francis Spellman and in 1960 received a Papal Coronation.

13 January: Our Lady of Victory

 MONG SHRINES DEDICATED to Our Lady of Victory, the one at Prague has become world-famous because it is also the home of the statue of the Infant of Prague.

The story of the shrine is an unusual one. In 1620 the Austrian Emperor Ferdinand II and Prince Maxmilian of Bavaria gained a major victory over a coalition of Protestant armies in the battle of the White Mountain near Prague. The previous day, Rev Fr Dominic of Jesus-Maria, a discalced Carmelite, had found in the castle of Strakowicz an image representing the Nativity of Christ. It showed the Blessed Virgin kneeling before her Divine Son, while St Joseph stood behind her holding a lantern. In the background were two shepherds. The Calvanists had shown their fanaticism by piercing the eyes of Mary and her spouse, St Joseph.

Carrying the picture to the camp, the monk held it up and urged the soldiers to restore Mary's honour. His words decided the hesitation of the generals and gave courage to the men. They adopted Mary's name as their battle cry and Mary blessed their efforts. In the moment of success, they hailed the painting as Our Lady of Victory and carried it in triumph into Prague, where their leaders adorned it with rich jewels.

In gratitude to God for his great success, and in recognition of the help given by Father Dominic, Ferdinand II founded several Carmelite monasteries, including one at Prague which was solemnly blessed under invocation of Our Lady of Victory. Before this time, however, Father Dominic had taken the picture of Our Lady of Victory to Rome where it was first venerated in the Basilica of St Mary Major, then carried—in the presence of Pope Gregory XV—to the church of St Paul near the Carmelite convent, on 8 May 1622. Pope Paul V subsequently changed the name of the church to Our Lady of Victory, and the feast was officially inaugurated.

The original painting was destroyed in a fire in 1833 and has been replaced by a copy. Another copy hangs in the church of

Our Lady of Victory in Prague, in a building erected in 1706 replacing the earlier church. From the Shrine of Our Lady of Victory in Prague, came to the entire world the devotion to the Infant of Prague.

Our need for Mary's help continues as long as we live, and so long, too, we need her guidance. The struggle between the forces of evil and the forces of good will continue until the end of time. The devil whose intelligence and power exceed those we can command in our own right, has an acute appreciation of the value of our souls bought with a great price. Our sure way to defeat him is to range ourselves under Mary's banner, to call on her to bring us victory, and to acknowledge her as Our Lady of Victory when she protects us from dangers and brings us triumphant through temptation.[12]

Prayer to Our Lady of Victory

O Victorious Lady, who has such powerful influence with your Divine Son in conquering the hardest of hearts, intercede for those for whom we pray, that their hearts may be softened by the rays of Divine Grace, and they may return to the unity of the true Faith, through Christ, our Lord. Amen.

14 January: Our Lady of Speech

 N THE YEAR 1514, Our Lady was venerated at a shrine near Montserrat, Spain. Her aid was invoked on behalf of a dumb man who went on pilgrimage there, and the Blessed Virgin miraculously restored his speech. From that time on she was given the title Our Lady of Speech. Here again the words of the *Memorare* were verified:

> Remember, O most gracious Virgin Mary, that never was it known that anyone who fled to your protection, implored your help or sought your intercession, was left unaided. Inspired with this confidence, I fly to you, O Virgin of virgins, my Mother; to you do I come, before you I kneel,

> sinful and sorrowful. O Mother of the Word Incarnate, despise not my petitions, but in your mercy hear and answer me.

When God was made man, it was she who gave voice to the Word. In the *Magnificat,* God the Holy Spirit, her mystical spouse, spoke though her. When Christ was a child, she was His voice. When Our Lord was a man, He spoke for himself, while His mother remained silent. After the Ascension, she again became His voice as she guided the infant Church through those perilous times. Over and over again the words of God came through her, for she is His Mediatrix of grace, the link between us and Him.

Vested with the almighty power of her Divine Son, Mary, imitating Him, visits the earth, going about doing good, granting petitions, supplying the needs of those who invoke her, and giving solace, comfort and aid to her children. She is indeed Our Lady of the Word; Mother of the Word Incarnate; "And the Word was made Flesh and dwelt among us," through her "Fiat."

As a consequence, even while on earth, His Mother's word had great influence upon Christ. "They have no wine," uttered in behalf of the embarrassed newlyweds at Cana, was all that was necessary to bring about her Sons' first miracle.

And so, down the ages, Mary hearkens to the words of her Calvary-born children and speaks in their behalf to Jesus. Her intercession, her word, her speech, is never in vain. Let us never cease to invoke this powerful protectress, who wants nothing more than to intercede for us, her children, before the throne of God.[13]

15 January: Our Lady of the Poor

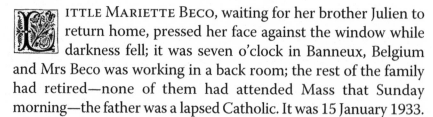 ITTLE MARIETTE BECO, waiting for her brother Julien to return home, pressed her face against the window while darkness fell; it was seven o'clock in Banneux, Belgium and Mrs Beco was working in a back room; the rest of the family had retired—none of them had attended Mass that Sunday morning—the father was a lapsed Catholic. It was 15 January 1933.

Suddenly Mariette called out, "Mother, there is a Lady in the garden. It is the Holy Virgin." Mrs. Beco scoffed at this. Taking a rosary Marietta had found on the road, she began to pray it. When Julien came home and heard what had happened, he said there was nothing in the garden; perhaps the icicles reflected weirdly and confused Mariette.

The parish priest was informed, but he did not set much store by the account, thinking the vision of Beauraing and Lourdes had led to an epidemic of visions. He sent word to Mariette to forget about it and not spread stories. The next morning, Wednesday, the priest was surprised to see Mariette at Holy Mass—she had quit school because she failed in her First Holy Communion examination three times, and after that had not gone to church anymore. That day Mariette went to school and for the first time in her life knew her lessons well.

The next evening she went into the garden, knelt and said the rosary; her father followed her with a coat which he threw around her shoulders. He tried to get the parish priest who was out, then called a neighbour, a practicing Catholic, and together they followed. The child was being beckoned on to the highway by the Lady, now known as Our Lady of Banneux, till they reached a spring, into which Marietta plunged her hands at the command of the lady, who said, "This spring is set aside for me. Good night!" Then she vanished.

When they reached home, the priest was waiting for them. Marietta described the Lady as similar to the Lourdes apparition:

> Her robe was long and white; she wore a blue belt and rays
> of light shone from her head. She was a little more than
> five feet tall; her right foot was bare and under it a golden
> rose. Her hands were raised to her breast on which was a
> golden heart. A rosary hung from her right arm.

There were six or seven more apparitions of Our Lady of Banneux: at one of these Marietta, on the advice of the priest asked the Lady her name, to which Our Lady of Banneux replied, "I am the Virgin of the poor" and leading the girl to a spring, said, "This spring is for all nations... for the sick... I would like a chapel built. I come to relieve suffering. Have faith in me and pray much. My dear child, pray hard... " At the end of each visit Mary would say *"Au revoir"* which means, "until we meet again" but at the last visit she said *"Adieu"* which means, "good-bye". She blessed Mariette then, at which the girl fainted. Mariette did not see the Lady depart.

The Beco family and many others became model Catholics. The chapel was built, and the spring became the site of numberless cures. During the German occupation of Belgium in 1942, the bishop encouraged the cult of Our Lady of Banneux, Our Lady of the Poor. In 1947, the bishop approved the devotion. In 1948 the cornerstone of a new basilica was laid; this was to supplant the small chapel. During the Second World War, Mariette married a Dutch salesman. During the Battle of the Bulge in 1944, an American chaplain found them and their fifteen month old baby living in a cellar of a small home occupied by American troops. Mariette Beco died 2 December 2011 at the age of 90. In 2008 she had made a final statement about her role in the apparitions: "I was no more than a postman who delivers the mail. Once this has been done, the postman is of no importance any more."[14]

16 January: Our Lady Refuge of Sinners

 HE WORST EVIL that can befall us is unquestionably sin, which makes us an object of abhorrence in the sight of God. God's infinite mercy has not only prepared for us a potent remedy against sin in the merits of Jesus Christ, our Savior, but it has also given us poor sinners a secure refuge in the assistance of Mary, Our Lady refuge of sinners. In the Old Law there were cities of refuge to which the guilty could flee for safety; in the New Law, Mary's mantle is for us that citadel of refuge for sinful souls. How can the Divine Wrath strike us, if we are covered by the mantle of Mary, the chosen daughter and the honoured Mother of God?

Our Lady refuge of sinners is thus not merely a pledge of our safety, but by her unrivalled sanctity, she is as earnest of pardon for all sinners who have recourse to her intercession. She not only disarms the just anger of God roused by our sins, but also obtains for her true devotees sincere and heartfelt conversion. All we need do is turn toward her with Faith, to obtain Divine Clemency and the means to rise from the mire of sin.

To be cleansed from sin and to be admitted again into the friendship of God is a grace beyond compare; but to be kept free from fresh falls is even more important, as our salvation depends entirely upon final perseverance. Mary, by her intercession, helps us detest past sins and faults; and keeps us from renewed relapses. Through God's permission we are tempted in all sorts of ways; but Mary's watchful assistance helps us put Satan to flight while she suggests to us, through our Angel Guardian, all manner of good thoughts and holy aspirations. More than ever at the hour of death, Mary shelters her devoted children, driving the Tempter far from us, and encouraging us to fight valiantly to the last gasp: "Holy Mary, Mother of God, pray for us sinners, now and at the hour of our death. Amen."[15]

17 January: Our Lady of Hope

URING THE WINTER of 1871 in the village of Pontmain, France, Eugène Barbedette was busy in his father's barn helping prepare the animal feed. He stood briefly in the open doorway, admiring the beautiful evening. Suddenly the gaze of the twelve year old was held there, for opposite the barn and in a framework of stars, stood a beautiful lady—motionless—smiling at him. "Do you see anything?" he shouted to the others, "Look, over there!"

"Yes," cried his brother Joseph, "a beautiful lady dressed in a blue robe with golden stars, yes, and blue shoes with golden buckles ... and, she has a golden crown which is getting bigger, and a black veil."[16] Since the father did not see her, he told the boys to get on with their work; then curiously, he asked, "Eugène, do you still see anything?" "Yes, she's still there," the boy answered and ran to fetch his mother; she saw nothing, but with a woman's intuition, she thought it might be the Blessed Virgin and assembling the family gently, all prayed five Our Fathers and Hail Marys in honour of the Mother of God. She called for a nun at the convent next door, who brought her two little charges with her, then later, Françoise and Jean-Marie, reaching the door of the barn, called out, "Oh, look at that lovely lady with the golden stars!" and clapped their hands with delight.

The news spread quickly, people gathered, with them the cure, M. Guerin. The Magnificat was intoned, and Eugène shouted, "Look what she is doing!" Slowly a great white streamer unfolded and in large letters they read: "Pray, my children, God will answer your prayers very soon. He will not allow you to be touched." The cure then intoned the hymn: "My Sweet Jesus ..." At that a red cross with the wounded body of Christ appeared before the Virgin, who held it. At the top in large red letters was written, "Jesus Christ."

The crowd burst into tears, while the cure ordered night prayers to be said; a white veil hid the vision, while our Lady smiled at the children, a smile which haunted them all through life with its beauty. Something of the sorrow of farewell was depicted on the faces of Eugene and Joseph, for the cure said quickly, "Can you still see anything?" "No, it is quite finished," they answered.

At the moment the message was being written in the sky, a messenger passing in front of the crowd had shouted, "You may well pray, the Prussians are at Laval." But they never entered it. On 17 January, at six o'clock at night, the very hour the Virgin appeared to the children of Pontmain, the division of soldiers, without apparent reason, received the order to retire. General Von Schmidt of the Prussian Army who was about to move on the city of Laval towards Pont-Main, received orders from his Commander not to take the city. On the evening of the ever-memorable 17 January 1871, the Commander of the Prussian forces, having taken up his quarters at the archiepiscopal palace of Le Mans, told Mgr Fillion, Bishop of that diocese: "By this time my troops are at Laval." On the same evening, the Prussian troops in sight of Laval stopped at half-past five, about the time when the Apparition first appeared above Pont-Main, a few miles off. General Schmidt is reported to have said on the morning of the 18th: "We cannot go farther. Yonder, in the direction of Brittany, there is an invisible 'Madonna' barring the way."

On 23 January, the armistice was signed at Versailles. After a long and searching inquiry, Mgr Wicart, the Bishop of Laval, proclaimed the authenticity of the vision, and at the very spot where Our Lady had appeared, a basilica was erected in honour of Our Lady of Hope of Pontmain. There the Queen of Heaven receives her countless children and gives them fresh hope in their trials, as she gave France peace in her hour of need. The basilica is a magnificent structure in the thirteenth century style, and one may still see the barn where Eugène and Joseph worked when Mary appeared.

Pope Pius XI established the Mass and Office in honour of Our Lady of Hope of Pont-Main. A final papal honour was given to Our Lady of Hope on 16 July 1932 by Cardinal Pacelli, who later became Pope Pius XII, by passing a decree from the Chapter of St Peter's Basilica that the statue of the Blessed Lady, Mother of Hope, be solemnly honoured with the crown of gold. The Lady then was crowned in the presence of archbishop, bishops, priests and the laity by Cardinal Verdier, Archbishop of Paris. The coronation took place on 24 July 1934.

18 January: Our Lady of Dijon

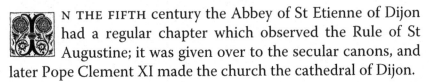 N THE FIFTH century the Abbey of St Etienne of Dijon had a regular chapter which observed the Rule of St Augustine; it was given over to the secular canons, and later Pope Clement XI made the church the cathedral of Dijon.

The image of Our Lady of Dijon in Burgundy was formerly named the "Black Virgin," and "Our Lady of Good Hope." In the year 1513, Mary miraculously delivered the city of Dijon, the ancient city of the Dukes of Burgandy, from the hands of the Swiss. The German and Swiss forces coming against them totalled 45,000 men, and although Dijon was well stocked for a siege, they only had perhaps 6,000 defenders. There were plenty of arrows, but little gunpowder, and most of the French cannon needed repairs.

The invading force was so sure of success that they there were columns of empty wagons pulled behind the army to bring back the loot they expected to take from the French towns and monasteries. The Monastery at Beze was not spared, as even dead monks were dug up in search of treasure.

The army arrived on 8 September, the solemnity of Our Lady's Nativity. There were so many men that the defenders saw nothing but a vast sea of shining armour wherever they gazed. The Swiss opened up with heavy cannon fire the next day, yet there were surprisingly few fatalities. When breaches were made in the walls and the enemy attacked, they were repulsed with heavy loss of life.

On Sunday 11 September, a procession was organized after Mass. The "Black Virgin" was carried through the streets as the French prayed to the Mother of God to spare them from their deadly enemies. The following day a treaty was signed, and the conflict ended unexpectedly. In thanksgiving for this favour, she was titled Our Lady of Dijon, and general procession to her shrine is made every year.

During the French Revolution the church suffered the outrage of being transformed into a forage storage house. Afterward, in atonement to Our Lady for this insult, the faithful of France rebuilt the shrine, and pleaded that the Holy See grant numerous relics and valuable keepsakes to be placed there. Our Blessed Mother responded to the generosity and love of the people by granting favours and cures and extending her God-given miraculous power over the people.

In 1944 the German army occupied the city of Dijon. The people turned to Mary, praying: "Holy Virgin, Compassionate Mother, you who protected our knights of old and who delivered our city from enemy attack, you maintained our ancestors in their times of trouble ... Our Lady of Good Hope, pray for us." On 11 September the Nazi army unexpectedly left Dijon.

19 January: Our Lady finds Jesus in the Temple

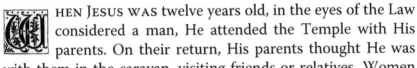 HEN JESUS WAS twelve years old, in the eyes of the Law considered a man, He attended the Temple with His parents. On their return, His parents thought He was with them in the caravan, visiting friends or relatives. Women were placed in the centre of the caravan; men and boys in the front of the back to protect the women. It was not until the end of the day that Mary and Joseph sought Jesus among their relatives and could not find him. Since they could not find him, they returned to Jerusalem in an agony of heart to search for their beloved Son.

On the third day with growing anxiety, they came to God's Temple to tell Him their sorrow and to plead for His mercy. Hardly had they returned to the Temple when they heard His voice, and God revealed to them the Child they had so diligently searched for all these worried days. Loving Mother that she is, Mary knew that her Son had good reason for his actions, but she was overcome with the pain of her emotions. Mary asked: "Son, why hast thou done so to us?" These words were forced from her by pain at the absence of her Son, Whom she loved above all things, and not by indignation, for He was blameless.

Christ was not unsympathetic to His parents' grief. He knew what they had suffered for three days, yet he had remained in Jerusalem because of His love of prayer and communion with His Heavenly Father. He also showed them, even then, some rays of His divinity, by which to make known that He had come for the glory of His Father, and to procure our salvation. The glory of

God and the salvation of our souls should be our chief object in life. So, He reminded his parents kindly that He must be about His Father's business, and they returned to their home, and He was subject to them.[17]

20 January: Our Lady of the Miracle

ARIE ALPHONSE RATISBONNE was born at Strasbourg France, on 1 May 1814. He was the son and heir of a wealthy, aristocratic family of Jewish bankers. When Alphonse Ratisbonne was still a child his older brother, Theodor, converted to the Catholic faith and became a priest. The family Ratisbonne reacted with hostility and horror. Alphonse resolved never to communicate again with his older brother, and developed a violent antipathy to the Catholic faith and to all things Catholic. In 1842, 28 years old, he was engaged to his own niece, Flore Ratisbonne, whom he planned to marry the following August.

He toured Europe, and in Naples he had mistaken the road and instead of coming to the reservation office for Palermo, as he intended, he arrived at the stage-coach for Rome. Even after he realized what happened, he remained there and booked his passage on the boat to Rome. He left Naples on the 5 January and arrived in Rome on the 6th, the feast of the Three Kings. On 8 January, Ratisbonne was called by name on the street. It was his old classmate from Strasburg, Gustavo de Bussières, a Protestant. The two eagerly rekindled their friendship. Later, when Alphonse calls on Gustave, he encountered the latter's older brother, the Baron Theodore de Bussières, a convert to Catholicism and a close friend of Alphonse's priest-brother. Alphonse felt instinctive abhorrence toward this zealous Catholic convert, but he knew the baron was an expert on Constantinople, which Alphonse plans to visit, so he agreed to call upon him for travel advice. De Bussières saw it as his mission to convert any unbeliever who crossed his path in life, to Catholicism. He and

Ratisbonne became friends, but Ratisbonne's sarcasm and blasphemy irritated him enormously.

Finally, the baron made an extraordinary proposition. "Since you abhor superstition and espouse such liberal views" he asked Alphonse, "would you consider submitting to a simple test?" "What test?" "To wear something I'm going to give you. It's a medal of the Holy Virgin. It appears quite ridiculous to you, no doubt. But as for me, I attach great importance to it." He showed Alphonse the Miraculous Medal attached to a cord. Alphonse was dumbstruck. He could scarcely believe the baron's impertinence. But as a man of the world, he didn't want to seem to be making too much fuss. So he consented, breezily quoting a line from *The Tales of Hoffman*: "If it does me no good, at least it will do me no harm." The baron's little daughter put the miraculous medal around Alphonse's neck. Alphonse burst out laughing: "Here am I, a Roman, apostolic Catholic!" But this was not enough for De Bussières. "And now", he said, "you must complete the test. Every morning and evening recite the Memorare, a short and efficacious prayer, which St Bernard composed to the Virgin Mary." Ratisbonne said: "Let it be! I promise to recite this prayer. If it will not do me any good, it will not do me any harm!"

In fact, the baron's relentless proselytism started to get on Alphonse's nerves. Far from drawing him towards Catholicism, it repelled him further. Yet the baron, undaunted, persisted, but did not rely on argument alone. He also prayed very hard, as did his friends, his fellow members of Rome's tight-knit community of aristocratic French expatriates. Notable among these friends was the Count Laferronays, ex-diplomat, once a notorious dissolute and licentious man and now a devout, fervent Catholic. Moved by the baron's pleas, the Count dropped into a church and fervently prayed more than 20 *Memorares* for the conversion of the young Jew. That very same evening, the Count suffered a fatal heart attack. After receiving his final Sacraments, he died piously, surrounded by his loving family.

At midday on 20 January 1842, when the Baron was arranging the funeral of his friend Count Laferronays in the church of Sant'Andrea delle Fratte in Rome he asked Ratisbonne to wait for him in the church. When the Baron came back to the church he found Ratisbonne on his knees in prayer. This sight moved him to tears. In Ratisbonne's own words:

> I was scarcely in the church when a total confusion came over me. When I looked up, it seemed to me that the entire church had been swallowed up in shadow, except one chapel. It was as though all the light was concentrated in that single place. I looked over towards this chapel whence so much light shone, and above the altar was a living figure, tall, majestic, beautiful and full of mercy. It was the most holy Virgin Mary, resembling her figure on the Miraculous Medal. At this sight I fell on my knees right where I stood. Unable to look up because of the blinding light, I fixed my glance on her hands, and in them I could read the expression of mercy and pardon. In the presence of the Most Blessed Virgin, even though she did not speak a word to me, I understood the frightful situation I was in, my sins and the beauty of the Catholic Faith.

The baron helped Ratisbonne outside and into his carriage. He took him to the Hotel Serny, where Alphonse was staying, and loosened his cravat so he could breathe. But Alphonse was still sobbing, clasping his Miraculous Medal, murmuring thanks to God. At last he turned to the baron, embraced him, and with a transformed face exclaimed: "Take me to a confessor! When can I receive baptism, without which I can no longer live?" "What has happened?" asked the baron. "What have you seen?" "That," said Alphonse, "I can reveal only on my knees and to a priest." So the baron took him to the Gesù, the Jesuit church, to see Father Villefort. There, Alphonse tried to explain himself, but he was still sobbing so hard that he was unintelligible. At last he calmed down, took the Miraculous Medal from his neck, held it up, and cried: "I saw Her! I saw Her!"

Alphonse Ratisbonne thought that his family would believe he was insane and would have ridiculed him. So he preferred to flee totally from the world, its chatter and its judgments. He entered the convent of the Jesuits to make a retreat under the guide of Father Villefort. On 31 January 1842, he received baptism, confirmation and his first Holy Communion from the hands of His Eminence Cardinal Patrizi, the Vicar of His Holiness. The following month, the Vatican held a canonical process to investigate the circumstances surrounding Alphonse's conversion. After a lengthy investigation and many depositions, it concluded that his sudden conversion was entirely miraculous; an act of God wrought through the powerful intercession of the Virgin Mary. In May 1842, only a few months after the apparition, a painting of the Madonna of the Miracle was placed for veneration in exactly the same spot and in the same form as she appeared. The canvas was painted by the artist Natale Carta, who according to tradition, followed the indications of Ratisbonne himself. In the same year, after a formal inquest concerning the apparition of 20 January, Cardinal Patrizi declared on 3 June 1842, that it was a divine miracle operated through the intercession of the Blessed Virgin Mary, and permitted the publication and spread of texts recording the miracle.

After his conversion Alphonse assisted his brother Theodor in founding the Sisterhood of Our Lady of Sion in 1843, was ordained priest in 1847, and entered the Society of Jesus. Desirous, however, to devote himself entirely to the conversion of the Jews, he left the society with the consent of Pope Pius IX, transplanted the Sisters of Sion to Jerusalem in 1855, and built for them in 1856 the large Convent of *Ecce Homo* with a school and an orphanage for girls. In 1860 he erected the Convent of St John on the mountain at Ain Karim, together with a church and another orphanage for girls. Here Alphonse laboured with a few companions (the Fathers of Sion) for the conversion of Jews and Muslims until his death. He died there on 6 May 1884. There were so many miracles operated by Mary in the church of St Andrea delle Fratte, that on 17 January

1892, Pope Leo XIII crowned the venerated icon with a diadem. On 25 April 1942, Pope Pius XII elevated the church to the rank of a basilica. On 12 March 1960, Pope St John XXIII elevated the basilica of Sant'Andrea delle Fratte to the rank of a cardinal's titular church. Pope St John Paul II visited this church on 28 February 1982.

21 January: Our Lady of Exile

RADITION TELLS US that St John took Mary to his house in Jerusalem after the death of Jesus. Mary pondered over the wonderful mysteries of her life; she prayed for the new child of hers, the Church; she helped the Apostles with her knowledge of her Son and with her prudent advice. Mary was to all during those long years a pillar of strength. Every day she received Holy Communion; she said again her "Ecce Ancilla" when her God incarnate was within her.

She had to nurse the new-born Church and strengthen the Apostles with her example and prayers; and supply them with many details of Her Son's Life. She had to establish her position as Mother of the Church. During those long years of exile, the Church learned to regard Mary as its Mother. Our Lord would give still more time to increase her merits by more suffering. Her crown was to be the most beautiful possible, and so she remained behind on earth suffering, which intensifies love, humility and submission of God's will.

Mother Mary still "walks the earth" as her many apparitions, especially of late years, testify. We are not alone in this vale of tears in this earthly exile, as our Mother is always with us. All we need do is keep our hand tightly clasped in hers, walk in her footsteps, remain securely under the protection of her mantle, and never fear, but be secure and safe until she clasps us in her arm eternally to lead us to the throne of her Son to enjoy the mansion He is even now preparing for us.[18]

22 January: Our Lady of Charity

 ILITIA CHIEF LUIS JIMÉNEZ DE ROJAS brought from Spain an image of Our Lady of Charity for the chapel at his hacienda El Chaparral, now the town of San Juan de los Morros in the state of Guarico, central Venezuela. In 1691, the hacienda burned down.

The picture of Our Lady was found in the ruins, intact, with its lamp still burning. This generated a surge of popular devotion, and on 22 January 1692, the Bishop of Caracas installed the image in the village church of San Sebastian de los Reyes and authorized the foundation of a Confraternity to undertake the construction of a new sanctuary. The large neoclassical Church of Our Lady of Charity was completed in 1725.

The Confraternity is still active. The Virgin of Charity shares annual festivities with St Sebastian co-patron of the town, whose feast day is 20 January. The image of Our Lady travels through the area ahead of time, tracing in reverse the pilgrimages to occur in her honour. On 21 January, a parade of offerings is brought to the Virgin's altar, followed by an evening serenade with traditional mariachi music, and on the 22 January, between 5 and 6 am, the morning procession takes place along all the streets of the city, accompanied by mariachis and brass bands.[19] Later the fiesta features craft sales, food, ball games, dancing, and concerts.[20]

23 January: Our Lady's Espousals

 T THE COUNCIL of Constance in 1416, John Gerson proposed that a votive Feast of the Betrothal of Mary Most Holy and St Joseph be observed mainly by priests on the Thursday of Advent ember week when the Gospel of the espousal would fit nicely. In 1474 Franciscan Bernardine of Bustis wrote an Office for the feast. By 1517 the Annunciation Sisters founded by St Jane of Valois already celebrated the feast. In 1537 the Franciscans adopted it to be celebrated on 7 March, and soon after the

Servites for March 8, and the Dominicans for 22 January. A 1550 work invites people in Holland to celebrate the recently instituted feast on 15 January. In 1684, Pope Innocent XI permitted its celebration in the empire of Leopold I, and later also in Spain. In both France and Canada it was observed on 22 January, while Polish confraternities celebrated 23 January. In 1725 Pope Benedict XIII extended it to the Papal States, setting the date for 23 January.

During the nineteenth and twentieth centuries various particular permissions have been given to celebrate the feast, usually on 23 January, but occasionally on other days. In 1840, for example, it was granted to the United States of America. The extent of usage merited its inclusion in editions of the pre-Vatican II Roman Missal for 23 January in the section for particular places.

Under Pope Blessed Pius IX, the Dioceses of Lausanne, Geneva, and Perpignan were allowed to celebrate the feast as a double major with the commemoration of St Joseph. The feast is listed in the 1848 martyrology of the Benedictine nuns of the Adoration of the Blessed Sacrament. In 1849 the feast was extended to the Kingdom of Saigon, and in 1850 to the Province of Oregon. Various dioceses were granted permission to add the commemoration of St Joseph to their celebration of the feast. At least since 1859 the feast is listed for 11 February in the Proper Office for the Archdiocese of Fribourg (and for 13 February in the 1894 edition). The feast and commemoration are contained in the calendar of St Martin's Monastery in Portugal, and in that of the Diocese of Cordoba, Argentina, both approved in 1878. For Cordoba, the feast is celebrated on 26 November, rather than 23 January as in the other instances listed.

During the pontificate of Pope Leo XIII, similar such permissions continued to be extended. Among the calendars approved with the feast and commemoration of St Joseph on 23 January were those of the Diocese of Rio de Janeiro, Brazil; the Martyrology of the Diocese of Fréjus-Toulon; the Capuchin Breviary; and the newly founded Swiss-American Benedictines. The Augustinian Canonesses of the Congregation of Notre Dame at Épinal,

France, and the Hungarian Cistercians were granted the same feast, but without explicit mention of the commemoration of St Joseph. In Spain, the Pious Society of Devotees of St Joseph in Barcelona, the Diocese of Huesca, and the Cistercian Nuns of Segovia all celebrated the feast on 26 November, and the first two of these were permitted an extrinsic celebration on the Last Sunday after Pentecost.

During the twentieth century the Feast of the Espousals on 23 January continued to be found in more particular calendars: St Mary Major Basilica in Rome, 1913; Marello's Oblates of St Joseph, 1921; the Oratory of St Joseph in Montreal, Canada, 1940; and Murialdo's Congregation of St Joseph, 1946. The Diocese of Zacatecas, Mexico, was granted the 26 November feast in 1958. In Vienna, Austria, the Piarist Church of the Espousals, which includes a Corradini sculpture of Mary and Joseph being blessed by the high priest, was named a minor basilica in 1949.

In 1961 the Sacred Congregation of Rites issued an instruction that removed from particular calendars numerous particular feasts, including the Feast of the Espousals of Mary and St Joseph, except in places where the feasts have a special connection with the place itself. In the post-Vatican II period of liturgical renewal, the feast is again being permitted for particular liturgical calendars. In 1989, for example, the Oblates of St Joseph obtained permission to celebrate on 23 January "The Holy Spouses Mary and Joseph" with the liturgical rank of "Feast", and full proper texts, including a preface:

> You give the Church the joy of celebrating the feast of the Holy Spouses, Mary and Joseph: in her, full of grace and worthy Mother of your Son, you signify the beginning of the Church, resplendently beautiful bride of Christ; you chose him, the wise and faithful servant, as Husband of the Virgin Mother of God, and made him head of your family, to guard as a father your only Son, conceived by the power of the Holy Spirit, Jesus Christ, our Lord.

24 January: Our Lady of Peace

UR LADY OF PEACE or Queen of Peace is a title of the Blessed Virgin Mary and she is represented in art holding a dove and an olive branch, symbols of peace. Her official memorial feast is celebrated on 24 January each year in Hawaii and some churches in the United States. Elsewhere, the feast is celebrated on 9 July. Our Lady Queen of Peace has been the patroness of the Catholic Church in Hawaii since 1827. The first Catholic missionaries to the Hawaiian Islands arrived at Honolulu Bay on 7 July 1827. These missionaries were members of the Congregation of the Sacred Hearts of Jesus and Mary and of Perpetual Adoration and upon their arrival in the islands dedicated their labours to the patroness of the Congregation, Our Lady Queen of Peace and placed the Islands under her protection. It was in her honour that these missionaries erected the first Catholic Church. Today, the Cathedral of Our Lady of Peace in Honolulu is the oldest Roman Catholic cathedral in continuous use in the United States.

There are three famous statues of Our Lady of Peace located in Paris and Honolulu. The original is a wooden carving located at a convent of the Congregation of the Sacred Hearts of Jesus and Mary in France. A larger replica in bronze was hoisted above the altar and sanctuary at the Cathedral of Our Lady of Peace. A third stands outside the cathedral on a pedestal. The original statue of Our Lady Queen of Peace is located in the Convent Chapel of the Sisters of the Sacred Hearts in Picpus, France. During the troubled days of the Commune, in 1871, the populace, incited by atheistic leaders, invaded churches, chapels and convents, destroying every emblem of religion that fell into their hands. The chapel of Our Lady Queen of Peace became their prey. The Superior, with tears in her eyes, begged them to spare their beloved shrine; and, strange to say, the rabble went away, leaving it unharmed. When the tempest of the persecution subsided, the statue was again returned to its usual place and honored and venerated by a phalanx of devout souls. On July 9, 1906, the statue of Our Lady Queen of Peace was solemnly crowned in the name of Pope St Pius X by his Eminence Cardinal Amette, Archbishop of Paris. Every year on July 9 the feast of Our Lady Queen of Peace is celebrated with great solemnity in the Congregation of the Fathers and Sisters of the Sacred Hearts of Jesus and Mary. During the troubled years of World War I, Pope Benedict XV added Our Lady of Peace to the Litany of Loreto, a sacred prayer in liturgy. Pope John Paul II consecrated and dedicated the Basilica of Our Lady of Peace of Yamoussoukro to Our Lady of Peace. It is the largest place of worship in Africa. Elsewhere throughout the world, there are parish churches named in honor of Our Lady of Peace in various forms, especially in Ireland and the United States.

We quote from the prayer to Our Lady of Peace of Pope John Paul II, which was formulated for the people of Oceania, but here has been adapted for the whole Church.

O Mary, Help of Christians, in our need we turn to you
with eyes of love, with empty hands and longing hearts.
We look to you that we may see your Son, our Lord.
We lift our hands that we may have the Bread of Life.
We open wide our hearts to receive the Prince of Peace.
Mother of the Church, your sons and daughters thank you
for your trusting word that echoes through the ages,
rising from a soul made full of grace,
prepared by God to welcome the Word to the world
that the world itself might be reborn.
In you, the reign of God has dawned,
a reign of grace and peace, love and justice, born from the depths
of the Word made flesh.
The Church throughout the world joins you in praising him
whose mercy is from age to age.
O *Stella Maris*, light of every ocean and mistress of the deep,
guide all peoples across all dark and stormy seas,
that they may reach the haven of peace and light prepared in him
who calmed the sea.
Keep all your children safe from harm
for the waves are high and we are far from home.

As we set forth upon the oceans of the world, and cross the deserts of our time,

show us, O Mary, the fruit of your womb,

for without your Son we are lost.

Pray that we will never fail on life's journey, that in heart and mind, in word and deed,

in days of turmoil and in days of calm, we will always look to Christ and say,

"Who is this that even wind and sea obey him?"

Our Lady of Peace, in whom all storms grow still,

pray at the dawn of the new millennium that the Church will not cease to show forth

the glorious face of your Son, full of grace and truth,

so that God will reign in the hearts of all peoples and they will find peace

in the world's true Saviour.

Plead for the Church that she may have strength

to follow faithfully the way of Jesus Christ, to tell courageously the truth of Jesus Christ,

to live joyfully the life of Jesus Christ.

O Help of Christians, protect us!

Bright Star of the Sea, guide us!

Our Lady of Peace, pray for us!

25 January: Icon of the Mother of God the Milkgiver

 HE MILKGIVER ICON of the Mother of God was originally located at the Lavra (monastery) of St Saba the Sanctified near Jerusalem.[21] Before his death in 532, St Saba, the holy founder of the Lavra, foretold that a royal pilgrim having the same name as himself would visit the Lavra. St Saba told the brothers to give the wonderworking icon to that pilgrim as a blessing.

In the thirteenth century, St Saba of Serbia visited the Lavra. As he approached the reliquary of St Saba the Sanctified, the saint's staff fell at his feet. The brethren asked the visitor his name, and he told them he was Archbishop Saba of Serbia. Obeying the instructions of their founder, the monks gave St Saba his staff, the "Milk-Giver" Icon, and the Icon "Of the Three Hands".

The holy archbishop took the icon to Hilandar on Mount Athos and put it on the right side of the iconostasis in the church of St Saba at the kellion of Karyes, which is attached to Hilandar. devotion to the Hilandar *Galaktotrophousa*, the Milk-Giver, spread throughout the Orthodox world, and particularly to Serbia. Stern and swarthy, she seems to embody the principle that hardship brings spiritual nourishment. On January 25, the Serbian Orthodox Church sings an Akathist in her honor, a long, 13-part prayer of praise and exultation. The icon reminds us of the reality of the Incarnation and of the Divine Motherhood of Our Lady as expressed in the Acathistos hymn:

> Immaculate one, you have received in your womb the Word Himself, and have borne the Sustainer of the universe; you have fed with your milk the Nourisher of creation![22]

26 January: Our Lady of the Waters

ONGMONG IS PART of a municipality in the United States territory of Guam composed of three separate villages (Mongmong, Toto and Maite), east of Hagåtña that experienced development after the Second World War. Mongmong was particularly popular during the early months of the year when people from all over the island would travel there to honour the village's patron saint *Nuestra Senora de Las Aguas*, or Our Lady of the Waters. They would pray to her for rain during the island's dry season.

In 1881, a man named James Young wrote to his sister in Australia telling her about the residents' devotion to the saint. He said people believed that this image of the Virgin Mary appeared to some villagers during a strong typhoon in 1850, and caused a perfect calm that saved their farm from destruction.

Although since World War II the Mongmong area is no longer dependent on farming, and few farmers still rely on Our Lady of the Waters for rain, the village still honours her as patron and presents her with annual offerings for a good harvest. Most of the official activities of the feast take place on the fourth Saturday in January. The archbishop comes to say the Mass, after which the boys of the confirmation class carry the statue in procession out to the road and back to the church, accompanied by Holy Communion candidates dressed as angels, along with priests, altar servers, and Knights of Columbus. The girls of the confirmation place the floral harvest offerings, while the rest of the parish joins in prayer. There follows an entire evening of feasting and entertainment in the community centre. On Sunday, the celebration continues privately as people visit family and friends.[23]

27 January: Our Lady of Life

HE TOWN OF MOUGINS is an ancient village located in the south of France, only a short drive from Cannes, and completely surrounded by dense forests; there are a variety of tall pines and other trees growing amidst the town's buildings. Like so many other places in Europe, the village was once also surrounded by a stone wall set with strong towers, though most of those walls have long since fallen down. Many of the charming older residences, however, are still in use opposite to newer dwellings.

Sometime during the eleventh century, a local nobleman gave the hill which overlooks the village to the monks of Saint Honorat, from the Isle of Lérins, who cared for the local populace until the time of the French Revolution. The monks built a chapel on the hill known as Saint Marie, though very little of that original structure still remains. The chapel of Sainte Marie was referred to for the first time in a Bull of Pope Alexander IV who confirmed it as a possession of the Abbey of Lérins, along with the Castle of Mougins with its three churches. The Chapel of Our Lady of Life, or *Notre Dame de Vie* in French, was rebuilt in 1654, and stands upon the former site of that much earlier church.

The hermitage of Notre Dame de Vie, Our Lady of Life, is located on a beautiful site still overlooking the village, set in a long meadow bordered by two rows of giant cypresses. There is a natural peace and tranquillity that seems to calm the soul at this place, which was once a site of many miracles.

The name of the first chapel was changed from Saint Mary to Notre Dame de Vie, Our Lady of Life. It served as a "chapel of respite," where babies born dead were laid out so that they could be baptized before burial if they showed signs of life. Notre Dame de Vie soon became famous throughout the area as a special sanctuary of grace, for if still-born babies were brought to the chapel, they would be miraculously brought back to life long enough to be baptized.

After such a respite, the parents of the infant who survived long enough to be baptized showed their gratitude to Our Lady by offering an ex-voto.[24] The walls of the chapel are covered with ex-votos, also for miracles in other circumstances such as people saved from drowning, shipwrecks, fires or diseases. In 1730, on the orders of Mgr d'Anthelmy, bishop of Grasse, the practice ceased, and by 1764, pilgrimages had been practically abandoned. During the twentieth century the church has been restored, the last time being in 2012 by the town of Mougins.

Devotion to Our Lady of Life is very important in an age prone to compromise human life at all its stages. Instead Our Lady helps us defend life from conception to its natural end.

28 January: Our Lady of Succour

N 1613 THE SPANISH GOVERNOR of Manila sent out a small fleet made up of two large galleys and several barques, to assist a neighbouring settlement which was under siege by pirates. The two galleys were named Our Lady of Guadalupe and Our Lady of Guidance.

The chief gunner on the Guadalupe was Francis Lopez, a man given to all kinds of wickedness. He had only one soft spot in his hard heart, and that was for Our Lady of the Rosary. Wicked as he was, he never neglected this offering to the Mother of Mercy. On the voyage in question, the Guadalupe struck a rock and sank and everyone had to swim for shore. Francis arrived safely, but promptly got embroiled in a free-for-all with the native galley slaves, who saw an opportunity to escape from the Spaniards. The slaves entrenched themselves behind the cliffs and rolled rocks down on their former masters. Francis was horribly wounded and left for dead, when the few survivors pulled away in a boat, sent from the Guidance.

For two weeks he lay helpless and in a frightful state from his wounds. He was surrounded by the dead, and deserted by the living. In his lucid moments he prayed to Our Lady of Succour, not to be delivered or for his heath to be restored, but for a priest. Francis was in no state to face God without confession, and he begged Our Lady of the Rosary to send him a priest.

Two weeks later, the other galley was in trouble and blown off its course. It was carried into the straits where the Guadalupe had gone down, and with all the efforts of the crew, it could not be steered around the cape. Finally the captain gave up, dropped anchor, and sent the crew ashore for fresh water. One of the sailors heard someone calling his name. The wounded man he found was almost too horrible to look upon, but his request was plain enough, "For the love of God, get me a priest!" The Franciscan chaplain of the Guidance was hastily summoned, and the man made his confession, and then died.

Favourable winds filled the sails of the Guidance, and in an hour the vessel was back on course. Back in Manilla, the sacristans were decorating the sanctuary for a feast. Dusting around the statue of Our Lady of the Rosary, one of the ladies noticed an odd fact. "His little shoes are wet and muddy," she said, pointing to the Infant, "and Our Lady's skirts are damp and full of wet sand, as though she had been walking on the beach!"

The prior, Father Michael Ruiz, was summoned to see the phenomenon. He confirmed that the Mother's robe and the Baby's shoes showed definite signs of a journey in a wet sandy place, and that the niche where the statue stood was perfectly dry. He carefully noted the day and the time, and summoned a visiting Franciscan who examined the statue and finally took the Baby's sandals to his room with him as a proof of the incident.

Weeks later when the Guidance came home, the story was put together. Our Lady of Succour had heard the cry of her wandering child, and no one ever doubted that the sand on her robe came from the beach where Lopez died, calling on her for help.[25]

29 January: *Our Lady of Châtillon-sur-Seine*

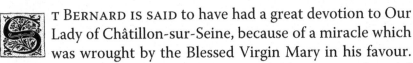

T BERNARD IS SAID to have had a great devotion to Our Lady of Châtillon-sur-Seine, because of a miracle which was wrought by the Blessed Virgin Mary in his favour. Bernard, the third of a family of seven children, was educated with particular care, because while yet unborn, a devout man had foretold his great destiny. At the age of nine he was sent to a famous school in France at Châtillon-sur-Seine, kept by the secular priests of Saint Vorles. He was an intelligent student, greatly devoted to the Blessed Virgin. He later wrote several books about the holy Mother of God, and it is thought by many that no one speaks as sublimely of the Queen of Heaven as he does. Mary appeared to Bernard as he wrote and inspired him with heavenly words and wisdom. The most hardened sinners, heretics and agnostics Mary brought to him and she proved a bulwark to his efforts to lead men to her and to Christ, her Divine Son.

Early in his adult life Saint Bernard became sick, so sick that he was preparing himself for death. Feeling useless and barren, his infirmity and the attendant pains he experienced increased to such a degree that Bernard asked two of his brethren to go to the church and beg for heavenly relief from God.

The Blessed Virgin Mary herself soon appeared to St Bernard, entering his cell attended by St Lawrence and St Benedict. All three approached Saint Bernard and touched the parts of his body where the pain was the most severe, bringing immediate relief. St Bernard had also been troubled with an intense flow of saliva which would not cease, and that trouble was also immediately ended. The saint was not completely cured, however, and although he did not die, it was yet some time before his health was completely restored to him. St Bernard used the time well, producing his first treatise on humility and pride, and his light began to shine as the morning sun.

30 January: Our Lady of the Rose

ISTORY SHOWS THAT the the rose is the favourite flower of Our Lady. In her apparition at Guadeloupe, she made use of roses as a sign of her presence and even arranged them with her own beautiful hands in the tilma of St Juan Diego. At La Salette she wore a profusion of roses in three garlands and had tiny roses around the rim of her slippers. She brought beautiful roses with her at Lourdes, Pontmain, Pellevoisin, Beauraing, and Banneaux. To Sister Josefa Menendez she showed her immaculate heart encircled with little white roses. Truly, she can be called the Madonna of the Rose.

In King's College Chapel, Cambridge, built by Henry VIII in memory of his father, there can be discerned, hidden in one of the Tudor rose-bosses on the walls, a small head of Our Lady which somehow escaped observation at the despoliation of images at the Protestant Deformation. Brother John, a clever carver, was hired to carve all of the roses; knowing of the king's quarrel with the pope, he secretly carved a tiny head of Mary, half-hidden within the rose petals in the upper tier of decorations, saying, "There you remain, Our Lady of the Rose, even if wicked men try to drive you and your Son from this Church." His words came true, when the place was stripped of every trace of Faith, the diminutive head of the Mother of God still remained.

Cardinal Newman says:

> Mary is the most beautiful flower ever seen in the spiritual world. It is by the power of God's grace that from this barren and desolate earth there ever sprung up at all flowers of holiness and glory; and Mary is the Queen of them all. She is the Queen of spiritual flowers; and therefore, is called the Rose, for the rose is called of all flowers the most beautiful. But, moreover, she is the Mystical or Hidden Rose, for mystical means hidden.[26]

But a rose has thorns, and so had the Mystical Rose—the sharpest for herself alone; so she could have compassion on our infirmities. Never did the breath of evil spoil the splendour of this Mystical Rose; never did God's lovely flower, the Madonna of the Rose, cease to give forth the sweet perfume of love and praise:

> There is no rose of such virtue
> As is the rose that bare Jesu;
> *Alleluia.*
> For in this rose contained was
> Heaven and earth in little space;
> *Res miranda.*
> By that rose we may well see
> That he is God in persons three,
> *Pari forma.*[27]

31 January: Our Lady of Hope

HE DEVOTION TO Our Lady of Hope in Brazil dates from its discovery. Pedro Álvares Cabral undertook his voyage to the Indies, which ended in the discovery of Brazil, carrying in his ship an image of Our Lady of Hope. Father Vaz Caminha, in one of his letters to the Portuguese king Dom Manuel I, related that the first Catholic Masses were said on Brazilian soil, 26 April and 1 May 1500, in the presence of a large cross and under the maternal gaze of the Mother of Hope. This image returned to Brazil in 1955 for the International Eucharistic Congress in Rio de Janeiro. A replica is found in the Brasilia Cathedral, and by the time Cidade da Esperança was established, 11 other Brazilian parishes claimed her as patron. Inaugurated 31 January 1966, Cidade da Esperança (City of Hope) was the first public housing development in the country, a model for those in other states. When the community was being planned, the Catholic women decided on the idea of building a church to Our Lady of Hope. The parish celebrates its patronal feast on the community's founding date.[28]

Notes

[1]   St John Damascene, *An Exposition of the Orthodox Faith*, Book 3, chapter 12.

[2]   See N. J. Santoro, *Mary In Our Life: Atlas of the Names and Titles of Mary, The Mother of Jesus and Their Place in Marian Devotion* (Bloomington, IN: iUniverse, 2011)), p. 502.

[3]   See M. Lamberty (ed.), *The Woman in Orbit: Mary's feasts every day everywhere* (Chicago: Lamberty, 1966), 4 January.

[4]   See *ibid.*, 5 January.

[5]   Vatican II, *Lumen Gentium*, 62.

[6]   Pope Benedict XVI, *Homily at Altötting* (11 September 2006).

[7]   See Lamberty, *The Woman in Orbit*, 7 January.

[8]   See *ibid.*, 8 January.

[9]   See *ibid.*, 9 January.

[10] See *ibid.*, 10 January.

[11] See *ibid.*, 11 January.

[12] See *ibid.*, 13 January.

[13] See *ibid.*, 14 January.

[14] See "Coronation at Banneux" in *Catholic Herald* (10 August 1956).

[15] See Lamberty, *The Woman in Orbit*, 16 January.

[16] Joseph Barbadette, who later afterwards became a priest of the Congregation of the Oblates of Mary Immaculate recounted: "She was young and tall of stature, clad in a garment of deep blue ... Her dress was covered with brilliant gold stars. The sleeves were ample and long. She wore slippers of the same blue as the dress, ornamented with gold bows. On the

head was a black veil half covering the forehead, concealing the hair and ears, and falling over the shoulders. Above this was a crown resembling a diadem, higher in front than elsewhere, and widening out at the sides. A red line encircled the crown at the middle. Her hands were small and extended toward us as in the 'miraculous medal'. Her face had the most exquisite delicacy and a smile of ineffable sweetness. The eyes, of unutterable tenderness, were fixed on us. Like a true mother, she seemed happier in looking at us than we in contemplating."

[17]   See Lamberty, *The Woman in Orbit*, 19 January.

[18]   See *ibid.*, 21 January.

[19]   Mariachi is a form of folk music from Mexico. Mariachi began as a regional folk style called "Son Jaliscience" in the centre west of Mexico originally played only with string instruments and musicians dressed in the white pants and shirts of peasant farmers. The word "mariachi" was thought to have derived from the French word "marriage", dating from the French intervention in Mexico in the 1860s, related to the music's appearance at weddings.

[20]   See J. L. Ramírez, "Celebraron 50 años de la coronación canónica de la Virgen la Caridad" in *Diario El Periodiquito* (22 January 2010).

[21]   A *Lavra* or *Laura* is a type of monastery consisting of a cluster of cells or caves for hermits, with a church and sometimes a refectory at the centre.

[22]   *Acathistos to the Most Holy Mother of God*, Ode 8, Troparion.

[23]   See "Mongmong honors Our Lady of the Waters" in *Central Weekly* (30 January 2008).

[24]   An *ex-voto* is a votive offering to God or a saint. It is given in fulfilment of a vow (hence the Latin term, short for *ex voto suscepto*, "from the vow made" or in gratitude or devotion. Ex-votos are placed in a church or chapel where the worshipper seeks grace or wishes to give thanks.

[25]   See Lamberty, *The Woman in Orbit*, 28 January.

[26]   Blessed J. H. Newman, *Meditations and Devotions* (London: Longmans, Green and Co, 1907), p. 66.

[27]   J. A. Fuller Maitland and W. S. Rockstro, *English Carols of the Fifteenth Century* (London: The Leadenhall Press, E.C., ca. 1891), Carol No. XIII, pp. 26–27, 54–55.

[28]   See Mgr Severino Bezerra, *Tribuna do Norte* (25 October 1964).

FEBRUARY

1 February: Icon of the All-Holy Consoler

HE MONASTERY OF the Holy Virgin of Kykkos is located at an altitude of approximately 1,200 metres, about one kilometre from mountain Kykkos, a 1,318 m high peak in the western part of the Troödos range. That peak is also known by the name Throni or Throni of Panagia. The Holy Monastery of Panagia of Kykkos was founded around the end of the eleventh century by Byzantine Emperor Alexios I Komnenos, and since then has housed a special icon of Our Lady. The tradition connected with this icon holds that the Archangel Gabriel gave Mary some wood from the Tree of Life. She gave it to St Luke, who used it to paint three images of her holding the Christ Child. When she saw the one now in Cyprus, she said, "May the grace of Him Whom I bore be with it." Luke sent the icon to the Christians in Egypt (or Antioch); from there it came to Constantinople in the 400s.

A virtuous hermit called Isaiah was living in a cave on the mountain of Kykkos in Cyprus. One day, the Byzantine governor of the island, duke Manuel Boutoumites, who was spending the summer at a village of Marathasa because of the heat of the season, went into the forest to hunt. Having lost his way in the forest he met hermit Isaiah and asked him to show him the way. The hermit who was not interested in the things of this world would not answer his questions. Boutoumites got angry at the monk's indifference and called him names and even maltreated him. Not long after, when the duke returned to Nicosia, he fell ill with an incurable illness by the name of lethargia.[1] In his terrible malady he remembered how inhumanly he had treated the hermit Isaiah and asked God to cure him so that he might go to ask the hermit personally for forgiveness; this favour was granted. However, God had appeared in front of the hermit and revealed to him that the very thing that had happened had been planned by the divine will and advised him to ask Boutoumites to bring the icon of the Virgin, that had been painted by the Apostle Luke, to Cyprus. The icon was kept in the imperial palace at Constantinople. When Boutoumites heard the hermit's wish he was taken aback because he considered the task impossible. Then Isaiah explained to him that it was a matter of the divine wish and they agreed to travel together to Constantinople for the realization of their aim.

Time was passing and Boutoumites could not find the right opportunity to present himself in front of the emperor and ask for the icon. For this reason he provided Isaiah with other icons and other necessary things and sent him back to Cyprus, at the same time placating him that he would soon see the emperor. By divine dispensation the daughter of the emperor had fallen ill with the same illness that had struck Boutoumites. The latter grasped the opportunity and went to see the Emperor Alexios III Angelos. He recounted to him his personal experience with the monk Isaiah and assured him that his daughter would be cured if he sent to Cyprus the holy icon of the Virgin. In his desperation the emperor, seeing that he had no other option, agreed. His daughter recovered instantly. The emperor, however, not wanting to be parted from the icon of the Virgin, called a first-class painter and ordered him to paint an exact copy of the icon with the aim of sending this one to Cyprus.

That evening the Mother of God herself appeared in a dream to the emperor and told him that her wish is for her icon to be sent to Cyprus and for the copy to be kept by the emperor. On the following day the royal boat with the icon of the Virgin departed for Cyprus where Isaiah was awaiting for it. During the procession of the icon from the coast to the Troödos Mountains, according to legend, the trees, participating in the welcoming ceremonies, were piously bending their trunks and branches. With patronage provided by the emperor Alexios, a church and monastery were built at Kykkos, where the icon of the Virgin was deposited. According to another tradition, still preserved by the people, a bird with human voice was flying around the area singing::

"Kykkou, Kykkou, Kykkos" hill
A monastery the site shall fill.
A golden girl shall enter in
And never shall come out again.

The "golden girl" is, without a doubt, the icon of the Virgin while the monastery is the Holy Royal and Stauropegial Monastery of Kykkos which has been sheltering the icon for over nine hundred years. Since 1576 the holy icon has been completely covered in silver and gold. A brocade veil over the Virgin's face depicts her hidden portrait.[2]

On 1 February 1997, a novice monk noticed that the Virgin and Child were both weeping on the icon of Panagia Paramythia, the All-Holy Consoler, in the Kykkos monastery. Off and on for a month, many witnesses, both monks and pilgrims, saw pine-scented tears flow down the holy faces. The icon, a 1500s copy of the one in Vatopedi Monastery on Mount Athos, was originally in the Monastery of the Virgin of Helicon three miles north, abandoned around 1800 and now a ruin. It hangs on the iconostasis near the Kykkiotissa, the ancient miracle-working icon of Kykko Monastery, held to have been painted by St Luke. The Abbot and Archbishop both said the tears were a sign from God, a call to repentance; and the Abbot promised to use any ensuing donations for the defence of Cyprus and rebuilding of the Helicon Monastery.

2 February: Presentation of the Lord

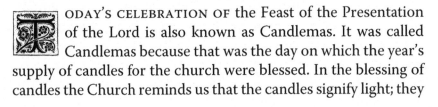 ODAY'S CELEBRATION OF the Feast of the Presentation of the Lord is also known as Candlemas. It was called Candlemas because that was the day on which the year's supply of candles for the church were blessed. In the blessing of candles the Church reminds us that the candles signify light; they

are blessed for the service of men, for health of body and soul, for those who desire to carry them in their hands with honour. Christ, the true Light and Fire of Charity, is asked to bless these candles; to dispel the darkness of night, to free us from the blindness of vice and to discern what is pleasing to Him and profitable for our salvation. Christians have been observing Candlemas since the fourth century. By the middle of the fifth century, candles were lit on this day to symbolize that Jesus Christ is the light of revelation and the hope of all peoples.

In Greek, this feast called (*Hypapante*), a Greek word meaning "meeting". This moment is the first encounter of Jesus, our Savior, with His people. Christ comes into the midst of the temple, the gathering place of all the people of God and even of some Gentiles assembled to pray and to fulfill the laws of God handed down by Moses. Jesus, too, wishing to be like us in all things, save sin, that He might sanctify every aspect of human life, enters the Temple carried by His mother and accompanied by St. Joseph to make the customary offering of two turtledoves or pigeons (see Leviticus 12:2-5). Mary, the all pure *Theotokos*, submits to the rite of Purification as an act of obedience to the customary laws. Jesus submits to the laws of God and customs so that He might illumine all human life for He is the Sun of Justice

Mary and Joseph followed the law prescribed for the Israelites and when the days were completed for their purification according to the law of Moses, they took Jesus up to Jerusalem to present Him to the Lord, just as it is written in the law of the Lord (see Luke 2:22-23). God had redeemed the Israelites from captivity in Egypt by killing all the first-born of the Egyptians, but he passed over the homes of the Israelites, who had marked their lintels with the blood of the lamb. For this reason God commanded: "Consecrate to me every first-born that opens the womb among the Israelites, both of man and beast, for it belongs to me" (Ex 13:2). We know that they are a poor family, because they do not make the offering of a lamb, but of two doves. The Holy Spirit moves many at this moment. Old Simeon is there to greet the holy family. This is another Visitation for Mary again presents Jesus to those awaiting His coming. Simeon knows it and in joy sings that hymn recited daily in Night Prayer:

> Now, Master, you can let your servant go m peace, just as you promised; because my eyes have seen the salvation which you have prepared for all the nations to see, a light to enlighten the pagans and the glory of your people Israel (Lk 2:29–32).

This prophecy reminds us that Mary is always to be associated with the destiny of Jesus, the one solitary partner of His lot, singled out to suffer with Him. Heresies that pierced the Son have transpierced the Mother. The early Church guarded the doctrines of Jesus by defining Mary's titles; today those who repudiate the honour of Mary, turn from the Son also. This feast reminds us how intimately Mary is associated with her Son in the work of Redemption. We welcome Her Child to our hearts with love and faith, we bless the Mother, too; for she "did not consider her own life when our nation was brought to its knees, but warded off our ruin, walking undeterred before our God" (Jdt 13:20).

We quote from a poem, "Our Lady of the Doves" by Cyril Robert:

Tis not the robin I hear today,
The robin with breast of red;
Ah, long the day since he fled away
From the fields now lying dead!
Tis not the thrush nor the nightingale,
Nor the lark that soars above;
But under the eaves in the wintry gale
I list to the cooing dove.
O dove at rest on the rooftree high,
O dove on the earth below,
Tis little ye know what ye tell to me
Of doves of the long ago!
For I close my ears to the city's roar,
And dream I am far away,
To stand at the mighty Temple's door

On the Presentation Day.
And I see the Mother with tender Child—
A mother, yet maiden, too—
Who stands in the ranks of the sin-defiled,
As Jehovah bade her do.—
A penny dove for a holocaust,
And a penny dove for sin,
Ah, cooing doves from the cages tossed,
What blessedness ye win!
For I see the blood of each gentle bird
Poured out the stones upon,
While the wondrous prophecies are heard
From Anna and Simeon.
Ah, Mother of God, in the Temple dim,
Who seest each bleeding dove,
I know thou art seeing the blood of Him,
Thine own little Bird of love!
O dove at rest on the rooftree high,
O dove in the city street,
I hark to the sound of your cooing cry,
And I find it wondrous sweet.
Ah; spring may come with the robin's trill
And the thrush's roundelay,
But never a bird my soul to thrill
As the doves of Candlemas Day.[3]

3 February: Apparition to Bl Elizabeth Canori Mora

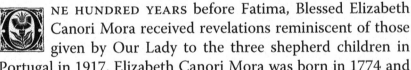NE HUNDRED YEARS before Fatima, Blessed Elizabeth Canori Mora received revelations reminiscent of those given by Our Lady to the three shepherd children in Portugal in 1917. Elizabeth Canori Mora was born in 1774 and lived in Italy until her saintly death in 1825. In 1807, then 3 February 1816 and 5 February 1825, Our Lady with the baby Jesus in her arms, appeared at her house in Rome.

At Christmas, 1816 Blessed Elizabeth saw Our Lady, who appeared extremely sad. Upon inquiring why, Our Lady answered, "Behold, my daughter, such great ungodliness." Blessed Elizabeth then saw apostates brazenly trying to rip her most holy Son from her arms. Confronted with such an outrage, the Mother of God ceased to ask mercy for the world, and instead requested justice from the Eternal Father. Clothed in His inexorable Justice and full of indignation, He turned to the world.

> At that moment all nature went into convulsions, the world lost its normal order and was filled with the most terrible calamity imaginable. This will be something so deplorable and atrocious that it will reduce the world to the ultimate depths of desolation.

Early in 1821, Our Lord also told of a future restoration in these terms:

> I will reform my people and my Church. I will send zealous priests to preach my Faith. I will form a new apostolate and send the Holy Spirit to renew the world. I will reform the religious orders by means of new holy and learned reformers... I will provide my Church with a new pastor, who is learned, holy and full of My Spirit. With holy zeal he will reform My flock.

When Pope Blessed Pius IX authorized Elizabeth Canori Mora's cause for canonization to proceed, for years, all her writings were scrupulously examined for doctrinal errors, to avoid the dangers of being misled by a false mystic. The ecclesiastical censor commissioned by the Holy See released his official judgment on 5 November 1900. It stated "there is nothing against faith and morals, and no doctrinal innovation or deviation was found". Elizabeth Canori Mora was beatified in 1994.[4]

4 February: Our Lady of Fire

 URING THE NIGHT of 3–4 February 1428, fire broke out in a school in Forlì (a small city southeast of Bologna, Italy) and burned over a period of a few days. The gathered townspeople were astonished to find, intact in the rubble, a woodcut of the Virgin and Child. This image had been the focus of devotion for the schoolboys, led by their teacher, Lombardino da Ripetrosa. By order of the city governor and the papal legate, the miraculous picture was moved to the cathedral the following Sunday. In 1636, a magnificent marble chapel was dedicated to Our Lady of Fire in the cathedral's left aisle.[5]

Throughout the region, her image was often reproduced on doorways and carts to protect against fire. The image of the Madonna of the Fire also appeared throughout and even beyond the city. It was printed in thousands of impressions, moulded into ceramic reliefs, painted on walls and monumental gates as well as on small pieces of cloth that her devotees carried. One small painting on panel was hung on an oak tree ten kilometres beyond Forlì's walls on the road to Tuscany. The painting began to work miracles in its own right, and a small roadside shrine was built there in 1629. By the early twenty-first century, the shrine was in disuse but in 2009, it was rebuilt.[6]

Our Lady of Fire (the Madonna del Fuoco) is the patron of Forlì, where her feast lasts from 4 February to the nearest Sunday. The city is ablaze with the blooms of yellow acacias, and stalls in the piazzas sell loaves of sweet Madonna del Fuoco bread baked with anise and raisins.

5 February: Our Lady of Perpetual Help

 URING A SMALLPOX EPIDEMIC, a copy of the Roman icon of Our Lady of Perpetual Help was installed in the church of St Francis in the Bel Air district of Port-au-Prince, Haiti. The icon was taken in procession to a neighbouring hill to bless the suffering city below. Haitians mark the date of 5 February 1882 as the end of the epidemic. Our Lady of Perpetual Help (in Creole, Nòtre Dam Pèpetyèl Sekou) became the official Patroness of Haiti in 1942. In 2007, the Catholic Church there celebrated the 125th anniversary of her miraculous intervention on 5 February. However, not long after the Haitian Catholic Bishops' Conference designated the church in Bel Air the National Shrine of Our Lady of Perpetual Help, it was destroyed in the earthquake of 12 January 2010. The Catholic bishops of Haiti renewed the consecration of their country to Our Lady of Perpetual Help on 8 December 2010. Haiti also honours Our Lady of Perpetual Help on her universal feast day of 27 June.

6 February: Our Lady of Louvain

AINT PETER'S CHURCH, or Sint-Pieterskerk, is the oldest church in Louvain, Belgium, having been founded in about 986. The first church burned to the ground, but the present Gothic style church was begun in 1425. The church suffered severe damage during both World Wars, as in 1914 the roof and nave were burned down, and in 1944 the north aisle suffered bomb damage.

The church of Saint Peter is the home of Our Lady of Louvain, or the Virgin of Louvain, a statue of the Blessed Virgin and her Divine Son, also called the *Sedes Sapientiae*, or Seat of Wisdom. The Virgin of Louvain was a wood statue of the Blessed Virgin Mary carved by Nicolaas De Bruyne in 1442. It is a larger facsimile of an earlier statue dating from the 13th century. That statue was completely destroyed during the Second World War, and not by the Nazis, but instead by allied bombs. It is a replica of Bruyne's famous statue that is currently on display in the church.

Sedes Sapientiae is a specific title for the statue of Our Lady of Louvain, but it is also a type of Christian iconography of the Blessed Mother which depicts the Blessed Virgin seated upon a throne with the Christ Child in her lap. This type of representation of the Blessed Mother became especially popular early in the 13th century, and the throne she sits upon usually has some depiction of lions and the Blessed Virgin's feet are usually shown resting upon a stool, and for good reason.

The "Seat of Wisdom" is a title of Mary that is found in the Litany of Loreto. In the eleventh century, Saint Peter Damian, said of the Blessed Virgin Mary that she is herself that wondrous throne referred to in the Book of Kings. In this he was alluding to Solomon's throne, the throne of the king renowned throughout history for his wisdom. His throne was of ivory overlaid with the finest gold.

> The throne had six steps, and bulls' heads at the back of it, and arms at either side of the seat; two lions stood beside the arms, and twelve lions stood on either side of the six steps. No throne like this was ever made in any other kingdom. (1K 10: 19–20)

Mary is descended from the noble lineage of David. As the Mother of God, the "Seat of Wisdom", the vessel of the Incarnation, who carried and gave birth to the second person of the Blessed Trinity, she herself is in a certain sense the throne upon which the Son of God reigns. This symbol, the *Sedes Sapientiae*, has become the seal for the Catholic University of Louvain. It bears the motto: *Universitas Catholica Lovaniensis. Sedes Sapientiae*, which is Latin for Catholic University of Louvain. Seat of Wisdom.[7]

7 February: Our Lady of Grace

 HERE HAVE BEEN miraculous images of Mary since the beginning of the Catholic Church, some of the very first ones, according to tradition, having been painted by St. Luke, the Evangelist. Since the earliest times, thousands of pictures and statues of the Blessed Virgin Mary have been carved, painted, or fashioned in some way, by all kinds of different people from around the world. Some of these pictures become famous, usually due to some form of miraculous intervention. One such picture is Our Lady of Grace also known as Our Lady of the Bowed Head, in the monastery church of the Carmelites in Vienna, Austria.

A Carmelite Monk, Venerable Dominic of Jesus and Mary, found the image in Rome in 1610. Father Dominic of Jesus and

Mary was born in 1559. He became a Carmelite at an early age, but desiring to live a stricter life, he joined the Discalced Carmelites founded by St. Teresa of Avila, and became its fifth General.) He was looking over an old broken down house which he wanted to convert into a Carmelite Monastery. Fr Dominic walked around the outside of the house and passed by a pile of garbage, but paid no attention to it. But as he entered the house and started looking over the rooms, suddenly he felt the urge to go back to the pile of refuse. Lighting his lantern, the good priest took a closer look at the heap of rubbish. Suddenly his eyes fell upon an old oil painting of the Blessed Virgin Mary! He was shocked! "Who would throw a beautiful picture of Our Lady in the rubbish", he wondered. Then Fr Dominic apologized to Mary, "I am sorry, dear Mother, that someone has treated your image in such a terrible manner. I will take it back to the monastery with me and fix it up, and I will give you the homage which you so rightly deserve."

After returning to the monastery, Dominic cleaned the picture and repainted the damaged parts. Now he could hang the picture up in his cell and give Holy Mary the devotion and attention which she deserved. He prayed to the Madonna with great confidence, asking her for many graces and blessings. One evening when he had just finished sweeping his cell, Fr Dominic noticed that the picture of Our Lady had some dust on it. He was crushed, "Oh, I'm terribly sorry my dearest Mother!" He exclaimed. "I humbly beg your pardon for forgetting to dust your picture." Then taking out his handkerchief he began to dust the picture saying, "O purest and holiest of Virgins, nothing in the whole world is worthy to touch your holy face. Dear Mother, I only have this coarse, old handkerchief and I beg of you to please accept my good will in dusting your image." Fr Dominic continued dusting the picture of Mary, when suddenly the face of Our Lady came to life! She smiled at the holy priest and nodded her head as a sign of thanksgiving. Dominic was afraid that what he was seeing was a trick of the devil. But Our Lady cleared up his doubts saying, "Fear not, my son, for your request is granted!

(Dominic had earlier requested a favour of her.) Your prayer will be answered and will be part of the reward, which you will receive for the love that you have for my Son Jesus and myself. Now Dominic I want you to ask me with all confidence, what favour you would like me to give you." The holy monk then fell upon his knees. "O my dear Mother, I offer myself entirely to you and to your dear Son Jesus, and I desire to do anything that you and Jesus will ask of me. O my Lady, I know that the soul of a benefactor is suffering in Purgatory. Would you please be so kind as to deliver this soul from the fires of Purgatory?" "Dominic, my son", Our Lady encouraged, "I will deliver this soul from Purgatory, if you will make many sacrifices and will have many Masses offered for this soul." Then the apparition of Mary faded away. The good monk hurried to do as Our Lady had asked.

Some time later, when all had been completed, he knelt again before the miraculous painting of Our Lady. Suddenly Mary appeared to him again, but this time she appeared with the soul of the special benefactor, whom she had delivered from Purgatory. The benefactor was grateful, "Thank you, Fr Dominic, for helping to release my soul from the fires of Purgatory with your prayers and sacrifices." "Dominic", Our Lady encouraged, "I would like you to ask me for more favours and blessings. I am the Mother of God and I delight in helping my children to obtain graces for their salvation." Fr Dominic thought for a moment and then spoke, "Dear Mother, would you please be so kind as to listen mercifully to the prayers of all those who will honour your image and ask for your help." Our Lady replied, "All those who ask for my protection and honour this picture with devotion will obtain an answer to their prayers and will receive many graces. Moreover, I will pay special attention to the prayers which are offered to me, for the relief of the souls in Purgatory." The vision of Our Lady soon disappeared and Fr Dominic thought about what he should do: "Our Lady made her promises to all who would honour and pray to her, before this miraculous image. Therefore, I can no longer keep this holy picture in my cell, I must have it put in a church, where the people can honour it." He then took the picture and had it placed in the Oratory of St Charles, which was attached to the Church of Santa Maria alla Scala, in Trastevere, Rome. Many people came to pray before the picture of Our Lady and it became a source of many graces and blessings. The holy image remained at the Oratory until Fr Dominic's death, which occurred in Vienna, on 16 February 1630.

Some copies of the miraculous picture were painted and soon they were honoured in many places. Maximilian, the Duke of Bavaria, had been one of Dominic's good friends, and also a friend of the Carmelites. One day he asked Fr Nicholas, the Vicar General of the Carmelite Order, if he could borrow the miraculous image of Mary. The priest said he could borrow it and the Duke was overjoyed. Arrangements were made, and Br Anastasius of St. Francis was chosen to take the holy picture to Munich, Germany. He had been Fr Dominic's travelling companion for over 15 years, and was most worthy of this honour. On 7 August 1631, Br Anastasius also wrote and signed a special document telling about all the things which Dominic had told him about the miraculous picture and all the miracles related to it. The Duke of Bavaria took the miraculous picture when it arrived in Munich, and kept it for a while. He then gave it to the Carmelite Priests in Munich, who received it with great joy.

Some time later, in 1631, the Carmelites loaned it to Emperor Ferdinand II. He was a very generous man, who founded the Carmelite Monasteries in Prague, Czechoslovakia, and Vienna, Austria. The Emperor and his wife, Empress Eleanor, were delighted when the picture of Our Lady arrived at the palace. They placed it in the palace chapel and had it richly adorned in a splendid fashion. Thus, they honoured the Queen of Heaven in a most glorious manner, a manner that she so much deserved. The Emperor had great confidence in "Our Lady of the Bowed Head", and always begged her to help him with all his difficulties. Ferdinand loved the Most Blessed Virgin very much and he is even supposed to have taken the picture with him every time he had to travel somewhere. Time passed, and one day the good Emperor died. Empress Eleanor then joined the convent of Carmelite Nuns, which she and her husband had founded in Vienna. The miraculous picture of Our Lady was also transferred to the convent, and Eleanor placed it in the chapel, over the main altar. When the Empress died in June 1655, the picture was given back to the Carmelite Fathers. Now the picture was back in a public church where people could pray before this miraculous image of Our Lady. Soon crowds of people were coming to pray before the holy picture. Our Lady did not forget her promise that: "All those who ask for my protection and honour this picture with devotion, will obtain an answer to their prayers and will receive many graces. I will pay special attention to the prayers which are offered to me, for the relief of the souls in Purgatory." When people prayed to Our Lady of the Bowed Head, she heard their prayers and granted them special favours and graces; souls were comforted or released from Purgatory, people were cured and sinners were converted. In time, a new Church and Monastery were built, and on December 14, 1901, the miraculous image of Our Lady was transferred to its new place of honour. Benefactors had built a beautiful altar in honour of Our Lady of the Bowed Head and the holy picture of Mary was placed by this altar. From here it can still be venerated by loving devotees and pilgrims. On 27 September 1931, it was solemnly crowned by Pope Pius XI—the 300th anniversary of its arrival in Vienna. The church can be found in Silbergasse, 35, Vienna, Austria.

Prayer

Virgin most holy, Mother of the Word Incarnate, Treasurer of graces and Refuge of sinners; we fly to your motherly affection with lively faith, and we beg of you the grace to do the will of God. Into your most holy hands we commit the keeping of our hearts, asking you for health of soul and body, in the certain hope that you, our most loving Mother, will hear our prayer. Therefore with lively faith we say: Hail Mary three times.

8 February: Our Lady of Trust

HE PICTURE OF Our Lady of Trust (*Madonna della Fiducia*) was painted by the great Italian painter Carlo Maratta (1625–1713), who was knighted by Pope Clement XI in 1704 and made court painter by King Louis XIV the same year. It is said that the renowned artist gave this painting to a young noble woman, who would become the Abbess of the Convent of Poor Clares of St Francis in the city of Todi. That Abbess, today known as Venerable Sister Clara Isabel Fornari, embraced a severe life of penance and was favoured with many mystical graces; she even received the Sacred Stigmata of Our Lord's Passion. Sister Clara Isabel had a great devotion to the Blessed Mother, like all the saints, and a very special attachment to this maternal image of Our Lady with the Divine Infant. For Our Lady had made a remarkable promise to Sister Clara Isabel that would win special graces for herself, her sisters and all those through the ages who would venerate this image. In Sister Clara Isabel's own words the special promise Our Lady made her with regard to this image was:

> My Heavenly Lady, with the love of a true Mother, assured
> me that She would give a special tenderness and devotion
> toward Her to everyone who contemplated this image.

Due to numerous cures and conversions worked through the intercession of Our Lady of Trust, copies of the portrait were made and circulated. One of these copies was placed in the small chapel of the Roman Major Seminary at the Lateran in Rome. The seminarians soon realized that their prayers and needs were always attended to by the *Madonna della Fiducia*.

Further, Our Lady of Trust protected them in times of crisis. She granted the seminarians full protection against the scourge of Asiatic flu, which claimed many lives in Rome in 1837, and again some 30 years later. During World War I, when over 100 seminarians were forced into the armed services of Italy, they placed themselves under her special care. All returned home safely. To repay the goodness of their Queen, the seminarians crowned both Mother and Child with golden jewelled diadems.

This image encourages and inspires that confidence. In keeping with the Renaissance style of depicting Our Lady and the saints as regional types, the Blessed Virgin, with her auburn hair, hazel eyes and soft complexion, appears as a northern Italian beauty. Serene and noble, She bears in her arms her great Treasure, Who has the commanding air of a Great Prince. With a surprising imperative gesture, Our Lord points directly to His Mother, as if to tell us, "If you would come to Me, go to her. For what she asks of Me, I will give her."

Pope Benedict XVI, speaking to the community of the Roman Major Seminary on the feast of Our Lady of Trust, said:

> It really is very beautiful and meaningful that you venerate the Virgin Mary, Mother of Priests, with the special title of Our Lady of Trust. It evokes a twofold meaning: the trust of the Seminarians who, with her help, set out on their journey in response to Christ who has called them, and the trust of the Church of Rome, especially that of her Bishop, which invokes the protection of Mary, the Mother of every vocation, upon this nursery-garden of priests.[8]

9 February: Our Lady of the Bells

 HE TOWN OF SAINTES was originally a thriving settlement in ancient Gaul (Gallia Aquitania) located along the Charente River. The town became known as *Mediolanum Santonum* once conquered by the Romans under Julius Caesar, and the remains of the triumphal arch of Germanicus and a large amphitheatre can still be seen there today.

The town, located in the Poitou-Charentes region of western France takes its name Saintes from a pious legend. According to this tradition, Mary Salome and Mary Jacob, accompanied by other disciples of Jesus Christ, were forced to flee the Holy Land about the year 45 AD. They left taking a boat with no sail, and were miraculously transported across the Mediterranean Sea, making land near the place which became known as Saintes Maries de la Mer. It is recorded that St Eutropius was a bishop there in the third century, and that the first cathedral was reconstructed by no less a personage than Charlemagne.

Norman invaders twice burned the town during the ninth century. Richard the Lionheart took refuge there against his father, and King Saint Louis IX defeated the English on the plains before the town. The Cathedral of Saint Peter, built in the twelfth century, was severely damaged by the Huguenots in the year 1568. Its bishopric was ended in 1790 as a result of the oppression of the French Revolution. The church is now reduced to being only an historical monument.

It is recorded that, long ago, on the octave day of the Purification,[9] the bells in the Cathedral of Saintes, France, rang out most sweetly of themselves. The sacristans, having run to the church, saw what appeared to be several unknown men holding lighted tapers and melodiously chanting hymns in honour of the Blessed Virgin, Our Lady of the Bells, who was venerated in a chapel of this church. Approaching softly, they—the men who had run to the church—begged the last of these men carrying lighted candles, to give them one in proof of the miracle they had witnessed. The light-bearers graciously complied. This taper, or candle, in remembrance of Our Lady of the Bells, is said to be preserved in that church up to this day.[10]

10 February: Our Lady of the Doves

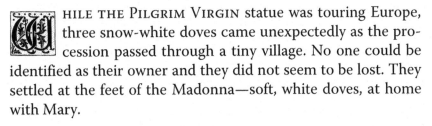 HILE THE PILGRIM VIRGIN statue was touring Europe, three snow-white doves came unexpectedly as the procession passed through a tiny village. No one could be identified as their owner and they did not seem to be lost. They settled at the feet of the Madonna—soft, white doves, at home with Mary.

Day by day as the pilgrimage drew near its destination of Bologna, Italy, the doves stayed on. They left the statue only for short flights, and never all at once. No minute passed that at least one of them was not at Our Lady's feet. When the procession neared the cathedral where the statue was to be enthroned, conjecture was made about the possible action of the doves. Eager eyes watched them as strong arms carried the Madonna to her pedestal in the sanctuary. Softly, the doves hovered over, undisturbed by the noisy devotion of the crowd of Latin enthusiasts for Our Lady—in Italy.

When the statue was finally set firmly and left free to them once more, the doves returned to their resting place, as before, at the feet of Mary. High Mass began at once. Through all the singing and incensing and preaching, the birds remained, watchful but not alarmed. Only as the Mass reached its climax at the Consecration did they stir. Then, as if by instinct, they left the statue and flew to the altar. Upon the high crucifix they perched for the rest of the Mass.

Then, at the end of Mass, with one accord they flew from the church and vanished. The doves of Mary had escorted her, Our Lady of the Doves, to the palace of the King. Earthly royalty selects eagles for insignia. Mary, Queen of Peace and Mother of the Prince of Peace, selects doves.[11] This type of incident has occurred several times, at a variety of different locations, in recent history.

11 February: Our Lady of Lourdes

N 1858, THERE LIVED in the village of Lourdes, a little peasant girl, Bernadette Soubirous, 14 years old, uneducated, simple, poor, good. On 11 February, she was sent with two more girls to collect wood. They walked to the Rock of Massabielle, where the two companions crossed a mountain stream; while Bernadette was removing her shoes to follow them she became conscious of a ravishing beautiful Lady, standing in the hollow of the rock, looking at her. Bernadette fell involuntarily upon her knees, gazing enraptured at the lovely Lady, who smiled lovingly at Bernadette and then disappeared.

The mysterious Lady from heaven appeared in all, eighteen times to the little girl and among other things told her to drink the water from a mysterious fountain which was not yet observed. Bernadette scratched in the sand at a spot indicated, and water began to trickle through the earth; after a few days there gushed forth every day 27,000 gallons of pure, clear spring water, and this water flows still.

Bernadette was asked by Our Lady of Lourdes, who always showed her a sweet heavenly courtesy, to request the priest to have a church built on the spot, that processions should be made to the grotto, that people should drink of the water. The main emphasis of her message was that the faithful should visit the grotto in order to offer prayer and penance for their sins and for those of the whole world.

On the 25 March 1858, in answer to Bernadette's inquiry, "Who are you?" the Lady answered, "I am the Immaculate Conception." This was remarkable as it confirmed the definition by Blessed Pius IX of the dogma in 1854. In 1862, the Bishop declared upon an exhaustive and scrupulous investigation, to the faithful, that they were "justified in believing the reality of the apparitions". In 1873, a basilica was built on top of the rock and in 1883 another church was built below and in front of the rock. From 1867 when records began to be kept till 1908, about 5,000,000 pilgrims had visited the grotto. Although Our Lady never at any time promised that pilgrims who visited the grotto would be healed of their physical ills, remarkable cures began at once and have continued ever since. Many of them are of such a character that they can be ascribed only to supernatural power. Bernadette died in 1879 at the age of 35, and was later canonized. The body of the blessed Saint can still be seen in its glass coffin, intact and incorrupt, looking as its photographs show, like a young woman asleep. The chair at which she prayed, the altar where she received her First Holy Communion, the bed in which she slept, the room in which she lived—all can be seen at Lourdes.[12]

Lourdes is one of the greatest Marian shrines in the world. Here, praying to Our Lady of Lourdes, one may obtain refreshment, courage, energy and inspiration to continue the age-old struggle of the great Catholic Faith against the forces of darkness and disintegration. This great shrine, all its miracles, and the streams of grace that are poured into the world through Our Lady of Lourdes, were made possible through the faithfulness and the sanctity of a little peasant girl. Since the appearances of Our Lady to young Bernadette in 1858, more than 200 million people have visited the shrine of Lourdes.

12 February: Our Lady of Argenteuil

N ABOUT THE YEAR 500, Clovis was the King of the Franks, but he was not yet a Catholic. Years passed as his wife Clotilda prayed for her husband to convert, yet always King Clovis demurred. Then one fateful day Clovis was engaged in a desperate battle, finding himself sorely tried. At the point of ruin he cried aloud to the God to assist him, promising to forsake his pagan gods if he were granted a miraculous victory. Looking up to heaven, Clovis cried:

> Jesus Christ, whom Clotilda declares to be the Son of the Living God, who it is said gives aid to the oppressed and victory to those who put their hope in You, I beseech the glory of Your aid! If You shall grant me victory over these enemies with that power which people consecrated to Your name say they have proved concerning You, I will believe in You and be baptized in Your name. For I have called upon my gods, but, as I have proved, they are far removed from my aid. So I believe that they have no power, for they do not succour those who serve them. Now I call upon You, and I long to believe in You—all the more that I may escape my enemies!

God was pleased to answer Clovis' petition immediately, for no sooner had he prayed than his enemies fled the field. Clovis won the battle, and he was a man of his word. Hating his former error, Clovis converted to the True Faith. He founded the original convent church at Argenteuil.

It is related in the Gospels that Christ's executioners played dice over His tunic. This tunic was originally documented as being seamless and of-a-piece, fitting the description found in the Gospel according to John (Jn 19:23–24). According to legend, that tunic was found in the fourth century by Saint Helena, the mother of Emperor Constantine. It was then kept at Constantinople until the eighth century. In the year 800, the Empress Irene of Byzantium offered Charlemagne the Holy Tunic at his coronation as Emperor of the West. The emperor then gave the relic to the priory of Argenteuil when his daughter, Théodrade, became abbess of the Monastery of the Humility of Our Lady of Argenteuil.

In the year 850 the Normans plundered the village of Argenteuil, including the Basilica of Saint Dennis, but the tunic was hidden in a wall before their arrival. When the abbey was rebuilt in 1003, the relic was restored. It is venerated until the 16th century when it was partially burned by Huguenots in 1567.

During the French Revolution the Benedictine priory was destroyed, and the relic then given to a parish church for safekeeping. In 1793, a priest found it necessary to cut it into pieces and bury them in his garden to protect them from profanation. In 1795, after the priest's imprisonment had ended, the Holy Tunic appeared again and the different fragments were sewn back together.

The Holy Tunic measures nearly 1.5 metres by 1 metre and the fibres are wool and of a very regular size. It is a soft, lightweight fabric, and the weaving is uniform and regular with a twisted "Z", made on a primitive loom. The tunic is remarkable for a tunic woven manually, as it is made without any seam, including the sleeves. The dark brown fabric is typical of the clothing in the early centuries of the Christian era. The fabric was dyed brown, using a method widely in practice at the time by people of modest means. The construction and dyeing show the tunic to date from the time of Christ. It is the garment worn by Christ after the Flagellation and along the road to Calvary as He carried His cross. Christ's blood and sweat thus impregnate the fabric. In 1985 a test was done showing the blood was type AB. Pollen common to Palestine has also been found in the fabric.

The relic was displayed again in the nineteenth century, and pilgrimages resumed. On the 13 of December in 1983, the parish priest of Saint Denis discovered the tunic had been stolen. On 2 February 1984, Father Guyard received a phone call from a stranger promising to return the treasure to the condition that their names would be kept secret. That same evening the tunic, with its case, was found in the Basilica of Saint Denis. The last solemn exposition of the tunic took place during the Easter holiday in 1984. In six days, approximately 80,000 people came to see the tunic. In honour of the Year of Mercy decreed by Pope Francis Mgr Stanislas LaLanne, Bishop of Pontoise and Guardian of the Holy Tunic announced that the relic was to be exhibited to the public for a very brief time: from 25 March to 10 April 2016.

13 February: Our Lady of Sant'Apollinare

SANT'APOLLINARE ALLE TERME is an eighteenth century former collegiate church of ancient foundation located in the Piazza di Sant'Apollinare n the rione Ponte in Rome. The church was described as being a small basilica, with a nave and aisles separated by arcades having re-used ancient columns. There was a transept, then an apse which contained a mosaic. In front of the church entrance was a loggia, on which was a venerated icon of Our Lady, which had been installed on the testamentary instructions of Cardinal William d'Estouteville in 1484, the year after his death. He had his Roman residence in a palazzo to the right of the church. The icon shows the (on the left) and St Peter, and is in a Mannerist style described as Roman-Umbrian.

In December 1494 the image was covered with a layer of dull and colourless plaster to hide it from the soldiers of Charles the VIII as well as to protect it from the dangers arising from the struggle between the Orsini and the militias of the Seneschal Belcari that were encamped in the portico. The fresco was subsequently forgotten through time. Some 153 years later on 13 February 1647 during a small earthquake, two boys and a soldier took refuge in the church loggia and saw the plaster coating covering the icon of Our Lady in the loggia fall off. The picture thus revealed became the focus of intense devotion on the part of the local faithful. The image was 'crowned' by the Vatican Chapter of the Vatican Basilica in 1653. At the base of the throne there is an inscription that is believed to have been appended during the plague of 1657:

> Our Lady, Reparatrix of our concord and that of all Christians, intercede for us before God to free us from the plague epidemic and from all evils present and to come. Amen.[13]

13 February is thus the liturgical feast day of Our Lady of St Apollinare, in memory of the rediscovery of her holy image in Rome.

14 February: Our Lady of Pellevoisin

HE LITTLE VILLAGE of Pellevoisin lies not far from Tours in France. It is in Berry, to the west of Châteauroux, in the Archdiocese of Bourges. In 1876 a young woman, Estelle Faguette, at the age of 33, lay dying of pulmonary tuberculosis, of an acute peritonitis and an abdominal tumour—with only five hours to live in the opinion of the doctors. However, on the 14 February, when all were expecting her death, Our Lady appeared near the sickbed. This occurred on three successive nights, and then, as Our Lady had promised, the sick woman was instantly cured on a Saturday. During the visits, Our Lady of Pellevoisin frequently spoke to Estelle, on the same theme she so often has expressed during the past hundred years:

> What afflicts me most is the lack of respect for my Son that people show at Holy Communion and the prayerful attitude that they adopt while their mind is really on other things. I mean this of people who make a show of piety.

For some months after her miraculous cure, Estelle continued to live quietly at Pellevoisin. She was at a loss to find the means of fulfilling the mission entrusted to her by Our Lady. Her heavenly visitor, however, was watching over her, and Estelle was to see her again and receive more detailed instructions as to what was required of her. On the feast of Our Lady's visitation in the same year, 1876, as Estelle was praying in her room, she was granted another vision. Our Lady, robed in white and wearing on her breast a white scapular with the image of the Sacred Heart of Jesus, appeared to her favoured friend. This was the first of a series of wonderful visions enjoyed by Estelle. Again and again Mary pointed to the great need for penance and expiation—a return to God.[14]

During one of these apparitions, Our Lady of Pellevoisin, taking her white scapular in her hand, held it before Estelle saying, "I love this devotion." Immediately Estelle knew that her life's work was to propagate devotion to the Sacred Heart by means of a scapular modelled on Mary's. On her last appearance, December 8th, Our Lady commanded Estelle to approach her Bishop and give him a copy of the new scapular:

> Tell him to help you with all his power, and that nothing would be more agreeable to me than to see this badge on each one of my children, in reparation for the outrages that my Son suffers in the Sacrament of His Love. See, the graces I pour upon those who wear it with confidence, and who help to make it known.

The Prelate in question, the Archbishop of Bourges, gave Estelle a favourable hearing and immediately set up a commission to investigate the whole matter. The result of all this was the establishment at Pellevoisin in 1894 by Pope Leo XIII of an Archconfraternity under the title of Mother of Mercy, Our Lady of Pellevoisin. The membership of this Confraternity had gone on increasing year after year, while Pellevoisin itself has become a center of pilgrimages for thousands of Mary's friends.

Estelle lived her quiet and peaceful life at Pellevoisin, neither desiring nor receiving any personal credit. She died in 1929. Although no formal approval has been granted acknowledging the authenticity of the events at Pellevoisin either by the local bishop at Bourges or by the Holy See, numerous acts at a secondary level of approval, including recognition of Mary's scapular request, have been granted. Pope Leo XIII, on 20 December 1892, by a *Motu Proprio* granted indulgences to encourage the pilgrimage to Pellevoisin, and on 4 April 1900, the Congregation of Rites issued a decree granting approval to the Scapular of the Sacred Heart.

On 17 October 1915, Pope Benedict XV commented that Our Lady had chosen Pellevoisin as a privileged place to dispense her graces. On 22 December 1922, the Congregation of Rites authorised a votive Mass of Our Lady of Pellevoisin to be celebrated on 9 September in the parish church and adjoining monastery. On 7 June 1936, via Cardinal Pacelli (later to become Pope Pius XII), Pius XI sent a painting of Our Lady of Pellevoisin as a gift to the Dominican community who were looking after the place of pilgrimage. On 7 December 1981, Archbishop Paul Vignancour established a medical commission to examine Estelle's apparently miraculous cure. On 6 September 1982, having received its report that the cure was indeed inexplicable in the light of present-day medical science, the Archbishop established a theological commission to consider whether this cure might appropriately be called miraculous. On 4 September 1983, while speaking at the annual pilgrimage to Pellevoisin, he announced the commission's

findings that Estelle's cure did indeed have a miraculous character. This was formally confirmed in writing on 8 September. On
19 September 1984, an Imprimatur was granted for a novena to
Our Lady of Pellevoisin.

Estelle Faguette addressed this prayer to our Lady in 1876,
begging for a cure as she was suffering greatly from peritonitis:

> Mother of Mercy, here I am once again at your feet
> You cannot refuse to hear me
> You have not forgotten that I am your child and that I love you
> From your Divine Son and for his glory grant me then the grace—
> Remember then the sufferings that you endured that night of the
> Savior's birth,
> when you had to go from door to door seeking shelter.
> Remember too what you suffered when Jesus was extended on the
> cross.
> I have confidence in you, O Mother of Mercy.
> If you will it, your Son will grant what I ask.
> Deign to listen to my supplications and repeat them to him.
> That he will grant me this grace—if such is his good pleasure, but
> may his will be done and not mine.
> May he grant me at least an entire submission to his designs.
> and that this will serve for my salvation and that of sinners.
> You possess my heart, O Mother Most Merciful, to do all that
> depends on me for your glory and that of your Divine Son.
> Take under your protection all those who are dear to me.
> O Blessed Virgin, grant that I will imitate your obedience and that
> one day in eternity I shall, with you, possess Jesus.

15 February: Our Lady of Paris

 HERE DOES NOT SEEM to be a great deal of information
about Our Lady of Paris; it is an ancient title, and can be
traced well back before the twelfth Century, when the
Cathedral of Notre Dame de Paris (Our Lady of Paris) was begun.
Some authorities say that veneration of the Blessed Virgin in Paris
can be traced to the first apostles of the city. Since Saint Paul was

in Gaul (France) during his travels, it may be assumed that this veneration dates to the first century of the Christian era. And if Mary was venerated in Paris at that early date, it is possible that she was, even then, known as Our Lady of Paris. Briefly, as long as Christian minds can be remembered, Paris was consecrated to the Virgin Mary, whom the inhabitants always venerated.

It is known that Our Lady of Paris was a church first built by King Childebert in the year 522. About the year 1257, the King Saint Louis IX assisted in the construction of a larger church carried on in the same place, on the foundations which King Philip Augustus had laid in the year 1191. The older church built by King Childebert, which had been dedicated to the Blessed Virgin, had became too ruinous to be repaired, so Maurice, Bishop of Paris, decided to rebuild it and at the same time adorn Paris with a Cathedral that would outshine all those which had hitherto been built anywhere.

Plans were drawn up during the reign of King Louis VII, and work had actually begun on Notre Dame de Paris, Notre Dame Cathedral, in 1162. The cornerstone was laid in the presence of Pope Alexander III. Notre Dame is a huge Gothic cathedral on the Île de la Cité, with beautiful flying buttresses to support the tremendous height of the walls, and are adorned with stylish gargoyles. It is home to a reliquary which contains Christ's Crown of Thorn. By the beginning of the fourteenth century, perhaps 1345, the cathedral was finished, virtually as it stands today. Some time during the building of the Cathedral, a statue of Our Lady was fashioned and installed in place.

As was typical, the cathedral was desecrated during the French Revolution, and many of the religious artefacts were lost to future generations.

> Rampaging regicides tore through the cathedral, plundering, pillaging, and desecrating its treasures in an attempt to eradicate religion in France. The rabble removed crosses and crucifixes and replaced statues of the Virgin Mary with Lady Liberty. They beheaded statues of the kings of Judah,

whom they mistook for French kings, on the façade. They
replaced the Mass with political rallies, dedicating the
shrine to the Cult of Reason and Cult of the Supreme
Being. They stole all the great bells except one (which was
kept as an alarm), and melted them down to make cannons. They turned the House of God into a food warehouse. Ultimately they intended to tear it down and sell it
off piecemeal as building materials, but Napoleon acted in
time to block that. Ever aware of the importance of
symbols, he decreed that it be salvaged and redecorated
for his coronation.[15]

The incredible stained glass windows were not destroyed in the
French revolution, including the spectacular "rose window" that
can still be seen today. Victor Hugo wrote about his beloved
church: "Assuredly, the Cathedral of Notre Dame de Paris is, to
this day, a majestic and sublime edifice."[16]

16 February: Our Lady of the Thorn

 N THE VIGIL of the Feast of the Annunciation, 24 March
in the year 1400, some shepherds tending their flocks
were attracted by a bright light coming from the Chapel
of Saint John the Baptist near Châlons-sur-Marne, France. As
they approached the light they saw that it was actually a thorn
bush fully engulfed in flames, and they discovered a statue of the
Blessed Virgin standing unharmed in the midst of the flames. In
fact, though the fire burned brightly, the branches and leaves of
the thorn bush were unaffected by the flames.

The miracle continued all that night and into the next day,
and news of the miracle spread quickly. Crowds of people
gathered around the burning bush that was so reminiscent of the
one witnessed by Moses on Mount Horeb. (Ex 3:1–6) St Gregory
of Nyssa sees in the Burning Bush (Ex 3:2) a prefiguration of
Mary's virginity. Like the bush which was aflame but not consumed, Mary brought the Light to the world but was not cor-

rupted, for the Light "kept the burning bush incorrupt; the sprout of her virginity was not withered by her childbearing".[17]

The Bishop of Châlons, Charles of Poiters, also witnessed the burning bush and the miraculous statue—both still unaffected by the fire. When the flames finally died down, the bishop reverently took the statue and carried it in his own hands to the nearby Chapel of Saint John. On the very site of the miracle, construction of a church was begun for the enshrinement of the miraculous statue. Since the church was built so rapidly—in a little over 24 years—a charming local legend claims that angels continued the work at night after the labourers had left for home.

Our Lady of the Thorn (Notre Dame de l'Épine) became a place of pilgrimage very rapidly. Today a minor basilica, the shrine proved to be so beautiful that the people considered it a worthy place to venerate the Blessed Virgin. The flamboyant Gothic church boasts majestic great doors, a splendid rosette decorating the principle entrance and two chiseled stone spires, rises high and imposing on the plain in Champagne.

During the terrors of the French Revolution, the statue of Our Lady of Thorns was removed from the main altar and hidden for safekeeping. After it had ended, the statue was brought back out for veneration. Many healings have also been reported at the shrine, many verified by physicians. The beautiful church of Our Lady of the Thorn has been recognized by several popes, including Pope Callixtis III, Pius II, and Gregory XV. Pope Leo XIII ordered the solemn coronation of the miraculous statue, saying,

> Yes, Our Lady of the Thorn will be crowned in my name.
> Prepare for her a diadem worthy of the Mother of God and
> the people whom she protects.

It is a place of grandeur where Christian souls can expand in adoration of the Son of God, and many are the pilgrims of all descriptions who have visited the shrine over the years, including Saint Joan of Arc in 1429. The basilica was classified a historic monument in 1840. In 1998 it was registered on the World

Heritage List by UNESCO under the title of "roads in France to St James de Compostela". Notre-Dame de l'Épine has always welcomed travellers and inspired writers, including Victor Hugo, Alexandre Dumas and Paul Claudel.

17 February: Seven Holy Founders of the Servite Order

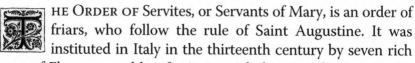 HE ORDER OF Servites, or Servants of Mary, is an order of friars, who follow the rule of Saint Augustine. It was instituted in Italy in the thirteenth century by seven rich men of Florence, and has for its special object meditation on the Dolours of the most holy Virgin, that its members may feel and share them with her, and propagate this devotion among the faithful.

The coming of the Friars took place in the very heart of the Middle Ages, along with other great founders like St Dominic (born 1170) and St Francis (born 1182); St Buonfiglio, the eldest of the Servites, was born in 1198. The special charism of each of the three Orders was closely allied to those of the others. St Dominic took the doctrine of Christ as his charge, to preach it everywhere, and set it forth in all its splendour; St. Francis embraced Christian morality, to practise it in all its heroism, and show the inexpressible sweetness which underlay its most austere observances. The Seven Holy Founders of the Servite Order, like loving and tender children, devoted themselves to Mary, who had borne Christ Himself in her immaculate bosom, Christ, source of all truth and principle of all good; to her, the inseparable coadjutrix of Jesus in the redemption of souls; to her who gave to the world the Word full of grace and truth, the Saviour sacrificed in His infinite love for the salvation and the blessing of all men. Thus while St Dominic and St Francis manifested Christ to those eager to know and to love Him, the seven Saints of Florence showed forth the sweet and radiant face of the Virgin, the Mother who from Bethlehem to Calvary encircles with her glory those who love her Son.

Between the years 1225 and 1227 these seven young Florentines joined the Confraternity of the Blessed Virgin—popularly known as the *Laudesi* or Praisers. It was a period when the prosperous city of Florence was being rent by political factions and distracted by the heresy of the Cathars who despied material creation; it was also a period of general relaxation of morals even where devotional practices were retained.

The eldest was Buonfiglio Monaldo, who became their leader. The others were Alexis Falconieri, Benedict dell'Antella, Bartholomew Amidei, Ricovero Uguccione, Gerardino Sostegni, and John Buonagiunta. They had as their spiritual director James of Poggibonsi, who was chaplain of the Laudesi, a man of great holiness and spiritual insight. All of them came to realize the call to a life of renunciation, and they determined to have recourse to our Lady in their perplexity. On the feast of the Assumption, as they were absorbed in prayer, they saw her in a vision, and were inspired by her to withdraw from the world into a solitary place and to live for God alone. There were difficulties, because, though three of them were celibates, four had been married and had ties, although two had become widowers. Suitable provision for their dependents was arranged, and with the approval of the bishop they withdrew from the world and betook themselves to a house called *La Carmarzia*, outside the gates of Florence, twenty-three days after they had received their call.

After many other difficulties, the group devoted themselves to prayer for light, and again they had a vision of our Lady, who bore in her hand a black habit while an angel held a scroll inscribed with the title of Servants of Mary. She told them she had chosen them to be her servants, that she wished them to wear the black habit, and to follow the Rule of St Augustine. From that date, 13 April 1240, they were known as the Servants of Mary, or Servites. One of the seven, Alexis Falconieri, died on 17 February 1310, so this day is the feast of the seven holy founders. This hymn is devoted to them:

The fathers lived a life in shade,
Yet seemed to Peter's vision seven
White glistening lilies for the Maid,
The Queen of heaven,

Through city streets, o'er hills and plains,
Upborne by love divine, they trod,
To fix in men the Mother's pains,
The swords of God.

This was the power in which they spoke,
Till each wild passion owned their sway:
They cheered the sad, from sinners broke
Their chains away.

Till at last the Virgin Queen
Led them to mansions in the sky,
Mansions where garlands aye are green,
And never die.

May they hear cries of all who pray,
And see how hard our earthly strife:
Aiding us onward to the day
When all is life.

Now to the Father thanks and praise;
To Thee, O Son, the same we send;
To thee, great Spirit, through all days,
World without end. Amen.

18 February: Mother of God, the Seeker of the Perishing

 N THE MID-EIGHTEENTH century, in the village of Bor of Kaluga governance, the pious peasant Theodotus Obukhov lost his way in a blizzard on the Feast of the Baptism of the Lord. His horse was exhausted and paused on the edge of an impassable ravine. Not seeing any way to save himself, Obukhov lay down in his sleigh, where he began to freeze. In these terrible moments he prayed with all his being to the Queen of Heaven for help, and he vowed that if he was rescued he would have a "Seeker of the Perishing" icon painted and donate it to the local church. Our Lady heard his prayer and helped him in a marvellous way. A certain peasant in the nearby village heard a voice outside his window saying "Take him." He went out and saw the half-frozen Obukhov on his sleigh. When he recovered his health, Obukhov immediately fulfilled his vow and commissioned a copy of the icon from the St George church in the city of Bolkhov in the Orlov governance.

From that time the Bor "Seeker of the Perishing" Icon was glorified by many manifestations of grace and miracles. There are other "Seeker of the Perishing" Icons: one manifested itself in 1770 in the village of Malizhino in Kharkov governance, and delivered the people from cholera three times; there was another in the village of Krasnoe in Chernigov governance, and another from Voronezh and Kozlov in Tambov governance. In the year 1835, at the Moscow Alexandrov Orphanage Institute, a church was consecrated in honour of the "Seeker of the Perishing" Icon. Of particular interest is the "Seeker of the Perishing" Icon in the Church of the Glorious Resurrection in Moscow. This icon had been transferred from the church of the Nativity of Christ to the Palashevska alley. Its final owner had become widowed and was on the verge of complete poverty.

Fervent prayer to the Most Holy Theotokos saved him from despair and arranged matters for his daughters. This man felt that he was not worthy to have this miraculuos icon in his house, so he gave it to the church. In 1812 the Palashevsk church was pillaged by the French. The desecrated icon was found broken into three pieces among the rubble. After the icon had been found, numerous miracles of healing took place. Brides entering into marriage pray before this icon that their marriage might be a happy one. People come to it, overwhelmed by drunkenness, perishing in poverty, suffering in illness, and they turn to the Icon

in prayer as to a Mother with her perishing children. The Queen
of Heaven sends down help and support for all:

> Seek us who are perishing, O Most Holy Virgin, chasten
> us not according to our sins, but as you are merciful in
> your love for mankind, have pity, deliver us from hell,
> sickness and necessity, and save us.

19 February: Our Lady of Good Tidings

N 23 DECEMBER 1563, the bishop of Luçon (a town in
the Vendée department of France) Jean-Baptiste Tierce-
lin, consecrated the church under the patronage of the
Blessed Virgin, Notre-Dame-de-Bonne-Nouvelle. This first
chapel under that patronage came into the world in the midst of
religious convulsions that were then taking place in Switzerland,
Germany, and England by the leaders of the Reformation, and
was an action courageously going against the tide. The religious
wars that began raging in France ten years after its erection began
to be another reason for some concern for faithful Catholics, but
the pilgrimages to the church of Notre-Dame-de-Bonne-Nouvelle continued undisturbed. From time immemorial there had
been venerated at Notre Dame a statue of the Blessed Virgin,
holding in her arm the Infant Jesus. Many went to her in
procession, especially children, who came each year to ask Mary
for perseverance after their first communion.

The revolutionary turmoil in France, which was to shake the
throne and the altar, also affected the parish of Our Lady of Good
Tidings. In 1790, the National Assembly decreed a new law in
which the church of Our Lady of Good Tidings was dissolved. As
the pastor, M. Fabre, had the courage to refuse the oath of the
Civil Constitution of the Clergy, he was thrown into the street.

A short time later, on 22 May 1791, the abbé Fourquet de
Damalis gathered in the church a large assembly of the faithful.
This occurred under the noses of twelve national guardsmen, and
so the police commissioner, a man named Cafin, arrived there

quickly. He asked the abbot why this meeting was taking place, and the priest answered him that he was explaining to the faithful the decrees of the National Assembly for the public good. The commissioner accepted the explanation, and since the meeting had been perfectly peaceful, the commissioner was obliged to agree to the monthly meetings and record it in his minutes.

One might think that worship would have been suspended at Notre-Dame-de-Bonne-Nouvelle during the Terror, but there is evidence to the contrary. As at Chartres, a great number of the faithful remained active and opposed the removal of the sacred ornaments of the church and defended their priests, and eager to fulfil their religious duties, they were not to be intimidated by the fear of imprisonment and even death. From the registry of marriages and baptisms, including a few that date back to 1793, we know that there were religious ceremonies such as baptisms and weddings held there secretly, sometimes in an oratory, sometimes in the church.

In the year 1818 a severe epidemic ravaged the country. The faithful vowed, with the agreement of their bishop, to go in procession to Our Lady of Good Tidings and celebrate in perpetuity the feast of the Visitation, which was the feast of the chapel. The procession took place, and God quickly put an end to the scourge of the plague. At about that time, a young boy began making regular visits to the church of Our Lady of Good Tidings, who was the patroness of the village. He was a poor boy materially, for Lempdes was one of the poorer villages in France, and he had been born into a peasant family that was struggling to eke out a living in the wreck of post-revolutionary France. He kept the faith, and when he grew up, this boy Jean-Baptiste Lamy was ordained a priest, eventually becoming the first Archbishop of Santa Fe, New Mexico.

20 February: Our Lady of Boulogne

NE DAY TOWARDS dusk in about the year 636, when Saint Audomare was bishop of the diocese, the people of Boulogne were gathered in a thatch-roofed chapel, located in the upper part of the city, when the Mother of God appeared and told the faithful to go to the river bank where a wonderful visitor was awaiting them. They ran to the designated place and found a boat without sails, oars, or sailors, on which stood a wooden statue of the Virgin, about one metre in height, holding the Child Jesus on her left arm. All this was diffusing an extraordinary impression of peace, calm, and happiness.

In the year 1104, Countess Ida de Bouillon, the mother of the famous Crusader Godfrey, King of Jerusalem, built a Romanesque church to house the statue. The construction work lasted 200 years and the Gothic choir was finished only in the beginning of sixteenth century. Already in the thirteenth century, it is said that Boulogne was similar to Lourdes in popularity. From the twelfth to the thirteenth century, pilgrims flocked to Boulogne, which became a stop on the road to Santiago de Compostela. One stopped in Boulogne, coming from England or the Netherlands, or returning to Spain or Italy. There exist many records of pilgrims from the famous Lanfranc, Archbishop of Canterbury, from Saint Bernard, and, in the Middle East, around 1050, from the bishops of Antioch and Mount Sinai. Later, in the thirteenth century, King Philip Augustus, Saint Louis, Henry III of England, and Francis I also visited the shrine. Many healings obtained through Our Lady of Boulogne were recorded in those times. Chaucer, in his famous *The Wife of Bath's Tale*, called Boulogne one of the most important shrines in Christendom.

The dedication of a new church built in honour of Our Lady of Boulogne was consecrated in the year 1469 by Bishop Chartier of Paris. The confraternity of Our Lady of Boulogne was so illustrious that six French kings chose to belong to it. The popularity of the Virgin of the Sea continued to increase until the year 1544, when the church was pillaged and the miraculous statue taken to England where it remained for many years. King Henry VIII is reported to have stolen the statue of Our Lady of Boulogne and taken it to England. After many negotiations, the French managed to get it back.

In 1553, the Emperor Charles V pillaged Therouanne, just outside Boulogne, which was the seat of the bishopric. Consequently the ordinary decided to reside in Boulogne and the church became a cathedral. During the sixteenth century, the period of the Wars of Religion, the Huguenots attacked Boulogne cathedral, breaking windows, burning the woodwork, and mostly directing their efforts to destroying the statue by fire, but in vain. The statue was finally thrown on a pile of manure and then down a well. The very devout wife of a Huguenot secretly withdrew it from the well and hid it in her attic, where it remained for over 30 years before it was returned to the cathedral. The statue was in very bad condition, but the continuation of miracles kept proving its authenticity. In 1630, Bishop Le Bouthiller rebuilt the cathedral.

The cathedral flourished until the French Revolution when the 1790 Civil Constitution of the Clergy brought it under government control. The miraculous statue of Our Lady of Boulogne was burnt in 1793. Its right hand, which had broken a little while before, is the sole vestige of the original statue, a piece of the hand can be found inside a copper reliquary under the dome. The cathedral served as an arsenal, warehouse, then sold to foreign traders, and it was demolished stone by stone.

Beginning in 1820, a priest, Fr Haffreingue, dedicated his life to rebuilding the cathedral, and he himself served as the architect, using as his inspiration St Paul's Cathedral in London and other major Roman basilicas. 160 men worked on the site, with whom he mingled willingly. He wanted the cathedral to be seen all the way from England and that it be like a permanent prayer lifted toward heaven for the unity of Protestant and Catholic communities, in a single Church. Fr Haffreingue was a very humble man.

On the outside, in front of the parvis,[18] is inscribed above the central portal "A Domino factum est" (This is the work of the Lord).

The terrors of World War II almost completely destroyed the statue. From 1943 to 1948, four reproductions of Our Lady of Boulogne (also known as Our Lady of the Great Return) were made, each mounted on a skiff. They toured nearly 750,000 miles across France, visiting 16,000 parishes and causing a surge of new faith, prayers and conversions in its path. The statue of Our Lady, carried as it stood in a boat, accompanied pleas for the deliverance of France, which took on a new sense in the context of World War II. One of these statues was taken to Walsingham, England in 1948 and carried in procession by the Cross-bearing pilgrimage when many other statues and images of the Virgin visited England.

21 February: Our Lady of Good Haven

N 1838, THE FORTY-EIGHT MEMBER CREW of a vessel which had just arrived at Paimpol, in Brittany, France, fulfilled a vow they had made on a most perilous voyage across the Atlantic, from Newfoundland, Canada. A terrific storm had broken, their sails were torn, and for three days they were in continual danger of finding a watery grave. The ship began to fill with water, and all hope of safety seemed lost, when the crew, by common consent, turned their eyes to Our Lady, Star of the Sea, and asked for good haven. They promised if she saved them, they would visit in the most devout and supplicant manner the church at Paimpol, where there is an image of Our Lady much venerated by the people. They had scarcely ended their prayer, when the weather became calmer and the waves began to subside.

Profiting by this providential change, they repaired their sails, and enjoyed a favourable wind till they reached the coast of Brittany. They landed in safety toward the decline of day, and their first act was to prostrate themselves on the ground, and give God thanks for their return. They then intoned the Litany of the Blessed Virgin, and advanced barefooted and bare-headed along the banks and through the streets of Paimpol, to the church of the Good Haven. The people gathered by the novelty of the sight, followed them. There were parents who went to give thanks to Our Lady of Good Haven for the return of their sons, and wives who thanked Mary for restoring their husbands to them. Tears streamed down every eye, and the immense multitude knelt down before the altar of that powerful Virgin, who had received from her Son power to command wind and wave.[19]

The torches shed a dim light on the recess of the sanctuary, where the image of the Blessed Virgin stood, Our Lady of Good Haven, whose inclined head and extended arms seemed to say to all, "Come to me, I am your Mother." These pious mariners with the most touching expression of sentiment, chanted the hymn, *Ave Maris Stella* in which they were joined in gratitude by the people.

> Bright Mother of our Maker, hail!
> Thou Virgin ever blest,
> The ocean's star, by which we sail,
> And gain the port of rest.

22 February: Our Lady of the Divine Tears

ERNUSCO SUL NAVIGLIO is a town about twenty kilometres from Milan. It was to become the place of foundation of the Institute of the Sisters of Saint Marcellina, popularly known as the Marcelline. In 1838, Monsignor Luigi Biraghi founded an institute of religious women, whose members would educate young people, and would thus help give a solid foundation to the family.[20] The college of Marcelline sisters of Cernusco was later used as a retirement home for the elderly and sick sisters. In 1922, a young nun was brought there, Sister Elisabetta Redaelli, suffering from frequent haemoptysis.[21] Until 1922 she had always been in good health. That year, however, at 25 years of age, she started suffering from meningitis. This was followed by pulmonary tuberculosis, progressive muscular paralysis and, within a year, total blindness.

On 6 January 1924, something occurred that changed the course of her life. At 10.30 that night, Sr Elisabetta's room-mates heard her speaking aloud. They thought she was talking in her sleep and did not disturb her. But she was not sleeping at all. She was conversing with a "beautiful lady" who had come to visit her, she said later. The lady comforted her, and encouraged her to bear all her suffering for the love of God. Sr Elisabetta said to her: "Oh dear Lady, you are so good; please pray for me. God will certainly listen to your prayers." "Pray, trust and hope. I will return on the night between the 22nd and the 23rd", the Lady said. For some reason Sr Elisabetta had understood, "on the night between the 2nd and the 3rd". "My dear Lady, please go and comfort also the other sick sisters as you have comforted me." The Lady smiled gently and disappeared.

The following month, on 3 February, Sister Elizabeth was found in tears: she had understood that the Lady would return from the 2nd to the 3rd of the following month, and she feared that the Lady had not appeared because she was not "good enough" as she repeated the other nuns. At 11:45 pm on 22 February, the day on which the doctor had already diagnosed her condition as desperate, she saw the supernatural visitor, recognizing her as Our Lady. She was wearing a light blue cloak and clutching to her heart the Child Jesus, and large tears flowed down His Face. He did not cry, though, because of the sins of the seer: "My Baby cries" said the Virgin with a rueful smile, "because He is not sufficiently loved, sought, desired even by the people that are consecrated to Him." Despite the fact that Sister Elizabeth had asked to be taken up to Heaven, because by now she felt she was a burden to the sisters, the heavenly visitor replied: "You must stay here, to recount this." Suddenly, the sick sister felt she should ask for a sign to be believed. Our Lady replied: "I restore you to health!" She then disappeared.

At this moment, Sister Elisabetta felt a terrible pain through her whole body, from the tip of her toes to her hands and up to the very top of her head. This was followed by a general feeling of well-being and life. She leaped from her bed and to the fearful, deeply moved sisters who had been watching and listening throughout, she shouted: "I am cured! I am cured! Our Lady has cured me!" It was about 12:15 am. The superior, Sister Emilia Gariboldi, who had witnessed the scene along with a nursing sister, but saw nothing and heard only the words spoken to her, heard these words as Sr Elizabeth jumped out of her bed: "I'm healed!" The whole house of Cernusco was taken by a whirlwind of joy as a result of this miracle, the news of which soon spread in the region. Sr Elizabeth, amazed by the commotion, said, "But Our Lady can do this and much more besides."

Sister Elizabeth, to escape the curiosity of the people, was sent to the Mother House in via Quadronno in Milan, where for many years she was dedicated to the schoolgirls. When people asked about the miraculous events, she skilfully turned the conversation around, faithful to her commitment not to divulge anything. The reason was that she wanted to distract attention from herself and rather focus on Our Lady. She died on 15 April 1984, after being brought back to Cernusco.

The infirmary room where the second appearance took place was made into a chapel; here a statue was placed that was very similar, but not identical, to the vision. At the base, protected by glass, one can see the exact spot where the Virgin rested her feet. The appearance was called "Our Lady of the Divine Tears", not because she was crying, but the Child she carried in her arms. Shortly after the eightieth anniversary of the apparitions, Cardinal Carlo Maria Martini authorized the naming of a parish in Cernusco with the title Our Lady of Divine Tears.

23 February: Our Lady, Covenant of Mercy

The Ethiopian and Eritrean Catholic and Orthodox Churches have a tradition that after Jesus's ascension, His mother went to Calvary to pray to Him for a favour, mindful of His words: "Ask and you shall receive." Jesus descended with a host of angels to ask what she wanted. Mary asked Him to save anyone who would pray or do works of charity in her name. Jesus's promise to do so is known as *Kidane Mehret,* the Covenant of Mercy, remembered on Yekatit 16 in the Ethiopian calendar. This usually corresponds to February 23 in the Western calendar; some churches celebrate the feast of *Kidane Mehret* on the nearest Sunday.

The Seven Salutations to the Covenant of Mercy

Salutation to you, O Covenant of Mercy, my hope, the justifier of the sinner, the seeker after the one sheep of the ninety-nine which had been lost.

Salutation to you, O Covenant of Mercy, you pillar set up by God; may you be a sign of salvation to all sinners, you whose love strengths us.

Salutation to you, O Covenant of Mercy, gold that embraces all riches, the storehouse of the poor and needy, and the wealth of Him who is in heaven.

Salutation to you, O Covenant of Mercy, who weighs the heavens in a balance ; my trust is in you, grant to me both the strife and the conquest of it.

Salutation to you, O Covenant of Mercy, hope of the kingdom of heaven; whosoever loves you shall live in hope until the resurrection of all mankind shall take place.

Salutation to you, O Covenant of Mercy. If I cannot justify myself by strivings and good works, let me rely upon you, O Virgin Covenant, to save my soul from perdition.

Salutation to you. Upon him who shall build a temple in the name of your Covenant, and upon those of us who pray in your name, O Mary, bestow a portion of your blessing, and make supplication unto your Good Son on our behalf. Amen.

24 February: Our Lady ends the Plague in Rome

N 24 FEBRUARY 591, Pope St Gregory the Great, having had the image of Our Lady *Salus Populi Romani* carried in procession, the plague ceased at Rome. The miseries that afflicted Rome in the year 591 were substantial. The Gothic

War between the Byzantine Empire and the Goths had substantially depopulated Italy, so much so that a Germanic tribe of Lombards had entered the peninsula and established their own kingdom. They were pagans and Arians who did not respect Catholics, burning the famous Benedictine monastery of Monte Cassino and pillaging the land at will.

This instability and warfare caused famine in large regions, though Rome was still able to obtain grain by sea. Then came earthquakes and flooding to further the suffering, and from this plague Rome was not immune. The banks of the Tiber overflowed, and when the waters did not recede, all of the low-lying lands became swamps that brought death and plague. The disease struck with such rapidity that the victim would often die shortly after realizing he had contracted the disease, although there were some who sickened but recovered. Our custom of saying, "God Bless you," to someone who sneezes came about at this time, for sneezing was one of the signs that someone had contracted the disease.

Pope Pelagius II died of the plague on 7 February 590. His successor was Pope Saint Gregory the Great, who was both a humble and pious man. It would be an understatement to say he did not want the honour of being the next pope, but he did do everything in his power to try to save his people. He understood that the plague was a chastisement from God, and encouraged the faithful to repent of their sins and pray for deliverance while he and the religious cared for the people of Rome.

Finally, Saint Gregory called for a procession to take place at dawn on 25 April. On that day the faithful first assembled in their groups throughout Rome and then walked through the streets of the city praying and singing as they approached the church of Saint Mary Major. The plague was so potent at that time that eighty people collapsed and died as they walked toward the meeting place.

Pope Saint Gregory met them upon their arrival, joining them in prayer as he took his place with them holding aloft the miraculous image of Our Lady, painted according to tradition by Saint Luke the Evangelist. As the procession neared the Vatican the participants all saw Saint Michael the archangel standing upon the cupola of Hadrian's mausoleum as he sheathed his flaming sword. It was a sign that the chastisement had come to an end, and at once the heaviness in the air abated and the air itself seemed to freshen and clear. Indeed, at that moment the plague ended as the faithful rejoiced and lifted up their voices to thank the Mother of God.

25 February: Our Lady of Great Power

UR LADY OF GREAT POWER is well known in North America, especially among the pupils of the Ursulines in Quebec. Generations of these, however, have dwelt within the walls of the Old Monastery during two centuries and more, since the arrival of the statue in the last years of the seventeenth century. In the annals of the Ursulines of the Sacred Heart at Perigueux, France, where the statue was solemnly crowned, we find the origin of the devotion. The devotion to Our Lady of Great Power began in the monastery of Issoudun. There a holy Ursuline nun, Mother Saint Peter, was inspired during her prayer to invoke Our Lady under this title. She spoke of her inspiration to her Sisters and her Superiors. The devotion was adopted with enthusiasm, and very soon it was decided that a statue be sculptured and a chapel built, dedicated to Our Lady of Great Power; she would henceforth be chosen as the first and principal Superior of the Monastery.

The feast of the dedication took place 25 February 1673, and was celebrated with great pomp, as the chronicle testifies:

> After High Mass two ecclesiastics carried the statue to the entry of the monastery where the nuns, in solemn procession, received it. It was placed on a richly decorated litter and, to the chanting of hymns, psalms and canticles, it was brought to the prepared chapel.
>
> When the same statue was raised on its pedestal, the superior laid the keys of the monastery, the seals and

constitutions at Our Lady's feet, begging her, in the name
of the community, to accept the gift of all hearts, and of
the entire monastery and to allow them to look on her as
their Superior forever. Each rendered homage while
hymns and canticles of thanksgiving were sung in Mary's
honour.

Ever after, when a superior was elected, the ceremony was
renewed and is still renewed in each Ursuline community
every year on a principal feast of the Blessed Virgin; though
homage is rendered only every three years, after the
election or nomination of superiors.[22]

The statue of Our Lady of Great Power was carried off and
profaned during the dark days of the French Revolution. It was
found and returned to the monastery at Perigueux; and the
devotion continued fervently until 1892, when the bishop of
Perigueux, in the name of the Sovereign Pontiff, placed a richly
jewelled crown on the head of the Mother and the Child, and
ratified the numberless and signal favours obtained through Our
Lady of Great Power.

Through the Ursulines in Quebec, the devotion soon spread
through North America. Before the altar in Quebec hangs the
famous votive light promised to be kept burning as a token of
thanks for favours granted to Mother Saint Agatha (Madeleine
de Repentigny). Relatives and descendants of this holy nun have
kept the lamp burning. One relative, Miss Anthon, had a new
lamp made, an artistic gem, the work of the celebrated ecclesiastical goldsmith Calliat of Lyon, France.

26 February: Our Lady of the Fields

 HE TITLE OF Our Lady of the Fields, or Notre-Dame des
Champs, and this devotion to Mary goes back to the
earliest days of Catholic life in France.

Our Lady des Champs, at Paris, was dedicated in pagan times
to Mercury. Saint Denis was the first Bishop of Paris. According

to tradition he drove the demons from the Temple of Mercury, the pagan goddess of agriculture, and placed therein an image of Our Lady modelled after Saint Luke's famous painting. The Temple was henceforth dedicated to the Blessed Virgin, whom Parisians have honoured for centuries under the title of Our Lady of the Fields. It is said that a picture of the Blessed Virgin is still to be seen there, on a small stone, a foot square, which was made along the lines of the image which Saint Denis brought to France.

King Robert the Pious (996–1031) rebuilt the church of Our Lady of the Vines on this spot to mark the place where St Denis had celebrated the Holy Mass. The Benedictine monks of Marmoutier then obtained permission to establish a Benedictine priory. Later in 1603, the Bendictines cede the priory to the Carmelites, who had come from Spain. This priory of Our Lady of the Field was one of the most celebrated sacred buildings during the reign of King Louis XIV.

Sadly, the French Revolution closed the priory, the church was destroyed, and there remained only the memory, perpetuated by the title Notre-Dame-des-Champs. In 1858 the parish of Our Lady of the Fields was erected in the form of a wooden chapel. On 17 March 1867 the foundation stone of the present church was laid, and on 31 October 1876 the church was blessed. On 25 March 1912 the new church of Notre-Dame des Champs in Boulevard du Montparnasse was consecrated by Cardinal Amette, Archbishop of Paris.

"I am the Flower of the field and the Lily of the valleys" (Sg 2:1), the Holy Spirit declares of the Blessed Virgin Mary. A flower of the fields has a simple beauty that charms us even more because it blossoms by itself without care or cultivation. Our Savior Himself marvelled at such a flower and of it He spoke these words of praise that have been repeated through the centuries: "See how the lilies of the field grow; they neither toil nor spin, yet I say to you that not even Solomon in all his glory was arrayed like one of these" (Lk 12:27). But lilies soon fade and roses are hardly open before they begin to shed their petals before the wind.

The beauty of Mary is not perishable; it remains ever fresh and unchanged in the valley of our exile.²³

27 February: Our Lady of Light

ARLY IN THE EIGHTEENTH CENTURY, a Jesuit, Father John Genovesi, lived in Palermo, Italy. At the beginning of his missionary career, he placed the souls over which he would have charge under the protection of the Blessed Mother, deciding to take with him on each of his missions an image of Mary. Not knowing which image of Our Lady to use, he consulted a pious visionary telling her to ask Our Lady what she desired. One day as this lady knelt in prayer, she beheld approaching her, the Queen of Heaven, surrounded by pomp, majesty and glory, surpassing anything else she had ever beheld in any of her visions. A torrent of light was shed from the body of the Virgin which was so clear, that in comparison with it, the sun seemed obscure. Yet, these rays were not painful to the sight; but seemed rather directed to the heart, which they instantly penetrated and filled with sweetness.

A group of Seraphs hovering in the air were suspended over their Empress and held a triple crown. The virginal body was clothed in a flowing robe, whiter than the snow and more brilliant than the sun. A belt inlaid with precious stones encircled Mary's beautiful form, and from her graceful shoulders hung a mantle of azure hue. Countless angels surrounded their Queen, but what most enchanted the contemplative soul, was the untold sweetness and grace and benignity shown in the motherly face of Mary. She radiated clemency and love. Our Lady told the pious woman that she wished to be represented as she was now under the title of Most Holy Mother of Light, repeating the words three times.

The Jesuit hired labourers to begin the work on the picture of Our Lady of Light, however neither the pious lady nor the priest were able to direct it, and the result was that after completion, it did not answer Our Lady's orders. Our Lady directed the woman to look at the image, and seeing the mistake, she again betook herself to prayer and asked Mary to help her. Mary appeared again, commanding the woman to supervise the work, giving directions, while Mary would aid in an invisible manner. Pleased by the finished work, Mary appeared over it, and blessed it with the sign of the cross.

This wonderful treasure is now in the city of Mexico in the cathedral of Leon, formerly known as the Jesuit Church. The back of the picture bears the authenticity and four signatures, including that of Father Genovesi, SJ. The painting was transferred from Palermo, Sicily, in 1702, and placed on the altar in Leon in 1732. The people of Leon have an innate devotion and great tenderness toward the Mother of God. In 1849 they solemnly promised before the picture to make Our Lady of Light the patroness of Leon. This promise was confirmed by Pope Pius IX; Leo XIII authenticated the crowning of the image of Our Lady of Light in 1902.[24]

28 February: Our Most Pure Lady of the Forty Hours

HE STORY GOES that in 1831 in Chile, fishermen found a chest floating in the sea; inside was a beautiful statue of the Virgin in a white robe and dark blue mantle. Devotion remained private for many years, but eventually grew to the point that the statue was moved to the local parish church of Santa Cruz in Limache near Valparaiso in Chile. Depending on the source, the Mary Immaculate of Limache became known as the Virgin of the 40 Hours after saving some sailors from a 40-hour storm, or because the statue was found after a 40-hour storm or again during the Forty Hours' Devotion of Eucharistic adoration at the church; or simply because such a devotion was held starting on the Friday before her feast. Now, a nine-day novena precedes the celebration in February, which of course is summertime in Chile. On the last Sunday of February, the statue processes through the city, passing the prison, whose inmates shout a greeting.

Notes

1   This could have been what we now call Myalgic encephalomyelitis or chronic fatigue syndrome (ME/CFS), a complex, chronic medical condition characterised by symptom clusters that include pathological fatigue and malaise that is worse after exertion, cognitive dysfunction, immune dysfunction, unrefreshing sleep, pain, autonomic dysfunction and also neuroendocrine and immune symptoms.

2   The monastery is widely known by the short name Kykkos, or as the Virgin of Kykkos. The origin of the name, which seems to date from the Byzantine era, is not known. One view is that it derives from the Kermes oak tree (*Quercus coccifera*), also called *kokkos*. Ephraim the Athenian, Patriarch of Jerusalem, seems to adopt this interpretation. In his work entitled *Description of the Venerable and Royal Monastery of Kykkos* (1751), he makes reference to mount Kokkos, subsequently renamed to Kykkos. On the other hand, tradition also associated the name Kykkos with the call of a bird, as mentioned in the verses cited above.

3   C. Robert, "Our Lady of the Doves" in *Mary Immaculate: God's Mother and Mine* (Poughkeepsie, New York: Marist Press, 1946).

4   See R. Laurentin and P. Sbalchiero, R. Etchegaray, *Dictionnaire des "apparitions" de la Vierge Marie: Inventaire des origines à nos jours méthodologie, bilan interdisciplinaire, prospective* (Paris: Fayard, 2012).

5   G. Bezzi, *Il fuoco trionfante: Racconto della traslatione della miracolosa imagine detta La Madonna del Fuoco, Protettrice della Città di Forlì* (Forlì: 1637), p. 8.

6   L. Pon, "Place, Print and Miracle: Forlì's Madonna of the Fire as Functional Site" in *Art History* 31 (2008), pp. 303–321.

7   See also the Feast Day of Our Lady, Seat of Wisdom on 8 June.

8   Pope Benedict XVI, *Discourse to the Community of the Roman Major Seminary on Occasion of the Feast of Our Lady of Trust* (25 February 2006).

9   The Feast of the Purification is now known as the Presentation of the Lord.

10   See M. Lamberty (ed.), *The Woman in Orbit: Mary's feasts every day everywhere* (Chicago: Lamberty, 1966), 9 February.

11   *Ibid.*, 10 February.

12   *Ibid.*, 11 February.

13   SANTA MARIA REPARATRIX NOSTRAE CONCORDIAE OMNIUM FIDELIUM CHRISTIANORUM TU INTERCEDE PRO NOBIS APUD DEUM UT LIBEREMUR A PESTE EPIDEMIA ET AB OMNIBUS MALIS PRAESENTIBUS ET FUTURIS. AMEN.

[14] In all there were to be fifteen apparitions of the Blessed Virgin to Estelle Faguette in 1876 in Pellevoisin, France. They were grouped in three phases of five, three and seven apparitions. The first five were associated with Estelle's illness and her extraordinary recovery. The second phase, in the summer of the same year, consisted of three apparitions from 1–3 July. Then there were a further seven between September and December 1876. It was in these later visions that Estelle was to receive her "mission" from Mary.

[15] J. A. Harriss, "Celebrating Our Lady of Paris" in *The American Spectator* (June 2013).

[16] V. M. Hugo, *Notre Dame de Paris* (New York: P. F. Collier & Son, 1917), Book 3, I.

[17] St Gregory of Nyssa, *De vita Moysis* in *PG* 44, 332.

[18] A *parvis* is the open space in front of and around a cathedral or church, especially when surrounded by either colonnades or porticoes.

[19] Lamberty, *The Woman in Orbit*, 11 February.

[20] Monsignor Luigi Biraghi (1801–1879) was spiritual director of the seminary of Milan and later doctor of the Ambrosian Library; he was beatified in 2006,

[21] Haemoptysis is the act of coughing up blood or blood-stained mucus from the bronchi, larynx, trachea, or lungs. This can occur with lung cancer, infections such as tuberculosis, bronchitis, or pneumonia, and certain cardiovascular conditions.

[22] Lamberty, *The Woman in Orbit*, 25 February.

[23] *Ibid.*, 26 February.

[24] *Ibid.*, 27 February.

MARCH

1 March: Our Lady of the Cross

HERE IS A SANCTUARY of Our Lady on the Bergamo Road, about a mile away from the city of Crema, Italy. The structure is a circular form, with four additions in the shape of a cross, which gave rise to the name: or Our Lady of the Cross. The sanctuary is located in a place where, in years gone by, there stood a dense little wood called *Il Novelletto*.

In the late fifteenth century, a young woman from a wealthy family named Caterina degli Uberti lived with her brother in the city of Crema. When she arrived at marriageable age, her brother induced her to wed one Bartolomeo Pederbelli; it was an unfortunate arrangement—Caterina was good and pious; Bartolomeo was quite the opposite, a criminal tending toward the wicked and corrupt. The marriage was unhappy for Caterina and uncomfortable for Bartolomeo—his rather crude and brutal ways shamed her, while her refined and holy life was a silent reproach to his somewhat scandalous mode of living.

So, after a year of turmoil, Bartolomeo decided to murder Caterina. Having made up his mind, he lost no time in carrying out his evil design. He suggested that they journey to Bergamo and visit his parents; she agreed, and in the late afternoon of 2 April 1490, they mounted their horses and set forth from the city. When they arrived at the wood about a mile from Crema, Bartolomeo left the highway and rode into the forest; Caterina was puzzled, but not knowing what else to do, followed him. When they reached the middle of the wood, Bartolomeo dismounted and made Caterina get down from her horse. Then, without warning, he drew his sword, raised it and fiercely brought it down, intending to split her head with one clean cut. Instinctively she drew up her arm to ward off the savage blow, and saved her head, but lost her right hand—the poor severed hand hung from the stump of her arm by a strip of skin, and Bartolomeo brutally tore it off and flung it to one side. He then slashed at her like a maniac until she fell to the ground in a pool of blood; thinking her dead, he leaped on his horse and fled.

Caterina was not dead, nor was she afraid to die, though she felt her time was short. With all her dying heart she wished for the Last Sacraments; so she prayed to the Mother of God, who heard her prayer. A glow of light pushed back the gathering darkness and a beautiful Lady approached her. Reaching down, the Lady, Our Lady of the Cross, took her by the arm and helped her rise—the blood stopped flowing and new life coursed through her mutilated body. The Lady bade Caterina follow her, but Caterina asked if she might look for her lost hand. The Lady promised it would be returned to her in due time. Taking Caterina to a hut, she told her these people would help her and then vanished. The kind peasants did all they could for Caterina, and the next morning they placed her on a rude stretcher and tenderly carried her back to Crema.

As they passed through the wood, one of the men found the severed hand and returned it to Caterina. They took her to the Church of St Benedict where Philip the priest, after hearing the story, anointed Caterina who died there. A doctor also examined her and a magistrate heard her account of what had happened. The story spread rapidly; some believed, others doubted that the Blessed Virgin worked such wonders.

An eleven year old boy, son of Francesco Marazzo living in Crema was plagued with an unhealable abscess on a foot, and begged to be taken to the wood to put his foot on the spot where Our Lady appeared. His mother and a group of relatives carried him there, and he was instantly cured, all traces of the abscess cleared up. Many other sick and infirm came also and were cured, and several miracles took place. The people erected a small chapel on the spot and placed in it a plaster image of Our Lady. More favours followed; many offerings were made by the faithful and in a few years a fitting sanctuary to the Madonna was completed by 1500. Later, a fine new statue of Mary was enshrined in the Sanctuary and on 4 September 1873 Our Lady of the Cross was crowned with a golden crown by Mgr Giuseppe Sanguettola. Pope Pius XII granted the church the dignity of a minor basilica with a Papal Bull dated 18 April 1958. On 20 June 1992 Pope St John Paul II visited the basilica.

2 March: Our Lady of Apparitions

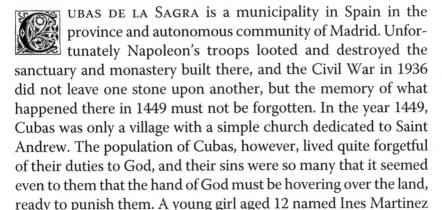 UBAS DE LA SAGRA is a municipality in Spain in the province and autonomous community of Madrid. Unfortunately Napoleon's troops looted and destroyed the sanctuary and monastery built there, and the Civil War in 1936 did not leave one stone upon another, but the memory of what happened there in 1449 must not be forgotten. In the year 1449, Cubas was only a village with a simple church dedicated to Saint Andrew. The population of Cubas, however, lived quite forgetful of their duties to God, and their sins were so many that it seemed even to them that the hand of God must be hovering over the land, ready to punish them. A young girl aged 12 named Ines Martinez (sometimes Yves or Agnes) who was of humble birth, fasted, confessed regularly, and prayed daily the 15 mysteries of the Rosary.

On Monday 3 March 1449, Ines was tending pigs on the outskirts of town in a place called Cecilia, when at noon a Woman appeared, a Lady bright and beautiful dressed in cloth of gold. She was surrounded by light, and asked Ines what she was doing there. Ines stated that she was tending the pigs. The Lady then said that the people were no longer keeping the fasts, and explained to Ines the necessity of fasting. The Lady said that the people of Cubas must change their ways, confess, and cease their debauchery and offences against God, or He would soon punish them. There would be a great pestilence that would come upon them from which many would die. Perhaps knowing the hard-heartedness of the people, Ines asked if she, too, or her mother and father, would die of this pestilence. She was told only that it would be as God desired. The Lady then disappeared.

At first Ines did not tell anyone of the incident, for she thought no one would believe what had happened. On Tuesday 4 March Ines was again tending the pigs, this time near the stream of Torrejon. At about the same time of day, at noon, just as the day before, the Lady reappeared. She asked Ines if she had told the people what she had been told to say, but Ines answered that she dared not to, for she suspected that she would not be believed. The Lady then commanded Ines to warn the people, and that if they did not believe, she would give her a sign. Ines asked the Lady who she was, but she said she would not tell her yet and then, once again, she disappeared. Finally Ines decided to tell her father, Alfonso Martinez, who did not give any importance to the events recounted by his daughter, but thought it a children's story, a story invented in the imagination of a young girl. He told Ines to be quiet when she tried to tell anyone about the warning.

On Friday 7 March, Ines was keeping the pigs in New Prado, when the Lady reappeared again as before. She asked Ines if she had told what she had been commanded to say. Ines answered that she had told her mother and father, and many others. The Lady told Ines to publish what she had said to all the people without any fear or trepidation. When Ines went home at the end of the day she told her parents what had happened. Her father told her she was lying and to "shut up," but her mother encouraged Ines, saying, "Well say it, just the same."

By Sunday 9 March, word had spread. A priest, Juan Gonzalez, with some other men, when to Ines' home and talked to her parents. Afterwards, the priest went to say Mass. Ines went out with the pigs, accompanied by her brother John, to a place called the Ciroleda. Ines' father left them and went to Mass. The Ciroleda was a watery meadow that the pigs liked. Ines left her brother after a time looking for one of the pigs that had slipped away, and soon lost sight of her brother. All by herself, she knelt on the soft earth, asking the Lady to return, even though she was afraid.

The Lady appeared again as before, telling Ines to rise. "Lady, who are you?" Ines asked. "I am the Virgin Mary", the Lady answered, and approaching Ines, took her right hand and squeezed her fingers and thumb together, making some kind of a sign. She then told Ines to go to the church and show the sign to the people as they left Mass. Ines told her brother to look after the pigs, and went to the church, arriving just as Mass was ending. She was crying, and went to kneel before the altar of Mary. There, she told everyone what had happened.[1]

We do not know what the sign was in Ines' hand, but whatever it was, the people examined her hand and many believed. The following day the priest led the notables of the town and the faithful in a procession to the place of the last apparitions, carrying a wooden cross. When they arrived, Ines walked forward alone with the cross. The Virgin Mary herself took the cross, telling Ines to have a church built there in her honour. The cross was permanently placed where the Virgin, Our Lady of Apparitions, had been last seen, and many miracles occurred there, including 11 people who were brought back to life. A church was begun shortly after the apparitions of the Virgin were approved. It stood for nearly five centuries, when it was destroyed in the 1936 fire, caused during the Civil War. Many of the nuns were martyred. In 1949 the reconstruction was begun and the current cross was placed in the same place where the first had been.

According to tradition, Ines spent the last years of her life in the monastery of Santa Maria de la Cruz after having had children and being widowed. It is said that anyone who goes to visit the place, with faith, receives special graces, and that miracles still occur there.

3 March: Our Lady of Angels

 N THE YEAR 1212, three merchants from Angers were passing through the forest of Bondy (near Paris) in France, when they were set upon by robbers. After being robbed, they were bound to trees and left to their fate. Since it was a wild and lonely place, known to be the haunt of robbers, their chances of rescue were few. They prayed earnestly to God and Our Lady, and, after a day and a night, angels came in visible form and released them.

The men discovered a spring near the place where they had been bound, which they considered to be miraculous. They determined to set up a shrine of Our Lady on the spot in thanksgiving for their deliverance. The first statue they set into the shrine was only intended to be temporary, to be used until something better could be made or purchased. However, almost immediately there began a stream of miraculous cures among those who prayed before the rough little statue. In the years that followed, fervent pilgrims thronged to the shrine, as evidenced by the numerous drinking vessels found during archaeological excavations carried out on the site.

The same statue remains today, but it has been richly clothed and decked with jewels. In 1260 the little chapel was enlarged to enclose also the spring. In 1663 the chapel was rebuilt and redecorated, and so remained until the French Revolution, when it was completely destroyed. However, after the Terror had passed, the chapel was rebuilt in 1808.

One of the many thanksgiving offerings in the chapel is a ship suspended above the altar, as an *ex-voto* from a group of sailors who were saved from shipwreck at the intercession of Our Lady.

On Sunday, 9 September 2012, the Diocese of Saint-Denis celebrated the 800th anniversary of the pilgrimage to Notre-Dame-des-Anges in Clichy-sur-Bois, under the leadership of Bishop Pascal Delannoy.[2] The pilgrimage to the small shrine always takes place on the second Sunday of September, and is thought by some to be the second oldest pilgrimage site in France.

4 March: Our Lady of Guard

 ATE ONE AFTERNOON during the thirteenth century, a solitary French fisherman was fishing off the harbour of Marseilles. Before he became aware of it, a terrific storm burst upon him. His boat tossed around like a shell, and filled with water faster than he could bail it out. His rudder was lost; his mast snapped. Cutting himself free from the rigging with a knife, he had saved himself temporarily from certain drowning. Still, everything looked hopeless, and he felt he could never get back to the harbour. The fisherman thought of the family he would never see again and cast a despairing look at the city, the huge rock standing like a sentinel or guard on the mountain which overtopped the city and harbour.

Dimly through the gloom he suddenly saw a solitary figure of a Lady, dressed in white, standing firmly on the very top of the rock. She seemed to be extending her hand as if she would help him to the shelter and safety of the harbour. At once it came to him that the Lady so calmly defying the wind and rain could only be the Blessed Mother, so he prayed to her to help him. Almost immediately his boat ceased its wild tossing, righted itself and pushed by a friendly gust of wind, raced into the calm water of the harbour until it drove onto the shore at the very foot of the mountain. Stepping onto the shore, the fisherman fell to his knees and poured out his thanks to the Blessed Virgin, and then hurried home to his worried family.

The story of his rescue through the assistance of Our Lady quickly spread throughout the port. It was remembered that other sailors, on numerous occasions during severe storms, had also seen the figure of the Lady on top of the rock. Always when she had appeared, the angry seas had calmed and their crafts had ridden safely into the shelter. Sailors who escaped a shipwreck gave thanks and deposited *ex-votos* at Notre-Dame of the Sea in the church of Notre-Dame-du-Mont.

However in 1214 Maître Pierre, a priest of Marseille, had already been inspired to build a chapel dedicated to the Virgin Mary on the hill known as La Garde, which belonged to the abbey of Saint-Victor. The abbot granted him permission to plant vines, to cultivate a garden there and to build a chapel.[3] The chapel, completed four years later, appears in a papal bull of Pope Honorius III dated 18 June 1218, listing the possessions of the abbey. After Maître Pierre died in 1256, Notre-Dame de la Garde became a priory. By the end of the sixteenth century the sailors also began making their thanksgiving to Our Lady at Notre-Dame de la Garde.[4]

The first chapel was replaced at the beginning of the fifteenth century by a larger building with a richly equipped chapel dedicated to Saint Gabriel.[5] On 3 January 1516 Louise of Savoy, the mother of Francis I of France, and his wife, Queen Claude of France, daughter of Louis XII, went to the south of France to meet the young king, fresh from his victory at Marignan. On 7 January 1516 they visited the sanctuary. On 22 January 1516 Francis also accompanied them to the chapel.[6]

During the French Revolution, after the barbarous execution of Louis XVI on the 21 January 1793, members of the Bourbon family were incarcerated for six months in the fortress of Notre-Dame de la Garde. Catholic worship was forbidden in France in November of the same year. The State seized all religious edifices. Everything the chapel contained then disappeared: the two statues of Our Lady (one in wood dating from the thirteenth Century and the other in silver from 1651), the bells, the altars the ex-votos.

After the Revolution, church services started again in Notre-Dame de la Garde in 1807. Joseph-Elie Escaramagne, an ex-sailor, gave to the sanctuary a statue of the Virgin bought at an auction sale: it is the statue of the "Vierge au bouquet" (Virgin with the bunch of flowers) which one can see behind the altar in the Crypt. For his part, the Fort Commander offered a small bell to the chapel. On the day the chapel of Notre-Dame de la Garde was reopened for worship, a procession started from Marseille

Cathedral, bringing to the sanctuary the statue that Escaramagne had bought.

Our Lady did not only help sailors, as was proved in the year 1832 when a severe epidemic of cholera struck Marseilles; the people decided to appeal to Mary. Forming a procession, they climbed the mountain, removed the statue from the chapel, brought it down, and solemnly carried it through the streets of the city. Almost immediately the epidemic waned, and in a few days vanished. So they called Mary, Our Lady of Help—the sailors called her Our Lady of Mariners.

Some years later, as the fame of the shrine on top of the mountain spread, with more and more people coming up to pay their respects. Work on a basilica was begun and the first stone was laid on 11 September 1853 by the Bishop of Marseilles, Mgr Eugène de Mazenod. The faithful made donations to finance the construction. However, during the early years, money often grew short and, on several occasions, work had to be interrupted. After 8 years work on the site, on the death of Mgr de Mazenod in 1861, the crypt in the rock had been excavated, but, of the church above, only the side-walls and the base of the bell-tower had been built. The vault of the nave, the dome and most of the tower remained yet to be constructed. The generosity of citizens of all religions and all social positions allowed completion of the work, from the Emperor Napoleon III and the Empress Eugénie, who visited Notre Dame de la Garde on September 9, 1860, to the poorest of Marseillais. Work was speeded up and, on 4 June 1864 the sanctuary could be consecrated, with an unfinished tower, by Cardinal Villecourt, member of the Papal Curia, surrounded by 41 bishops.[7]

The basilica suffered during the Second Word War. Between 2000 and 2008, under the direction of the architect Xavier David, many restoration projects began on the sanctuary. These involved work both to the interior and to the exterior. The lighting system was very much improved, bringing out the true value of our magnificent mosaics.[8]

In Marseilles today, the hill of Notre Dame de la Garde is topped by a beautiful basilica. The interior has a multitude of sailors' votive offerings, and model ships are hung in all parts of it in sign of thanksgiving for all the mariners who have been assisted by their heavenly Mother. A golden statue of the Virgin and Child suitably dominates the city from its place on top of the western tower.

5 March: Our Lady of Good Help

OR OVER 350 YEARS, the Chapel of Notre-Dame-de-Bon-Secours, a jewel of history and heritage, has made its way into the hearts of generations of visitors and pilgrims. As you step into the church, you will immediately notice the peaceful atmosphere and feel a palpable link to Montreal's past. The church has been the sanctuary for seamen leaving Montreal for the seven seas. A wooden chapel was built in 1657; replaced in 1675 by a building whose foundations serve the present church which was erected in 1771. Over the entrance is an inscribed message: "If the love of Mary is graven in your heart, forget not a prayer in passing."

On the walls are mosaics of Marguerite Bourgeoys, who inspired the first chapel; and of Maisonneuve, founder of Montreal, said to have felled the first oak for the chapel. Saint Marguerite Bourgeoys was the founder of the Congregation of Notre Dame. When she returned from France in 1673 she brought back with her a wood statue of Our Lady of Good Help. It can still be seen in the reliquary on the gospel side of the altar, for when the church burned in 1754, the statue was saved from the fire. This is not to say that someone took the statue from the church, for after the fire had ravaged the original chapel, the statue was found uninjured among the smouldering embers that remained.

The mortal remains of Saint Marguerite Bourgeoys were interred in the sanctuary of the church in the year 2005, the 350th anniversary of Notre-Dame-de-Bon-Secours. She rests now at the feet of the statue she herself had brought from France. In 1849 the Bishop of Montreal placed a statue of the Blessed Virgin, Star of the Sea, atop the tower facing the harbour. For this reason, the chapel is also known as the Sailor's Church. There are votive offerings, carved ships, models of sailing ships suspended from the vault of the chapel in thanksgiving to the Blessed Virgin for her assistance in their safe return from the sea.

6 March: Kozelshchansk Icon of the Mother of God

HE KOZELSHCHANSK ICON of the Mother of God is of Italian origin and was brought to Russia by one of Empress Elizabeth's (1741–1761) maids of honour, who was Italian. The maid married a records clerk of the Zaporozhsky-Cossack army, Siromakh, and the icon went to the Ukraine with them. During the nineteenth century it belonged to the family of Count Vladimir Kapnist, who lived in the village of Kozelschina, lying in the Poltava governance. During Cheesefare Week in the year 1880, Maria, the daughter of Vladimir Kapnist, dislocated some bones in her foot.[9] The local doctor said the problem was not serious. Dr Grube, a noted surgeon in Kharkov, agreed with the diagnosis, and he applied a plaster cast to Maria's foot. He also prescribed hot baths and iron supplements. To lessen the discomfort of the foot while walking, a special shoe was made with metal bands that went around the girl's leg. Lent passed, but the girl did not feel any relief.

After Easter, Maria's other foot became twisted and then both shoulders and her left hip became dislocated, and she developed pain in her spine. The doctor advised Count Kapnist to take his daughter immediately to the Caucasus for the curative mineral waters and mountain air. The journey to the Caucasus and the curative treatments caused even greater affliction. The girl lost all feeling in her hands and feet, and did not even feel pinches. Because of the advanced degree of the illness, and since therapy was not helping, they were compelled to return home. In the month of October, the father journeyed with his sick daughter to Moscow. Here he consulted specialists, who declared that they could do nothing for Maria.

The parents and their sick daughter began to despair. However, an unexpected opportunity for help came in the form of a foreign professor of medicine. Since it would be some while before his arrival in Moscow, the sick girl asked to return home. The Count sent her back to the village, and his wife promised to bring their daughter back to Moscow when he received news of the the professor's arrival. On 21 February 1881, they received a telegram saying that the professor had arrived in Moscow. On the day before the appointment, Maria's mother suggested that she pray before the family icon of the Mother of God. She said to her daughter, "Masha [a diminutive form of Maria], tomorrow we go to Moscow. Take the icon, let us clean its cover and pray to the Most Holy Theotokos that your infirmity be cured." The girl, who had no confidence in earthly physicians, placed all her hope in God. This icon had long been known as wonderworking. According to Tradition, young women would pray before it to have a happy family. It was also the custom to clean the cover of the icon, and the one praying would wipe it with cotton or linen. 21 February in the Old Calendar now corresponds to 6 March, the Feast Day of the healing icon.

Pressing the holy icon to her bosom, the sick girl, with the help of her mother, cleaned it and poured out all her sorrow and despair of soul to the Holy Mother of God. All at once, she felt strength return to her body and she cried out loudly, "Mama! Mama! I can feel my legs! I can feel my hands!" She tore off the metal braces and bandages and began to walk about the room, while continuing to hold the icon of the Mother of God in her hands. The parish priest was summoned at once and celebrated a Service of Thanksgiving before the icon. The joyous event quickly became known throughout all the surrounding villages. The Countess and Maria went to Moscow and took with them the holy icon of the Mother of God. News of the healing quickly spread about Moscow and people began to throng to the hotel, and then to the church, where they had brought the icon.

The icon continued to work several more healings. When the family returned home to Kozelschina, people had already heard about the miracles of the Kozelschansk icon of the Mother of God in Moscow, and many came to venerate the icon. It was no longer possible to keep the icon at home, so by the order of Archbishop John of Poltava, the icon was transferred to a temporary chapel on 23 April 1881. Every day from early morning, services of Thanksgiving and Akathists were celebrated before the icon.[10] In 1882 a chapel was built on the grounds of the estate, and then a church. Following a decision of the Holy Synod on 1 March 1885, a women's monastery was established, and on 17 February 1891 it was dedicated to the Nativity of the Most Holy Theotokos. At present, the Kozelschansk Icon is in the Krasnogorsk Protection women's monastery (Kiev diocese). In the lower left corner of the icon is a table with a cup and a spoon. It is believed that this symbolizes the Mother of God as a "bowl for mixing the wine of joy".[11]

7 March: Our Lady of Quetzaltenango

CCORDING TO TRADITION, the Spanish were carrying the image of the Virgin of the Rosary to the capital of Guatemala, but took a rest stop in the city of Quetzaltenango while crossing the high plains. When the time came to leave, the image became too heavy for the oxen to pull its cart. Spanish and local people tried repeatedly to move it but could not. When they turned the cart around, the weight lessened; and everyone understood that the Virgin wanted to remain in Quetzaltenango.

The image was consecrated on 20 January 1781 by Archbishop Cayetano Francos y Monroy in the cathedral there. Devotion intensified after 18 April 1902, when at 8:00pm the San Perfecto earthquake struck. Constant tremors provoked a fire which consumed most of the church that housed the statue. When the flames finally reached the Our Lady's altar, residents rescued it and placed it in the bandstand in the park. The townspeople who were there knelt immediately and began to pray to the Virgin Mary, and the aftershocks subsided. The city thanked Our Lady of the Rosary for its survival. Xela (as Quetzaltenango is usually called), now the second most important city in Guatemala, celebrates its patron in late September and early October, with festivities culminating on 7 October, feast of Our Lady of the Rosary. On 7 March 1983, Pope St John Paul II crowned the statue during his pastoral visit to the native communities of the Department in the plains of Olintepeque.

> Remember that the Son of God came to us in the Person of Jesus, our Saviour, by means of a woman, the Virgin Mary. She is our sister and our Mother. The Mother of each of us and of the Church. I know that you love her and invoke her, full of confidence. I beg her to protect you. She will protect your homes; accompany you in your work; in your trials and joys; in life and in death. May Mary give you Christ and always be your beloved Mother. Amen.[12]

8 March: Our Lady of Tears

 N 1928, IN THE CITY OF CAMPINAS, São Paulo State, Brazil, Amália Aguirre was one of the founding members of the Missionaries of Jesus Crucified, taking the name Sister Amália of the Scourged Jesus, and gaining fame when she developed stigmata, which later healed. The following year, kneeling before the Blessed Sacrament in prayer for a relative's dying wife, Sister Amália asked Jesus what she could do to help the young mother. She received the answer, "Ask me for the sake of my mother's tears", and received three prayers:

> O Jesus, look upon the tears of the one who loved You most on earth, and loves You most ardently in heaven.
> O Jesus, listen to our prayers, for the sake of the tears of your most Holy Mother.

O Mary, Mother of Love, Sorrow and Mercy, we beseech you to unite your prayers with ours so that Jesus, your Divine Son, to whom we turn, may hear our petitions in the name of your maternal tears, and grant us, not only the favours we now ask, but the crown of everlasting life.

Four months later, Our Lady appeared.

It was 8 March 1930. I was in the chapel kneeling on the steps of the altar, as I suddenly felt myself being lifted up. Then I saw a Woman of unspeakable beauty approaching me. She wore a violet robe, blue mantle, and a white veil draped over her shoulders. Smiling, she floated in the air towards me, holding a rosary in her hands, which she herself called a *corona* (crown, circle, rosary). Its beads shone like the sun and were as white as snow. Handing me this rosary she said to me, "This is the rosary of my tears, which is being entrusted by my Son to His beloved Institute as a portion of His inheritance."

Our Blessed Lady told Sister Amalia how to say the rosary of her tears, replacing the Our Father, Hail Mary, and concluding prayer of the standard rosary with the three prayers given by Jesus.

My Son wants to honour me in a special way through these invocations, and so, He will grant all graces that are begged for the sake of my tears.

On 8 April 1930, Sister Amália again saw the Blessed Virgin Mary, who revealed a medal of Our Lady of Tears. On the front, around a picture of Mary holding the rosary, are the words, "O most sorrowful Virgin, your tears overthrew the infernal empire." On the reverse is an image of Jesus with the inscription, "By your divine gentleness, O manacled Jesus, save the world from the error that threatens it." In 1934, the founder of her Institute Mgr Francisco de Campos Barreto, Bishop of Campinas, gave an Imprimatur to the Rosary of Tears and recommended use of the medal, saying it had already worked many miracles in Brazil and Europe.

9 March: Our Lady of Miracles

N THE MORNING of 9 March 1510, in the village of Motta di Livenza, near Trevisio in the Veneto region of Italy, Giovanni Cigana, aged 79, went to enlist a friend's help ploughing his field. On the way, he stopped to pray at a wayside shrine, saying seven Our Fathers and seven Hail Marys. Walking on, he was surprised to see a beautiful girl in white seated on the green wheat. "God give you a good day", he said. "A good day and a good year" she answered. They spoke a little, when suddenly he had an understanding that this was the Most Holy Mother of God and fell to his knees. The radiant girl stood up and asked that he, his family, and the people of Treviso fast for three Saturdays in repentance to obtain Christ's pardon for their sins, and that a church be built on the site.

"My Lady, no one will believe me" the old man remarked. "This evening, I'll give you a sign in the sun", she replied. After his friend agreed to plough the field, Cigana went home and told the story. That evening, the sun appeared blood red. Within a few days, the people of the area had built a wooden church, soon known as Our Lady of Miracles for the many blessings dispensed there. On 16 September 1513, a new stone church was consecrated, placed under the care of the Friars Minor of the Observance. During the Napoleonic era, it was one of the few convents to escape suppression, and in 1875 was granted the title of minor Basilica. a It was granted the status of becoming a National Monument in 1877.

The sanctuary celebrates the feast of the Our Lady of Miracles annually on 9 March, and kept its 500th anniversary in 2010.[13]

10 March: Our Lady of the Oak

HE CITY OF VITERBO is located at the foot of Mount Cimino in the province of Rome. At one time in Viterbo there was a certain man named Mastro Baptist Magnano Luzzante, who was a very God-fearing devotee of the glorious

Virgin Mary. He hired a painter named Monetto in the year 1417 to paint an image on a tile of the blessed Virgin Mary holding her Son in her arms. Mastro Baptist then lovingly laid the tile on an oak tree that stood at the edge of his vineyard, near the road leading to Bagnaia and along which robbers often awaited to attack unwary travellers.

The image remained there for about 50 years under cover of the oak's branches, and after a while only a few women who passed by ever stopped to say a prayer and to admire the beauty of a natural tabernacle that a wild vine, which had embraced the oak, had created. During this period a hermit of Siena, Pier Domenico Alberti, whose hermitage was at the foot of Palanzana, went around the countryside and the nearby towns of Viterbo, saying, "Between Bagnaia and Viterbo there is a treasure."

Many people, driven by greed, started digging there but found nothing and asked for an explanation from the hermit. Domenico then brought them to the oak tree chosen by the Virgin and pointed to the real treasure, Our Lady. He told them of the day he had decided to take away the sacred image to his hermitage, and of how it had returned to the oak.

Dominico was not alone in this experience. A devout woman named Bartolomea often walked past the oak tree and stopped each time to pray to Our Lady. One day she also decided to take the tile to her home. After saying her evening prayers, Bartolomea went to bed, but woke up in the morning to find the image missing. She at first thought that her family had taken it to place it somewhere else, but upon learning that this was not so, she ran to the oak tree and saw what she had already guessed had happened: the tile had miraculously returned to its place amid the tendrils of the vine. Bartolomea tried to take the image home again, but always the sacred image returned to the tree. At first she did not say anything to anyone to avoid being taken for being mad.

Then, in 1467, during the month of August, the whole region was struck by the greatest scourge of those times: the plague. Everywhere the bodies of the dead lay in the deserted streets, and there was great weeping and mourning. Some then remembered the image painted on the humble tile, and, as if driven by an inexplicable force, went to kneel beneath the oak. Nicholas of Tuccia, an historian, said that on one day 30,000 people went there to beg for mercy. A few days later the plague ceased, and then 40,000 of the faithful came back to thank the Virgin Mary. The people of Viterbo were led by their bishop Mgr Pietro Gennari, and many also came from other regions.

In early September of the same year another extraordinary event happened. A good knight of Viterbo had many enemies, as will often happen to a follower of Christ. One day he was surprised by his enemies outside the walls of Viterbo. Alone and unarmed, and having no way to deal with the mortal danger, he fled into the nearby woods. Fatigued and desperate to reach his destination, the knight heard the cries of the enemy draw nearer and nearer. Eventually he arrived at the oak with the sacred image of Mary, where he fell at her feet with great faith and embraced the trunk of the tree, putting his life into the hands of his Heavenly Mother. The knight's enemies reached the oak, but were surprised that they could no longer see the knight. They began to look behind every tree and bush, but not one could see him since he had disappeared before their very eyes. Failing to find him after a long time spent in searching, they gave up in disgust.

Then the knight, after thanking the Virgin Mary, returned to Viterbo and told everyone what had happened. Bartolomea heard his tale, and encouraged by his words, she described the miracles to which she had been a witness. They told everyone what had happened to them with so much enthusiasm, faith and devotion that the stories spread like wildfire, and many people, coming from the most diverse regions of Italy, flocked to the feet of the oak to implore help from the Blessed Virgin.

It was decided to build an altar, and then a wooden chapel before Pope Paul II gave the necessary permission to build a small church in 1467. Many popes and saints have been devotees of the image, including St Charles Borromeo, St Paul of the Cross, St

Ignatius Loyola, St Crispin of Viterbo, and St Maximilian Kolbe, among many others. On 20 January 1944, during the bombing of Viterbo, a squadron of 12 bombers headed for the oak, but upon arriving at their destination, inexplicably veered to the right and the bombs dropped did not destroying anything apart from the asylum which was empty. The remains of the bombs, 3 large chunks, are kept behind the altar of the Madonna.

In 1986, Pope St John Paul II proclaimed Our Lady of the Oak Patroness of the new diocese of Viterbo, formed from the union of those of Viterbo, Tuscania, Montefiascone, Acquapendente and Bagnoregio.[14] Pope Benedict XVI visited Our Lady of the Oak on 6 September 2009, and invoked her with this prayer:

> Holy Virgin, Our Lady of the Oak,
> Patroness of the Diocese of Viterbo,
> gathered together in this Shrine
> consecrated to you,
> we extend to you a plea and
> a confident prayer:
> Watch over the Successor of Peter
> and over the Church
> entrusted to his care;
> watch over this diocesan community
> and its pastors,
> over Italy, over Europe and
> over the other continents.
> Queen of Peace, obtain for us
> the gift of harmony and peace
> for all peoples and all mankind.[15]

11 March: Our Lady of the Forests

ALPHONSUS I WAS the first king of Portugal, and his wife, Queen Matilda, better known as Mafalda of Savoy (1125–1158), married him in the year 1146. She was the daughter of Amadeus III of Savoy, count of the Holy Roman German

Empire, and a sister to Blessed Umberto. Matilda died young, long before Alphonsus was king—yet her life still had great significance.

Alphonsus I was almost constantly at war with the Moors of Andalusia, and Portugal did not become formally recognized as an independent kingdom until 1179, when Alphonsus I was recognized as king by the pope. Perhaps there was a crisis during these years of upheaval when Queen Matilda was forced to hide in a forest with a cherished image of the Blessed Virgin Mary.

Although little is known of Queen Matilda, it is believed that she built a small abbey chapel in honour of the Blessed Virgin in the outskirts of Fatima in a place called the Rock of Fatima. There was also an attached monastery at this site that was built by the Cistercians, although nothing remains of that monastery now and its foundations have become the floor for the parish church at Fatima. Built in the 18th century, it was originally called Our Lady of the Rosary.

One of Queen Matilda's descendants was Blessed Margaret of Savoy, who founded a convent for women. On 16 October 1454, Blessed Margaret was present in the Monastery of Saint Mary Magdalene of the Dominican nuns of Alba, south of Turin, Italy, when her dying cousin, Sister Filipina, spoke aloud the names of the saints who came to assist her on her way to heaven. Sister Filipina revealed during that last ecstasy that in the future there would be terrible wars, and that there would be a monster who would rise in the East as a scourge of all mankind. He would eventually be slain by Our Lady of the Holy Rosary of Fatima. She said: "A statue of the Most Holy Virgin will speak about very grave future events, for Satan will wage a terrible war. But he will lose because the Most Holy Virgin Mother of God and of the Most Holy Rosary of Fatima, more terrible than an army in battle array, will defeat him forever." After saying this, Sister Filipina died in the arms of the holy foundress, Blessed Margaret. The documents attesting to these events surfaced in the year 2000, but it should be borne in mind that this revelation took place nearly 500 years before the Marian apparitions of Our Lady of Fatima at the Cova da Ira.[16]

12 March: Our Lady of Fourvière

OURVIÈRE IS AN ANCIENT SITE, now part of the Historic Site of Lyons World Heritage Site declared by UNESCO in 1998. Fourvière Hill was originally the location of the Roman Forum and a temple. Early Christians expressed their faith on this hill (Saint Pothin was martyred there), placing themselves under the protection of Mary from the beginning.[17] As early as 1168, a Christian chapel was built on the hill, which by that time had already become a Marian shrine. The chapel was dedicated to the Virgin Mary and to the medieval English Saint Thomas Becket (1118–70), who had been martyred shortly before. The chapel contained a statue of the Black Virgin.

On 29 April 1552, Huguenots destroyed the chapel and its Black Virgin statue. The Catholics of Lyon replaced both soon afterwards.In 1638, a serious epidemic of scurvy affected the children in the city and nothing seemed to be able to stop it, people decided to go on procession to Fourvière. The sickness then gradually disappeared and never came back. During an outbreak of black plague, on 12 March 1643, city officials made a vow to the Virgin Mary to erect two statues in her honour and on September 8, feast of her birth, to make a pilgrimage to her shrine to celebrate Mass and donate seven pounds of candles and a gold écu. The epidemic which continued to ravage France ended in Lyon that year, and pilgrims began flocking to Fourvière.

In 1832, the neighbouring departments were hit by cholera which threatened the city of Lyons. The archbishop commanded that public prayers were made. Once more spared by the scourge, the Lyonnais thanked the Virgin Mary by painting a huge painting (le "tableau d'Orsel"), that is now placed at the back of the Basilica.

On 23 July 1816, twelve Marist aspirants, priests and seminarians, climbed the hill to the shrine of Our Lady of Fourvière and placed their promise to found the Society of Mary (Marists) under the corporal on the altar while Jean-Claude Courveille celebrated Mass. On 21 January 1851, Peter Julian Eymard prayed at the

Shrine of Our Lady of Fourvière and was inspired to found the Congregation of the Blessed Sacrament.

In 1851, church leaders decided to replace the chapel's dilapidated bell tower with a new one, topped with a statue of the Virgin overlooking the city. Local sculptor Joseph Fabish, who later made the Virgin's statue at Lourdes, created the 18' gilt bronze image. Because his workshop flooded, installation was postponed from 8 September to 8 December, feast of the Immaculate Conception. When stormy weather that night prevented fireworks, devout citizens put lights in all their windows in the Virgin's honour. In memory of that event, Lyon celebrates a Festival of Lights on 8 December each year.

In 1870, citizens turned again to Our Lady for help, against an imminent Prussian invasion. When their prayers were answered, they decided to build a basilica on the holy hill. Building started in 1872 and finished in 1884, but the lavish mosaic decoration took another 80 years to complete. Its dedication anniversary is celebrated annually on the Saturday after the second Sunday of Easter. In the Basilica crypt are located images of the Virgin representing the various ethnic groups of the area. The Portuguese statue of Our Lady of Fatima is particularly venerated.[18]

13 March: Our Lady of the Empress, Rome

N THE CHURCH of St Gregory on the Caelian Hill there is an image of Our Lady before which Pope Gregory the Great prayed. A tradition records that, in the year 593, this image spoke to Saint Gregory the Great. We do not know what Our Lady said to Pope Gregory, but we know a little of what he said about her. He was imbued with Marian devotion, as can be seen from some of his writings. In speaking of the Blessed Virgin Mary at the Marriage at Cana Pope Gregory declared this profound intuition, which effectively indicates Mary's cooperation in the Redemption:

At the marriage, when the Virgin Mother said that wine was wanting, He replied, "Woman, what have I to do with you? My hour is not yet come" (Jn 2:4). For it was not that the Lord of the angels was subject to time, having, among all things which He had created, made hours and times; but, because the Virgin Mother, when wine was wanting, wished a miracle to be done by Him, it was at once answered her, "Woman, what have I to do with you?" As if to say plainly, That I can do a miracle comes to me of my Father, not of my Mother. For He who of the nature of His Father did miracles had it of His mother that He could die. Whence also, when He was on the Cross, in dying He acknowledged His mother, whom He commended to the disciple, saying, "Behold your mother" (Jn 19:27). He says, then, Woman, what have I to do with you? My hour has not yet come. That is, "In the miracle, which I have not of your nature, I do not acknowledge you. When the hour of death shall come, I shall acknowledge you as my mother, since I have it of you that I can die."[19]

14 March: Virgen del Carmen, Chile

 N 11 FEBRUARY 1817, General O'Higgins proclaimed Our Lady of Mount Carmel "Patrona Generalísima de las Armas de Chile", protector of the liberation army. However, a year later, Spanish forces pushed the Chileans back to Santiago, where on 14 March 1818, residents and clergy joined the revolutionaries in requesting heavenly help, vowing that on the spot of a decisive victory for freedom they would build a shrine to Our Lady of Mount Carmel. Their prayers were shortly answered at the battle of Maipú on 5 April. The first stone of the Chapel of Victory was laid that November, but because construction was intermittent for lack of funds, it was not inaugurated until 1892. And then in 1906, an earthquake nearly destroyed it, and another earthquake damaged the rebuilt church in 1927. On 16 July 1944, the first stone of a new, larger shrine was laid on the battlefield. Designed by Chilean architect Juan Martínez of quake-resistant reinforced concrete, the late deco-style building is the tallest church in the country. On 24 October 1974, the Votive Temple of Our Lady of Mt. Carmel opened beside the mossy old chapel. Pope John Paul II named the Sanctuary a Minor Basilica on 27 January 1987. It houses a statue of the Virgin of Carmel said to have been carried into the decisive battle and found on the field after the victory. It is a candle-bearer image, with carved wooden head and hands mounted on a clothed framework.

Pope St John Paul II crowned the statue of Our Lady of Maipú on 3 April 1987, during his apostolic visit to Chile:

> Virgin of Carmel of Maipú,
> Queen and Patroness of the Chilean people!
> We entrust the Church to your maternal heart
> and all the people of Chile:
> the pastors and the faithful,
> all the sons and daughters of this nation.
> Under your maternal protection,
> may Chile be united in its common home,
> a country reconciled in forgiveness
> and in forgetting wrongs,
> in the peace and love of Christ.
> You are Mother of the true life,
> teach us to be witnesses to the living God,
> of the love which is stronger than death,
> of the forgiveness which forgets wrongs,
> of the hope which looks to the future
> to build, in the strength of the Gospel,
> the civilization of love in a homeland reconciled and at peace.[20]

On the weekend after 14 March, Maipú celebrates the *Fiesta de la Promesa* with traditional music and dances in the plaza outside the church. It also hosts thousands of pilgrims on 16 July, Solemnity of Our Lady of Mount Carmel, a national holiday in Chile.

15 March: Our Lady of the Rosary, Qatar

ATAR IS A PENINSULA bordering Saudi Arabia, with an area of 22,000 square kilometres, and 350,000 inhabitants. It gained independence on 3 September 1971. The region is mostly a desert. The meagre incomes earned by traditional occupations rearing of camels, pearl fishery, production of dates and dry fish were given a boost by the discovery of oil in 1949. The oil is collected from the well in Dukhan and piped to Umm Said, which serves both as a harbour and refinery centre. The Sheikhdom is ruled by the hereditary monarch of a royal family, which concentrates all power in its hands according to a constitution written in 1970. Doha is the Capital. The missionaries used to visit the Christian communities of Qatar from Bahrain. A permanent presence began with Fr Adriano Benini in December 1970.

When Bishop Gremoli made his first pastoral visit in July 1976 he found a large community of Christians. In 1978 Fr Adriano was succeeded by Fr Kevin Mulhearn an English diocesan priest. He was able to gather a community of 5,000. Besides conducting services in the capital, Doha, Fr Kevin extended his pastoral care, in continuance of the work of Fr Adriano, to Dukhan—the oil centre and Umm Said—the refinery 50 km. from Doha. He organised services in private homes as it was impossible to have a church.

In 1980 Fr Kevin was replaced by Fr Timothy Cestello, an American Capuchin who was deported by the authorities a few months later. In the meantime, the Catholic population had increased to 6,000, composed of people of many countries, but most of them (nearly 90%) from India. As permission for a resident priest could not be obtained, Fr. Kevin returned for a time. He remained in Doha for six months, entrusted with the responsibility of preparing lay ministers. In this he was eminently successful. When he left Qatar for good on 26 May 1981, there was a good organisation to carry on the pastoral care of the Catholic communities.

On 4 November 1981, the Apostolic Vicar succeeded in finding a priest to reside in Qatar. He was Fr Gerard Dunne of the Mill Hill Fathers and British by nationality, and this had the right to reside in the country for a month, the priest was. In spite of his age (he had spent many years in Kenya and Borneo), he undertook the task of remaining in Doha for a month, leaving it for a couple of hours, and returning to start another period of stay, thus making the most of the concession granted to British subjects.

The government, while tolerating the presence of a priest in the country, would not permit a fixed place for the celebration of the liturgy. Thus began the house Masses, with small domestic congregations actively participating in the Eucharistic Sacrifice with exemplary piety. Fr Dunne left Qatar on 16 August 1986. He was succeeded by Fr Lesek Wisniewski, a British priest of Polish origin. Young and enterprising, he has given a great impetus to religious services, and organised catechism classes for children. He left for England in July 1989, and was succeeded by Fr John Van Deerlin.

Finally on 14 March 2008, the first Christian church in the emirate of Qatar opened, dedicated the next day to Our Lady of the Rosary by Cardinal Ivan Dias of India and Bishop Paul Hinder, apostolic vicar of Arabia. Because of its location in an Islamic state, by permission of the ruler and on land donated by him, it is not a typical Catholic church. The large, modern building has no exterior cross or other sign of Christianity, and the biggest day for worship is Friday, not Sunday. Before entering the Blessed Sacrament chapel, visitors remove their shoes, as they would at a mosque. There is a 24-hour police guard outside the church. Our Lady of the Rosary Church serves a cosmopolitan congregation with masses in nine languages and two rites. Many of the parishioners are from India, and the pastor, Capuchin Franciscan Tomasito Veneracion, is from the Philippines.[21]

16 March: Our Lady of the Fountain

 MPEROR LEO I, also known as Leo I the Thracian, Leo the Great, was the emperor of the Byzantine Empire from the year 457 until 474. Leo had begun with a career in the military, eventually rising to the rank of tribune in 457. When the emperor then reigning died, Leo was acclaimed the new emperor. It is interesting to note that he is considered a saint in the Orthodox Church.

According to the legend, the future Emperor Leo I of the Byzantine Empire was a good and pious man long before he became Emperor. One day in his travels he had come upon a blind man, who, being tormented with thirst, begged Leo to find water to quench his thirst. Feeling compassion for this man, Leo went in search of a source of water, but found none. As he was about to cease his search, he heard a voice telling him: "Leo, you do not need to tire yourself for there is water nearby."

Leo looked again, but still found no water. Then he heard the voice again, this time telling him:

> Emperor Leo, enter into the deepest part of the woods and you will find a lake; draw some cloudy water from it with your hands and give it to the blind man to quench his thirst, then anoint his darkened eyes with the clay and you will immediately know who I am, for I have dwelt in this place for a long time. Build a church here that all who come here will find answers to their petitions.

Leo found the lake, and did as he was instructed. As soon as the blind man's eyes were anointed, he received his sight. Leo became emperor a short time later, and then built a large and beautiful church in honour of the Blessed Virgin at that place just outside the Golden Gate near the Seven Towers district. Many miracles began to occur there, including resurrections from the dead, through the intercession of the Mother of God. When this church was damaged by earthquakes, it was rebuilt by subsequent emperors who also experience miraculous healings.

The church was razed to the ground when Constantinople fell to the Turks in the year 1453. The material that remained was taken to be used to construct the mosque of Sultan Beyazid. Even then people continued to come to the place seeking relief, for the spring remained intact beneath the ruins. The shrine had twenty-five steps going down to it, and a window in the roof above from which it received a little light.

In 1821 the shrine was destroyed during the Greek War of Independence. In 1833 the Sultan Mahmud allowed the Orthodox Christians to rebuild the shrine. Later, on the night of 6 September 1955, the Turks killed the abbot and the shrine was desecrated and burned to the ground. The shrine has since been restored yet again, but appears nothing like it once had in the distant past. Nevertheless, it is said that the water from the spring still has healing properties.

17 March: Our Lady of Ireland

URING THE DIFFICULT times of the persecution by Oliver Cromwell, one of the bishops forced to leave Ireland was Mgr Walter Lynch, Bishop of Clonfert. He took the painting of Mary, Comforter of the Afflicted, with him into exile. In Vienna he met the bishop of Györ, Hungary, who invited him there. He finally came to Hungary in 1654. He was kindly received by Mgr John Pusky, Bishop of Györ, and eventually became auxiliary bishop of the Diocese, where he served until his death in 1663.

Ten years later Bishop Lynch planned to return to his native land. Almighty God prevented this; during his dying hours he gave to the Bishop of Györ his only material treasure— the picture of Our Lady of Ireland. Soon after, as a memory of the Irish Bishop, the picture of Our Lady was hung on the wall of the Cathedral at Györ.

Some years passed, and on the feast of Saint Patrick, 17 March 1697, while large numbers of the faithful were present in the Cathedral, an awe-inspiring event took place. A bloody sweat was observed to come over the figure of the Blessed Lady in the picture. Drops of blood fell onto the Infant Jesus; as the bleeding continued for three hours. Linen towels, which are still retained under glass at her shrine, were used to wipe the blood from the perspiring face.

In the archives of the Cathedral of Győr, there is a document written in 1697 on parchment, relating this event. It is signed not only by the clergy and the laity who were present at the Mass, but by the mayor and members of the city council, by the governor, by Lutheran and Calvanist preachers, and by a Rabbi—over one hundred signatures represent eye-witnesses to the miracle. The weeping continued after the tears were wiped off and the picture removed from its frame. Some people connected this with a law passed later that year in Dublin banning Catholic bishops from Ireland. In 1767, the Weeping Virgin Mary was set in a magnificent baroque altarpiece. Against a dark background, the Madonna looks down at the baby asleep on a little bed, neatly tucked between two sheets and a red brocade spread, with his head on two pillows. His chest and arms are bare. She wears a pinkish grey veil over brown hair and a blue mantle over a terracotta robe. In 1874, Pope Pius IX granted a plenary indulgence on the feasts of Saint Patrick and the Assumption, before which feast public novenas are held.[22]

18 March: Our Lady of Sorrows

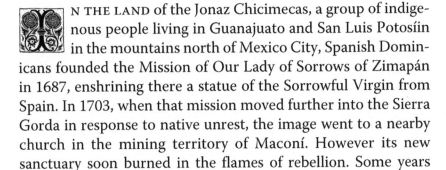 N THE LAND of the Jonaz Chicimecas, a group of indigenous people living in Guanajuato and San Luis Potosíin in the mountains north of Mexico City, Spanish Dominicans founded the Mission of Our Lady of Sorrows of Zimapán in 1687, enshrining there a statue of the Sorrowful Virgin from Spain. In 1703, when that mission moved further into the Sierra Gorda in response to native unrest, the image went to a nearby church in the mining territory of Maconí. However its new sanctuary soon burned in the flames of rebellion. Some years

later, a Dominican friar found the old statue in the ruins. Fray Luis de Guzmán, sent by the Viceroy to pacify the area and subdue the Jonaz, placed the recovered statue in a nearby church. In the late 1770s, Franciscan Fray Guadalupe Soriano moved it to a new mission at Bucareli, and then to the Mission of Santo Domingo de Soriano, near present-day Colón, where it worked many miracles and attracted so many pilgrims that a larger shrine became necessary. The first stone was placed on 19 March 1880, which was Friday of Sorrows that year, *Viernes de Dolores*, the Friday before Palm Sunday, when many Spanish communities honour Our Lady of Sorrows. Bishop Manuel Rivera Muñoz consecrated the new church on 18 March 1912.

In 1964, the statue was canonically crowned in a huge ceremony by authority of Pope Paul VI. In 2009, during an even more spectacular ritual, the shrine received Pope Benedict XVI's designation of Minor Basilica. Over the centuries, so many people had left ex voto offerings in thanks for answered prayers that in 2006 the shrine opened a Museum of Miracles next to the Basilica. In 2007, the Gutiérrez Hernández family brought a metal painting, commissioned by local artist Alejandro Padilla González, illustrating the dramatic story of their daughter María José: in 2004, the girl fell into a well when no one was looking, and by the time another child saw her floating body it was lifeless, swollen, and purple. All attempts to resuscitate the girl failed until the stricken family called on the Most Holy Mother of God. When she finally came to in the hospital, María José said that the woman who saved her was the little Virgin of Sorrows. In a neighbouring state, a woman dying of AIDS saw news of the miracle on television and begged to be taken to the shrine in Colón, where she recovered so completely that she went back to work and commissioned Padilla González to paint a tribute in thanks. Over the entrance to the Museum of Miracles are the words of the angel Gabriel to Mary: "For nothing is impossible to God"(Lk 1:37).[23]

19 March: Our Lady of the Cape

UR LADY OF THE CAPE SHRINE is Canada's National Shrine to Our Blessed Mother. It is located at Trois-Rivières, in the district of Cap-de-la-Madeleine. The city of Trois-Rivières is in the Province of Quebec, half-way between Montreal and Quebec City. The very first church of Cap-de-la-Madeleine was a small wooden structure built in 1659. Father Paul Vachon, its first resident pastor, instituted the Brotherhood of the Rosary in 1694. In 1714 construction began of the second parish church that was opened for worship in 1720, replacing the first small wooden church. This second church, presently called the Old Shrine, and made with fieldstones, is still the oldest church in Canada in which Mass is celebrated daily.

Following Father Vachon's death in 1729, there was a period of 115 years without a resident pastor. Consequently, without the guidance of a pastor and the more or less sporadic celebration of the holy sacrifice of the Mass, the parish was in great need of a spiritual renewal. Father Luke Desilets was sent to the little town of Cape de la Madeleine in 1864. One evening in 1867 Father Desilets went into his church and found, before the statue of the Virgin, a small pig with a rosary between its teeth. "There", the priest said, "men drop their beads, but the very beasts pick them up!" He knelt before the statue and promised to spend the rest of his life spreading devotion to the rosary. Immediately afterward there was a remarkable rebirth of piety among his people.

In time there was need for a larger church at the Cape. The men of the parish crossed the river, quarried and prepared the stones for the new edifice. The parish could not afford a barge to bring the stones across the river, and the river is so wide and swift at the point that it does not freeze every year. Beginning in November, 1877, the parishioners recited the Rosary every Sunday after High Mass in petition for freezing weather. The beginning of March they became discouraged, but the pastor himself continued to pray.

On the evening of 14 March, a warm wind began breaking up the ice farther down the river. It came floating in huge chunks. Ice accumulated behind the cape. By 16 March, it formed a mass reaching almost from shore to shore. All that night in the bitter cold more than 50 men worked to reinforce the causeway. The work was dangerous because the current was swift and much of the ice was soft. Far into the morning a dim light shone from one of the rectory windows. "There is nothing to fear", the men said to each other. "The Curé is reciting his beads. His Aves are holding us up." From then on the causeway of ice was called the Bridge of Rosaries.

For eight days the men brought the stones over the Bridge of Rosaries on their sledges; pools swirled a few feet from the path across the ice, but there were no accidents. On the eighth day the weather turned warmer; the stones had been hauled. Father Desilets ordered the work to stop; in the afternoon the passage was swept away. The new church was built, and the ancient chapel dedicated to the Queen of the Rosary, on 22 June 1883. On dedication evening Father Desilets and two other priests knelt in the church where that day the statue of the Virgin had been moved from the side to the main altar. That evening Pierre Lacroix from Trois-Rivières, a handicapped man, came to pray and asked for the assistance of Father Frederic Janssoone OFM, and Father Luc Desilets to help him into the church. As the three men were praying, suddenly Father Desilets got up to ask Father Frederic if he could see the same thing he was seeing. Father Frederic answered that "Yes, the statue has opened its eyes, hasn't it?" Pierre Lacroix also noticed this. Both priests got up, moving from spot to spot while still looking at the statue to make sure that they were really seeing this. Father Frederic often spoke of this event saying that the eyes of the statue were wide opened; that they stayed opened for about five to ten minutes; that her eyes were dark, well formed and in perfect harmony with the rest of her face; that she had the face of a living person; that her look changed his life forever. He never stopped talking about this wonderful event of the Blessed Mother. Father Desilets died a month later, his work was accomplished.[24]

The miraculous statue called Our Lady of the Cape, was crowned in 1904 by authority of Pope St Pius X. In 1909 the Bishops of Canada proclaimed the chapel to be a National Shrine to the Blessed Virgin. The construction of the Basilica began in 1955 and it was inaugurated in 1964; it can seat 1660 persons. On 10 September 1984, Pope St John Paul II was welcomed by a crowd estimated at 75000 persons and declared:

> For as long as there has been evangelization here, there has been devotion to Mary. How indeed can one announce and realize the Son's work without turning to the Mother, without admiring her openness and her faith, without imploring her intercession? This very ancient shrine of Notre-Dame-du-Cap is evidence of the fact. I too am happy to have come here as a pilgrim. Pilgrims come here from the whole of Quebec, from other provinces, from every part of Canada. Times of pilgrimage are high points in the Christian life, opportunities for community and personal prayer and that in a spirit of freedom and simplicity not always found at home. They are occasions for a return to the sources, in search of the Word of God. We come here to lay our concerns and our requests at Mary's feet, with a confidence pleasing to God.[25]

20 March: Our Lady of Calevourt

HE IMAGE OF OUR LADY OF CALEVOURT, at Uckelen, near Brussels began to work miracles in the year 1451, which led to the determination to build a magnificent chapel in honour of Our Blessed Lady, in the year 1623, which the Infanta of Spain, Isabella Clara Eugenia, devoutly visited in the same year. The statue is of the Blessed Mother standing with her Divine Child reclining on her right arm, His feet supported by the left hand of His mother. Our Lady holds a key and a large rosary.

This image of Our Lady is known under various titles, due to the fact that Mary gives aid, even miraculous aid, when specifically called upon for help. Our Lady of Calevourt is perhaps better known as Our Lady of Good Success, or Our Lady of Aberdeen. During the Protestant Reformation, the figure was taken to Flanders and hidden away by a Catholic family to protect it from profanation; in due course it fell into the hands of Protestants. This family received numerous graces and blessings which they attributed to the presence of the holy image in their house. They were reconciled to the Church as a result.

In 1623 a Spanish captain was given the statue with instructions to place it into the hands of Archduchess Isabella. The arrival of the statue in Brussels took place with several incidents. The same day the ship arrived, the Infanta Isabella won a battle against the Hollanders. The Princess sent the statue back to Brussels, providing the necessary funds for a sanctuary she intended to be called Our Lady of Aberdeen. The townspeople greeted the statue enthusiastically with a procession and placed it in the chapel, but when the victory became known, the name of the sanctuary was changed and dedicated instead to Our Lady of Good Success.

From that time on the statue of Our Lady travelled from place to place, but always her image was saved. During the Terrors of the French Revolution the statue was given to an English Catholic who kept it safe until 1805, when it was restored to Belgium. A few years later the Protestants forced the image to be transferred to a parish church in Finistère, where the image now reigns peacefully over her beloved people.

21 March: Kursk Root Mother of God

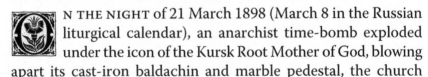 N THE NIGHT of 21 March 1898 (March 8 in the Russian liturgical calendar), an anarchist time-bomb exploded under the icon of the Kursk Root Mother of God, blowing apart its cast-iron baldachin and marble pedestal, the church

windows, and the cupola. However, the precious image and its glass cover remained unharmed. This widely revered Orthodox icon had resided for hundreds of years in Kursk in western Russia.

At the time of its discovery on 8 September 1295, after Tatar devastation, the area was a depopulated wilderness.[26] Some men had come from Rylsk, around 75 miles southwest, to hunt game there. One of them noticed the icon lying face down at the root of a tree, and when he lifted it up, a spring gushed forth. The hunter built a chapel for the image near the spot, where the number of pilgrims and miracles soon multiplied. When the prince of Rylsk tried to move the icon to a finer church there, it repeatedly returned to its place in the forest. In 1597, the Tsar decided to rebuild the city of Kursk and founded the Kursk Root Hermitage (monastery) at the site of the chapel. When Tatars destroyed the hermitage in 1611, the icon went to Moscow until 1618, when the monastery was rebuilt. After that, annual processions commemorated the icon's return from Moscow to Kursk: on the ninth Friday after Easter, it was carried from the Kursk Cathedral of the Sign to the rural Hermitage, remaining until September 13, when it returned to the city.

Following the Russian Revolution, Orthodox bishops took the icon to Serbia in 1919. In 1920, the counter-Revolutionary White Army brought the icon to their Crimean stronghold. After their defeat, the Kursk Root Icon returned to Serbia until 1944, when it accompanied Orthodox clergy into exile, moving through many countries in Europe and finally to New York, where since 1957 it has resided in the Church of the Mother of God of the Sign in New York City, Cathedral of the Russian Orthodox Church Outside of Russia. It often tours the Russian diaspora, and visited Russia itself in 2007. The Kursk Root Mother of God is an icon of the "sign" type, with the child in front of his mother facing the viewer, often in a roundel. Its main feast day is celebrated on November 27 in the Julian calendar or December 10 in the Gregorian.

22 March: Our Lady of the Seven Veils

 N THE CATHEDRAL of Foggia one can find an ancient and mysterious image of the Blessed Virgin Mary. This icon, called Our Lady of the Seven Veils, once caused Saint Alphonsus to go into ecstasy. As a young priest, St Pio of Pietreclina would make a visit to this image every day.

In eleventh century Italy, Foggia was a tiny town perched around the Tavern of the Owl. One day in 1062 some local farmers saw three flames over a small pond or bog. Intrigued, they dug where the miraculous fire had been and discovered a large "table" buried in the mud. They realized that this "table" was actually a Byzantine icon that had remained somewhat preserved despite being soaked in water and mud. The image was cleaned and then cloaked with new veils. The icon was then placed in the local Tavern of the Owl for veneration. Soon the tavern became a place of pilgrimage.

In 1080 Robert Guiscard built a church to honor the sacred image. In 1172 the church was expanded by William II "the Good" of Sicily. The "face hole" is all that one can now see of the original wooden icon. It is black and the face is now indiscernible. However, on Maundy Thursday of 1731, the Virgin Mary's white face appeared in this portal, which was usually black and dark. Saint Alphonsus Liguori heard about apparition and went to Foggia to venerate the Immaculate Mother of the Saviour. He also received an apparition of the Virgin's face in the small black portal. He described the Blessed Virgin's face on that occasion as a girl of 13-14 with a white veil. The apparitions of the Virgin's face on the icon continued until about 1745; Foggia's patronal feast 22 March commemorates them

As the city grew larger, the church was decorated and enriched. The Normans, Swabians, Angevins, Aragonese, Spaniards, and Bourbons considered the church to be one of the most important in Italy. It has served as the site for several royal weddings. Today, the image is said to be covered in seven layers of precious metal and embroidered material—hence the name Our Lady of the Seven Veils.

23 March: Our Lady of Ujarrás

JARRÁS VALLEY IS in the midst of the Cordillera de Talamanca and the Central Volcanic Chain of Costa Rica, made up of alluvial soil. This piece of territory was inhabited by natives governed by Chief Guarco, with the arrival of the Spaniards, suffered the ravages of domination. In the sixteenth century, a native Huetar Indian was fishing at the mouth of the Pacuare River, when he saw a wooden box that drove the waves toward the shore; he picked up the box without opening it and brought it to his people. When reached Ujarrás, wanting to continue to Cartago, he could not lift the box because it had become so heavy that even with the help of other Indians it was impossible to move. Confused he went to the Franciscan convent in Cartago, where he told the monks what was happening. They opened the box, and found inside it a beautiful image of the Virgin Mary. At the same time they realized that the image desired to remain there, so, between 1575 and 1580, they erected a hermitage made of straw and indigenous people called the image Virgin Mary as "The Queen of the Valleys".

Over the years the image attained fame due to many miracles that it performed for the villagers. When the English pirate Henry Morgan attacked the village in 1666, the Virgin Mary came to their rescue to repulse the attack. Then on 16 February 1723, the Irazu volcano erupted shaking he city of Cartago, covering everything with ashes. Such was the alarm of the people that they immediately prayed with devotion to Our Lady of Ujarrás, and the fury of the volcano subsided. Also, in January 1725, the Ujarrás valley was hit by very bad weather, but despite the rain, the men worked at their tasks and the women at their household chores. When the church bells rang in a sad and unusual tone, all the people ceased their work and headed towards the church.

Meanwhile, the priest and the sacristan were even more intrigued as the bells rang on their own and no one had touched them. The bells stopped ringing, and then started again after a moment of quiet. By that time, the whole town was gathered at the church praying. Then, the peal ceased a second time, and in the same manner began to restart; at this point everyone understood the sign and fled to the mountains. A rumbling sound was then heard in the mountains and soon the whole valley was covered with water, like a waterfall, causing one of the largest floods that took place in the valley. The people concluded that Our Lady had rung the bells to save her people, so when everything returned to normal, they took the image in procession to Cartago, where feasts were held in thanksgiving for Mary's care.

In 1833, the village was subject to a devastating flood which led to the government passing a decree to move the village to a safer place. The church in Ujarrás has since been restored, and was built with limestone. The Virgin of the Holy Conception of Ujarras, Holy Patron of the Colony, was originally installed in the church. However, the image was moved to the new township to the Sanctuary of Paradise. The image has pleasant features on its face and hands and is well preserved.

24 March: Our Lady of the Flowering Thorn

ROM THE INFANCY of the Church, images of our Blessed Lady have been in use among the faithful, to enkindle and to keep alive in their hearts a tender devotion to the mother of God. When the barbarians overran the Roman Empire, the Christians, fearful of profanation, hid these statues of the Blessed Virgin in the most secret recesses of caves and forests. The Huns and Vandals spared neither age nor sex, and when the tumult of war had subsided, few or none remained to withdraw those statues from their hiding places; and they rested until the providence of God made many of them be discovered and often in a miraculous manner. Our Lady of the Flowering Thorn was one of these, and the marvellous circumstances of the discovery are thus related.

On the western side of the Jura in France, there once stood an old baronial residence. Its noble owner had heard the voice of St Bernard calling through the length and breadth of the land, to the rescue of Jerusalem and of the holy sepulchre. Among those heroes of the Crusades, fell the lord of this castle on the Jura, leaving a widow to mourn her loss while she rejoiced in his gain. Their names have been lost in the lapse of ages; he is only remembered as the crusader, she as the saint. It was on one of those days when winter, about to leave the earth, seems to cast himself into the bosom of spring, that our saint was walking along the avenue of her castle, her mind full of pious meditation. She had reached the termination of the avenue, when her eye was attracted toward a thorny bush, laden with the richest blossoms of spring.

She hastened towards it, doubtful whether the flakes of snow had not deceived her; but no, she found it crowned with a multitude of little white stars shaded with crimson rays, and she carefully broke off a branch to hang up in her oratory, over an image of the Blessed Virgin which she had venerated from childhood, and she joyfully returned towards the castle, carrying her innocent offering. She went every day to gather a fresh garland to adorn the statue of her mother Mary. Now it happened that one day, being very busy in relieving the wants of the poor who came to her for alms and kind words, she could not go to gather her garland before the shades of evening had covered the earth, and as she approached the thicket an uneasy feeling came over her, occasioned by the increasing darkness. She was thinking that it would be difficult to gather the flowers, when a calm clear light seemed to overspread the bushes. Startled at the sight, and fearing that robbers might be lurking there, she paused for a moment, but remembering she had never once omitted to bring her offering, she boldly ventured forward, though it was with a trembling hand she plucked the branch that seemed as if it bent towards her. She saw something mysterious, and, the following evening she went to the thicket, accompanied by a faithful servant and her old chaplain. The soft light was seen as they approached, becoming every instant more bright and vivid. They stopped, they fell upon their knees, for it seemed to them that this light came from heaven. Then the good old priest arose, and moved with reverential step toward the thicket, chanting a hymn of the Church; he put aside the branches which appeared to open of their own accord, and a little image of the Blessed Virgin, simply carved by unskilled though pious hands, was found in the midst of the bushes, and it was from this statue that the light emanated. "Hail Mary, full of grace", said the priest, kneeling before the image, and at that moment a melodious murmur was heard through the surrounding woods, as if the chant had been taken up by the choirs of angels. He then recited litanies and after repeated acts of veneration, he took the statue in his hands to carry it to the castle, and fixed a niche for it in the chapel. There the noble lady and her retinue watched and prayed until midnight.

In the morning, however, the statue had returned to the thorn tree. The Lady feared in her humility that her own unworthiness sent the statue from her; but the chaplain assured her that Our Lady simply wanted to be honoured in the place that she herself had chosen. A chapel was built around the thorn-tree to Our Lady of the Flowering Thorn, and the statue was left in its original spot. Its fame spread all over Europe, and for many years pilgrims turned from the more famous pilgrim roads to seek out the narrow gorge where Our Lady of the Thorn held court, and sprigs of the favoured tree withered on many a chapel wall throughout Christendom. Nuns, too, came to the favoured spot, and the noble lady gave them her house for a cloister and built there an abbey church. She herself joined the nuns and after a holy life, died at the foot of Our Lady's altar. Now grasses creep for many centuries over the stones worn smooth by sandaled feet of consecrated nuns, and the pilgrims ways are lost in the brush and the thorn. Still, each spring, till Time is no more, the thorn trees bloom, and white petals testify to those who will listen, to the tale that no scientist would believe, the story of Our Lady of the Flowering Thorn.[27]

25 March: The Annunciation of the Lord

 HE SOLEMNITY OF the Annunciation is one of the most important Feasts of Our Lady in which we celebrate the great Mystery of the Incarnation, the Word made flesh. Also known as Lady Day, it falls nine months before Christmas, in accordance with the ancient tradition that the angel's words came true, and Jesus was conceived, as soon as Mary assented. "I am the handmaid of the Lord: be it done to me according to your word" (Lk 1:38), Our Lady replied to the angel Gabriel; modern theology makes much of Mary's "Fiat" as an exemplary alignment of human will with God's, demonstrating the power of free will when unconditionally agreeing to the divine plan: Gabriel's words "troubled" Mary, but her consent made possible Christ's Incarnation, just as His agonized assent in Gethsemane made possible our Redemption. This joyful feast usually occurs during the penitential season of Lent. Here are the meditations of St Gregory Thaumaturgus, bishop of Neo-Caesarea in Pontus, now in Turkey, on this great celebration:

> Today are strains of praise sung joyfully by the choir of angels, and the light of the coming of Christ shines brightly upon the faithful. Today the glad spring-time is around us, and Christ the Sun of righteousness has beamed with clear light in our midst, and has illumined the minds of the faithful. Today is Adam made anew, and moves in the choir of angels, having winged his way to heaven. Today is the whole circle of the earth filled with joy, since the sojourn of the Holy Spirit has been realized to men. Today the grace of God and the hope of the unseen shine through all wonders transcending imagination, and make the mystery that was kept hid from eternity plainly discernible to us. Today are woven the chaplets of never-fading virtue. Today, God, willing to crown the sacred heads of those whose

pleasure is to listen to Him, and who delight in His festivals, invites the lovers of unswerving faith as those He has called and His heirs. The heavenly kingdom urgently summons those who love celestial things to join the divine service of the incorporeal choirs. Today did Gabriel, who stands by God, come to the pure Virgin, bearing to her the glad Annunciation, "Hail, you who are highly favoured!" Mary asked herself what this greeting could mean, but the angel said to her, "Mary, do not be afraid; you have won God's favor. Look! You are to conceive in your womb and bear a Son, and you must name Him Jesus. He will be great and will be called Son of the Most High. The Lord God will give Him the throne of his ancestor David; He will rule over the House of Jacob for ever and His reign will have no end." Mary said to the angel, "But how can this come about, since I have no knowledge of man?" The angel answered, "The Holy Spirit will come upon you, and the power of the Most High will cover you with its shadow. And so the Child will be holy and will be called Son of God."[28]

26 March: Our Lady of Soissons

N THE YEAR 1128, a plague afflicted the city of Soissons. For six consecutive days the victims went to the shrine of Our Lady and called out to her for help. The Blessed Virgin Mary appeared to them, accompanied by heavenly hosts of angels. Immediately the people who witnessed the miracle and believed were healed. The Bishop asked all who were healed to make a novena of thanksgiving and to kiss the slipper of the Holy Virgin kept in the church.

A rustic servant of one of the knights of Soissons, a man named Boso, came to the church for the festival which was to follow the novena. While his companions gave gifts and talked of the slipper of Our Lady, he gave nothing and scoffed at the idea, muttering, "You are very foolish to believe this to be the Virgin's slipper. It would have rotted long ago." At these words Boso's irreverent mouth was drawn toward his ear with such sharp pain that his eyes seemed to slip out of his head. A tumour appeared and covered his face, making it seem inhuman. Roaring and writhing, he threw himself before the altar of Our Lady, begging for help, as he had offended the Mother of God, and he knew there was no one else who could heal him.

The abbess, a woman named Mathilda, took the slipper and made the sign of the cross over the victim. Immediately he began to heal. The punished scoffer repented and gave himself up to the service of the Church of Soissons. Many—the lame, the blind, the deaf, the dumb, the paralytics, were healed at the shrine. The Abbey was once the largest in France, famous for its rich collection of relics, including the "Lady Slipper", but all that remains today of the abbey is a ruined wall with two arches, as the rest was methodically razed during the French Revolution.[29]

27 March: The Seven Sorrows of Our Lady

HE FRIDAY OF Sorrows is a solemn pious remembrance of the sorrowful Blessed Virgin Mary on the Friday before Palm Sunday at the end of the fifth week of Lent It is traditionally known as Our Lady in Passiontide. In certain Catholic countries, especially in Mexico, Guatemala, Italy, Peru, Brazil, Spain, Malta, Nicaragua and the Philippines, it is seen as the beginning of the Holy Week celebrations and termed as Viernes de Dolores (Friday of Sorrows). It takes place exactly one week before Good Friday, and concentrates on the pain that the Passion of Jesus Christ caused to his mother, the Blessed Virgin Mary, who is venerated under the title Our Lady of Sorrows.

Traditionally, this suffering was not limited to the passion and death event; rather, it comprised the sorrows of Mary, which were foretold by the priest Simeon who proclaimed to Mary: "This Child is destined to be the downfall and the rise of many in Israel, a sign that will be opposed and you yourself shall be pierced with a sword so that the thoughts of many hearts may be laid bare" (Lk 2:34–35). These seven sorrows of our Blessed Mother included the flight of the Holy Family into Egypt; the loss and finding of the Child Jesus in the Temple; Mary's meeting of Jesus on His way to Calvary; Mary's standing at the foot of the Cross when our Lord was crucified; her holding of Jesus when He was taken down from the cross; and then our Lord's burial. The prophesy of Simeon that a sword would pierce our Blessed Mother's heart was fulfilled in these events. For this reason, Mary is sometimes depicted with her heart exposed and with seven swords piercing it. More importantly, each new suffering was received with the courage, love, and trust that echoed her Fiat, "let it be done unto me according to your word", first uttered at the Annunciation.

This Feast of Our Lady of Sorrows grew in popularity in the twelfth century, and by the fourteenth and fifteenth centuries, the feast and devotion were widespread throughout the Church. In 1482, the feast was officially placed in the Roman Missal under the title of Our Lady of Compassion, highlighting the great love our Blessed Mother displayed in suffering with her Son. The word compassion derives from the Latin roots *cum* and *patior* which means to suffer with. Our Blessed Mother's sorrow exceeded anyone else's since she was the Mother of Jesus, who was not only her Son but also her Lord and Saviour; she truly suffered with her Son. In 1727, Pope Benedict XIII placed the Feast of Our Lady of Compassion in the Roman Calendar on Friday before Palm Sunday. In 1668 the feast in honour of the Seven Sorrows was set for the Sunday after September 14, the Feast of the Holy Cross. The feast was inserted into the Roman calendar in 1814, and Pope Pius X fixed the permanent date of September 15 for the Feast of the Seven Sorrows of the Blessed Virgin Mary, now simply called the Feast of Our Lady of Sorrows.

28 March: Our Lady of Bocciola

 N A WARM spring day almost five centuries ago, on the 28 March 1543 to be precise, Giulia Manfredi, a young shepherdess, deaf since birth, was tending her family's cows and their few sheep at pasture on the green patch of land near her house, in the hills of the eastern part of Lake Orta, at an altitude of 500 meters above sea level and in the municipality of Ameno, near Novara in Piedmont, Italy.

Like every other day the girl stopped to pray silently in front of the little chapel dedicated to Our Lady and the Infant Jesus; that day among the branches of a wild plum tree (a whitethorn, referred to as "bocciolo" in the local dialect) growing nearby the chapel, the Virgin Mary appeared and promised the young girl that she would be taken up into heaven; she asked her to let people know that, in return for the grace she was about to bestow, she wished to be solemnly honoured in that same place every Saturday afternoon.

"They won't believe me", Giulia said to the Virgin, who told her to have faith; when the poor young girl got home she realised she had been granted the gift of speech and while she was telling everybody all about the apparition, the church bells, though nobody had touched them, began to ring festively. News of the prodigious apparition quickly spread far and wide and Our Lady of Graces has attracted the faithful in large numbers ever since, from every village in the Alps and particularly from the Vallese area. From that day forward, as the Sanctuary's annals may confirm, many miracles have taken place, such as people whose lives have been saved in accidents and the seriously ill who have made a complete recovery.

The building of a place of pilgrimage began in 1628 at the site of the apparition to replace the original little chapel; it stands there today in its typically neoclassical style and sombre colonnade in pink granite while a few fragments of the wild plum tree on which

Our Lady appeared are kept inside it. The church was honoured by Pope Gregory XVI in 1844 with the official title of Sanctuary.

29 March: *Our Lady in Aracoeli*

T MARY OF the *Ara Coeli* (Altar of Heaven) is the name of a Basilica in Rome. It dates to the sixth century, and is located on the highest point of Capitoline Hill, on the site where a Sibyl is supposed to have prophesied to Emperor Augustus the birth of Christ.

> At a certain time during the reign of Caesar Augustus (born 63 BC—died 14 AD) the Roman Senate, wishing to vest him with a supreme honour, resolved to proclaim him god. This pleased his vanity, but for some strange reason, he advised the senate to withhold the honour until he consulted the Sibyl of Tivoli regarding it. She requested him to give her three days before she answered, during which she invoked "those on high" to enlighten her. After the three days she said to the emperor, "Augustus, most powerful sir, hearken! There is no one should be called god unless he is God' you are only a man, though famous. Another, who is truly God is about to descend upon the earth and He will assume flesh in the womb of a most Pure Virgin." Then a brilliant light shone forth from the sky; it churned and swirled, forming a halo. Within its centre Augustus saw a most beautiful Lady with a Baby in her arms. She stood upon a splendid white altar and her figure was surrounded by little angels and from heaven a voice rang out, "This is the promised young girl who will give a Savior to the world, and that is the altar of the Son of God." Overcome by the marvellous sight, Augustus fell to his knees, with his forehead to the ground, remained a long time in silent adoration of the Mother and Child. He announced to the Senate and all the people that he must renounce the title they proposed, and told of his vision. Then he commanded that an altar be erected on the Capitoline Hill dedicated to the Only-Begotten Son of God

and His Mother. This legend is inscribed on the wall of the
chapel of St Helena. The image of the Madonna of Ara
Coeli was crowned on 29 March 1636.[30]

The chapel of St Helena in this church is supposed to be on the
very spot where the prophecy was made and where subsequently
Augustus erected an altar to the First-Born of God. On the high
altar of the church is the Madonna of the Altar of Heaven, an
image in Byzantine style. By the 500s, Greek monks had built a
church there. In the 1200s, Franciscan friars built the present
church in honour of the belief that Our Lady, holding the divine
Child, appeared to Augustus there. On the high altar is an icon
said to be by St Luke and to have come from Jerusalem, by way
of the Chalkoprateia Church of the Theotokos in Constantinople,
to Rome in the 400s. The present image is a copy, dated to the
late 1000s, closely resembling the ancient Madonna di San Sisto
in the Dominican Convent on Monte Mario. It is an icon of the
Hagiosoritissa variety, showing Mary without child, her hands in
an intercessory gesture: Our Lady the Advocate. During the
plague of 1348, the image was processed through the streets of
Rome. The plague ended swiftly, and the great staircase leading
to the church was dedicated that same year in thanksgiving. On
29 March 1636, the Madonna d'Aracoeli was solemnly crowned.
French troops stole the crown in 1797; it was replaced in 1938.
On 30 May 1948, the Roman people were consecrated to the
Immaculate Heart of Mary before the icon.

The Church of Our Lady in Ara Coeli is a great gathering place
for Roman children during Christmas time. The attraction is a
life-size statue of the Christ child, carved by a Franciscan monk
living in Jerusalem in the fifteenth century, and made of wood
from the Mount of Olives in Jerusalem. Being unable to finish it,
the monk set it aside in a corner of his cell until he could get the
proper colour of paint; that night, the angels came and finished
it for him. Later the monk was recalled to Rome and he carried
the statue with him, unfortunately his ship ran into a storm and
was wrecked near the port of Livorno. The statue was lost, but

floated to the shore where it was recovered and eventually found its way to the Church of Our Lady in Ara Coeli.

30 March: The Risen Christ appears to Our Lady

ESUS'S APPEARANCE TO his Blessed Mother after His resurrection, is evidenced by a well-established tradition of the event, even though it does not appear anywhere in the New Testament accounts concerning the risen Jesus. The first Western reference to Jesus appearing first to His mother appears to be St Ambrose. In his treatise on the excellence of virginity Ambrose suggests that it confers a special integrity of faith: since "virgins merited seeing the resurrection of the Lord before the apostles".[31] He seems to imply here that all the women who visited the tomb on the Sunday morning were virgins;[32] but he goes on then to contrast the Virgin Mary with Mary Magdalene: "Mary saw the resurrection of the Lord; she was the first to see and believe. Mary Magdalene also saw, but she hesitated."[33] It could be that Ambrose was also introducing a distinction between Mary's faith and the Magdalene's doubt to reconcile the non-biblical tradition of Jesus's first appearing to His Mother with the statement in Mk 16:9 that Jesus "first appeared to Mary Magdalene".

A fifth-century author, Sedulius, maintains that in the radiance of His risen life Christ first showed himself to his Mother. In fact, she, who at the Annunciation was the way He entered the world, was called to spread the marvellous news of the Resurrection in order to become the herald of His glorious coming. Thus bathed in the glory of the Risen One, she anticipates the Church's splendour.[34] In the Middle Ages, Ludolf of Saxony's *Vita Christi* ('Life of Christ') was an important source of the tradition of the risen Jesus appearing to His Mother. This Cistercian writer devoted a whole chapter to enquiring how the Lord Jesus appeared to His Mother.[35] He describes how the women going to the tomb to anoint the body of Jesus did so with His Mother's permission.[36] He later observed that it seemed surprising that

Mary did not go with the women and suggested as possible reasons for this that it would have been too much for her, and that out of concern for her, John, to whom she had been entrusted by Jesus, would not permit her to go, adding finally that "the blessed Virgin knew that He was not there, but had risen immortal and incorruptible". For "while our Lady was praying and gently weeping, suddenly the Lord Jesus came" and appeared to His mother. She embraced Him, "her mourning transformed into happiness", and sharing their joy they sat and conversed about what had happened to him and what he had been doing since, while she reassured herself that his sufferings were really over.[37] Finally, Ludolf observed, unlike Jesus's other Easter appearances, which were aimed at proving His resurrection from the dead, "He appeared first of all to His Virgin Mother, not to prove His resurrection but to delight her at the sight of Him."[38]

In Spiritual Exercises, St Ignatius places Jesus's appearance to His mother as His first after the resurrection.[39] After Jesus had been laid in the tomb, Mary "alone remains to keep alive the flame of faith, preparing to receive the joyful and astonishing announcement of the Resurrection."[40] It seems reasonable to think that Mary, as the image and model of the Church which waits for the Risen One and meets Him in the group of disciples during his Easter appearances, enjoyed a personal contact with her risen Son, so that she too could delight in the fullness of paschal joy.[41]

31 March: Our Lady of the Rose

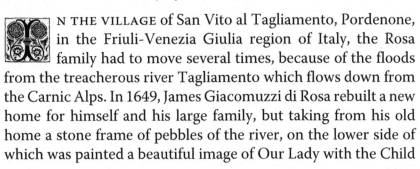 N THE VILLAGE of San Vito al Tagliamento, Pordenone, in the Friuli-Venezia Giulia region of Italy, the Rosa family had to move several times, because of the floods from the treacherous river Tagliamento which flows down from the Carnic Alps. In 1649, James Giacomuzzi di Rosa rebuilt a new home for himself and his large family, but taking from his old home a stone frame of pebbles of the river, on the lower side of which was painted a beautiful image of Our Lady with the Child

in her arms. In breaking down the old house, that frame with the image of the Virgin had fallen but had not broken. Therefore he decided to place the frame in his new home, right at the entrance, on the porch. The family often gathered in prayer before that image. Nevertheless, both he and and many of his fellow country folk had the bad habit of swearing against God with blasphemous phrases during the day while working in the fields, complaining about their hard life, about the inclemency of the place, after the famine and plague.

On 2 February 1655, the Feast of the Presentation of Jesus in the Temple, James Giacomuzzi di Rosa and his large family was in church for religious services. Mariute, his daughter of eight and a half years, stayed at home with her aunts, as she suffering from epilepsy. Suddenly the aunts saw the gaze of Mariute fix on the image of the Virgin, and as the girl approached the Madonna painted on the wall, her face lit up as if in ecstasy. Her aunts, surprised at what was happening, waited for her to recover and then bombarded her with questions. Mariute reported the words of the apparition, with great serenity and sweetness: "All should refrain from the sin of blasphemy." The girl was also cured of her epilepsy.

When her father recounted this episode in the village, many did not believe the story of her father but a Franciscan priest, Father Vitale Vitali, made a careful investigation of the facts and of Rosa, concluded that the Blessed Virgin had indeed appeared and spoke to the girl Mariute Giacomuzzi di Rosa. On the evening of 31 March 1655, the image was transported to the church of San Nicolò by a pair of yoked oxen followed by the parish priest and the people, with banners and torches. They were accompanied by three angels illuminating the sky. Many miracles followed and 150 years later a new church was built.

During the Second World War, the sanctuary was destroyed and the image was twice lost and then miraculously found unharmed. After the war, rebuilding was planned and begun and finally on 28 August 1960, the miraculous image of Our Lady of the Rose was triumphantly taken to the magnificent new sanctuary accompanied by throngs of the faithful.

Notes

1   See W. A. Christian, *Apparitions in Late Medieval and Renaissance Spain* (Princeton NJ: Princeton University Press, 1989), pp. 57–86.
2   See http://paroisse-clichy.pagesperso-orange.fr/pelerinage-2012.html. The Apostolic Nuntio, H. E. Mgr Luigi Ventura noted in his sermon on that occasion: "Depuis huit siècles, en ce lieu qui conserve la mémoire du jour où les trois marchands angevins ont été providentiellement libérés des liens par lesquels les bandits les avaient destinés à une mort certaine dans l'obscurité et la solitude de la forêt, le peuple chrétiens vient puiser à la même source de grâces, et Clichy-sous-Bois est ainsi devenu l'un des buts de pèlerinage les plus anciens de France."
3   Abbé G. Arnaud d'Agnel, *Marseilles, Notre-Dame of Garde* (Marseilles: Tacussel, 1923), pp. 13–15.
4   See Régis de la Colombière, *Notice sur la chapelle et le fort de Notre-Dame de la Garde* (Marseille: Typographie Veuve Marius Olive, 1855), p. 3.
5   F. Hildesheimer, *Notre-Dame de la Garde, la Bonne Mère de Marseille* (Marseille: Jeanne Laffitte, 1985), p. 17.
6   R. Levet, *The Virgin of the Guard within the Fortress, Four centuries of cohabitation between Church and Army on a hill of Marseilles (1525-1941)*, (Marseilles: Tacussel, 1994), pp. 14–15.
7   See http://www.notredamedelagarde.com/The-building-of-a-new-sanctuary.html.
8   See *ibid.*
9   Cheesefare Week, also known as *Maslenitsa* (Máспеница), Butter Week, or Pancake week, is celebrated during the last week before Great Lent— that is, the seventh week before Easter. Cheesefare roughly corresponds to the Western Mardi Gras or Shrove Tuesday, except that Orthodox Lent begins on a Monday instead of a Wednesday, and the Orthodox date of Easter can differ greatly from the Western Christian date.
10   The Akathist hymn is one of the most well-loved services of devotion in the Eastern Churches. Although there is some debate concerning the particulars of its authorship, many scholars agree with the pious tradition which states that the original Akathist of Our Lady was composed in the imperial city of Constantinople, "the city of the Virgin", by St Romanos the Melodist, who died in the year 556. The Akathist Hymn has proved so popular that many other hymns have been written following its format, particularly in the Russian Orthodox Church. These include Akathists to

Our Lord Jesus Christ, to the Holy Cross, and to various saints. The word "akathistos" literally means "not sitting", namely standing; normally all participants stand while it is being prayed.

11   *Akathist of the Theotokos*, Ikos 11. See also https://oca.org/saints/lives /2014/02/21/100578-icon-of-the-mother-of-god-kozelshchansk.

12   Pope St John Paul II, *Discourse to the indigenous peoples at Quetzaltenango* (7 March 1983), 6.

13   See www.santuariomotta.it.

14   See Pope St John Paul II, Apostolic Constitution *Viterbiensis* (27 March 1986): "Novam dioecesim sub protectione ponimus beatissimae Virginis Mariae a populis appellatae «S. Maria della Quercia»."

15   Pope Benedict XVI, *Prayer to Our Lady of the Oak Tree* (6 September 2009).

16   L. Dufaur, "The Triumph of Fatima: Foreseen Nearly Five Centuries Before the Apparitions of 1917" in Crusade Magazine (September/October 2004), pp. 5–9.

17   St Pothin was bishop of Lyons, the immediate predecessor of St Irenaeus, and was martyred in 177 AD:

18   See www.fourviere.org/en.

19   Pope Gregory the Great, *Registrum Epistolarum*, Book 10, Letter 39 to Eulogius, Patriarch of Alexandria.

20   Pope St John Paul II, *Dedication of the People of Chile to Our Lady of Mount Carmel*, National Sanctuary of Maipù, (3 April 1987), 4.

21   See www.rosarychurchqatar.com.

22   See J. Smith, "The Irish Madonna of St Stephen's" (18 December 2006) on http://catholictoledo.blogspot.it/2006/12/irish-madonna-of-st-stephens.html.

23   See www.basilicadesoriano.mx.

24   See https://sanctuaire-ndc.ca/en.

25   Pope St John Paul II, *Message on visit to the Old Shrine at Notre-Dame-du-Cap* (10 September 1984).

26   The Tatars are a Turkic people living in Asia and Europe who were one of the five major tribal confederations (khanlig) in the Mongolian plateau in the 12th century AD. The name Tatar first appears in written form on the Kul Tigin monument as TaTaR. Historically, the term "Tatars" was applied to a variety of Turco-Mongol semi-nomadic empires who controlled the vast region known as Tartary. More recently, however, the term refers more narrowly to people who speak one of the Turkic languages.

27   See "Legend of Our Lady of the Flowering Thorn" in *The Sacred Heart Review* 9/26 (20 May 1893), p. 10.

28   St Gregory Thaumaturgus, *The First Homily on the Annunciation to the*

Holy Virgin Mary.

[29]   See M. Lamberty (ed.), *The Woman in Orbit: Mary's feasts every day everywhere* (Chicago: Lamberty, 1966), 26 March.

[30]   Account from Lamberty (ed.), *The Woman in Orbit*, 29 March.

[31]   St Ambrose, *De virginitate*, 3 in *PL* 16, 269.

[32]   Mt 28:1 refers to Mary Magdalene and another Mary, but Mk 16:1 identifies them as Mary Magdalene and "Mary the mother of James and Salome".

[33]   St Ambrose, *De virginitate*, 3 in *PL* 16, 270.

[34]   Cf. Sedulius, *Paschale carmen*, 5, 357–364 in *CSEL* 10, 140f.

[35]   Ludolf of Saxony, *Vita Christi*, part 2, chapter 70 (Salzburg Universität: Institut für Anglistik und Amerikanistik, 2006), vol. 4, pp. 698–700.

[36]   *Ibid.*, p. 698.

[37]   *Ibid.*, pp. 699–700.

[38]   *Ibid.*, p. 700.

[39]   See St Ignatius, *Spiritual Exercises*, nos. 218-224, 299.

[40]   Pope St John Paul II, *Discourse at the General Audience* (3 April 1996).

[41]   Pope St John Paul II, *Discourse at the General Audience* (21 May 1996).

APRIL

1 April: Our Lady of Tears

ALSO KNOWN AS the Weeping Madonna of Syracuse, Sicily, this plaster hanging wall plaque depicts the Immaculate Heart of Mary in the style of the 1950s. Like many others just like it, it was mass-produced in a factory in Tuscany and shipped to various locations throughout the world. This particular plaque of Our Lady of Tears was purchased for a wedding gift for Antonina and Angelo Iannuso who were married on 21 March 1953.. The couple would later admit that they were not devout, but they liked the plaque and placed it on the wall over their bed.

When Antonina discovered she was with child, she was unfortunately afflicted with toxemia that caused her to convulse at times and experience some blindness. At three in the morning on Saturday, 29 August 1953, Antonina suffered a seizure that left her blind. By 8:30 that morning her sight was restored; when she was able to see, her eyes were on the Madonna, which, to Antonina's amazement was weeping effusive tears. At first the others thought she was hallucinating due to her illness, but Antonina insisted she wasn't. Her family looked again and they could see the tears run down the Madonna's cheeks and onto the bed. The neighbours were brought in and they confirmed the tears.

The plaque of Our Lady of Tears was publicly displayed, convincing even the sceptics of the prodigy as many of the sick were miraculously healed of their ailments. Some of the tears were collected for scientific examination, and the findings were as follows:

> The liquid examined is shown to be made up of a watery solution of sodium chloride in which traces of protein and nuclei of a silver composition of excretory substances of

the quanternary type the same as found in the human secretions used as a comparison during the analysis... The appearance, the alkalinity and the composition induce one to consider the liquid examined analogous to human tears.

The report was dated September 9, 1953 and signed by the examining doctors. The Archbishop of Palermo, Ernesto Cardinal Ruffini stated:

After careful sifting the numerous reports, after having noted the positive results of the diligent chemical analysis under which the tears gathered were examined, we have unanimously announced the judgment that the reality of the facts cannot be put in doubt.

From the time Antonina Iannuso first saw the tears, she recovered completely from severe toxemia and gave birth to a healthy son on 25 December 1953. Pope Pius XII, in a radio broadcast on 17 October 1954 said:

We acknowledge the unanimous declaration of the Episcopal Conference held in Sicily on the reality of the event. Will men understand the mysterious language of those tears?[1]

The little house where the Madonna first wept, is now a sanctuary where Mass is constantly celebrated. The image itself is enshrined above the main altar of the Sanctuary of Our Lady of Tears, built especially to accommodate the crowds that continue to gather to pray before the holy image.[2]

On 6 November 1994, Pope St John Paul II, declared during his homily the homily at the dedication of the Shrine to Our Lady of Tears:

Tears of Mary belong to the order of signs: they testify to the presence of the Mother in the Church and in the world. A mother cries when she sees her children threatened by some evil, whether spiritual or physical. Sanctuary of Our Lady of Tears, you are born to remind the Church of the weeping Mother. Those who are oppressed by awareness of sin are welcomed here and experience the riches of God's mercy and forgiveness! The tears of their Mother Mary lead them here. They are tears of sorrow for those who reject God's love, for broken families or those in difficulty, for toady's youth threatened by the consumer society and often disoriented, for the violence that still sheds so much blood, for the misunderstanding and hatred that causes such deep divisions between peoples and nations. They are tears of prayer: prayer of the Mother who gives strength to every other prayer and supplicates even for those who do not pray because they are distracted by so many other interests, or because they stubbornly closed to the voice of God. They are tears of hope, that dissolve the hardness of hearts and open them to the meeting with Christ the Redeemer, the source of light and peace for individuals, families, society as a whole.[3]

2 April: Our Lady of Light

UR LADY APPEARED in Zeitoun, Cairo, Egypt hovering above Saint Mary's Coptic Church, a shrine dedicated to the Holy Family, who according to tradition rested in that place during their stay in Egypt. The apparitions took place at night, and Our Lady was always surrounded by light.

At 8:30 pm on Tuesday 2 April 1968, an hour and a half after sunset, the mechanics and drivers of the garage were all alarmed by some disturbance in the street. The workmen ran to the street. They saw a young lady dressed in white walking on the church dome. They thought that she was about to throw herself down. So they cried: "Be careful. Take care, you may fall down, wait." As the dome is curved, no human being can walk on it. Then some of the pedestrians who stood to watch the scene cried "Virgin Mary, Virgin Mary." As the garage workmen who were watching the apparition were all Muslims, they looked on keenly and they all became extremely astonished. The Lady who appeared in a luminous body, moved on the dome and bowed and knelt before

the cross. The traffic in Tumanbay Street was stopped and a big crowd of people stood to watch the apparition. The workmen of the garage who were on duty at that particular time all gave reports that ascertained and confirmed their witness as they all gave the same particulars as also did Father Constantine Moussa, the priest of the church. The first man who saw her, a Muslim, Farouk Mohammed Atwa, was undergoing a series of operations for a case of gangrene. The following day when he went to hospital for his scheduled operation to amputate his finger, he was certified completely healed.[4]

Thus began three years of almost nightly visits by Mary, visits heralded by extraordinary lights and immense clouds of incense. She was seen sometimes vaguely, often quite clearly, smiling, bowing, waving an olive branch, blessing, praying deeply, holding fast or kneeling before the Cross of her Son. These apparitions, often lasting throughout the night, were photographed, televised, witnessed by millions, written about in the international secular and religious press, and seen by both religious and political dignitaries such as Abdu Nasser, president of Egypt and self-proclaimed Marxist.[5] Among the witnesses were Orthodox, Catholics, Protestants, Moslems, Jews and non-religious people from all walks of life. The sick were cured and blind persons received their sight, but most importantly large numbers of unbelievers were converted.[6]

Spellbound people, often rooted to the ground, prayed the Rosary and sang Christian hymns. Muslims chanted, "Mary, God has chosen You ... He has chosen You above all women", from the Koran. Some saw nothing. Many, many more saw it all, taking in her radiance hour after hour, watching and praying, going home to rest, and returning—only to find Her still there, watching and praying over them!

The head of the Coptic Orthodox Church of Alexandria, His Holiness Pope Kyrillos VI appointed a commission of high-ranking priests and bishops to investigate the apparitions, and on Saturday, 4 May 1968, the Coptic Orthodox Church officially confirmed the apparitions after thorough investigation (see official report below). His Holiness Pope Kyrillos VI also assigned the responsibility of documenting the apparitions and accompanying miracles to a special committee headed by Anba Gregorios, bishop of postgraduate studies, Coptic culture and scientific research. The apparitions were also approved by the local Catholic Patriarch, Cardinal Stephanos I, who stated that the apparitions of our Lady at Zeitoun were beyond any doubt and were seen by many of his trustworthy Coptic Catholic faithful. The Rev Dr Henry Ayrout, the rector of the Catholic Collège de la Sainte Famille (Jesuit order) in Cairo also declared his acceptance of the miraculous apparitions of Virgin Mary, saying that whether Catholic or Orthodox, we are all her children and she loves us all equally and her apparitions at the Zeitoun Coptic Orthodox Church confirmed this idea. Rev. Dr. Ibrahim Said, head of all Protestant Evangelical Ministries in Egypt at the time of the apparitions, affirmed that the apparitions were true. Catholic nuns from the Sacré-Coeur order also witnessed the apparitions and sent a detailed report to the Vatican. On the evening of Sunday, 28 April 1968, an envoy from the Vatican arrived, saw the apparitions and sent a report to His Holiness Pope Paul VI in Rome.

In Arabic, "Zeitoun" translates to "olive", a fact not lost on the onlookers, who witnessed Mary holding an olive branch on many occasions. Today, when Christians—Coptic and Catholic alike—are subject to persecution and martyrdom from radical Islam, many look to the unity Our Lady inspired at Zeitoun, and pray to Mary's intercession that someday, peace will return to the Holy Family's place of refuge.[7]

3 April: Our Lady of the Oak

N THE SEVENTEENTH century, near Maisières, Doubs, Franche-Comté, France, a statue was placed near a tree. During the ensuing years, many miracles had been reported there and it became a popular place to pray. Over the years, the tree actually grew around the statue, finally encasing it to the point where it could no longer be seen. Then came the French Revolution, when churches were desecrated and the Church persecuted. In order to deceive the authorities, a man had placed a similar statue in another tree in the valley, so that when the authorities came, chopped down the tree and desecrated the statue, it was the new one and not the original.

And, so it was to the grand-daughter of that courageous man, (a devout Catholic girl named Cecile), that the Blessed Mother chose to reveal herself, and the location of the statue. In 1803, when Cecile and a friend were returning home from the First Communion Mass, and walking along, they saw a lady who was surrounded by young women, all of whom were carrying candles. The woman stopped in front of an oak tree, and suddenly the other young women that had been with her were gone. Next to the tree Cecile saw a statue with lighted candles on each side. However, her friend saw nothing. Running to a nearby house, she recounted the story, which was met with disbelief. When she told her father, Monsieur Seure about the experience, he told her to stop telling such stories as they were not true.

Little was said after that, until, on the Feast of the Assumption that same year, an event occurred that would change everyone's opinion. Cecile's father, his 3 daughters, and a labourer were walking past the same tree on their way to Mass. Cecile's younger sister, Marguerite, mentioned that this was the tree where Cecile had claimed to see the vision earlier that year. As he looked over towards the tree, Cecile's father saw light shining from the tree trunk; however, as Mass was about to begin they hurried on the church. After Mass, they returned to the oak with an axe to see what was inside the tree. By now the entire village had assembled to watch, and when Monsieur Seure cut into the tree, he found a small earthenware statue of the Blessed Mother.

Under the authority of the Archbishop, the Church began an official investigation in 1844. After interviewing over 40 people, the Archbishop proclaimed the vision to be "worthy of belief".[8]

4 April: Our Lady of Grace

HE CHAPEL OF Notre-Dame de Grâce (or Our Lady of Grace) which is about 2.5 km outside the town centre up the hill of the Côte de Grâce et Le Mont Joli. The hill overlooks the estuary of the River Seine with views of Le Havre, le Pont de Normandie and over Honfleur itself.

The original chapel was built in 1023, during the times of Richard II, Duke of Normandy, after the Virgin Mary had saved him from the perils of the sea. However, following a cliff fall in 1538, where the chapel was destroyed, the church was rebuilt in the early 1600s by the sailors and fishermen of the town. It was then pillaged during the French Revolution and later restored. It is dedicated to the Our Lady of Grace and is filled with all kinds of marine memorabilia and is still used regularly to offer prayers and thanks for the safe return of the town's fishing and sailing community. The gilt wood statue of Our Lady of Grace, from around 1700, surrounded by cast-off crutches and ex votos commemorating Our Lady's help at sea, was crowned 19 June 1913.[9] In June 1887, Thérèse of Lisieux in the company of her father and her sisters Léonie and Céline, went on pilgrimage to Notre-Dame de Grace to plead with Our Lady to gain permission for her to enter Carmel.

From top of the little mountain which the church crowns, the mouth of the Seine is visible, and then, in the distance, the ocean, with its long waves of dark green, which receives in its bosom the river of blue waters. Two roads lead to the chapel: the one rough and rocky, the other smooth and even. In earlier times the inhabitants of Honfleur took delight in pointing out Our Lady of Grace, in reducing its steepness, in covering it with small, fine sand, so that a gracious princess, who had made herself beloved in these parts by her generous bounty, might be able to ascend it without fatigue, when she went to offer her prayers and vows to the Blessed Virgin.

5 April: Our Lady of Divine Providence

HE SHRINE OF Our Lady of Divine Providence, or the Santuario della Madonna della Divina Provvidenza, is located in a rural district of the diocese of Fossano, Italy, called Cussanio. Fassano lies in Piedmont in the province of Cuneo. According to tradition, in the year 1521 the Blessed Virgin Mary appeared to a deaf mute shepherd, Bartolomeo Coppa. The first apparition occurred on 8 May when she cured Bartolomeo of his disability and told him to preach penance to the inhabitants of Fossano.

In a second apparition on 11 May, the Blessed Virgin brought Bartolomeo three loaves of bread and again asked him to preach penance to the people of Fossano. The locals, however, only ridiculed the visionary. A short time later, however, a plague broke out among the Fossanesse, who only then had recourse to Our Lady. After having been granted respite from the plague through the intercession of the Blessed Virgin Mary, the grateful people of the region had a chapel built which was known as Our Lady of Divine Providence. This chapel was later replaced with a larger church between 1634 and 1642.

In 1600 the Augustinian Brothers of the Congregation of Genoa came to Cussanio and the friars built the great monastery complex next to the sanctuary. During the French Revolution the convent and church were suppressed and the buildings forcibly abandoned. Later, in the year 1872, the bishop Mgr Emiliano Manacorda, a personal friend of Saint John Bosco, arrived at the diocese and claimed ownership of the monastery that had been wrongfully confiscated by the state and decided upon the complete renovation of the sanctuary. Work began shortly after 1875 and continued for about twenty years, and included the elevation of the majestic dome and the reconstruction of the entire façade. The nave was extended, two aisles built and the interior was adorned with altars, sculptures and paintings.[10]

6 April: Mater Admirabilis

 HE CATHOLIC UNIVERSITY of Ingolstadt was founded in 1472. One of its most illustrious professors of Theology was Dr Johannes Eck, famous for his disputations against Martin Luther. Some time later a Jesuit College was instituted at the University, with the help of St Peter Canisius. In 1570, St Francis Borgia, Superior General of the Jesuits, sent to the Jesuit College in Ingolstadt one of seven copies of the Image of Our Lady of the Snows (enshrined in the Basilica of St. Mary Major at Rome; also called *Salus Populi Romani*—Salvation of the Roman People), the painting of which had been permitted by Pope St Pius V. These were not exact copies; rather the stark iconic look of the original had been somewhat softened.

Mary's image, thus enshrined in Ingolstadt, became a favorite place of prayer of a pious young Jesuit, Father Jakob Rem, who was stationed at nearby Dillingen. This religious, a fellow-novice of St Stanislaus Kostka, was illustrious for his eminent virtues and, above all, for his devotion to Our Lady. He sought to instill in all his students a deep love for the Rosary—a love which was undoubtedly increased due to the well-known influence this devotion had in the victory at the Battle of Lepanto in 1571. While yet a novice in Rome, Father Rem had become acquainted with the Marian Congregation, a lay apostolate which had been founded by a Flemish Jesuit, Johann Leunis, in 1562.

As the Protestant revolution raged on, the staunchly Catholic Duke Albrecht encouraged everything which would help preserve Catholic faith and morals in Bavaria. Thus, when Father Rem established the first Marian Congregation on German soil, at Dillingen in 1574, his efforts were met with much enthusiasm. It was at the request of St Peter Kanisius that Father Rem established a second Marian Congregation in Ingolstadt in 1577. Its members would meet in the chapel where the copy of Our Lady of the Snows was enshrined.

After being transferred to Ingolstadt, Father Jakob Rem gathered the most elite and fervent members of the Marian Congregation. With them he formed, in 1595, the *Colloquium Marianum* (literally the Marian Conversation or Marian Conference); so-called because its members bound themselves always to try to say something in praise of Mary in their daily conversations, and because they would give and listen to conferences and have discussions about devotion to Mary in their meetings. The majority of the future spiritual and intellectual leaders of the Catholic Counter-reformation were members of the Colloquium Marianum. Indeed, due to the efforts of Father Rem and the Colloquium Marianum, Ingolstadt became a centre of Marian devotion, which was to have a profound influence, not only in Bavaria, but also throughout Europe.

On 6 April 1604, Father Rem, together with the members of the Colloquium, were chanting the Litany of Loreto in Our Lady's chapel, as they were accustomed to do at their meetings. Father Rem had previously formed a great desire, out of pious curiosity, to know which of Our Lady's titles were most pleasing to her. On this day, as the chanting continued, Father Rem was lifted from the ground in ecstasy and beheld the Mother of God in a vision. She made known to him that the title *Mater Admirabilis* was especially pleasing to her, as it summed up all of her graces and privileges. Just as the vision ended, the cantor sang the invocation, *"Mater Admirabilis"*, and all responded, *"Ora pro nobis"*. Father Rem instructed the members to repeat the invocation two more times.

It was not long before the reason for this three-fold invocation became known, not only to the members of the Colloquium, but also to Father Rem's superiors. Soon it became the custom, at Ingolstadt and other places throughout Bavaria and Germany, to repeat this invocation three times whenever the Litany of Loreto was chanted. It was thus that the copy of Our Lady of the Snows at Ingolstadt became known as *Mater Ter Admirabilis* ("Thrice Admirable Mother" in English). The image of the Thrice Admirable Mother was later copied many times. Many missionaries took copies on their journeys and reported miraculous happenings through the intercession of the Thrice Admirable Mother.[11]

7 April: *Our Lady of Puig*

 HE FORTRESS AND THE CHURCH of Our Lady of Puig are a short distance outside Valencia in Spain; both date from Roman times, when a temple of Venus stood on the hill overlooking the pleasant valley. At the coming of Christianity in around 306 AD, it was turned into a monastery. Early in history they acquired the image of Our Lady of Puig, in bas-relief, carved on a slab of marble, which was said to have formed part of the tomb of the Blessed Virgin Mary. How it got to Spain is not known with certainty, though the pious insist that it was brought there by angels. It was the principal object of devotion at the shrine, which thrived and grew beautiful until the ancient kingdom of the Visigoths fell to the Muslim invaders in the eighth century.

In the year 712 AD the monks sadly buried their treasure to hide it from desecration, along with the church bell, under the floor of the monastery, and fled for their lives. After five centuries the Moors were expelled from Valencia, and the plaque of Our Lady of Puig played a part in its liberation. King James I of Aragon, victorious in other parts of Spain, moved on Valencia with his armies. The Moors, in an effort to trick the Christians into sending their troops to the wrong place, moved to attack the ancient fortress of Puig. This was done with great secrecy, but Our Lady warned the Christians and helped them to win the desperate battle.

Saint Peter Nolasco, who helped to found the Society for the Redemption of Captives (the Mercedarians) under Our Lady's guidance, was in Puig when the battle took place. One of the soldiers came to him and reported that when he had been on night guard he had seen strange lights over the old ruined church of Our Lady of Puig; sometimes the stars seemed to come down from the sky and circle around the building. Especially on Saturday nights there were bright lights around the mount of the church.

Saint Peter suggested to the king that all the soldiers should receive the Sacraments and pray to know what God was trying to tell them. After this had been done, he led them to the top of the hill and directed them to dig under the floor of the old monastery. Here they found the plaque and the bell, buried for 500 years, but unharmed. The plaque was first carried to the chapel of the castle fortress. As soon as possible a new church was built on the mountain and given into the charge of the Mercedarians under Saint Peter Nolasco. The ancient bell which was dated as being cast in 660, was placed in the tower of the church. This bell was said to be powerful against storms and always rung of its own accord in time of trouble. In 1550 the bell broke and a new one was cast from the fragments of the old one.

The church built by Saint Peter Nolasco was called "the angelic chamber" because angels were often heard singing there in the night, especially on Saturdays. Our Lady of Puig has been the patroness of Valencia for hundreds of years, and as recently as 1935 was honoured by the Spanish Armies who have carried her image in so many successful battles. She was at that time named as a General in the Army and invoked as patroness in the Christian struggle against Communism.[12]

8 April: *The Mother of God of Boronyavo*

 ORONYAVO IS A SMALL TOWN in the eastern part of Trans-Carpathia, not far from the junction of the Hungarian and Romanian borders with Ukraine. It is in a mountainous area known as the Hutsul Region or Hutsylchyna, a district of rugged heights with a distinct culture and dialect. The small church is surrounded by fields in a valley of these mountains, and was defended against Communist destruction by devout Greek Catholic faithful of the area.

The church and monastery date back for centuries, and a small community of monks has lived here since the 1500s at least. After the Union of Uzhorod in 1646, whereby the local Orthodox Church entered into union with the Roman Catholic Church, the monks came under the Rule of Saint Basil. The Austrian Emperor Joseph II saw no need for small, contemplative communities in his empire, and the monks of Boronyavo were forcibly dispersed by imperial decree in 1771. The men went to live in caves in the hills, and one of them, Kozak, was gifted with a vision of the Holy Mother of God holding in her arms the Infant Jesus, Saviour of the world, when he went to take water from a spring. Mary told him that she was pleased with their continued faithfulness to their vows, and Kozak paintedthe icon from his memory of the vision.

The icon was enshrined in the chapel, which had been spared destruction by the imperial forces by the intervention of townspeople throughout Trans-Carpathia who loved the monks. Immediately God began to work miracles in the church, including the dramatic conversion of an atheist and many healings. Huge pilgrimages began to the shrine, particularly on the feast of the Annunciation (March 25), Saint Elias (July 20), and the Dormition or Assumption of the Virgin (August 15), which is the largest of all the pilgrimages.

After the Soviet conquest of 1944-1945, and Czechoslovakia's forced cession of the entire province to the USSR, the native Greek Catholic Church was bitterly persecuted by the Soviets. The monastery was closed, the monks arrested, and plans set to destroy the entire site. However the icon of Our Lady was taken away to the city of Chust and hidden in an apartment there, and the local peasants regularly defended the buildings against destruction, even when bulldozers were brought in. Many people were arrested, but the church was never given over to Orthodox use, and it survived Soviet rule. Barbed wire was wrapped around the site of the shrine, and people would tie rags as a sign of their prayers onto the wire in defiance of the guards.

On 8 April 1991, after three years work of restoration, the church was re-dedicated. Bishop Ivan Semedi of the Greek Catholic Eparchy of Mukachevo stepped aside at the altar to allow the former superior, arrested in 1946 and sent to the Siberian gulags, to come forward and offer the first public Divine Liturgy. The icon was enthroned above the Royal Doors of the iconostas in 1992, back where it belonged at last.[13]

9 April: Our Lady of the Thorn

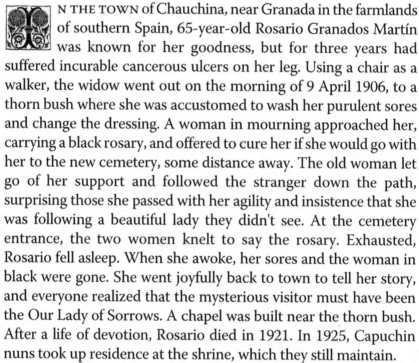 N THE TOWN of Chauchina, near Granada in the farmlands of southern Spain, 65-year-old Rosario Granados Martín was known for her goodness, but for three years had suffered incurable cancerous ulcers on her leg. Using a chair as a walker, the widow went out on the morning of 9 April 1906, to a thorn bush where she was accustomed to wash her purulent sores and change the dressing. A woman in mourning approached her, carrying a black rosary, and offered to cure her if she would go with her to the new cemetery, some distance away. The old woman let go of her support and followed the stranger down the path, surprising those she passed with her agility and insistence that she was following a beautiful lady they didn't see. At the cemetery entrance, the two women knelt to say the rosary. Exhausted, Rosario fell asleep. When she awoke, her sores and the woman in black were gone. She went joyfully back to town to tell her story, and everyone realized that the mysterious visitor must have been the Our Lady of Sorrows. A chapel was built near the thorn bush. After a life of devotion, Rosario died in 1921. In 1925, Capuchin nuns took up residence at the shrine, which they still maintain.

Meanwhile, around 1918, in the city of Granada, devout José Farrugia perceived his antique statue of Our Lady of Sorrows telling him, "Take me to Chauchina!" After the third request, he visited the town some 10 miles away, and on learning about the apparition there, donated the image to the shrine. When Rosario saw it she exclaimed, "She looks so much like the Good Woman!"

Dating from around 1600 and much restored, the tearful image was canonically crowned 9 September 2006. Chauchina celebrates Our Lady of the Thorn on 9 April every year, with rosaries, confessions, Masses, floral offerings, and a procession to the cemetery, where everyone who has made a vow takes turns carrying the statue.

10 April: *Our Lady of Naval*

F ALL THE famous Marian images in the Philippines, La Naval stands alone as a native Virgin. Although her clothes mark her readily as a product of the seventeenth century Spanish Golden Age, her oriental features reflect the uniqueness of her position as a truly indigenous queen of the Philippines. In 1593, on the death of his father, the Spanish Governor General Luis Perez Dasmarinas commissioned Captain Hernando de los Rios Coronel to have a Marian statue sculpted. He wished to give a religious imprint to his regime in the Philippines. A non-Catholic Chinese sculptor was found to make the statue. This sculptor later became a convert through the intercession of Our Lady.

The beautiful image was presented to the Manila Dominicans and enshrined in the old Santo Domingo Church. The image is nearly 2 metres tall and is made of hard-wood, with an ivory face and hands. Over three centuries have mellowed the ivory to a delicate brown. The Oriental-Philippine face is almond-shaped, with high-set cheekbones and slanting eyes. The image is dressed as a royal lady of the palace of King Philip of Spain. On her left arm, she holds her beloved Holy Child Jesus. With her right arm, she holds a royal sceptre and staff and her Rosary. The statue is covered with jewels, tributes from her throngs of devotees through the ages. Each jewel has its own story. The halo is surrounded by 24 stars, and she wears a queenly crown.

In the Philippines of 1646, there were not only hostile Muslims in the South, but also Dutch and English privateers who wanted the riches of the archipelago and who wanted to replace Catholicism with Dutch Protestant Calvinism. During this year, there were five bloody naval battles between the greatly outnumbered Spanish, Catholic Philippine forces and the Dutch marauders. Only fifteen of the defenders of Manila were lost in all of the battles. The Dutch, then political enemies of the Spanish, retreated, and never again threatened to destroy the integrity of the islands by annexing them to the Dutch East Indies.

Before each of the battles, the intercession of Our Lady was fervently sought. Crew members—Spanish soldiers, religious, and Filipinos—vowed special homage to Our Lady for a victorious battle. True to their Latin heritage and Catholic identity, the victorious defenders petitioned official Church recognition and declaration of the naval victories of 1646 as miracles worked by the Mother of God. The Ecclesiastical Council in Cavite, with the help of doctors of theology, canonical experts, and prominent religious, deliberated and examined written and oral testimonies from all eye-witnesses. Finally, on 9 April 1662, the Council ordered that the five naval victories of 1646 be declared as miraculous,

> granted by the Sovereign Lord through the intercession of the Most Holy Virgin and devotion to her Rosary, and decreed that the miracles be celebrated, preached and held in festivities and to be recounted among the miracles wrought by the Lady of the Rosary for the greater devotion of the faithful to Our Most Blessed Virgin Mary and Her Holy Rosary.

After the 1896 Revolution, the large processions in Our Lady's honour were toned down, but never suspended. In 1906, La Naval was crowned canonically by the Papal Legate. In 1941, her shrine in the old Santo Domingo Church in Manilla was bombed. La Naval was safely hidden for a time in the old church's vault, and later transferred to the chapel of the University of Santo Tomas. Here, thousands of her devotees flocked to honour her in her third Centennial in 1946. In 1952, the cornerstone was laid for a new shrine at the Santo Domingo Church in Quezon City.

In 1954, in a boat shaped carriage, Our Lady of La Naval was led in solemn procession by the Philippines hierarchy, public officials, priests, nuns, and thousands of devotees to her new home. This shrine was declared by the Philippine bishops as the national shrine of the Queen of the Holy Rosary of the Philippines. During her celebration in October of 1973, La Naval was acknowledged as the patroness of the capitol city of the Philippines. In 1974, she was enshrined in a safer vault-altar because of recent sacrilegious robberies of churches and sacred images in the area. In 1985, a year long celebration was held in the Philippines for the Marian year. Shortly thereafter, in February of 1986, Cardinal Jaime Sin, archbishop of Manilla, called for "people power" in a pastoral act designed to avoid bloodshed. The phenomenon surfaced, and people armed only with the weapons of love—rosaries, icons of Jesus and Mary, flowers and food—were able to stop tanks and troops in battle gear. Rosary vigils and nightly processions of a replica of the antique image of La Naval were led by the Filipino Dominicans outside the gates of the Presidential palace.

Prayer

La Naval de Manila, Queen of the Most Holy Rosary of the Philippines, Mirror of Justice, help us to pray for the greatest victory, the victory of Your Son's Peace in the Philippines and the entire world. We ask you to help us remember that one of your most blessed titles is Queen of Peace.

11 April: Our Lady of Mekong

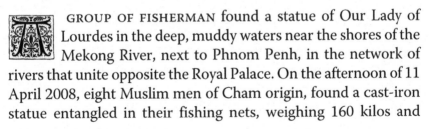 GROUP OF FISHERMAN found a statue of Our Lady of Lourdes in the deep, muddy waters near the shores of the Mekong River, next to Phnom Penh, in the network of rivers that unite opposite the Royal Palace. On the afternoon of 11 April 2008, eight Muslim men of Cham origin, found a cast-iron statue entangled in their fishing nets, weighing 160 kilos and

measuring a metre and a half in height. It had been in the river for at least 33 years, since the beginning of the regime of Khmer Rouge.

Not knowing what to do with it, they sold it for $7 US dollars to some local inhabitants that intended to recycle it and use it for raw material. Some Christian people who happened to pass through the area immediately recognized it as a statue of the Blessed Virgin Mary. Thus, it was passed to new owners, from the parish of Areaksat, being sold at $1,000 US dollars, which immediately translated into 10 sacks of rice. It seems that its new owners did not want to make a business deal with a sacred image. The statue is now at the parish of Our Lady of Peace. The Christian community has immediately expressed its gratitude to the poor family, for having donated the statue.

For some time now, the account of the statue's appearance in the river has been circulating around Phnom Penh. In this month of May, consecrated to the Virgin, the faithful take her daily offerings and flowers. Especially on Sunday, numerous Christians come together to pray before the image of Our Lady of Lourdes, that has been named, Our Lady of Mekong. At present, the origin of the statue is completely unknown. With the conquest of religious houses during the war, the statue was surely thrown into the waters, where it remained 33 years. The parish of Areaksat, near to the site of the statue's appearance, was not located there during wartime, but 2 kilometres away from the site. Some of the area's elderly people were questioned regarding the statue, but they have been unable to recognize it or offer information as to its location before it was thrown into the Mekong River.[14]

12 April: Our Lady of the Revelation

RUNO CORNACCHIOLA, though raised a Catholic in Rome, grew not only to detest everything Catholic, but also nursed a deep hatred for the Catholic Church and vowed action in order to bring her down. Bruno's hatred was not helped by the fact that he grew up poor and kept bad company with unruly boys of his own age. After receiving only a rudimentary education Bruno joined the military which seemed to suit his need for constant excitement and fed his need to hate someone or something. One would think that with such hatred eating at his very soul, Bruno would be a lost cause, but God, "desires all men to be saved and to come to the knowledge of the Truth" (1 Tim 2).

Bruno decided to go and fight in the Spanish civil war; though he had no particular ideology Bruno fought simply for the love of it. When he arrived in Spain Bruno met up with a Lutheran man who convinced Bruno that the Catholic Church was the cause of all the world evils and needed to be destroyed, most especially the Pope. These words fed Bruno's already active hatred of all things Catholic, and he vowed then to one day kill the Pope. This was no empty threat for while in Spain Bruno bought a dagger in order to carry out this evil deed. Bruno was not a good husband and constantly beat his wife, he also threw out any statues or other religious items from his home. The Cornacchiola household was certainly not a happy one, as his wife lived in fear everyday of her life and the children suffered as they themselves were beaten and witnessed their father's violence towards their mother.

Bruno demanded that his wife leave the Catholic Church and join a Protestant Church, and under great duress Bruno's wife did just that but only after she had applied conditions that Bruno would make the Nine Fridays devotion. Bruno scoffed at this challenge but did as his wife suggested, and so Iolanda left the Catholic Church and joined her husband in the new Protestant Church, though she was sorely grieved at taking this action.

Bruno eventually found a steady job as a tram conductor in Rome, but this brought no relief to the family as Bruno's violence intensified against Iolanda and his children who had to deal with his abuse and drunkenness. However, Iolanda did not give up hope and constantly prayed for the salvation of her husband and the well-being of their children. This man's heart was so full of hate that he soon became an avowed communist much to his wife's distress.

One day while he was preparing an anti-Church and anti-Mary speech, Bruno took his children to the park near Tre Fontane where he sat and wrote notes on his speech as his children played ball. As Bruno prepared his notes he could hear his children gleefully playing together, this did not deter Bruno from his course. Only when the children cried out that they had lost their ball, Bruno with great irritation left his notes and began to help his children look for it. While Bruno and his children were searching for the ball, Bruno could hear his son Gianfranco say over and over 'oh beautiful Lady, beautiful Lady'. Very much in fear for his son Bruno searched for Gianfranco and found him kneeling transfixed before the small grotto, soon all three of Bruno's children knelt in awe at the sight of this most beautiful Lady. Bruno immediately tried to get his children away from the Grotto but to no avail, he as strong as he was could not lift his own little ones. Finally Bruno yelled, 'God help us!'

Upon yelling this out, Bruno could finally see what his children were seeing, as two hands reached out and touched his eyes he gradually saw before him the most beautiful woman he had ever seen. He also felt a welling of great inner joy at the sight of his most gracious and lovely Woman. Bruno like his children could not move or remove his eyes away from this glorious woman who was wearing a green mantle over a white dress with a rose sash tied at her waist. Her expression was one of deep sadness and Bruno felt immediate compunction over the sad look in her eyes, but still he could not tear his eyes away from such a sight as this most wondrous Lady.

Bruno also noticed that the beautiful and sad Lady held a book in her hands which she cradled close to her heart and beneath her feet was a broken crucifix on top of a black cloth. Bruno could hardly believe what he was seeing but he could not move as he listened to Our Lady speak to him. She bent a little towards Bruno and said these words to him,

> I am she who is related to the Divine Trinity. I am daughter of the Father, Mother of the Son, and Spouse and Temple

of the Holy Spirit. I am the Virgin of Revelation. You have persecuted me, now is the time to stop! Come and be part of the Holy Fold which is the Celestial Court on earth. God's promise is unchangeable and will remain so. The nine First Fridays in honour of the Sacred Heart, which your faithful wife persuaded you to observe before you walked down the road of lies, has saved you.

Our Lady continued to instruct Bruno as she said, "Live the divine doctrine. Practise Christianity. Live the Faith ... The Hail Marys that you pray with faith and love are like golden arrows that go straight to the heart of Jesus." She added: "Pray much and recite the Rosary for the conversion of sinners, of unbelievers and of all Christians."

Bruno was stunned at her words and a transformation began to take place within the heart of this man who had been driven by hate but had now been touched by Divine Love through the help of Our Lady. Bruno's heart began to beat with the chorus of love rather than the loud and raucous diatribe of hate, a miracle had happened within the soul of this one man which would affect his life forever.

Our Lady also had further messages for this simple man, "I promise this special favour: With this sinful soil I shall perform great miracles for the conversion of unbelievers and of sinners ... Science will deny God and will refuse His calls." Our Lady then spoke of her Assumption into Heaven, "My body could not and did not decay. I was assumed into Heaven by my Son and the angels." The Blessed Mother also instructed Bruno with a special message for the Holy Father himself, "You must go to the Holy Father, the Pope, the Supreme Pastor of Christianity, and personally tell him my message. Bring it to his attention. I shall tell you how to recognize the one who will accompany you to see the Pope."

After this message Our Lady disappeared leaving a pungent scent of roses, Bruno was almost in shock at what he had seen and heard, he would never be the same again. Upon returning home, Iolanda could smell the scent of roses and when she enquired the children blurted out that they had seen a most beautiful lady, Iolanda with tears in her eyes forgave her husband as Bruno begged her forgiveness for his vicious behaviour towards her and their children.

The Roman Church authorities also carried out an investigation, and the cult of the Virgin of Revelation was approved with great speed by the Vicariate of Rome. As the number of pilgrims grew, the area around the grotto had to be altered to make it safer and more accessible. A special statue, representing Mary during the apparition, was blessed by Pope Pius XII on 5 October 1947, and then taken in procession, amidst huge crowds, from St Peter's Square to Tre Fontane.

Bruno was indeed a changed man and he with his entire family re-converted back to the Catholic Faith which filled his wife's heart with great joy. Never again would Bruno raise his hand in violence against his family. It would take two years before Bruno could fulfil Our Lady's request when he and a group were invited to pray the Rosary in private with Pope Pius XII on 9 December 1949. After completing this most holy prayer the Pope then asked if anyone wished to speak with him. Bruno immediately raised his hand and with great sorrow he knelt before the Pope and begged his forgiveness for his years of hatred and his intention to kill this holy man of God, the Pope unhesitatingly gave Bruno his forgiveness.

The Franciscan Conventual Friars Minor were given custody of the grotto in July 1956, and asked to construct a chapel at the site, in addition to administering the shrine. Since then, a prayer to the Virgin of Revelation has been given an imprimatur by the Vicariate of Rome, and the cult was so well recognized that, during Vatican II, numerous prelates went to Tre Fontane to pray. In 1987, on the fortieth anniversary of the apparition, Cardinal Ugo Poletti, the Cardinal Vicar of Rome, and thus the Pope's official episcopal representative for the diocese, came to the shrine to celebrate Mass. However, a definitive judgement, either positive or negative in regard of Tre Fontane, has not been made.[15] On Friday 22 June 2001 at 12 noon, Bruno Cornacchiola died; it was the Solemnity of the Sacred Heart of Jesus.

13 April: Our Lady of Mantua

HE PRESENT SHRINE to Our Lady of Mantua was built by the Gonzaga family in the year 1460. It harbours a miraculous painting of the Blessed Virgin Mary holding the baby Jesus that is known to have been venerated since about the year 1000. Originally known as Our Lady of the Vows, the painting is crowned today. According to tradition, the history of the site dates back to Saint Anselm. At that time the Blessed Virgin had promised her protection for the city. Starting in 1477, word spread that before the image numerous miracles had occurred, so that by then substantial offerings began to pour into the church (hence the name of Our Lady of the Vows).

After the plague of 1630, which had overwhelmed the city and its territory, the princess Maria Gonzaga, regent of the duchy, desired to entrust herself, her dynasty, and the state to the protection of the Blessed Virgin. The princess was determined to place herself, her son Charles II and the states of Mantua and of Monferrato under the special protection of Our Lady. She ordered that the image of Mary should be carried in procession through the streets of the city, and asked that the image be solemnly crowned in the Basilica of Saint Andrea, as the Queen of Mantua. The solemn crowning of Our Lady of the Vows was strongly urged by the pious princess Maria Gonzaga in the year 1640, when the dam of the Po River in Italy broke. The coronation took place with great solemnity on 28 November 1640.

Since then, the church and the painting of Our Lady of the Vows were described as Crowned (*Incoronata*), and the annual festival was fixed on the first Sunday after the feast of Saint Martin, November 11. On this occasion, but also during the month of May, which is traditionally dedicated to Marian devotion, the *Incoronata* is exposed in the cathedral, covered in sumptuous dresses dating from the seventeenth century. The three following centenary years in particular saw an unanimous and grateful expression of love on the part of the Mantuans, who still venerate the Madonna *Incoronata*, the Madonna who said, "Mantua is mine, and as mine I will always defend it."[16]

14 April: Our Lady of Guam

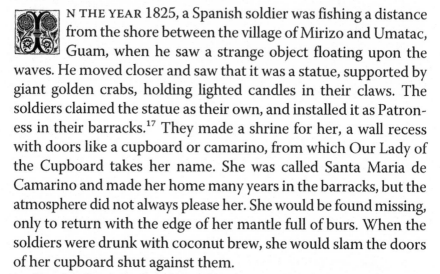N THE YEAR 1825, a Spanish soldier was fishing a distance from the shore between the village of Mirizo and Umatac, Guam, when he saw a strange object floating upon the waves. He moved closer and saw that it was a statue, supported by giant golden crabs, holding lighted candles in their claws. The soldiers claimed the statue as their own, and installed it as Patroness in their barracks.[17] They made a shrine for her, a wall recess with doors like a cupboard or camarino, from which Our Lady of the Cupboard takes her name. She was called Santa Maria de Camarino and made her home many years in the barracks, but the atmosphere did not always please her. She would be found missing, only to return with the edge of her mantle full of burs. When the soldiers were drunk with coconut brew, she would slam the doors of her cupboard shut against them.

On the fourteenth of April one year during the early nineteenth century, the statue left the barracks for the cathedral of Agana, when a great earthquake occurred, terrorizing the natives and destroying their homes. It is believed that on that day she deserted the uncouth soldiers and showed herself to be the Patroness of the people and of Guam in particular. Many miracles of protection are attributed to Our Lady of Guam on this day.

On the eve of this day the people place a lighted candle outside their tight-closed shutters; they do this in memory of their Fathers who made the promise to Santa Maria de Camarino. In 1825 and again in 1834, they vowed to celebrate yearly a special feast for her protection from the earthquake the typhoon. On its part the miraculous statue has seen to it that no devout life has since that time been lost. Earthquakes and typhoons have come and left destruction, yet they have never taken one life or harmed the children of Santa Maria de Camarino, Our Lady of Guam.

When American marines and soldiers during the latter part of July 1944, captured the island of Guam, the native population was for the most part Catholic. The Faith was brought there by Spanish priests who accompanied Magellan when he sailed around the world. The natives are called Charmorros, offspring of Spanish and Micronesian ancestors, and make up the people of the Mariana Islands. They know the American way of life, since they have lived for more than fifty years under the benevolent guidance of the Stars and Stripes. And Mary, Our Lady of Guam, Our Lady of the Cupboard, loves them and protects them.

Our Lady of Guam, the miraculous statue to which the natives have such deep devotion, is about one metre high, all ivory from the delicate classical face of Our Lady to the hem of her exquisite gown. She has a head of brown hair, adorned with a beautiful crown, and golden rings hang from her tiny ears. Flags of various nations have flown over the royal coconut trees of Agana: admirals and governors have come and gone, and each in his proper time has departed. Spanish architecture has had its day, and the Seabee buildings mushroomed all over the island. Yet, Santa Maria de Camarino abides through all changes to cherish her strangely chosen people. She reigns affectionately in the hearts of the people, the natives, as their Queen and Patroness.

The statue was stolen from the Basilica in 1968, on 9 May 1971, and on 28 December 1992 but successfully retrieved each time. The Archbishop believes that the thefts of Our Lady were motivated not by the promise of monetary gain, but by proximity to the miraculous. "All of the people who took the statue did it to be close to her. They were troubled people who hoped that having her near would somehow caused her to perform a miracle."

15 April: Our Lady of Nicaragua

 ERNARDO MARTINEZ WAS a very simple, middle-aged rancher with great humility. In the valley of Cuapa, Nicaragua, he took care of the small sacristy. From the time he was a young boy, he had done the cleaning in the chapel, opened doors for services, prepared for all celebrations, rang the bells and led the Rosary hours all without pay. Bernardo's grandmother had been very devout, and she taught him to have a great love for Our Holy Mother Mary, and the Rosary. Bernardo was very poor, owning a single calf and bathing in a nearby stream.

On two different nights in April of 1980, Bernardo had gone to the sacristy, where he found the lights turned on. Bernardo was sure some of the local women had left the lights on, and he had lightly scolded them. Then, on the night of 15 April 1980, Bernardo saw the glow of the lights from the sacristy, and entered to turn them off. What he found instead, was not the sacristy lights on, but the statue of the Virgin Mary illuminated all by itself. Because of Bernardo's humility and simplicity, he thought that the statue lit up because Mary was angry at him for blaming some of the women for leaving the lights on. He decided to ask their forgiveness because he was so moved at seeing the statue illuminated. After this public apology, Bernardo told all the people who were there praying the Rosary what he had seen. However the people and even the local priest ridiculed him.

On 8 May 1980 Bernardo went out to go fishing. Returning from this fishing trip he saw two lightning flashes. On the second flash the Virgin Mary appeared to him. He felt immobilized and could not run or shout, but he was surprised that he felt no fear. He thought that he might just be envisioning the same statue in his mind—and perhaps was dreaming, but when he passed his hand over his eyes and looked again, he saw that she had human skin and eyes that moved and blinked. "She is alive!" he thought to himself—because his tongue would not move to speak. He felt numb—his lower jaw and tongue were stiff as if asleep. His whole body was immobilized—only his thoughts in his mind could be active. She was so beautiful, wearing a long white dress with bare feet resting upon an extremely white cloud. She had a celestial cord around her waist, long sleeves, and a veil of a pale cream colour with gold embroidery covering her. She extended her arms and rays of light, "stronger than the sun", emanated from her hands. The rays touched his chest, and he was able to speak again, so he asked her name. He saw her move her lips and say that her name was Mary. He knew she was alive and real because she actually responded to him, and encouraged him to pray the rosary and promote peace saying: "Make Peace. Don't ask Our Lord for peace because, if you do not make it, there will be no peace." At this time, Nicaragua was going through a civil war. The Sandinista government was facing armed opposition from the Contras. Bernardo Martinez claimed that the Virgin Mary ordered him to burn bad books, which was interpreted to mean Marxist books.

Our Lady asked that the Rosary be prayed always and not only in the month of May; furthermore Mary added that prayers should not be rushed or said in a mechanical fashion. She instructed Bernardo to read the Scripture passages that go along with the mysteries of the Rosary. Our Lady then said:

> Nicaragua has suffered much since the earthquake. She is threatened with even more suffering. She will continue to suffer if you don't change. Pray! Pray, my son, the Rosary for all the world. Tell believers and non-believers that the world is threatened by grave dangers. I ask the Lord to appease His Justice, but if you don't change, you will hasten the arrival of a Third World War.

Our Lady appeared again three further times, on 8 June, 8 July On 13 October a large glowing circle appeared above the ground in front of fifty people that had gathered to say the Holy Rosary. Everyone saw the light that came from the sky—a single ray—like a powerful spotlight that illuminated the circle in front of them. Then the people noticed that a circle had also formed in the sky. The circle began to radiate all the colours of the rainbow (at exactly 3:00 pm) which danced about the sky. One could feel a small breeze that moved softly. All of a sudden, there was a lightning flash, the same as the other times, then, a second flash. Our Lady then appeared on her little cloud which rested above a pile of flowers that the group had brought. She extended her hands, and rays of light reached out to everyone, causing some to cry with joy. Bernardo begged her to appear to all of those present as they did not all believe in his vision. Mary's face became pale and her clothes turned grey, appearing as Our Lady of Sorrows, and she spoke thus:

> It saddens me to see the hardness of those persons' hearts. But you will have to pray for them so that they will change. Pray the Rosary. Meditate on the mysteries. Listen to the Word of God spoken in them. Love one another. Love each other. Forgive each other. Make peace. Don't ask for peace without making peace, because if you don't make it, it does no good to ask for it. Fulfil your obligations. Put into practice the Word of God. Seek ways to please God. Serve your neighbour—as that way you will please Him. They ask of me things that are unimportant. Ask for Faith in order to have strength so that each can carry his own cross. The suffering of this world cannot be removed. That is the way life is. There are problems with the husband, with the wife, with the children, with the brothers. Talk, converse, so that the problems will be resolved in peace. Do not turn to violence. Never turn to violence. Pray for faith in order that you will have patience. You will no longer see me in this place.

As she departed, the little cloud seemed to be pushing her back up to Heaven. At this, the messages from Mary were completed. The local bishop of Juigalpa, Mgr Monsignor Vega, published his approval of these apparitions on 13 November 1983. On 10 June 1994, Bishop Robelo of Leon authorized of the accounts of the apparitions entitled *Let Heaven and Earth Unite!* compiled by Stephen and Miriam Weglian.[18] In 1995 at the age of 64 years, Bernardo Martinez was ordained a priest in the Cathedral of León, Nicaragua; he died in 2000.

16 April: Our Lady of Victories of Saint Mark

N THE YEAR 1683 a formidable army of well over 100,000 Turks invaded Austria and laid siege to Vienna for the second time. The city was strategically located in Europe, and the Ottoman Turks had been pressing further and further into Christendom over the preceding centuries. If they could take Vienna, it would open up all of Europe to them.

Unfortunately, Europe was not united against the invader. The various Protestant groups despised their Catholic neighbours more than they feared the Turk, and favoured doing nothing as the Catholics fought alone to save Europe. In fact, the Ottoman Empire had been supporting the Protestants, and encouraged them to revolt and rebel against their lawful government, which weakened Christendom and obviously played into the hands of the Turks. It went so far that they actually promised their Protestant dupes that they would be given the "Kingdom of Vienna" if they should help defeat them.

Suffering under an intense siege, Vienna was on the point of surrendering to the enemy. The people were filled with fear and anxiety, for had this happened, the Turks would easily have invaded the rest of Europe, and filled it with blood and strife. From all parts of the Catholic world prayers were offered to the Queen of Heaven, that she intercede and avert this disaster. Our Lady, Consoler of the Afflicted, did not fail her people.

The pious and valiant Catholic King of Poland, John Sobieski, with an army seemingly inadequate to the need, bravely marched against the enemy. Even though his army was tiny in comparison to the multitudes that awaited him, there was no one else who could come to the aid of Vienna. When John Sobieski came in sight of the Turkish camp, before beginning battle, he ordered Holy Mass to be celebrated, at which he himself served; then he begged the celebrant to bless the whole army.

Full of confidence in the help of Mary Most Holy, Our Lady of Victories, King John Sobieski manfully threw his forces into the conflict. Initiating what would be the largest cavalry charge in history, King John led his now legendary Winged Hussars into the face of the enemy like a host of avenging angels, disrupting the enemy formations and breaking their lines. The enemy, though far more numerous, turned and fled, while the king's army were masters of the field. The rejoicing of Christians was great at this news, and from all Christendom fervent prayers were offered to the Blessed Mother, Our Lady of Victories, in thanksgiving for her protection.

Pope Innocent XI, reigning at the time, placed all his trust in the Blessed Virgin Mary. He had vowed to institute a feast in her honour, if she would liberate the Church from this terrible danger. In fulfilment of this vow, he extended to the whole Catholic world the solemnity of the feast of the Holy Name of Mary, which had up to that time only been observed in particular churches. The famous image of Our Lady of Victories is the one which Emperor John Zimiarnes and John Commenus carried in a triumphal car after having besieged the enemy. The image is now borne in procession at Vienna to obtain rain or fine weather, as the need may be.[19]

17 April: Our Lady of Arrabida

 HE SHRINE OF Our Lady of Arrabida is popular with sailors and with all those who travel by water. It owes its beginnings to a miraculous occurrence during the sixteenth century, near Setubal in Portugal. An English merchant named Hildebrand was standing off the entrance to the Tagus River when a fierce storm caught his ship and immediately plunged him into the dangerous waters at the mouth of the river. The ship was in great danger and the merchant, being a pious Catholic, knelt before a picture of Our Lady which he always kept on board his ship.

Soon after he began praying a bright light was seen shining through the darkness and the ship came to rest in calm waters.

When daylight came, it could be seen that the vessel was safely anchored at the foot of a very steep wooded mountain. Hildebrand went back below decks to kneel before the image of Our Lady in thanksgiving, when he found that it was no longer there. Since he had seen the light coming from the direction of the mountain the night before, the merchant went on land and climbed the steep trail to the top. There, at the very summit of the mountain, amid the dense woods, was his picture of Our Lady, before which he had prayed in his hour of need. Greatly moved, the merchant finished his business as soon as possible in England and returned to Portugal. He gave away his goods to the poor and settled down in a small hermitage at the top of the mountain, where the picture had indicated that Our Lady wished a shrine to be.

The shrine is there today, and still popular with all who travel by water. Numerous votive tablets surround the picture, testifying to miracles worked by Our Lady of Arabida for those who come to her in need. Sailors going on a long voyage usually go for a farewell visit on departure and return to give thanks when they come back.[20]

18 April: Mother of God of Kasperov

ACCORDING TO TRADITION, the Kasperov Icon of the Most Holy Theotokos had been brought to Cherson from Transylvania by a Serb at the end of the sixteenth century. Passing down from parent and child, the icon had come to belong to a certain Mrs Kasperova of Cherson in 1809.

One night in February of 1840 she was praying, seeking consolation in her many sorrows. Looking at the icon of the Virgin, she noticed that the features of the icon, darkened by age, had suddenly become bright. Soon the icon was glorified by many miracles, and people regarded it as wonder-working.

During the Crimean War (1853–1856), the icon was carried in procession through the city of Odessa, which was besieged by enemy forces. On Great and Holy Friday, the city was spared.

Since that time, an Akathist has been sung before the icon in the
Dormition Cathedral of Odessa every Friday.

The icon is painted with oils on a canvas mounted on wood.
The Mother of God holds Her Son on her left arm. The Child is
holding a scroll. St John the Baptist is depicted on one side of the
icon, and St Tatiana on the other. These were probably the patron
saints of the original owners of the icon.

19 April: Our Lady of Máriabesnyő, Hungary

 N THE 1750s the third wife Terezia Klobusiczky of Antal
Grassalkovich I, the ruler of the region of Gödöllő, about
30 kilometres north-east of Budapest became fatally ill.
At this time the Count made a resolution that if his wife recovered
he would build a church in honour of the Blessed Virgin Mary.
When the work was started stonemason János Fidler saw a vision
and heard the words: "If you dig among the ruins of the church
where once the main altar stood you will find a beautiful object."
On the following day, 19 April 1759 he started to search at the
location described, and at a depth of two spades he found a
beautiful statue of the Virgin Mary, which was an 11cm high
carved piece of ivory from the eleventh or twelfth century.

Antal Grassalkovich decorated the statue from his family
treasury with two crowns and a belt of precious stones, and it is
also adorned with the gift of a gold ring from the Austrian
Emperor Franz Josef I. The statue was placed in a silver house
behind crystal glass in the chapel, which was completed by 14
August 1761. Due to increasing demand the church was continuously extended and was consecrated on 17 March 1771. The
news of the miraculous find of the country's smallest devotional
statue spread quickly and Máriabesnyő became a place of pilgrimage. Even today several hundred thousand people visit it every
year, asking for the graces of the Holy Virgin Mother. Starting
from early times very many prayers were answered and miracles

took place here. The small expressions of thanks located in the area around the altar bear witness to this.

Count Grassalkovich entrusted the care of the shrine to the Capuchins in 1763. The church was renovated by the order in 1912 and then in 1942, but in 1950 when the orders were disbanded by the Communist regime, they were forced to abandon it. After the fall of the Iron Curtain the capuchins returned to Máriabesnyő, which became the second most visited Virgin Mary shrine in Hungary in the twentieth century.

Pope Benedict XVI with the decree of the Congregation for the Divine Worship and the Discipline of the Sacraments issued on 2 May 2008 raised the Máriabesnyő chapel to the rank of minor basilica.

20 April: Our Lady of Schier

RNAUD SCHIER IS remembered as being the odd son of the Bavarian House of Schier. Sullen and disgruntled, he angrily left the dining hall before the meal was finished. It would prove to be his last meal. His parents had decided to give up their castle, which Arnaud had hoped would be his heritage, for the honour of the Blessed Virgin Mary. He did not favour the idea of giving the castle to the Virgin, and no one had even thought to ask him his opinion.

Slamming the door, he wandered into the darkness of night alone, caring little if anyone should overhear his repeated objections. The more he thought about it, the angrier he became. Why did the family wish to give up the ancestral home? And for a shrine to Our Lady at that! Arnaud wanted no more of this continued discussion on the subject. On he walked, oblivious of where, nursing his grievance against the Mother of God. He was last seen by a servant waiving his hands in the air and bemoaning his loss, wondering what he should do.

Arnaud had forgotten that his chief concern should have been to seek after perfection. Children will usually imitate their parents after initially watching them and then conversing with them. Parents who are a fine Christian example, such as Arnaud's parents, should have had children who would also seek to imitate their Divine Master. The surest route is with the help of God's grace, but also through the intercession of His Most Holy Mother.[21]

21 April: Our Lady of Betharram

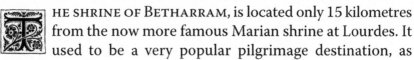 HE SHRINE OF BETHARRAM, is located only 15 kilometres from the now more famous Marian shrine at Lourdes. It used to be a very popular pilgrimage destination, as according to St Vincent de Paul, Betharram was once the second most popular place of pilgrimage in France. The river Gave, beside which the shrine is located, is the same river whose waters flow past Lourdes.

The shrine of Our Lady of Betharam is famous for no less than three miracles attributed to the Blessed Virgin Mary. According to tradition, one day in 1503 there were some shepherds leading their flocks along the bank of the river Gave when they suddenly observed an extremely bright light coming from the rocks. When they drew nearer, they found a beautiful statue of the Blessed Virgin. Learning of the incident, the people in the nearby village of Lestelle decided to construct a chapel to house the statue. Due to space limitations, the chapel was initially planned for the opposite bank from where the statue had been found. Once the statue was placed there, however, they found that it would always return on its own to the other side of the river where it had originally been found. The faithful then understood that the Blessed Virgin desired that the chapel should be built where the statue had been found, and so it happened.

The next miracle occurred in the year 1616 when some peasants from the village of Montaut were returning home from the fields at the end of the day. A rushing storm suddenly appeared, with fierce winds that threatened Betharram. In fact, the labourers saw that there was a tornado in the storm that beat against the great wooden cross that had been erected at the summit. The cross fell, but then was encircled by a radiant aura of dazzling light before standing again on its own in its former position.

The third miracle is the one after which the shrine is named. A young girl fell headfirst into the Gave when trying to pick a flower along the bank. The water runs fast in deep in this area, and the girl was on the verge of drowning when she cried aloud to Our Lady of Betharram at the nearby shrine. The Blessed Virgin appeared standing on the bank holding the Divine Infant, who held a branch which he extended to rescue the girl. After her miraculous rescue, the girl offered a golden branch to the shrine as an *ex-voto* offering. "Betharram" means "a beautiful branch" in the local dialect, and thus became the name of the shrine.

Many other wonders occurred; at one point between the years 1620 and 1642 there were 82 documented miracles involving the blind who received their sight, the paralysed who regained the use of the limbs, and those instantly cured of cancer. The cross on the summit that the winds could not destroy was finally destroyed by the folly of man during the French Revolution. The property was unlawfully confiscated and the chaplains expelled. However the priest St Michel Garicois restored the shrine and helped needy people. He took St Bernadette Soubirous into his confidence. She frequently visited the shrine of Betharram, and the rosary beads that Bernadette used when praying with the Blessed Virgin during the first apparition at Lourdes had come from the Betharram shrine. St Michel Garicois alone believed Bernadette's accounts of the apparitions at Lourdes. Garicois founded the congregation of the Priests of the Sacred Heart, or the Betharram Fathers; he was canonized in 1947.

Pope St Pius X was known to be very devoted to Our Lady of Betharram. He offered her two magnificent golden crowns made up of branches woven together. This prayer accompanying the inscription stated: "May the Son and His Mother accept our gifts and by appeasing our hopes and desires may they gain for us one day the crown of glory which cannot tarnish."

22 April: Our Lady of the Jesuits

T ALL THE KEY MOMENTS in the birth of the Society of Jesus, Our Lady was present: when Ignatius Loyola left his old life behind him, he made a vigil before the Black Madonna on the eve of the feast of the Annunciation in 1522; he made his first vows on the feast of the Assumption, 1534; and when he celebrated Mass for the first time, it was in the church of St Mary Major on Christmas Day, 1538. Seven months after the official approval of the Society by Pope Paul IV, Ignatius and his first five companions celebrated this new birth by making their vows together at Our Lady's altar in the Basilica of St Paul Outside-the-Walls, on 22 April 1541. Ignatius had been elected the first general two weeks earlier and so it was he who celebrated that Mass. As Mary had helped bring Jesus to birth so she, too, helped bring to birth this community of brothers and priests who would be her Son's Companions.

The beautiful, late-medieval image of Our Lady of the Way was in a small chapel where Ignatius often used to pray; and when the newly-founded Society of Jesus was able to build her first church, the Gesù, they did so on the grounds of this earlier chapel. Ignatius preserved the image and it is now in the north chapel of the church of the Gesù. It is a symbol not only of the Mother—the one who helps bring Jesus to life—but also of the Mother who accompanies her Son and His followers on their way, on our journey together, to the Father. Mary is there, journeying with us. The prayer which accompanies this beautiful image is also one which alludes to Mary not only as our Mother but also as the one who accompanies us on our journey. Mary, Mother of a pilgrim people. As Pope Benedict XVI prayed: "May Mary continue to watch over the Society of Jesus so that every member may carry in his person the 'image' of the Crucified Christ, in order to share His Resurrection."[22] The Jesuits now celebrate Our Lady of the Way on 24 May.

23 April: Our Lady of Ardents

UR LADY OF ARDENTS is a small, charming red brick church in the lower part of town in Arras, France. It was built in the beautiful style unique to the twelfth century in order to celebrate the appearance of the Blessed Virgin, and to commemorate the miraculous assistance she gave to the people then living in the region. According to tradition, a terrible epidemic ravaged the countryside in that year 1105, and everyone felt that they were in the clutch of Death. The evil of Ardent was a disease causing a kind of gangrene in the limbs, and the strange sickness caused terrible suffering in all parts of the body, and laid low both men and women, and even their children throughout the whole of the area.

There were at that time two minstrels, one named Itier, who was from Tienen in Flemish province of Brabant, and the other called Norman, who lived in the Chateau de Saint-Pol. They were in a blood feud, as Norman had killed Itier's brother. One night they both had the same dream: the Virgin Mary, dressed in white, appeared to them and told them to go to the cathedral. Norman, who was closer, arrived first. As he entered the cathedral he saw all the patients who had taken refuge there. He found the bishop and told him of the apparition, but Bishop Lambert thought that Norman was mocking him and sent him away. Itier arrived the following day and also spoke to the bishop. When the bishop told Itier that someone named Norman had come to tell him of the same vision, Itier asked where he was, because he intended to kill him to avenge his brother's death. Bishop Lambert then understood that the Blessed Virgin had sent the two men to be reconciled. The bishop spoke to each separately and then put them in each other's presence and asked them to give each other the kiss of peace and then spend the night in prayer inside the cathedral.

On Pentecost Sunday, 28 May 1105, at about three o'clock in the morning, the Virgin Mary appeared to the two minstrels in the Cathedral. Norman and Itier witnessed a sudden light as the

Blessed Virgin descended from the height of the nave, carrying a lighted candle in her hands. She gave the men the candle intended for the healing of the sick, and explained to them what they must do. A few drops of the wax that fell from the candle were to be mingled with water, giving it miraculous properties for the people to drink. All who believed were healed. The two minstrels, now brothers, distributed the miraculous water and the epidemic was stopped, for the patients would regain their health after they drank of the water mixture.[23] There were many prodigies of healing that went on for hundreds of years, especially with wounds, inflammations, and ulcers. All of this shows how reconciliation and prayer are pleasing to God and can bring about great miracles, such as curing diseases, ending natural disasters, as well as ending or preventing wars.

The bishop of Arras desired to build a church worthy of Our Lady of Ardents and to receive the relic of the Holy Candle, and the church was consecrated in 1876 just before the definitive establishment of the Third Republic. This relic, the Holy Candle, can still be seen today. On the eve of Corpus Christi and the four following days, the Holy Candle is lit and shown to the people.

24 April: Our Lady of Bonaria

HE SHRINE OF Our Lady of Bonaria (Good Air) dates back to the latter years of the fourteenth century, at Cagliari, on the island of Sardinia. According to tradition, on 25 March 1370, a ship ran into a terrific storm at a spot some miles off the coast of Sardinia while en route from Spain to Italy. Soon the ship seemed in imminent danger of sinking, and the sailors in a last desperate effort to save her, began to get rid of the cargo.

When they heaved a certain large packing case into the sea, the waves immediately died down and the sea became calm. The sailors knew the ship had been miraculously saved and attempted to regain the last crate, followed it for some time. Unable to retrieve it, the sailors returned to their original course. The case floated away, and pushed by the tides, eventually landed on the shore of Sardinia at the foot of a hill called Bonaria. A large crowd ran down to the beach when the crate washed ashore, eager to see what it contained. Some tried to open it, though no one was able to pry off the lid. Others tried to carry it from the waves, but could not do so, for the crate was too heavy. One of the children suddenly cried out: "Call for the Mercedarian Friars!" They came and raised the heavy crate without any difficulty, and took it to their church, where it was opened in the presence of a large group of people. To the surprise of all, they found it contained a beautiful statue of the Virgin and Child. In her right hand the Virgin held a candle which was still lit.

In this way a prophesy was fulfilled—the church had been build around 1330 by Father Carlo Catalan, while he was the ambassador to the Argonese Court. At the dedication he told the monks, "A Great Lady will come to live in this place. After her coming, the malaria infecting this area will disappear and her image will be called the Virgin of Bonaria." So when the statue floated in from the sea, and the Fathers placed it in their church, remembering what Father Carlo had said, they named it "Our Lady of Good Air," or "Our Lady of Bonaria." Due to the miracle, devotion to the Virgin spread quickly, especially among sailors who took the Blessed Virgin for their protector and carried her devotion far and wide.

The statue is in coloured wood, probably of Spanish workmanship. Pope Pius X in 1908, declared Our Lady of Bonaria the patron Saint of Sardinia. Most recently, on 7 September 2008, Our Lady of Bonaria was visited by Pope Benedict XVI in honour of the first centenary of her announcement as the Patron Saint of Sardinia, and he gave Our Lady of Bonaria a Golden Rose.

In 1536, Spanish explorer Pedro de Mendoza found and named the port of Buenos Aires in Argentina. His company included a Sardinian squire, two friars of the Order of Mercy, and an image of Santa María del Buen Ayre. Navigators had already claimed Our Lady of Good Air as patron, spreading her fame from her original Mercedarian shrine of Bonaria in Sardinia, off Italy, to Mendoza's homeland of Andalusia in southern Spain. Perhaps in recognition of her assistance to mariners, her title altered in Argentina and some other places to Nuestra Señora de los Buenos Aires, Our Lady of Good Winds.

Meanwhile, no church in Buenos Aires was dedicated to Our Lady of Good Air or Winds, although there were images of her in the Cathedral and other churches. With the backing of Sardinian immigrants, the church of Nuestra Señora de los Buenos Aires, begun in 1911, was inaugurated on 3 December 1932, almost 400 years after Mendoza gave her name to the Argentinian capital. By then April 24 had become the liturgical feast day of Our Lady of Good Winds.

25 April: Mary, Mediatrix of all Graces

NEAR THE CLOSE of the Second World War, the parish priest of Pfaffenhofen, Germany, Father Martin Humpf, together with several parishioners, promised to build a chapel in Our Lady's honour, if she would preserve the town from harm. On 25 April 1946, Father Humpf, his sister Anna, and a pious young woman aged 22, Barbara Ruess, began searching for a suitable place to build the promised chapel. They found what appeared to be a very suitable place, but Father Humpf wished out loud that they could be given some sort of sign of Our Lady's will. The three prayed the Rosary and then began to dig a hole in order to plant there a small picture shrine on top of an ornamented stick. The picture so happened to be one of the copies of the Thrice Admirable Mother of Schönstatt. While they were digging, Barbara heard someone call her name. When Barbara went to see who it was, she saw and spoke with a beautiful Lady, whom the others could not see or hear. The Lady identified herself only as "the Sign of the Living God", saying that there would be peace when all men believed in her power of intercession. As she disappeared, she said, "The peace of Christ be with you, and with all who pray here." This is the origin of the name given to the place of the apparitions—for Marienfried means Marian peace. Our Lady heard their prayer and the town was spared.

In this first apparition an angel had appeared, and Mary was addressed as the great Mediatrix of Graces. On 25 May, Barbara and Anna went again to Marienfried in order to ornament the little shrine with fresh flowers. The two lingered there to pray, when the Lady appeared again to Barbara. She gave a lengthy message to Barbara and said she would return on June 25. Angels would also play a prominent role in this latter apparition, surrounding the Blessed Mother and kneeling before her in profound reverence and then worshipping the Holy Trinity.

During the final apparition, the Lady acknowledged that many had honoured her with the title Mater Admirabilis. She lamented, however, that although she had already given so many signs and spoken to the world so often, most people had not taken them seriously. She added that she would work her wonders in secret, in the souls of her children. Men should not expect further signs and wonders. Barbara asked the Lady (whom she was convinced was the Blessed Virgin Mary), if she wanted the promised chapel to be built there. The Lady said, "I have fulfilled your request; keep your promise here." Then Barbara asked what image should be used in the chapel. The Lady pointed to the picture of the Thrice Admirable Mother and told Barbara that they should use that image, for already many people had offered prayers and sacrifices before that image, and she willed that many more would come and do the same.

The Virgin was described as "unspeakably beautiful and brilliant, a blinding vision of most pure light and radiance … above her head were brilliant rays forming a three-tiered crown." When she lifted her hand to give a blessing she became incredibly brilliant and transparent. She was so bright that Barbara was unable to look at her. The messages from the Blessed Virgin at Marienfried have much in common with those of Fatima. Besides the appearance of angels preceding the visitation of the Mother of God, many of the same exhortations that were directed to the three children at Fatima were also made here by Our Lady.

The importance of the Rosary was highlighted as well as the need to live a life of holiness, sacrifice and consecration to the Immaculate Heart of Mary. The Blessed Virgin stated the great importance of offering acts of love, praise and adoration to God the Father and the Most Holy Trinity. Our Lady also underscored the great truth that she is Mediatrix of All Graces, and declared that "it is the will of the Father that the world acknowledge this position of His Handmaid."

Although the apparitions of Marienfried are not approved, they are likewise not condemned and have the status of not giving signs or evidences of supernaturality.[24] While not affirmed, the apparitions are not denied and the faithful are free to make pilgrimage to the Marian site, as underscored by the Bishop of Augsburg on 20 March 2000.

26 April: Our Lady of Good Counsel

UR LADY OF GOOD COUNSEL (*Mater boni consilii*) is a title given to the Blessed Virgin Mary, related to a miraculous painting now found in the Augustinian church at Genazzano, a town about twenty-five miles southeast of Rome. The church had been entrusted to the order in 1356, and it was the Augustinian Order which subsequently contributed most to the spread of this particular devotion internationally. According to tradition, in the year 1467, in the midst of the festivities for the Feast of St Mark, the townsfolk suddenly heard beautiful music. A mysterious cloud was then said to have descended and obliterated an unfinished wall of the parish church. Suddenly, the bells of the old tower began to ring by themselves, and the other bells of the town rang miraculously in unison. In front of the populace, the cloud dissipated and a beautiful fresco was revealed, which was paper-thin and no more than eighteen inches square, of the Blessed Virgin Mary and the

Christ Child. Two foreigners named Giorgio and De Sclavis entered the city among a group of pilgrims that had come from Rome. They wore strange clothes and spoke a foreign tongue, saying they had arrived in Rome earlier that year from Albania. While most people had refused to believe their story, it had a special significance for the inhabitants of Genazzano.

January of 1467 had seen the death of the last great Albanian leader, George Castriota, better known as Scanderbeg. Raised by an Albanian chief, he placed himself at the head of his own people. Subsequently, Scanderbeg inflicted stunning defeats on the Turkish army and occupied fortresses all over Albania. With Scanderbeg's death, the Turkish army poured into Albania, occupying all its fortresses, cities and provinces with the exception of Scutari, in the north of the country. However, the city's capacity to resist was limited, and its capture was expected at any moment. With its fall, Christian Albania would be defeated. Faced with this prospect, those who wished to practice their faith in Christian lands began a sad exodus. Those two men, Giorgio and De Sclavis also studied the possibility of fleeing, but something kept them in Scutari, where there was a small church, considered the shrine of the whole Albanian kingdom. In this church dedicated to the Annunciation, the faithful venerated a picture of Our Lady which had mysteriously descended from the heavens two hundred years before; according to tradition, it had come from the East. Having poured out innumerable graces over the whole population, this church became the principal centre of pilgrimage in Albania. Scanderbeg himself had visited this shrine more than once to ardently ask for victory in battle. Now the shrine was threatened with imminent destruction and profanation. The two Albanians were torn by the idea of leaving the great treasure of Albania in the hands of the enemy in order to flee the Turkish terror. In their perplexity, they went to the old church to ask their Blessed Mother for the good counsel they needed. That night, the Consoler of the Afflicted inspired both of them in their sleep. She commanded them to prepare to leave their country, which they would never see again. She added that the miraculous fresco was also going to leave Scutari for another country to escape profanation at the hands of the Turks. Finally, she ordered them to follow the painting wherever it went. The next morning, the two friends went to the shrine. At a certain moment they saw the picture detach itself from the wall on which it had hung for two centuries. Leaving its niche, it hovered for a moment and was then suddenly wrapped in a white cloud through which the image continued to be visible.

The pilgrim painting left the church and the environs of Scutari. It travelled slowly through the air at a considerable altitude and advanced in the direction of the Adriatic Sea at a speed that allowed the two walkers to follow; after covering some twenty-four miles, they reached the coast. With unbounded confidence, Giorgio and De Scalvis walked on the waves of the Adriatic Sea. Without stopping, the picture left the land and advanced over the waters while the faithful Giorgio and De Sclavis continued to follow, walking on the waves much like their Divine Master had done on Lake Genesareth. When night would fall, the mysterious cloud, which had protected them with its shade from the heat of the sun during the day, guided them by night with light, like the column of fire in the desert that guided the Jews in their exodus from Egypt. They travelled day and night until they reached the Italian coast. There, they continued following the miraculous picture, climbing mountains, fording rivers and passing through valleys. Finally, they reached the vast plain of Lazio from where they could see the towers and domes of Rome. Upon reaching the gates of the city, the cloud suddenly disappeared before their disappointed eyes. Giorgio and De Sclavis began to search the city, going from church to church asking if the painting had descended there. All their attempts to find the painting failed, and the Romans incredulously regarded the two foreigners and their strange tale. Shortly thereafter, amazing news came to Rome: a picture of Our Lady had appeared in the skies of Genazzano to the sound of beautiful music and had come to rest over the wall of a church that was being rebuilt. The two Albanians rushed to find their country's beloved treasure miraculously suspended upon the wall of the chapel where it remains to this day. Although some inhabitants found the strangers' story difficult to believe, careful investigation later proved that the two were telling the truth and that the image was indeed the same one that graced the shrine in Scutari.

Soon after the appearance of the image at Genazzano, many miracles were attributed to the intercession of Our Lady of Good Counsel. Because of this, Pope Paul II ordered an investigation and the results have been preserved. A commission of enquiry determined that a portrait from the church was indeed missing from the church in Albania: an empty space the same size as the portrait was displayed for all to see. Such was the holy image's reputation that Pope Urban VIII made a special pilgrimage to Genazzano in 1630, invoking the protection of the Queen of Heaven, as did Pope Blessed Pius IX in 1864. On 17 November 1682, Blessed Pope Innocent XI had the picture solemnly crowned. Among her noted devotees have been St Aloysius Gonzaga, St Alphonsus Liguori and Blessed Stephen Bellesini. The Feast of Our Lady of Good Counsel is celebrated on 26 April. The small Scapular of Our Lady of Good Counsel (the White Scapular) was presented by the Hermits of St. Augustine to Pope Leo XIII, who, in December 1893, approved it and endowed it with indulgences.

Prayer to Our Lady of Good Counsel
Composed by Pope Pius XII

> O Holy Virgin, to whose feet we are lead by our anxious uncertainty in our search for and attainment of what is true and good, invoking you by the sweet title of Mother of Good Counsel. We beseech you to come to our assistance, when, along the road of this life, the darkness of error

and of evil conspires towards our ruin by leading our minds and our hearts astray.

O Seat of Wisdom and Star of the Sea, enlighten the doubtful and the erring, that they be not seduced by the false appearances of good; render them steadfast in the race of the hostile and corrupting influences of passion and of sin.

O Mother of Good Counsel, obtain for us from your Divine Son a great love of virtue, and, in the hour of uncertainty and trial, the strength to embrace the way that leads to our salvation. Supported by your hand we shall thus journey without harm along the paths taught us by the Word and example of Jesus our Saviour, following the Sun of Truth and Justice in freedom and safety across the battlefield of life under the guidance of your maternal Star, until we come at length to the harbour of salvation to enjoy with you unalloyed and everlasting peace. Amen

27 April: Our Lady of Spain

HE ONE AND only Lady of Spain, is a black Madonna who reigns from the lofty heights of Montserrat. The Virgin smiles down from her place of honour above the main altar of the Basilica of Montserrat. The statue is known as La Moreneta means the Little Black One. The statue is four feet high and made of wood, blackened from the smoke of innumerable candles which have burned before her through the ages. Our Lady of Moreneta is seated upon a chair and holds her Divine Child who has a pine-cone in His left hand. Our Queen is clothed in a golden mantle, a tunic and a veil of various colours; the Infant wears a simple tunic, and He and His Mother wear matching wooden crowns. The miraculous statue reposes upon a gleaming throne of marble, and over all, the sunlight diffuses glow.

The origin of the statue and the manner in which it first came to a lowly grotto in the mountainside is not clearly known. A legend recounts that in the year 880, on a Saturday night when the sun was going down over Montserrat, some young shepherds saw a bright light coming down from the sky, accompanied by beautiful music. The following Saturday they returned with their parents, and the vision came to them again. On the following four Saturdays the Rector of Olesa went with them, and everyone saw the vision. Then the statue of Our Lady was found in a cave in the mountains. A great monastic centre was founded in the same cliffs in the eleventh century and the small black statue of Our Lady drew the kings of Aragon, the monarchs of Spain, Emperor Charles V, saints, and celebrities, as well as ordinary people to the steep mountain. Here arduous pilgrimages terminated, and here wondrous miracles were wrought.

As the fame of La Moreneta spread, her original chapel underwent many transformations before the basilica was constructed in the sixteenth century. Now the first chapel is called the holy grotto and is decorated within with marble, fine tapestries, and two altars; one to Saint Scholastica, the other to Saint Benedict.

Montserrat, which means "Saw-tooth Mountain," was chosen by Our Lady for her shrine is believed to have an intrinsic holiness. Rebuilt after the Napoleonic and Civil Wars, the Abbey and Sanctuary of the Mother of God of Montserrat host some two million pilgrims a year. The shrine celebrates her feast day on 27 April with liturgical ceremonies, folk music, and dances.

> O Virgin resplendent, here on the high mountain gleaming with shining wonders, where believers from everywhere ascend; with your peaceful, holy eye behold those bound in the bond of sin; let them not suffer from the blows of the nether world, but by your prayer let them be reckoned with the blessed.[25]

28 April: Our Lady of Quito

 HIS MIRACULOUS IMAGE of Our Lady of Quito currently in the capital of Ecuador is said to date from the first Spanish settlement there in the year 1534. At the very least, it has certainly been venerated there for a long time, and is popularly called by the people of Quito Our Lady of the Earth-quake. The painting represents the Sorrowful Mother, and in the early years of the twentieth century, devotion to Mary under the title of Our Lady of Quito was introduced into England by the Servite Friars in London. Pope Saint Pius X accorded them an indulgence for those who should pray before her picture, and the devotion was greatly promoted in England by the Sisters of the Holy Child Jesus, Mother Cornelia Connelly's congregation. The original image at Quito was solemnly crowned in 1918.

On 20 April 1906, thirty-six boys attending the boarding school of the Jesuit Fathers at Quito, Ecuador, together with Father Andrew Roesch, witnessed the first miracle of this famous picture of Our Lady. While in the refectory they all saw the Blessed Mother slowly open and shut her eyes. The same miracle occurred no less than seven times after that, in favour of the boys at the school, but this time in the chapel to which the picture had been taken.

Ecclesiastical authorities soon investigated these incidents and finally concluded by ordering the picture to be transferred in procession from the college to the church of the Jesuit Fathers. Once at the church the prodigy was repeated several times before large crowds, and many, many conversions took place because of these miracles. At one time the wonder continued for three consecutive days. At Riobamba, before a faithful reproduction of Our Lady of Quito, the same wonder was seen by more than 20 persons, including the president of the city. In Quito this picture is known as the Dolorosa del Colegie.[26]

29 April: Our Lady of Faith

UR LADY OF FAITH is not a common title of the Blessed Virgin Mary in England, but in several places just across the channel in Belgium and France, this is a very tender designation of Our Lady. The title originally goes back to the discovery of a terracotta statue of Our Lady and Child hidden deep in an oak tree which was felled in 1609 between the Belgian city of Dinant and the nearby village of Foy. It seems that the statue had originally been placed on the outside of the tree which had subsequently grown around it.

Following the discovery of the statue which was first of all replaced in a niche in a neighbouring oak tree people began to visit, pray and experience various gifts of grace, including some miraculous healings. In due course the statue was moved first to the chapel of the local castle and then to a special sanctuary built on the site of the original oak. The church of Notre-Dame-de-Foy is still a pilgrimage centre today. This is in the French-speaking part of Belgium where "foy" is an old spelling of the word "foi" (faith). From quite an early date, copies of the statue were made and these too became focuses of devotion where they were set up, most notably in Amiens, where Our Lady of Faith has a special commemoration on 29 April.

Of all the images made of wood modelled after the original Madonna, the most famous perhaps is the one that is kept today at the cathedral of Amiens. The statue was placed in the church of the Augustinian religious at the beginning of the year 1629, whose monastery was located in the parish of Saint Michael. Starting 3 May of that year, wonderful miracles began to occur, and soon the Bishop of Amiens, Francois Le Febvre de Caumartin, formed a commission to study and conduct the necessary investigations. He ended by canonically recognizing devotion to the image and published four major miracles which had occurred, including the most striking being the resurrection of a dead child. The child had fallen into a pit and been buried for several hours. The devout Christians who struggled to rescue him did all in their power to revive him, but to no avail. Finally, the people took the child before the statue of Our Lady of Foy and knelt to pray with confidence for Our Lady's intercession. Immediately the child showed signs of life and awakened as if from sleep.

A ship's captain related that his vessel had recently sunk, and that the sailors and passengers aboard had all perished. The captain alone remained struggling against the swells, without hope of rescue, and recalled that he himself was near death. In his pressing moment of need he had recourse to Our Lady of Faith, and vowed to make a pilgrimage to the church if he should live. Although he was three leagues from Gravelines, he was instantly transported to the shore and hastened to fulfil his vow.

In the year 1636 noble ladies were frequently seen with their maids of honour praying before the holy image, and Cardinal Richelieu attended the litanies that were sung every day in this blessed sanctuary. In addition, the confraternity established in honour of Our Lady of Foy, included a number of high-ranking personages, including King Louis XIII, Anne of Austria, King Louis XIV, Queen Marie-Therese, King Louis XV, as well as the members of the noblest and most illustrious families of Picardy.

The image of Our Lady of Foy was hidden to protect it from the impious during the time of the French Revolution. Afterwards, the image was returned to the church, but the little Madonna became lost in the vastness of the cathedral, and received the homage of only a few souls who knew and remembered. In 1878, Bishop Louis-Désiré-César Bataille celebrated Mass at Notre-Dame de Foy, and restored this devotion. Soon the chapter of canons, supported by the bishop, asked the Pope to deign to open the treasure of indulgences. Many devotions and pilgrimages were once again made in her honour, and candles were constantly kept burning before her image.

30 April: Our Lady of Africa

N OUR DAY, we tend to think of North Africa as being under the dominion of Islam, but in the second century AD the region was part of the Roman Empire, and by the third century, under the Emperor Constantine, it began to become Christian. This was once the land of Saint Augustine, and it remained Christian until the Arab invasions in later centuries. The French were established in these parts early in the nineteenth century.

In Algiers, there was an ancient shrine, dedicated to the Immaculate Conception. It was originally a small statue of the Madonna, set in a frame of shells at a spot often visited by Barbary robbers. Fishermen came there to pray for safe voyages. In time, the grotto became a chapel and eventually a large church. There was, of course, no church in Algiers when the first bishop arrived, and the local population was hostile to the French. The first Bishop of Algiers, Mgr Antoine-Louis-Adolphe Dupuch (13 September 1838–9 December 1845), was without a church, funds or residence and was surrounded by Muslims whose hostility was evident and whose friendship had to be won. As he had no money to build a church, Bishop Dupuch went back to France to appeal for any assistance. The Sodality of Our Lady in Lyon had a bronze statue of the Immaculate Conception that they offered to the bishop on the understanding that she would be the Protectress of both the Muslims and the natives. It was brought from France in 1840 and was for some time entrusted to the Cistercian monks of Staouëli.

A great miracle made the revered chapel even better known. Archbishop Lavigerie (1825–1892) of Algiers was on his way to Rome accompanied by seven hundred soldiers, priests, and a Trappist abbot when their ship was caught in a violent storm. The crew despaired of the ship's safety. The archbishop had promised the Mother of God a pilgrimage to the shrine of Our Lady of Africa if she would save them. The ship was saved and the promise was kept. The Basilica of Our Lady of Africa, or Notre Dame d'Afrique, was eventually built, and is situated on a height overlooking the Bay of Algiers. It took fourteen years to construct in an attractive Neo-Byzantine style, and was consecrated in the year 1872: this now houses the crowned statue of Our Lady. Later, Cardinal Lavigerie, founder of the White Sisters, enshrined it in the new basilica at Algiers, where on 30 April 1876 the image was crowned with great splendour. Pope Blessed Pius IX donated the golden diadem with precious stones that Mary, Consolation of the Afflicted, now wears. The statue donated by the sodality became known as Our Lady of Africa, and the statue venerated in Algiers today is this same bronze image, very dark in colour, but with European features.

Pilgrims began to come to venerate the image where the lame, the blind, and the crippled were miraculously healed, and sailors came also to beg for protection of their long and perilous voyages. The walls of the basilica are now covered with votive offerings testifying to the assistance the faithful had received from the Mother of Mercy. At the shrine there are many Muslim pilgrims as well as Christian ones. To the faithful Muslim she is *Lala Meriem*, she who bestows her favours. The Holy See has entrusted the care of the sanctuary to the congregation of White Sisters of Africa.

Prayer to Our Lady of Africa

Our Lady of Africa, mother of the human family,
Be mindful of your African children,
at home or dispersed on other continents.
You who are full of grace,
look upon all those who do not know Jesus,
the Son sent by the Father.
May his light draw them and make them
receptive to the gift of Faith.
You, who are one with Christ
In suffering and in glory,
Be mindful of those assailed by trials,
That they may discover
His liberating Passover, and live by it in hope.
You who turned to Jesus
When the wine of joy ran out
Be mindful of peoples in distress,
that justice and peace may prevail
In a united world where Charity reigns.
You who, in the midst of the Apostles,

Received the breath of the Spirit
Be mindful of the apostles of today.
May they announce the Word with assurance
And proclaim it by their lives.
May young people hear the call of Christ
And follow him with joy.
Our Lady of Africa, Queen of the universe,
Be mindful of humanity on the way.
May Christ your Son, gather all peoples
In the unity of his Spirit
To the glory of the Father
For ages to come. Amen.

Notes

1   Pope Pius XII, Radio broadcast (17 October 1954).
2   See www.madonnadellelacrime.it.
3   Pope St John Paul II, *Homily at the Dedication of the Sanctuary of Our Lady of Tears*, Syracuse, Sicily (6 November 1994).
4   See P. LaFave, "When Mary Returned to Egypt" in *The Christian Review* (21 January 2016).
5   See *ibid.*
6   See www.zeitun-eg.org/zeitoun1.htm.
7   See LaFave, "When Mary Returned to Egypt".
8   See R. Laurentin, P. Sbalchiero, R. Etchegaray, *Dictionnaire des "apparitions" de la Vierge Marie: Inventaire des origines à nos jours méthodologie, bilan interdisciplinaire, prospective* (Paris: Fayard, 2012).
9   See S. Lavergne, *Notice historique sur la chapelle de Notre-Dame-de-Grâce de Honfleur* (Honfleur: Charles Lefrançois,1865).
10 See M. Lamberty (ed.), *The Woman in Orbit: Mary's feasts every day everywhere* (Chicago: Lamberty, 1966), 5 April.
11 See "The Shrines of Mater Admirabilis" in *Our Lady of Fatima Crusader Bulletin* Vol. 45, No. 140.
12 See Lamberty, *The Woman in Orbit*, 7 April.
13 See the website of the The Mission Society of the Mother of God of Boronyavo: www.missionboronyavo.org/shrine.html.
14 Fides News Agency, *Bulletin*, 21 May 2008.

[15] This is probably due, at least in part, to the character of Bruno Cornacchiola; it seems that he went on to claim a total of 28 further apparitions by 1986, with messages which became increasingly apocalyptic in tone, including predictions of various evils which have not materialized. It also seems that he has not been completely truthful in his biography. This is like the tragic history of Mélanie at La Salette; her initial experience was trustworthy, but she allowed events to go to her head in later years.

[16] See Lamberty, *The Woman in Orbit*, 13 April.

[17] Historians surmise that the statue might have come from a Spanish galleon, *Our Lady del Pilar* 1673, that ran aground and sank in the treacherous waters outside the reef of the Cocos Islands, Southern Guam.

[18] See M. and S. Weglian, *Let Heaven and Earth Unite* (Milford, OH: Faith Publishing Company, 1996).

[19] See Lamberty, *The Woman in Orbit*, 16 April.

[20] See *ibid.*, 17 April.

[21] See *ibid.*, 20 April.

[22] Pope Benedict XVI, *Discourse to the Fathers and Brothers of the Society of Jesus* (22 April 2006).

[23] See I. Couturier de Chefdubois, *Mille pèlerinages de Notre-Dame, région A: Normandie, Artois et Picardie, Île-de-France, Maine, Anjou, Orléanais, Blésois et Touraine, Poitou, Vendée, Aunis et Saintonge, Bretagne* (Paris, Éditions Spès, 1953), pp. 58–60.

[24] For the expression *non constat de supernaturalitate* see Congregation for the Doctrine of the Faith, *Norms on the Manner of Proceeding in Judging Alleged Apparitions and Revelations* (1978).

[25] From the *Llibre Vermell de Montserrat*, 1399: "O Virgo splendens hic in monte celso miraculis serrato, fulgentibus ubique quem fideles conscendunt universi, Eia, pietatis oculo placato, cerne ligatos fune peccatorum ne infernorum ictibus graventur sed cum beatis tua prece vocentur."

[26] See Lamberty, *The Woman in Orbit*, 28 April.

MAY

1 May: Our Lady, Queen of the May

HE MONTH OF May is flower-bedecked, and to add to its loveliness it is dedicated to the most beautiful flower of all, Mary, the Mother of God; no month could be more fitting for her. She is Mary, Our Lady Queen of May. May devotions have a splendour all their own. Garlands of flowers, petal-strewn processions culminating in the crowning of her image, are all forms of homage to Our Queen. As Newman pointed out:

> Why is May chosen as the month in which we exercise a special devotion to the Blessed Virgin? The first reason is because it is the time when the earth bursts forth into its fresh foliage and its green grass after the stern frost and snow of winter, and the raw atmosphere and the wild wind and rain of the early spring. It is because the blossoms are upon the trees and the flowers are in the gardens. It is because the days have got long, and the sun rises early and sets late. For such gladness and joyousness of external Nature is a fit attendant on our devotion to her who is the Mystical Rose and the House of Gold.[1]

The Litany of Our Lady offers a list of the most meaningful titles the Church could bestow on any creature. As all good earthly queens look to the welfare of their subjects, so does Mary on a much grander scale care for us. She is the summit of kindness and consideration. Though Queen of Heaven, there is no doubt that when this earth was privileged to have her as a dweller, Mary, Our Lady Queen of May, was the most humane of human beings, even through blessed far beyond our capacity to conceive of it.

Although she is Queen of the Universe, she does not enjoy the loyalty of all and must suffer the indifference of those who do not deign to pay her homage. Above everything, she sorrows to see so many deny her Son. Catholic devotion to Mary is found on all the virtues which human nature should and would possess, but seldom does. Mary is worthy of the admiration which devout people give her. Hers is a heart adorned as no other heart, with tenderness for the sinner Her Divine Son died to save; with meekness to confound the proud, with kindness toward human frailty; with love for all, because God has loved them first.

Mary's holiness and purity are the special object of our devotion; a purity that become the special object of our devotion; a purity of soul and body that we should revere and strive to imitate. Sin and Satan were never a part of Mary's life. Would that we could say the same! Not for a moment was there ever any difference between her will and that of the Most High. Not for a moment was there anything in Mary that could in any way displease her Lord. Of all God's creatures, Mary is indeed all fair, the beloved of the Almighty. During this month dedicated to her, let us admire the sinlessness of God's Mother, of our own Heavenly Mother. With God's grace and Mary's assistance and intercession, we can achieve that purity of soul that is pleasing to her and to her Son.

> Bring flow'rs of the fairest,
> Bring flow'rs of the rarest,
> From garden and woodland
> And hillside and vale;
> Our full hearts are swelling,
> Our Glad voices telling
> The praise of the loveliest
> Rose of the vale.
> O Mary! we crown thee with blossoms today,
> Queen of the Angels, Queen of the May,
> O Mary! we crown thee with blossoms today,
> Queen of the Angels, Queen of the May.[2]

2 *May: Our Lady, Queen of the Rosary and Peace*

 HE SMALL TOWN of Itapiranga in northern Brazil, about 650 miles southwest of Sao Paulo and about 880 miles from Rio de Janeiro, with a population of 8,000 people, is located in the midst of a tropical jungle known more for its wildlife than anything else until 2 May 1994. On that date a woman named Maria do Carmo was praying her rosary when she saw a beautiful girl of about seventeen who appeared holding Maria's son, who had died in a tragic accident in 1989 at the age of 11. The Lady identified herself as Queen of the Rosary and Peace, the Blessed Virgin Mary. Much like Fatima, her messages stressed the need for conversion, praying the Rosary, Mass, Confession and Holy Communion and penance to save the world mired in unbelief and sin. She and Jesus urged devotion to St Joseph's Most Chaste Heart.

Several apparitions took place on the following few days where the Blessed Mother warned against the evils of abortion. On 11 May 1994, Jesus appeared to Maria and spoke of adultery and cohabitation as grave sins. There were apparitions in Itapiranga from 1994–1998 in which St Joseph appeared along with Mary and Jesus, often with Saint Joseph holding the infant Jesus in his hands in addition to the Blessed Mother. The visionary was Edson Glauber, another son of Maria do Carmo.

In January 2010, the local Bishop of the Apostolic Prelature of Itacoatiara, Dom Carillo Gritti, after much study, prayer, reflection, observation and seeing the growth in the faith life of thousands, issued a Decree of Worship favouring the Itapiranga appearances and in an earlier document deemed it of "supernatural origin".[3]

3 *May: Our Lady of Czestochowa*

 ORTHEAST OF THE ancient city of Krakow, Poland, is the small town of Czestochowa. To every Pole the name means one thing—Mary's Sanctuary. On a nearby hill—

the Bright Hill, Jasna Gora in Polish—the Monks of St Paul the Hermit have a monastery. In the chapel of Our Lady in their monastery church, is the famous painting of the Blessed Virgin. This painting of the Mother of God holding the Child Jesus in her arms, bears the title, Our Lady of the Bright Hill (Jasna Gora) she is the Patroness and Protectress of the Poles; the Queen of the Crown in Poland.

The history of Our Lady of Czestochowa is the history of Poland. Traditional holds that this picture of Mary was painted by St Luke the Evangelist on a piece of wood cut from the table of the Last Supper. It was the Christians of Jerusalem who presented this picture to St Helen, the mother of Constantine. She in turn gave it to her son and so it was put in his palace at Constantinople. The salvation of this city while besieged by the Saracens was ascribed to Our Lady's intercession. The Byzantine Emperors showed great devotion for this picture and were able to hide it during the Iconoclast (breaking of images) persecution, thus saving it from destruction at the hands of the heretics who tried to destroy all statues and images. In 989, upon the marriage of Princess Anna, the sister of the Emperor, to Prince Vladimir of Kiev, the picture of Our Lady of Czestochowa was a wedding gift taken to her, to the Ukraine.

In the fourteenth century the picture was again in danger due to the Tartar raids. In a dream the wish of Our Lady was made known to Prince Ladislaus of Opol and in fulfillment of it, the holy image was taken to Jasna Gora. At that time the monks of St Paul the Hermit were invited to come from Hungary and be the custodians of the shrine. During the Hussite persecution, heretics plundered the monastery and the church. They hurled the precious image of Our Lady of Czestochowa to the ground and it was broken into three pieces. But when they tried to carry it off, the wagon bearing the image could not be moved. In rage one of them drew a sword and struck Our Lady's cheek twice. As he raised his arm a third time he fell dead on the spot. Seeing this, his comrades fled in terror.

Under King Ladislaus II of Poland a commission of artists restored the painting but no effort on their part could remove the sword strokes which remain to this day. These artists at the time placed a silver background over the upper part of the picture on which five scenes were engraved. These are: the Annunciation, the Adoration of the Christ child, the Scourging at the Pillar, Christ mocked by the soldiers, and St Barbara, to whom Poles have a great devotion.

On 1 April 1656, King Jan Casimir proclaimed the Mother of God the Queen of the Polish Crown and the shrine of Jasna Gora at Czestochowa its spiritual capital. In 1923, Pope Pius XI designated 3 May as the Feast of Our Lady, Queen of Poland. The Kings of Poland were especially devoted to Our Lady of the Bright Hill; at her shrine they and their people sought intercession in all needs of the nation. In danger from the Turks, during invasion by Swedes, under siege by Prussians, Austrians and Russians, after the partition of Poland in 1795, during the German invasion of 1939, and then under Communism, the hearts of Poles have always turned to Our Queen. Her shrine at Jasna Gora is for them a symbol of their faith and hope.

Tradition holds that, in 1920, when the Russian army was massing on the banks of the Vistula river, threatening Warsaw, an image of the Virgin was seen in the clouds over the city. The troops withdrew on seeing the image. There have been reports for centuries of miraculous events such as spontaneous healings occurring to those who made a pilgrimage to the portrait. On 4 June 1979, on his first visit as Pontiff to Poland, still under Communist oppression, Pope St John Paul II made an act of consecration to Our Lady at Czestochowa and said: "I who am the first servant of the Church offer the whole Church to you and entrust it to you here with immense confidence, Mother."[4]

Prayer

O Mary, our dear Lady of Czestochowa, look graciously upon your children in this troubled and sinful world. Embrace us all in your loving and Motherly protection. Protect our young from godless ways; assist our dear ones grown old with age to prepare for their journey home; shield our defenceless unborn from the horrors of abortion, and be our strength against all sin. Spare your children from all hatred, discrimination and war. Fill our hearts, our homes and our world with that peace and love which comes only from your Son, whom you so tenderly embrace. O, Queen and Mother, be our comfort and strength! In Jesus' name we pray. Amen.

4 May: Our Lady of Salvation

HE SHRINE OF the Our Lady of Salvation rises on the slopes of Mount Ginestra, in the village of Cori, in the province of Latina. In its current form, it was built in 1639, but already in 1537 it was consecrated previously in honour of the Madonna of the Broom Tree, but this title was changed to Our Lady of Salvation. The sanctuary came about following the apparition of the Blessed Mother who, in 1521, aided a 3-year-old girl by the name of Oliva Iannese.

On Saturday 4 May 1521 Oliva, got lost on the mountain while in search of her mother. Soon after she was overwhelmed by a storm and in that moment a beautiful Lady appeared to her who said to her: "I am the Virgin Mary." The Celestial Mother remained with her for eight whole days, day and night, after which she showed her the road back to town and soon after was found by some ladies who had gone to collect some fresh herbs on the mountain. The Virgin disclosed to the fortunate little girl a venerable image and made the consoling promise to offer special help to whoever ascended the mountain of the broom trees to venerate her.

During the eight days, an extraordinary fact occurred each time that Oliva was hungry; the Blessed Mother put her finger in the girl's mouth and every type of hunger or thirst passed. At the end of the storm, Maria Fantetti, Onorata Maggi and Onorata

Gabaluzzi went up the mountain of the broom trees to make bouquets of fresh herbs and find the lost Oliva. Her parents believed Oliva to be already dead, and she was led back to her family home to the joy and excitement of everyone.

Later, Oliva, having revealed the wonders of the mountain of the broom, died consumed by the great desire of seeing again her beautiful Lady. The people of Cori found the miraculous image of Our Lady which was subsequently enshrined in the Sanctuary of Our lady of Salvation. The adventurous and providential loss of Oliva on the mountain of the broom trees, with all the miraculous events that followed, were formerly submitted to judgement by the Curia of the local bishop in 1577 with a process requested by the two officials of the Shrine at the time and on 20 September 1778 the image discovered at the site of the apparition was solemnly crowned by a decree approved by Vatican authority. On the site the first church was consecrated in 1537 to Our Lady of the Broom. The numerous miracles attributed to the Virgin in the following years led in addition to the change of the title to Our Lady of Salvation, and to the construction of a new larger church, consecrated in 1639. The feast is kept on the second Sunday of May.

5 May: Our Lady of Europe

 IBRALTAR TAKES ITS name from the phrase Gibel Tarik, which means "the Mountain of Tarik", and commemorates the capture of the peninsula by the Mauritanian warrior Tarik Ibn Zayid in 710. Moslem troops built a fortress and a mosque at Europa Point at the southernmost part of Gibraltar, located just across from the North African coast. The Catholic Monarchs of Spain were acutely aware that the reconquest of Catholic Spain could never be fully achieved so long as Gibraltar remained in Muslim hands. The Rock of Gibraltar formed the bridge between Europe and Africa ensuring a steady flow of Muslim troops into Spain.

In 1309, nearly six hundred years later, the Spanish King Ferdinand IV finally succeeded in capturing Gibraltar and in so doing expelled the Muslims from the Rock. Following his victory, the King gave thanks to God Almighty and, as tradition recounts, he dedicated the Continent of Europe to the Mother of God, giving her the title of Our Lady of Europe. At the same time, he converted the ancient mosque at the southernmost tip of the Rock into a Christian Shrine and it is believed that a statue of Our Lady, sculptured in limestone, was venerated there.

The Muslims recaptured Gibraltar in 1333, and the Christian population left the Rock, carrying whatever they owned, including the limestone statue of Our Lady of Europe. In 1462, Henry IV, grandson of Ferdinand IV, recaptured Gibraltar once more and restored the devotion begun by Ferdinand to Our Lady of Europe in 1309. Since the original stone statue could not be found, he commissioned a new one, this time depicting the Virgin sitting on a chair holding the Child Jesus. This statue was to be venerated at the Shrine.

The Shrine was ransacked by Barbarossa's Turkish pirates in September 1540 and badly mutilated the statue of Our Lady of Europe. It was eventually restored in Seville and brought back to the Shrine. In 1704, during the War of the Spanish Succession, Anglo-Dutch troops captured Gibraltar. The civilian population, once again left Gibraltar, taking with them the statue of Our Lady which had once again been mutilated. Only in 1864 was the statue returned to Gibraltar, thanks to the efforts of Bishop Scandella, after 160 years 'in exile' in Algeciras, Spain. The statue of Our Lady of Europe was crowned by His Holiness Pope St John Paul II during Bishop Caruana's *Ad Limina* visit to Rome in 2002.

In 2008, Bishop Caruana requested the Holy See to authorised a Jubilee Year to be celebrated on the seventh centenary of the foundation of devotion to Our Lady of Europe. The authorisation was duly granted by the Pope Benedict XVI and the Bishop Caruana opened the Jubilee Year on 12 May 2008, with a Solemn Mass. On 5 May 2009, the feast day of Our Lady of Europe, a solemn High Mass took place in a marquee outside the Shrine. The statue of Our Lady of Europe was brought in procession from the Shrine at Europa Point. During the Mass, the Shrine and the Diocese of Gibraltar received the Golden Rose, a rare gift bestowed by the Pope. The Continent was re-consecrated to Our Lady of Europe.

6 May: Our Lady of Miracles, Rome

HE CHURCH OF Our Lady of Peace, or Santa Maria della Pace in Rome was built by Pope Sixtus IV after the city of Rome had been under siege by the Duke of Calabria. The pope had made a vow that he would build a new church in Rome in honour of Our Lady if peace could somehow be re-established between his Papal States and the cities of Florence, Milan and Naples. Construction actually started in 1482 as an act of thanksgiving to the Blessed Virgin, but the work was not completed until the time of Pope Innocent VIII.

According to various traditions, the particular site for the church was chosen because of an incident in which a drunken soldier had stabbed a statue of the Madonna in the breast, at which the figure had started bleeding as if it were alive. There is also another tradition that perhaps a stone was thrown at the image of Our Lady of Miracles that currently hangs over the high altar in the church of Our Lady of Peace, which subsequently started bleeding. In any event, the church was in fact built on the foundations of an earlier church known as Saint Andrea de Aquarizariis (Watercarriers).

The venerated painting of Our Lady of Miracles depicts the Blessed Virgin holding the Divine Child. It currently hangs over the high altar at the church, which was specifically designed by Carlo Maderno to display and enshrine the famous painting. The now famous image was once believed to have been venerated in the portico of Saint Andrea de Aquarizariis. There is also another

famous fresco inside the church known as the Four Sibyls, which
was painted by Raphael in the year 1514.

7 May: The Seven Joys of Mary

ORRESPONDING TO THE feast of the seven sorrows of
Our Lady, observed on 15 September, there is also the
feast of her seven joys. The first of the seven joys of Mary
was the Annunciation: "The Immaculate Virgin Mary joyfully
conceived Jesus by the Holy Spirit." In the first chapter of Saint
Luke, we read how the Angel Gabriel came from God and told
the Virgin Mary that she was to be the Mother of God. Imagine
the joy in the heart of Mary to learn from the messenger of the
Almighty that she, who was willing to be but a handmaid or
servant in the household of the Lord, was now to be really the
Mother of God. What joy and happiness at the greeting of the
angel. What joy to know that now within her womb she carried
the Son of God.

The second great joy of Mary was the Visitation. "The Immaculate Virgin Mary joyfully carried Jesus visiting Elizabeth."
Charity and love inspired this visit. How happily our Blessed
Mother must have made her way over the hills to the distant
home of her cousin Elizabeth, who also was with child, the future
John the Baptist. Womanlike, Mary wanted to tell her cousin and
share in the joys of an expectant mother. What an inspiration
and joyful example to all the mothers in the world.

The third of the seven joys of Mary life was the Nativity. "The
Immaculate Virgin Mary joyfully brought Jesus into the world."
Everyone who has ever experienced the bliss of Christmas has
had just a faint echo of Mary's joy when she gave birth to Christ.
Every mother shares that joy. Mary experienced it in all her
innocence and sweetness. She experienced the holy happiness of
bringing into the world the Son of God, who was to be the
Redeemer and Saviour of all men.

The fourth joy of Mary was that of the Epiphany, which we might express in these words: "The Immaculate Virgin Mary joyfully manifested Jesus to the adoration of the Magi." Every mother is happy when she can show her child to others. Every mother is joyful when friends or acquaintances or even chance visitors comment about her child, praise it, and even bring it gifts. That was the happy experience of Mary when the three Wise Men came thousands of miles to adore and honour her Child, to bring gifts to her Boy.

The fifth of the seven joys of Mary, our Blessed Mother, is what she experienced when she finally found Jesus after His three-day loss in the temple. "The Immaculate Virgin Mary joyfully found Jesus in the temple." To have her child with her is a mother's joy. However, to find a child that is lost is a greater joy because of the contrast to the sorrow of separation. Mary experienced such a bliss when she found Christ in the temple teaching and listening to the doctors, the learned professors of the law.

The sixth great joy of the Blessed Mother was the one she experienced upon seeing Jesus after His resurrection. "The Immaculate Virgin Mary joyfully beheld Jesus after His resurrection." Words fail in expressing the happiness of the Mother of God when she saw her Son risen from the grave, saw Him in the full beauty of manhood, saw the Boy whom she had brought into the world, had reared and trained and taken care of for so many years. Her joy, by way of contrast with the grief of the first Good Friday, was supreme.

The seventh of the seven joys of Mary, and the crowning joy, was that Mary had when she was taken up into heaven and crowned Queen of heaven and earth. "The Immaculate Virgin Mary was joyfully received by Jesus into heaven and there crowned Queen of heaven and earth." No human pen, no human brush can express or picture the joy in Mary's heart when she was finally reunited with her Son in the bliss of the beatific vision. Neither can we express in words the happiness in her heart when she was crowned, rewarded by her Divine Son who made her the Queen of this world and of the heavenly court.

> By the crib wherein reposing,
> with His eyes in slumber closing,
> lay serene her Infant-boy,

> Stood the beauteous Mother feeling
> bliss that could not bear concealing,
> so her face o'erflowed with joy.

> Oh, the rapture naught could smother
> of that most Immaculate Mother
> of the sole-begotten One;

> When with laughing heart exulting,
> she beheld her hopes resulting
> In the great birth of her Son.

> Who would not with gratulation
> see the happy consolation
> of Christ's Mother undefiled?[5]

8 May: Our Lady of Pompeii

OMPEII IS A ruined Roman city near Naples in the Italian region of Campania, in the territory of the commune of Pompeii. This city was destroyed by the volcanic eruption of Mount Vesuvius in 79 AD. The city that developed about a mile from these ruins was also subjected to tragedy when it was ravaged in 1659 by a widespread epidemic of malaria that killed most of the population. Bartolo Longo was born in 1841 in Laziano, Italy as the son of a doctor and a devout Catholic mother. His mother ensured from an early age that Bartolo developed a great love for Our Lady through praying the Rosary. In 1871, Bartolo became a third order Dominican and took the name Brother Rosary. In 1872, Bartolo arrived in marshy Pompeii, accompanied by two armed escorts to protect him from bandits that overran the area. He was shocked and filled with great pity at the ignorance, poverty, and lack of religion of the inhabitants of the area. He was also struggling with his own doubts about his Christian faith. While walking through the parish on 9 October, he distinctly heard a voice say to him: "If you seek salvation, promulgate the Rosary. This is Mary's own promise". His generous heart was moved, and he promised Our Lady to do all in his power to promote devotion to the rosary among the people of the area. To this end, he set up rosary festivals, with games, races, and even a lottery to attract the people. He started restoring a dilapidated church in October of 1873 and sponsored a festival in honour of Our Lady of the Rosary. In 1875 Longo obtained a well worn painting of Our Lady of the Rosary from a convent in Naples and raised funds to get the image restored so as to locate it in the church.

A young girl from Naples, Fortuna Agrelli, was suffering from a painful, incurable disease. She had been given up by the most celebrated physicians. On 16 February 1884, the afflicted girl and her relatives commenced a novena of Rosaries. The Queen of the Holy Rosary favoured her with an apparition on 3 March. Mary, sitting upon a high throne, surrounded by luminous figures, held the Divine child on her lap, and in her hand a Rosary. The Virgin Mother and the holy Infant were clad in gold-embroidered garments. They were accompanied by St Dominic and St Catherine of Siena. Fortuna marvelled at the beauty of Mary and asked her as "Queen of the Rosary," for her cure. Mary replied that, since she had called her by a title that was so pleasing to her, she could not refuse her request; she then told her to make three novenas of the Rosary to obtain all she asked for. The child was indeed cured, and soon after Mary appeared to her again saying: "Whosoever desires to obtain favours from me should make three novenas of the prayers of the Rosary in petition and three novenas in thanksgiving." This is how the Rosary Novena devotion to Our Lady originated.

In 1883, a sanctuary was built for the image and consecrated in 1891. Many miracles are attributed to the intercession of Our Lady of Pompeii. The image of Our Lady of Pompeii represents

Our Lady of the Rosary as Queen of Heaven. She and her Son, Jesus, are handing out rosaries to Saint Dominic and Saint Catherine of Siena. The Pompeii portrait is derived from the Eastern icon style of the sixth century. On 21 October 1979, Pope John Paul II visited Pompeii. The gathering was a national pilgrimage to Our Lady of Pompeii. On 26 October 1980, Bartolo Longo was beatified by John Paul II and called "Man of the Rosary" and the "Apostle of the Rosary".

9 May: Our Lady of Solitude

OCAL LEGEND RELATES that Antiguan carver Pedro de Mendoza (d. 1662) ran out of paint the night before he was to deliver the statue of Most Holy Mary of Grief. He went to bed leaving her face unfinished and woke in the morning astonished to find that the work had been completed without his help. In any case, the Virgin has a rich, deep complexion to complement her ineffably sad expression. After the statue was damaged in the 1976 earthquake, restorers had trouble matching the colour of her face.

Our Lady of Solitude (*Virgen de la Soledad*) represents the mourning Mother of the crucified Jesus, between Good Friday and Easter. Soledad is often translated solitude. The Holy Mother is "lonely", missing her Son; she is Our Lady of Grief. In the inland city of Antigua Guatemala, as in Spain, a Catholic confraternity carries her statue through the streets in procession on Good Friday and on Holy Saturday. Along with another highly revered statue, representing the recumbent Entombed Lord, *El Señor Sepultado*, Our Lady of Solitude moved to the church of the Escuela de Cristo in 1664 from the Veracruz Chapel nearby. Founded by the Franciscans in 1543, the Escuela de Cristo now houses a Franciscan seminary.

On 9 May 1999, Mgr Próspero Penados del Barrio, Archbishop of Guatemala City, consecrated the statue of Our Lady of Solitude, as the Entombed Lord statue had been consecrated 20 years before.

In Guatemala, the consecration of a sacred image is more than a simple blessing such as priests offer when such a work is installed. Like the ritual coronations of images common in other Catholic countries, it signifies a special relationship between the community and the saint represented. Like the sacrament of confirmation, consecration is always performed by a bishop, in the context of a Mass, using the consecrated oil known as chrism. Recalling Jacob's anointing of the stone on which he had dreamed of the heavenly ladder (Genesis 28:10–22), the bishop anoints the image's forehead, hands, and feet, and crosses of gold or silver are affixed to its hands as a permanent sign of consecration. There were two such consecrations in Guatemala in the 1700s, and then in the twentieth century many more took place. Now there are some 30 consecrated images in the country. Antigua commemorates the Virgin of Grief's consecration with an annual procession on Mother's Day, the second Sunday in May.

10 May: Our Lady of Pew

 UR LADY OF Pew is strongly connected withy the Dowry tradition in England. The origins of the name "pew" are obscure, but there is good reason for associating it with the French puissant ("powerful"), as it was common to anglicize French words, and an Englishman would probably pronounce this word as "pewssant" anyway. Moreover, there is the association of the French shrine of Our Lady of Le Puy, and, as some contend, the Latin *podium* ("strong support") is the origin, the connection with the hill shrine of Le Puy as a strong-point further connects with the idea of power, and with Our Lady's title *Virgo Potens*.[6] Other commentators link the expressions Pew with "puits" for wells, as there were no less than four wells beside St Stephen's chapel in the royal palace of Westminster. The nineteenth century antiquary Edmund Waterton suggested that the word might have been taken from Our Lady of Pity, shortened by a careless scribe to "pty" and then to "pui".[7] In any case the first chapel of the *Pieu*

or Pew was on the south side of that of St Stephen's in the royal palace of Westminster, the site of Cotton-gardens.[8]

More familiar to us today is the shrine in the Abbey Church. The Palace shrine, rebuilt after a fire in 1452, survived the Reformation, but was finally destroyed by fire in 1834. The Abbey shrine had been established in an unprecedented way. The Chapel of Henry VII being the original Lady Chapel (in the apse beyond the high altar), the little shrine which has now become the focus of attention began with a widow's benefaction for the soul of her husband. The Countess of Pembroke (whose husband Aylmer de Valence, Earl of Pembroke, has a fine effigy in the Chapel of Saints Edmund and Thomas) established a mortuary chapel for daily Masses for her husband next to the Chapel of St John, and she presented the Abbot of Westminster with an alabaster statue of Our Lady. This is probably how the Abbey chapel came to be, because the monks of Westminster had just lost a battle with the canons of St Stephen's with regard to ecclesiastical jurisdiction in the Palace of Westminster, and thus were debarred from the Palace shrine of Our Lady of Pew. The Abbot therefore apparently lost no time in establishing with the Countess' gift a secondary shrine of Pew which, unlike the other, with its restriction to courtiers, would be accessible to all. The Countess' will, proved in 1377, records that the statue of Our Lady was already in position at the secondary shrine of Pew. And, according to the Sacrist's Roll of 1378–80, the image of the Blessed Mary called "Le Puwe" was already much in evidence.

In 1381, England was ravaged by the Peasants' Revolt, when the introduction of the poll tax caused the south-eastern counties to rise in open rebellion. Jean Froissart gives a vivid description of the manner in which the young King Richard II of England prepared to meet the rebels, led by Wat Tyler, at Smithfield:

> Richard II on the Saturday after Corpus Christi went to Westminster, where he heard Mass at the Abbey with all his Lords. He made his devotions at a statue of Our Lady in a little chapel that had witnessed many miracles and

where much grace had been gained, so that the Kings of
England have much faith in it.[9]

Thus King Richard II knelt amidst a great throng of his subjects
to re-dedicate England to Mary, as her Dowry. Richard made at
least two pilgrimages at this time to Our Lady's Shrine in
Walsingham and to that of St Edmund at Bury. The saintly
Edmund, king of East Anglia, where Walsingham was situated,
had been martyred for the faith by the Vikings in the 9th century.
In the [Wilton] diptych (above) the three "dowry kings", as they
are known, are depicted with St John the Baptist, Richard's special
patron. Another chronicler, Strype, described the event thus:

> On the coming of the rebels and Wat Tyler, the same King
> went to Westminster... confessed himself to an anchorite;
> then took himself to the chapel of Our Lady of Pew; there he
> said his devotions, and went to Smithfield to meet the rebels.

The outcome of the meeting was favourable with Wat Tyler
throwing down his arms and taking up the King's colours.
Naturally the King and Court regarded this as a miracle wrought
by the Holy Virgin, and therefore set about encouraging her
veneration at Westminster. After his success in quelling the
rebels, and their acceptance of the standard of the realm, Richard
returned to meet his mother at Westminster and to give thanks.
Froissart records the young King's words as follows: "Yes, Madam
... rejoice and praise God, for today I have regained my kingdom
which I had lost." And he placed the Kingdom under Our Lady's
protection, in thanksgiving for having regained it:

> Dos tua Virgo pia Haec est, quaere leges O Maria, This is
> your Dowry, O Holy Virgin, therefore rule over it, O Mary.

From this and other evidence, we learn that the Pew Chapel had
already been in existence for some time before Richard II's
reign.[10] What, therefore, was the situation which occasioned
Richard II's re-ordering of the shrine? In the answer to this
question lies the clue to the origin of England's title, *Dos Mariae,*

"Mary's Dowry".[11] The original shrine, as we stated, was housed in a chapel within the Palace of Westminster attached to the Collegiate Church of St Stephen. This shrine survived the Reformation, but, as already explained, was finally destroyed in the fire of 1843. Today its exact location may be determined by the site of the Speaker's House next to the now restored Church of St Stephen. It was to this greater shrine that the sovereigns of England went to beseech the help of Our Lady, but the little chapel in the Abbey survives with evidence to show that it was patronized by at least one sovereign in particular.[12]

The royal chapel of St Stephen to which was annexed the smaller chapel called Our Lady of the Pew had been converted into the Parliament by Edward VI, and the paintings on the wall were covered over with oaken panels. In 1800, when the Act of Union united the English and Irish Parliaments, some alterations had to be made to the chamber. When the panelling was taken off the wall, paintings were revealed in the interstices, which were as fresh and clear as the day they had been covered up, owing to their being protected from the air. According to the parliamentary reports of the time, behind the Speaker's chair was a picture of the Virgin and Child with St Joseph bending over them, and King Edward III and his Queen and his sons and daughters making an offering to Our Lady. Fr Bridgett attempts to explain the significance of this image:

> It may either have commemorated an historical event, or its execution may be considered an historical event in itself. It is not, nor does it record an act of private devotion... Acolytes were holding lighted tapers and two angels were represented as taking part in a solemnity. It is the consecration of England, through its Sovereign to the Blessed Virgin. It was before the eyes of every King and noble until hidden by Edward VI.[13]

The Abbey shrine is probably more significant as evidence for England's title, *Dos Mariae*, as its existence as a shrine dates from the time of Richard's successful bid to keep his throne, and it is probably a grateful monarch's gift to his people who did not have access to the greater shrine within the Palace. Moreover, the traces of painting on the walls of this little chapel are irrefutable evidence of King Richard's patronage, as there are on the east wall remnants of the King's "white hart" badge. Therefore, what was originally a chantry chapel, the King by all accounts transformed into a public shrine dedicated to Our Lady of Pew. This was the lesser shrine, but perhaps the more significant, as its foundation marked the gratitude of King Richard to Our Lady for the safe return of his realm, in offering it to her as her dowry.

11 May: Our Lady of Aparecida

NE MORNING IN October of 1717, Dom Pedro de Almedida, Count of Assumar, was on his way to the state of Minas Gerais from Sao Paulo. He would have to pass by Guarantinqueta, a small city in the Paraiba river valley. The people of Guarantinqueta decided to hold a great feast to honor the Count, and a lot of fish would be needed. Among the fishermen were three men who always prayed to Our Lady of the Immaculate Conception—Domingos Garcia, Joco Alves, and Felipe Pedroso. Before going out to fish, they asked God to help then in this difficult task, to find enough fish at this time when no fish were available. Felipe knelt and prayed, along with his companions, "Mother of God and our Mother, we need to find fish!"

After many hours of catching nothing, the fishermen were very depressed. Joco Alves cast his net once more near the Port of Itaguagu, but instead of fish, he hauled in the body of a statue. The three cast their net again, and brought up the statue's head. After cleaning the statue they found that it was Our Lady of the Immaculate Conception. Naming their find Our Lady *Aparecida* (She who appeared), they wrapped it in cloth and continued to fish.

They very carefully washed the statue and saw that it was Our Lady of the Immaculate Conception. They wrapped her in some cloths and continued to fish. Domingo commented, "We worked all night and have found no fish!" Felipe had a proposition: "Let's continue to fish with faith in the Virgin Aparecida (who appeared)." From this moment on, the net became very full with fish. This was the first miracle of Our Lady of Aparecida. Felipe Pedroso, partner of Joao Alves, took the statue to his house and started the veneration of Our Lady with his family and neighbours. In 1732, he moved to Porto Itaguassu and took the statue to its first shrine, which was built by his son Atanasio. Travellers spread out the fame of Our Lady Aparecida and the pilgrims started to come. The people decided to build a bigger church in the top of a hill near Porto Itaguassu to shelter the statue. The church was opened in 1745 when the statue was brought in from its former site and the village of Aparecida was born, as a district of Guaratingueta.

In 1846, work began on the construction of a new church, completed in 1888, and the statue was transferred to it. In 1904 by order of the Holy Father, the image was solemnly crowned. In 1909 the church was raised to the level of a minor basilica; in 1930 Pope Pius XI promoted it to a Basilica and officially declared Our Lady of Aparecida the Patroness of Brazil.

Our Lady of Aparecida has been specifically targeted on several occasions by the Protestants in Brazil, as on 16 May 1978, a Protestant attempted to steal the statue, taking it from its niche and casting it on the ground when he was stopped by guards and parishioners. Since the statue is made of clay, it was smashed into many pieces and took a great effort on the part of talented artisans to repair.

Pope Bl Paul VI granted the sanctuary its first golden rose on 12 August 1967. Pope St John Paul II elevated and consecrated formally as a Basilica on 4 July 1980. Pope Benedict XVI granted its second golden rose on 12 May 2007. On the occasion of World Youth Day, Pope Francis visited the basilica on 24 July 2013, venerated the image of Our Lady of Aparecida and celebrated Mass there.

Prayer

O incomparable Lady of the Aparecida, Mother of God, Queen of Angels, Advocate of Sinners, Refuge and Consolation of the Afflicted and Troubled, most holy Virgin, full of power and goodness, look favourably upon us, so that we may be helped by you in all our needs. Remember, most clement Mother of Aparecida, that it has never been known that anyone who sought your help, invoking your name and imploring your singular protection, was ever abandoned. Encouraged by this confidence, I turn to you, accepting you for once and always as my Mother and protector, my consolation and guide, my hope and light at the hour of my death. Please, Lady, free us from everything that might offend you and your most holy Son, my Redeemer and Lord Jesus Christ. Blessed Virgin, keep this your unworthy servant and this house and those who live here from plague, hunger, war, assault, lightning, storms, floods, accidents and other perils and bad things that might plague us. Sovereign Lady, please guide us in all spiritual and temporal things; free us from the devil's temptations so that, following the way of virtue and by the merits of your purest virginity and the most precious Blood of your Son, we may be able to see, love and enjoy you in the eternal glory, for ever and ever. Amen.

12 May: Our Lady, Mother of Mercy

HIS MEMORIAL OBSERVES an extraordinary event that occurred in Rimini, Italy, in 1850, in the church of St Clare, staffed by the Missionaries of the Most Precious Blood. In a painting of the Virgin Mary, under the title of Mother of Mercy, the eyes of the image were seen moving by countless citizens and visitors. The pupils of the eyes of this sacred image were raised up toward heaven and then lowered toward the faithful. At times the eyes were shining like stars, other times as if shedding tears. The face would appear sometime rose-coloured and then pale. The miracle was immediately submitted to the

Bishop for the proper investigation; he declared the authenticity of the motion of the eyes that had taken place for several months, from 12 May to December 1850.

As St Bernard of Clairvaux wrote:

> Why should a frail human being be afraid of approaching Mary? There is nothing harsh and fear-provoking in her: she is gentleness personified who offers everyone milk and wool. Consider carefully all the accounts of the Gospel: should you discover in Mary a trace of anger, of harshness, or even a slightest sign of disinterest, then, yes, you might well have your doubts and be afraid to approach her. But if you discover her to be, as she is, full of holiness and grace, of meekness and mercy, then be grateful toward the One who, with the most loving condescension, has granted us such a Mediatrix worthy of the greatest trust. After all, since she became all things to all people, she made herself debtor of boundless charity to the wise as well as to the ignorant. She opened to all her merciful heart, so that all could receive comfort: freedom for the slave, healing for the sick, relief for the down-trodden, forgiveness for the sinners, grace for the righteous, joy for the angels. Mary does not inquire about our past merits, but she is considerate and loving toward all; in her great love she responds to the needs of all. She is that woman, promised ages ago by God, who by her virtue would have crushed the head of the old serpent: this one with deceit had tried to allure her, to no avail. Mary, alone, has routed out all perverse heresies. The heretics were exposed and silenced; and all generations call her blessed. Let us cast ourselves at Mary's feet; let us prostrate ourselves with immense devotion before her. Let us keep hold of her and not let go of her until she has blessed us; she is very powerful. Like the fleece of Gideon which is between the dew and the chaff, as the woman in the Book of Revelation who is between the sun and the moon, so Mary stands between Christ and the Church.[14]

Prayer

All-holy Father,
hear the prayers of your children,
weighed down by our sinfulness,
as we turn to you and call upon the merciful love
that moved you to send your Son as Saviour of the world
and to enthrone holy Mary as queen of mercy.
We make our prayer through our Lord Jesus Christ, your Son,
who lives and reigns with you and the Holy Spirit,
one God, for ever and ever.[15]

13 May: Our Lady of Fatima

 N 13 MAY 1917, in Portugal, Our Lady of Fatima appeared to three children in a place called Cova da Iria, outside the hamlet of Aljustrel, very close to Fatima. It was at noon, and the children were shepherding sheep. Suddenly there was lightening, and the children, thinking that it was going to rain, began to run. Then, just above a holmoak tree, they saw a beautiful Lady formed of light, holding a rosary in her hand.

Our Lady of Fatima asked the children if they would pray and make sacrifice for sinners, and if they would come to this same place on the thirteenth of each month for five months. The children agreed and Lucía said "Yes." Only Lucía spoke to Our Lady of Fatima, the others listened. According to Lúcia's account, Mary confided to the children three secrets, known as the Three Secrets of Fatima. She exhorted the children to do penance and to make sacrifices to save sinners. Most important, Lúcia said Mary asked them to say the Rosary every day, reiterating many times that the Rosary was the key to personal conversion and world peace. This was the beginning of a new life for the children, for their sole purpose was now to pray and make sacrifices for sinners. They would give their lunch to the sheep as a sacrifice, and perform other acts of mortification. The children noted that the beautiful Our Lady of Fatima was sad, and they were sad also because of Our Lady of Fatima's sadness.

Many young Portuguese men, including relatives of the visionaries, were then fighting in World War I. Thousands of people flocked to Fatima and Aljustrel in the ensuing months, drawn by reports of visions and miracles. On October 13, 1917, the final in the series of the apparitions of 1917, a crowd believed to be approximately 70,000 in number, including newspaper reporters and photographers, gathered at the Cova da Iria in response to reports of the children's prior claims that on that day a miracle would occur "so that all may believe". It rained heavily that day, yet, countless observers reported that the clouds broke, revealing the sun as an opaque disk spinning in the sky and radiating various colours of light upon the surroundings, then appearing to detach itself from the sky and plunge itself towards the earth in a zigzag pattern, finally returning to its normal place, and leaving the people's once wet clothing now completely dry. The event is known as the "Miracle of the Sun".

Columnist Avelino de Almeida of *O Século* (Portugal's most influential newspaper, which was pro-government in policy and avowedly anti-clerical), reported the following

> Before the astonished eyes of the crowd, whose aspect was biblical as they stood bare-headed, eagerly searching the sky, the sun trembled, made sudden incredible movements outside all cosmic laws-the sun "danced" according to the typical expression of the people.

Eye specialist Dr Domingos Pinto Coelho, writing for the newspaper Ordem reported:

> The sun, at one moment surrounded with scarlet flame, at another aureoled in yellow and deep purple, seemed to be in an exceeding fast and whirling movement, at times appearing to be loosened from the sky and to be approaching the earth, strongly radiating heat.

The special reporter for the 17 October 1917 edition of the Lisbon daily, *O Dia*, reported the following:

> The silver sun, enveloped in the same gauzy grey light, was seen to whirl and turn in the circle of broken clouds... The light turned a beautiful blue, as if it had come through the stained-glass windows of a cathedral, and spread itself over the people who knelt with outstretched hands... people wept and prayed with uncovered heads, in the presence of a miracle they had awaited. The seconds seemed like hours, so vivid were they.

Francisco died in 1919 and Jacinta in 1920, both from disease. When Our Lady of Fatima appeared to Jacinta, she gave her information about her death. "You will die in a hospital, away from your family, alone." Jacinta's death was as Our Lady of Fatima had said. Lucía took the name Sister Maria Lucía of the Immaculate Heart of Mary when she became a Carmelite nun.

On 13 May 1981, there was an assassination attempt on the life of Pope John Paul II. Shortly afterward His Holiness read the dossier concerning Fatima. Coinciding with the beatification on 13 May 2000, of Jacinta and Francisco, the Holy Father released the third part of the secret. This third part of the secret had been given to the children on 13 July 1917, was written by Sister Lucía in 1944. Popes have shown exceptional favour toward Fatima, Pius XII, Bl Paul VI, St John Paul II, Benedict XVI and Francis in particular making a visit to the shrine. In a rustic setting, pilgrims hear the message repeated that Mary spoke to the children: prayer, works of penance, recourse to her Immaculate Heart.

14 May: Our Lady of Bavaria

LSO KNOWN AS Our Lady of Altötting, the shrine of the Chapel of Grace in Bavaria lies amid the mountains about three miles south of Oberammergau in upper Bavaria. The miraculous healings that have occurred there are so numerous that the shrine is thought of today as the "Lourdes of

Germany". There are many votive offerings that have been left at the shrine as testimony of graces received and miraculous healings.

A Benedictine monastery was founded there in 1330 by the Emperor Ludwig IV, who established a community of twelve knights with their families to guard the place. However, it is the Capuchin friars who have served the shrine now for centuries, among them Brother Conrad of Parzham (1818–1894), who acted as porter for over forty years.

What is perhaps the most famous miracle occurred in the year 1489. A young boy had drowned, and his mother, full of faith, brought his body to lay at the feet of the image of the Mother of God, seeking a miracle. She was not disappointed, as her son was restored to life before many witnesses. From that time on, the chapel became a popular place of pilgrimage.

The emperor Ludwig gave a small statue of the Mother of God, carved in Italy: this image is a Black Madonna of great antiquity (possibly about 1330), carved from lime wood. The place was soon famous both for its shrine of Mary and the learning of the monks. In 1744 the medieval church was burnt down, its successor being built and decorated in the German baroque manner. The chapel has an unusual octagonal shape, and it is thought to be the oldest Marian shrine in Germany. The other buildings had been remodelled mostly as they appear today.

A century later the abbey was suppressed, with other Bavarian religious houses; but it was restored in 1904, and Our Lady is still a resort of pilgrims. This great sanctuary has a truly magnificent mountain setting. Pope St John Paul II visited the shrine in 1980, accompanied by Cardinal Joseph Ratzinger, who was born in the nearby town of Marktl am Inn. Then Pope Benedict XVI went there in 2006, leaving the episcopal ring he had worn while Archbishop of Munich. The ring is now a part of the sceptre held by the Blessed Virgin.

15 May: Our Lady of the Most Blessed Sacrament

 HIS FEAST, WHICH providentially falls on the same day as that of Our Lady of Fatima, was started by St Peter Julian Eymard (1811–1868), of France, who had a strong devotion to the Holy Eucharist and to Our Lady and began his priestly life in the Society of Mary. His heart burned with the desire to establish perpetual adoration of Jesus in the Blessed Sacrament exposed upon a royal throne and surrounded by a large court of adorers. On 2 February 1851, at the shrine of Fourvière, the most Blessed Virgin had enabled him to understand its necessity. She said: "All the mysteries of my Son have a religious order of men to honour them. The Eucharist alone has none ..."

After several years of prudent reflection and interior combat, encouraged by Pope Blessed Pius IX, Eymard founded the Congregation of the Most Blessed Sacrament at Paris on 13 May 1856. The title of Our Lady of the Blessed Sacrament was first given to Mary by St Peter Julian Eymard in May 1868, while speaking to his novices. A few years later he described what her statue should look like: "The Blessed Virgin holds the Infant in her arms; and He holds a chalice in one hand and a Host in the other." He exhorted them to invoke Mary: "Our Lady of the Blessed Sacrament, pray for us who have recourse to thee!" Later, Blessed Pius IX enriched the invocation with indulgences. Twice, St Pius X did the same. On 30 December 1905, he granted a 300 days indulgence to the faithful who pray: "Our Lady of the Most Blessed Sacrament, pray for us." "This title, Our Lady of the Blessed Sacrament, is perhaps the most meaningful of all", said St Pius X. In 1921, the Sacred Congregation of Rites authorized the Blessed Sacrament Congregations to celebrate each year, on the 13 May, a solemn commemoration of the Blessed Virgin, with the intention of honouring Mary under the title of "Our Lady of the Most Blessed Sacrament." This Feast is still celebrated today with great joy by all the spiritual sons and daughters of St Peter Julian Eymard. Pope Blessed John XXIII confirmed the title of

Our Lady of the Most Blessed Sacrament when he declared St
Peter Julian Eymard a saint on 9 December 1962, at the close of
the first session of the Second Vatican Council.

Prayer to Our Lady of the Most Blessed Sacrament

O Virgin Mary, Our Lady of the Most Blessed Sacrament, the
glory of Christians, the joy of the universal Church, and the hope
of the world, pray for us. Kindle in all the faithful a lively devotion
to the most Holy Eucharist, so that they may be worthy to receive
Holy Communion every day. Our Lady of the Most Blessed
Sacrament, pray for us. Let us with Mary Immaculate adore,
thank, supplicate, and console the most sacred and beloved
Eucharistic Heart of Jesus.

16 May: Our Lady appears to Saint Catherine

AINT CATHERINE OF Alexandria, also known as Saint
Catherine of the Wheel, was the beautiful daughter of
King Costus and Queen Sabinella of Alexandria, who at
a young age decided to remain a virgin until and unless she should
meet someone who exceeded her in status and political position,
as well as beauty, intelligence, and wealth. She decided upon
Christ, who reigns over us all, for "His beauty is more radiant
than the shining of the sun, His wisdom governs all creation, and
His riches are spread throughout all the world."

While yet a teenager, Saint Catherine received a vision of the
Blessed Virgin Mary and Her Divine Son Jesus Christ. In this
vision, the Mother of God gave Catherine to her Son in a mystical
marriage. Mystical marriage is in some senses very similar to a
marriage ceremony, as Christ presents the chosen soul with a ring
that is often visible to others, and often there are saint and angels
present. There have been well over 70 documented mystical
marriages with saints, and although the action is mysterious and
not well understood, it appears that Christ gives special attention
to these saints. Saint Teresa of Avila explained that it was the

highest state a soul could achieve in this life, and represents a transforming and constant union with the Blessed Trinity.

Saint Catherine was martyred by the Roman Emperor Maxentius when she refused his proposal of marriage. Again, according to tradition, her body was taken by angels to Mount Sinai where a church and monastery were built in her honour. Saint Catherine's relics were rediscovered about the year 800, and it was said that her hair was still growing and that there was a continuous stream of oil coming from her body that was found to have miraculous healing properties. Saint Edward the Confessor was said to have collected some of that oil and taken it back to England with him.

17 May: Our Lady of the Steps

ESTLED AT THE foot of Gruyères Hill, in the Canton of Fribourg, Switzerland, a chapel overlooks the terraced deposits of the Saane River known as Les Marches, the Steps. Documentary evidence of a chapel here dates to 1572, and inside is a 28-inch high statue of Our Lady of the Steps, a standing Virgin and Child in the late Gothic style of the 1400s.

The present building goes back to 1705, the work of three brothers, all priests, from a family of cheese merchants. Dom Nicolas Ruffieux, protonotary of Broc, decided to build the most beautiful chapel in the country. His brother Jean-Jacques, parish priest of neighbouring Gruyères, took on the project with a third brother's help. In 1721, the Commune of Broc added the enclosure and the lime trees that still shade the courtyard.

On 17 May 1884, a healing occurred at Notre-Dame des Marches, the first of several in the 1880s, which turned the rural chapel into a place of pilgrimage. Stricken with a spinal malady, Léonide Andrey, 22, had been unable to walk for six years. She was carried to Mass at the chapel and walked home easily afterwards. By the 1930s, the sanctuary was known as the "little Lourdes of Fribourg". Two main pilgrimages were established:

one in September, initially termed the "anti-alcoholic pilgrimage", and one on a Wednesday in spring, the Pilgrimage of the Sick.

18 May: Our Lady of Skępe

HE BERNARDINE MONASTERY in Skępe, Poland, was founded in the early 16th century. In 1508–1510 a stone church of the Annunciation of the Virgin Mary was built; in the 18th century it was rebuilt in the Baroque style. On its main altar stands the statue of Our Lady of Skępe famed for its miraculous powers. According to tradition, local inhabitants, including shepherds, kept seeing "an extraordinary light" at this location; some said they saw Our Lady surrounded by choirs of angels, and that her footprints remained on the stone. At the time there was a plague in the area; sick people began to be brought to Skępe and were miraculously healed.

Pilgrims began coming to the apparition site, and many reported cures. A calvary was erected at the stone. A pilgrim named John, from Pobiedziska near Gniezno, reported a vision in which Our Lady told him that the proprietors of Skępe should build a chapel there. Castellan Nicholas Kościelecki took this to heart, and with his wife Catherine built a wooden chapel dedicated to the Annunciation of the Blessed Virgin Mary. In 1496, in thanks for regaining the use of her legs, their daughter Sophia had a metre–high wooden statue brought from Poznań for the shrine. The statue depicts Our Lady expecting Jesus, with her hands folded in prayer. In 1498, Bernardine Fathers came to care for the chapel and pilgrims. The statue became famous for the graces it bestowed and was instrumental in the development of the veneration of Our Lady of Skępe —Queen of Mazovia and Kuyavia.

Nicholas' uncle, Bishop Kościelecki, dedicated a new brick church there in 1511, which was remodelled in Baroque style over the next two centuries. Regional pilgrimages took place annually on 8 September, feast of the Nativity of Mary. By authority of the Vatican, Fabian Pląskowskiego, Auxiliary Bishop of Chełmno, crowned the statue on Pentecost Sunday, 18 May 1755. In 1980, the crown was stolen, and the Bernardine Fathers arranged for a new one. Bogdan Sikorski, Bishop of Płock, recrowned the image on 8 September 1984. The Blessed Mother of Skępe is also known as Queen of Masovia and Kuyavia and Pregnant Mother of God. Childless couples visit the shrine to enlist her help with conception.

19 May: The Sorrowful Mother

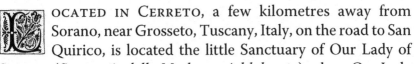 OCATED IN CERRETO, a few kilometres away from Sorano, near Grosseto, Tuscany, Italy, on the road to San Quirico, is located the little Sanctuary of Our Lady of Sorrows (*Santuario della Madonna Addolorata*), where Our Lady appeared to the shepherdess Veronica Nucci. The apparition took place on the afternoon of 19 May 1853, while Veronica, aged 12, looked her sheep in the country together with her brother, Giovanni Battista.

On that day it began to rain and Veronica went with her brother and her sheep towards a hut, to find a safe place to shelter. Suddenly, in the midst of fields, she saw a kneeling woman. She was dressed in a white dress embroidered with red flowers, with a black-shiny belt at the waist, a blue mantle descending from head to foot and, on her head, there was a golden crown with a cross in the middle. The Lady, who had her hands open as in supplication, called her, made her kneel beside her and invited her to pray together. Veronica saw that she was crying and so she asked her why; the Lady replied:

> I weep for so many sinners. Do you see how much is it raining? The sins are more than the drops of water falling. My Son has His hands and His feet nailed and five open wounds. If the sinners do not become good people, He wants to bring about the end of the world.

Then, the Lady recommended that she recite every day seven times the Our Father, the Hail Mary and the Glory Be in honour of the Blood of Jesus which was shed, five times the Our Father, the Hail Mary and the Glory Be in honour of the five Wounds of Our Lord and, finally, seven times the Our Father, the Hail Mary and the Glory Be in honour of Our Lady of Sorrows.

Our Lady left Veronica after having told her to tell everything to her mother, who was to publicly reveal what her daughter had experienced. For the time that Veronica remained next to Our Lady, she was not at all touched by the rain; once she came home, she found her mother ill and even if she did not immediately recount her extraordinary experience, everybody at home were surprised at seeing her dry, despite the heavy rain. The next day Veronica told her mother and other people what she had experienced; they were all astonished. The news of the apparition of Our Lady immediately spread to the nearby villages; the next morning many people went to Veronica's house to hear from her in person what had happened; but one of her cousins decided to take a wooden cross and going out: everyone followed him in silence. The cross was planted at the spot of the apparition and there everyone noticed with amazement the footprints of a kneeling person on the wet ground. Veronica had told the truth. In the days following the apparition, news about it spread and crowds went to Cerreto, not only from the near villages but also from other parts of Tuscany, from Rome and other areas.

The Church authorities began investigations into the event and Veronica was questioned by the parish priest of Sorano and then, by the bishop of Sovana and Pitigliano, Monsignor Francesco Maria Barzellotti. The latter informed Pope Bl Pius IX of the event, asking him the permission to build a chapel in the place of the apparition. After having examined the information provided by the bishop, the Pope recognized the apparition and, with a letter dated 13 August 1853, authorized the building of the chapel of Cerreto. On 9 November 1854, the investigations on the apparition of Our Lady finally concluded, confirming the supernatural origin of the event.

Meanwhile, it had become necessary to protect Veronica, as everyone wanted to see her, listen to her, and touch her. So, she gladly accepted to enter the monastery of the Poor Clares in Ischia di Castro. Here, Veronica of Our Lady of Sorrows took her vows and lived in an exemplary way: she experienced some further apparitions and it is also said that she performed some miracles. On 9 November 1862, Sister Veronica died after months of infirmity due to various diseases: first, inflammation of the bronchial passages, then abscesses in the armpits, lower abdominal pain, fever and loss of appetite. During those months, Sister Veronica patiently experienced her sufferings with an ineffable resignation.[16]

The day after her death, her body was exposed at the Monastery of Ischia di Castro and many believers came, trying to get a little piece of the dress or a flower on her coffin to be preserved as a holy relic. It is said that some sick believers were healed after having taken the relics from the body or after having prayed for her intercession. The construction of the church at Cerreto was only completed in 1864. A continuous stream of pilgrims came to Cerreto in the early years, but then started to fade. Only on the occasion of the 125th Anniversary of the Apparition in 1978 the Bishop Mgr Giovanni D'Ascenzi examined the documents relating to the event and declared the church of Our Lady of Sorrows of Cerreto a Diocesan Sanctuary; in 1992 the remains of the body of Sister Veronica Nucci, the shepherdess to whom Our Lady appeared, were brought to the church. The sanctuary was entrusted to Carmelite nuns, whose convent adjoining the church was built in 2000; the name is significantly *Janua Coeli*, meaning Gate of Heaven.[17]

20 May: Mother of God of Zhyrovichy

Zhyrovichy is in the Grodno region of eastern Belarus, which belonged to the Grand Duchy of Lithuania at the time when this episode occurred.[18] One night around 1500, some shepherds noticed a wild pear tree radiating light, whose source in the branches turned out to be a jasper oval, about the size of a child's hand, carved with the image of a woman and child and the Slavonic inscription, "More honourable than the cherubim, And more glorious beyond compare than the seraphim, In virginity you bore God the Word; True Mother of God, we magnify you." The portrait was recognizable as an Eleousa or Tenderness type of icon, with the Child's cheek pressed against His Mother's, and the words as the refrain of the Magnificat.

The herders took their find to the landlord, Alexander Soltan, who put it in a chest, but when the object reappeared in the forest, Soltan built a wooden church there. Some fifty years later, it burned down. Subsequently, some children passing the spot saw a radiant woman holding the stone icon. When their parents returned there with the priest, she had vanished, but the icon was there on the rock where she had been sitting. A new church was built of stone, to which pilgrims flocked from all over Lithuania and Ukraine.

In 1558 the shrine became famous for a miracle of resurrection. Doctors had given up on gravely sick Iryna, 17, prescribing a pilgrimage to Zhyrovichy as a remedy of last resort. But when the family arrived at the shrine, the girl was already dead. Her parents decided to bury her there. Three days later, at the funeral, Iryna astonished the mourners by rising from her coffin to kneel before the icon. She became a nun at a convent in Pinsk, where she served as abbess for many years. In 1575, the lord of Zyrovichy established an Orthodox monastery at the shrine. In the early 1600s, the monastery came under Basilian monks of the new Greek Catholic rite. A copy of the stone image was brought to Rome, where it is revered as the Madonna del Popolo in the Church of Saints Sergius and Bacchus. In 1730, Athanasius Sheptitsky, Greek Catholic Metropolitan of Kiev and Galicia, solemnly crowned the Mother of God of Zhyrovichy with a Roman crown blessed by Pope Benedict XIII. In the 1800s, the monastery returned to Orthodoxy.

In 1915, the icon was moved to the crypt of St Basil's Cathedral on Red Square in Moscow. Smuggled out of the Soviet Union in a shipment of jam, it returned to the Grodno diocese in 1938, missing most of its ornaments. It is now in the Church of the

Exaltation of the Cross in Holy Dormition Monastery in Zhyrov-ichy. The Russian and Belarusian Orthodox Churches celebrate the feast of the Mother of God of Zhyrovichy on 20 May or 7 May in the Julian calendar.

21 May: Our Lady of Czechia

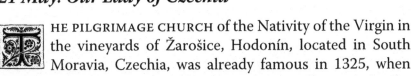 HE PILGRIMAGE CHURCH of the Nativity of the Virgin in the vineyards of Žarošice, Hodonín, located in South Moravia, Czechia, was already famous in 1325, when Elisabeth Richeza, Queen of Bohemia, donated a statue. The one-and-a-half metre wooden image was carved from a single trunk, possibly by an artist at the Cistercian monastery she had recently founded in Brno, from which she also brought monks to care for the shrine. This classic Gothic Madonna, with the long hair of a virgin and the head covering of a matron, dressed as a medieval queen in gilded robes, became the subject of legend.

During the siege of Vienna in 1529 Turkish forces invaded Moravia. The story goes that with two other officers the pasha entered the church and made fun of the statue, poking it, until he saw it weep.[19] Then he too began crying, and, suddenly blind, asked the priest on duty to pray for him, promising to become a Christian if he regained his sight. The Turkish leader stayed in Žarošice, took instruction, received baptism, and then recovered his vision. He became a hermit in the service of Our Lady's church—the only one left intact in the area—and was buried there.

In 1645, the Swedes invaded. As with other churches in Mora-via, they plundered the Virgin's shrine. However, their wagon stopped along the way and would not go forward until they unloaded the statue in the forest. Some time later, a youth named Joseph Nemec was walking there when he saw a radiance in the undergrowth and heard a voice say, "Joseph, take me with you." He fetched a grape bin from his parents' house in the village of Archlebov, nine miles west of Žarošice, brought the statue home, and set it in a niche by the door. At night, it shone so brightly that neighbours thought the house was on fire. In the morning, it was gone. Young Nemec found it in the same place he had the day before, and this time decided to return it to Žarošice.

As part of a modernizing campaign, Habsburg Emperor Joseph II dissolved the Cistercian monasteries in 1782 and banned pilgrimages in 1785. Nevertheless, pilgrims went to Žarošice on 11 September 1785 as they always had on Golden Saturday, the Saturday after the Feast of Mary's Nativity. Finding the shrine closed, they broke in, took the statue, and carried it to the Parish Church of St Anne, which has been its home ever since. On Golden Saturday, St. Anne's still hosts the annual pilgrimage, with Masses, processions and prayers. Pope John Paul II crowned the beloved statue of the Mother of God on 21 May 1995.

22 May: Our Lady of Laus

ITUATED IN DAUPHINÉ, in southern France at the foot of the Alps, just southeast of Gap, is the vale of Laus. Its name means lake in the local dialect as there once was one at the bottom of the basin. In 1666 the hamlet held twenty households scattered in little huts. The inhabitants had built a chapel dedicated to the Annunciation, Notre-Dame de on Recontre (Our Lady of the Good Encounter). It was here that Our Lady chose to appear in another Good Encounter, several times to to a humble, unschooled girl, Benoite Rencurel: "I asked my Son for Laus for the conversion of sinners, and He granted it to me" said the Blessed Virgin to the young shepherdess.

Benôite Rencurel was an orphan, born on 16 September 1657, in Saint-Etienne d'Avancon. After her father died when she was only 7 years old, she helped her family by serving as shepherdess for a neighbour. Benôite had not learned to read or write; her only source of education was the parish church and the sermons she heard at Mass. In May 1664, she saw a beautiful lady holding a child in her arms and standing on a rock in the valley of Laus, where Benôite was guarding her neighbour's flocks and praying the Rosary. Her simple response, offering to share the hard bread she had to eat after softening it in the nearby fountain, made the beautiful lady smile. Her desire to hold the little child made the lady smile again, but she left without saying a word.

Over the next four months, the beautiful lady, whose name Benôite did not know, returned daily to instruct her on her mission. Benôite told her neighbour about the lady, and the neighbour did not believe her. Following Benôite to the valley one day, she heard the lady—although she did not see her—warn Benôite that her neighbour was in spiritual danger: "She had something on her conscience" and needed to confess her sins and do penance, because she took the name of Our Lord in vain. Benôite's neighbour took this message to heart and did penance for the rest of her life.

Benôite finally asked the Lady who she was. "My name is Mary", she replied. Mary called on Benôite to pray for sinners and work for their conversion. She asked Benôite to meet her at a chapel in Laus which was to be used as a shrine. Once the diocese recognized the authenticity of the apparitions, the same chapel was replaced by a larger church, the present shrine church. The miraculous healings with the oil from the sanctuary lamps continued, drawing more and more pilgrims to Laus. At the present time, more than 120,000 travel there yearly. The Catholic philosopher Jean Guitton called it "one of the most hidden and powerful shrines of Europe".

Like all visionaries, Benôite knew suffering and misunderstanding. After all, she was a simple peasant instructing priests on how to welcome penitents with kindness and charity in the Sacrament of Penance to encourage them to confess their sins and repent. Benôite also urged young girls and older women to be modest, sometimes correcting their dress or behaviour. She became a Third Order Dominican and received visions of Jesus in His passion from 1669 to 1679. Among these five visions, Jesus told her once, "My daughter, I show myself in this state so that you can participate in My passion." Benôite mystically participated in the sufferings of Christ for 15 years, enduring great pain starting every Thursday evening and continuing until Saturday morning. On Christmas Day 1718, she received holy Communion; on the feast of the Holy Innocents, she went to confession, received extreme unction and died.

In May 2008, Bishop Jean-Michel di Falco Leandri, the bishop of Gap in the French Alps, celebrated a special Mass to announce the Vatican's approval of Marian apparitions in that diocese that occurred between 1664 and 1718. Bishop di Falco Leandri, in addition to urging the Vatican approval of the apparitions—the first approval in this century and the first approved in France since Lourdes—has also supported the cause for Benôite's canonization.[20] On 3 April 2009, Pope Benedict XVI recognized the heroic virtue of Benôite Rencurel, proclaiming her Venerable.

23 May: Our Lady of Grace, Aés

N 23 MAY 1575, as widow María Saínz de Quijano prayed the rosary while watching sheep on Hediilla Mountain, at Aés in the Cantabria region in the north of Spain, she saw Our Lady appear "with such great splendour that I didn't dare look at Her Majesty, and she said I should ask the curate of the place to build a chapel in that spot and put in it an image of the Virgin of Grace and one of St Lawrence". To the woman's objection that people wouldn't believe her, the Virgin answered that she would make them believe.

When the woman started to get up, she found she could not, and stayed there, calling for her daughter Juana. Some neighbours passing by found Juana, who carried her mother home on her back. María asked Juana to get the local priest. She told him what had happened, and he then told his superior, the vicar of the valley, who dismissed it with a laugh, saying the shepherdess must have been dreaming. A few days later the vicar passed through that place with his servant, who said, "Sir, they say the Virgin recently appeared to a woman in this spot." The vicar laughed again, and was suddenly struck blind. The servant led him home. In fear and remorse, the vicar dictated a letter to the Archbishop, asking him to order construction of the chapel so that he would regain his sight.

The Archbishop ordered workers to began cutting wood for construction. They cut some from high on the mountain and some from lower down, at the apparition site. However, they couldn't move the wood from the heights, although they moved that from the lower site easily. Records in the National Archives of Spain, don't specify whether the seer and the vicar recovered, but presumably they were among the first to receive the graces of the Virgin of Aés. The chapel has been rebuilt and renovated several times over the centuries, most recently in 1993. An annual pilgrimage to the mountain shrine outside the village of Aés on 23 May, the apparition anniversary, draws participants from the entire valley.

24 May: Our Lady, Help of Christians

OPE SAINT PIUS V gave Mary the title *Help of Christians*, after the victory of the Christian fleet over the Turks at Lepanto on 7 October 1571, and he added this invocation to her litany. In 1624, the Catholics of Passau in Bavaria enshrined a fifteenth century picture of Mary Help of Christians in a newly built sanctuary to Our Lady under this title. Pilgrims to the Shrine traditionally uttered the aspiration: *Maria, hilf* (Mary, help). A Confraternity of Mary Help of Christians was founded by Capuchin Friars at Munich, Germany, in 1627. It was approved by Pope Urban VIII. The first Italian centre was erected in Turin in 1657 and had its own chapel at the church of Saint Francesco di Paolo. The feast of Our Lady, Help of Christians, was later instituted by Pope Pius VII. By order of Napoleon, the Pope had been taken prisoner on 5 July 1808, and held at Savona and Fontainebleau. In January 1814, after the battle of Leipzig, he was brought back to Savona and set free on 17 March, the eve of the feast of Our Lady of Mercy, the patroness of Savona. The journey to Rome was truly a triumphal march with the Pontiff, who attributed the victory of the Church to the Blessed Virgin, after so much agony and distress. He visited many of her sanctuaries on the way, crowning her images, and entered Rome on 24 May 1814 to enthusiastic crowds. To commemorate his own sufferings and those of the Church during his exile he extended the feast of the Seven Dolours of Mary to the universal Church on 18 September 1814.

When Napoleon left Elba and returned to Paris, Murat was about to march through the Papal States from Naples. Pius VII fled to Savona on 22 March 1815, where he crowned the image of Our Lady of Mercy on 10 May 1815. Following the Congress of Vienna and Battle of Waterloo, he returned to Rome on 7 July 1815. To give thanks to God and Our Lady he instituted the feast of Our Lady, Help of Christians for the Papal States on 15 September 1815; it is now celebrated on 24 May, the anniversary of his first return. The dioceses of Tuscany adopted it on 12 February 1816, and it spread over nearly the entire Latin Church. It is the patronal feast of Australasia, and is celebrated with great splendor in the churches of the Fathers of the Foreign Missions of Paris. It has attained special celebrity since Saint John Bosco dedicated the mother church of his congregation at Turin to Our Lady, Help of Christians. The Salesian Fathers have carried the devotion to their numerous establishments, and prayers for her intervention are credited with the miraculous cure of Blessed Artemide Zatti.

Prayer of St John Bosco to Our Lady, Help Of Christians

Most Holy Virgin Mary, Help of Christian,
how sweet it is to come to your feet
imploring your perpetual help.
If earthly mothers cease not to remember their children,
how can you, the most loving of all mothers forget me?
Grant then to me, I implore you,

your perpetual help in all my necessities,
in every sorrow, and especially in all my temptations.
I ask for your unceasing help for all who are now suffering.
Help the weak, cure the sick, convert sinners.
Grant through your intercessions many vocations to the religious life.
Obtain for us, O Mary, Help of Christians,
that having invoked you on earth we may love and eternally thank you in heaven. Amen.

25 May: Our Lady, Mediatrix of All Graces

 FTER THE DOGMATIC DEFINITION of the Immaculate Conception in 1854 and the definition of papal infallibility by the First Vatican Council in 1870, interest in Marian doctrines was stimulated. Pope Leo XIII's series of Marian encyclicals in the 1880s and 1890s prompted René-Marie de La Broise (1860-1906), a French Jesuit and professor at the *Institut Catholique* of Paris, to publish in 1896 the first explicit proposal for a papal definition about Mary's role in the distribution of all graces, such as Mary's intercession or mediation of all graces, or her spiritual motherhood. Later, François Xavier Godts (1839-1928), a Belgian Redemptorist, published the first treatise in 1904 promoting the dogmatic definition of Mary's universal mediation. At the same time as these theologians were making their scholarly proposals, a Belgian Carmelite superior, Mother Madeleine of Jesus (1862-1946), received mystical visions from Jesus asking for the dogmatic definition of His mother's mediation. In 1906, when the newly appointed Archbishop of Malines, Belgium, Désiré Joseph Mercier (1851–1926) visited Mother Madeleine, she asked him to speak to Pope Pius X about making this dogmatic definition. Although Mercier simply replied that he would consider it, from 1907 to 1914, he began speaking publicly of Mary as "Distributrix of divine graces," "Mother of divine grace" and "Mediatrix."

After Germany invaded Belgium in 1914, Cardinal Mercier made a public vow to Jesus and to Mary. Although the details are uncertain, it appears that Mercier promised, if Belgium would be liberated from German occupation, that he would at least "ask the pope to institute a special feast in honour of Mary Mediatrix because it was to her all-powerful mediation that we entrusted the outcome of our prayers" and perhaps even to do all he could to bring about the dogmatic definition of Mary's universal mediation. Mercier worked to fulfil his vow by pastoral letters and petitions to the pope. These prayers and petitions yielded results. In 1921, Pope Benedict XV made 31 May the feast of Mary, Mediatrix of All Graces, complete with its own Mass and Office, for Belgium and all the dioceses that would request it. Capitalizing on his international fame gained during World War I, Mercier promptly invited all bishops of the world to ask for the feast, and so many requested it that the feast became almost universal. In printings of the Roman Missal from that date until 1961, the Mass of Mary Mediatrix of All Graces is found in the appendix for Masses for use in Some Places. Now that the Visitation of Our Lady is kept on 31 May, the celebration of her Mediation could be kept on 24 May.

St Louis-Marie Grignion de Montfort remarked thus about Mary Mediatrix:

> The plan adopted by the three persons of the Blessed Trinity in the Incarnation, the first coming of Jesus Christ, is adhered to each day in an invisible manner throughout the Church and they will pursue it to the end of time until the last coming of Jesus Christ. God the Father gathered all the waters together and called them the seas (*maria*). He gathered all his graces together and called them Mary (Maria). The great God has a treasury or storehouse full of riches in which he has enclosed all that is beautiful, resplendent, rare, and precious, even his own Son. This immense treasury is none other than Mary whom the saints call the "treasury of the Lord". From her fullness all men are made rich. God the Son imparted to his mother all that he

gained by his life and death, namely, his infinite merits and his eminent virtues. He made her the treasurer of all his Father had given him as heritage. Through her he applies his merits to his members and through her he transmits his virtues and distributes his graces. She is his mystical channel, his aqueduct, through which he causes his mercies to flow gently and abundantly. God the Holy Spirit entrusted his wondrous gifts to Mary, his faithful spouse, and chose her as the dispenser of all he possesses, so that she distributes all his gifts and graces to whom she wills, as much as she wills, how she wills and when she wills. No heavenly gift is given to men which does not pass through her virginal hands. Such indeed is the will of God, who has decreed that we should have all things through Mary, so that, making herself poor and lowly,, and hiding herself in the depths of nothingness during her whole life, she might be enriched, exalted and honoured by almighty God. Such are the views of the Church and the early Fathers.[21]

26 May: Our Lady of Caravaggio

 N ITALIAN SHRINE to Our Lady of Caravaggio near Milan is said to have its origin in 1432, when the Mother of God is reported to have appeared in a vision to a sick peasant woman and pointed out to her a healing stream, where the woman was cured and may other miracles and cures were effected. The apparition that took place on 26 May 1432 near the Lombard town of Caravaggio, where the famous painter was to live in the following century.

Giovannetta, the pious daughter of Pietro Vacchi, intended to become a nun, but her father had different ideas; to please him, she married a farmer named Francesco Varoli. The marriage was unhappy—Francisco was an unpleasant fellow and made life miserable for his wife. On 26 May 1432, although Giovannetta was not feeling well, Francesco sent her out to the fields to cut grass for his cattle. After gathering a large bundle of fodder, she sat down to rest; perhaps she slept a little, for when she lifted her head, the Blessed Virgin Mary stood before her and told the woman to be of good heart, her troubles would soon be over. Jesus was displeased by the sins of the people, but Giovannetta could obtain mercy for them if they repented and changed their ways—otherwise Christ would punish them all. Mary also said she wished a church built in that spot in her honour—she charged Giovannetta to make known her wishes to all the people and promised if they obeyed, she would bless them with many favours and miracles; then Mary vanished. However, as a memento of her appearance Mary left behind the imprint of her feet in a stone upon which she had stood, and from beneath the stone a spring of pure water gushed.

Giovannetta hurried to the village of Caravaggio and told everyone of the apparition and the things the Our Lady had confided to her; few believed her; rather, they greeted her story with scorn and derision. Some time later, some of the people chanced to bathe in the stream flowing from beneath the rock and were amazed to find their aches and pains had mysteriously vanished. Others followed and the same thing happened to them. Then, they remembered Giovannetta's story of the apparition and began to believe her. The incident spread far and wide, and the people, assisted by Filippo Maria Visconti, Duke of Milan, built a shrine at the place of the vision.

As great crowds came to the shrine to offer homage to Our Lady, the sanctuary was too small to accommodate them; so, in 1575, Charles Borromeo (who later became a saint) employed the celebrated architect, Pellegrino Pellegrini to enlarge it. Later additions and changes were subsequently carried out, resulting in the present sanctuary. A statue of Our Lady of Caravaggio was placed in the enlarged sanctuary—this statue depicts Our Lady blessing Giovannetta; it supposedly occupies the very spot on which the Virgin stood during the apparition; and from beneath Mary's feet, the little stream of water still flows.[22]

27 May: Our Lady of La Codosera

L A CODOSERA IS a district of the province of Badajoz, in Estremadura, situated north-west of Badajoz, at the border with Portugal. In May 1945, precisely at the end of the Second World War, the Our Lady of Sorrows appeared in Codosera to two seers independently in the same spot of Chandavila.

On 27 May 1945, around three o'clock in the afternoon, the little Marcelina Barroso Exposito and her cousin Agustina Gonzalez (both from La Codosera) were on their way to the nearby hamlet of El Marco to carry out an errand for the mother of Marcelina. After having covered about three kilometres, while passing through the area called Chandavila, Marcelina noticed a dark swelling that was protruding from a chestnut tree, at a distance of about seventy metres to the right of the footpath. At the time, she did not pay any attention to it, but on her way back she wondered if the object were still there. As if gently urged by an interior force, she approached to see it better. She was astonished to see clearly the image of the Most Holy Sorrowful Virgin, enveloped in luminous rays, as high as halfway up the trunk of the chestnut tree, by profile, with a halo of brilliant stars, a black mantel embroidered with stars, hands joined, and a most beautiful face in which was reflected a sadness both human and divine.

As soon as the vision disappeared, the girl instinctively began running toward the village together with her cousin who, however, had seen nothing. Having arrived at home, she sought to keep silent, but she could not and so she recounted to her mother what had happened to her; naturally, word spread very rapidly throughout the neighbourhood.

The event was repeated on the morning of 4 June, nine days after the first apparition. Our Lady appeared again to the young Marcelina near Chandavila and told her to return that evening to perform a sacrifice in the presence of all those who would come with her. The young girl obeyed and that evening, in the presence of a thousand people, both Spanish and Portuguese, she fell into ecstasy, stirring up a great commotion. The girl was about seventy metres from the chestnut tree when, suddenly, in the blue of the sky, Our Lady of Sorrows appeared to her, slowly descending until she remained in front of the tree, in the same position in which she had seen her the first time. The Virgin invited the girl to move, on her knees, the distance that separated them. The girl was not convinced, and so the Sorrowful Mother encouraged her by saying: "Be not afraid. Nothing will happen to you. I will arrange in front of you a carpet of branches and grasses so that you will not get hurt." Departing from across the creek, the girl began to move on her knees towards Our Lady. Her mother, Augustina, who was present at the scene, fainted. For about ten minutes she remained kneeling near the tree. Then the chestnut opened slightly and within it appeared a beautiful church, adorned with precious lamps. On the altar, the Virgin Mary appeared, indicating to the girl to dip her fingers into the holy water font and make the Sign of the Cross, a gesture that was repeated by all those present.

After the apparition, the Virgin descended from the altar piece and asked her if she desired to go away with her. The young girl replied: "Yes, Lady, now" and the Most Holy Virgin smiled, embraced her and kissed her forehead. The girl felt on her face the caress of the mantle of the Mother of God. The Virgin expressed the desire that a chapel be built there in her honour. Upon coming out of the ecstasy, Marcelina went back to speak with her friends. On the knees of Marcelina there were no marks or scratches, in spite of having travelled seventy metres on her knees; many young people (and the parish priest of La Codosera, Juan Antonio Galan y Galan) attempted to do it, but were forced to give up because of the cuts and wounds.

Marcelina encountered the Virgin other times, on several occasions in the company of other people, among whom was her teacher, Josefa Martin. She studied in a convent of nuns in Villafranca de Los Barros (Badajoz) and afterwards she entered as a religious into the Congregation of the Sisters of the Company of the Cross, 2 August 1975, in Seville, where she dedicated herself to the care of the sick, of orphans, of the poor, and of the elderly, with the name of Sister Mary of the Mercy of the Cross. Today she is in a cloistered convent in Ciudad Real.

Afra Brigido Blanco (born 21 January 1928) at the age of seventeen years, on 30 May 1945 (Feast of Corpus Christi), at three o'clock in the afternoon (the same time of the apparitions to Marcelina), decided to go with her friends to Chandavila. Upon arrival she thought she could see, in the dark clouds, something that resembled a chapel and, more clearly, the precise form of a cross. The following day, at the same time, in the same place many people were already gathered. She sat down in front of the chestnut tree of the apparitions and saw emerge from the dark clouds a dark figure that, little by little got closer to her, allowing a glimpse of the profile of the image of the Sorrowful Virgin, with her face turned to the right. Very emotionally touched by this vision, Afra fainted, and upon regaining consciousness, she decided to return home with her friends. A few days later, her paternal grandmother passed away. She dressed in mourning and left the house very little. In the face of insistence from her friends, however, she let herself be convinced to return to Chandavila, upon permission from her mother, Cipriana. On 17 June when, sitting on one of the chestnut trees in front, she again saw the apparition, in the identical form as the previous time. She entered into ecstasy and began to travel the bed of the creek on her knees. The Virgin asked her to get up and to continue walking up to the chestnut. Arrived there, she knelt down and began a conversation with the Virgin. The Virgin told her that she would always be near her, told her a secret, predicted great sufferings, and at the end told her to give a kiss on her behalf to little Marcelina (who was present) and to make the Sign of the Cross, which the young girl did in that very instant. During successive apparitions, the Virgin asked her to recite the Holy Rosary and to have a hermitage built on the site of the apparition, in addition to a sacrifice, that of singing in the solemn Mass of the 4 September, wish that was realized thanks to the spontaneous suggestion of the pastor of La Codosera. Afra and other friends, including Marcelina, remained in Villar del Rey from the Sunday 21 July, to the 24, vigil of Saint James, and that same Sunday they visited the convent of Our Lady of the Incarnation or of Rivera, patroness of the region, and they returned every day, morning and evening, to give thanks for the favour received.

During one of these visits (Monday 22 July), while the Stations of the Cross were being celebrated, Afra entered into ecstasy during the Eleventh Station of the Cross, situated to the side of the epistolary, almost at the centre of the convent, and she saw the Calvary of Our Lord Jesus Christ and His crucifixion, and she felt profound pain in the palms of her hands. Alter this event, first some lesions appeared on her hands with an incision in the centre in the shape of a nail, and then another wound in her ribcage that shed blood, causing her great suffering, and finally lesions on her feet. With the passing of time, the wounds of the feet and hands became larger until they went all the way through her limbs, from front to back, with the appearance of a deep incision on her back. The blood flowed principally on Fridays. Afra was subjected to medical examinations and to specialized treatments from a hospital attendant, but the wounds did not heal. It is interesting to underscore that the wounds had a pleasant perfume. Afra lived and worked in a hospital in Madrid, dedicating herself to works of charity, until she died, on 23 August 2008, at the age of 80 years, after a long and agonizing malady.

For La Codosera, these occurrences were exceptional and extraordinary, for the conversion of the souls that followed, but also because they gave rise to the construction of a little chapel that covers and encloses within a fenced area the chestnut tree where the apparitions of the Virgin took place and a larger church, in which is displayed a statue of Our Lady of Sorrows, corresponding to the description given by the visionaries, and brought to life by a very devout Marian artist, Fr Genaro Lazaro Gumiel, who presented it as a gift to the Shrine, the construction of which began on the 27 May 1947. Despite all this, the bishop of Badajoz has not yet officially declared on these matters, but has however given permission for the construction of the Shrine, and for the devotion. Each year, on the 27 May, a festive pilgrimage occurs to which many people participate, coming from the entire region and from nearby Portugal.

28 May: Our Lady of the Ukraine

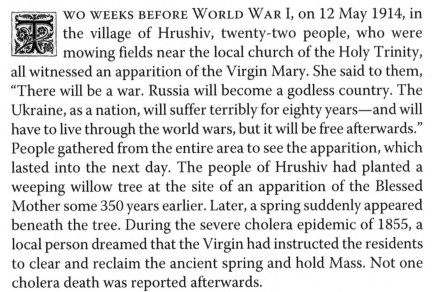 WO WEEKS BEFORE WORLD WAR I, on 12 May 1914, in the village of Hrushiv, twenty-two people, who were mowing fields near the local church of the Holy Trinity, all witnessed an apparition of the Virgin Mary. She said to them, "There will be a war. Russia will become a godless country. The Ukraine, as a nation, will suffer terribly for eighty years—and will have to live through the world wars, but it will be free afterwards." People gathered from the entire area to see the apparition, which lasted into the next day. The people of Hrushiv had planted a weeping willow tree at the site of an apparition of the Blessed Mother some 350 years earlier. Later, a spring suddenly appeared beneath the tree. During the severe cholera epidemic of 1855, a local person dreamed that the Virgin had instructed the residents to clear and reclaim the ancient spring and hold Mass. Not one cholera death was reported afterwards.

Then, on 26 April 1987, seventy-three years after 1914 and exactly one year after the Chernobyl nuclear reactor disaster, a bright light covered the church of the Holy Trinity and the surrounding area. A television program even recorded part of this light phenomenon. From within this "impressive silver dazzle" over the church, the Virgin Mary appeared and floated above the cupola of the church.

She first appeared to Marina Kizyn, age 12, who immediately called her mother and a few neighbours. Soon, hundreds and then thousands came from all over Russia to see the apparitions which continued every day until 15 August 1987. It is estimated that a total of 500,000 people had seen her by the time these apparitions ended. On most days the crowd might reach as many as 45,000 to 70,000 people at one time. Neither the Soviet militia nor the KGB could begin to manage the crowds. The Virgin Mary was even seen by the KGB agents. Many priests (from underground Catholic churches) came and celebrated as many as ten Holy Masses per day in front of the church. Many messages were documented:

> I have come on purpose to thank the Ukrainian people because you have suffered most for the church of Christ in the last 70 years. I have come to comfort you and to tell you that your suffering will soon come to an end. Ukraine will become an independent state.

> Forgive your enemies. Through you and the blood of martyrs will come the conversion of Russia. Repent and love one another. The times are coming which have been foretold as being those in the end times. See the desolation which surrounds the world ... the sin, the sloth, the genocide. Pray for Russia. Oppression and wars continue to occupy the minds and hearts of many people. Russia, despite everything, continues to deny my Son. Russia rejects real life and continues to live in darkness. If there is not a return to Christianity in Russia, there will be a Third World War; the whole world will face ruin.

Our Lady predicted that the Ukraine would "suffer terribly for eighty years" before gaining independence, she was extremely close in her prediction. The Ukraine had its declaration of independence ratified in Kiev on 24 August 1991—some 77 years after Blessed Mary's prediction in 1914!

29 May: Our Lady, Queen of Apostles

 Y AN OLD TRADITION, the Saturday after the Ascension is kept as the Feast of the Blessed Virgin Mary, Queen of the Apostles. The title refers to a particular episode in the life of Our Lady described in the reading from the Acts of the Apostles. After the Ascension, the apostles returned to Jerusalem, went to the upper room where they were staying, and: All these with one accord devoted themselves to prayer: together with the women and Mary the mother of Jesus, and with His brothers.

The apostles understood better than anyone else the great privileges of Mary. They realized her sanctity; they recognized her virtues; they knew how she had cooperated in the work of redemption; they knew how Jesus loved her. During the public life of Christ they were closely associated with the Blessed Mother. They were with her through the suffering of our Lord. With Mary they persevered in prayer in the upper room, waiting for the coming of the Holy Spirit. During this long association, even before the death and resurrection of Jesus, the apostles came to know her as their Queen and Mother.

Great must have been her zeal and joy when she could preach Christ crucified, living in herself, as she abode, during the years in pagan Ephesus with the Beloved Disciple. Her Son was no longer a hidden God, but One on High, risen from the dead. Mary perhaps converted many by her spotless life, where the virtues of a Christian shone the more gloriously because set in a pagan land.

Mary is Queen of the Apostles in another sense. The apostles were zealous but they had their defects. They sometimes showed lack of courage, faith, humility and meekness. Mary, on the contrary, had every virtue in perfection, especially those of the true missionary-zeal and the spirit of sacrifice. Mary merited the title Queen of Apostles by years of exile in foreign countries among pagans. She saw mission life in all its phases.

We need the example and inspiration of Mary to convert the world. We need her virtues to win the world to her Son. It will strengthen all who are interested in spreading the Faith, to reflect that Mary spent so many of her days on earth among the heathen. Thank God, our missionaries, our modern apostles, our priests and sisters and brothers, and lay people in the missions, take her for their model.

Devotion to Mary as Queen of Apostles is an ancient practice for the Church. God continues to give all graces through Mary, just as He willed that Christ should come to us through Mary: He was "born of a woman" (Galatians 4:4). Christ began his apostolate through Mary at Cana; the mission of the apostles was begun through Mary in the cenacle. Mary is Queen of Apostles because she was chosen to be the Mother of Jesus Christ and to give Him to the world; she was made the Apostles' Mother and our own by Our Savior on the Cross; she was with the Apostles while awaiting the descent of the Holy Spirit, obtaining for them the abundance of supernatural graces they received on Pentecost. Likewise through the centuries all apostolates have received their origin and strength through Mary. Without God nothing exists; without Mary, nothing in Christ and in the Church. The title of Queen of Apostles appears in the Litany of Our Lady.

In several religious Congregations, the Blessed Virgin Mary is especially venerated and invoked under the title of Queen of Apostles, including the Pallotines, the Marianists, and the congregations founded by Blessed James Alberione (the Society of St Paul, the Daughters of St Paul, and several others). In the twentieth century, Blessed Alberione promoted this devotion in a particular way. The feast of the Queen of Apostles was established on the first Saturday after the Ascension by the Sacred Congregation of Rites at the request of the Pallottine Fathers, and a liturgical feast is kept in certain calendars on this day. As Mary remained with the first Apostles, to care for, encourage and pray for them, we know that she is with the Church now. And, as we give her Son, the Word of God, to the modern world, we can count on her special care and intercession to make our apostolic efforts fruitful, for the glory of God and the good of her children on earth.

Prayer

O Virgin most pure, noble Queen of Martyrs, Morning Star, safe refuge of sinners, rejoice for the days in which you were teacher, comforter and Mother of the apostles in the cenacle, to invoke and receive the divine Paraclete, the Spirit with the seven gifts, Love of the Father and of the Son, transformer of the apostles. By your all-powerful intercession and by your humble and irresistible prayers, which always move God's heart, obtain for me the grace to realize the value of every human person, for whom Jesus Christ shed his most precious blood. May each one of us be enthusiastic about the beauty of the Christian apostolate. May the charity of Christ urge us on. May the spiritual misery of poor humanity move us. Grant that we may feel in our hearts the needs of childhood, of adolescence, of adulthood, of old age. Grant that vast Africa, immense Asia, promising Oceania, troubled Europe, the two Americas may exercise a powerful attraction on our souls. Grant that the apostolate of example and word, of prayer and the press, of films, radio and television, of the souls in purgatory, may conquer many generous persons, even to the point of the most heroic sacrifices. O Mother of the Church, O Queen of Apostles, our Advocate, to you we sigh, mourning in this valley of tears.

30 May: Our Lady of the Sacred Heart

 HEN HITLER'S ARMIES defeated the French and entered the city of Paris during the latter part of 1939, a young woman, Maria Hendizabal, fled from France to live in Mexico. Arriving at Vera Cruz, she went to the Mexican capital to make a new home. Among her few possessions she had a large picture of Our Lady of the Sacred Heart which she wished to give to some church for safekeeping, since she would be obliged to live in a small town and expected to have nothing more than a small room for herself. Fr Juan Gomez of the Church of San José (Saint Joseph) allowed her to place the image on the wall of the sacristy on 2 February 1940.

That very same evening a nine year old boy, who was afflicted with infantile paralysis, was immediately cured after praying before the lovely image of Our Lady of the Sacred Heart. The youth left his crutches on the floor of the vestibule and hurried home to tell his mother. The news of his cure spread rapidly and the next day hundreds of the faithful visited the church, where before, there was never an attendance of more than a hundred at Sunday Mass. This cure was followed by others, and day by day the crowds grew larger.

After a week the pastor had to take the picture down from the wall of the sacristy and place it in the front of the church where it could be more easily viewed by the crowds clamouring to see it. Since Mexico is rich in silver, the usual way of acknowledging favours is to make a gift of precious silver. At present the entire left wall of the church is covered with silver remembrances donated by the recipients of favours received from Our Lady of the Sacred Heart.

In the sixty-some years that the shrine of Our Lady has existed, thousands of cures have been performed through the intercession of the Our Lady. These cures have been verified by affidavits signed by reliable physicians in the presence of notaries; the documents may still be seen in the present day at the shrine. One father, in gratitude for the cure of his daughter, had a silversmith make a new frame for the picture.[23]

31 May: The Visitation

HE ACCOUNT OF the Visitation of Our Lady to Saint Elizabeth is well known: When Saint Gabriel the Archangel appeared to Our Lady during the Annunciation, he informed her that her cousin, Saint Elizabeth, was with child. Our Lady travelled to Saint Elizabeth's house, to care for her until her son, Saint John the Baptist, was born. Although Our Lady had already conceived the Child Jesus, she had not told anyone.

Nevertheless, Saint Elizabeth knew by inspiration that the Child Jesus was in Our Lady's womb. Thus, she greeted Our Lady, saying: "Blessed are you among women and blessed is the fruit of your womb" (Luke 1:42). When Our Lady spoke to her, Saint John the Baptist heard Our Lady's voice, was sanctified by it and leapt for joy, inside Saint Elizabeth's womb.

This feast is of medieval origin, it was kept by the Franciscan Order before 1263, and soon its observance spread throughout the entire Church. Previously it was celebrated on 2 July. Now it is celebrated between the solemnity of the Annunciation of the Lord and the birth of St. John the Baptist, in conformity with the Gospel accounts. Some places appropriately observe a celebration of the reality and sanctity of human life in the womb.

St Ambrose remarks concerning this important event in the life of Our Lady:

> Notice the contrast and the choice of words. Elizabeth is the first to hear Mary's voice, but John is the first to be aware of grace. She hears with the ears of the body, but he leaps for joy at the meaning of the mystery. She is aware of Mary's presence, but he is aware of the Lord's: a woman aware of a woman's presence, the forerunner aware of the pledge of our salvation. The women speak of the grace they have received while the children are active in secret, unfolding the mystery of love with the help of their mothers, who prophesy by the spirit of their sons. The child leaps in the womb; the mother is filled with the Holy Spirit, but not before her son. Once the son has been filled with the Holy Spirit, he fills his mother with the same Spirit. John leaps for joy, and the spirit of Mary rejoices in her turn. When John leaps for joy Elizabeth is filled with the Holy Spirit, but we know that though Mary's spirit rejoices, she does not need to be filled with the Holy Spirit. Her son, who is beyond our understanding, is active in his mother in a way beyond our understanding. Elizabeth is filled with the Holly Spirit after conceiving John, while Mary is filled with the Holy Spirit before conceiving the Lord. Elizabeth says: "Blessed are you because you have believed."[24]

Pope St John Paul II links Mary's role of Mediatrix with the event of the Visitation:

In the Visitation, the Virgin brings Christ to the Baptist's mother, the Christ who pours out the Holy Spirit. This role of Mediatrix is brought out by Elizabeth's very words: "For behold, when the voice of your greeting came to my ears, the babe in my womb leaped for joy" (Lk 1:44). By the gift of the Holy Spirit, Mary's presence serves as a prelude to Pentecost, confirming a co-operation which, having begun with the Incarnation, is destined to be expressed in the whole work of divine salvation.[25]

Notes

1   Bl John Henry Newman, *Meditations and Devotions*.

2   Marian hymn written by Mary E. Walsh

3   J. Pronechen, "Major Apparitions of St Joseph Are Approved" in *National Catholic Register* (5 August 2016).

4   Pope St John Paul II, *Act of Consecration to the Mother of God* (4 June 1979).

5   Jacopone da Todi (1230–1306), *Stabat Mater speciosa*.

6   See M. Elvins, "The Origin of the Title 'Dowry of Mary' and The Shrines of Our Lady at Westminster". Appendix in *Catholic Trivia, Our Forgotten Heritage* (Leominster: Gracewing, 2002).

7   See A. Vail, *Shrines of Our Lady in England* (Leominster: Gracewing, 2004), p. 212.

8   Cotton House, the town house of Sir R. Cotton, founder of the Cotton Library, was near the West end of Westminster Hall.

9   J. Froissart, *Chroniques de France, d'Engleterre et des païs voisins*, c.76.

10 M. T. Elvins, *Catholic trivia: our forgotten heritage* (Leominster: Gracewing, 2002), p. 138.

11 *Ibid.*, p. 139.

12 *Ibid.*

13 T. B. Bridgett, "England's Title: Our Lady's Dowry: its history and meaning" in *The Church of Old England* vol. lll (CTS: London, 1894), pp. 15–16.

14 St Bernard, *Sermon of the Twelve Stars*, 2.

15 Collect from the Proper of Feast Days, *Missal for the Congregation of the Missionaries of the Precious Blood*, 12 May.

16 See R. Laurentin and P. Sbalchiero, *Dictionnaire des "apparitions" de la Vierge Marie* (Paris: Fayard, 2007), p. 160.

17 See www.monasterocarmelitane.it/santuario/.

18 The name Жырóвічы is transliterated variously: Zhirovichi, Zhirovits, Zhirovitsy, Zhuravichi, Zhyrovichy, Žyrovičy, Żyrowice.

19 A pasha was a higher rank in the Ottoman Empire political and military system, typically granted to governors, generals, dignitaries and others.

20 See S. A. Mann, "Who Is Our Lady of Laus? 'My name is Mary'" in *The Catholic Answer* (28 March 2014).

21 St Louis-Marie Grignion de Montfort, *True Devotion to Mary*, 22–25.

22 See M. Lamberty (ed.), *The Woman in Orbit: Mary's feasts every day everywhere* (Chicago: Lamberty, 1966), 26 May.

23 See *ibid.*, 30 May.

24 St Ambrose of Milan, *Commentary on the Gospel of Luke*, 2.

25 Pope St John Paul II, *Discourse at General audience*, 2 October 1996.

JUNE

1 June: Our Lady of Turzovka

THE MESSAGES GIVEN to Matúš Lašut which he reportedly received from the Virgin Mary at Turzovka, in former Czechoslovakia, now Slovakia, in 1958, have yet to be approved by the Church. The apparition is a strong candidate for future recognition, due to the various miracles and healings reported at this site. It can sometimes take many years for Marian apparitions to achieve formal Church approval. So while any apparitions still awaiting Church approval should always be considered with discernment, they need not be entirely dismissed either.

Matúš was by all accounts a simple man. From the age of five, when his mother died, he'd learned to bear hardships as a normal part of life. He grew up tending cows, often sleeping with them in the barn on a bed of straw. During the years of violent transition that his country went through—from an independent Czechoslovakian nation to a Nazi puppet state to a Communist satellite of the Soviet Union—Matúš always worked the land quietly as a woodcutter, until he was promoted to the respectable position of forest ranger by the local government.

His faith was simple also. Without a mother to instruct him, he had nevertheless learned the basics of being Catholic. He knew the Our Father and the Hail Mary and he understood a few points of the catechism. He followed the Church's requirements regarding his marriage and the baptism of his children but he wasn't so fervent when it came to Mass and confession and communion, not to mention charity for his fellow men. He didn't particularly like many people but the ones he disliked he made certain they knew it. His faith wasn't lacking so much as it was lazy. Yet Matúš retained throughout his life an aspect that was characteristic of all Slovakians regardless of status, a second-natured devotion to Mary.

On 1 June 1958 Matúš was making his rounds on Okruhla, a mountain near the village of Turzovka. As usual, just before 9 am, he stopped at a spot on the side of the mountain called Zivcak (literally meaning "at the picture"). On a pine tree by the side of the trail was an icon of the Mother of God of Perpetual Help and it was here that he knelt to pray:

> I quickly prayed the Our Father and Hail Mary, but before I finished, at the end of Hail Mary, all of a sudden I spotted a short flash of light on my left side. I looked in that direction and to my amazement I saw at a distance of approximately 12 meters, a statue of Our Lady of Lourdes about two meters above the ground as if on a mound... A faint gust of wind coming from the east slightly moved her veil to reveal on the left side of her head a lock of light chestnut-coloured hair... I realized that this was no statue but a living being standing on a tiny cloud as if it was made from a mist.

Matúš went on to describe her as having folded hands and wearing a crown of twelve stars. Her hair fell over her shoulders from beneath a gold-edged veil of white that stretched to her feet. A blue girdle, also edged with gold, cinched her snowy-white dress. On each foot rested a rose of gold.

Hanging over her right arm was a rosary that reached to her knees—white beads for the Hail Marys and gold ones for the Our Fathers. Interestingly, though the vision indeed strongly resembled Our Lady of Lourdes, the rosary that she held was of five decades, not the six decade one described by St Bernadette.

A field of white roses suddenly appeared below the Lady and surrounding it was a white picket fence; three of the boards were loose. The lady looked at Matúš and pointed to where there was a little hammer and some nails. Matúš immediately understood that she wanted him to repair the fence. Unquestioningly, he bent down and set to work. Upon completion, the lady seemed pleased.

She then smiled at Matúš, held out her arm and gently shook the rosary she was holding. He knew that she was asking him to pray the rosary—only Matúš had never learned that special prayer of Our Lady. Before his embarrassment overtook him, the Lady turned her head in the direction of the tree where her icon stood. Matúš followed her glance. Before the pine was a canvas showing a map of the world and below it was a black screen.

The map depicted was not unusual in that the oceans between the continents were blue and the land was variously coloured green and yellow. Matúš was made to understand that the green signified nations that were good, pleasing to God. The yellow were those countries that had abandoned Him. At first, the colours were stable but soon they began to blur and shift until the entire map was yellow. Little explosions erupted on the map, first on the coasts and in the oceans. Eventually the whole world was in flames. On the black screen below the image, these words appeared:

Repent! Pray for priests and the religious! Pray the Rosary!

Frightened and confused, Matúš looked back at the Lady. She motioned for him to look above her and a flash of lightning cracked the sky in the shape of a triangle. From the hole in the sky, Christ emerged in all His majesty, wearing a long white robe and with a red cape draped over his shoulder. Under his left arm he carried a cross and in the middle of his chest there pulsed an image of his Sacred Heart. Three brilliant rays shot forth from the Heart. Two passed by each side of Matúš but centre one flashed right through him and he shut his eyes and collapsed to the ground.

He awoke to the sound of bells. They were the bells of the nearby church announcing the Angelus—it was noon—he had been there for three hours. He sat up and looked around. The map was gone, as were the flowers and the fence. And the Lady was gone too, but on a rock just below where she had appeared, lay her rosary. He picked it up and began to pray. The Glorious Mysteries formed miraculously on his lips.

When Matúš finished his rosary, the understanding came to him that the three fence-boards that the Lady had asked him to repair were indicative of the repairs that he needed to make in his own life. They were his three main shortcomings and he was supposed to fix them through the prayer of the Holy Rosary, the receiving of the Sacraments frequently, and a friendship with all people.

> After the apparition, I felt a great infusion of faith. First of all, I had to make peace with people whom I had come into conflict with. I would like to have avoided it but felt I had to do this. After returning from the mountain that very evening I went to beg forgiveness from all those people in Turzovka and the surrounding area. I did it as if against my own will. I took me until late in the night. People were surprised, some laughed at me, others thought that I had gone insane. The next day in the morning, I made confession and went to communion. From that time on, I was released from all my illness; first of all from heavy cough which had troubled me for many years and which the doctors claimed to be incurable.

He told no one of what he had seen. Matúš was visited six more times at Zivcak by the Lady. Each time she appeared the same way, as Our Lady of Lourdes, and each time a vision was given to him in the same way, on a screen with words subtitled below it. Each vision dealt with the sinful condition of the world and the coming of a divine chastisement that could only be put off through prayer and penance. He gave a general description of some of his visions but he also saw specific names, places, and dates which he would keep secret from everyone except the Holy Father. The Vatican has never made these revelations public, probably as the events are still under review. On the seventh and final appearance on 14 August 1958, she came under the title of the Immaculate Conception.

During the time that Matúš was having his visions, people began to notice a marked change in him. They pestered and questioned him until finally he broke his silence and told his story. On 8 September, the feast of the Nativity of Mary, a thousand people accompanied him on a visit to the icon on the hill. There, he surprised his new friends by announcing that in three days, he would be imprisoned.

That night, a police car stopped at his front door. Neighbours flocked to Matúš' house and prevented him from being taken away but he was ordered to appear at the police station the next day on charges of inciting insurrection. The communist authorities were not about to brook any supernatural resistance to their authority. He did as ordered, and two days later they decided it would be better to classify him as mentally ill; he was confined to a psychiatric hospital "for his own protection".

Matúš Lasut was moved in and out of various prisons and hospitals by the "committees" in charge of his case. He faced nineteen separate investigations and signed 120 sworn testimonies. During the course of his investigation, he was often subject to twice-daily interrogations as well as torture.

After five years, Matúš Lasut was finally released from prison but lived under constant surveillance for the rest of his life. Left half-blind and nearly toothless from the torture inflicted upon him, he went right back to his mountain. He found that despite attempts by the police to deter pilgrims by cutting down trees and burning images of the Holy Virgin, the site of the apparitions was growing dearer and stronger in the hearts of his countrymen every day. In fact, visitors from other parts of Czechoslovakia began to trickle in to Turzovka and soon they followed by Austrians and Germans and others. Many offered money to Matúš but he never accepted a penny, preferring to live out his life in poverty.

However the story of Our Lady of Turzovka doesn't end there. The remainder of the story begins with a man named Jaroslav Zaalenka. He had a dream in which a beautiful Lady told him to go up to the mountain (Okruhla) and dig. Not understanding what he was supposed to do, he didn't follow her directions until after the third night of the same dream. He brought his shovel to the mountain and wandered around looking for a place he should dig. At a loss for guidance, he picked a random place that wasn't too rocky. No sooner had he begun when the lady from his dream suddenly appeared and spoke to him. "Not here," she said, "but over there, where you see those ferns." He walked over to the ferns and set his shovel below the roots. As his foot pushed the shovel into soft ground, the ferns vanished and water began to bubble up. He turned to look back at the lady but she was gone. Six more springs formed on the mountain over the ensuing years when there had never been a single one recorded in its history.

Nuns, priests, doctors, engineers, and people from all walks of life swore to the healing effects of this water. Lung cancer. Blindness. Paralysis. Soon, upon request, jars of the water were being sent to Rome. The prophecy reportedly made by the visionary and stigmatist Therese Neumann to Slovakian Bishop Mgr. Karol Kaspar in the 1920's had apparently been fulfilled: "In a few years, you will have in Slovakia another Lourdes where you will go on pilgrimages." Even the name of Padre Pio was brought into the mix after he wrote in a letter to a Slovakian Jesuit priest, "Turzovka—ít is an authentic apparition. In time, it will become the Slovak Lourdes!"

Turzovka grew beyond control. Visions and voices and unexplainable events spread like a contagion among those who visited the site. There doesn't seem to have been an "industry" that profited from the appearance of Our Lady. Nothing but good seems to have come of it. And nothing contrary to the Faith.

One of the more tender stories , of typically Slovakian flavour, regards a bus filled with passengers that stopped at Cadca, a village about 10 kilometers from Turzovka. A barefooted woman with a rosary in her belt boarded the bus. "Where are you going?" the driver asked her. "Turzovka", she replied. The driver calculated the fare and handed her a ticket but the woman said that she had no money to pay for it. One of the passengers offered to pay her fare but the woman smiled at him and said she couldn't accept his offer because he already had three children at home for whom he must care.

The driver, feeling pity for the woman, then offered to pay for her himself. He was taken aback when she told him that she could not accept his help either because although he was not married, she knew that wanted to be. He did indeed need to save every coin for the hard times that he would soon be facing. By this time, the passengers had begun to pay attention. One of them came up with the idea for everyone aboard to each pay a tiny portion of her fare. The lady agreed to this but before she took a seat, someone insisted that she first show her identification as no one had ever seen her in those parts before. The lady looked at the bus driver and announced that her ID was in his pocket. The surprised driver reached into his jacket. All that was there was a holy card picturing the Holy Virgin. The woman disappeared before their eyes.[1]

Perhaps the greatest miracle to occur though, was that Slovakia and its faithful devotion to the Mother of God, survived through decades of relentless persecution to outlast the Soviet Union. After the communists departed, the dream of millions finally came true. A permanent shrine was finally permitted at the site of the apparitions in 1993.

2 June: Our Lady of Edessa

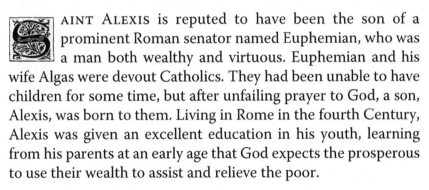 AINT ALEXIS is reputed to have been the son of a prominent Roman senator named Euphemian, who was a man both wealthy and virtuous. Euphemian and his wife Algas were devout Catholics. They had been unable to have children for some time, but after unfailing prayer to God, a son, Alexis, was born to them. Living in Rome in the fourth Century, Alexis was given an excellent education in his youth, learning from his parents at an early age that God expects the prosperous to use their wealth to assist and relieve the poor.

When Alexis grew up, Euphemian and his wife Algas chose what they thought would be a good spouse for their son. His bride to be is said to have been a member of the Roman imperial family, but Alexis wanted to give his life to God, and did not wish to be married. In obedience to the wishes of his parents, Alexis did marry, but after the ceremony, by divine inspiration, he removed his wedding band and gave it back to his bride. Apparently Alexis' bride had consented to this, and so Alexis left Rome in secret and took ship to Syria. He then journeyed to Edessa, where, although he had once been very rich, he began living the life of a common beggar at the entrance to a church dedicated to the Blessed Virgin Mary, Our Lady of Edessa. Not knowing the circumstances of his disappearance, his family searched for him in vain for many years.

Saint Alexis was content to live a beggar's life, surviving off the meagre alms he obtained each day after praying before the image of the Blessed Virgin at the shrine. He spent much of the rest of his time caring for the sick and infirm at Edessa's hospital. He never spoke of himself, or of the life he had left behind, and there were none to whom he ever revealed his name.

One day the image of Our Lady venerated by Saint Alexis spoke to a sacristan, defending the saint while also revealing that Alexis was a man of God, and making known his holiness to all the people of Edessa. Saint Alexis, seeing himself as nothing but a lowly beggar, found he was suddenly venerated as a holy man. Humbled by the revelation of Our Lady of Edessa, he fled the city for a place where he could remain unknown. He boarded a ship to Tarsus, but a storm forced the ship to the Italian coast. Seeing the hand of God in this, and following divine inspiration, Saint Alexis returned to his boyhood home on Aventine Hill in the city of Rome.

The parents of Saint Alexis were still alive, but they did not recognize their own son in the ragged beggar he had become. He who was heir to a noble title and magnificent property was given modest employment and a miserable corner beneath the stairs where he could sleep. He revealed himself to no one, and never asked for anything more. Saint Alexis spent the remaining 17 years of his life as a stranger in his own home, suffering the contempt and buffets of his father's servants in patience and humility.

When Saint Alexis died, the church bells rang of their own accord. Pope Innocent I was celebrating Mass when he was interrupted by an unseen voice telling him to "Seek the man of God." The Roman Emperor joined Pope Innocent in the search, and the two, guided by the mysterious voice, found the body of Saint Alexis where he had expired under the staircase. When Saint Alexis was found he held a scroll detailing the account of his life that God had commanded he put down in writing, and this document also revealed his identity. Alexis' parents were deeply saddened to learn that the beggar who had lived beneath the stairs and eaten the scraps from their table had actually been their own son, though they also realized that he was a saint who had suffered all for the love of God. Saint Alexis was first buried in Saint Peter's Basilica, though his remains were later transferred to the church of Saint Boniface on the Aventine Way in Rome. There is an enclosed display which shows the very staircase beneath which Saint Alexis once slept.[2]

3 June: Our Lady of Sasopoli

HE SANCTUARY OF Our Lady of Sasopoli, is some 1700 feet above sea level on one of the hills in the range of Mount Giove, twelve miles northwest of Florence, Italy. In ancient times, a little shrine stood on a hill and it contained a tablet depicting the Blessed Virgin and the Child. Since the plaque is, according to experts, a work of the Giotto School, it must have been made some time between 1300 and 1490. Giotto was himself in Florence in 1300, 1302, 1307, and 1334, and died in 1336.

Many people came to pray at the shrine and among these were two young shepherdesses of the Ricovera family. On 2 July 1490, the two girls were praying at the shrine. As their father was gravely ill, they were imploring the Virgin to restore him to health. They heard a sound and looking around, they saw sitting on a nearby stone a lovely Lady with a child in her arms. Before they recovered from their surprise the Lady spoke to them. She told them not to be afraid and not to worry, that she was the one to whom they had been praying so fervently, and that she wished to have a church built on that spot in her honour. She asked them to go and bring their father, as she wished to speak to him.

The girls told the Lady that their father could not come because he was so sick; he could not even get up out of his bed. But she assured them that he was now well again and that they should go and get him. Obeying, the girls hurried to their home and found their father completely recovered. They returned with him to the shrine; the Lady was still sitting on the stone. She told the father of her wish that a church be built on that spot. The man and his daughters spread the story of his recovery and of how the Virgin had appeared, but very few believed them and nothing at all was done about the church.

Later, on 15 August, the feast of the Assumption, when a large number where gathered at the shrine, the Virgin appeared for the third time. She told them she was displeased at the delay and demanded that they get busy and build her a church. This time they believed her and started to work. However, since the ground around the stone on which she had appeared seemed too steep to attempt to put a building there, they started to lay the foundation at a place some few hundred feet away. However, when the masons arrived for the work the following morning, they found the walls they had laid the day before were demolished and the stones strewn around. After this happened several times, they decided that the Virgin did not want the church built there, but over on the spot where the stone was. So they bowed to the inevitable and with great labour, levelled off the ground around the stone, and there erected the church in honour of Our Lady of Sasopoli. Since the Virgin had appeared on the stone, and moreover, insisted that the church be erected on that very spot, it was natural the church and the image be called Madonna del Sasso or Our Lady of Sasopoli, Our Lady of the Stone.[3]

4 June: The Immaculate Heart of Mary

HE FIRST KNOWN PRAYER invoking the Heart of Mary, was composed in 1184 by Ekbert of Schonau, in what is now Germany, and calls on all to praise the happiness of Our Lady's heart, whence our salvation flowed. At the Cistercian monastery of Helfta, a centre of women's spirituality in the 13th century, interest in the devotion was promoted by its renowned visionaries, Mechtild of Hackeborn and Gertrude the Great. Medieval Franciscan theologians, especially St Bernardine of Siena, wrote of Mary's heart as a "furnace of divine love". The most notable advance in devotion to the heart of Mary can be attributed to St John Eudes, who composed texts for a proper Mass and office, which he hoped would be adopted by the universal Church.

At the beginning of the nineteenth century, the Apostolic See first approved the liturgical context by which the Immaculate Heart of the Virgin Mary is given due honour. Pope Pius VII instituted the feast of the Most Pure Heart of Mary, to be celebrated in a devout and holy way by all the dioceses and religious congregations which had requested it. Later, Pope Pius IX added the proper Office and Mass. But the ardent zeal and hope, which had arisen even in the seventeenth century and had grown day by day, that this feast should be given greater solemnity and be extended to the whole Church, was graciously fulfilled by Pope Pius XII in the year 1942, during the Second World War. In 1942, the twenty-fifth anniversary of Fatima, Pope Pius XII consecrated the world to the Immaculate Heart of Mary. That same year, he assigned the feast day to 22 August, the octave of the Assumption. On 4 May 1944, he extended the Feast of the Immaculate Heart of Mary to the Universal Church. Pope Pius XII first consecrated the Church and the world to the Immaculate Heart of Mary on 31 October and again, solemnly, on 8 December 1942. With the liturgical reforms of the Second Vatican Council, the memorial of the Immaculate Heart of Mary was transferred to the Saturday following the feast of the Sacred Heart of Jesus.

St John Eudes writes as follows of the Immaculate Heart of
Our Lady:

> The first foundation and the primary source of the devotion
> to the most holy Heart of Mary is the adorable Heart of the
> Eternal Father and His unfathomable love for the Blessed
> Mother of His Only-begotten Son. This infinite love induced
> our Heavenly Father to give us many beautiful images and
> figures of the most worthy Heart of His holy Mother.
>
> God the Father, to whom we assign by appropriation the
> creation of the world, together with the establishment and
> fulfilment of the Old Law, was pleased to foreshadow, in
> every part of the universe and in all the mysteries, sacrifices
> and ceremonies of the Old Testament, His only Son
> through whom He created and willed to renew all things.
> Likewise, the Eternal Father lovingly prefigured, both in
> the visible world and in the rites of the Mosaic Law, Mary,
> the woman chosen from all eternity to be the Mother of
> the adorable Redeemer. St John Damascene says that the
> earthly paradise, Noah's ark, the burning bush, the Tables
> of the Law, the Ark of the Covenant, the golden vessel
> containing the manna, the golden candlesticks in the
> Tabernacle, the table with the loaves of proposition,
> Aaron's rod, the furnace of Babylon, were all figures of the
> incomparable Virgin Mary.
>
> The Eternal Father did not content Himself with prefigur-
> ing the person of His Son Jesus in His prototypes, Abel,
> Noah, Melchisedech, Isaac, Jacob, Moses, Aaron, Joshua,
> Samson, Job, David and many other holy persons who lived
> under the Old Law, which preceded His Son's appearance
> on earth. God also wished to give us several beautiful
> representations of His mysteries in detail, such as His
> divine espousal of human nature in the Incarnation, His
> Passion, Death, Resurrection and Ascension.
>
> In like manner, God the Father was not satisfied to
> foreshadow and represent the person of the Mother of His
> Beloved Son merely in the person of Mary, sister of Moses,

in the Prophetess Deborah, wise Abigail, chaste and generous Judith, beautiful and compassionate Esther, and many other valiant women. Beyond this, the Eternal Father designed to entrust to us special pictures and images of the mysteries and qualities of His incomparable Mother, her virtues and even the more noble faculties of her virginal body. Several passages of Sacred Scripture reveal these pictures, especially the twenty-fourth chapter of Ecclesiasticus, and the Canticle of Canticles, where her Immaculate Conception is represented by the lily growing among thorns without being wounded by them. But above all else, Our Heavenly Father has willed to place before our eyes a wealth of beautiful figures and marvellous representations of Mary's most holy Heart. He has done this to show us how much He values and cherishes this lovable Heart and because the rare and wondrous perfections that fill it are well-nigh innumerable and can be represented and described only through a great number of figures and symbolic pictures.[4]

5 June: Our Lady of Help

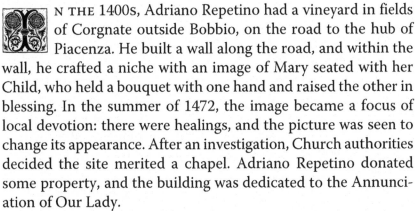 N THE 1400s, Adriano Repetino had a vineyard in fields of Corgnate outside Bobbio, on the road to the hub of Piacenza. He built a wall along the road, and within the wall, he crafted a niche with an image of Mary seated with her Child, who held a bouquet with one hand and raised the other in blessing. In the summer of 1472, the image became a focus of local devotion: there were healings, and the picture was seen to change its appearance. After an investigation, Church authorities decided the site merited a chapel. Adriano Repetino donated some property, and the building was dedicated to the Annunciation of Our Lady.

On 5 June 1611 miracles resumed. The picture was found covered in sweat, and healings multiplied. The bishop named the wonder-working image the Blessed Virgin of Help. A larger, finer church, begun in 1621, was finally consecrated on 13 July 1738,

and construction continued into the 1800s. Built over the old, the newer shrine houses the processional statue of Our Lady of Help, modelled on the miraculous fresco in the old shrine below.

In thanksgiving for her protection during World War II, the town of Bobbio named Our Lady of Help its principal patron in 1947, when the image was officially crowned. In 1970 Pope Paul VI elevated the church to the rank of Minor Basilica. The shrine celebrates May as Mary's month, closing the events on the evening of May 31 with a solemn procession through Bobbio, where all the churches are lit up and open for the occasion. On 5 June, anniversary of the miracles of 1611, the shrine celebrates the Feast of Our Lady of Help with a solemn Mass.[5]

6 June: Our Lady of China

UR LADY OF CHINA appeared near Beijing, in a village named Tong Lu. A Poor Mission was started there by the Vincentian Fathers. It was perhaps the poorest place in the whole region, formerly called "the place of beggars". In 1900, there were some seven hundred Christians gathered about the little hamlet. However, the anti-colonialist and anti-Christian members of the Boxer Rebellion tormented China from the 2 November 1899 to the 7 September 1901. They had many political issues but they also opposed religion and often attacked the missions. They sacked the foreign embassies and committed so many atrocities that the Alliance of the Eight Nations, which included the United States of America mobilized twenty-thousand armed troops to defeat the rebels. Nevertheless, during their activity in 1900, ten thousand rebels attacked the small impoverished village of Dong Lu.

While they fired their weapons on the frightened crowds of Christians, suddenly the aggressors began to fire into the air. When they saw that their attack was not giving the expected result, they stopped. It was then that the people saw in the sky a vision of the Virgin Mary, surrounded by a resplendent light, together with Saint Michael the Archangel and his hosts. The rebels, to their great surprise and dismay, were driven out of the village by Saint Michael. Grateful for the protection received by Our Lady, the inhabitants of the village built a beautiful church in her honour. At the time, the pastor had a painting that depicted the Virgin dressed in the imperial garb of the Dowager Empress Tzi-His, while Baby Jesus wore precious imperial attire. The painting was hung in the church of Dong Lu where pilgrims began to venerate it in 1924; this image was to be officially approved with the name of Our Lady of China. It was blessed by Pope Pius XI in 1928, in response to the requests presented by the Synod of Chinese Bishops that was held in Shanghai in 1927, the first national conference of bishops of the country.

The little church was recognized in 1932 by Pope Pius XI as an official Marian Shrine. In 1941 Pope Pius XII proclaimed the second Sunday of May as the special feast day of Our Lady of China and approved its insertion into the liturgical calendar.[6] The Tong Lu church was completely destroyed by Japanese bombs during the Second World War, or by the Chinese Communists, but the picture of Our Lady of China remains intact because only a copy of the picture was used in the church. The original was hidden in the wall behind the copy, and this was recovered and found intact. It is now in possession of Chinese priests who carry out their activities in secret.

As recently as 23 May 1995, Our Lady appeared again. Over 30,000 Catholics from the unofficial (underground) Church had gathered for Mass at the Donglu Shrine, on the vigil of the Feast of Our Lady, Help of Christians. There were four bishops of the unofficial Church concelebrating the Mass and nearly 100 unofficial priests standing in the open field. Suddenly, during the opening prayer and again during the consecration, the people observed the sun spinning from right to left, similar to the phenomenon observed at Fatima. The centre of the sun was covered by a sacred Host, from which shone rays of various colours. Within minutes, the sun changed colour, first yellow, then red, blue, violet, orange

and other hues. orange, Subsequently. the people saw diverse
apparitions in the nucleus of the sun: the Holy Cross, the Holy
Family, Our Lady of China and the Holy Eucharist. At times the
sun approached the crowd and then it retreated. The phenomenon
lasted approximately twenty minutes.

Prayer

Hail, Holy Mary, Mother of Our Lord Jesus Christ, Mother of all
nations and all people. You are the special heavenly Mother of
the Chinese people. Teach us your way of total obedience to God's
will. Help us to live our lives true to our faith. Fill our hearts with
burning love for God and each other. Stir up in our youth an
unconditional giving of self to the service of God. We call on your
powerful intercession for peace, reconciliation and unity among
believers and the conversion of the unbelievers in China and
throughout the world, for God's mercy is our only hope. Our Lady
of China, Mother of Jesus, hear our petitions and pray for us.
Amen.

7 June: Our Lady of the Valley

UR LADY OF THE VALLEY or Marienthal, as the monastery is called, is located on the north bank of the Rhine
River in Germany, not far from from Mainz. According
to legend, someone in the early years of the thirteenth century
placed a wooden statue of the Blessed Virgin in the recess of a
hollow tree—the statue represented Our Lady of Sorrows, with
the wounded Body of Christ from the Cross held in her arms.

Soon the people of the neighbourhood came to pray before
the little statue framed by the niche of the tree, and reports began
to circulate of cures obtained through the intercession of Our
Lady. One day a blind man came to pray before the image. He
regained his sight. The story of this outstanding favour quickly
spread far and wide and pilgrimages began to come to Marienthal
from all parts of Germany.

Shortly thereafter people erected a church—probably in 1225—and in it enshrined the statue. As the fame of the place grew, the grateful recipients of Mary's favours began to speak of the statue as Our Lady of Marienthal. Later a much larger church was built and the statue was transferred to it. Our Lady of the Valley, Marienthal is still a place of renowned pilgrimage, and the Franciscans look after the shrine.[7]

8 June: Our Lady, Seat of Wisdom

EAT OF WISDOM means Temple or Throne of Wisdom. This name is most appropriate to Mary, for Wisdom is a Scriptural name of Our Lord. In the Books of Wisdom of the Old Testament all the beautiful things which are said of Wisdom apply to a Divine Person. Wisdom in these Books is not a mere abstract concept or figurative expression, but the Eternal Word, the Second Person of the Most Holy Trinity. When, therefore, we see an image of Mary with the Infant Jesus in her arms or seated on her knee, we have an answer to the question— why is Mary called the Seat of Wisdom? "Wisdom has built herself a house," says the Holy Spirit in Sacred Scripture. This house, this temple of Wisdom, was, and ever is, Mary.

The phrase *Sedes Sapientiae*, which was characterized in the 11th and 12th centuries, by St Peter Damian and Guibert de Nogent as likening Mary to the Throne of Solomon, refers to her status as a vessel of the Incarnation, carrying the Holy Child. In June 2014, a statue of Our Lady, Seat of Wisdom, created by the renowned English sculptor Peter Eugene Ball, was been given to Merton College, Oxford, to celebrate its 750th anniversary.

When Jesus Christ, Who is the Second Person of the Blessed Trinity, the Eternal Wisdom of the Father, took up His dwelling in Mary, He made Her His Temple when He became Man. While He was a little Baby, seated on His Mother's knee, she was in literal truth His throne and temple. We, too, each one of us, are temples of Wisdom, "temples of the Holy Spirit," as St Paul says. Wisdom is one of the Seven Gifts of the Holy Spirit.

Every time we receive Holy Communion, we become the throne or temple of Our Lord in a most real, physical way; each one of us is then really and truly a "Seat of Wisdom," a throne or temple of Jesus.

"Wisdom has built herself a house." "He Who created me rested in my tabernacle." She is the "Wise Virgin." Nevertheless heavenly wisdom is very different from worldly wisdom. Worldly wisdom teaches us to seek after the "good" things of this life—money, position, power, pleasure. Heavenly Wisdom, on the contrary, teaches us to hold all these material goods as inferior to the good of the soul, to eternal life. Happy we are if we always have recourse to Mary, the Seat of Wisdom, and thus make it, as it were, as sure as possible for us to act on the principles of heavenly wisdom!

How much must Mary have learned from Jesus, the Eternal Wisdom of the Father, during all those years she lived with Him in such close and tender intimacy? The secrets of His Kingdom in Heaven and on earth, His Church, the Mysteries of Faith, the Sacraments, grace, the world of souls, the future of the Church, Her share in His work and Kingdom—all these she learned. He, "the true Light, which enlightens every man who comes into this world", was unveiled to her as never to a creature before or since. Of her could be said what God said of His servant Abraham: "Can I hide from Abraham what I am about to do?" No wise and learned doctor of the Church ever had such light as Mary, the Seat of Wisdom, on all the wonders of the Kingdom of God. She is ever ready to share Her wisdom with the least of us; we have only to ask Her, and She will give us of the treasures of Her wisdom.

Prayer

O God, infinitely wise, in order to raise fallen man you decreed that the Virgin Mary should be the dwelling place of your Wisdom. Through her intercession may we avoid the spirit of pride and, following her example, serve you with a true spirit of humility.

9 June: Our Lady of Grace

 IGH UP IN the Sabine Mountains of Italy, at Mentorella, about 65 kilometres southeast of Rome, stands the ancient and venerable shrine of Our Lady, Mother of Grace. The place and shrine of Mentorella are considered sacred because as a tradition tells us at the great cliff just behind the shrine, the miraculous conversion of Placid, an officer in the army of Trajan, who was later to be called St Eustace, took place. He beheld there, it is said, Our Lord crucified between the antlers of a great stag, which as a huntsman he had pursued.

The Shrine of Our Lady of Mentorella, Mother of Grace, was built about a thousand years ago though various religious objects of religion contained there are much older. The statue of Our Lady encased in glass and placed upon the marble baldachino of the main altar, dates back at least to the twelfth century. Mentorella's greatest claim to renown lies in the fact that the shrine is a place of pilgrimage and of special devotion to the Blessed Mother of God. The original church was built by Constantine and consecrated by Pope St Sylvester. The seventeenth century Jesuit scholar Father Anthanasius Kircher, believed that Mentorella was one of the 12 abbeys founded by St Benedict and that he lived in the adjacent cave for up to two years.

In 1857 Pope Bl Pius IX placed Mentorella under the care of the Congregation of the Resurrection. In 1864, the Holy Father ceded the Sanctuary of Mentorella to the Congregation of the Resurrection in perpetuity.

The shrine acquired greater fame as the secret hermitage of Pope St John Paul II, which he had already visited before he was elected Pope. After his election, the first place to which he travelled, on 29 October 1978, was Mentorella. He spoke these words to those who had come out to greet him:

> From the opening of the Second Vatican Council, I have had the opportunity of staying in Rome several times, both for the work of the Council and for other tasks entrusted

to me by Pope Paul VI. On the occasion of these stays in Rome, I have often visited the sanctuary of Our Lady of Mentorella. This place, hidden among the mountains, has particularly fascinated me. From it, one's eyes can range over and admire the magnificent view of the Italian landscape. I came here again a few days before the last Conclave. And if today I have wished to return, it is for various reasons, which I will set forth now.

We read in the Gospel of St Luke that Mary, after the Annunciation, went to the hill country to visit her kinswoman Elizabeth. When she arrived at Ain-Karin, she put her whole soul into the words of the canticle which the Church recalls every day in Vespers: "Magnificat anima mea Dominum"—"My soul magnifies the Lord". I wanted to come here, among these mountains, to sing the "Magnificat" in Mary's footsteps.

This is a place in which man opens to God in a special way. A place where, far from everything, but also at the same time close to nature, one can speak confidentially to God himself. One feels within one what is man's personal call. And man must glorify God the Creator and Redeemer; he must, in some way, become the voice of the whole of creation in order to say, in its name, "Magnificat". He must announce the "magnalia Dei", the great works of God, and, at the same time, express himself in this sublime relationship with God, because in the visible world only he can do so. Therefore the Pope, as the Vicar of Christ on earth, wishes in the first place to unite with all those who strain towards union with Christ in prayer, wherever they may be: as a Bedouin in the steppe, or the Carmelites or Cistercians in deep enclosure, or the sick on a hospital bed in the sufferings of the death agony, or a person in activity, in the fullness of life, or oppressed and humiliated individuals everywhere.[8]

10 June: Our Lady of Cranganore

N KERALA, INDIA stands the church and the shrine of Our Lady of Cranganore, which it is asserted was built by one of the three Kings who visited the Divine Child and His Blessed Mother. India was one of the countries that had the privilege of receiving the light of Faith at the dawn of Christianity.

History relates that St Thomas the Apostle came to India at Cranganore (Kodungallur) in 52 AD. There the Christians are still known as St Thomas' Faithful. Kerala, as the place is also known, is cut off by the mountain ranges from the rest of India, and has held firmly to the Faith, regardless of the rest of the continent. The deep spirituality of the Catholics evidences their great love for the Mother of God; Nala-bat as the country is also called, may be translated as Mary's country, Mary's namesake. It is believed that when St Thomas came to Cranganore, he brought with him a picture of Our Lady, painted by St Luke; this was lost after St Thomas' martyrdom, but later discovered in a cave at Little Mount, Madras, near the scene of his death.

In 1498 when the Portuguese arrived in Cranganore, they were surprised to find so many churches dedicated to Our Lady. St Francis Xavier found the people of Cranganore very strong in faith and devoted to Mary; he spared no pains to encourage their devotion to the Mother of God. One may wonder why devotion to Mary took root and blossomed so strongly in Kerala. Perhaps the reason for such spontaneous devotion is to be found in the position of the mother in the Hindu family. For while love, obedience, devotion and dependence on one's mother are natural to all peoples and nations, in Cranganore the exalted position of the mother assumes singular, if not unique, proportions. The mother is everything in the family; to depend on her is a deep-rooted tendency of all children in Kerala. Much more than the father, the mother is the breadwinner of the family. She owns, buys, and sells property and governs the house without any consultation with the father; he may frequently be away, but she always remains at home in the house. Her brothers have no right to property, only a living allowance and accommodations. Now this matriarchal system has been carefully guarded by the majority of Hindus. It lies at the very heart of traditional way of life in Kerala; a time-honoured custom which has helped to give Marian devotion an easy welcome and speedy growth.

11 June: Our Lady of Awaiting

HE VILLAGE OF MAGHDOUCHE is inhabited by 5000 Melkite Catholics. It is located on a hill south east of the Biblical city of Sidon where Jesus often preached. At the entrance of the village, there is a high tower with a statue of the Virgin on the top; this is the sanctuary of Our Lady Of Mantara. The centre of the sanctuary is a natural cave, where according to tradition, Our Lady waited for her Son Jesus Christ while he was preaching in Sidon, a pagan Phoenician town where Jewish woman could not go. The old Roman road from Jerusalem to Sidon passed through Caesarea Philippi (now called Marjayoun) and through the village of Maghdouche. That is why it was called Mantara which means "awaiting".

Emperor Constantine's wife Helena replaced Astarte's shrine there with one to the Holy Mother, donating to it an icon and altar furnishings. Three centuries later, after takeover by an intolerant Arab ruler, Christians sealed up the cave and fled Maghdouché. The people of Maghdouché did not return to their ancestral home despite the arrival of the Crusaders in Sidon; these latter spent most of the 12th and 13th centuries in the shadow of Magdhdouché without ever suspecting the sacred cave's existence even though they built a small fort, called La Franche Garde, within metres of the hidden entrance to the cave.

In 1683, descendants of the exiles returned to their homeland under the more tolerant Prince Fakhreddin II (1572–1635). On 8 September 1721, when a goat fell through a gap in the porous limestone, its young herder made a rope from vine twigs, tied it to a tree, and followed the animal into the hole, but the rope broke. The boy fell into the darkness, where eventually he made out the golden glimmer of an icon of the Madonna and Child. On seeing the image, the Melkite Catholic clergy recognized it as St Helen's icon. Christians now celebrate its rediscovery annually on 8 September, Feast of Our Lady's Nativity. A cathedral was added to the site in 1860 and a modern tower topped with a bronze statue in the 1960s. On 11 June 1911, some 400 people saw a silent, luminous apparition of the Madonna and Child near the cave. Our Lady of Awaiting is invoked for the healing of eye diseases and the protection of children, so the shrine is a popular site for infant baptisms.

12 June: Our Lady of Akita

 N THE JAPANESE town of Yuzawadai located less than 90 miles from the city of Sendai, where a tsunami took place on 11 March 2011, is the site of the miraculous statue of Our Lady of Akita and the apparitions of Our Lady that took place there. A few pious women known as the Institute of the Handmaids of the Holy Eucharist were leading a quiet, hidden life of prayer in Yuzawadai just outside of Akita, when they welcomed into their novitiate Sister Agnes Katsuko Sasagawa, who was then 42 years old and a convert from Buddhism. When she entered on 12 May 1973, Agnes was totally and incurably deaf, however she was blessed with various mystical favours; soon this convent would become so well-known that their little chapel would attract pilgrims from around the world.

The extraordinary events began on 12 June 1973, when Sr Agnes Sasagawa saw brilliant rays emanating from the tabernacle as she knelt in prayer. The same thing happened again the next two days. Sixteen days later, on 28 June 1973, a cross-shaped wound appeared on the inside of Sister Agnes' left hand. It bled profusely and was very painful. On 6 July, Sr Agnes heard a voice coming from the statue of the Blessed Virgin Mary in the chapel where she was praying. The statue was carved from a single block of wood from a Katsura tree and is three feet tall. Our Lady spoke to Sister Agnes and asked her to pray for the reparation of sins and to consecrate herself to the Eucharistic Lord. This was only the beginning of many mysterious happenings occurring with the statue. On the same day, a few of the sisters noticed drops of blood flowing from the right hand of the statue. On four occasions, this blood flow was repeated. The wound on the hand of the statue remained until 29 September, when it disappeared. On that day, the sisters noticed the statue had then begun to "sweat", especially on the forehead and neck. Two years later, on 4 January 1975, the statue of Our Lady began to weep. It continued to weep at intervals for the next 6 years and eight months. It wept on 101 occasions.

Including the message of 6 July, Sister Agnes Sasagawa received three messages from Our Lady of Akita. The last of them is chilling in light of the recent events in Japan. The Blessed Mother said:

> As I told you, if men do not repent and better themselves, the Father will inflict a terrible punishment on all human- ity. It will be a punishment greater than the deluge, such as one will never have seen before. Fire will fall from the sky and will wipe out a great part of humanity, the good as well as the bad, sparing neither priests nor faithful. The survivors will find themselves so desolate that they will envy the dead. The only arms which will remain for you will be the Rosary and the Sign left by my Son. Each day, recite the prayers of the Rosary. With the Rosary, pray for the Pope, the bishops and the priests. The work of the devil will infiltrate even into the Church in such a way that one will see cardinals opposing cardinals, and bishops against other bishops. The priests who venerate me will be scorned and opposed by their fellow priests. The Church and her altars will be vandalized. The Church will be full of those who accept compromises and the demon will press many priests and consecrated souls to leave the service of the

Lord. The demon will rage especially against souls consecrated to God. The thought of the loss of so many souls is
the cause of my sadness. If sins increase in number and
gravity, there will no longer be pardon for them.

In his pastoral letter dated 22 April 1984, Bishop John Ito, the
Ordinary of the Diocese of Niigata, wrote a pastoral letter in
which he approved the apparitions In the following terms:

After long prayer and mature reflection, I hand down the
following conclusions in my position as Bishop of Niigata:

1. After the investigation conducted up to the present day,
I recognize the supernatural character of a series of
mysterious events concerning the statue of the Holy
Mother Mary which is found in the convent of the Institute
of the Handmaids of the Sacred Heart of Jesus in the Holy
Eucharist at Yuzawadai, Soegawa, Akita. I do not find in
these events any elements which are contrary to Catholic
faith and morals.

2. Consequently, I authorize, throughout the entire diocese, the veneration of the Holy Mother of Akita, while
awaiting that the Holy See publishes definitive judgment
on this matter. And I ask that it be remembered that even
if the Holy See later publishes a favourable judgment with
regard to the events of Akita, it is a question only of a
private Divine revelation. Christians are bound to believe
only content of public Divine revelation (closed after the
death of the last Apostle) which contains all that is necessary for salvation. Nevertheless, the Church, until now, has
equally made much of private Divine revelations as they
fortify the faith.[9]

Four years later, on 20 June 1988, during Bishop Ito's visit to Rome,
at the Congregation for the Doctrine of the Faith His Eminence
Cardinal Joseph Ratzinger did not give any judgment on the
reliability or credibility of the messages of Our Lady. According to
the transcription of the meeting, he simply affirmed that "there
are no objections to the conclusions of the pastoral letter".[10]

13 June: Our Lady of the Blessed Sacrament

ATHER LEO HEINRICHS was born on the Feast of the Assumption, 1867, in Oestrich, now a part of Erkelenz, Westphalia, Germany and given the name of Joseph. When he joined the Franciscans, their friary had left Germany as a result of the persecution under Otto von Bismarck. The friars had emigrated to Paterson, New Jersey, and Heinrichs took the name of Brother Leo before being ordained a priest on the Feast of the Immaculate Conception, 1890.

Father Heinrichs served in various positions in the New York and New Jersey area between 1891 and 1907. When he was pastor at Paterson, smallpox broke out and he was known to spend many hours at a nearby "pest house" tending to the sick and the dying. In September 1907, the Provincial Chapter appointed him pastor of St Elizabeth's parish in Denver, Colorado where he arrived on 23 September. He had only 5 months to live and had received permission to leave for Germany to visit his family who had not seen him for over twenty years. However, he had a class of children preparing for their first Holy Communion and he was determined to give them First Communion on 7 June 1908.

A week before his death, Father Leo told the Young Ladies' Sodality: "If I had my choice of a place where I would die, I would choose to die at the feet of the Blessed Virgin."[11] On 23 February 1908, this martyr for the Faith was due to offer the 8 am Sunday Mass at St Elizabeth of Hungary church but asked to switch to the earlier Mass so he could attend a meeting. Thus he the 6 am Mass that morning, known as the working man's Mass. Among those at Mass that morning was fifty-year-old Giuseppe Alia, who had recently immigrated from Italy. Alia arrived before Mass and was seated in the third row, in front of the pulpit.

During Communion, Alia knelt at the Communion rail and received the Host. Then, however, he spat it into his hand and flung it at Father Leo's face. The Host fell to the floor as Alia drew his gun aiming at Father Heinrich's heart. As an altar boy screamed the man opened fire. The dying priest exclaimed, "My God, my God!" before falling to the floor. Before he died, he placed the ciborium on the step of Our Lady's altar, and managed to place two fallen Hosts back into the ciborium before strength left him and with his last bit of strength he pointed to the spilled Hosts that he was now too weak to pick up. Rose Fisher, an eyewitness, reported that Father Leo died smiling, at the foot of the Blessed Virgin's altar just as he had always wanted. Father Wulstan Workman, who had switched with Father Leo for the later Mass, administered the Last Rites. Father Wulstan told the Denver Post, "I would have been killed and he would be alive now. There is one way to solve the affair that I can see, and that is that God chose the better man."

Father Leo's body was transported to New Jersey for burial in a Franciscan cemetery. Guiseppe Alia attempted to flee the Church, but E. J. Quigley, a conductor for the Denver & Rio Grande Railroad, caught him. Then, Patrolman Daniel Cronin, an off-duty Denver police officer placed him under arrest and took him into custody. At the police station, Alia boasted of his anarchist ideology:

> I went over there because I have a grudge against all priests in general. They are all against the workingman. I went to the communion rail because I could get a better shot. I did not care whether he was a German priest or any other kind of priest. They are all in the same class ... I shot him, and my only regret is that I could not shoot the whole bunch of priests in the church.[12]

Alia was tried, convicted, and sentenced to death by hanging within weeks of the shooting. Shortly before the execution, a Franciscan priest from St Elizabeth's visited Alia in prison. Infuriated, Alia cursed and swore at him. Alia never expressed any remorse, and, despite the pleas of the friars at St Elizabeth's, he was hanged at the Colorado State Penitentiary in Canon City. Alia's last words, reportedly, were "Death to the priests!"

The coroner discovered that Father Leo secretly practiced an extreme form of mortification. Around the priest's waist the skin was calloused and scarred, but showed no sign of infection. None of his fellow priests had any idea of Father Leo's self-inflicted penances, which he adopted perhaps to help him master his quick temper. When the friars entered Father Leo's room after his death, they also found that he slept on a wooden door.

In Germany, Erkelenz has named a street after Fr Leo Heinrichs. The process of beatification has been open in Rome since 1938 and his tomb in Totowa, Holy Sepulchre Catholic Cemetery, remains a place of veneration. Saint Elizabeth of Hungary still stands, and also serves the Russian Catholic community in Denver.

Mary is indeed Our Lady of the Blessed Sacrament. Through Mary all God's gifts come to us, especially that greatest gift, the Holy Eucharist. The Body of Our Lord, which becomes present on the altar during Holy Mass; which is given to us in Holy Communion; which remains in the tabernacle day and night, is the same Body that was born of the Virgin Mary. We cannot separate the Mother from her Child. We cannot separate Our Lady from Our Lord in the Holy Eucharist. We honour Mary along with her Son; we stand by our Eucharistic King and the Lady who stands first in His court.

14 June: Our Lady of the Trellis

 N 14 JUNE 1234, at Lille in northern France, 53 cripples were cured upon praying before the statue of Our Lady of the Trellis, installed behind a latticework fence in St Peter's Collegiate Church. A procession, founded in 1270 by Countess Margaret of Flanders, in honour of the statue of the Virgin Mary is held annually on the second Sunday after Pentecost to commemorate the miracles.[13] Saved during the destruction of St Peter's Church in the French Revolution, the statue was later moved to St Catherine's Church.

Devotion to Our Lady of the Trellis revived in the mid-1800s, and a grand neo-Gothic church arose in her honour, where the statue was installed in 1872 and canonically crowned in 1874. After the theft of the original in 1959, sculptor Marie Madeleine Weerts carved the image now displayed in Lille's Catholic Cathedral, the Basilica of Notre-Dame de la Treille.

15 June: Our Lady of the Taper

HE ORIGINAL IMAGE of Our Lady is believed to have originated in Arras, where Flemish wool traders established links with the market town of Cardigan. According to tradition, a statue of Our Lady of the Taper was found on the Welsh coast, standing near the sea. It was a simple little statue of the Blessed Virgin, her Son on her arm, with a burning taper in her other hand. Devotion to the image of Our Lady of the Taper began immediately. In 1158 a special chapel was finally built to accommodate Our Lady of the Taper, as the people began to understand that the Virgin Mary wished it to be there. The shrine is known to have been a place of pilgrimage long before the twelfth century.

The first church was part of a Benedictine Priory, and the monks lived there until 1538 when the infamous Oliver Cromwell had the monks evicted and destroyed the ancient statue, as he had ordered all images of Our Lady should be sent to London to be destroyed, and the devotion was unfortunately all but forgotten.

An examination of the statue by Bishop Barlow was made on 16 March 1538, and stated:

> the image now situated in the church of Cardigan which is used for a great pilgrimage to this present day was found standing upon the river Teifi and her son upon her lap and the same taper burning in her hand. The said image was carried to Christ Church of Cardigan and the image would not tarry there but was found three or four times in the place where is now built the Church of Our Lady, and the

> taper burning in her hand which continued burning the
> space of nine years without wasting.

As Bishop Barlow noted, several times the statue of Our Lady of the Taper was brought into Christ Church, Cardigan, but always it mysteriously returned to the seashore.

Bishop Petit sought to restore the shrine in the nineteenth century, and Dom Vincent Dapre, OSB, was commissioned to create a new statue using the only known description of Our Lady of the Taper, written by an Anglican, the Reverend Silas M. Harris. In 1956 the new state was placed in Cardigan as thousands of the faithful gathered to witness in a great procession. That statue, however, was not robust enough to withstand the years,

On 18 May 1986, the Church of Our Lady of the Taper, was inaugurated as the National Shrine for Catholics in Wales. In order to mark this occasion in a fitting way, it was decided to commission a new statue. Hence, Mother Concordia, a Benedictine nun, cast the statue in bronze and Pope St John Paul II blessed the first taper candle that was to be lit in the hand of Our Lady of the Taper. He then signed a Letter affirming that the medieval Shrine of Our Lady of Cardigan was the National Shrine of Our Lady for Wales by the solemn placing there of a new statue of Our Lady of the Taper.[14]

16 June: Our Lady of Rocamadour

ROCAMADOUR (Rocamador in Occitan) is a commune in the Lot department in southwestern France. According to the founding legend, Rocamadour is named after the founder of the ancient sanctuary, Saint Amator, identified with the Biblical Zaccheus, the tax collector of Jericho mentioned in Luke 19:1–10, and the husband of St Veronica, who wiped Jesus' face on the way to Calvary. Driven out of Palestine by persecution, St Amadour and St Veronica embarked in a fragile skiff and, guided by an angel, landed on the coast of Aquitaine, where they met Bishop St Martial, another disciple of Christ who was preaching the Gospel in the south-west of Gaul.

After journeying to Rome, where he witnessed the martyrdoms of St Peter and St Paul, Amadour, having returned to France, on the death of his spouse, withdrew to a wild spot in Quercy where he built a chapel in honour of the Blessed Virgin, near which he died a little later. This site became a sanctuary, but after the fervour of the Middle Ages, Rocamadour, as a result of war and the French Revolution, had become almost deserted. Nevertheless it remained in the minds and hearts of the explorers of the New World.

Jacques Cartier is considered by Canadians not only as the "discoverer", but also one of the founders of Canada, at the start of the French occupation of three-quarters of the continent. On 16 May 1535, Jacques Cartier took a fleet of three ships, the *Grande Hermine*, the *Petite Hermine* and the Hermérillon, and left for New France on a mission from the King of France to complete the discovery of the Western Lands. Locked in the ice of the St Lawrence river in mid-February of 1536, Jacques Cartier and his companions were threatened by a deadly epidemic of scurvy. In the crypt of the church of Saint Francis of Assisi, the men invoked the Blessed Virgin Mary under her title of Our Lady of Rocamadour, and then they made a pilgrimage with Our Lady's image placed on the branches of a tree.

Cartier then met some North American Indians who explained to the men how to brew the herb tea with the needles and bark of the aneda tree, a Canadian white cedar tree.[15] After losing 25 men from the epidemic, all the crew members were cured by drinking this tea. Jacques Cartier himself admitted to "a true and clear miracle". The crypt became therefore the Canadian shrine of Our Lady of Rocamadour, and became the first destination of Marian pilgrimages in Canada. Then, on 31 May 1998, Our Lady of Rocamadour became the patron of the parish of Limoilou in Quebec City. In 2006, a young French priest from Rocamadour (France) decided to offer an ex-voto to the Cardinal of Quebec City. At present the two shrines, separated by an ocean, are joined by fraternity.

17 June: Our Lady of the Forest

 RITTANY IS AN AREA noted for its pilgrimages, and that of Folgoët is one of the foremost of them. In the year 1419 a church took the place of a small chapel of Our Lady in the Forest of Lesneven, and it became a famous pilgrim-shrine. In 1380 there lived near Lesneven a good old man named Solomon (Salaün). He had no one to care for him, lived alone, and did not associate with any person; he walked with his eyes to the ground, but his heart was in Heaven.

As the years went by, old and crippled as he was, he might be seen every evening hobbling to the chapel of the Blessed Virgin where he spent most of the night in prayer after the villagers had returned to the warmth and security of their own homes. He was a simple man of the woods, and here, where the chapel of Our Lady of the Forest was later built, he slept in the open under an oak tree near a fountain. Solomon loved to swing from the branches of a tree that hung over the fountain, all the while singing praise to Our Lady at the top of his voice. He begged for bread each day to obtain his meals, and in doing so he was often laughed at, jeered at and otherwise mistreated by the small boys.

One day, while the villagers were on their way to the chapel for the celebration of All Saints, they found the old man in the snow dying of exposure. They tried to help him, but it was too late for their kindness, as the old man soon died with the words "Ave Maria" on his lips. The "fool of the wood" had finally gone to his Queen in Heaven. Legend further relates that he was buried in an out-of-the-way place in Lesneven, for he had no family to mourn him.

When spring came, a snow-white lily rose from the outcast's grave, and on the delicate petals of the lily, in letters of gold, the words "Ave Maria!" could be seen. The grave was opened, and it was soon discovered that the lily had taken root in the mouth of the penniless old hermit. News of the miracle drew crowds to the scene, and a church was built to honour Our Lady of the Forest.

The grave of the simple hermit can still be seen nearby, and visited even in our day. It is marked by four simple stones.

After a chequered history, the shrine fell into decay and was destroyed by fire during the French Revolution. It was restored by the people in 1818 and the venerated image of Our Lady was brought back and crowned in 1888: it is it was made from kersanton granite. The pilgrimage has grown in popularity ever since, and has been described as follows:

> They file past, one after another, and their hearts beating in their anxious breasts, find peace once they have kissed Our Lady. Presently, carried by the arms of six or eight men, this block of stone crowned with gold will go forward into the crowd of people gathered there. Behind the colourful banners, behind the bishops giving benedictions, there she will go, Our Lady, bearing, in the name of all her beloved, the cry of all her Salaüns, of all those poor and simple folk who, in the middle of the banquet of their life, "have no more wine".[16]

18 June: Maria Taferl

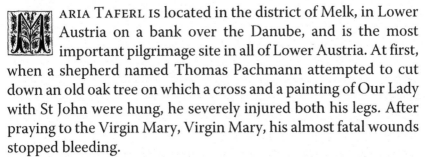 ARIA TAFERL IS located in the district of Melk, in Lower Austria on a bank over the Danube, and is the most important pilgrimage site in all of Lower Austria. At first, when a shepherd named Thomas Pachmann attempted to cut down an old oak tree on which a cross and a painting of Our Lady with St John were hung, he severely injured both his legs. After praying to the Virgin Mary, Virgin Mary, his almost fatal wounds stopped bleeding.

Later, in 1641, Alexander Schinnagl suffered from depression. He received from a friend, a carver of wood, a small statue of the Pietà in walnut. While he slept, in the middle of the night, he heard a voice: "Alexander, do you want to be healed? Then take my statue and bring it to Taferlberg at Marbach on the Danube, then leave it under an oak tree." The man did so, took the statue and placed it in the hollow of an oak tree there, replacing the cross which had by now become rotten. After a few days he recovered.

Between 1658 and 1661 were seen near the oak numerous apparitions of red and white figures, which, in the light of day as the darkness of the night, hovering in the air, some went to the edge of the woods. During the night the stars illuminated the statue with heavenly light and several candles burned before they appeared. Many people of all ages, even other religious confessions, witnessed these miraculous phenomena. The Bishop of Passau organized a commission of inquiry which interviewed fifty-seven people who then confirmed under oath what they had seen. Recognizing the phenomena as supernatural, in 1660 he set the first stone of the sanctuary. The church building was erected between 1660 to 1710.

The church is also a kind of information treasure chest about its pilgrims, their origins, and their number. Within it are the ex-votos of the pilgrims, who came on account of illness and were cured. The pilgrimage is still very active. The murdered Archduke Franz Ferdinand of Austria and his family lived in the nearby Artstetten Castle and is known to have regularly attended Mass at Maria Taferl. Maria Taferl became a minor basilica in 1947.

19 June: Our Lady of Phileremos

WHEN THE KNIGHTS Hospitaller of St John of Jerusalem were driven from the Holy Land by the Muslims, they eventually emigrated to the island of Rhodes in the Mediterranean in the early 14th century. There they found, on Mount Phileremos, a chapel dedicated to Mary under the title of Our Lady of Phileremos. Within the chapel was an icon of Our Lady of Phileremos, said to have painted by St Luke the Evangelist, the "Painter of the Virgin". The icon was very antique and has been in this place since time immemorial. Local tradition has handed down several accounts of different miracles attributed to Our Lady under this title.

The founder of the chapel had been a rich man, who climbed up the hill to a place where the ancient Phoenicians had built a temple to one of their pagan solar divinities, which lay in ruins. For reasons unknown to us, he climbed the hill to commit suicide. There, on this hill haunted by the demons of paganism, the desperate man was about to carry out his reprehensible plan, when "a Lady, all bathed in white light", appeared to him; and by the gentleness of her smile and the imparting of heavenly grace, the man had a complete change of heart. Converted and repentant, he chose to live on the spot where Our Lady appeared to him. Here it was that he built a chapel in her honour and enthroned in a place of veneration the icon of Our Lady that he had brought from Jerusalem.

Veneration of the icon spread quickly over the island and the population used to visit it piously. Its fame as a wonder-working image became well known all over the Aegean. As soon as the Knights arrived, they became very devoted to Our Lady of Phileremos, whose name became their war cry. They built a large monastery next to the chapel and two new chapels were added to the sanctuary by Grand Master, Pierre D'Aubusson after the siege of 1480, in thanksgiving to Our Lady of Phileremos from preserving them from the Muslim attackers. When, at length, they were finally forced off the island by the Muslims, they took their "most precious possession" with them. When the departing fleet got under way, with only a few surviving Knights aboard, no standard was hung, except one banner on the ship of the Grand Master, the banner of Our Lady of Phileremos, with these simple words: "In my misfortune, you are my hope."

20 June: Our Lady of Luxembourg

CCORDING TO PIOUS TRADITION, in 1624 a student of the Jesuit College, established in Luxemburg in 1607, went for a walk along the banks of the Alzette River which ran outside the city walls. Arriving at a place called Rocks of Crispinus, he saw in the hollow of an oak tree, a statue of the Virgin and Child. He told some of the other students, and together they took the statue and placed it on the altar in their church. The next morning it had disappeared. It was afterward found in the hollow of the same oak. Once more they carried it to the church, but it again disappeared.

Then the Jesuits decided that Our Lady wished to be honoured in that particular spot of the oak tree, so they built a chapel and enshrined the statue in it, giving it the name of Our Lady, Consoler of the Afflicted. The shrine became a centre of devotion; numerous miracles reputedly took place there, and many pilgrims visited the shrine.

During the French Revolution the Duchy of Luxembourg became involved in the struggle. In 1795 the capital was taken, all the churches desecrated and the chapel of Our Lady was totally destroyed. The statue was saved by some quick-thinking soul and hidden in the vault of the Church of the Immaculate Conception. After the Revolution was over, the statue was again available for public veneration, the church rebuilt and the image restored to it. A larger church had to be built, and today Our Lady resides in the enlarged cathedral shrine. This destination is now the site of an important annual pilgrimage to Our Lady of Consolation, each year during Eastertide, and it has been attended by the Grand Ducal Family for several generations.[17]

21 June: Our Lady of Matarieh

N THE THIRTEENTH CENTURY, devotion started at a spring in Matarieh five miles northeast of Cairo where the Holy Family is said to have stayed while on their flight to Egypt.[18] The miraculous fountain is said to have been started by Our Lady's prayers, when she fled to Egypt with Saint Joseph, her spouse, and the Divine Child, to escape Herod's wicked designs. St Peter Chrysologus explained that this journey was so arduous that the very angels were struck with wonder when they beheld the Saviour required to make it.

It is held by tradition that at Matarieh the Blessed Virgin, Our Lady of Matarieh, washed the swaddling clothes of the Infant Jesus and bathed him. It still displays miraculous powers. The city is by some called the City of the Fountain in remembrance of Our Lord Jesus Christ, who used it as a bath. The spring had already been famous among the ancient Egyptians, who believed that the Sun-god, Ra, bathed his face there when he rose for the first time. People still call it the Holy Fountain, and at the Feast of the Epiphany a vast number of people are said to flock there from all nations to wash themselves in its water.[19]

22 June: Our Lady of Ta' Pinu

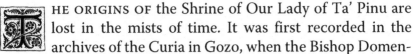 HE ORIGINS OF the Shrine of Our Lady of Ta' Pinu are lost in the mists of time. It was first recorded in the archives of the Curia in Gozo, when the Bishop Domenico Cubelles paid a visit to the chapel. This noted that the chapel had just been rebuilt and that it belonged to the noble family named Gentili. In 1575 the apostolic visitor Pietro Duzina was delegated by Pope Gregory XII to visit the Maltese Islands. In his pastoral visit to the church, he found that the chapel was in a very bad state. He ordered the church to be closed and demolished and its duties passed to the parish church, now the Cathedral of the Assumption of the Blessed Virgin Mary of Gozo. When demolition began the workman broke his arm while striking the first blow. This was taken as a sign that the chapel should not be demolished. The church was the only chapel on the island to survive Duzina's decree also ordering the demolition of other similar chapels. Pinu (Philip) Gauci became the procurator of the church in 1598 and its name was changed from of the Gentili to "Ta' Pinu", meaning "Of Philip". In 1611, Gauci offered money for its restoration and the chapel was rebuilt, with a stone altar erected and funds for liturgical services provided. Gauci also

commissioned the painting of the Assumption of Our Lady for the main altar which was finished in 1619 by Amadeo Perugino.

The chapel again fell into disrepair over the centuries. On 22 June 1883, Karmela Grima (aged 40) heard a woman's voice coming from it on her way home from the nearby fields: "Come, because it will be another year before you will be able to return." After Karmela knelt to pray in the chapel, the voice said, "Recite three Hail Marys in honor of the three days my body remained in the tomb" (before being assumed into heaven). Very soon the pious woman fell ill, remaining bedridden over a year without telling anyone about the voice. In 1885, she told a friend, Francesco Pinelli, who revealed that about the same time he also had heard a woman's voice, asking for devotion to the "hidden wound" of her Son from carrying the cross. When Francesco's mother was miraculously healed after praying to Our Lady of Ta' Pinu, the isolated chapel began attracting pilgrims. Soon a better building was needed, and a new church, begun in 1920, was finally consecrated in 1932.

Pope St John Paul II celebrated Mass at the shrine during his visit to the island of Gozo on 26 May 1990. On 18 April 2010, when visiting Malta, Pope Benedict XVI donated and placed a Golden Rose in front of the devotional image of Our Lady Of Ta' Pinu which was brought over from Gozo to Malta for this special occasion. The Pope invited everybody to pray to her under the title Queen of the Family. Pope St John Paul remarked:

> This morning, we celebrate our communion with the Church of every time and place, that Church of which the Blessed Virgin Mary stands out as the pre-eminent member. At this venerable Shrine of Our Lady Ta' Pinu, we give thanks to our Lord Jesus Christ for the loving presence and protection of his Virgin Mother which the Church in Malta and Gozo has experienced throughout its history. For centuries, the faithful of these islands have drawn near to Mary in prayer and have sought her loving intercession to aid them in their needs and to comfort them in their

distress. In calling Mary blessed among women, they have echoed the words of the Angel Gabriel at the Annunciation (Lk 1:28), and fulfilled the prophecy which she herself uttered to her kinswoman Elizabeth: "From this day forward all generations will call me blessed" (Lk 1:48). In a very special way, Mary has been the patroness of the Christian families of Malta and Gozo as they have sought to fulfil their unique role in God's plan for the salvation of the human race. We may be confident that with a mother's love Mary has not failed to intercede for generations of parents and children, inspiring in them that fear of the Lord which is the beginning of wisdom (cf. Ps 110:10) and accompanying them on their pilgrimage of faith.[20]

23 June: Our Lady, Cause of Our Joy

HE TITLE OF MARY CAUSE OF OUR JOY IS one of the most beautiful from the Litany of Our Lady. The sorrow brought into the world by Eve's disobedience has been changed into joy by the obedience of the New Eve, the Blessed Virgin Mary. The prophet Zechariah foretold this as he spoke God's words: "Sing and rejoice, O daughter of Zion! See, I am coming to dwell among you, says the Lord" (Zc 2:10). The angel Gabriel repeated this call to rejoice when he spoke to Mary at the Annunciation and told her she was to conceive the Messiah, the Son of God. This great joy was communicated by Mary to Elizabeth at the Visitation. At that joyful encounter, even the unborn infant John the Baptist leapt for joy in his mother's womb. Mary, on that occasion, sang the beautiful canticle of joy, the Magnificat: "My soul proclaims the greatness of the Lord; my spirit rejoices in God my Saviour."

Our Lord came into the world to bring peace and joy to the human family. At His birth, He filled the humble shepherds outside Bethlehem with joy. At His resurrection, He brought joy to the disciples, and, at His Ascension, He left the apostles in great joy. Now, from His place at the right hand of the Father, He sends joy upon the Church through the gift of the Holy Spirit, the Spirit of love and joy.

Without Jesus, who has saved us from sin and hell, there would be no joy for us, neither in this world nor in the next. Mary's consent was necessary that Jesus become our Redeemer. She cooperated in the redemption by her full and free consent to deliver Jesus to death for us. All the joys that come to us through the Divine Kingdom of Grace, the Sacraments, and the Church, pass through the hands of Mary. When we get to Heaven we shall see how her prayers, her maternal solicitude, her powerful help, followed us in every step of our lives; how she interceded for us in our sorrows that we might receive comfort and consolation; how she presented our petitions to her Son, and helped to get our prayers answered; how she saved us from temptations and falls: how she, the Star of the Sea, piloted us through countless storms and shipwrecks on the sea of life.

True joy is something deep, quiet, lasting; not fleeting, exciting, deceptive, like pleasure. It is peace of soul, contentment of heart, deep enduring satisfaction which comes when we refuse God nothing; when we are faithful to conscience, to our duty, to principles; when we make God the centre of our lives. True Joy is found only in Jesus. Only God is our True Joy. Mary is the Cause of Our Joy. She alone can make us truly happy, if we cling to her, honour her, imitate her, consecrate our lives, all our loved ones, all we have and do, all our merits to her, in her and through her. Our search for joy can be found, in the quietest and most ordinary life, if our hearts are rightly focused on God through Mary.[21]

24 June: Our Lady of Medjugorje

N 24 JUNE 1981, young Mirjana Dragicevic and Ivanka Ivanković reported seeing an apparition of the Virgin Mary at a village in what is now in Bosnia-Herzegovina. The following day another vision was reported, this time also witnessed by four other young people:, Marija Pavlović Jakov

Colo, Vicka Ivanković, and Ivan Dragicevic. The children claim that they saw an apparition on the hill Crnica (on the place called Podbrdo); the alleged apparition was a white form with a child in her arms. Surprised and scared, they did not approach. The next day at the same time four of the youths returned, and were later joined by the other two.

For several years the six visionaries reported seeing daily apparitions from the Virgin Mary. It has been reported that Our Lady of Medjugorje has been appearing daily to three of these visionaries ever since, some say that they have stopped having daily apparitions. At the time of the first alleged apparition Vicka Ivanković was sixteen years old. She claims to have prayed with Our Lady and talked to her; she also claims to have been given nine "secrets". Her "prayer mission", said to have been given by the Blessed Virgin Mary, is to pray for the sick. Vicka says that her daily apparitions have not yet stopped. Vicka claims to have received a biography of Mary's life, contained in two hand written notebooks, which Vicka has said will be published when the Blessed Virgin Mary tells her to do so. Vicka Ivanković continues to meet with pilgrims to Medjugorje, which she has done for over twenty one years. Vicka is often called "the smiling visionary" because she always has a smile filled with joy on her face.

Regarding her alleged visions, Vicka once stated:

> Before, I prayed from pure habit. Now I've turned completely to prayer. I commit my life completely to God. I feel sorry for those who do not believe in God, because Our Lady wants no one to be lost. We can help each other find the right way to God. It's up to the people to obey the messages and be converted. Great things are happening here: Our Lady is among us. She wishes to attract everyone to Her Son. That's the reason She has been coming so long and so often. Here, everyone feels the nearness and the love of God. As role model and example, Gospa (Mary) began, in January 1983, to tell me Her life story, which took over two years.

The basic message of Our Lady is: "I have come to tell the world that God exists. He is the fullness of life, and to enjoy this fullness and peace, you must return to God." Since the apparitions began in 1981, approximately 40 million people of all faiths, from all over the world, have visited Medjugorje and have left spiritually strengthened and renewed. Many bring back stories of miracles in the form of healings (of mind, body and spirit), supernatural visual signs, and deep conversions back to God.

On 17 March 2010, Pope Benedict XVI set up a commission to examine the apparitions of Medjugorje, and this commission concluded its work on 17 January 2014. It seems that the commission noted a very clear difference between the beginning of the phenomenon and its subsequent development, and therefore decided to issue two distinct votes on the two different phases: the first seven presumed appearances between 24 June 24 and 3 July 1981, and all that happened later. The first seven appearances seem genuine, but what happened later may not have been. After examining the report of the commission and the opinions of the members of the Congregation for the Doctrine of the Faith, the Pope decided to entrust to the Polish Archbishop Mgr Henryk Hoser a special mission of the Holy See to acquire more in-depth knowledge of the pastoral situation. It is possible that the parish at Medjugorje could be made into a pontifical sanctuary. By summer 2017 the Polish Archbishop will deliver the results of his work with which the Pope will make a decision.[22]

25 June: Our Lady of the Little Well

WENTY-THREE YEAR OLD Franz Forell brought to Wemding, Bavaria, a statuette of the Virgin Mary from Rome. He placed her on a pedestal at his house and it soon became an object of veneration by many faithful. A Protestant gentleman, living in Wemding, near the house of Forell, was suddenly cured from terrible headaches when he invoked the help of Mary. Soon the news spread and and a intense flux of pilgrimages began to the house of young Franz. The comings and goings of pilgrims, devotees and curious, in this private home was frowned upon by Church authorities; then an agreement was reached to place the miraculous image of the country estate next to the church, but there it was forgotten. Although Franz left Wemding for ever in 1681, his relatives held the image of Mary with the Jesus child on his left arm in high esteem.

Father Reinhard Köhler, Franz Forell's brother-in-law, was on his way home from a night-time urgent call, when suddenly a type of invisible wall blocked his way at the Schiller's brook, where water collected below a spring. Full of fear, he made a vow to build a chapel for the forgotten image of the Virgin Mary, if he could pass. The path immediately cleared and in 1692 the priest fulfilled his promise

On 25 June 1735, Maria Regina Forell, the fifteen-year-old granddaughter of Franz Forell, brought flowers to the statue of Our Lady and placed it between her fingers. Immediately after the image of the Mother of God turned her head and moved her eyes. Several other people noticed the miraculous image of Mary changing facial features. With the news of these phenomena, the number of pilgrims increased, and soon the chapel became too small. On 28 August 1746 the colour of Our Lady's face changed and she turned her eyes towards the city (seventy-three witnesses testified to this in writing), and the cornerstone was laid for the construction of a new church. After the consecration of this church, 107 miraculous cures from various diseases of the eyes took place.[23] In 1998, Pope St John Paul II declared the church a minor basilica.

26 June: Our Lady of Mylapore

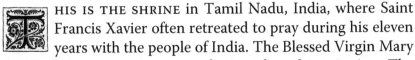 HIS IS THE SHRINE in Tamil Nadu, India, where Saint Francis Xavier often retreated to pray during his eleven years with the people of India. The Blessed Virgin Mary was Francis' constant source of strength and inspiration. The

image before which Saint Francis used to pray is called Mylai Matha in Tamil, or Our Lady of Mylapore in English. It is an ancient statue about one metre tall, and Our Lady of Mylapore can still be venerated at the church.

The church of Saint Thomas of Mylapore contains Mary's shrine. According to tradition, the Apostle St Thomas came to India in 52 AD. Due to his success making converts to the true Faith, he was persecuted and finally martyred in the year 72 AD. Saint Thomas is buried at the shrine of Our Lady of Mlyapore, and there are also relics of Saint Francis Xavier.

According to tradition, there was a church in Mylapore going back to the first century, built by St Thomas. At that time, there was a huge log that had washed down the river to a place where it blocked the water and caused massive flooding. The local king was at a loss to remove the blockage, but having heard that St Thomas was a miracle worker, asked him for his assistance. St Thomas prayed and then touched the log, which made it so light that the king's men were suddenly able to easily pull it clear from the river. The king, in thanksgiving, gave the massive log to St Thomas, who used the wood he obtained from it to construct his church.

The famed traveller Marco Polo visited the shrine in 1292, and by 1500 thought the church was deemed comparable to the Church of Saint John and Saint Paul in Venice, but by the time the Portuguese came in 1517 the shrine was nothing but ruins. The good people knew that they were Christians, and nothing more; but they had Mary as their Mother, and she cleared the way into their hearts for the zealous Francis to sow the seed of Christ's Gospel. It was at Mary's shrine that Francis obtained the miraculous favours to raise the dead, cure the sick, convert sinners and bring to Christ thousands of souls. Regardless of where his journeying took him, Francis always returned to his Lady of the Wayside at Mylapore. Our Lady of Mylapore was his most beloved Mother and from her he received consolation and strength, spiritual delights second only to the joys of Paradise.[24]

The image of Mylai Mytha is taken around in a chariot in procession on every second Saturday of the month.

27 June: Our Lady of Perpetual Help

 HE PICTURE OF OUR LADY of Perpetual Help is painted on wood, with background of gold. It is Byzantine in style and is supposed to have been painted in the thirteenth century. It represents the Mother of God holding the Divine Child while the Archangels Michael and Gabriel present before Him the instruments of His Passion. Over the figures in the picture are some Greek letters which form the abbreviated words Mother of God, Jesus Christ, Archangel Michael, and Archangel Gabriel respectively. In 1498, the picture of Our Lady of Perpetual Help was located in a church on the island of Crete, in Greece. The picture had been there for some time and was known to be miraculous.

One day a merchant from Crete stole the image of Our Lady. He hid the picture among his possessions, boarded a ship and set out to sea. When a great storm arose the terrified sailors begged God and Our Lady to save them. Their prayers were heard and they were saved from shipwreck. A year later, the merchant went to Rome with the picture. There he contracted a disease and became terribly sick. He asked his Roman friend to take care of him. The merchant grew worse and realized that he would soon die. He called on his friend and with tears in his eyes, begged his friend to do him one last favour. When the Roman promised to do so, the weeping merchant continued, "Some time ago I stole a beautiful, miraculous picture of Our Lady from a church in Crete! You will find it with my belongings. I beg you, please place it in some church where the people will give it much honour." In time the merchant died. The Roman found the picture and showed it to his wife. She wanted to keep the picture, so she put it in her room. One day, the Blessed Virgin appeared to the Roman saying, "Do not keep this picture, but put it in some more honourable place." However, the Roman did not do as Our Lady asked him and kept the picture.

Some time later Our Lady begged him a second time not to keep the picture, but to place it in a more honourable place. Again, he did not do as Our Lady asked him to do. Then the Blessed Virgin appeared to the Roman's six-year-old daughter, and told her to warn her mother and her grandfather saying, "Our Lady of Perpetual Help commands you to take her out of the house!" Finally, after many delays, the Virgin Mary appeared to the little girl a second time, "Our Lady of Perpetual Help commands you to tell your mother, to place my picture between St Mary Major and St John Lateran, in the church dedicated to St Matthew the Apostle!"

The mother did as she was told and sent for the Augustinian Fathers who were in charge of that church at that time. Then on that very day, 27 March 1499, the picture was taken to the church of St Matthew the Apostle on the Esquiline Hill, one of the seven hills in Rome. It was placed between two beautifully carved columns of black Carrara marble above a splendid white-marble altar. Crowds flocked to this church, and for nearly three hundred years many graces were obtained through the intercession of the Blessed Virgin. The picture was then popularly called the Madonna di San Matteo. When the French invaded Rome in 1812 and destroyed the church, the picture disappeared; it remained hidden and neglected for over forty years, but a series of providential circumstances between 1863 and 1865 led to its discovery in an oratory of the Augustinian Fathers at Santa Maria in Posterula. Pope Blessed Pius IX, who as a boy had prayed before the picture in St Matthew's church, became interested in the discovery and in a letter dated 11 December 1865 to Father General Mauron, CSSR, ordered that Our Lady of Perpetual Succour should be again publicly venerated in Via Merulana, and this time at the new church of Saint Alphonsus. The ruins of San Matthew were in the grounds of the Redemptorist Convent. This was only the first favour of the Holy Father towards the picture.

He approved of the solemn translation of the picture (26 April 1866), and its coronation by the Vatican Chapter (23 June 1867). By a decree dated May 1876, the Pope approved of a special office and Mass for the Congregation of the Most Holy Redeemer.

Prayer

Oh Mother of Perpetual Help, grant that I may ever invoke your powerful name, the protection of the living and the salvation of the dying. Purest Mary, let your name henceforth be ever on my lips. Delay not, Blessed Lady, to rescue me whenever I call on you. In my temptations, in my needs, I will never cease to call on you, ever repeating your sacred name, Mary, Mary. What a consolation, what sweetness, what confidence fills my soul when I utter your sacred name or even only think of you! I thank the Lord for having given you so sweet, so powerful, so lovely a name. But I will not be content with merely uttering your name. Let my love for you prompt me ever to hail you Mother of Perpetual Help.

28 June: Institution of the Angelus of Our Lady

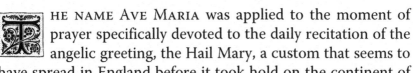 HE NAME AVE MARIA was applied to the moment of prayer specifically devoted to the daily recitation of the angelic greeting, the Hail Mary, a custom that seems to have spread in England before it took hold on the continent of Europe. Toward the end of the 11th century, the Normans invaded and occupied England. In order to ensure control of the populace, the Normans rang a curfew bell at the end of each day reminding the locals to extinguish all fires, get off the streets and retire to their homes. While not intended to encourage prayer, this bell became associated nevertheless with evening prayer time, which included saying the Hail Mary. Once the curfew requirement ended, a bell continued to be rung at the close of each day and the term curfew bell was widely popular, although in some areas it was known as the "Ave" or the "Gabriel" bell. Around 1323, the Bishop of Winchester, and future Archbishop of Canterbury,

Bishop John de Stratford, encouraged those of his diocese to pray the Hail Mary in the evening, writing:

> We exhort you every day, when you hear three short interrupted peals of the bell, at the beginning of the curfew (or, in places where you do not hear it, at vesper time or nightfall) you say with all possible devotion, kneeling wherever you may be, the Angelic Salutation three times at each peal, so as to say it nine times in all.[25]

In Italy, practice of reciting the Hail Mary three times in a row dates back at least as far as the 12th century, and St Anthony of Padua (1195–1231) strongly recommended it. This devout practice was a great favourite also of St Mechtilde of Helfta (1241–1298) in her *Revelations*. St Bonaventure, in a Chapter of the Order of the Friars Minor in 1269 proposed they recite these three Hail Marys in the evening after Compline, meditating on the mystery of Christ's Incarnation, urging at the same time that the recitation be preceded always by the ringing of a bell so that the brothers and all the faithful nearby would know that it was time for the Hail Mary.[26]

As time passed, in the Christian lands, the practice was repeated first in the early morning, and then at midday. Testimonies to the noon recitation are found around 1413 in Czechoslovakia and in 1423 in Cologne. The institution of the Angelus occurred June 28–29, about 1456 by Pope Callistus III. The Turks had been threatening Serbia and it was the Pope's request that the faithful recite the Angelus for the safety of Christendom against the Turks, and for peace.

Pope Sixtus IV, in 1475, was the first to endow the recitation of the Angelus at noon with an indulgence. This indulgence was confirmed and extended by Pope Leo X in 1517 to whoever recited it in the morning, at noon, and in the evening, and Pope Pius XI (1922–1939) seems to have been the last one to grant an indulgence.

29 June: Our Lady and St Peter

N THIS EARTH, Our Lady and St Peter surely were very close in their love and service of the Saviour. Moreover, as St Pio of Pietrelcina humorously recounts, they also exercise their ministry in the heavenly court:

> Our Lord walks through Paradise, and He encounters the faces of many sinners worthy of hell and not of Paradise. He calls St Peter and warns him to be more attentive not to let anyone into Paradise who is not worthy. St Peter promises to be more vigilant and attentive.
>
> The next day, Our Lord takes another walk, and again He encounters many sinners. He calls St Peter again, and this time severely admonishes him. St Peter feels humiliated, and promises Him the maximum vigilance.
>
> But the next day, the same thing happens: Our Lord encounters new sinners in Paradise. This time He calls St Peter, determined to punish him and snatch the keys of Paradise away from him. But St Peter knows how to defend himself, because he discovered the way in which sinners are entering Paradise; and he relates to Our Lord that, in the dark of the night, while all are sleeping, Our Blessed Lady opens the doors of Heaven and lets in those sinners. "Well", St Peter concludes, "with Your Mother, I cannot do anything"; and Our Lord adds: "And neither can I!"[27]

30 June: Our Lady, Queen of the Holy Mountain

N THE SPRING of 1539, a shepherd girl named Ursula Ferligoj brought her village a message which she related Mary had given her on the high mountain west of the town of Svetogorska Kraljica, Nova Gorica, Slovenia. The message ran: "Tell this community that they should build me a church here and come to ask for graces." Local officials responded by jailing the seer, but she escaped repeatedly. Pilgrims began visiting the mountain, now on the border of Italy and Slovenia but then under Austrian rule, where they built a wooden chapel at the apparition site. Italian sculptors provided a statue modelled on Ursula's description.

In 1540, the provincial governor gave permission for a church. When digging the foundations, workers discovered a stone inscribed with the Hail Mary and other remains of a previous place of worship on the site, probably destroyed in the Turkish invasion of 1470.

In 1544 the Catholic patriarch of Aquileia donated the painting on the main altar, by Venetian artist Jacob Palma the Elder. It was canonically crowned Queen of the Holy Mountain in 1717, and in 1748 Pope Benedict XIV ordered that the coronation should be remembered annually in the Patriarchate of Aquileia on the third Sunday after Pentecost. Since then, local believers have called this *Kronanca*, or Crowning Day. However, in 1786 Emperor Joseph II had the church and monastery auctioned off, along with many others, in an effort to modernize his domains. In 1793, not long after taking power, his son Francis II agreed to the renovation of the sanctuary and the return of the sacred image to the Holy Mountain.

In 1907, Pope St Pius X designated the church a minor basilica. Later, during World War I, the friars fled with the painting to Italy; the shrine complex was reduced to rubble. In the 1920s, under Italian rule, it was rebuilt; the friars and the holy image returned. In 1943, after partisans imprisoned the friars, Italian clergy removed the painting for safekeeping. Used as a fort by German forces in 1944, the shrine itself remained unharmed. Clouds foiled an aerial attack planned for 29 April 1945. After the war, the friars and the painting returned, and then the area became part of Yugoslavia. Now part of Slovenia, the Holy Mountain remains a pilgrimage destination despite periods of official disapproval.

Notes

[1] P. Heintz, *A Guide to Apparitions of Our Blessed Virgin Mary* (Sacramento, CA: Gabriel Press, 1995), pp. 248–254.

[2] See M. Lamberty (ed.), *The Woman in Orbit: Mary's feasts every day everywhere* (Chicago: Lamberty, 1966), 2 June.

[3] See Lamberty (ed.), *The Woman in Orbit*, 3 June.

[4] St John Eudes, *Admirable Heart of Mary*, Part Two, Chapter I.

[5] See M. Tosi, *Il santuario della Madonna dell'aiuto* (Bobbio: Edizioni Columba, 1975).

[6] See N. J. Santoro, *Mary In Our Life: Atlas of the Names and Titles of Mary, The Mother of Jesus, and Their Place in Marian Devotion* (Kansas City, MI: iUniverse, Inc, 2011), pp. 396–397.

[7] See the website franziskaner-marienthal.de.

[8] Pope St John Paul II, *Discourse during his pilgrimage to Mentorella* (29 October 1978).

[9] Bishop John Shojiro Ito, *Pastoral Letter* (22 April 1984).

[10] S. M. Paci, "The Tears of Akita" in *30 Days* (July–August 1990), pp. 42–43.

[11] See A. M. Santarelli, *The Life of the Servant of God Rev. Fr Leo Heinrichs, OFM* (New York: Franciscan Press, 1926), p. 25.

[12] See K. Schiffer, "108 Years Ago, This Priest's Murder at Mass Shocked the U.S." in *National Catholic Register* (23 August 2016).

[13] M. Harris, *Sacred folly: A new history of the Feast of Fools* (Ithaca, NY: Cornell University Press, 2011), chapter 24 "Our Lady of the Trellis"

[14] See J. Jones, "Christ the Light of the World" in *ORE* (11 August 2010), p. 5.

[15] Aneda is generally believed to have been *Thuja occidentalis*, a common tree in Quebec also known as Arborvitae. However, historian Jacques Mathieu has argued at length that aneda was more likely *Abies balsamea*, given that tree's role as a traditional remedy and given the much higher vitamin C content of its needles. See J. Mathieu, *L'annedda: L'arbre de vie* (Septentrion: Quebec, 2009).

[16] D. de Lafforest, *Les mares de Septembre: récits de Bretagne* (Sint-Genesius-Rode: Longue Vue, 1998).

[17] See Lamberty (ed.), *The Woman in Orbit*, 20 June.

[18] See P. M. Julien, *Der Muttergottesbaum in Matarieh* (Regensburg 1906); O. F. Meinardus, *Das Heilige Land—Aud den Spuren Marias von Nazareth* (Frankfurt, 1998).

[19] See Lamberty (ed.), *The Woman in Orbit*, 21 June.

[20] Pope St John Paul II, *Homily at Mass at the Shrine of Our Lady Ta' Pinu* (26 May 1990), 2.

[21] See Lamberty (ed.), *The Woman in Orbit*, 23 June.

[22] See A. Tornielli, "Medjugorje; the findings of the Ruini report" in *Vatican Insider* (16 May 2017).

[23] See G. Hierzenberger and O. Nedomansky, *Tutte le apparizioni della Madonna in 2000 anni di storia* (Casale Monferrato: Piemme, 1998⁶).

[24] See Lamberty (ed.), *The Woman in Orbit*, 26 June.

[25] See D. D. Emmons, "What Is the Angelus?" in *The Catholic Answer* (4 April 2011).

[26] See G. Luppino, "Short History of the Angelus" in *ORE* (4 September 2002), p. 6.

[27] Cited in S. M. Manelli, *Devotion to Our Lady: The Marian Life as Taught by the Saints* (New Bedford, MA: Academy of the Immaculate, 2001), pp. 75–76. Obviously the story is not intended to foster presumption on the part of the believer but rather hope in Our Lady's intercessory power.

JULY

1 July: Our Lady of the Precious Blood

EVERY SUPERNATURAL GRACE coming to mankind after the Fall of Adam, flows from the Sacrifice of Christ on the Cross. Almighty God could have made some other arrangement, but as a matter of fact, He did require the sacrificial shedding of the Blood of Christ for the restoration of fallen man to the order of grace. The Sacrifice is the price which God demanded; it is the price which the Redeemer paid. To this Sacrifice, the Blessed Virgin has a most intimate and singular relationship because of which we may rightly call her Our Lady of the Precious Blood.

For a sacrifice in the strict sense, there must be a priest who offers and a victim which is offered. In the Sacrifice of Redemption, Christ Himself is both the priest and the victim. The very coming of the Redeemer as Priest and Victim and therefore also the fruits of His Sacrifice, were dependent upon Mary's consent and cooperation. At the time of the Annunciation she gave her consent to become the Mother of Jesus, that is, of Him who would save His people from their sins. He was to save them in the manner in which God had predetermined, namely, by His whole lifework, but especially by His Sacrifice upon the Cross. "Be it done to me according to Your Word", is the reply of Mary to the Angel. Thus she gave her consent to all the events of His life, including the Sacrifice, at least implicitly at the Annunciation and explicitly as the plan of God unfolded itself. She is not the Mother of a Son who became a Priest independently of her after His birth, for Jesus was conceived as a priest. As a Priest He was born and was nourished and clothed and sheltered by Mary.

However, this Priest is also the Victim. Thus, as only His Mother could, Mary prepared the Priest and Victim for the

Bloody Sacrifice of Redemption. With Him she also offered the Sacrifice by sharing His sorrow and suffering by perfectly uniting her intention with His and by resigning herself perfectly to the will of the Father.

Furthermore, as God called Mary to be most intimately and uniquely associated with her Priestly Son in the acquiring of grace, He also associated her with Him in the dispensing of grace. This fact is succinctly expressed by Pope St Pius X when he writes:

> By reason of this communion and sorrow between Mary and Christ, she merited to be called most rightly the Restorer of a lost world and therefore the Almoner of all the gifts which Jesus earned for us by His Death and His Blood.[1]

Since, then, Mary prepared the Priest and Victim for the bloody Sacrifice of Redemption; since with Him she offered the Sacrifice on the Cross; and since with Him she dispenses the graces merited by this Holy Sacrifice, we may very appropriately call her Our Lady of the Precious Blood.

Prayer

Remember, O Lady of the Precious Blood, the sorrowful shedding of the Blood of your Jesus and the most bitter tears you mingled with His Redeeming Blood. In the name of the Blood of the Victim of Reparation and of your holy tears; in the name of the seven swords which pierced you heart, by which you became the Mediatrix of all graces for the human race and the Queen of Martyrs, have pity on my soul and on all its miseries; have pity on sinners and on the innocent souls they seek to pervert; have pity on the poor, the sick, the infirm, on all their sufferings, both physical and moral; have pity on the agonizing, especially upon those who, except for your intercession, would leave this world without being purified in the Blood of the Lamb. By the Blood of your dying Son, by His inexpressible Sufferings, by His last plea to His Father on behalf of mankind, by His ignominious Death and by the perpetuation of His holy Sacrifice of the altars, that I beg you not to reject my supplications, but graciously to hear them. Amen.

2 July: Our Lady of Virtues

HE VIRTUES OF the Most Holy Mother of God are first prefigured in the Books of the Patriarchs and the Kings of God's people. Mary could not fail to inherit all the glory of her ancestors, because not only did their blood flow in her veins, but Mary regarded them as models of virtue. It is an incontestable truth that Mary's faith was stronger than Abraham's; her obedience greater than that of Isaac; and her gifts of gentleness and piety finer than those of Jacob. Her purity transcended that of Joseph; her courage that of David; and her wisdom that of the great and peace-loving Solomon. Thus it necessarily follows that Mary is called the Mother of Mankind, as well as the First of All Women and, like Sara, the Mother of all Believers. The beauty of Rachel, the fertility of Lia, the integrity and valour of Debora; the zeal, the fearlessness, the saintliness of Judith, the prudence and the happiness of Esther—all these admirable qualities we find united in our Queen as the line of all her ancestors meet in her, for which they were formed and whom they prefigured.

These great men and women, so renowned in the Ancient Law, were models for Mary. Their virtues shone in her soul with such added, unbelievable splendour, that there was the same difference between Mary and her models that there is between a real man and his portrait, between the architect's plan for a palace and the palace itself, between a shadow and the object which caused it.

> Love the lovable Mother of God; love her tenderly and constantly. Honour her before men; speak of her with reverence and zeal. Read about her often; perform works of piety in her honour. Finally, pray often to her; ask for sentiments as tender as those which the most devoted and the most celebrated of her followers had for her, and all

the virtues which made those followers so pleasing to her; so that, with Mary's help her glory may in part at least be yours when you give up your soul with the name of Mary on your lips. Then, the Gates of Heaven cannot fail to swing wide without delay, as the ark was opened for the dove which appeared bearing an olive twig in its beak. In order to have that name which will bring us such happiness and salvation, on our lips, when we are dying, we must have it constantly in our hearts while we live.[2]

3 July: Our Lady of Mount Athos

OUNT ATHOS OR AGION OROS, as it is locally known, is the oldest surviving monastic community in the world. It dates back more than a thousand years, to Byzantine times. It is a unique monastic republic, which, although part of Greece, it is governed by its own local administration. It occupies the best part of the Athos peninsula in Halkidiki.

The tradition of Mount Athos is linked with the Mother of God. Returning from Ephesus and Antioch, the Mother of God then remained in Jerusalem for a considerable period. During this time, St Lazarus, (whom the Lord had raised from the dead on the fourth day of his repose according to John 11:14–44), was living on the island of Cyprus. The Apostle Barnabas had consecrated him as bishop. Now St Lazarus had a great longing to behold the Theotokos who he had not seen in a long while. However, he dared not enter Jerusalem for fear of the Jews, who still sought him. The Theotokos learned of this and wrote to St Lazarus, the true friend of her Son, a letter wherein she comforted him. She asked him to send a ship to her that she might visit him in Cyprus, for she would never demand of him to come to Jerusalem for her sake. When the holy Lazarus read her letter, he was filled with tremendous joy and, at the same time, he wondered at her great humility.

Without a moment's delay, he sent a ship for her together with a letter of reply. Whereupon, the Theotokos together with

Christ's beloved disciple, John, and others, who reverently accompanied them, set sail. It is said that she had sewn St Lazarus an *omophorion* (a bishop's stole, pall) with *epimanikia* (cuffs) and that she wished to present them to him personally. The year was 52 A.D. The Virgin Mary and her company set sail from the Holy Land on a bright and glorious day. As the ship parted from the shore, the Virgin prayed to her almighty Son that He pilot their vessel, according to his will. It happened that, after a time at sea, a violent sea storm raged and the sailing vessel was forced off course. By divine intervention, as the storm abated, they found themselves outside the port of Clemes (Clementos) on Athos.

At that time, Athos was inhabited by pagan tribes. In ancient times, the citizens of that region were mostly young virgins dedicated to the goddess Diana and destined to become priestesses to serve in the idolatrous temples of Greece. To this purpose, young girls were sent there from all parts of Greece. It was forbidden, under penalty of death, for men to enter. When the ship carrying the Virgin Mary approached Athos, Jupiter's statue, at the top of the mountain fell and shattered to pieces in a thunderous noise. The presence of this statue is mentioned in ancient history. Plutarch and Anaximander and others also mention that at the top of Athos there was a great gold-ivory statue of Jupiter which, instead of eyes, bore two large gems, reflecting the starlight. Emitting flashes by night, they served as lighthouses to the seaman sailing around Athos.

It is said that Our Lady's group came ashore close to the present Monastery of Iveron which is situated above a picturesque inlet on the northeastern side of the peninsula. There, the holy Virgin rested for a while, overwhelmed by the beauty of the place, she asked her Son to give her the Mountain, despite the fact that the inhabitants were pagans. A voice was then heard saying: "Let this place be your inheritance and garden, a paradise and a haven of salvation for those seeking to be saved." The Virgin then brought to mind the words of the Archangel Gabriel, who told her some twenty years earlier, after Pentecost, that her lot would be a Macedonian peninsula, Mount Athos. Thus it was consecrated as the inheritance and garden of the Mother of God, and immediately acquired the name *Aghion Oros* or Holy Mountain, because Our Lady the Holy Theotokos chose this Mountain and placed it under her own protection. Upon asking and receiving Athos as a heavenly gift, in that very moment, the ground shook and the pagan statues in all the temples fell prostrate and broke into pieces. Then, even the trees of the peninsula bent forward, as though offering veneration to the Theotokos who had reached the port of Clemes.

On the peninsula there was a pagan temple and shrine of Apollo. Diabolical works such as fortune telling, divination and witchcraft took place there. All the pagans greatly honoured this place as one chosen by the gods. In fact, people from all over the world gathered there to worship. There, they would receive answers to their questions from the diviners. Therefore, when the Mother of God entered port, and all their idols had collapsed, shouting, confusion and uproar were heard from all the idols in Athos. Cries could be heard, saying: "Men of Apollo, go to Clemes harbour and welcome Mary, the Mother of the Great God Jesus!" Thus, all the demons inhabiting the idols, forced against their will, could not resist the power of God and they proclaimed the truth.

Whereupon, all the inhabitants of Athos hastened from all parts to that port. Once there, they welcomed the Theotokos. Meeting her with honour, they took the Theotokos, St John and all their fellow passengers to the common hall, called the Synagogeion (meeting house or assembly room). They then asked her, "What God did you bear and what is His name?" Opening her divine lips, Mary explained, in detail, to the people everything about Christ. The natives diligently posed questions concerning the mystery of providence in the divine Incarnation. They even wondered at how she, a Hebrew woman, explained everything to them in the Greek language. As a result of all the awesome and supernatural occurrences coinciding with her arrival, they believed. Upon being catechised by her teaching, they accepted the Christian faith. They then fell down to the ground and worshipped the God Who was born of her and showed great respect to the Virgin who bore Him in the flesh. The Mother of God also worked many miracles on the Holy Mountain. After their baptism, she appointed a leader and teacher for the newly-illumined from among them.[3]

4 July: Our Lady of Divine Love

 HE HISTORY OF the Sanctuary of Our Lady of Divine Love dates back to the 13th century when in this area of the Roman Campagna there stood a kind of fortress belonging to the Savelli-Orsini family, called the Castel di Leva (Leva Castle). On one of the towers of the castle there was a votive image of the Virgin Mary, portrayed as sitting on a throne and holding the child Jesus in her arms. A dove descends upon her as a symbol of the Holy Spirit, who is indeed Divine Love. The image, which was frescoed in those same times, was much venerated by the local shepherds.

In the spring of 1740 a wayfarer on his way to Rome, while approaching the tower, was attacked by a pack of dogs and was on the point of being killed. The wretched man saw the holy image and cried out for help to the Mother of God. Immediately the dogs calmed down and fled into the countryside. On account of this prodigy, on 5 September of the same year the image of Mary was removed from the tower and transferred to a nearby estate called "La Falconiana", where a small church dedicated to St Mary ad Magos stood. Five years later, on 19 April 1745, the image was brought back to its ancient location, where meanwhile a church had been erected which before long had been consecrated in 1750 by Cardinal Carlo Rezzonico; who later became Pope with the name of Clement XIII. From that time pilgrimages began, which became more and more numerous and still continue today.

On 24 January 1944, Rome was in serious danger of being destroyed during the Second World War. The image of Our lady was moved into the city and brought in pilgrimage to various churches. In the last of these churches, that of St Ignatius, on 4 June 1944 the Roman people, in order to obtain the liberation of the city, made a vow to Our Lady to renew their lives, to erect a new sanctuary, and to carry out charitable work in her honour. The Virgin Mary performed the miracle, and Rome was saved. On 11 June 1944, Pope Pius XII went to the Sanctuary to pray together with the Roman faithful, and conferred the title of "Saviour of the City" on Our Lady of Divine Love.

In 1991 work was begun on the construction of a new shrine, which was solemnly consecrated by Pope St John Paul II on 4 July 1999. The Pope declared in his homily:

> Today, the dedication of this new shrine partially fulfils the vow which the Roman people, at the request of Pope Pius XII, made to Our Lady of Divine Love in 1944, when the allied troops were about to launch their final attack on Rome, then occupied by the Germans. Before the image of Our Lady of Divine Love, the Romans prayed on 4 June of that year for the safety of their city, promising Mary that they would change their moral conduct, build the new Shrine of Divine Love and open a charitable institution in Castel di Leva. That same day, a little more than an hour after the vow had been read, the German army withdrew from Rome without offering any resistance, while the allies entered through Porta San Giovanni and Porta Maggiore and were welcomed with exultation by the Romans.
>
> Today the shrine is a reality and the charitable institution is nearly finished: a home for the elderly not far from here. But the Roman people's vow included a promise to Blessed Mary that is unending and much more difficult to fulfil: the change in moral conduct, the constant effort, that is, to renew life and make it conform ever more closely to Christ's. Dear brothers and sisters, this is the task that the sacred building dedicated to God today recalls.
>
> These walls surrounding the sacred space where we are gathered, and even more, the altar, the great multi-coloured

stained-glass windows and the other religious symbols, are meant as signs of God's presence among his people. A presence made real in the Eucharist, celebrated every day and kept in the tabernacle; a presence which shows itself living and life-giving through the administration of the sacraments; a presence which can be continually experienced in prayer and meditation. May this presence be a constant call to conversion and fraternal reconciliation for everyone![4]

Every Saturday night, from Easter until the end of October, a night Pilgrimage on foot takes place, covering a distance of about 15 kilometres. It sets out at midnight from Piazza di Porta Capena, Rome, and reaches the Sanctuary at 5 o'clock on Sunday morning. A similar night Pilgrimage is carried out on 7 December, on the eve of the feast of the Immaculate Conception. The night pilgrims walk along the famous Via Appia Antica (old Appian way) until they reach the church of *Quo Vadis*, then they turn on to the Via Ardeatina and continue their way, walking over the Catacombs of St Callistus and past the Mausoleum of the Ardeatine Caves (Fosse Ardeatine). They bring their personal intentions to the feet of the Virgin, along with the necessities, the hopes and the mission of the Church of Rome and of the Eternal City.

5 July: Our Lady of the Little Hands

 HE TITLE DERIVES from the Cistercian monastery (Nuestra Senora de las Mañitas) in Lima, Peru, and the miraculous events that tradition says occurred at the monastery on 5 July and commemorated annually on that date. The episode recounts the gift of rings from the hands of the image of the Blessed Mother to two young girls.

Las Mañitas is a song in musical verse of which one translation that has been offered is:

These are your good morning greetings,
like the ones that King David sang.
We sing you this song with love

and we sing these morning greetings for you.
Arise my love arise my lovely, see how the dawn
now breaks.
The birds are singing sweetly and now the sun is up.
How beautiful is the morning on the day that you were born.
They day you were born all of the flowers came in bloom.
On the day of your baptism, all of the birds were singing.[5]

6 July: Our Lady of Joy

 ROM THE HILLS of Laon where the cathedral lifts its towers adorned with stone-carved oxen in homage to the men who labour below—one can see for miles and miles over the immense plain, to the village of Liesse, in northern France. In this village there is a shrine dedicated to Our Lady of Joy. Here the village church is naturally everything. The church transports one back to the thirteenth century. Directly in front of the choir screen are four statues. They are the three knights of d'Eppes and the Princess Ismoria, and their story is the story of the church.

During the time of the Crusades about the year 1134, these three knights, brothers from this part of the country, dedicated themselves, heart and soul, to God's cause to fight in Palestine against the Saracens. In a daring raid at Bersake they were taken prisoners and carried off to Egypt. There the Sultan used every means at his disposal to make them apostatise: he starved them, sent his most learned men to discuss with them; but all to no avail. Then he decided to send his beautiful and intelligent daughter, the Princess Ismoria to charm them with her wit. She went to the prison where a discussion was opened, but she was won over by the conviction and constancy of these noblemen, who repeatedly mentioned the Blessed Lady and her Child. Ismoria longed to see a picture or some sort of image of Mary. Would they be able to make her a representation of that Lady?

One of the knights, without reflection, promised to do so; but when she brought wood and carving utensils, they realized they could not—none of the knights had ever carved before. What were they going to do? They spent the night in prayer, pleading with Our Lady to do something about it. The next morning they found a luminous statue of the Virgin and Child near the wood to be used. When the princess returned and saw the beautiful refulgent statue, her mind and heart were open to the truth and she no longer doubted the faith of the Christian knights. "If you give me the statue", she cried, "I shall become one of you. The knight gladly gave it to Ismoria, who carried it to the palace. The next night she saw Our Lady in a vision, who told her to change her name to Mary, to free the imprisoned knights, and to flee with them. The prison was miraculously opened and the four escaped to France; while en route they passed through untold dangers, unchallenged and unseen.

On the banks of the Nile they found a young man waiting to take them over the river in his boat. Once across, he suddenly disappeared. Fatigued, they decided to rest before pushing on farther. During their sleep they were miraculously transported to France and the knights awoke to find themselves near their home in Picardy. They went to the castle accompanied by the princess. On the way, Ismoria suddenly found the statue too heavy to carry. They interpreted this as a sign from Heaven that Mary wanted her statue left at this spot. The princess was kindly received by the mother and brothers of the knights, and after adequate instruction, was baptized by the bishop of Soissons.

Later, a chapel was built on the spot where the statue had been left. The church took on the name of Our Lady of Joy, because of the wonderful adventures of the three knights and Ismoria. Great miracles were performed and countless graces were obtained through the intercession of Our Lady of Joy, to whose shrine both the great and the humble went: St Joan of Arc, Francis I, Louis IX, XIII, XIV, Marie Antoinette, Blessed Mary of the Incarnation, the pious Olier, St John Baptiste de la Salle, St Benedict Joseph Labre, saints and sinners alike.[6]

7 July: Sweet Mother of the Woods

 HE IMAGE OF the Sweet Mother at Hertogenbosch, in the north Brabant province of the Netherlands, was an object of derision when it was first heard of, in 1380. However, those who mocked it were afflicted in various ways until it was repaired.[7] The image had been found dirty and damaged, in a builder's shed; but it soon became celebrated for the wonders connected with it. 481 miracles took place through Our Sweet Lady including the the the following remarkable story:

> On 24 December, Albrecht, the son of Albrecht Loze van Dynter, who lives in Schijndel, was on his way from Flanders to the town of Zevenbergen when he was taken for a spy and arrested. As soon as he called on the Virgin Mary of Den Bosch, the iron chains with which he was bound fell apart. He jumped from the tower where he was jailed. He landed in the canal and reached the land unharmed. Out of gratitude he went on pilgrimage barefoot and dressed in woollen clothes. The last mile he walked without any clothes.

The statue of Our Sweet Lady is of oak is nearly four feet tall and is of an unusual pattern: Our Lady stands upright, while her forearms are extended at right angles to her body. The Child is balanced on her left hand and in her right she holds an apple.

At the Reformation the statue was taken to Brussels for safety. The statue had to be hidden to keep it safe, and so was placed in a chest and secreted out through the town gates. It was then taken to St Geradus's church in Belgium before being taken to Koudenberg church in Brussels. In 1853, when the Church of the Netherlands was officially restored, the Catholics of Den Bosch received back their Cathedral. Then, it took the prolonged efforts of Bishop J. Zwijsen, the bishop of Hertogenbosch, to have the beloved statue of Our Sweet Lady returned to his cathedral in 1878. It was crowned by the grateful bishop in the name of Pope Leo XIII that same year, and the feast is 7 July with proper Mass and Office in certain places. The fraternity of Our Sweet Lady has taken care of the statue, the shrine and its activities since 1837.

8 July: Our Lady of Kazan

HIS MIRACULOUS ICON, also known as the Theotokos of Kazan, is thought to have originated in Constantinople in the 13th century before it was taken to Russia. When the Turks took Kazan in 1438, the icon may have been hidden. Czar Ivan the Terrible liberated Kazan in 1552, and the town was destroyed by fire in 1579.

The icon was eventually found in the ruins of a burnt-out house at Kazan on the River Volga on 8 July 1579. According to tradition, the location of the icon was revealed during a dream by the Blessed Virgin Mary to a ten-year-old girl named Matrona. Matrona told the local archbishop of her dream, but he did not believe her. There were two more similar dreams, after which Matrona and her mother went to the place indicated by the Blessed Virgin and dug in the ruins what had been a house until the uncovered the icon. It appeared untouched by the flames, with the colours as vivid and brilliant as if it were new. The archbishop repented of his unbelief and took the icon to the Church of St Nicholas, where a blind man was cured that very day. A copy of the icon was sent to Ivan the Terrible, who had a monastery built on the site where the icon had been found. Matrona, as well as her mother, then joined the religious community that was installed there.

In 1612, St. Sergei was said to have appeared to Bishop Arseni. The saint—who had died in 1392—told the bishop that the Lady of Kazan would intervene in battle. Hence, the icon was brought to lead the troops of Prince Pozharski that were trying to free Moscow. True to the prophecy, on 27 November 1612, the Kremlin was liberated.

Ever since, whenever Russia had to go into battle, the Virgin of Kazan or one of its copies was carried in front of the army.

Later, the Virgin also rescued Russia from Napoleon's troops. In September 1812, Marshal Koutesov took the icon from Moscow's Cathedral and rallied his troops to cut off Napoleon's supply routes. As such, the icon is often considered to be a "palladium", an image upon which the safety of a city or a country—Mother Russia—was said to depend.

At the time of the Russian Revolution, the basilica housing the icon was destroyed, apparently to prove that God did not exist. As great sledges and rams knocked down the church, loudspeakers blared: "You see, there is no God! We destroy the church of the so-called protectress of Russia, and nothing happens!" A green plot of grass in front of Lenin's tomb marked the site where the Basilica of Our Lady of Kazan had once stood as the national Marian Shrine of Russia. It is uncertain what happened to the icon afterwards. Some argue that it was sold by the Emperor's family to sustain itself in exile (a hope that never materialised for them), and others say that the icon was sold to help pay for the Bolshevik Revolution. In any case, the icon apparently reached Western Europe in 1935.

It seems that on 23 September 1953, the English adventurer "Mike" Mitchell-Hedges purchased the icon. Between 1953 and 1965, the precious relic hung in the home of Anna Mitchell-Hedges, Mike's daughter. By the convergence of various data this icon would be the original and not one of the many copies that were made.[8] Meanwhile, in 1964–1965, a special pavilion was erected at World Trade Fair in New York to house the icon so that people could come to admire it. On 4 October 1965, Pope Bl Paul VI came to bless the icon. The night of 13 September 1965, the pavilion had been filled with members of the Blue Army, led by the Bishop of Fatima himself. It appears that the entire night was spent in adoration and prayer for the conversion of Russia and world peace. Blue Army groups around the world, in many cities, held similar all night vigils on that same date. The Blue Army learned about the opportunity to purchase the icon in January 1970. Anna Mitchell-Hedges demanded $125,000 for the relic—a most reasonable price.

Once the icon was purchased, it was taken to Fatima. Russia's most precious relic now hung in the very place where Our Lady had predicted the evils of communism. The Soviet communist regime then suggested that the icon was not the original one. The Soviet powers were perfectly aware that the icon was courting a date with destiny and became extremely nervous. What happened next was that the icon went to the Vatican to the private quarters of Pope John Paul II. After surviving the assassination attempt on 13 May 1981, the Pope became convinced that his life had been saved by the intervention of Our Lady herself, and believed that the Third Secret of Fatima had predicted his survival. When he discovered the icon in 1991, during one of his many visits to Fatima, he realised that it was most important. Pope St John Paul II asked to have it transferred to the Vatican, where it was installed in the papal apartments. In 1993, the Blue Army consented to this transfer.

In 1989, when communism had collapsed, Metropolitan Alexy of Leningrad, the future Patriarch Alexis II of Moscow, visited Seattle and had dinner with Father Frederick Miller, then-executive director of the Blue Army. The meeting could be seen as the first step in a process that might see the return of the icon to Russia. Little happened for a decade, but after Vladimir Putin's visit to the Vatican in 2003, it became obvious that the seriously frail and aging pope would not be invited to Russia any time soon. Thus, Pope John Paul II consented in a lower key process in which a Vatican missionary would present the icon to the Russian Church.

In late August 2004, the Pope said goodbye to the icon in an incense-filled Liturgy of the Word celebration inside the Vatican. "How many times have I prayed to the Mother of God of Kazan," he remarked about the icon that had hung over his desk in the papal apartments for the past ten years, "asking her to protect and guide the Russian people and to precipitate the moment in which all the disciples of her Son, recognizing themselves as brothers, will know how to reconstruct in fullness their compromised unity." He then handed the icon over to two emissaries, Cardinals Walter Kasper and Theodore McCarrick, the then archbishop of Washington, who took it to Russia.

Interestingly, Cardinal Walter Kasper, the president of the Pontifical Council for Christian Unity, stated that the icon was

> a symbol of the new Europe and its formation, of which Russia is a part... Our Lady of Kazan is the protector of Europe and its Christian roots. After two world wars, and the phenomena of secularisation, Europe needs to be founded again in the faith.

On 26 August 2004, the Virgin of Kazan went on display in St Peter's Basilica. Two days later, it was delivered to Moscow. Cardinal Walter Kasper handed the icon back to the Russian Orthodox Church in a ceremony at the Kremlin's Cathedral of the Assumption, as a personal gift from Pope St John Paul II.

About one year later, Patriarch Alexis II and Mintimer Shaymiev, the President of Tatarstan, placed it in the Annunciation Cathedral of the Kazan in the Kremlin. The Virgin of Kazan was back where she belonged—and where she had conquered, it seemed, the forces of communism. Before the revolution, perhaps still, sometimes a Russian mother would give a copy of this picture to her daughter at her wedding, as a blessing on her and her new home.

9 July: Our Lady of the Atonement

T THE LAST SUPPER, Our Lord prayed "That all may be one." At the foot of the Cross, Mary shared in the redemption for all mankind. The title of Our Lady of the Atonement is a title of unity. One of the most unusual facts about this title is that devotion to Mary under this name began outside of the Catholic church.

The Rosary League of Our Lady of the Atonement was formed in 1901 with the purpose "to pray and work for the restoration of Mary's Dowry, England, to our Virgin Queen, the Holy Mother of God". Later, the object of the League became more extensive and included not only the conversion of England but the entire world. The league was formed by Father Paul Wattson and Mother Lurana Mary Francis White, members of the Anglican communion until they, with fifteen others, were received into the Catholic Church in 1909. The little community grew, and is now known as the Franciscan friars and sisters of Graymoor. In 1919, Pope Benedict XV gave his approval and apostolic recognition to the title of Our Lady of the Atonement.

In the beautiful representations of Mary under this title, she wears a red mantle, symbolizing the Precious Blood of which she was the Immaculate source, and by which she was made immaculate. It was by the shedding of this most precious blood that the redemption of the world was accomplished. She wears a blue inner tunic, and she holds the infant Jesus in her arms. The child Jesus is depicted holding a cross, the symbol of His suffering and glory.

The concept of Our Lady of the Atonement includes two parts. First, it emphasizes Mary's role as Coredemptrix in the mystery of the Cross. Second, it points to Mary's role in effecting the unity or At-one-ment of men with God. Mary co-operated with Christ as no other creature did, in His work of reconciling man with God. In honouring Mary with this title, we remember her with gratitude and love for the great gift of her Son to us, just as Christ in His death on the cross, gave Mary to us to be our Mother.

Mary is Our Lady of Unity, Our Lady of the At-one-ment. Even those who are separated from the Church still have a claim upon her charity, and she longs to unite them to her Divine Son. Just as the father's heart went out to his prodigal son in love and forgiveness, Mary's Immaculate Heart reaches out to her children who have wandered from the Father.

Prayer

We salute you, Holy Mary, Daughter of God the Father, and entreat you to obtain for us a devotion like your own to the most sweet Will of God.

We salute you, Virgin Mother of God and Son, and entreat you
to obtain for us such union with the Sacred Heart of Jesus that
our own hearts may burn with love of God and an ardent zeal for
the salvation of souls.

We salute you, Immaculate Spouse of God the Holy Spirit, and
entreat you to obtain for us such yielding of ourselves to the
Blessed Spirit, that He may, in all things, direct and rule our hearts
and that we may never grieve Him in thought, word or deed.[9]

10 July: Our Lady of Aberdeen

 HE MEDIAEVAL STATUE of Our Lady of Aberdeen is
approximately one metre high, probably carved in linden
wood, and painted. It was also decorated with silver and
gold. Our Lady carries the Christ Child in her arms and holds a
sceptre. She wears an open crown and the Child has the closed
imperial crown. The crowns and sceptre are silver and may not
the original ones. It is commonly described as being carved in the
Flemish tradition and even to have come from Flanders, but there
is no reason to suppose that there were no capable sculptors in
the North East of Scotland, though all the evidence of their work
disappeared at the time of the Reformation.

The original medieval statue is said to have stood in either the
Cathedral of Saint Machar or the Mother Kirk of Saint Nicholas
in Aberdeen in the time of Bishop Gavin Dunbar of Aberdeen
(1514–1531), and it was credited with miraculously directing him
to the spot where the new bridge over the River Dee should be
built. Whatever its history up to that point, it is fairly certain that
a finer silver Madonna replaced it in its favoured position and it
was given as a gift by Bishop Dunbar to the new chapel, which
stood by the new Bridge of Dee (1527). Here travellers to the city
could pause after their dangerous journey and give thanks to the
Virgin for their safe arrival.

Our Lady also appeared to Bishop Dunbar, while he was
praying before the statue of Our Lady. She told to him apostasy

had caused the calamities of his country, but being the last Catholic bishop of the city he would be saved. At the beginning of the Scottish Reformation (c. 1559) many religious objects from churches in Aberdeen and the St Machar's Cathedral in Old Aberdeen were given for safe keeping to Catholic sympathisers. It is claimed that the statue was in the hands of a Catholic family, the Gordons of Strathbogie, until 1625. It was then sent to the Low Countries by a William Laing, thought to be the Procurer for the Kings of Spain to the Infanta Isabella Clara Eugenia in Brussels. In Scotland, the Catholic Church celebrates 9 July as Our Lady of Aberdeen.

11 July: Our Lady of Good Success

WO SPANISH FRIARS, Brothers Gabriel de Fontaned and Guillermo de Rigosa travelled to Rome to meet the Pope for the approval of their order, the Order of Minims for the Service of the Sick or The Order of Saint Francis of Paola. As they were passing through the town of Traigueras (under the jurisdiction of Tortosa in the Principate of Catalonia), a furious storm descended upon them. The brothers prayed for God's guidance and help. Immediately they saw a mysterious light coming from a cave in a cliff. Climbing up, they entered and found a beautiful statue of the Virgin Mary holding the Baby Jesus in her arms. They reported being surrounded by shimmering lights and fragrant scents. As no one claimed the statue, the two carried it with them, hoping that the Blessed Mother would help in obtaining approval for their order.

On arriving in Rome in 1607, the brothers were concerned about obtaining papal approval. However, Pope Paul V on hearing the story of their journey, knelt before the statue and placed his pectoral cross around its neck. As he embraced and kissed the statue, he said:

> Look Brothers! She is smiling! Why does she smile like this? What good success you have had on this journey!

There is no doubt that Our Lady has deigned to protect
and support you in your work. Therefore it will not be me
that will go against her. May all of your efforts obtain good
success!

He then blessed the statue and christened her Our Lady of Good
Success. The image was placed in the Royal Hospital of Madrid,
where it became famous for the numerous favours granted by
God through Our Lady. In 1641, King Philip III ordered the
construction of the church of Our Lady of Good Success, which
enshrines the image.

The invocation to Our Lady of Good Success was not long in
making its way across the ocean to the New World. The Blessed
Virgin deigned to favour the Convent of the Immaculate Conception in Quito, Ecuador, in a very special way by means of this
particular avocation. In an apparition to Mother Mariana de Jesus
Torres, the Blessed Virgin appeared and asked that a statue be
made of her under the title of Good Success. She should be made
just as she appeared there, with the Child Jesus in her right arm,
and the Abbess' crozier and the keys of the Convent in her right
hand. She should be placed above the Abbess chair in the upper
choir because she desired to be Abbess of that Convent until the
end of time. And so the Virgin of Good Success of Quito appears
with the crosier in her right hand, instead of the sceptre that she
carries in Madrid.

Mother Mariana also received apparitions with specific warnings and predictions, mentioning the 20th century in particular
which matches with our own experience. Here is a portion of the
message of Our Lady to Mother Mariana on 21 January 1610:

As for the Sacrament of Matrimony, which symbolises the
union of Christ with His Church, it will be attacked and
deeply profaned. Freemasonry, which will then be in
power, will enact iniquitous laws with the aim of doing
away with this Sacrament, making it easy for everyone to
live in sin and encouraging the procreation of illegitimate
children born without the blessing of the Church. The

Catholic spirit will rapidly decay; the precious light of Faith will gradually be extinguished until there will be an almost total and general corruption of customs. Added to this will be the effects of secular education, which will be one reason for the death of priestly and religious vocations.

In Ecuador and Spain, the feast day of Our Lady of Good Success is celebrated on 2 February, the day she appeared to Mother Mariana along with the archangels and St Francis of Assisi.

12 July: Our Lady of Kherson

RADITION MAINTAINS THAT a holy icon of Our Lady had been brought to Kherson in Ukraine from Transylvania by a Serb at the end of the sixteenth century. Passing down from parent and child, the icon had come into the hands of a certain Mrs Kasperova of Kherson in 1809. One night in February of 1840, in a village on the banks of the Dniepr river, she was praying, seeking consolation in her many sorrows. Looking at the icon of the Virgin, she noticed that the features of the icon, darkened by age, had suddenly become bright. Soon the icon was glorified by many miracles, and people regarded it as wonder-working.

During the Crimean War, the procession moved to the city of Odessa, which, though besieged by enemy forces, remained unharmed. Thereafter, the Kasperov Icon has made an annual rotation among Odessa, Kherson, and the towns of Nikolaev and Kasperovka. 11 July (29 June in the old calendar), the icon's last day in Kherson, is celebrated as its feast, along with October 1 and the Wednesday after Easter. The icon is painted with oils on a canvas mounted on wood. The Mother of God holds her Son on her left arm. The Child is holding a scroll. St John the Baptist is depicted on one side of the icon, and St Tatiana on the other. These were probably the patron saints of the original owners of the icon.

13 July: Our Lady of Chartres

HARTRES IS NOT ONLY the oldest shrine in France, but also—in all probability—the oldest Marian shrine in the world. It has pre-Christian origins, like the Athenians' "altar to the unknown god" and was dedicated to the Virgin who would bring forth a son, at least a century before the birth of Christ. About 100 years before Christ, an image of a woman seated on a throne with a child on her knees was honoured there. Under it was placed the sign, "The virgin who will give birth to a god." The early Christians at Chartres understood this to be a prophecy, albeit from within a pagan tradition, about the Virgin Mary.

Even before the Gothic cathedral was built, Chartres was a place of pilgrimage, albeit on a much smaller scale. During the Merovingian and early Carolingian eras, the main focus of devotion for pilgrims was a well, into which it was believed the bodies of various local early Christian martyrs had been tossed. There have been at least five cathedrals on this site, each replacing an earlier building damaged by war or fire. Nothing survives of the earliest church, which was destroyed during an attack on the city by the Danes in 858. In 1140, Christians were returning from the first crusade with new Byzantine dignity added to their idea of the kind of art demanded for the veneration of royalty. In 1144 men began building, with rich and poor alike putting their strength and their possessions into the work. The result is still standing, as strong as the moment it was consecrated in 1260—an architectural marvel that makes people gaze in admiration.

Chartres is the court where Mary sits enthroned beside her Son, receiving her subjects, turning peasant pilgrims into lovers of the beautiful, turning crusty scholars, come to see about some detail, into romantic dreamers at her feet. Mary sits above the southern door, crowned and robed and sceptred like an eastern empress; Christ sits above the central door, not as Judge but, like Mary, a triumphant benevolent sovereign and long lean figures of kings, queens, saints and prophets stand with oriental dignity, lining the columns of the doorways like courtiers attendant on a king and a queen. The windows above depict the Passion of Christ. The Cathedral of Notre-Dame of Chartres is probably the most beautiful gothic church in the world; in its crypt is the shrine of Our Lady Underground, in the choir, a statue of Our Lady of the Pillar, a reputed garment of Mary's is preserved in the treasury. Kings and princes, popes and prelates, saints and sinners, thousands after thousands of ordinary people have come here on pilgrimages for seven hundred years. Miracle upon miracle has been the response to their faith, their confidence and their ardent prayers.[10]

14 July: Our Lady of Canòlich

CCORDING TO PIOUS TRADITION, on 14 July 1223, a shepherd was tending his flock near the village of Canòlich in southern Andorra, when suddenly a bird with brilliant plumage landed on an outcrop. The shepherd approached, caught the bird with no trouble, and carried it to his house. The next day the bird had disappeared, and again he found it in the field. The sequence recurred three times, but the last time, the shepherd found an image of the Virgin Mary in a niche in the rock.

In response to this prodigy, the people of Sant Julià de Lòria parish decided to build a shrine to the Virgin where her statue was found. Nothing remains of that church; the present sanctuary, containing a baroque altarpiece from a previous shrine, dates from the 1970s. The Romanesque image of the Mother of God of Canòlich resides in the parish church of Sant Julià y San Germà in the urban centre of Sant Julià de Lòria: a wooden statue from the late 1100s, with original polychrome, crowned by the Vatican in 1999. On the last Saturday in May, parishioners gather in Sant Julià de Lòria for morning fireworks and Mass in honour of Our Lady. Then the celebration moves to Canòlich, with Masses at the sanctuary, dancing, and blessing and distribution of bread.[11]

15 July: Our Lady of Molanus

 N THE YEAR 1099, the Christian armies arrived at Jerusalem, overjoyed that they had survived to reach their objective. Their joy nearly turned to despair, however, as they ran short of food and suffered greatly with a plague during the siege of the city. The leaders of the crusade realized that they could not win without seeking Divine Assistance. It was agreed by all that they should march together barefoot around the city while singing litanies to the Blessed Virgin Mary. This they did, as the Jews had done centuries before at Jericho, while praying, fasting, and giving alms.

Eight days later, Godfrey of Bouillon was the first to breach the walls and set foot in Jerusalem, which was then swiftly taken. The Turks were finally defeated after what had been a long and difficult siege, and the First Crusade ended with a Christian victory. Now that the city was in Christian hands, the Crusaders desired that they should have a king for the new Kingdom of Jerusalem. The nobleman Raymond of Saint Gilles was offered the crown, but he refused, as it did not seem proper to him to be named king in that holy place. Next, Robert Courte-Heuse also refused. Finally, Godfrey of Bouillon, who had so distinguished himself in the taking of Jerusalem, was asked to accept the crown.

Godfrey of Bouillon was a good man, the son of Blessed Ida of Bouillon, whose father was the Duke Godfrey of Lorraine, himself a descendent of Blessed Charles the Great. Although Godfrey agreed to be made king, still, as they were about to crown him King of Jerusalem, Godfrey pushed aside the crown, saying, "I cannot wear a diadem in the place where my Lord wore a crown of thorns." Instead, as he had prayed at Our Lady at Boulogne-sur-mer before leaving on the Crusade, he credited the Blessed Virgin Mary with the victory, and symbolically gave the crown to Our Lady of Molanus.

After the victory, clad in white garments, the crusaders expressed in solemn procession, hymns and prayers, their gratitude to the Mother of God for giving them this singular victory over the enemies of the Church. The annual celebration in remembrance of the victory occurred every 15 July with a Mass offered to Our Lady of Molanus.

16 July: Our Lady of Mount Carmel

NINE CENTURIES BEFORE Christ, the great prophet Elias went to the heights of Carmel to beg God to send rain after three and a half years of drought. In answer to his prayers Elias saw a small cloud rise out of the sea—a promise of the Immaculate Virgin Mary who would give us her Son to save mankind from the punishment of original sin. At the time of the Crusades there were hermits living on Mount Carmel in imitation of Elias. In their midst was a chapel dedicated to Our Lady. To the medieval members of the Order, Mary was the Gracious Lady who protected them from danger, who won for them the favour of Christ, her Son.

This feast has its origin in the apparition of Our Lady on Mount Carmel in Israel to St Simon Stock, a Carmelite, on 16 July 1251 when he was 86 years old. In response to his appeal to Our Blessed Mother for help for his oppressed Order, Mary appeared to him holding a Brown Scapular in her hand. Mary said to him: "Receive, my beloved son, this habit of your order: this shall be a privilege for you and for all Carmelites; whosoever dies clothed in this shall never suffer eternal fire." This was truly a great gift and a great promise from the Mother of God.

Indeed, the Order of Carmelites takes its name from Mount Carmel, which was the first place dedicated to the Blessed Virgin Mary, and where a chapel was already erected in her honour before her Assumption into heaven. St Simon Stock had entered the Carmelite Order in Kent, England, when he was 40 years old. He was sent to Mount Carmel in the Holy Land where he led a life of prayer and penance until he and most of his brother religious were forced to leave by the Muslims. The group sailed for England. At a General Chapter which was held in Aylesford, Kent, in 1245 St Simon was unanimously elected Prior General of the Carmelite Order. For over 700 years, the Brown Scapular of Our Lady of Mount Carmel has been one of the most precious gifts and highly-indulgenced sacramentals of the Church. It is in reality a garment, given to us by Our Blessed Mother which makes us her special children.

The second promise Mary made is known as the Sabbatine Privilege. Here, Our Lady promised scapular-wearers who perform certain additional acts in her honour prompt delivery from Purgatory, especially on the Saturday after death. We believe that God grants all graces through His Mother. Mary showed herself to St Bernadette at Lourdes for the last time on 16 July; in her last vision at Fatima, she appeared as Our Lady of Mount Carmel. We quote here from the Sequence of the Feast.

Sequence

> Flower of Carmel,
> Tall vine blossom laden;
> Splendour of heaven,
> Childbearing yet maiden.
> None equals thee.
>
> Mother so tender,
> Who no man didst know,
> On Carmel's children
> Thy favours bestow.
> Star of the Sea.
>
> Purest of lilies,
> That flowers among thorns,
> Bring help to the true heart
> That in weakness turns
> and trusts in thee.
>
> Hail, Gate of Heaven,
> With glory now crowned,
> Bring us to safety
> Where thy Son is found,
> true joy to see.

17 July: Our Lady of Campitelli

HE SANCTUARY OF Sancta Maria in Campitelli is one of the most celebrated of Rome. In this church, a precious image is venerated that was transported from the portico of the palace of the Roman noble lady, St Galla, to whom the Virgin herself appeared on 17 July 524. After the death of her husband, Galla had dedicated her life to the poor. Then she found an image of Our Lady in her porch; the icon is on 25 centimetres high. Galla immdeiately went to the Lateran palace to tell Pope John I, who blessed the Roman people with this icon, and a terrible plague which had afflicted them was overcome. Mention is made of the miraculous appearance by Pope Gregory the Great. The image is known as Our Lady in the Portico, or the Madonna del Portico.

The church where the icon was kept was known as Santa Galla Antiqua, and it used to be located just north of the Piazza Bocca della Verità and west of the Via Petroselli. However, in 1656 (or 1658) the icon of Our Lady at the (now demolished) church of Santa Galla Antiqua in the direction of the Bocca della Verità was believed by many people to have miraculously halted an epidemic, after it had been carried through the streets of the city in expiation. Pope Alexander VII agreed that a new church should be built by the city as a shrine for the icon. The consecration of the new church only took place in 1728. The icon of Our Lady of Campitelli is surrounded by an ornate shrine, and there is a stairway behind the display that allows a closer inspection of the famous icon. It is not open to the general public. Many times the sacred image of Our Lady of Campitelli has been carried in procession through the streets of Rome to invoke Our Lady's protection against pestilence, epidemics and earthquakes. Since the time of the Old Pretender, whose son Henry Benedict Cardinal Stuart was Cardinal Deacon of the church from 1747 until his death in 1807, the church has been a centre of devotion for the conversion of England.

18 July: Our Lady of Good Deliverance

AINT-ÉTIENNE-DES-GRÈS WAS LOCATED on the Rue Saint-Jacques, on the site of the present Faculty of Law. It was one of the early centres of Christianity in Paris and stood on the site of an oratory erected by St Denis to St Stephen, and its foundation dates to around the sixth century. Saint-Étienne was one of five Merovingian churches marking the road from Paris to Orleans. The original church was destroyed by the Vikings, but rebuilt in the 11th century. Canons were installed in 1045 to serve the church and pray for the king. It became a parish sometime before 1080, but the parish was absorbed by St Benedict's between 1195 and 1205. The Chapter existed until 1790. The collegiate church was demolished in 1792.

The church notably contained a Black Madonna, the Notre Dame de Bonne Délivrance (Our Lady of Good Deliverance), also known as the Black Madonna of Paris. The statue dates from the 14th century, replacing an 11th-century version. It is 150 centimetres tall, and made from painted limestone. The Virgin wears a white veil and dark blue mantle ornamented with fleurs-de-lys over a red robe. The Royal Confraternity of Notre Dame de Bonne Délivrance was established in 1533. Louis XIII and Anne of Austria were members. The shine was visited by many notable French saints, including Vincent de Paul and Francis de Sales—it was in front of the statue that de Sales recited the Memorare, and made his religious conversion.

In 1703, a young seminarian named Claude Poullart des Places gathered a dozen of his companions at Saint-Étienne-des-Grès and consecrated the group to the Virgin; that act was the beginning of the Congregation of the Holy Ghost. Other notable pilgrims to the statue—some before the Revolution, some after—have included Claude Bernard, Jean-Jacques Olier, John Bosco, Prosper Guéranger, and Madeleine Sophie Barat. When the church was destroyed during the Revolution, all its contents were sold; the statue was saved by a pious rich woman named Madame de Carignan. De Carignan was arrested during the Reign of Terror, and she would pray to Our Lady in prison with others who had been arrested for their faith. When de Carignan was freed in 1806, she gave the statue to the Sisters of St Thomas of Villeneuve, who had been imprisoned with her. The statue is still located in the chapel of the Congregation of the Sisters of St Thomas of Villeneuve in Neuilly-sur-Seine. The feast of Our Lady of Good Deliverance is kept on 18 July.

19 July: Our Lady of the Miracle

HE FRANCISCAN FRIARS who accompanied the Spanish Conquest to Peru hung an image of the Immaculate Conception over the door of their first church in Lima. On missionary journeys around the region, they would take the image which they called "La Misionera" with them. They were in the Inca capital of Cusco on 23 May 1536 when, during the rebellion of Manco Inca against the two-year Spanish regime, natives trapped many Spaniards in a hut and set fire to the straw roof. *La Misionera* was seen by all to leave her place inside and to appear above the burning building together with St James the Greater. The fire ceased, and all were saved. In honour of this event, the Spanish built the Church of the Triumph, now an adjunct of the Cusco cathedral.

Back in Lima, after the Franciscans surrounded the little chapel with a big monastery complex, the image over the door was gradually forgotten. By the 1600s, it had one regular devotee, a poor woman. One day she heard Our Lady speak: "You alone, daughter, among all the people here, visit me and pray to me. One day I will repay you." After the woman told saintly Brother Juan Gomez, he often remarked, "Lima does not recognize the great good it has in this miraculous image, but soon it will know."

On 27 November 1630, when most of the people of Lima were attending a bullfight in the main square, a violent earthquake struck the city. All were terrified, for it seemed certain that they would perish. But those near the Franciscan Church saw the image of Our Lady turn in the direction of the Blessed Sacrament, with her hands held in suppliant gesture. Abruptly, the earthquake stopped. Several hours later, when the Franciscan community had gathered before the miraculous image to give thanks, the prodigy was renewed. The statue turned again to its former position, smiling graciously.

Now called Our Lady of the Miracle, the statue was housed in a magnificent new church. In 1835, the church burned down. Only the statue remained intact. On 19 June 1953, the papal nuncio crowned the miraculous statue. The feast of Our Lady of the Miracle is on 27 November, anniversary of the 1630 earthquake.

20 July: Our Lady of Caversham

HE ORIGINS OF the Shrine of Our Lady in Caversham are a mystery. We know that by the time of the Norman Conquest there was a shrine chapel beside the River Thames, containing a statue of Our Blessed Lady, and that pilgrims came there to pray. For many years it was believed that the Shrine was part of the church of St Peter's and that the Shrine was situated close to the present Caversham Bridge. However, there is now evidence that suggests that the Shrine was part of the Manor of Caversham which was situated near the present Dean's Farm.

The reason why people came on pilgrimage is not clear. The first definite historical record is from the year 1106, when Duke Robert of Normandy presented to the Shrine a relic of Christ's Passion which he had brought back from the First Crusade. In 1162 the care of the shrine was entrusted to the Augustinian Canons of Notley Abbey, near Aylesbury, one of whom was always resident at Caversham as the Warden of the Shrine. Although the great Reading Abbey was only a short distance away across the Thames it never owned or controlled the Shrine. However the Abbey did help build the first bridge over the river, with a chapel to the Holy Spirit on the Reading side and another dedicated to St Anne on the Caversham side; there was also a holy well, known as St Anne's Well, still to be seen today at the top of Priest Hill, Caversham.

Throughout the Middle Ages the fame of Our Lady of Caversham spread throughout the country and pilgrims came not only to pray, but also to present votive offerings to the Shrine, so that by the 15th century the statue was plated in silver. In 1439 Isabella Beauchamp, Countess of Warwick, left 20 pounds of gold to be made into a crown for the statue. Kings and Queens of England travelled up river from Windsor to visit the Shrine, the last being Queen Catherine of Aragon who came on 17 July 1532 to pray to Our Blessed Lady while Henry VIII pressured her for a divorce.

Henry's break with Rome led to the destruction of all religious houses and shrines so, on 14 September 1538, John London, the government agent, arrived at Caversham and in a single day closed down the Shrine, stripped it bare of all its religious property and ended over five hundred years of religious devotion. The statue was sent up to Thomas Cromwell in London where it was burnt.

Revival of devotion to Our Lady of Caversham began in 1897, the year following the foundation of the Parish of Our Lady and St Anne. Fr Haskew, the parish priest, wrote the first account of the Shrine in modern times. When a new bridge was built in the 1920s, stones from the foundations of the original bridge chapel were given to the parish to be incorporated into a restored shrine. At that time there was a fine white marble statue of Our Lady and Child given to the church to encourage devotion to Our Lady; it is now in the church, in the Cenacle.

In the Marian Year of 1954 the then parish priest, Fr William O'Malley, decided that a suitable shrine should be built. A stone chapel, in the Norman style was built, and a large oak statue of Our Lady and Child, about 500 years old, from Northern Europe, was purchased, reputedly found in an antique shop in London. This lovely statue shows Mary nursing the infant Christ; her cloak is gilded, her dress, originally blue and silver, and her face are now dark with age, but her look of tender and dignified love is truly beautiful, inspiring and prayerful. The renewed Shrine of Our Lady of Caversham was solemnly blessed and dedicated by Archbishop Francis Grimshaw of Birmingham in 1958. The stone floor of the chapel is below the level of the church to allow for better viewing of the statue from the body of the church, and also so that passers-by may kneel at an angled window outside the church, to see the statue without entering. To complete the link with the medieval shrine, in 1996, to celebrate the centenary of the parish, a gold and silver crown was made for the statue, and blessed by Pope St John Paul II during a parish pilgrimage to Rome. The statue was solemnly crowned by the Papal Nuncio, Archbishop Barbarito, on 20 July 1996. Today groups and individuals come regularly to pray to Our Blessed Mother at her Shrine. During the Millennium Year the Shrine was one of the recognised places to obtain the Jubilee Year Indulgence.[12]

21 July: Our Lady of Mercy

 NE THING MOVED Catherine McAuley, the foundress of the Sisters of Mercy, to action—the pity of God. Her heart was touched by the misery of the poor of Dublin. Poverty of body was equalled, among many of them, by poverty of soul. The youth, brought up in the slums, were especially susceptible to the loss of the faith that had defied centuries of persecution.

There was, her practical soul pondered, only one remedy. If there might be a group of women who would educate themselves to the works of mercy among these people, some of the corporal and spiritual misery would be lifted. To feed the hungry, to give drink to the thirsty, to clothe the naked, to shelter the homeless— this she planned first; then, when the needs of the body were cared for; to instruct the ignorant, to counsel the doubtful, to pray for the living and the dead.

For a patroness of this venture, as old as Christendom itself, she had not far to look. Our Lady had been a Mother to her all her life, especially since her parent's death. The title, Mother of

Mercy, had been dear to her when she learned of the ancient Order of Mercy that had ransomed the captives of the Turks, giving not only money for their return to Europe and their families, but often substituting for them, going into harsh captivity in the place of others—and all this in the name of Mary, Queen of Mercy, the Pitiful One. She would call her co-workers Sisters of Mercy, modelling her life and theirs on Our Lady. With her and in her spirit, they would perform the works of mercy wherever the Holy Spirit led them.[13]

22 July: Our Lady of the Rocks

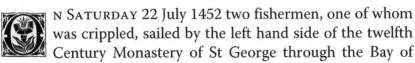 N SATURDAY 22 July 1452 two fishermen, one of whom was crippled, sailed by the left hand side of the twelfth Century Monastery of St George through the Bay of Kotor in Montenegro, and passed a small crag jutting out of the water. On it was a painted icon of the Virgin Mary and Child. As they got closer, the crippled fisherman put one arm out from the boat and lifted the icon from the crag. He took it home with him and thought nothing else of it until the next morning, Sunday, when he became aware of two things. First, the icon of the Mother and Child was missing, and second, he was no longer crippled. He ran to tell the priest of the miracle, but with no proof of the icon little could be done aside from offering prayers of gratitude to Our Lady who he believed had saved him.

However just a few months later, as the two brothers were passing again by that small rocky crag in the bay, the fisherman once again spotted the miraculous icon and this time, upon landing in Perast, he ran straight to the priest. "This is the icon. This is the reason I could run here. This, Father, is the source of my miracle." It was decided that a shrine to the miraculous Virgin Mary was to be founded upon that very same crag on which the icon was found. Old, unused sailing boats were gathered in the bay as well as huge rocks from the area. A procession began in the direction of the crag and once it arrived the boats and rocks were sunk to the bottom of the sea until an island was formed. Over time, the islet gradually emerged from the sea. The custom of throwing rocks into the sea is kept alive even to this day. Every year at sunset on 22 July, an event takes place in which local residents take their boats and throw rocks into the sea, widening the surface of the island.

The first known church was built on the islet in 1452. Unfortunately it was plundered and burnt down by pirates before being replaced in 1632 by the Venetian settlers as the present Church of Our Lady of the Rocks; it was upgraded in 1722. Over 2,500 votive silver tablets are housed at the Church, depicting tales of the threats the sailors survived whilst away from the Bay of Kotor, and how Our Lady rescued so many people from danger at sea.

23 July: Our Lady, Mother of Divine Grace

HIS FEAST IS particular to the Carmelite Order and is octave of the Solemnity of Our Lady of Mount Carmel. We honour Mary as Mother of Divine Grace since she is the Mother of the Son of God, the Author of Grace. Tradition ascribes to Mary the titles Mother of Divine Grace, Mother most amiable, Mother most admirable, Mother of Mercy. God has chosen her to be treasurer and dispensatrix of all His graces. Since Mary has formed the Head of the predestined, Jesus Christ, it pertains to her to form also the members of the Head, who are the true Christians. She has received from God a special power to nourish souls and to make them grow in Him. St Augustine says that the predestined in this world are enclosed in Mary's womb and that they come to the light only when their good Mother brings them forth to eternal life. It is to her that the Holy Spirit has said "Take root in my elect" (see Ecclesiasticus 24:12) —roots of deep humility, of burning charity and of all the virtues.

Hymn

Virgin resplendent in the court of heaven,
Carmel's rare beauty and all mankind's glory,

hear us, dear mother, as our voices humbly
tell your love's story.

Gifts beyond reckoning you pour out in bounty,
rich rain of blessing dropped on hill and meadow
where you still shelter your devoted offspring
in Carmel's shadow.

Grant then your favour, quick to heed and answer,
may these our fervent prayers win grace like starlight,
keen, constant, tracing out a way to heaven
through our profound night.

Stay with us, Mary, on this holy mountain;
so may our love refreshed with heavenly showers
thrive like a garden and provide your altar
with wreaths of flowers.

Ever in kindness strengthen and sustain us,
lightening our burden with a mother's blessing,
that we may share the Father's life and splendor
past dispossessing.

Praise God who made us, God whose goodness crowned you
queen of creation, dear above all other,
and gave you to us, Lady of Mount Carmel
and Virgin Mother. Amen.

24 July: Our Lady of Prémontré

HE ORDER OF Canons Regular of Premontré, also known as the Premonstratensians, White Canons, or the Norbertines, are a religious order founded at Prémontré in 1120 by Saint Norbert, who later became the Archbishop of Magdeburg. Saint Norbert was not a particularly pious young man until he had an encounter with God similar to that of St Paul. While riding through the countryside one bright day in the year 1115, Norbert had not gone far with the sky darkened due to a sudden storm. A bolt of lightning struck the ground near Norbert, causing his mount to rear and throw him to the ground. Norbert lay unconscious for some time, but when he awoke he went to his knees, calling out: "Lord, what dost thou wish that I should do?" A voice was heard to respond: "Avoid evil and do good."

After that, Norbert was a changed man, determined to obey the heavenly command. He made a spiritual retreat and became a priest, giving away his estates and retiring to a life of rural solitude, applying himself to a life of prayer and contemplation. Saint Norbert left his hermitage from time to time to preach in France, Belgium and Germany, begging for his bread along the way. In time, a few good men were drawn by his sanctity and began to follow him.

During this time Saint Norbert befriended Saint Bernard of Clairvaux, and it is thought that Saint Bernard's example inspired Saint Norbert to form a similar community for canons. A remote place in the marshy forested lands of Premontre was selected to be the place where they decided to make their place of retreat, devoting themselves to the chanting of the Divine Office, prayer and meditation. Soon they had a simple monastery and church in the wilderness.

Saint Norbert had a tender devotion to the Blessed Virgin Mary. She herself, Our Lady of Premontre, appeared to him in a vision, giving Norbert the white habit that he and his brothers in religion were to wear. In only a few years there were nine houses and the order had papal approval from Pope Honorius II. By the middle of the 14th century there were over 1,300 monasteries and 400 convents stretching from Palestine to Norway while nourishing all of Christendom. This was the time of the High Middle Ages, creating the cradle for Western Civilization.

A little below Lancaster, England, stand the ruins of what was once Cockersands Abbey, also known as Our Lady of the Marshes, and Our Lady of Prémontré, because the Premonstratensians were responsible for its erection, changing the bleak and barren lands into fertile profitable ones. When the dissolution of the Lancashire monasteries began in 1537, the Abbey seal was broken and the gold and jewels stolen by King Henry VIII.

Furniture and goods were sold, and the monks' quarters stripped of their lead and left to fall into ruin, and decay.

Since this monastery had been dedicated to Mary, at least one monk was set aside as the "Mary priest" whose special duty it was to offer daily or two or three times a week a votive Mass in honour of Our Lady of Premontre. He also rang the "Mary Bell" morning and evening and kept her shrine decked with flowers and lights and saw that the best vessels and finest linens were used on her feast days. Going on a pilgrimage to Mary's shrine, people would be "measured" for a candle by taking their length and breadth in the form of a cross and candles were made to equal the sum of these two numbers. The candles were coiled and carried to burn either in supplication or thanksgiving before Our Lady's image. On her feast days large candles, "wreathed with flowers" were burned in profusion. They were called "Gaud-candles" meaning joy and beauty.

Hough de Pourte in 1318 left a yearly rent "to maintain a 3-pound candle to burn before Our Lady's altar daily at her High Mass," whilst John Baret at Bury requested in his will that at his burial and Requiem Mass five men should follow the coffin dressed in black to represent the five wounds of Our Blessed Lord, and five women dressed in white to represent the five joys of Our Blessed Lady. Each "must hold a candle of clean wax." Another man left a half acre of ground to purchase "Lady" candles to burn yearly to "lighten Our Lady's way." Countless more of these requests could be enumerated.

Candles and light are symbolic. A light is put to the wick – the hard wax melts and overflows and is drawn downward with blessing from Our Lady; the light illumines our darkness of mind and soul – when our hearts are lit with God's love and that of His Blessed Mother, they soften, become filled with God's grace and light, and inevitably shine before men. May the candles of Our Lady of Prémontré continue to lighten Our Lady in our souls and make us more and more Mary-like each day. May the number of votive Masses in Mary's honour increase and may there be again those who will be proud to style themselves "Mary priests." May hearts glow with love of her. Only through her intercession may we ever hope for the conversion of our land which is so rapidly falling prey to the mighty evils of these modern times in which we all need our Heavenly Mother more than ever before in the world's history. Our Lady of Prémontré, ever enlighten our way![14]

25 July: Our Lady of Lac Bouchet

HE SAGUENAY FJORD is an ancient glacial valley located in the province of Quebec, Canada, that has been overrun with sea water. In 1828 a surveyor, Joseph Bouchette, ventured into the region for the purpose of collecting data for topographical maps. It was during this expedition that he found a suitable site for a future village, which Pascal Dumais and his family later settled. This marked the founding of the village of Lac-Bouchette, with more and more people coming to settle in the area until the village had 300 inhabitants around the year 1888.

A man named Charles Napoleon Robitaille, a salesman who travelled the roads in and around Quebec. During the winters he would have to cross frozen rivers, and it was in the winter of 1878 while trying to cross the Saguenay River that the ice broke under the weight of his horse and sleigh. Pulled beneath the surface of the icy waters, Charles was alone and completely helpless. Knowing he was dying, he implored the Blessed Virgin Mary to save him. Charles miraculously survived, and managed to escape from the river with his life. He knew Our Lady had assisted him, and so to honour Mary and her recent apparition at Lourdes, he asked Louis Jobin to create a huge statue of the Blessed Virgin sculpted in the image of Our Lady of Lourdes. He envisioned the statue in the heights overlooking the mouth of the river. The statue Jobin sculpted became known as Notre-Dame du Saguenay.

The finished statue is an impressive 10 metres high, and weighs 3 tonnes. Sculpted of solid white pine, it was then sheathed in lead to protect the statue from the harsh weather. Hauling such a huge statue into place was a difficult task in the late nineteenth century. After being constructed, it was broken down into 14 separate pieces and then hoisted into place to be put together again. On the right side of the base of the statue, the sculptor affixed a lead plate on which is written: "Louis Jobin, Quebec." The statue made him the most famous sculptor of the time, and the statue has become a regional landmark, with visitors from the world over assembling at her feet to sing the Ave Maria.

In 1889 the mission church of Saint Thomas Aquinas was built, and the next year Father Joseph Ironwood became the first pastor. A second church was soon built, in 1898, as the population increased dramatically. Now, on the north shore of Lake Bouchet, in the province of Quebec, there stand the buildings of a friary and the sanctuary of Our Lady of the Sagueney. In 1920, Father Elzéar Delamarre built a house and a private chapel dedicated to Saint Anthony of Padua on the site, which later became known as the hermitage of Saint Anthony and is one of the national shrines in Quebec. So began the pilgrimage-shrine that has since grown steadily in popularity. After Father de Lamarre's death in 1925, the Capuchin Franciscans took over the property, built their house and church there, and ministered to the thousands of pilgrims who sought out the sanctuary.

26 July: Our Lady of Faith

LESSED IS SHE who has believed: with these words, Elizabeth welcomes the presence of Mary in her house. Our Lady's life fulfilled the true goal of all living: her great achievement was to do the will of God—her vocation, as ours, is to live by faith. Every appearance of Mary on the Gospel scene has some connection with the will of God, starting with her words to the Archangel Gabriel: "Behold the handmaid of the Lord; be it done unto me according to your word" (Lk 1:38). During Christ's infancy we have no recorded words of Mary, but her actions expressed her magnanimous faith. When the shepherds and the

Wise Men came, she pondered things in her heart. When after forty days she brought her Child to the Temple and was told by Simeon of the "sword of sorrow" that would pierce her heart, she accepted, as also when the will of God was made known to St Joseph for the escape into Egypt, and later for their return to Nazareth.

When the twelve-year old Boy Jesus remained behind in the Temple; she accepted in humble submission to God's will His mysterious answer: "How is it that you sought me? Did you not know that I must be about my Father's business?"—"she kept all these things carefully in her heart" (Lk 2:49, 51). Mary walked by faith and she lived by it. She had to make acts of faith each day to accept the divinity of her Son, flesh of her flesh. With the exception of the Annunciation, the great signs given were for others, not for her—there was no need for extraordinary things to make Mary's faith grow. During Jesus' boyhood, when He, "advanced in wisdom and age and grace before God and men" (Lk 2:52), she too advanced in wisdom and age and grace before God and men, particularly so in her faith. When the public life of Christ began, Mary was there at Cana as well as at Calvary. Christ's pronouncement, "Blessed are they who hear the word of God and keep it" (Lk 8:21), perfectly expresses Mary's perfect faith-life.

The Magnificat is Our Lady's hymn of thanksgiving to God; she is blessed in her maternity as well as in her spiritual motherhood at the foot of the Cross:

> Yes, truly "blessed is she who believed"! These words, spoken by Elizabeth after the Annunciation, here at the foot of the Cross seem to re-echo with supreme eloquence, and the power contained within them becomes something penetrating. From the Cross, that is to say from the very heart of the mystery of Redemption, there radiates and spreads out the prospect of that blessing of faith It goes right hack to "the beginning", and as a sharing in the sacrifice of Christ—the new Adam—it becomes in a certain sense the counterpoise to the disobedience and disbelief embodied in the sin of our first parents. Thus

teach the Fathers of the Church and especially St Irenaeus: "The knot of Eve's disobedience was untied by Mary's obedience; what the virgin Eve bound through her unbelief, the Virgin Mary loosened by her faith."[15]

Mary's supreme achievement in life was to hear the word of God and to do it. She had to walk in faith. Faith is the "evidence of things that do not yet appear" (Heb 11:1). Mary's life was a steady progress of faith as God communicated to her more and more of His secrets.

> Mary is thus the icon of the disciple, of the believing and prayerful woman who knows how to accompany and encourage our faith and our hope in the distinct stages we must go through. In Mary we find the faithful reflection not of a poetically sweetened faith, but of a strong faith especially at a time when the sweet enchantments of things are broken and there are contradictions in conflict everywhere. And we will certainly have to learn from that strong and helpful faith that characterised and characterises our Mother; to learn from this faith that knows how to get inside history so as to be salt and light in our lives and in our society.[16]

Faith will one day give place to sight in the joy of the vision of paradise; for Mary, our Mother, the timeless woman, is to be found at the side of Christ, body and soul, in heaven. Mary's concern in Heaven is the same she had on earth—to do the will of God, and by her prayers, by her living presence, she is still advancing the salvation of all her children, of all of us, in Heaven.

27 July: Our Lady of a Happy Death

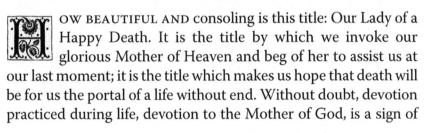 OW BEAUTIFUL AND consoling is this title: Our Lady of a Happy Death. It is the title by which we invoke our glorious Mother of Heaven and beg of her to assist us at our last moment; it is the title which makes us hope that death will be for us the portal of a life without end. Without doubt, devotion practiced during life, devotion to the Mother of God, is a sign of

predestination and, as such, assures for us at the hour of death the assistance of this divine Mother. Mary could not abandon at this supreme moment anyone who has faithfully called upon her during life. Besides this devotion, in keeping us away from evil, draws us both strongly and calmly to the practice of the Christian virtues; in addition, it is incompatible with a life of sin and vice. It is therefore, like a remote but extremely efficacious preparation for our passage from time to eternity. That is why it is said that to serve Mary is to gain control over the devil; it is likewise written that a true servant of Mary cannot perish because, devotion to this Mother of the Divine, in keeping us virtuous, gives us a certain pledge that Heaven will be ours. Death is the crowning of life: a good life cannot end in eternal loss.

Besides, there are other particular reasons, for which Mary's assistance is especially assured to us at the hour of death; and this assistance, provided we prove ourselves worthy of it, is bound to procure for us the special grace of a holy death. Those reasons are: Mary has merited by her own death (which is the ideal of the death of a Christian) the power of helping her faithful servants at the moment of the great passage from life to eternity. Having assisted her Divine Son in His agony and till His death on the Cross, she has received from Him the mission of assisting us equally during our agony and the hour of our death. She will exercise on our behalf the office of a Mother, at this supreme moment.

These considerations will enable us to know and to appreciate better, all that we owe to our Heavenly Mother. It is through Mary that Jesus was given to us, when He came, a tiny infant in the infirmity of human flesh, wrapped in swaddling clothes, in order to save us; it is equally through Mary that on the last day we hope to see face to face this same Jesus surrounded by the glory of the Father—the source of eternal happiness to us: "And after this our exile, show unto us the blessed fruit of thy womb, Jesus."[17]

28 July: Our Lady of the Gate of Dawn

 UE TO FREQUENT attacks on the Lithuanian lands from the Tatars and regular conflicts with the Grand Duchy of Moscow, in 1503 Grand Duke Alexander of Lithuania granted the city of Vilnius a privilege to build fortifications of brick and stone around the entire city. Of the nine gates that were once part of the defensive walls encircling the old, medieval city of Vilnius, only one remains. Built between 1503 and 1522, the Gate of Dawn is one of Vilnius' most important religious, historical, and cultural monuments. It owes its significance to the fact that the chapel built over its arch is home to the icon of the "Blessed Virgin Mary, Mother of Mercy"also known as "Our Lady of the Gate of Dawn." In the 16th century, it was common for people to place religious artefacts in city gates. The purpose was to not only protect the city from enemies, but also to bless travellers who were leaving the city. For this reason, the icon was hung in the small chapel built over the Gate of Dawn.

The Chapel was not the first home of the painting of Our Lady of Mercy. At first, Our Lady's image was hung on the inside of the gateway in a small niche as a counterpart to the depiction of the Saviour of the World on the outside. The painting did not have either a suitable chapel or any adornments that are typical of wonder-working images. The Discalced Carmelites arrived in Vilnius in 1626, and they were given a piece of land to build a church and a convent near the Gates of Dawn. The church which was consecrated only in 1654 and dedicated to St Theresa of Avila. In 1668, the city's authorities entrusted the Carmelites with the care of Our Lady's painting and in 1671, a wooden chapel was built to house the image. After the chapel was renovated in 1927, Our Lady was crowned by the townspeople and Pope Pius XI bestowed the title of Mother of Mercy on the image. Painted on eight joined oak boards by an unknown artist in the 1620s, the icon had been covered with silver and gold around 1671. It is an unusual image, for in this painting Mary is not depicted holding her infant Son. Instead, she is alone and pregnant, praying as she crosses her hands over her chest.

From the beginning, so many miracles were attributed to the intercession of Our Lady the Mother of Mercy that news of her power spread quickly. The chapel walls are covered with votive offerings—expressions of gratitude left behind by those whose prayers have been answered, who have received Divine favours through the intercession of Our Blessed Mother.

In 1655 the Russian army set fire to the city of Vilnius and most of the town was destroyed. The fire lasted seventeen days. However, the image above the Gate of Dawn survived without any damage. This strongly encouraged the people's devotion toward it and attracted many pilgrims. Since then it is considered a miraculous symbol of Lithuanian and Polish independence.

In 1671, a small two-year old child fell sharply from the top floor on to the stone ground below, and when he was lifted from the ground he was dead. The mourning parents took their child to the picture of Our Lady in deep faith that their prayers would indeed be answered. The next day they found their child full of health without the slightest injury to his body or the least bruise.' In gratitude to the Holy Mother of God for this favour and in eternal remembrance of the miracle, a plaque showing the incident was hung in the chapel on May of the same year.

In 1702, Vilnius was captured by the Swedish Army during the Great Northern War. The Swedes, who were Protestants, mocked the painting, forbade songs and prayers, and caroused around the Gate of Dawn. One soldier even shot at the painting (the bullet hole can still be seen on the right sleeve). In the early morning of Great and Holy Saturday, the heavy iron gates fell and crushed four Swedish soldiers—two died instantly and two later from their injuries. The next day, Easter Sunday, the Lithuanian Army successfully counter-attacked near the gate. The commander, grateful for the victory, bestowed a large silver votive offering upon the chapel.

In May 1715 when a fire destroyed the wooden chapel, the image was rescued and placed in the church at the monastery until a new chapel was built on the original site in 1726. The wall was destroyed, in 1795, during the years Russia occupied Lithuania. The only thing that remained standing was the Gate of Dawn shrine. The shrine grew in popularity over the years, but in 1944, the Soviets put an end to religious services at the shrine. When Lithuania declared its independence, forty-five years later, services were resumed.

The Gate of Dawn is also significant because of its connection to the life of St Maria Faustina and the Feast of Divine Mercy. She lived in Vilnius from 1933 to 1936, and she often came to the gate of Dawn to pray. The Feast of Divine Mercy was celebrated for the first time on 28 April 1935 at the Gate of Dawn. It was also here that the image of the Divine Mercy was first displayed for public veneration at the conclusion of the Jubilee of the Redemption of the World (26–28 April 1935). The festival of Our Lady the Mother of Mercy is now the most important celebration in the Diocese of Vilnius and is celebrated for a week in the second half of November.[18]

During his visit to Lithuania, Pope St John Paul II, recited the Rosary on 4 September 1993 and addressed the people in these words:

> For many centuries, this shrine has seen many pilgrims who daily bring their joys and woes to Our Lady of Mercy. For that reason, the gates have become a meeting place between the faithful and the Mother of Christ and His Church, and a symbol of unity for the faithful from Lithuania, Poland, Belarus, Ukraine and many other countries; this is a place where Christians can share their common faith as brothers and sisters in the presence of the Virgin Mary to express their common hope and charity.

Prayer

O my Mother, the Blessed Virgin Mary, I offer myself entirely to your grace and to your overwhelming mercy today and forever, but mostly at the hour of my death do I dedicate myself to you. To thee do I dedicate my body and soul, all my happiness and hope, all my sorrows and sufferings! I offer my life and the end of my life to your holy hands so that through your merits all my deeds and acts go according to your holy will and according to the will of your sweetest Son! Amen.

29 July: Our Lady of Ephesus

N THE SCRIPTURES, Mary is last seen praying with the Apostles before Pentecost: "With one heart all these joined constantly in prayer, together with some women, including Mary the mother of Jesus, and with his brothers" (Ac 1:14). Among the Apostles she was closest to St John who had been entrusted to her by her Son dying on the Cross. St John, author of the Gospel, is said to have spent his last years in Ephesus. Although early traditions, through the Middle Ages, placed the Virgin Mother's final days on earth in Jerusalem, the idea that she accompanied the Beloved Disciple to Ephesus had gained currency by 1670, when Venerable Maria d'Agreda wrote of it in *The Mystical City of God*.

In the 1820s, stigmatic Blessed Anne Catherine Emmerich, from her sickbed in Germany, saw detailed visions of the lives of Christ and His Mother, which poet Clemens Brentano recorded. The *Life of the Blessed Virgin Mary* was published in 1852, after both Emmerich and Brentano were dead. Blessed Catherine envisioned Mary's stone house, built by St John over a stream, to be part of a small Christian community on a wild, overgrown height nearer to the sea than Ephesus. In 1891, Sister Marie de Mandat-Grancey, at the Daughters of Charity mission in Smyrna (Izmir), convinced two French Lazarist missionaries, Fathers Henri Jung and Eugene Poulin, to climb Mount Koressos near

Ephesus to check reports of an old structure corresponding to the mystic's vision. On 29 July, they found a ruined chapel which fit Blessed Catherine's description uncannily. It turned out that local tradition held it to have been the house of Mother Mary (Meryem Ana), near the sacred spot from which she was assumed into heaven. A year later, foreign Catholics were joining the local pilgrimage to Mount Koressos for the Feast of the Assumption on August 15. Lazarist Fathers came to renovate the building and manage the site, which they still do. The August gathering also attracts Muslims as well as Christians.

In 1914 Pope St Pius X granted a plenary indulgence to those who visited the shrine. Pope Pius XII reconfirmed this indulgence in 1950 after the definition of the dogma of the Assumption, and Blessed Pope John XXIII reconfirmed it again in 1962. Bishop Roncalli (later Pope St John XXIII) had visited this house, as did his successors to the papal throne. On 26 July 1967, Pope Paul VI visited the house of Our Lady. Pope St John Paul II travelled to the site on 30 November 1979 to confirm the belief that this was indeed the home of the Mother of God. Pope Benedict XVI celebrated Mass at the House of the Virgin Mary in Ephesus on 29 November 2006. Reflecting on his visit, Pope Benedict remarked:

> The Shrine of Mary's House stands in a pleasant place called the Hill of the Nightingale which overlooks the Aegean Sea. This is a small and ancient chapel, built to contain a cottage which, according to a very old tradition, the Apostle John had built for the Virgin Mary after taking her with him to Ephesus... Archaeological research has shown that from time immemorial the site has been a place of Marian worship which is also dear to Muslims, who go there regularly to venerate the One they call "Meryem Ana", Mother Mary. In the garden in front of the Shrine, I celebrated Holy Mass for a group of the faithful who came from the neighbouring city of Izmir, from other parts of Turkey and from abroad. At Mary's House we truly felt at home, and in that atmosphere of peace we prayed for peace in the Holy Land and throughout the world.[19]

30 July: Our Lady of Safe Delivery

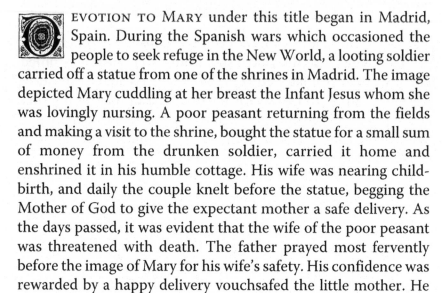EVOTION TO MARY under this title began in Madrid, Spain. During the Spanish wars which occasioned the people to seek refuge in the New World, a looting soldier carried off a statue from one of the shrines in Madrid. The image depicted Mary cuddling at her breast the Infant Jesus whom she was lovingly nursing. A poor peasant returning from the fields and making a visit to the shrine, bought the statue for a small sum of money from the drunken soldier, carried it home and enshrined it in his humble cottage. His wife was nearing childbirth, and daily the couple knelt before the statue, begging the Mother of God to give the expectant mother a safe delivery. As the days passed, it was evident that the wife of the poor peasant was threatened with death. The father prayed most fervently before the image of Mary for his wife's safety. His confidence was rewarded by a happy delivery vouchsafed the little mother. He named the statue accordingly, the Mother of Safe Delivery.

The news spread rapidly, and Mary's devotees under similar circumstances as the peasant's wife, frequented the home; until it became too small to accommodate all. A chapel was built, and later a church—that of St Martin. The statue was removed with great pomp; nobility and peasant alike knelt in prayer in their personal and family needs. Our Lady recognized all as her children, bestowing safe deliveries where requested.

In the 1620's the Spanish colonists, as a sign of their love for the nursing Mother of Jesus Christ, established the first sanctuary dedicated to the Blessed Virgin Mary in what is today the United States. It was established in the same place where the first Mass had been celebrated years before, at the Mission of the Name of God, in St Augustine, Florida. The rustic chapel and several others, built after were destroyed by the artillery in the first days of the colony, and later by hurricanes. The actual chapel was built in 1915, and there a replica of the rustic statue is exposed. Many mothers go to the sanctuary of Our Lady of the Milk at St

Augustine to ask for the blessing of maternity, beseeching Our Lady for her intercession, in order that God may obtain for them a good delivery, as well as joyful and pious children.

31 July: Our Lady of the Slain

 UR LADY OF THE SLAIN is a statue located at a Cistercian monastery in Ceiça, near Coimbra, in Portugal. It is piously believed that this image was brought directly from heaven to be given to the Abbot John, who was the uncle of King Afonso I of Portugal. The statue earned its unique title through many spectacular miracles. It is best known for the fact that life was restored to several persons who had been murdered. Interestingly, in memory of these miracles, those who had been raised from the dead would bear, from that time forward, a red mark upon their throats, like that which was seen on the throat of the image.[20]

King Afonso I, the Conqueror, (also known as Afonso Henriques), was the first king of Portugal and a lifelong sworn opponent of Islam. He spent 46 years as king of Portugal waging war against the Moors in order to drive the invaders from his land. He was also known for his piety and great love for God. A relative of Saint Bernard of Clairvaux, he bestowed many privileges and benefits to the religious orders and built Alcobaça Monastery for the Cistercian Order. He was responsible for the foundation of several monasteries and convents, and was favourable especially toward the Cistercians.

King Afonso was not a stranger to the miraculous. Before the battle of Ourique, when Afonso was to meet in battle an overwhelming army of five Moorish kings, he prayed that God would give him the strength to defeat his enemies. He fell asleep, and in his dream a mysterious old man entered his tent to him to advise him that it was God's will that he would be victorious in the coming engagement against the Moors. Afterward, he was awakened by his guard, who told him there was an old man waiting outside who wished to speak to him. King Afonso bade him enter, and was started to see it was the old man from his dream. The old man said: "Alfonso, have confidence, because you will conquer and destroy these infidel kings, you will smash their power and the Lord will appear to you." He then instructed the king to leave his camp that night, without any attendant, at the sound of the church bell ringing from the old man's hermitage.

It was dark, and the night seemed ominous and strangely vacant when King Afonso heard the mournful toll of the bell. He took up his sword and shield and mounted his horse to ride alone from the camp. A heavy cloud cover blotted out the light of the moon and stars when suddenly an intense beam of light illuminated the night from the East, and in this resplendent light a Cross appeared bearing the crucified Christ. King Afonso dismounted and prostrated himself before the image of the King of Kings when he heard a voice telling him that he would indeed be victorious against the Moors. Trusting in God, King Afonso went into battle and won an impressive victory against the five kings. It is said that Saint James, the Moorslayer, appeared during the battle to guarantee the victory of the Christian army. King Afonso went on to win other great battles against the Moors, doubling the size of the kingdom of Portugal that he had founded.[21]

Notes

[1]   Pope St Pius X, *Ad diem illum*, 13.

[2]   See M. Lamberty (ed.), *The Woman in Orbit: Mary's feasts every day everywhere* (Chicago: Lamberty, 1966), 8 February.

[3]   See Mother Mariam, *The Life of The Theotokos* (Holy Apostles Convent and Dormition Skete: 1989).

[4]   Pope St John Paul II, *Homily at the dedication of the new sanctuary of Our Lady of Divine Love* (4 July 1999), 4.

[5]   N. J. Santoro, *Mary In Our Life: Atlas of the Names and Titles of Mary, The Mother of Jesus, and Their Place in Marian Devotion* (Kansas City, MI: iUniverse, Inc, 2011), p. 335.

[6]   See Lamberty, *The Woman in Orbit*, 4 July.

7   Santoro, *Mary In Our Life*, p. 122.

8   See P. Coppens, "A supernatural icon for Mother Russia" in *Atlantis Rising* 87 (May–June 2011).

9   Prayer composed by Father Paul Wattson.

10   Lamberty, *The Woman in Orbit*, 13 July.

11   M. O'Neill, *365 Days with Mary* (Salt Media, 2016), 14 July.

12   See http://www.ourladyandstanne.org.uk/the-shrine/history.

13   See Lamberty, *The Woman in Orbit*, 21 July.

14   See *ibid.*, 23 July.

15   Pope St John Paul II, *Redemptoris Mater*, 19. See St Irenaeus, *Adversus Haereses* III, 22, 4.

16   Pope Francis, *Homily for Feast of Our Lady of Guadalupe* (12 December 2016).

17   See Lamberty, *The Woman in Orbit*, 27 July.

18   See S. van der Sloot, "Our Lady of the Gate of Dawn" in *Swords of Truth* (16 November 2015).

19   Pope Benedict XVI, *Discourse at General Audience* (6 December 2006).

20   See *Cistercian Chronicle*, Book VI, cc. 27–28.

21   See Lamberty, *The Woman in Orbit*, 31 July.

AUGUST

1 August: Our Lady of Compassion

HIS TITLE SUMMARIZES Mary's compassion, pity or grief on Calvary and was very common in medieval England, but is now experiencing a revival. On 21 May 2017, the Bishop of Shrewsbury, Mgr Mark Davies, blessed a new shrine dedicated to Our Lady of Pity within the grounds of his cathedral. The pertinent image ultimately became the Pietà as we now know it: Our Blessed Lady holding the afflicted Body of her dear Son, as He was taken down from the Cross, lying in her lap. The devotion to Mary's sorrows had its origin in meditation on Our Lady and St John standing at the foot of the Cross on Calvary, her "compassion" in the deepest meaning of the word, "suffering with".

Our Lady of Pity is first found in the writings of St Anselm of Canterbury around 1109, and other monks of his age, then in an office attributed to St Bonaventure and was later developed by such mystics as Blessed Henry Suso, Tauler, Gerson, and St Bridget. Many hymns were devoted to the theme of which few are now remembered, except the *Stabat Mater*, and the theme inspired many pictures and statues, especially in the form of the Pietà.

The convent of Our Lady of Compassion (*Nuestra Señora de la Piedad*) in Mexico dates back to the year 1595. Don Luis de VelascoII, when he was Viceroy of New Spain, had as his confessor a Dominican, Fray Cristobal de Ortega, who also acted as his financial adviser. In gratitude for the friar's diligence and loyalty to his interests for many years, Don Luis presented the Dominican Order with the convent on 12 March 1595. Shortly afterward, a Dominican religious and a lay brother went to Rome on business for the Order, and were commissioned him to bring back a painting of Our Lady of Compassion.

On arrival, the religious asked an artist of great merit to accept the commission. The painter agreed, but would not set a date upon which he would undertake to have the picture ready. Very soon the religious would have to return to Mexico. Finally he could wait no longer. With some misgivings he visited the studio. Had the painting been finished? "Finished?" retorted the artist, with haughty indifference. "Why, I have scarcely begun to make a sketch of it!" The poor friar did not know what to do. His superiors had ordered him to leave for New Spain the following morning. For some time he stood in thought, and at last he said: "I will take back the sketch, at least, so that they may see it is no fault of mine." "And what good will a simple sketch do?" asked the painter. "In Mexico, we shall find someone who can finish the painting." "Only one brush can complete this picture," replied the painter; "mine!" "But I mean, with the help of God!" burst out the friar. These words, uttered with such simple faith, shook the artist from his indifference—something that even a bag of gold pieces would not do—and he handed over the sketch.

A month later, the friar and his lay brother companion were in mid-ocean, bound for New Spain. Suddenly a storm arose, the like of which in ferocity and intensity the crew and passengers had never before experienced. Advised by the Dominican priest that they should entrust their prayers to Our Lady, Star of the sea, the passengers and crew promised a sanctuary to the Virgin Mother in Mexico should they be saved. At once the storm began to subside, and soon the sea was calm again. The grateful crew and passengers, mindful of their promise, made generous offerings. Shortly thereafter the ship arrived at Veracruz, and the two Dominicans made their way overland to Mexico City. Their fellow religious at the Convent of La Piedad were considerably chagrined to learn the inconsequential outcome of the friar's business with the Roman artist. Some complained that they might have secured a suitable painting in Mexico, for a fraction of the cost, and much more quickly. Others said it might be a chastisement from God for their vanity in choosing a famous artist to do the work. With many misgivings, they set about opening the crate in which the sketch had crossed the ocean. As they were unrolling the canvas, signs of colour were seen, but they assumed that some paint had adhered to it in the artist's studio. Their astonishment increased as they continued unwrapping the canvas, and when it was exposed to view, they gazed at it in silence, unable to take their eyes from the painting. For painting it was, of extraordinary beauty and perfection, depicting the Mother of Jesus holding her crucified Son.

They were so absorbed in the painting that it was some time before they saw that the two newly returned religious were still on their knees before the picture, overcome by the marvellous outcome of events. When they were at last able to speak, they related the circumstances in which they had acquired a rough sketch for the painting. They added the tale of the storm at sea and the near-shipwreck. They told how the crew and passengers had come to them with the promise to build a shrine for the Virgin if she spared their lives. When they had concluded their recital, all agreed that the hand of God had played a part in the supernatural affair of the painting. From that time the religious of the Convent of La Piedad preached devotion to Our Lady in her image. Notable miracles have been worked through her intercession, and many of the most outstanding have been certified by formal process before the ecclesiastical tribunal. This venerable image today hangs in the new sanctuary of Our Lady of La Piedad, and it has been raised to the status of a Minor Basilica.[1]

2 August: Our Lady, Queen of the Angels

THE CLOSE CONNECTION between the Blessed Virgin Mary and the Holy Angels is one we see throughout her life on Earth: at the Annunciation, the Nativity of her Divine Son, her Assumption into heaven, and finally her Coronation as Queen of Angels and Men. The first invocation of her as Queen in her Litany is as "Queen of Angels". She is the Mother of Christ, who created the angels, for as St Paul says, "in Him were created all things in heaven and on earth: everything visible and everything invisible, thrones, ruling forces, sovereignties, powers—all things were created through Him and for Him" (Col 1:16). St John of Damascus observed: "Mary was made the Queen of all creatures, because she was made the Mother of the Creator." She is their queen, because, as she is elevated far above them in dignity and glory, they look up to her with the greatest reverence. She is their queen, because her Son Jesus Christ is the restorer not only of earth but heaven; God has willed "to reconcile all things to him, everything in heaven and everything on earth, by making peace through his death on the cross" (Col 1:20). By Christ's redemptive power, those seats of glory which were vacated by the disobedience of the fallen angels, are filled up; and the angels—whose charity is great in proportion to their closeness to God, Who is charity itself—rejoice at the elevation of every child of Adam, who, through Christ is raised to the glory which their unfaithful companions forfeited.

The feast of Our Lady Queen of Angels dates back to before the days of St Francis. It is first mentioned in the year 1045, when it was called the Chapel of Our Lady of the Angels; the locals had heard angels singing there, and immediately thought of the Assumption. By the time St Francis arrived in 1207 the church had fallen into disrepair. Jesus appeared to Francis there and asked him to repair his church. Francis thought the Lord meant the physical building which he immediately began to do. Only later did Francis realize the Lord meant that he was to repair the Church as a Community of believers. In this little chapel known as the *Portiuncula* (or little portion) Francis received his vocation to follow Christ and it was here in 1208 that he founded his order of Franciscans and then later the Poor Clares and here he held several chapters or meetings of the community. In 1226 he died in an adjoining room to the chapel. One can still visit the original chapel which is now entirely enclosed and covered by a much larger church building on the plain at the foot of the hill leading to Assisi. The contemplation of Mary forms a portion of the beatitude of the angels. As they admire God's works in proportion to their excellence, so they find in Mary—the most excellent of God's creatures—more subject for admiration, than in the contemplation of the immense orbs of light with which the fiat of the Creator has studded the heavens, or all the created glory of that Paradise, which St John describes in the Apocalypse, under such glowing imagery. They find more subject for the exercise of their sublime intelligence, in contemplating her instrumentality in the mystery of the Incarnation, and in the other mysteries of her life, than they do in considering all the other wonders of God's providence on his creatures. If the faithful servants of Mary on earth have felt their hearts inflamed by the consideration of the amiableness and beauty of the celestial queen; what must be the feelings of those blessed spirits, who see her, as she is, and whose superior nature renders them more capable of appreciating the wonders of God's grace in her than we can possibly be. It is not, then, without reason, that the church says that the angels of God rejoiced at the Assumption of this heavenly queen. "Mary is assumed into heaven: the angels rejoice."

Mary's title as "Queen of angels" should remind us, that we also are destined to enjoy the society of angels, and with them admire the wonders of God's power in this heavenly queen. We should remember that God has deputed some of these heavenly spirits to be the guardians of people on earth, according to the Psalmist: "For you has he commanded his angels, to keep you in all your ways. They shall bear you upon their hands lest you strike your foot against a stone" (Ps 91:11-12) as also the words of Christ: "See that you never despise any of these little ones, for I tell you that their angels in heaven are continually in the presence of my Father in heaven" (Mt 18:10). Each one of us has one of these guardian angels, to protect us in dangers and assist us in difficulties. When we invoke Mary as Queen of angels, the thought of our future companionship with them for eternity should make us endeavour to lead lives of angelic innocence. Gratitude for the care they take of us, and for the desire they have for our salvation, should produce in our souls a desire of attending to all the holy inspirations, which they communicate to our souls; that thus we may prove ourselves faithful servants of the queen of angels, and prepare for the high destiny, that awaits us, of enjoying God in their company for a blessed eternity.

3 August: Our Lady of Bows

 UR LADY OF BOWS was a Marian shrine in London. It is related that in the year 1071 Mary's image there had been carried away by a storm, together with more than 600 houses. It fell uninjured with such violence that it broke into the pavement, and sunk more than 20 feet into the earth, whence it was never possible to draw it out. There is a church currently in London named Saint Mary-le-Bow that was constructed in about 1080 by the Archbishop of Canterbury. It is a Norman church which may have replaced a previous structure of Saxon origin, and that building may have been destroyed in a storm in 1071.

What is certain is that a terrible tornado struck the city of London on 23 October 1091, based on a 12th century chronicle.[2] It was recorded that there was a great wind and a tornado from the south that killed two men and lifted the roof and rafters of the church so high that when they fell the rafters were driven so far into the earth that only a seventh or eighth part of them remained visible. The rafters were nearly 30 feet long. It is also mentioned that the rafters could not be pulled back out of the ground, and so were sawed off at ground level and left.

The church of Saint Mary-le-Bow takes its name from the unusual Norman arches, or bows, which were considered a novelty.[3] The church is thought to be built above a crypt from a much earlier age. Sir Christopher Wren, who rebuilt the church after it was destroyed in the Great Fire of 1666, felt it was of Roman origin, and wanted it used as a burial chamber. At that time the only access to the crypt was by a trapdoor with a ladder, although later a staircase was constructed to assist access.

Besides the tornado that struck the church in 1091, there was a fire in 1196. A tower of the church collapsed in 1271, and the church was completely destroyed in World War II before being rebuilt in 1964. There is a saying that to be a true Londoner, a Cockney, one must be born within hearing distance of the bells of Saint Mary-Le-Bow. It is now an Anglican church.[4]

4 August: Our Lady of Dordrecht

 UR LADY OF DORDRECHT, in Holland, is located at the west end of the Voorstraat, and is also known as Grote Kerk or Onze Lieve Vrouwekerk (Church of Our Lady). The name of Dordrecht comes from the informal name of Dordt given to the town by its inhabitants, combined with "drecht", which means "ford". It became a major market city due to its strategic location.

According to tradition, it was built by Saint Sauters, also known as Saint Sura, in about the year 1300, on the spot designated by an angel, as it is said, who was sent by the Blessed Virgin. Saint Sauters is said to have planned on building the church when she only had three small coins in her purse. Afterwards she received the crown of martyrdom in the same church where the shrine was erected, as Saint Sauters was said to have been murdered by the builders of the chapel out of greed because of her supposed wealth. A legend recounts that Saint Sauters rose from the dead after her murder. There is a painting of Saint Sauters in the Church of Saint Nicholas holding a church in her hands as she looks up at a statue of the Blessed Virgin holding the Infant Jesus on her right arm.

To render her memory more celebrated, God caused a fountain to flow, after her death, which, through the intercession of the Saint and recourse to Our Lady, cured fevers. The healing water soothes troubled minds, brings relief to aching brows and strength to weakened limbs, as Mary's sick children come for aid to her. Dordrecht is the oldest city in Holland, having been granted city rights by the Count of Holland, William I, in the year 1220. The church was built in the Gothic style, and is the only one in Holland with stone vaulting. The tower, at over 122 meters tall, is the still the tallest structure in the city. A total of 49 bells were installed in the year 1949. Charles the Bold, the last Valois Duke of Burgundy, is buried in the choir space behind the high altar.

In 1568, the Dutch revolted against Spain and King Philip II, and nearly all of Holland met at Dordrecht for what was called the First Assembly of the Free States. The church was already the home of Michelangelo's sculpture known as the Madonna and Child, which had been donated to the church in the year 1514. Thankfully, it somehow survived the ravages of the French Revolution, as was returned to the church after being stolen by Nazis in World War II.[5]

5 August: Our Lady of the Snows

MPOSSIBLE AS IT IS for snow to fall during August in Rome, history tells of such a snowfall on the night of 5 August 352 in the Eternal City. There lived in Rome a nobleman, John and his childless wife, who had been blessed with much of this world's goods. They chose the Mother of God as the heir to their fortune, and at the suggestion of Pope Liberius, prayed that she might make known to them how to do this by a particular sign. In answer, during the night of August 5 the Virgin Mother appeared to John and his wife and also to the Holy Father, Pope Liberius, directing them to build a church in her honour on the top of the Esquiline Hill. The sign that John and his wife had requested was that snow would cover the crest of the hill.

Snow rarely falls in Rome even in the deepest of winter, but the flakes fell silently during that night, blanketing the peak of the historic hill. In the morning the news quickly spread and crowds gathered to throng up the hill and behold the white splendour. The snow had fallen in a particular pattern, showing the outline of the future church. When it became known that the snow was a sign from Mary, the people spontaneously added another to her long list of titles, Our Lady of the Snows.

The church built by John and his wife in honour of Our Lady of the Snows, restored and enlarged at various times was known by different names: the Basilica of Liberius, Saint Mary of the Crib because it enshrines relics of Christ's Crib; lastly, Saint Mary Major, to distinguish it from the many other Roman churches dedicated to the Mother of God; Major, means Greater. There is an image revered as Our Lady of the Snows, which is believed to have been produced by St Luke the Apostle. Saint Mary Major is one of the four basilicas in which the pilgrims to Rome must pray in order to fulfil their pilgrimage.

The white blanket of that August night fittingly symbolizes Mary, pure as the driven snow; her blessings and graces, numerous and varied as the falling snowflakes. Science tells us that every snowflake is different in form and make-up: size, outline, structure, ornamentation, are all without limit, infinite in wondrous beauty, startling complexity, perfect symmetry as they fleet, dancing down from the sky. What a wonderful figure of the blessings Mary obtains for us! Snow changes the face of the earth, painting even a field of mud with a white coat. The grace of God won through prayer to Mary, also changes the face of the earth.

Snow preserves the heat of the earth, protects vegetation, supplies moisture with slow effectiveness. Grace serves similar purposes: it preserves the warmth of God's love in our hearts; it protects the soul from the chill of temptation and sin; it nourishes the soul with new life. We see a further symbolism in this feast. There are millions living in lands of ice and snow who have not come to the knowledge of Mary and her Divine Son. We might ask that with the actual snowflakes, she shower down upon them the graces of the True Faith.[6]

6 August: Our Lady of Grace

 N 6 AUGUST 1936, Maria da Luz Teixeira, 13, and Maria da Conceição, 16 (a poor girl living with the Teixeira family), were gathering castor beans on Guarda mountain in the Cimbres district, 15 miles from Pesqueira, Brazil. There was a flash of light and then Maria da Conceição said, "Look, there's an image that looks like Our Lady." Maria da Luz saw it too, up on a rock. They ran home and told Maria da Luz's parents. At her mother's insistence, Artur Teixeira climbed the hill with the girls, who reached the spot long before he struggled up through the brush. He saw nothing unusual, but at his suggestion, the girls together asked the image, "Who are you?" "I am Grace."

They asked what she wanted. "I've come to warn of three punishments sent by God. Tell the people to pray much and do penance." After this the girls returned to the site daily, where they prayed with a growing crowd of pilgrims. On 9 August, the crowd demanded a sign; reluctantly, the girls asked for one. The next day, they found water flowing from the rock and two sets of footprints embedded in stone, one an adult's and one a child's. The apparition confirmed they belonged to her and her Son. The bishop conducted an investigation. Maria da Luz described Our Lady of Grace as "similar to Our Lady of Mount Carmel in Pesqueira Cathedral, but her mantle is blue and her dress cream, with a belt. She has a little child in her left arm, and both have very beautiful crowns on their heads." Eventually the Virgin told her that the people's response had been sufficient to avert the three chastisements, sometimes identified as armed bandits (particularly the notorious Lampião, killed by police in 1938) and the coming of World War II or a Communist regime to Brazil. Maria da Conceição died young.

In 1940, Maria da Luz joined the Religious of Christian Instruction, taking the name Sister Adélia. Pilgrims continued to visit the shrine at the apparition site, where 296 carved stone steps lead to a statue of Our Lady of Grace (as depicted on the Miraculous Medal, without the Child, not as the girls saw her), and to report healings there. In 1966, the Vatican approved the Guarda apparitions. Sister Adélia has since participated in some events at the shrine, including the anniversary pilgrimages of 1985 and 1986, and reported some new messages from Our Lady. On 13 October 2013 (day of the last Apparition of Our Lady in Fatima) Sister Adélia died at the age of 91. Because the original site is located in the Xukuru Indian reservation, an area of constant conflict, the city and diocese of Pesqueira have built a new shrine to Our Lady of Grace, with a grotto and chapel, on a Calvary shrine hill closer to town.

7 August: Our Lady of Schiedam

CHIEDAM LIES IN South Holland, and tradition relates that a sculptor arrived in Schiedam with a wooden statue of Mother and Child, which he intended to sell at a fair in Antwerp.. For an inexplicable reason, it became impossible for the vessel to leave its mooring. More than 20 sailors struggled to set the ship free but without success. Their efforts soon attracted a crowd, which found great amusement at their difficulty. The unusual situation required an investigation, and as a result, attention was drawn to the statue and its sudden increase in weight.

The statue that had become heavy as soon as it was on board ship suddenly became light when the merchant agreed to take it ashore. As the sculptor disembarked among the acclamation of the people, the boat sailed away without the slightest difficulty. It was everywhere declared that the mysterious event indicated that the Blessed Virgin was intent on having her statue remain in Schiedam. When the parish priest was informed of what had taken place at the dock, he also agreed that the statue must remain in their city.[7]

The city of Schiedam is well known for the miraculous statue, but its fame seems to rest more on its famous resident, St Lydwina. She was born in Schiedam, Holland, in 1380 to a poor family. As a child St Lydwina was drawn towards the Mother of God and prayed a great deal before the miraculous image of Our Lady of

Schiedam. During the winter of 1395, when St Lydwina was 15 years old, she went ice skating with friends and had an accident on the ice causing her to fall over and to break a rib on her right side. This was the start of great illness and suffering for her. She eventually became paralysed except for her left hand. Gangrene appeared in the wound and then began to spread. She experienced great pain, which went on for several years. No medical skill was able to help her. God, however, rewarded St Lydwina with the wonderful gift of prayer and visions. She fasted severely and gained the ability of bringing healing to others who suffered.

On the morning of Easter day 1433 she was in deep contemplation when she received a vision of Jesus coming towards her to administer the Last Rites. Lydwina was canonised by Pope Leo XIII in 1890 and is officially the patron saint of ice skaters. During the Reformation, the original statue was destroyed, but a replica was made that has proved to be enormously popular.

8 August: Our Lady of Cuba

ROUND 1608 TWO BROTHERS, Rodrigo and Juan de Hoyos, and a ten-year-old slave boy named Juan Moreno, left Santiago del Prado (modern El Cobre, named after the copper mines), Cuba in search of salt to preserve meat for the copper miners. Halfway across the Bay of Nipe they put in for the night to wait out a strong storm. The next morning a small white bundle floating across the water toward them. It turned out to be a statue of Our Lady. It was attached to a board, was completely dry, and bore the inscription "I am the Virgin of Charity" ("Yo Soy la Virgen de la Caridad"). A shrine was built immediately, and instantly became a pilgrimage destination.

Overjoyed by what they had discovered, they hurried back to Barajagua, where they worked. They showed the statue to a government official, Don Francisco Sánchez de Moya, who then ordered a small chapel to be built in her honour. One night, Rodrigo went to visit the statue, but discovered that the image was gone. He organized a search party, but had no success in finding Our Lady of Charity. Then, the next morning, she was back on the altar, as if nothing had happened. This was inconceivable as the chapel had been locked. This event happened three times. The people of Barajagua came to the conclusion that Our Lady wanted to be in a different spot, so they took her to El Cobre. She was received with much joy in El Cobre, and the church there had its bells ring on her arrival. It was at this point that she became known as "Nuestra Señora de la Caridad del Cobre" or "Our Lady of Charity of El Cobre". Much to the dismay of people in El Cobre, the disappearance of the statue continued to occur. One day, a young girl named Jabba was playing outside, pursuing butterflies and picking flowers. She went towards the mountains of the Sierra Maestra, where she came across the statue on top of a small hill. In the end, the Virgin was taken to the spot where Jabba had discovered her, and a church was erected for the statue.

Before the famous image on 19 May 1801, a royal edict from king Charles IV of Spain decreed that Cuban slaves were to be freed from the El Cobre copper mines. At the request of the veterans of the War of Independence, Our Lady of Charity was declared the patroness of Cuba by Pope Benedict XV in 1916. Then image was solemnly crowned, at the request of Pope Pius XI, during the Eucharistic Congress at Santiago de Cuba in 1936. Pope Paul VI raised her sanctuary to the status of a minor basilica in 1977. Pope St John Paul II solemnly crowned her again in 1998. Pope Benedict XVI awarded a Golden Rose in honour of the image and her shrine on 27 March 2012. Pope Francis enshrined a brass statue given to Pope Benedict XVI by Cuban bishops (in May 2008) within the Gardens of Vatican City in August 2014. The image is 13th among the 14 Marian images that shall be permanently enshrined in the gardens in 2016 by the Pontifical mandate of His Holiness.

Prayer

Most Holy Mother of Charity who came to us as a messenger of peace across the sea. You are the Mother of all Cubans To you we come, Most Holy Mother of God to honour you with love as your children. To your motherly heart we entrust our desires and hopes our work and our prayers. We pray for our torn country that we may be able to build a nation based on peace and unity. We pray for our families that they may live in fidelity and love. We pray for our children that they may grow strong in spirit and in body. We pray for our young people that their faith may increase, as well as their attachment to the truth. We pray for the sick, the homeless, the lonely, the exiled, and for all suffering souls. We pray for the Catholic Church in Cuba, for its mission, for its priests, deacons, religious and laity. We pray for the victory of justice and love in our country. Mother of Charity! We place ourselves under your mantle of protection! Blessed are you among women and blessed is the fruit of your womb, Jesus! And to Him be the glory and the power now and forever. Amen.

9 August: Our Lady of Nagasaki

 N 1571, THE port of Nagasaki was established by Portuguese traders, Jesuit missionaries, and a wealthy convert, Omura Sumitada. Most of its inhabitants were Catholic. But in 1587, Japanese nationalist leader Toyotomi Hideyoshi banned missionaries. For the next three centuries, Nagasaki's Catholic community was repeatedly suppressed and persecuted. After the Japanese government revoked its ban on Christianity in 1873, many exiles returned to Nagasaki and began building a cathedral in the Urakami district under the direction of Father Pierre Fraineau of the Missions Etrangères de Paris. Consecrated in 1914, but not completed until 1925, the handmade brick cathedral was the largest Catholic church in Asia. In 1929, a wooden statue of the Immaculate Conception, carved in Italy after Murillo's painting in the Prado, was placed over the altar.

On 9 August 1945, the US aircraft *Bockscar* dropped an atomic bomb that destroyed much of Nagasaki, killing over 70,000 people and levelling the cathedral while priests were hearing confessions.

That Autumn, Trappist monk Kaemon Noguchi, a native of Urakami just discharged from military service, found the blackened head of Our Lady's statue in the rubble and took it back to his monastery in Hokkaido. In 1975, he returned it to Nagasaki. The Virgin's head was on display at Junshin Women's College, the Urakami Cathedral Hall of the Believers, and the Atomic Bomb Museum before returning to the Cathedral—rebuilt in 1959—where it has remained in its own chapel since 2000. A new chapel in the cathedral was dedicated 9 August 2005, on the 60th anniversary of the bombing.

Knowing that the inscrutable will of God permitted even such sufferings as the atom bomb, to come to His beloved children, Mary would not stop it. But that did not mean her Motherly care did not instantly bend to the stricken city, to Nagasaki, which was the ancestral seat of Japanese Catholicism where so many of her children cried day and night. Somehow this cloud of suffering must be pierced by the great fire of love.[8]

10 August: Our Lady of the Crag

N 10 AUGUST 1685, Bernardino Rodríguez de León saw a great and unusual radiance that was not the natural light of day in the peaks east of Bogotá. On approaching, he realized the light was coming from an image of an angel, the Virgin and Child, and St Joseph, outlined in the living rock. News of the discovery soon spread through the capital, and after an investigation, the Archbishop authorized construction of a chapel on the mountain and public veneration of the images on the Sunday before Ash Wednesday of 1686.

The thatched chapel collapsed in 1714, and a sturdier stone one took its place. Mysteriously, people began to see Our Lady's face change expression at times: sad, tearful, joyous. On 8 May 1716, the left wall of the chapel collapsed to its foundation, after only 150 days. It was decided to move the images from the mountain. In early June, stonemason Luis de Herrera began separating the images from the underlying rock. Legend relates that when he finished, a bird flew out. The images were cleaned, polished, and touched up to make the figures and clothing more distinct. They still weighed 750 pounds. In November, men carried them on their shoulders to the plain, where they were greeted with rejoicing and dancing. Another straw shelter protected the statues until completion of a new chapel in 1722. Now a national monument, Our Lady of the Crag is still an active church and an archdiocesan sanctuary.

11 August: Our Lady, Highest Honour of our Race

 UR LADY IS CENTRAL in God's work of salvation, as seen in the clear light of Scripture and Tradition. Now, since the beginning and throughout all time but especially in the modern age freedom has been the great dream of humanity.[9] However how that freedom is used is important; in Mary's case her use of freedom makes her also the highest honour of our race.

Mary's greatness lies above all in her free and unreserved openness to God. She not only hears the word but "keeps" it (cf Lk 11:28). Our Lady conceived Christ in her heart before she enclosed him in her womb. her greatness resides also in her spiritual maternity, in freely welcoming God's will, and then also in her physical maternity. She freely renews this commitment time and again. She "ponders" the Word (cf Lk 2:19, 51), while not always understanding it (cf Lk 2:50), and freely embraces it, making it life of her life.

In her choice of the supreme good, namely God Himself, by a will unhindered by selfishness, Mary achieves the greatest freedom ever attained by a human creature. She is therefore a model of authentic human freedom. Mary overturns the widespread notion of freedom as "doing whatever I like, regardless of anything". By showing the fruitfulness of self-surrender to the divine call, she continually reminds her children of the unlimited horizons of love they may freely embrace, thereby making superlative use of their freedom.

12 August: Our Lady of the Swan

OT LONG AFTER founding the city of Loja, Ecuador in 1548, the Spanish colonized a mountain area 45 miles away, naming it El Cisne, or The Swan. In 1594, a drought and plague of rats destroyed crops in the region. Threatened with famine in addition to pressure from the Spanish, the local Indians had decided to emigrate in search of a better land, when an apparition of the Virgin Mary changed their minds.

A young native woman herding sheep to pasture met with a most lovely Lady crowned with fragrant roses who stayed with her, conversing about God while the flock grazed. "Confide in me, because I am going to help and protect you so you will never be hungry again. Here I want to assist you. Build a shrine in this place, where I will always be with you", Our Lady said. The people built the church, and rains fell. 12 October 1594, is sometimes given as the apparition date, sometimes as the end of the drought. 12 October, feast of the Virgen del Pilar, has long been a Marian holy day in Spanish-speaking countries.[10]

The natives of El Cisne commissioned a statue from Diego de Robles of Quito, already known for the image of Our Lady of Quinche, another popular Ecuadoran Virgin with indigenous ties. Carved of oak, the statue of the Virgen del Cisne, stands about 30cm tall, holding the Child in her left hand and a sceptre in her right. The statue was canonically crowned on 8 September 1930. A new shrine begun in 1934 was consecrated on 12 August 1979, attended by a crowd of regional clergy and officials. Annually in mid-August, thousands of pilgrims accompany the Virgen del Cisne on a three-day journey to the Cathedral in Loja, where the statue remains before returning to the Basilica of El Cisne on 1 November.

13 August: Our Lady, Refuge of Sinners

HEN WE READ in spiritual writers that Jesus keeps the Kingdom of Justice for Himself and gives over the Kingdom of Mercy to Mary, we ought not to misinterpret them so as to imagine an opposition between Jesus and Mary. They are not working at cross-purposes. Mary wishes what God wishes. What these pious authors mean is that sinners generally find it hard to understand that Jesus, our Judge, can be both infinitely just and infinitely merciful. Thinking of Jesus only as their just Judge, they often lack the confidence needed for sincere repentance and amendment of life. God has therefore, condescended to their weakness by willing that His Holy Mother should serve as Queen of Mercy and Refuge of Sinners—so as to inspire confidence in those who are in most need of God's mercy.

No one could have yearned for the return of sinners as much as Jesus yearns. He died on the Cross for them. "God so loved the world that He gave His Only-Begotten Son." He is our ultimate Refuge. So when we give to Our Lady that consoling title, "Refuge of Sinners," we see in her one who loves the lost sheep, as Jesus loves them. We see her as the great intercessor with Him, as she prays for them in conformity with the Divine Will. The power of prayer is a fact, but it is a mystery. We know that Mary has great power with Jesus, and that she loves us because God loves us, and intercedes continually that not one of us may be lost. She is our refuge, our advocate, because God wants us to come to Him through her, since every grace He gives us is given through her hands. He uses her as the instrument of mercy as He uses her to dispense all His graces. She is our friend at court, whom He wishes to be counsel for us.

St John Damascene calls Mary a city of refuge to all who flee to her. This idea of a city of refuge is an old Scriptural fact calling attention to the humanity, the pity, of the old Jewish Law, which established certain cities of refuge where criminals might find escape from the arm of the authorities. The Jewish idea was brought into Christianity. One of the beautiful customs in the Middle Ages was "the right of sanctuary," by which those who ran foul of the law could not be taken so long as they remained in the Church, or sanctuary. This history of the cities of refuge, or sanctuary, is recalled in Our Lady's title "Refuge of Sinners"—a place to which we may run, using the sanctity of her presence to plead with the Omnipotent Judge. It is a logical following out of the truth that Mary cooperated in the Redemption, which saved us from sin. That does not mean that she is tolerant of sin. She knows what it cost her Divine Son in pain and sorrow. However, though she hates sin, she loves the sinner, for she sees in him the possible saint; so loving him, as every mother loves the wayward child, she pursues him, weeps over him, as Monica wept over Augustine, and pleads with him to come back home.

Dating back to the time of St Germanus of Constantinople in the eighth century, this title is associated with the image of Mary as the New Eve. Where Eve was responsible for the suffering of humans since their fall from Heaven, the Virgin Mary is viewed as the source of all healing. She is the new Eve who cannot eliminate the damage created by Eve, but who can limit it. Mary was a Refuge of Sinners from the very beginning. We can easily believe that it was her prayers that obtained the conversion of the Good Thief. She was for him, as St Bernard calls her, "the ladder of sinners," the ladder by which he mounted to his cross. We, too, are thieves who have robbed God of His glory, but there is the same hope for us in her maternal love. "Pray for us sinners"—is our constant cry, and it is one prayer we know is being answered by that Mother of ours every minute of our lives.[11]

Prayer

O God, you reconciled the world to yourself by the precious blood of your Son, and in your merciful design made the Virgin Mary the Refuge of Sinners. Through her loving intercession, may we receive the pardon of our sins. Through Christ Our Lord. Amen.

14 August: Our Lady of Scex

OLLOWING THE MARTYRDOM of Saint-Maurice at the end of the third century, the Celtic village of Acaunus became an important place for pilgrimage on the via Francigena connecting Canterbury to Rome. The Abbey of Saint-Maurice was founded in 515 by Sigismond, king of the Burgundians, and is one of Switzerland's first monasteries. It immediately became an important site and helped to shape the region's history. It remains of central spiritual importance today. St-Maurice offers visitors the chance to discover new dimensions: a future that grows out of the past.

Nestled in a rocky escarpment (in French called a *scex*, pronounced "she") over 100 metres above the town and Abbey of Saint-Maurice, the Chapel of Our Lady of Scex was founded by Benedictine hermit, and later abbot, St Amatus in 611. Amatus was of a noble Roman family and his father had consecrated him even as a child to the monastic life. In the chapel, extensively remodelled in the 1700s and 1950s, an enthroned Virgin and Child from the 1200s occupies a niche high above the altar. Both of the painted wood figures wear crowns, and the Virgin holds an orb, possibly a fruit signifying her role as the New Eve. Among the many ex-votos present in the chapel, one recalls that in 1722 a young roofer, Pierre-François Seydoux, who was working with his father on roof repairs in the chapel fell from where he was working, but special protection preserved him from all harm. He got up, looked for his hat, and went up to join his father. He subsequently worked as a stonecutter and porter at the abbey for a few years, and died on 22 February 1756 at the age of 46.

In 2011, the chapel of Our Lady of Scex celebrated the 1400th anniversary of its foundation. On 14 August each year , the night before the Solemnity of the Assumption, pilgrims gather for prayers at the Abbey Basilica, then climb the 484 steps to the chapel for Midnight Mass.

15 August: The Assumption of the Blessed Virgin Mary

 HE DEVELOPMENT OF the doctrine of the Assumption of Mary, was a rich pilgrimage for the Church. A common Patristic theme is that the doctrine of the Second Eve implies assumption as the final and complete victory of the woman. Next, Mary in her predestination is always associated with her Son. Further, Mary's Immaculate conception and sinlessness imply exemption from corruption in the grave, and so lead to her immediate resurrection and glory. Another concept is that the perpetual virginity of Our Lady, as fleshly incorruption, involved exemption from physical corruption after death. A further argument is that the filial piety of the divine Son implied that He would grant her the favour of the Assumption, if it were otherwise possible and fitting. Mary at her death was more exalted in dignity than other creatures will ever be. If, then, other Christians are destined to he bodily with Christ in heaven, this must have applied to Mary straightway after her death. Finally, the woman of the Apocalypse is already seen in her glory, after being carried by eagle's wings.[12]

After many requests, in 1950 Pope Pius XII solemnly defined a dogma which had been believed by the Church for well over a thousand years. The definition was of great historical significance. In took place in the middle of a century when the sacredness of the human body was denied theoretically and practically at many levels. In the first half of the twentieth century it was denied politically in the totalitarian systems of Marxism and Nazism which denied the sacredness of the body in theory and in the slaughter of millions in the gulags and concentration camps. In the second half of the twentieth century, the assault on the sacredness of the human body was taken a step further through the massacre of untold millions through abortion and euthanasia, and also through sacrilegious experiments carried out on embryos to say nothing of genetic engineering and attempts to clone the human being. All of this is counterbalanced by the

Church's affirmation that Our Lady was assumed body and soul to the glory of heaven. The Church, which believes in the resurrection of the body, believes that this same body has been created in the image and likeness of God, and is called to a supernatural destiny in Christ.

The Assumption can also be understood in light of the mystery of the Church. In the most Blessed Virgin Mary, the Church has already reached that perfection whereby she exists without spot or wrinkle (cf. Ep 5:27), however, the faithful still strive to conquer sin and increase in holiness.

> In the meantime the Mother of Jesus in the glory which she possesses in body and soul in heaven is the image and beginning of the Church as it is to be perfected in the world to come. Likewise she shines forth on earth, until the day of the Lord shall come (cf. 2 Pet. 3:10), a sign of certain hope and comfort to the pilgrim People of God.[13]

For Our Blessed Lady, Our Lady there is no "intermediate eschatology", namely there is no "period" of waiting between death and the General Judgement for the body and soul to be reunited, and this sets her apart from us.

The Assumption of Mary shows that God's plan is now realised not only in Christ the bridegroom, but also in the bride, signified by the Church, recapitulated in Mary.[14] Thus the Assumption is an exaltation of woman, in contrast to all ancient and modern paganism. If the power of sin has served to oppress women, the Assumption shows how God has empowered a woman for the spread of holiness. The Assumption is a triumph for the nobility of maternity and also of virginity. The Assumption is also an indication of the glory which awaits the body of the Christian, who in this life has been the home of the Body of Christ in the Eucharist. Finally, the Assumption indicates the glorification of the poor and their liberation from oppression, in the fulfilment of the words of the Magnificat: "The Almighty has done great things for me: Holy is His Name" (Lk 1:49). The Assumption of Mary is "the glorious culmination of the mystery of God's preference for what is poor, small, and unprotected in this world, so as to make God's presence and glory shine there." It offers "hope and promise for the poor of all times and for those who stand in solidarity with them; it is hope and promise that they will share in the final victory of the incarnate God."[15]

16 August: Our Lady of Torcoroma

 N THIS DAY in the highlands of northeastern Colombia, the people of Ocaña celebrate Our Lady of Graces, whose image appeared over 300 years ago beneath the bark of a tree. In 1709, a man named Cristóbal Melo, who maintained a sugar mill and small farm, which he worked personally with a grown son went, accompanied by his son, each with his axe, to look in the mountains for a log suitable to carve into a mill trough. Climbing up the hill called Torcoroma, which is in sight of the city, he found one that seemed to meet his needs. They put their axes to it, and when it fell to earth, they measured it, and seeing that it wasn't large enough, left it and continued looking for another in those mountains. In this effort he passed an entire year, and the need for the trough increased as the time of sugar cane processing neared, and not having found a tree that suited him he resolved to make do with the one he had cut on Torcoroma. He returned there in 1710 in the company of his son, and cut it to its greatest length, and then told his son to strip the bark off the top. Having lifted the rough bark, Cristóbal saw formed in low relief in the sapwood an image of Our Lady, in the form and dress of the Immaculate Conception: in the detached bark the same image was engraved where the other was embossed, and with great silence they brought both pieces to their mill, and from there to their house in the city, where they revered them until the following year, 1711, when the miracles worked by Our Lady became known.

As word of the find spread and miracles began to occur, the parish priest of Ocaña investigated and authorized private veneration. Around 1716 the bishop conducted his own favourable investigation, naming Pascuala Rodríguez, Melo's wife, as caretaker of the treasure and altar linens. He gave permission for a chapel at the apparition site, but when none materialized, he had the wooden image moved to the main church in Ocaña, where it still occupies a chapel in what is now St Anne's Cathedral. Cristóbal Melo kept the mirror image of bark. When at last the chapel was built on Torcoroma, in 1882, the bark image was moved there. Our Lady of Torcoroma is an *acheiropoieta* image, not made with hands—like the Mexican Virgin of Guadalupe, but more deteriorated.[16] The mountain sanctuary is known for its spring waters with curative powers.

In 1906, Pope St Pius X authorized a Mass proper to Our Lady of Graces of Torcoroma, which has been her title ever since. 16 August 1711 has traditionally been commemorated as the day when the Melos found the relief in the tree, although historians now agree, that it was more likely the date when the image was enshrined in Ocaña. The tercentennial was celebrated in 2011, with a shower of flowers and papal crowning of Our Lady's image.

17 August: Our Lady of Assiut

ESIDENTS OF ASSIUT, Egypt were awakened in the middle of the night of 17 August 2000 by an exceptionally bright light coming from Saint Mark's Coptic Orthodox Church. Those who looked toward the church saw an apparition of Our Lady between the church's two towers, accompanied by large, glowing white doves (a traditional symbol of peace and the Holy Spirit) flying around her. The figure of Mary emanated a brilliant white light, and so did the halo around Mary's head. Witnesses said they smelled the fragrance of incense (which symbolizes prayers from people travelling to God in heaven) while they watched the apparition.

The apparitions continued on various nights over the next several months, until January 2001. People often gathered outside the church at night to wait to see if an apparition would occur.

Since the apparitions usually took place in the middle of the night, those hoping to see them often camped out overnight on the local streets or on nearby rooftops. While they waited, they prayed and sang hymns together. Our Lady most often appeared with the white dove birds flying nearby, and sometimes flashing blue and green lights appeared over the church as well, drawing the attention of people miles away.

Thousands of people witnessed the apparitions, and many recorded them. Some took video that they then posted on the Internet; some took photos that were published in newspapers. Although Mary did not speak during the Assiut apparitions, she did gesture toward people in the crowd. It appeared as if she was blessing them. People also reported that, during some of the church's liturgies, light would emanate from a picture near the altar that showed Mary with a dove above her head, and the light would sometimes flow down out of the picture. Each time afterward, those outside the church would report seeing lights flashing above the church building. Lights are spiritual symbols that can mean life, love, wisdom, or hope.

The main miracle associated with the apparitions of Our Lady at Assiut is the powerful way it inspired peace between people of faith who had been in conflict with each other in Egypt. Christians and Muslims, who both honour Mary as the mother of Jesus Christ and as an extraordinarily faithful person, had been at odds in Egypt for years. After Mary's apparitions in Assiut, relationships between many Egyptians of both faiths were marked by peace rather than hostility, for a while—just as they improved for a while after Mary's apparitions in Zeitoun, Egypt from 1968 to 1971, which also featured doves flying around the figure of Mary.

The Coptic Orthodox Church declared the apparitions themselves to be miraculous in that they were supernatural events with no natural explanation. Before the apparitions, Assiut was already a place of pilgrimage, because it was a place reportedly visited by Our Lady, Jesus, and Saint Joseph while they lived in Egypt for a while to escape from King Herod.

18 August: Mother of Our Creator

HE DOCTRINE OF GOD as our Creator is that which most fills us with awe and reverence towards Him and a sense of our own utter nothingness. The great God Who made us, Who has absolute and entire control over every part of our being, and everything belonging to us, and before Whom we are but as little grains of the dust of which we are made! That the great Creator should be her very own Child, absolutely dependent on her for His being, His life, His support, His food—can we ever realize how great must be her power, when the very God Who had made her put Himself completely in her power? "He Who created me rested in my tabernacle." Even on earth, in the days of their poverty, Our Lord showed Mary the greatest respect. At a simple suggestion from her, "they have no wine" (Jn 2:3) He brought forward the time of His miracles, and worked His first wonder. He even told her that His hour had not yet come, and yet because it was His Mother who asked, He did what she desired: He changed the water into wine. Thus would He show us what was the reverence of the Creator for His Mother.

The Son never refuses the Mother anything she seeks, as St Bridget learned in a revelation, when she heard Jesus saying to Mary: "Ask Me for anything; your request can never be in vain." This is the beautiful reason He gave: "Because you never refused Me anything on earth, I will refuse you nothing in Heaven." However we must ourselves ask her help, as Christ has indicated: "Ask, and it will be given to you; search, and you will find; knock, and the door will be opened to you" (Mt 7:7). We must exert ourselves to ask for graces. God is so good that He gives us many, many graces that we do not ask for; but the more we ask, the more we shall receive. "He has filled the starving with good things" (Lk 1:53), Mary herself tells us. Grace comes to us through fervent prayer.

Go then, with all confidence to Mary, the Mother of Our Creator, and ask for whatever you desire, be it little or great; she does not mind whether our requests are little or great, for she can do all. You will never be refused, no matter what your trouble is. "Let us, then, have no fear in approaching the throne of grace to receive mercy and to find grace when we are in need of help" (Hb 4:16). The tabernacle where the Creator rested is that "throne of grace". By Mary's help you will be helped, for she, being the Mother of the all-powerful Creator, is omnipotent by her intercession.

19 August: Our Lady of Saint-Hospice

T JEAN-CAP-FERRAT IS a village in the Alpes-Maritimes province in south-eastern France on the Mediterranean coast; it is located on a promontory of the same name that juts out into the sea. about two miles south-west of Beaulieu. Out from the centre of the village on a peninsula is Pointe Ste-Hospice and the chapel of St Hospice. St Hospitius (or Hospice) was born in Egypt, and migrated to Gaul. He lived as a hermit in the ruins of an old tower on St Hospice Point, wearing heavy iron chains, living off bread and dates even outside penitential seasons. He foretold the invasion of Gaul by the Lombards. A Lombard patrol around 575, finding Hospitius loaded with chains and living in isolation, decided he was some type of criminal; Hospitius agreed that he was a terrible sinner, with a litany of offences to his shame. Convinced he was a danger of some sort, one of the soldiers raised his sword to kill the old hermit; the soldier's sword arm became paralysed, moving again only after Hospitius made the sign of the cross over it. The soldier was converted on the spot, and spent the rest of his life in service to God. Hospitius foretold the hour of his own death, spent his last hours in prayer, took off his chains, and passed on.

Fort St Hospice was built on this spot in 1561 by Emmanuel-Philibert of Savoie. The Duke of Berwick razed it to the ground in 1706. St Hospice. a hermit friar, lived in the ruins of an old tower on the peninsula in the sixth century. The chapel was built in the 17th century on the remains of the Tower of Saint Hospice as it was called. The site is also the location of a military cemetery for many of those who died during the First World War. There is also a very large statue of the Blessed Mother in bronze, over ten metres in height that was installed in 1903. This huge statue depicts the Blessed Mother standing and holding the Christ Child in her right arm. with a sceptre in her left hand. Christ holds a globe in His left hand and the cord to a tablet in His right. Both figures have very pleasant expressions and both are crowned in line woven bronze. The immense size of the statue can easily be appreciated by its position neat to the outside walls of the chapel, and has no pedestal.

20 August: Our Lady of Valaam

 NE OF THE greatest treasures in the possession of the Monastery of New Valaam in Heinävesi, Finland is the wonder-working icon of the Mother of God of Valaam. Painted on lime wood, image depicts the Virgin Mary as a full-length figure standing on a cloud with lowered gaze, clothed in a bright red cloak and a dark turquoise garment. She is holding the Christ Child, who is dressed in a thin, pale yellow smock, on her left arm. With her right hand, she points to Christ, in the style of the "hodigitria" icons of the Mother of God. Christ blesses with His right hand and holds an orb, surmounted by a cross, in His left hand, signifying that He is the Creator of the world and King of all. According to the inscription, the icon was painted in 1878, the work of the monks of Valaam.[17] It is customarily attributed, however, to Father Alipy, one of the leading iconographers at the original Valaam Monastery in Lake Ladoga in Russian Karelia. Father Alipy painted the icon only a few years after he arrived at the monastery, before he had become a novice there. He was tonsured to monastic orders in 1884 and ordained as priest in 1893.

Following the conventions of the late 19th century, the icon was painted in a "naturalistic" style, employing a technique that combined the use of tempera and oils. Originally, the icon was to have been placed in the Valaam Monastery's Church of the

Dormition. This never occurred, however, and subsequently the icon was misplaced. In 1897, the icon was rediscovered and gained its miracle-working reputation on the strength of a succession of visions of the Mother of God experienced by an elderly woman with serious rheumatoid arthritis, Natalia Andreyevna Andreyeva, who was cured of her illness.

Despite the Valaam Monastery's long history, it had never had an icon of the Mother of God of its own design, although Father Alipy's icon came to occupy such a position in subsequent years. In the turmoil of World War II, the icon was transported to safety in Finland, along with many other treasures from Valaam and the majority of the monks. It now occupies a prominent position in the Church of the Transfiguration of Our Lord at the New Valaam Monastery. In 1987, the bishops of the autonomous Orthodox Church of Finland established an annual feast in the Valaam Icon's honor on August 7 in the Julian calendar. The *troparion* and *kontakion* for the feast were written by the late Archbishop Paul of Finland. On 29 July 2005, the Valaam Icon of the Mother of God was brought for the first time to North America by His Eminence, Archbishop Leo of Karelia and All Finland.

21 August: Our Lady of Knock

N THE EVENING of 21 August 1879, Mary McLoughlin, the housekeeper to the parish priest of Knock, County Mayo, Ireland, was astonished to see the outside south wall of the church bathed in a mysterious light; there were three figures standing in front of the wall, which she mistook for replacements of the stone figures destroyed in a storm. She rushed through the rain to her friend Margaret Byrne's house.

After a half hour, Mary decided to leave and Margaret's sister, Mary, agreed to walk home with her. As they passed the church they saw and amazing vision very clearly: Standing out from the gable and to the west of it appeared the Blessed Virgin, St Joseph and St John. The figure of the Blessed Virgin was life-size, while the others seemed to be neither as large nor as tall. They stood a little away from the gable wall about two feet from the ground. The Virgin was erect with her eyes toward Heaven, and she was wearing a large white cloak, hanging in full folds; on her head was a large crown.

Mary Byrne ran to tell her family while Mary McLoughlin gazed at the apparition. Soon a crowd gathered and all saw the apparition. The parish priest, Archdeacon Cavanaugh, did not come out, however, and his absence was a disappointment to the devout villagers. Among the witnesses were Patrick Hill and John Curry. As Patrick later described the scene: "The figures were fully rounded, as if they had a body and life. They did not speak but, as we drew near, they retreated a little towards the wall." Patrick reported that he got close enough to make out the words in the book held by the figure of St John. An old woman, named Bridget Trench, drew closer to embrace the feet of the Virgin, but the figure seemed always beyond reach. Others, out in the fields and some distance away, saw a strange light around the church. The vision lasted for about three hours and then faded.

The next day a group of villagers went to see the priest, who accepted the their report as genuine; he wrote to the diocesan Bishop of Tuam; then the Church set up a commission to interview a number of the people claiming to witness the apparition. The diocesan hierarchy was not convinced, and some members of the commission ridiculed the visionaries, alleging they were victims of a hoax perpetrated by the local Protestant policeman! However the ordinary people were not so sceptical, and the first pilgrimages to Knock began in 1880. Two years later, Archbishop John Joseph Lynch of Toronto made a visit to the parish and claimed he had been healed by the Virgin of Knock.

In due course many of the witnesses died. But Mary Byrne married, raised six children, living her entire life in Knock. When interviewed again in 1936 at the age of eighty-six, her account did not vary from the first report she gave in 1879. The village of Knock was transformed by the thousands who came to commemorate the vision and to ask for healing for others and themselves.

The local church was too small to accommodate the crowds. In 1976 a new church, Our Lady Queen of Ireland, was erected. It holds more than two thousand and needs to—for each year more than a half million visitors arrive to pay their respects to the Blessed Virgin. Ireland West Airport Knock serves the needs of the pilgrims coming from abroad.

The Shrine at Knock is open all year round. In 1994, three life-sized statues were erected of Our Lady, St Joseph and St John. On 30 September 1979, Pope St John Paul II visited the shrine to commemorate the centenary of the apparition. During that historic visit, the Pope addressed the sick and nursing staff, celebrated Mass, established the shrine church as a basilica, presented a candle and the Golden Rose to the shrine and knelt in prayer at the apparition wall.

22 August: Our Lady, Queen of Heaven

ROM THE EARLIEST centuries of the Church, Christians have addressed suppliant prayers and hymns of praise to the Blessed Virgin Mary, and the hope they have placed in the Mother of the Saviour has never been disappointed. They have looked upon her as Queen of Angels, Queen of Patriarchs, Queen of Prophets, Queen of Apostles, Queen of Martyrs, Queen of Virgins. Because of her eminence, She is indeed entitled to the highest honours that can be bestowed upon any creature. Saint Gregory Nazianzen called her Mother of the King of the entire universe, and the Virgin Mother who brought forth the King of the entire world. Mary is Queen principally through her influence over her Son and the guidance of her children towards salvation. The *Salve Regina* and other antiphons expressed these ideas, and Mary is invoked as Queen of Mercy, whose prayers are all-powerful. Pope Pius XII, in his Encyclical *Ad coeli Reginam*, indicated as the basis for Mary's Queenship in addition to her motherhood, her co-operation in the work of the Redemption.

The Pope recalls that Mary, Queen of heaven and Sovereign of the world, was first the sorrowing Mother near the Cross of our Lord Jesus Christ. He then established an analogy between Mary and Christ, which helps us understand the significance of the Blessed Virgin's royal status. Christ is King not only because He is Son of God, but also because He is the Redeemer; Mary is Queen not only because she is Mother of God, but also because, associated as the new Eve with the new Adam, she co-operated in the work of the redemption of the human race. The feast was celebrated on 31 May before the liturgical reform of Vatican II, but is now seen as linked to Our Lady's Assumption and is thus celebrated on the octave day of that feast.

Pope Pius XII's Prayer to Mary, Our Queen

From the depths of this vale of tears
where sorrowing humanity makes weary progress,
through the surges of this sea of ours,
endlessly buffeted by the winds of passion,
we raise our eyes to you,
O most beloved Mother Mary,
to be comforted by the contemplation of your glory
and to hail you as Queen of heaven and earth,
Queen of mankind.

Reign, O Mother and Queen,
by showing us the path of holiness
and by guiding and assisting us
that we may never stray from it.

In the heights of heaven
you exercise your primacy
over the choirs of angels
who acclaim you as their sovereign,
and over the legions of saints
who delight in beholding your dazzling beauty.
So, too, reign over the entire human race,
above all by opening the path of faith
to those who do not yet know your Divine Son.

Reign over the Church,
which acknowledges and extols your gentle dominion
and has recourse to you
as a safe refuge amid the calamities of our day.
Reign especially over that part of the Church
which is persecuted and oppressed;
give it strength to bear adversity,
constancy never to yield under unjust compulsion,
light to avoid falling into the snares of the enemy,
firmness to resist overt attack,
and at every moment unwavering faithfulness to your
kingdom.

Reign over men's minds,
that they may seek only what is true;
over their wills,
that they may follow solely what is good;
over their hearts,
that they may love nothing but what you yourself love.

Reign over individuals and over families,
as well as over societies and nations;
over the assemblies of the powerful,
the counsels of the wise,
as over the simple aspirations of the humble.

Reign in the streets and in the squares,
in the cities and the villages,
in the valleys and in the mountains,
in the air, on land and on the sea;
and hear the pious prayers of all those who recognize
that yours is a reign of mercy,
in which every petition is heard,
every sorrow comforted,
every misfortune relieved,
every infirmity healed,
and in which,
at a gesture from your gentle hands,
from death itself there arises smiling life.

Obtain for us,
that all who now in every corner of the world
acclaim and hail you Queen and Lady
may one day in heaven enjoy the fullness of your kingdom
in the vision of your Divine Son, who with the Father and the Holy
Spirit,
live and reign forever and ever. Amen.

23 August: Our Lady of Rhodes

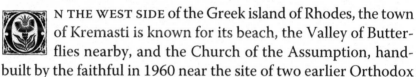 N THE WEST SIDE of the Greek island of Rhodes, the town of Kremasti is known for its beach, the Valley of Butterflies nearby, and the Church of the Assumption, hand-built by the faithful in 1960 near the site of two earlier Orthodox churches. The wonder-working and grace-flowing icon of our Most Holy Lady the Theotokos and Ever-Virgin Mary called "Katholiki" is kept in this church. It took the name "Katholiki" during the sovereign rule of the island by the Knights of Saint John, because it received universal honour by both the Orthodox residents and by the Latin conquerors.

This large icon, which dates to the end of the fourteenth or beginning of the fifteenth century, depicts the Most Holy Theotokos seated on a throne holding as an Infant the incarnate Son and Word of God, the Lord Jesus Christ. On either side of the Mother of the Lord stand two Angels in reverence. According to local tradition, it is a replica of an older icon, called "Ktitorissa", which was a fresco on the wall of the first Temple, built after the miraculous finding of the icon of the Mother of God in that place.

Witnesses say that on the 25 November in the year 1935 the shrine that contained the sacred icon burst into flames; the cause was unknown and the church was completely burned. The bells of the Temple rang without the intervention of human hands during the night and the residents ran to the Temple to see what happened. With horror they saw the icon of the Theotokos on top of burning coals and, when they lifted it, they were amazed to see that while the wood on the back had been burned, while miraculously the colours remained unchanged. This was confirmed with admiration by the restorers of the icon in 2010.

During the last restoration the shrine was moved, revealing behind the icon the old fresco "Ktitorissa", affirming as true the local oral tradition of generations past. In 1926 the icon had been decorated with a silver mantle made in Smyrna. The have been countless miracles performed over the centuries of the wonder-working icon by the grace of the Most Holy Theotokos, who is revered by all and ever-venerable, a sacred refuge and gratuitous physician to the sick, a comfort of the oppressed and hope of those who resort with faith and reverence and seek the maternal provision and perception of the most blessed Mother of God. On 23 August each year naval officers carry the Our Lady's image in procession.

Prayer

Today O Theotokos we honour Your revered icon, the wonder-working Katholiki, singing a hymn with gladness, as a source of life-bearing sanctification, giving forth streams of divine grace, to those who cry out: Rejoice, the boast of Rhodes.

24 August: Our Lady, Health of the Sick

 UR LADY WAS WELL USED to the sick-bed and the death-bed. There is silence in the Gospels about most of the details of her life, only those which concern the vital facts of her cooperation in the Incarnation and Redemption are recounted So much is told, however, that we know something about her love and her dedication, as wife and as mother.

St Joachim and St Anne, the parents of Our Lady took good care of their Heaven-sent child. It was but a fair return that she take care of them, who were already old when she was born. It is no stretch of imagination for us to see Mary waiting hand and foot on the old couple, sitting by their sick-bed and folding their hands in death. More so even was Our Lady's care of St Joseph. Their mutual love was the greatest the world has ever seen. St

Joseph is the Patron of the dying because Jesus and Mary sat by his sick-bed, his death-bed. Mary wet his parched lips, smoothed his pillow, kept vigil through the night, folded his hands, and closed his eyes. Maybe memory of that, she is first called "Health of the Sick", that her love followed Joseph to the grave and after.

However Mary was consecrated "Health of the Sick" as Mother of God. Jesus was immune to sickness and death, but He willed suffer the Passion and die. Who can try to estimate the source of strength Mary was to Him in His dereliction, in His scourging, His crowning with thorns, His way of the Cross, and finally in the three-hour passion and death? Every line of the *Stabat Mater* is in a sense a commentary on her title "Health of the Sick", with its final prayer for a happy death, applying to us:

> Christ when Thou shalt call me hence,
> be Thy Mother my defence;
> be Thy Cross my victory.
> While my body here decays,
> may my soul Thy goodness praise,
> safe in Paradise with Thee.

And "Health of the Sick" (*Salus Infirmorum*) primarily means our eternal health, our eternal salvation—for "salus" means not only "health", but "salvation".

That Mary should have a special love for the sick was necessary if she was to follow the example of Jesus. He was the Divine Physician for bodies as well as souls. To narrate the many cures of the sick, by Him and His Disciples, would be to quote most of the Gospels and the Acts of the Apostles. He had come to destroy sin; He had sympathy for the sickness, which man had brought upon himself by Original Sin. The healing of the sick man was not only a proof of His Divine Mission, a proof that He was Lord of Life and Death, and therefore God, but also a work of pure Mercy, the compulsion of His love. His love for the sick was so great that He instituted the Sacrament of the Sick, one of the purposes of which is to restore the body to health, if it is to the spiritual benefit of the patient.

Through all the ages of Christianity, Our Lady has been the constant nursing-mother at the sick-beds of her children. It would be impossible to number, let alone name, the shrines where she has established her hospital. At every one of these shrines, she has worked miracles of healing. Lourdes is the most notable, because it is of our day, but there were many in ages past no less famous than Lourdes. The miracles already wrought there are innumerable. There is no doubt that she has chosen certain places to be specially dedicated to her—Lourdes, Le Puy, La Salette, Fatima, Altötting, and innumerable others, but her help is not confined to any one place. Every sick-bed is her shrine, every hospital is her basilica.

Health of body, yes; Mary wants us to have that, as her Divine Son gave health of body. But most of all, she wants for us health of soul. Mary, who cooperated in the Redemption, wants to see us healed of the disease of soul. There is an old Irish prayer that runs "O Lady, Physician of the most miserable diseases, behold the many ulcers of my soul." So St Simon Stock called her "Medicine of sinners" and St Ephraem called her "Robust health for those who have recourse to her." Thus the Church applies to her the words of the book of Proverbs: "For whoever finds me finds life, and obtains the favour of the Lord" (Pr 8:35).[18]

Prayer

Virgin, most holy, Mother of the Word Incarnate, Treasurer of graces, and Refuge of sinners, I fly to your motherly affection with lively faith, and I beg of you the grace ever to do the will of God. Into your most holy hands I commit the keeping of my heart, asking you for health of soul and body, in the certain hope that you, my most loving Mother, will hear my prayer.
Into the bosom of your tender mercy, this day, every day of my life, and at the hour of my death, I commend my soul and body.
To you I entrust all my hopes and consolations, all my trials and miseries, my life and the end of my life, that all my actions may

be ordered and disposed according to your will and that of your Divine Son. Amen.

25 August: Our Lady, Queen of Martyrs

HE CHURCH HAS CROWNED MARY, not only with a crown of twelve stars but also with a crown of thorns, in calling her the Queen of Martyrs. Thus in the Communion Verse for the Feast of Our Lady of Sorrows we pray: "Happy the Blessed Virgin Mary, who without death obtained the palm of martyrdom at the foot of the Cross of the Saviour." The spiritual writers say the same. St Bernard has this to say:

> O Blessed Mother, a sword has truly pierced your soul!... So deeply has the violence of pain pierced your soul, that we may rightly call you more than a martyr for in you participation in the passion of the Son by far surpasses in intensity the physical sufferings of martyrdom.[19]

The pure body of Our Lady was exempt from physical degradation. By her Immaculate Conception she was free from bodily ills. If she died it was not from sickness or physical disintegration, the result of original sin, but from love. Somehow we shrink from the very thought of seeing that holy body of hers hurt in any way. It was to be all fair from the beginning and throughout eternity. However, there is a martyrdom besides that of the body; it is the martyrdom of the soul. We know that by our own experience. We have ceased to feel bodily pain at times when an overwhelming grief has rushed upon our heart. The death of dear ones, disgrace, disappointment, worries, so pierce our heart with pain, that we ignore the wounds or sickness that would otherwise lay us low physically. It is easier to bear the cut of the sword than dishonour. A broken heart is not as easily mended as a maimed body. If we are subject to this martyrdom of soul, we can easily understand how fittingly the title martyr is given to Our Lady, who endured suffering more than sufficient to cause her death, had not God saved her from the physical consequence of that agony. She was willing to shed her blood. God spared her that, but He did not free her from martyrdom.

Our Lady cooperated in the Redemption, not only in preparing her Son for the Sacrifice, but in associating her life with His. That association was effected first of all by her sanctity, and then by her martyrdom, which was indeed, the flowering of her sanctity, her will to be conformed in all things to His will. To conform to Him, she had to suffer. She knew what she was taking upon herself when she consented to become the Mother of God. God did not trap her. Mary knew the Scriptures, knew the Prophecy of Isaiah about the Man of Sorrows. God clarified that to her, so that she foresaw all the pain which association in the most intimate way with the suffering Christ would entail upon her. In the moment of her consent she became the Queen of Martyrs. St Gabriel brought a sword sheathed in the Annunciation lily.

Thus from the beginning Mary was vowed to a life of martyrdom. Some even go further and say that, with the infused knowledge which she had at the first moment of her existence, she foresaw all that she would be called upon to undergo, and hence was a martyr even then. However her actual martyrdom—it was a long, slow process—began on the Annunciation. Over the day of the Annunciation was the shadow of Good Friday. But before Good Friday would come there were a thousand pains to be endured, pains of fear for the life of her Child, pains over the sins of men, which were the cause of the terrible woes He must endure. To get at the real heart of Mary's life, you must appreciate her hatred of sin. She, the sinless one, knew that all the pain she was enduring, and would endure, was part of the fight for the conquest of evil, and for that reason she was glad to welcome any suffering her Son would ask her to bear.

No sooner did she hold Jesus in her arms than she had to accept the sword of sorrow. Simeon, with his prophecy, thrust his two-edged sword mercilessly; Herod, with his threats on the life of the Child and with the forced flight into Egypt, thrust his sword exultingly; and in the three days' loss she suffered the deepest of all pains, because it was the Hand of Love that forged the sword. These sorrows up to the time of the Passion were but her apprenticeship. The true accolade of martyrdom was given to her when the King of Martyrs took His crown and His throne. Pain did its best to crowd all it could into those few hours. It was not enough for the Mother to be compelled to meet her Son on the way to execution. That is one of the most excruciating agonies of Mary, to see Him bruised and beaten and bloody, needing her so, yet unable to go to Him and comfort Him. The eyes of Jesus alone touched her, but they flashed a sword that buried itself in her Heart. Now the swords leapt from a million scabbards until one great sword, the hilted sword of the Cross, dug into her Heart and cut it in two. It was still there when she held His lifeless body in her arms, that new sword of desolation, still there when she laid Him in the tomb, that sword of abandonment. The sword of the Cross was ever present till the very day of her Assumption. It was a long martyrdom, and an intense martyrdom. "To what can I compare or liken you, daughter of Jerusalem?", says the Church, applying to her the Lamentations of Jeremiah (Lm 2:13). "Who can rescue and comfort you, young daughter of Sion? For huge as the sea is your ruin: who can heal you?" (Lm 2:13). This is not mere sentimentality. If there is one thing that is common to the meditations of these graduates of the School of Pain, it is the realization of the illimitable immensity of the suffering of the Mother of God. Their findings are all summed up in the pronouncement of St Bernardine of Siena, that if her pain was subdivided and parcelled among all creatures, they would perish instantly.

We shudder today as we read of the sufferings of the martyrs of the early ages, of Saints Lucy and Agnes and Agatha, of those flayed alive, the human torches, the beast-devoured, the racked, the torn, the mutilated; of the martyrs of the Elizabethan persecutions; of the poor starved Irish martyrs who in Penal days called Our Lady, "Queen of the Poor;" they had good right to claim her as their own in calling her "Queen of Martyrs". Martyrs all, martyrs in every age, every land, but little martyrs by the side of her, for as St Anselm says: "Whatever cruelty was exercised upon the bodies of martyrs was light, nothing, compared to her passion."

The most famous church dedicated to Our Lady of Martyrs is the Pantheon at Rome. It was originally built by Marcus Agrippa in 25 BC, as a temple of Jupiter, Venus, Mars, and all the false gods. In 609 or 610 AD it was consecrated to God by Pope St Boniface IV in honour of the Blessed Virgin Mary and all the Martyrs.[20]

26 August: Our Lady of Minsk

HE MINSK ICON of the Most Holy Theotokos was brought by the holy Prince Vladimir from Korsun in the Crimea and placed in Kiev's Cathedral of the Tithes. This church was consecrated in 996. In the year 1500, during the capture of Kiev by Khan Mengli-Gyr, a certain Tatar stripped the cover and adornments from the icon, and threw it into the Dniepr River. After a while it was found floating in the River Svislocha, near Minsk.

Surrounded by an extraordinary light, the icon was brought to shore and taken to the church of the Nativity of the Most Holy Theotokos, in the estate of the princes of Minsk in Belarus; this occurred on 13 August 1500. The Minsk Icon was brought to the Uniate Monastery of the Holy Spirit in 1616, and returned to the Orthodox in 1839. The church of the Holy Spirit Monastery became an Orthodox cathedral, which was dedicated to Saints Peter and Paul. During the spring of 1922, Soviet forces confiscated the icon of the Mother of God. Then in 1936 Petropavlovsy Cathedral was blown up by the Soviets power and the icon was found in the local history museum. In 1941 an orthodox Minsk woman Varvara Slabko managed to ask German occupation forces for the miracle-working icon, and an icon painter restored it. Later in 1945 the icon of the Mother of God was taken to the Cathedral of the Holy Spirit. Finally, in 1992 one of the leading masters of Belarus, Peter Zhurbey, restored the icon. Every Friday, an Akathist hymn is celebrated before the holy icon, and many miracles have been recorded.

27 August: Our Lady of Dzublyk

N 27 AUGUST 2002, two girls—Olena Kuruts, aged 10, and Mariana Kobal, aged 9—went to fetch water at Dzublyk spring in the Carpathian foothills of western Ukraine. As one was drawing water, the other shouted, "Look who's behind you!" They saw a beautiful white lady standing on a flower-strewn hovering cloud. Frightened of this possible apparition, the girls hurried home with their water, but the Lady accompanied them on her floating cloud. On hearing the story, Olena's parents scolded her, but Mariana's father Petro, a Greek Catholic priest, cautioned them to make the sign of the Cross if they saw the apparition again.

That evening when the girls went to get Olena's little sister from kindergarten, the Lady on the cloud reappeared, making the sign of the Cross herself after they did so. Thus reassured that the vision was not an evil spirit, Olena and Mariana asked her name. She answered that she was the Virgin. The girls began seeing and conversing with her every day. She asked that their parents go pray at the countryside spring, and that Father Petro tell the bishop about the apparitions, which he did. The bishop travelled to their village and questioned the girls in his car, requesting that they ask the Lady for a sign to show that the events were from God. After speaking with her on the spot, they answered that the greatest sign was that people were flocking to pray at the spring. Happy with this reply, the bishop conducted the first liturgical service at Dzublyk on 31 August, only four days after the apparitions began. But that bishop died a year later, and other church authorities were dubious.

The Ukrainian Greek Catholic Synod issued letters to all parishes discouraging pilgrimages to Dzublyk. However, after the seers visited Pope St John Paul II at the Vatican in 2003, and following successful negotiations by a supportive monk, the hierarchy relented, allowing the building of a church complex and monastery at the apparition site. Meanwhile, there were miracles: pilgrims also saw the Virgin, as well as solar phenomena; a large cross bled; lapsed believers returned to Greek Catholic practice. Mariana stopped seeing the apparitions, but Olena continued to meet often with pilgrims and report frequent meetings with the Mother of God. For a time, she experienced the pain of Christ's crucifixion. The shrine hosts big pilgrimages on the 27th of each month, with fireworks on the apparition date, 27 August. In 2012, the sanctuary celebrated the tenth anniversary of Our Lady's appearance.

28 August: Our Lady of Kiev

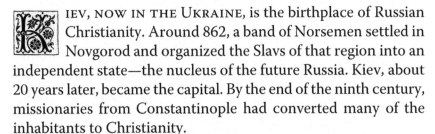 IEV, NOW IN THE UKRAINE, is the birthplace of Russian Christianity. Around 862, a band of Norsemen settled in Novgorod and organized the Slavs of that region into an independent state—the nucleus of the future Russia. Kiev, about 20 years later, became the capital. By the end of the ninth century, missionaries from Constantinople had converted many of the inhabitants to Christianity.

During the three succeeding centuries, Kiev became the intellectual and religious centre of the country, and numerous convents and monasteries arose in Kiev and the surrounding territory. One of these was staffed by the Dominicans. To it there came in the early years of the thirteenth century a Dominican Father by the name of St Hyacinth, who had a burning ambition to convert the pagans and infidels of China, Mongolia and outer Russia (the Tartars), to the Christian faith. In this dedicated task he made numerous journeys, mostly by foot, into the far countries lying beyond Kiev.

In 1240, St Hyacinth had just completed a magnificent church at Kiev, in Poland, which he dedicated to the Most Holy Mother of God. One day as he had just finished the celebration of Holy Mass, it was announced to him that the Tartars, the most implacable enemies of the Christian name, had reached the walls of the town, and were endeavouring to force an entrance. The

Saint was much surprised at this information, but he did not allow himself to be disturbed. He feared less the ruin of the city and the church than the outrages without number which these barbarians would inflict on the innocent people, and the sacrileges they would commit against holy things, especially the Most Holy Sacrament of the altar. He had removed the Sacred Host from the Tabernacle and was hurrying down the aisle when he heard a voice call out, "Hyacinth, are you going to leave me here at the mercy of the Tartars?" The voice seemed to be coming from the statue of the blessed Virgin on one of the side altars. Hyacinth stopped and turned his gaze toward the statue which was of alabaster, fairly large in size, and obviously much too weighty for one man to carry. What should he do? Then the voice spoke again: "Take me with you, Hyacinth, I will make the burden light". So, holding the Blessed Sacrament in one hand he picked up the statue with the other, and, to his surprise, found he could easily carry it. Leaving the church, he fled from the city, and saved the Blessed Sacrament and the statue of Our Lady from harm.

Eighty years later after the Mongols had been driven away, the statue was returned to Kiev. That city became the centre of great devotion to the Blessed Virgin, and it was natural that people soon gave the statue the name of Our Lady of Kiev. The statue was later taken to a Dominican convent in Lwow. What has happened to it since the Communists took over Lwow, is unknown. But surely, Our Lady still pleads to each one of us, "Take me with you; I will make the burden light." She will always make all our burdens light and bearable, as long as we keep her with us always and everywhere.[21]

29 August: Our Lady of Velankanni

LONG THE COAST of the Bay of Bengal, 250 km south of the city of Madras in Tamil Nadu, lies Velankanni, a small town of just five thousand inhabitants, where every year over twenty million pilgrims arrive, from every corner of

India and other countries of the world. They come devoutly every year to visit and to pray in this place, known and venerated as the Lourdes of the East.

There are three officially recognized apparitions at Velankanni. The first one dates to the beginning of the sixteenth century. Towards dawn a Hindu boy was going from Velankanni to Nagapattinam to deliver the milk to his master, as he did every morning. Taken by an unusual drowsiness he took a nap and upon reawakening he saw a Lady of remarkable beauty, who was carrying in her arms a child of divine appearance. The boy was surprised when the Lady asked him for some milk for her child. With reverence and fear, the youth offered his full container and when he reached his master, he apologized for his tardiness and for the shortage of milk. At that moment there were also other people present listening to the story, when suddenly, amid everyone's general astonishment, milk began to flow out spontaneously from the container. Thus the boy and his master, also a Hindu, returned to the small lake of the first apparition and Our Lady appeared again. The event became known among the nearby Catholic community who called that lake "Matha Kalum", meaning the "Little Lake of Our Lady".

Towards the end of the sixteenth century the second apparition of the Virgin Mary occurred to a twelve-year old Tamil boy, lame since birth, son of a poor widow who sold butter in Velankanni. The relatives of the boy had sought help to cure his infirmity from a wealthy benefactor, who however never decided to take action On the day of the apparition the boy saw a very clear light appear in front of him and, in the light, he saw a Lady of incomparable grace with a beautiful Child in her arms. The Virgin asked him for some butter for her Child, and the boy gave it to her. Then Our Lady requested him to recount what happened to the wealthy Hindu man of the nearby town, Nagapattinam, asking him to build a chapel in the place of her apparition. The boy did not immediately realize that while the Lady was talking, his legs were healing. He got up immediately and ran very fast to that man to accomplish the task. That man too had had a vision the day before, in which the Virgin Mary asked him to build a chapel for her. Soon afterwards, they went together to the place of the apparition. The Hindu benefactor was also cured of the dropsy from which he suffered; later he converted to Catholicism. Afterwards the chapel became a place of devotion to Our Lady called "Arokia Matha", meaning "Mother of Good Health".

The third miracle, which occurred in the seventeenth century, involved some Portuguese merchants who were on a journey from China to Ceylon, when they encountered a violent storm and invoked the protection of Our Lady, the Star of the Sea. During the storm they made a vow: if they were saved they would build a church dedicated to the Virgin Mary, wherever they would reach shore. The stormy sea became calm, and their ship docked near Velankanni; later they were led by local fishermen to the chapel, that was still a hut. They transformed the chapel into a stone structure, dedicating the church to "Our Lady of Health". Nowadays the celebrations for the feast at the sanctuary begin on 29 August and end on 8 September which is also the Feast of Our Lady's Birthday.

30 August: Our Lady of Deliverance

 N A STORMY NIGHT a man was driving with great difficulty a truck containing a heavy load of wine, close to the church of Eland in Germany. It was dark and a strong wind was blowing, the storm raged, and every moment it seemed harder to guide the heavy load along the almost impossible road. Now and then the man stopped, gazing into the darkness to see if he could find any hope of shelter. No sound but the echo of his own voice answered his cries for help. All remained desolate, dark, terrifying. No friendly light, no barking dog, no sign of a homestead was to be found. The storm kept lashing harder and harder. The lonely traveller grew more terrified when the truck suddenly sank in a deep place, and all his efforts could not move it from the spot! Loud were his cries for help, but they remained unanswered.

In his anguish he at last cried out to the Mother of God, the hope of the despairing, to help him and deliver him from this danger. Suddenly he heard a rustling in the thicket and the form of a woman glided out of the darkness, a brilliant light floated round her; then the radiant figure approached the sunken truck, and with one touch of her hand it was drawn out of the deep mire. Thrilled by the vision, the man fell on his knees and poured out his heart to his Heavenly Deliverer, expressing his regret that he had no means to make an offering to her chapel close by. At this, she touched a thorny shrub, and instantly leaves and buds burst forth; the whole shrub was loaded with lovely lilies, breathing forth a wondrous and unknown perfume.

The Queen of Heaven, for it was she, broke off one of the lilies and formed a chalice; as the man wondered if he might fill it with wine from his casks, the vision vanished. The man drove on to the chapel at Eland and entered to thank God for his deliverance, when lo! He recognized in the painting of Our Lady over the altar his gracious Deliverer, and placed the lily-chalice as an offering on her shrine. The fame of the miracle spread throughout Germany, and the Chapel of Our Lady became one of the most frequented shrines. Thus was one more example given to men of the sweet amiability, and readiness to help all in need, of Our Mother, Lady of Deliverance.[22]

31 August: Our Lady of the Well

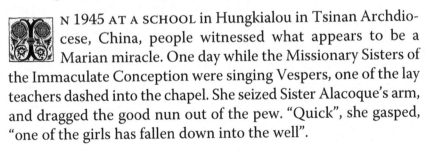N 1945 AT A SCHOOL in Hungkialou in Tsinan Archdiocese, China, people witnessed what appears to be a Marian miracle. One day while the Missionary Sisters of the Immaculate Conception were singing Vespers, one of the lay teachers dashed into the chapel. She seized Sister Alacoque's arm, and dragged the good nun out of the pew. "Quick", she gasped, "one of the girls has fallen down into the well".

Sister Alacoque hurried to the well. Peering down, she saw to her amazement, the little girl with head just above the water. Her hands were folded and she was praying: "Holy Mother, save me! Holy Mother, save me!" It took fifteen minutes for the workmen to arrive. Chain and rope were then lowered into the well. The little girl slipped her foot into a loop of the chain, grasped the rope with both hands and was drawn out of the well.

The girl's story was this: "When I fell into the well, I went way, way down under the water." Her hair was dripping wet.

> I called on our Blessed Mother to save me, and right away I was lifted to the surface. I found something solid under my feet, so that I could stand with my head above the water. I kept on asking Our Lady to help me, until they pulled me out of the well.

Later, the workmen measured the depth of the water: it was a sheer fall of fourteen feet![23]

Notes

[1] J. C. Cruz, *Miraculous Images of Our Lady: 100 famous Catholic statues and portraits* (Charlotte, NC: TAN Books, 2012), chapter 74 "Our Lady of Compassion".

[2] This was the first documented tornado in British history. From accounts of the damage, meteorologists estimate that this tornado would have rated T8 on the tornado scale, which runs from T1 to T10. If so, winds of up to 240 mph would have struck the city.

[3] The title is also known as Sancta Maria de Arcubus.

[4] See N. J. Santoro, *Mary In Our Life: Atlas of the Names and Titles of Mary, The Mother of Jesus, and Their Place in Marian Devotion* (Kansas City, MI: iUniverse, Inc, 2011), p. 387.

[5] See M. Lamberty, *The Woman in Orbit: Mary's feasts every day everywhere* (Chicago: Lamberty Co, 1966), 4 August.

[6] See *ibid.*, 5 August.

[7] See Cruz, *Miraculous Images of Our Lady*, chapter 83 "Our Lady of Schiedam".

[8] See Lamberty, *The Woman in Orbit*, 9 August.

9   See Pope Benedict XVI, *Discourse at Roman Major Seminary* (20 February 2009).

10   See the description of Our Lady of Pilar on 12 October below.

11   See "Refuge of Sinners" in *Salve Maria Regina*, Volume 53, No. 171 (Winter 2013).

12   See Rv 12:14.

13   Vatican II, *Lumen Gentium*, 68.

14   See G. Gozzelino, *Vocazione e destino dell'uomo in Cristo* (Leumann: Elle Di Ci, 1985), pp. 151–152.

15   I. Gebara and M. C. Bingemer, *Mary, Mother of God, Mother of the Poor*, vol. 7 of *Liberation and Theology* (Tunbridge Wells: Burns and Oates, 1989), pp. 120–121.

16   Acheiropoieta, from the Medieval Greek (ἀχειροποίητα), meaning made without hands, are Christian icons which are said to have come into existence miraculously, not created by a human agency. Invariably these are images of Jesus Christ or the Virgin Mary. The most notable examples that are credited by tradition among the faithful are, in the Eastern Church the Mandylion, also known as the Image of Edessa, and the Hodegetria (depending on the version of their origin stories followed—in many versions both are painted by human painters of Jesus or Mary while alive), and several Russian icons, and in the West the Shroud of Turin, the Veil of Veronica, Our Lady of Guadalupe, and the Manoppello Image.

17   The monastery had been originally established on Valaam, which is an archipelago in the northern portion of Lake Ladoga, lying within the Republic of Karelia in the Russian Federation.

18   See *Salve Maria Regina*, Volume 52, No. 170 (Autumn 2012).

19   St Bernard of Clairvaux, *Sermon on the Sunday in the Octave of the Assumption*, 14.

20   See *Salve Maria Regina*, Volume 54, No. 178 (Autumn 2014).

21   See Lamberty, *The Woman in Orbit*, 28 August.

22   See Lamberty, *The Woman in Orbit*, 30 August.

23   See Lamberty, *The Woman in Orbit*, 26 September.

SEPTEMBER

1 September: Our Lady of Olives

N A PLEASANT valley of France there lies a little city where, by the favour of God, lightning never falls. This privilege, unique in the world, dates back to the time when the church of Murat (Cantal) was burned by lightning except for a wooden statue of the Virgin Mary. In 1493, and ever since, the town has been known as Our Lady of Olives. The Virgin Mary is the Olive recalled in the scriptures: "I have grown tall as a palm in En-Gedi, as the rose bushes of Jericho; as a fine olive in the plain, as a plane tree, I have grown tall" (Si 24:14).

The medal of Our Lady of Olives, offers those who wear it protection from lightning wherever they may be during a storm. The second privilege of the medal is to protect women who are about to become mothers and to assist them in the hour of deliverance. Those who are afflicted with sickness and who pray to the Divine Mother, are promptly relieved. The image was crowned on 18 June 1881, by an apostolic brief issued by Leo XIII in May 1878. Immediately after his baptism, Dom Afonso de Santa Maria, Prince of Beira, Duke of Barcelos (born 25 March 1996), the eldest son and heir of Duarte Pio, Duke of Braganza, the current pretender to the throne of Portugal was consecrated at Guimarães to Our Lady of the Olive Tree, where his ancestor John I, had been to thank her for his victory at the battle of Aljubarrota, in 1385

Prayer

Kneeling at your feet, we pray you Virgin Mary, that through your intercession, a new generation there may be born who will unite all hearts and souls in the same faith and the same charity. We pray you "Divine Olive of Peace", to implore God that harmony may reign between nations, that true liberty be given to all people, that heresies and all false doctrines condemned by the Pope may disappear. We pray that all the treasures of the Divine Heart be showered upon all people and that we be preserved from all harm. Pray for us, help us and save us. Amen.

2 September: Our Lady of the Mountain

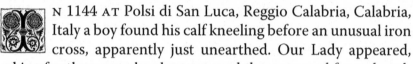 N 1144 AT Polsi di San Luca, Reggio Calabria, Calabria, Italy a boy found his calf kneeling before an unusual iron cross, apparently just unearthed. Our Lady appeared, asking for the young herder to spread the news and for a church to be built on the spot, about a kilometre high in the mountains. In 1560, a chest was found floating in the sea to Bagnara. Taken ashore, it was found to contain a stone statue of Our Lady. When the chest was placed in a cart, the oxen suddenly took off for the mountain pass, and nothing more was heard of the statue until it turned up in the heart of Aspromonte, at the place where a calf had found a cross and Our Lady had requested that a church be built. The sanctuary there became a place of pilgrimage.

Every year on 2 September, people from all over Calabria and Sicily would make the 24-hour trek, enlivened by dances and ballads, along the rugged path to Polsi, where they would greet Our Lady with gunshots on their arrival. Pilgrims still make the journey—though now they can also travel by road or train—they can spend the night in one of the hostels near the shrine. On 3 September, a wooden statue of the Virgin Mary is carried in procession. The stone statue is only taken from its place on the main altar every 25 years or in special circumstances. Also known as the Mother of the Good Shepherd, Our Lady of the Mountain was crowned in 1881 and 1931 and on 2 September 1981.

3 September: Madonna dei Monti

ET IN THE CHARACTERISTIC alleys of the Monti neighbourhood of Rome, the church of Santa Maria ai Monti
is one of the most interesting examples of the transition
between Renaissance and Baroque architecture.

Devotion to the Madonna dei Monti dates back to the 16th
century, when miraculous events took place inside the remains
of an abandoned 13th century Poor Clare convent, then reduced
to a complex of houses and storage rooms. This convent was
founded in 1223, during the lifetime of St Francis, but in 1308 the
nuns moved to San Lorenzo in Panisperna nearby, which was a
properly-built monastery instead of a large house. The dwelling
that they left behind was turned into a barn, but an icon of Our
Lady painted on a wall in the hayloft managed to survive for 350
years. There, on 26 April 1579, after several mysterious earthquakes occurred in the hayloft, a 15th century fresco painting
representing the Virgin Mary with Child and Saints was rediscovered and, according to the tradition, it became responsible
for some other miracles. Some workmen engaged in demolishing
the derelict structure heard a voice saying "Don't harm the child".
Looking at the wall, they found the painted-over icon which
immediately became a focus of veneration by locals. After a blind
old woman called Anastasia recovered her sight while praying
before it, so much money was donated in the same year (1579)
that a new church could be built immediately from scratch.

Upon popular request, Pope Gregorio XIII decided to built a
new church on the site in order to celebrate the re-discovery of
this miraculous image. Designed by Giacomo della Porta, this
became the church of Madonna dei Monti, in the central district
that occupies three of Rome's seven hills. Installed on the high
altar in a magnificent setting, the image was crowned on 3
September 1632. and even nowadays a copy of this sacred picture
is taken in procession on 26 April every year.

4 September: Our Lady of a Happy Journey

E ARE ALL on a journey, a journey to Heaven, our eternal home. On the way we must detour occasionally to be "about Our Father's business". These side-jaunts are little diversions made happy in the knowledge that we do all for the Love of God.

Our Blessed Lady is our model in this as in all other matters; she too, as we know from Holy Scripture, went on happy journeys to do the will of God and aid in our redemption. Her presentation in the Temple—mutually joyful and sacrificing for her and her parents; her Visitation after the angel's visit to her at the Annunciation, joyful to Elizabeth, and to John the Baptist, who, as Scripture tells us "leaped for joy" in his mother's womb; in response to the edict of Augustus, the arduous but happy journey to Bethlehem when Mary was with Child; the anxious hands of Herod, mingled with the happy assurance of safety; the destitute, but eager and joyful return to Nazareth; the loss-resulting journey to the Temple when Jesus was twelve years old, and the joy of finding Him among the doctors in the Temple; the happy participation in the unique miracle at the wedding feast of Cana; the three journey-filled years of Christ's public life as Mary followed with joyful love and humility His every action; the soul-crushing death-march to Calvary, consoled by His infinite Love for us her children; the unparalleled, bereaved, lonely, return from His borrowed grave, happy in the thought that now He could suffer no more; the joyful trips to His post-resurrection rendezvous with those He loved; the thrilling trip to the Mount of the Ascension; the relaxing journey with John to her new home in Ephesus; and, finally, her ecstatic entrance into Heaven.

Regardless of the fact that this is a "vale of tears" in which we journey on, all sorrow can be turned into joy here below, if we, handclasped with Mother Mary, walk along at Mary's side on life's journeyings and find happiness as she did, in doing the Father's will.[1]

5 *September: Our Lady of Galloro*

 HE LITTLE TILED PICTURE of Our Lady, found in 1621 at Galloro, in Ariccia in the Alban Hills marked the site of an older Church built there in her honour and long since ruined, probably by one of the periodic invasions by foreign troops.

The tile was discovered by a small boy named Santi Bevilacqua, who was and orphan and lived with his uncle at Ariccia. Santi had been sent to watch the sheep, and was in the nearby brambles picking berries when he saw a low stone wall half-hidden in the brush and decided to investigate. He followed the wall and at one point fell into the brambles. When he picked himself up, he saw a picture of the Madonna painted on the wall. Being a pious child, he knelt and said a prayer; then, the following day he returned with a bouquet of flowers.

Soon a number of his friends were coming with him to the Madonna in the woods. They brought flowers and sang hymns as they went along. This did not impress the neighbours, who feared for their fruit with so many children passing by. Finally, the children set about making a path that would let them into the brambles by an easier way, and in the course of their construction unwisely set fire to the brush. Quite a fire ensued and they were forbidden to go into the brush or into the woods to play.

Sometime after this Santi was playing in his carpenter shop and fell asleep in a corner near a pile of timber. The lumber fell on him as he slept and he awoke only in time to cry out to the Madonna of the Woods to save him. His frightened uncle, unpiling the timber, discovered the boy unhurt and demanded to know who had saved him. The boy told him again about the Madonna at Galloro. The uncle made inquiries, and found that there was indeed a wall there which had once formed part of a church. There was an attractive little tile on one side of it, showing the Madonna. He set about rebuilding the church.

Research revealed that the tile had been painted by a monk of Grottaferrata and that the church had been a pious venture of a good woman. There had been a dispute of the ownership of the land, and the church was abandoned. The years had converted the site into a wilderness again.

Santi's uncle with great perseverance and with the help of the Madonna, got the funds together and started rebuilding the church. Others helped, and in time a chapel was build, and also a home for priests. Santi went there to live, so that he could serve Masses at the shrine. Plague and cholera passed by Galloro when people prayed at the shrine of Our Lady. These and other miracles endeared her to the people, and it is still a place of pilgrimage, Our Lady of the Woods.[2]

6 September: Our Lady of the Light

UR LADY OF THE LIGHT (*Nostra Signora della Luce*) is a church in the Trastevere region of Rome. According to some sources there was a very old church on the site, dating from the third or fourth century and consecrated by Pope Julius I. The older church used to be known as San Salvatore in Corte. It used to be a parish church, but parochial responsibilities were transferred to San Crisogono in 1596.

The church's name of Santa Maria della Luce comes from a miracle that took place nearby in the year 1730. A young man, depressed because he was unable to find work, was about to commit suicide by throwing himself off the bridge into the Tiber when he saw a bright image of the Blessed Virgin on a wall. He changed his mind, and found a job within days. Later, a blind man got the use of his eyes back thanks to the same image, which was named Our Lady of the Light. The image was transferred to the church, which as a result was rebuilt and rededicated. The icon of Our Lady of Light is now enthroned above the high altar.

7 September: Our Lady of the Legion

 HE FIRST MEETING of the Legion of Mary took place in Dublin, Ireland on 7 September 1921, founded by Catholic layman and Servant of God Frank Duff (1889–1980) as an organization for women. In 1929, the Legion opened to men, and in 1931, it came to the United States. There are now over 3 million members worldwide. The Legion is organized along the lines of the Roman Army; members belong to local Praesidia which meet weekly for prayer and planning, with three administrative levels between them and the Concilium in Dublin. All Praesidia have a priest as spiritual director, but otherwise the Legion and its officers are Catholic laity. Each member promises to say daily prayers, attend weekly meetings, and perform two hours of service per week.

The purpose of the service is both to help the Church and community and to fulfil the baptismal promises of its members by performing the traditional Works of Mercy, both corporal (feed the hungry, give drink to the thirsty, clothe the naked, shelter the homeless, visit the imprisoned, visit the sick, bury the dead) and spiritual (admonish the sinner, instruct the ignorant, counsel the doubtful, comfort the sorrowful, bear wrongs patiently, forgive all injuries, pray for the living and the dead).

Prayer

O Lord, all hearts are in Your Hand
You can bend, as it pleases You,
the most obdurate, and soften the most hardened.
Do that honour this night through the Blood, merits, wounds,
names and inflamed Hearts of Your Beloved Son and His Most
Holy Mother by granting the conversion of the whole world.
Nothing less My God, Nothing less because of Mary Your Mother
and because of Your might and Your Mercy.

8 September: The Nativity of Our Lady

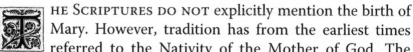HE SCRIPTURES DO NOT explicitly mention the birth of Mary. However, tradition has from the earliest times referred to the Nativity of the Mother of God. The earliest document commemorating the feast comes from the sixth century. Indeed the Feast of Our Lady's Nativity was celebrated historically before that of her Immaculate Conception. It is likely that this feast originated in Jerusalem since there is evidence, in the fifth century, of a church dedicated to St Anne, located north of the Temple in the neighbourhood of the Pool of Bethesda. Sophronius, the Patriarch of Jerusalem, affirmed in the year 603 that this was the location of Mary's birth.

Some people think that the date of 8 September was chosen to celebrate the Nativity of Mary since the civil year began in Constantinople on 1 September. The date was chosen since it was symbolic that the "beginning" of the work of salvation should be commemorated near to the beginning of the new year. The Solemnity of the Immaculate Conception of Mary, was later fixed at 8 December, nine months prior to her birth. The Nativity of Our Lady was introduced in Rome from the Eastern Church in the seventh century. The Syro-Sicilian Pope St Sergius I, who reigned from 687–701, decreed that a litany and procession be part of the liturgical celebration of this feast day. Paschasius Radbertus (died 860) wrote that this feast of Mary's Nativity was being preached throughout the universal Church and it became a holy day of obligation in the West by the year 1007. In Medieval times, the feast marked the end of the time when all were obliged to help on the communal harvest. After Our Lady's Birthday, which was a holiday, each man could work on his own little cottage plot and harvest his own garden crops for his family.

We cite here a prayer of St Anselm which praises Our Lady's Birth:

> Grant that I may praise you, O sacred Virgin; give me strength against your enemies, and against the enemy of

the whole human race. Give me strength humbly to pray to you. Give me strength to praise you in prayer with all my powers, through the merits of your most sacred Nativity, which for the entire Christian world was a birth of joy, the hope and solace of its life. When you were born, O most holy Virgin, the world was illuminated. Happy is your stock, holy your root, and blessed your fruit, for you alone as a virgin, filled with the Holy Spirit, merited to conceive your God, as a virgin to bear Your God, as a virgin to bring Him forth, and after His birth to remain a virgin. Have mercy therefore upon me a sinner, and give me help, O Lady, so that just as your Nativity, glorious from the seed of Abraham, sprung from the tribe of Juda, illustrious from the stock of David, announced joy to the entire world, so may it fill me with true joy and cleanse me from every sin. Pray for me, O Virgin most prudent, that the beautiful joys of your most helpful Nativity may remit all my sins. O holy Mother of God, flowering as the lily, pray to your sweet Son for me, a wretched sinner. Amen.

9 September: Our Lady of Puy

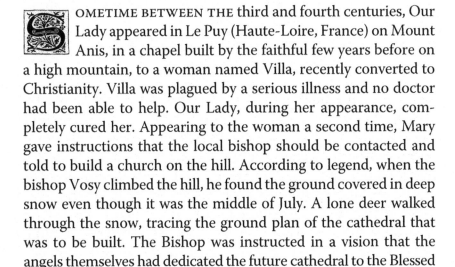 OMETIME BETWEEN THE third and fourth centuries, Our Lady appeared in Le Puy (Haute-Loire, France) on Mount Anis, in a chapel built by the faithful few years before on a high mountain, to a woman named Villa, recently converted to Christianity. Villa was plagued by a serious illness and no doctor had been able to help. Our Lady, during her appearance, completely cured her. Appearing to the woman a second time, Mary gave instructions that the local bishop should be contacted and told to build a church on the hill. According to legend, when the bishop Vosy climbed the hill, he found the ground covered in deep snow even though it was the middle of July. A lone deer walked through the snow, tracing the ground plan of the cathedral that was to be built. The Bishop was instructed in a vision that the angels themselves had dedicated the future cathedral to the Blessed Virgin, whence the epithet "Angelic" given to the cathedral of Le

Puy. Convinced by these miracles of the authenticity of Mary's wishes, the bishop completed construction of the church by AD 430. Soon this sanctuary became very popular, as proved by a text of Gregory of Tours in 591. The Emperor Charlemagne and many kings of France went there to pray to Our Lady.

In 1051, Pope Leo IX wrote "In this sanctuary on Mount Anis more than anywhere the Blessed Virgin Mary has received veneration, honour, and the love of a great many believers in the country." Louis IX met James I of Aragon there in 1245, and in 1254 when passing through Le Puy on his return from the Holy Land he gave the cathedral an ebony image of the Blessed Virgin clothed in gold brocade, one of the many dozens of venerable Black Virgins of France. It was destroyed during the Revolution, but replaced at the Restoration with a copy that continues to be venerated. Le Puy marks one starting-point for the pilgrim route to Santiago de Compostela, a walk of some 1600 km.

The celebration of the Great Jubilee of Our Lady of the Puy-en-Velay (France), one of the oldest in the history of the Church, is decreed by the Pope, when 25 March, solemnity of the Annunciation, falls on Good Friday. The Jubilee begins on that date and ends on 15 August. The previous Jubilee was held in 2016, and the next will be held in 2157.

10 September: Our Lady of Nazaré

N THE EARLY MORNING of 14 September 1182, Dom Fuas Roupinho, magistrate of Porto de Mós, Portugal, was out hunting on his domain, near the coast, when he saw a deer which he immediately began chasing. All of a sudden a heavy fog rose up from the sea. The deer ran towards the top of a cliff and Dom Fuas in the midst of the fog was cut off from his companions. When he realised he was on the edge of the cliff he recognised the place. He was next to a small grotto where a statue of Our Lady with the Enfant was venerated. Thus he prayed out loud to Our Lady to help him. All of a sudden his horse miraculously stopped at the end of a rocky point suspended over the void, the Bico do Milagre (Point of the Miracle), thus saving the rider and his mount from a drop of more than 100 metres, a fall that would certainly have caused their death.

Dom Fuas dismounted and went down to the grotto to pray and give thanks for the miracle. Then he ordered his companions to fetch masons in order to build a small chapel over the grotto so that the miraculous image could be easily venerated by all and as a memorial to the miracle that saved him. Then before walling up the grotto the masons destroyed the existing altar where amongst the stones they found an ivory chest containing some relics and an old parchment describing the story of the little wooden statue, one palm high, of Our Lady seated feeding the baby Jesus seated on her left leg. According to the document, the statue seems to have been venerated since the beginning of Christianity in Nazareth, in Palestine. According to oral tradition, the holy icon was sculpted by St Joseph the carpenter, in Nazareth, when Jesus was still a baby. A few decades latter St Luke the evangelist, painted it. So, it may well be the most ancient image venerated by Christians. It was rescued from the iconoclasts in the fifth century by the monk Ciriaco. It was he who brought it to Iberia, to the monastery of Cauliniana, near Mérida, where it remained until 711, the year of the battle of Guadalete, when the Christian forces were defeated by the Moorish invading army coming from north Africa. When the news of the defeat arrived at Mérida, the friars of Cauliniana prepared to leave their monastery. Meanwhile, the defeated king, Roderic, who was able to flee the battlefield alone and disguised as a beggar anonymously asked for shelter at the monastery. When he asked one of the friars, Frei Romano, to hear his Confession he had to tell who he really was. Then the friar suggested they flee together taking with them an old and holy image of Mary with the Child Jesus venerated at the monastery.

So the statue of Our Lady of Nazaré, which received its name from the village in Holy Land where it was first venerated, was brought by friar Romano and by king Roderic to the Atlantic coast. When they reached their destination they settled in an empty hermitage on the top of a rocky hill, the Monte de São Bartolomeu, and there they stayed for a few days. They then decided to separate and live by themselves as hermits. The friar took the image and settled in a little grotto, on the edge of a cliff above the sea, next to the hill where the king went on living. A year went by and Roderic decided to leave the region. Friar Romano stayed in his hermitage above the sea until he died. The holy statue, a black Madonna, stayed on the altar where he left it until 1182, when Dom Fuas, after the miracle, moved it to the chapel built over the grotto as a memorial to the event that saved his life. Thus the chapel was named Capela da Memória (Chapel of the Memory).

In 1377, because of the increased number of pilgrims, king Fernando had a church built near the chapel, and transferred the statue there. At the end of the sixteenth century this church underwent the first of a series of reconstructions and enlargements. The existing building is now the result of several interventions from the sixteenth to the nineteenth centuries that give it a very unusual character. This church or sanctuary is named Santuário de Nossa Senhora da Nazaré (Sanctuary of Our Lady of Nazaré). The holy image is now on display in the main chapel in a small niche above the altar that can be accessed by a staircase leading from the sacristy. The yearly festival takes place from 8–12 September.

11 September: Our Lady of Hildesheim

 NOBLE YOUTH named Eskil was sent by his father, the prince, to Hildesheim, a city of Saxony, to study; but he gave himself up to a disorderly life. He fell dangerously ill and received Extreme Unction. While in this state he had a vision; he found himself shut up in a fiery furnace, and believed himself already in hell; but he seemed to escape from it by a hole, and took refuge in a great palace, in a room of which he saw the most Blessed Virgin Mary, who said to him: "Presumptuous man how do you dare to appear before me? Depart from here, and go to that fire which you have deserved." The young man then besought the Blessed Virgin to have mercy on him; and then addressed himself to some persons who were there present, and implored them to recommend him to Mary. They did so, and the Mother of the Divine replied to them: "But you do not know the wicked life that he leads, and that he does not even deign to salute me with a Hail Mary." His advocates replied, "But, Lady, he will change his life"; and then the young man added, "Yes, I promise in good earnest to amend, and I will be your devout servant." The Blessed Mother's anger was appeased, and she said to him, "Well, I accept your promise; be faithful to me, and meanwhile, with my blessing, be delivered from death and hell." With these words the vision disappeared.

Eskil returned to himself, and, blessing Our Lady related to others the grace which he had received, and from that time he led a holy life, always persevering in great devotion to the Mother of God. He became archbishop of Lund in Sweden, where he converted many to the Faith. Towards the end of his life, on account of his age, he renounced his archbishopric, and became a monk in Clairveaux, where he lived for four years, and died a holy death. He is numbered in the Cistercian annals amongst the Cistercian Saints.

Most certainly God will not condemn those sinners who have recourse to Mary, and for whom she prays, since He Himself commended them to her as her children. This most benign Lady only requires that the sinner should recommend himself to her, and purpose amendment of his life. The Blessed Virgin told St Brigid:

> However much a person sins, I am ready immediately to receive them when they repents; nor do I pay attention to the number of their sins, but only to the intention with which they comes to me: I do not disdain to anoint and heal their wounds; for I am called, and I am truly, the Mother of Mercy.[3]

12 September: The Holy Name of Mary

 HE BEAUTIFUL MEMORIAL of the Holy Name of Mary originated in 1513 at Cuenca in Spain, and was assigned with its own Office to 15th September, the octave day of Mary's Nativity. In 1622 it was extended to the Archdiocese of Toledo by Gregory XV and it was granted to all Spain and the Kingdom of Naples in 1671. This feast was extended by Pope Innocent XI to the whole Church in 1683, that the faithful might in a particular manner recommend to God on this day, through the intercession of the Blessed Virgin, the necessities of His Church, and render Him thanks for His gracious protection and numberless mercies. What brought about the institution of this feast was the desire of all Christendom for a solemn thanksgiving which would commemorate the deliverance of Vienna, obtained through the intercession of Our Lady, after the city had been besieged by the Turks in 1683.

The object of the feast is the Holy Virgin bearing the name of *Mirjam* (Mary) in Hebrew, which is said to mean "Star of the sea," a most fitting name for the Virgin Mother. She may well be compared to a star; for, as a star beams forth its rays without any diminution of its own light, so too the Virgin gave birth to a Son with no loss to her virginity. The departing rays do not lessen the star's brightness, nor Mary's Son her inviolate maidenhood. She is, therefore, that noble star risen from Jacob and raised by nature above this great and wide sea. She shines with merits, she enlightens with her example. The Church, cast about upon the sea of this world in storms and tempests looks to the splendour of this star.

St Alphonsus de Liguori wrote these lovely words about the power of Her Name:

> After the most sacred name of Jesus, the name of Mary is so rich in every good thing, that on earth and in heaven there is no other from which devout souls receive so much grace, hope, and sweetness. Hence Richard of St Laurence "encourages sinners to have recourse to this great name,"

because it alone will suffice to cure them of all their evils; and "there is no disorder, however malignant, that does not immediately yield to the power of the name of Mary." The Blessed Virgin herself revealed to St Bridget "that there is not on earth a sinner, however devoid he may be of the love of God, from whom the devil is not obliged immediately to fly, if he invokes her holy name with a determination to repent."

On another occasion she repeated the same thing to the saint, saying, "that all the devils venerate and fear her name to such a degree, that on hearing it they immediately loosen the claws with which they hold the soul captive." Our Blessed Lady also told St Bridget, "that in the same way as the rebel angels fly from sinners who invoke the name of Mary, so also do the good angels approach nearer to just souls who pronounce her name with devotion." Consoling indeed are the promises of help made by Jesus Christ to those who have devotion to the name of Mary; for one day in the hearing of St Bridget, He promised His most holy Mother that He would grant three special graces to those who invoke that holy name with confidence: first, that He would grant them perfect sorrow for their sins; secondly, that their crimes should be atoned for; and, thirdly, that He would give them strength to attain perfection, and at length the glory of paradise. And then our Divine Saviour added: "For your words, O My Mother, are so sweet and agreeable to Me, that I cannot deny what you ask."[4]

13 September: Our Lady of Zell

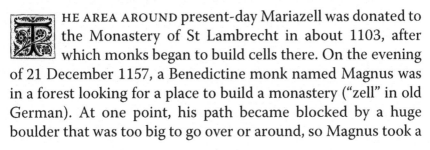 HE AREA AROUND present-day Mariazell was donated to the Monastery of St Lambrecht in about 1103, after which monks began to build cells there. On the evening of 21 December 1157, a Benedictine monk named Magnus was in a forest looking for a place to build a monastery ("zell" in old German). At one point, his path became blocked by a huge boulder that was too big to go over or around, so Magnus took a

small wooden statue of the Virgin Mary he had in his knapsack, knelt in prayer, and asked the Virgin Mary for guidance.

Soon there was a great rumble and the rock split in two, allowing him to pass through. Magnus placed the statue reverently on a white branch and soon after, he and some of the local people built a small chapel to house the statue. Word of the miraculous statue of the Virgin quickly spread across the countryside, and the chapel had to be periodically expanded to accommodate the growing crowds.

In 1200, the chapel was enlarged to a church and in 1335, Henry I expanded the church after experiencing a miraculous cure. Still more pilgrims began to visit after about 1330, when a Zellfahrt was introduced as a form of atonement for criminals. In 1363, Louis I of Hungary replaced the church with an even larger one in thanksgiving for a victory. The Gothic church was expanded by Ferdinand III, and given the requisite Baroque makeover, in 1643. This is the church that still stands today. By 1699, almost 400,000 pilgrims flocked to the shrine of Our Lady of Mariazell each year. However, in 1783, Emperor Joseph II dissolved the Mariazell monastery in Mariazell, and in 1787, he completely banned pilgrimages there. The restrictions were later lifted.

To mark the 750th anniversary of the shrine's founding, Pope St Pius X granted a plenary indulgence to those who visited Mariazell in 1907. The same year, the statue of Our Lady of Mariazell was crowned and the church was designated a Minor Basilica. The first non-Austrian pilgrimages to Mariazell came from Hungary, followed soon after by Croatia, Slovakia, Bohemia, Germany, and other Central European countries. Our Lady of Mariazell came to be known by the titles "Great Mother of Austria, Great Lady of Hungary, and Great Mother of the Slavic People." The Shrine of Mariazell celebrated its 800th anniversary in 1957 and Pope John Paul II visited on pilgrimage on September 13, 1983. Restorations have been underway since 1992. Today the shrine receives around a million pilgrims each year.

Prayer

O Mary, we call upon you.
You are the Great Mother of Austria,
the Mother of the Slavic peoples.
You offer a safe haven for the exiled;
you bring freedom and consolation to prisoners.
We ask you holiest of all virgins,
to guard innocence and purity.
Helper us in all our needs,
assist us in danger when we call upon you.
O Mary, guardian of the German Lands,
we pray that you may banish the scourges of war and bring peace
to all believers.
Through your powerful intercession,
console the disillusioned,
bring back the erring,
comfort the sick,
and give hope to sinners.
Great Mother Mary,
Our Lady of Mariazell,
bless and protect the people who honour you. Amen

14 September: Our Lady of Einsiedeln

 N THE NINTH CENTURY, the monk St Meinrad, of the family of the Counts of Hohenzollern, left one of the local monasteries to built a hermitage in the Swiss wilderness that would later become Einsiedeln. He took with him a miracle-working statue of the Virgin Mary given to him by the Abbess Hildegarde of Zürich. He soon became well-known in the local village for his kindness and holiness, and received many visitors and gifts.

On 21 January 861, two thieves murdered Meinrad for the treasure in his hermitage. According to legend, the murderers were apprehended after two ravens followed them into town and

drew attention to them with loud squawking. In 940, a small group of Benedictine monks transformed Meinrad's little hermitage into the Lady Chapel. The chapel is said to have been consecrated by Christ himself on September 14, 948. The bishop who was to consecrate the new site had a vision in which the church was filled with a brilliant light as Christ approached the altar; the next day, when he went to perform the ceremony, he heard a voice saying the chapel had already been divinely consecrated. The miracle was confirmed by Pope Leo VIII 16 years later in a papal bull.

St Meinrad had the Black Madonna statue (its dark colour traditionally explained by years of candle smoke) as part of his altarpiece; after his death it was placed in the Lady Chapel for veneration. Many miracles were attributed to the intercession of Our Lady of Einsiedeln, and pilgrimages to Einsiedeln began shortly after 1000 AD. Throughout the Middle Ages, as many as 50,000 pilgrims streamed into the monastery each week.

Since 1620 the Benedictine abbey of Einsiedeln has been a school of theology for its own clerics, those of other abbeys, and students training to become priests. The small school has had 30 students at the most at one time. Despite temporary setbacks to the pilgrimage tradition during the Reformation and especially the major destruction during the French Revolution, Einsiedeln continues to receive about 200,000 pilgrims each year.

15 September: Our Lady of Sorrows

RADITIONALLY, THE SEVEN SORROWS OF MARY comprise the prophecy of Simeon (Lk 2:33–35), the flight into Egypt (Mt 2:13–15), the loss of the Child Jesus in the Temple (Lk 2:41–52), the meeting of Jesus and Mary on the Way of the Cross (Jn 19:17), the Crucifixion (Jn 19:25–30), the taking down of the Body of Jesus from the Cross (Jn 19:31–37), and the burial of Jesus (Jn 19:38–42). The prophecy of Simeon in one sense marked the start of Mary's participation in Jesus' redemptive Passion:

> When David, in the midst of all his pleasures and regal grandeur, heard, from the Prophet Nathan, that his son should die, he could kind no peace, but wept, fasted, and slept on the ground. Mary with the greatest calmness received the announcement that her Son should die, and always peacefully submitted to it; but what grief must she continually have suffered, seeing this amiable Son always near her, hearing from Him words of eternal life, and witnessing His holy demeanour! Abraham suffered much during the three days he passed with his beloved Isaac, after knowing that he was to lose him... Not for three days, but for three and thirty years had Mary to endure a like sorrow![5]

During the Passion and Death of Christ, every torture inflicted on the body of Jesus, was a wound in the heart of his Mother. In this sense, Our Lady suffered more than a martyr. This is a new kind of martyrdom, a Mother condemned to see an innocent Son, and one whom she loves with the whole affection of her soul, cruelly tormented and put to death before her own eyes.[6]

The Feast of Our Lady of Sorrows grew in popularity in the 12th century, although under various titles. Some writings would place its roots in the eleventh century, especially among the Benedictine monks. The first altar to the *Mater Dolorosa* was set up in 1221 at the Cistercian monastery of Schönau. The formal feast of the Our Lady of Sorrows was originated by a provincial synod of Cologne in 1423 and its object was the sorrow of Mary during the Crucifixion and Death of Christ. Before the sixteenth century this feast was limited to the dioceses of North Germany, Scandinavia, and Scotland.

After 1600 it became popular in France and was set for the Friday before Palm Sunday. By a Decree of 22 April 1727, Pope Benedict XIII extended it to the entire Latin Church, under the title of the Seven Sorrows of Our Lady. In 1668 a second, separate feast was granted to the Servites, for the third Sunday in September. By inserting the feast into the General Roman Calendar in 1814, Pope Pius VII extended the celebration to the whole of the

Latin Church. It was assigned to the third Sunday in September. In 1913, Pope Pius X moved the feast to September 15, the day after the Feast of the Cross. It is still observed on that date. In 1969 the Passion Week celebration was removed from the General Roman Calendar as a duplicate of the feast on 15 September. In some Mediterranean countries, parishioners traditionally carry statues of Our Lady of Sorrows in processions on the days leading to Good Friday.

We would propose that the celebration of Our Lady of Sorrows be now restored to the Friday before Palm Sunday, and 15 September be considered the feast of Our Lady Corredemptrix.

16 September: Our Lady of Gietrzwałd

IETRZWAŁD LIES AMONG gentle hills along the river Giłwa in north-eastern Poland. On one of these hills is the Marian shrine, now a big pilgrimage complex. Founded in May 1352, by a charter established the village of Gietrzwałd as a Marian shrine. A wooden chapel was erected and Father Jan Sterchen carried out his ministry there. During the wars between Poland and the Teutonic Knights, the village and the chapel were destroyed. In the 15th century a shrine with no aisles was erected on the stone foundation. In 1500 the shrine was consecrated, under the title of the Nativity of Our Lady, by Auxiliary Bishop Jan Wilde.

In the 19th century, Father Jozef Jordan expanded the church and the shrine acquired the present shape of the Roman cross in the place of the previous rectangle. It is also during this time that the wooden tower was demolished and replaced with brick spire with a gothic capping. On 27 June 1877, Our Lady appeared for the first time to Justyna Szafrynska (13) when she was returning home with her mother after having taken an examination prior to receiving the First Holy Communion. The following day Barbara Samulowska (12) also saw the Bright Lady sitting on the throne with Infant Christ among Angels over the maple tree in front of the church while reciting the rosary. The girls asked "Who are you?" she answered, "I am the Blessed Virgin Mary of the Immaculate Conception!". "What do you request, Mother of God?", they asked, the answer was: "I wish you recite the rosary everyday!"

On 1 July 1877, the children from the parish in Gietrzwałd received their First Holy Communion. Justyna asked during the prayer of Rosary under the maple-tree "Who are You?", and the Holy Mother answered: I am The Most Holy Virgin Mary Conceived Immaculate!" On 3 July, the girls asked the Holy Mother whether the sick people who came there, would be healed?" The Holy Mother answered: "A miracle will take place, and after that the sick people will be healed", and later said: "Let the sick people pray the Rosary". On 8 September 1877, at about seven o'clock in the evening the Holy Mother blessed the nearby spring and said the words: "Now, the sick people can take this water for their healing". Pilgrims have been taking healing water from the spring ever since. On 16 September, at about five o'clock in the evening the Holy Mother blessed her own statue in the small chapel, and after that she blessed all the people. At the end, she said: "Pray the Rosary zealously!"

Bishop Filip Krementz, administrator of the diocese, requested a detailed report from the parish priest, and sent delegates to Gietrzwałd to observe the state and behaviour of the visionaries in the course of apparitions, to prepare the record of their testimonies and to collect observations from pilgrims and clergy. The bishop's delegates confirmed that the apparitions did not appear fraudulent and that the girls behaved normally. They reported that the girls did not seem to be seeking profit or acknowledgement and possessed modesty, sincerity and simplicity. The last apparition took place on 16 September 1877. In 1878, after receiving the results of the commissions to examine authenticity of the apparitions, Bishop Filip Krementz promoted the publication in German and in Polish of the study by Father Franciszek Hipler entitled *The Apparitions of Our Lady in Gietrzwałd to the Catholic People According to the Official Documents.*

In September 1967 the Primate of Poland Cardinal Stefan Wyszynski visited the shrine to commemorate the ninetieth anniversary of the apparitions and crowned the miraculous icon. At the same time, the Holy See approved the liturgical celebration of Our Lady of Gietrzwald for the diocese of Warmia on 8 September. On 2 February 1970, Pope Bl Paul VI elevated the church in Gietrzwałd to the rank of Basilica Minor. Finally, on 11 September 1977, for the centenary of Our Lady's apparitions in Gietrzwałd, many of faithful gathered with the representatives of the Episcopal Conference of Poland headed by Cardinal Karol Wojtyła who prayed:

> Remember, Blessed Virgin Mary, no one has heard that anybody who has entrusted his needs to your maternal kindness has been disappointed. Therefore, full of trust in face of pleading might of your heart, we are laying down in your generous hands, the health of your servant and our Primate. Look at his loyalty and devotion, with which he has been serving you for many years as priest and bishop, and restore in full his strength so that he may see your glory in the days of the jubilee of the basilica of Our Lady of Czesto-chowa and direct the Church in Poland for many years.

On the same day, the decree of the Bishop of Warmia, Mgr Jozef Drzazga, was read approving the devotion to Our Lady's apparitions in Gietrzwałd as not contradicting Christian faith and morals and recognizing the miraculous and divine nature of the events.

17 September: Our Lady of the Burning Bush

S t Catherine's Monastery on Mount Sinai is home to a plant said to be the original bush that Moses saw flaming in the presence of God. In its Chapel of the Burning Bush an icon depicts the Virgin and Child in the fiery bush, with Moses kneeling barefooted between her and St Catherine. The "Unburnt Bush" Icon of the Most Holy Theotokos is based on the miracle witnessed by Moses in the Old Testament.

In Chapter 3 of Exodus God calls Moses on Mount Horeb (Sinai) from the midst of a bush which "was burning, yet it was not consumed" (Ex 3:2). Moses is informed that he will lead the Hebrews out of their slavery in Egypt, and then God tells him His name, "I am Who am" (Ex 3:14).

The Church has always regarded the Unburnt Bush on Horeb as a type of the Most Holy Theotokos giving birth to the Saviour Christ, while remaining a Virgin. This imagery is to be found in the Church's hymnography, and also in iconography. One of the earliest depictions of the Mother of God as the Unburnt Bush shows her holding her divine Son in the midst of a burning bush. Moses is shown to one side, removing his sandals, for that place was holy (Ex 3:5). Most icons now depict the bush in a symbolic fashion. There are two overlapping diamonds: one red (representing the fire), the other green (representing the bush), forming an eight pointed star. The Theotokos is shown in the centre. In the four corners of the green diamond are the symbols of the four Evangelists: a man (Saint Matthew), a lion (Saint Mark), an ox (Saint Luke), and an eagle (Saint John). These symbols are derived from Ezekiel 1:10 and Revelation 4:7. Archangels are depicted in the four corners of the red diamond.

The design of the icon has become more complex over time. Sometimes archangels are depicted along with Moses and the burning bush (Ex 3:2), Isaiah and the seraphim with the burning coal (Is 6:7), Ezekiel and the gate through which only the Lord may enter (Ez 44:2), and Jacob with the ladder (Gn 28:12). The Theotokos is shown holding Jacob's ladder which leads from earth to heaven. Sometimes the Root of Jesse (Is 11:1) is shown in the centre of the icon's lower border. The Russian Orthodox Church honors the Unburnt Bush Icon of the Most Holy Theotokos on the same feast day as Moses: 4 September in the old calendar, 17 September in the new.

18 September: Our Lady of Consolation

HE BAROQUE MARIATROST (Our Lady of Consolation) Basilica on top of the Purberg hill in Mariatrost, a district of Graz, is one of the most famous pilgrimage sites of Styria in Austria. At the origin of the shrine is the story of a nobleman, Hans von Wilfersdorf, who had a crippled daughter. He went to visit his brother who gave him a Cistercian statue of the Madonna and Child, and vowed to make a precious garment for the statue if the child was healed. His prayer was answered soon thereafter in 1676. In 1714, the Emperor Charles VI laid the first stone of the Baroque basilica on 18 September. Despite the closure imposed by Joseph II, Our Lady has always worked many miracles, as evidenced by the ex-votos kept by the Franciscans who have been the caretakers of the shrine since 1846.

The ceiling frescoes inside the church are particularly noteworthy. Two massive 61 meter-high towers anchor the church and cupola at the eastern end of the structure and can be seen from far away. The front of the church is accessed through a set of stairs called the Angelus Steps. To this day the Basilica of Maria Trost is the second most important pilgrimage church (after Mariazell) in the Austrian province of Styria. Declared a Minor Basilica by Pope St John Paul II on 28 October 1999, Mariatrost celebrates its patronal feast on 8 September, the Nativity of Our Lady.

19 September: Our Lady of La Salette

WO YOUNG SHEPHERDS, Maximin Giraud (11) and Melanie Mathieu (14), were headed for high pastures in the French Alps on Saturday, 19 September 1846. They came from non-practicing Catholic families, disregarded church bells, and were not serious about their religion. Suddenly, around 3 pm, they became stunned and mesmerized by a large, glowing circle of light—"like the sun"—shimmering like a diamond. Then it began to open, revealing a weeping woman inside, bent forward with her face buried in her hands, and her elbows resting on her knees, sitting on a large rock. The glowing globe faded away and the woman stood up, revealing her exquisite beauty in a long white dress that seemed to glitter with small pearls of light. She wore a translucent white headdress with a tall crown underneath. Across her shoulders was a shawl trimmed with roses. A large yellow apron was tied around her waist. A cross hung on a chain around her neck. The following details were extracted from the exact text written in 1878 by Melanie:

> The sight of the Holy Virgin was itself a perfect paradise. She was all beauty and love. The sight of her overwhelmed me. Everything radiated the majesty, the splendour, the magnificence of a Queen beyond compare. The word LOVE seemed to slip from her pure and silvery lips. She appeared to me like a good Mother, full of kindness, amiability, of love for us, of compassion and mercy. She had a beautiful crucifix hanging from her neck (the brightness in which she was enveloped seemed to come from the crucifix). At times the Christ on her cross appeared to be dead. At other times, He appeared to be alive—His head erect, His eyes open ... He appeared to speak ... showing that He was on the Cross for our sake.

> The Holy Virgin was crying nearly the whole time she was speaking to me. Her tears flowed gently, one by one, down to her knees. Then—like sparks of light—they disappeared. They were glittering and full of love ... The eyes of our Mother cannot be described in human language ... They appeared thousands of times more beautiful than the rarest diamonds and precious stones. In her eyes, you could see paradise. They drew you to her.

Then the Blessed Virgin spoke these words: "Come to me, my children. Do not be afraid. I am here to tell you something of the greatest importance." As they approached, the globe of shimmering light enveloped all of them.

If my people will not obey, I shall be compelled to loose my Son's arm. It is so heavy, so pressing, that I can no longer restrain it. How long have I suffered for you! God is being dishonoured with swearing. The price for such abuse would be costly. If the harvest is spoiled, it is your fault. A great famine is coming. Many young children will die from a serious disease.

Woe to the inhabitants of the earth! God will exhaust His wrath upon them. The leaders of the people of God have neglected prayer and penance, and the devil has bedimmed their intelligence. They have become wandering stars which the serpent will drag along with his tail to make them perish. ... There will be bloody wars and famines, plagues and infectious diseases. There will be thunderstorms which will shake cities, earthquakes which will swallow countries. Voices will be heard in the air. The fire of heaven will fall and consume three cities.

In the year 1864, Lucifer, together with a large number of demons, will be unloosed from hell. They will put an end to faith, little by little, even in those dedicated to God. Several religious institutions will lose all faith and will lose many souls. Evil books will be abundant on earth, and the spirit of darkness will spread everywhere a universal slackening in all that concerns the service of God.

The true faith of the Lord having been forgotten, they will abolish civil rights as well as ecclesiastical. All order and all justice will be trampled underfoot, and only homicides, hate, jealousy, lies, and dissension would be seen without love for country and family. All the civil governments will have one and the same plan—which will be to abolish and do away with every religious principle, to make way for materialism, atheism, spiritualism, and vice of all kinds.

The earth will be struck with calamities of all kinds. There will be a series of wars until the last war, which will then be fought by the ten kings of the anti-Christ, all of whom will have one and the same plan. Before this comes to pass,

> there will be a time of false peace in the world. People will think of nothing but amusement. The wicked will give themselves to all kinds of sins. And so, my children, make this known to all my people.

Then she turned and spoke to each child individually without the other being able to hear her. When asked if they prayed, they admitted "hardly ever". She encouraged them to do so every night and morning with at least an Our Father or Hail Mary during the day if rushed. She impressed Maximin with recounting an incident with him and his father, word for word, when he thought they had been alone. Then she turned and left, gliding over the ground and rising into the air in the globe of light again.

Upon returning to their families, their story seemed fantastic, yet, their details matched perfectly, and their manner was so sincere. Despite pressures, bribes, and threats from townspeople, they stuck to their story. About a week later, a spring gushed forth out beside the rock upon which the Virgin had sat. This place had only collected water previously whenever snows melted or after heavy rains. But now, the spring flowed steadily, incessantly, and fully—even in dry weather conditions. And it has never stopped since that time. Numerous miraculous cures have been attributed to the water.

On the anniversary of the sighting, 50-60,000 people gathered and celebrated Mass at the site. Twenty-three people reported miraculous cures. The Vatican approved this apparition in 1851. A Basilica was eventually built on the original site, high in the Alps, in 1879 where their visitation took place. Mary had correctly prophesied the great famine in Europe and the decline of religion and morals in the world. She also accurately predicted the American Civil War and the "great war" (World War I) that would follow.

Memorare to Our Lady of La Salette

Remember, Our Lady of La Salette, true Mother of Sorrows, the tears you shed for us on Calvary. Remember also the care you have taken to keep us faithful to Christ, your Son. Having done so much for your children, you will not now abandon us. Comforted by this consoling thought, we come to you pleading, despite our infidelities and ingratitude. Virgin of Reconciliation, do not reject our prayers, but intercede for us, obtain for us the grace to love Jesus above all else. May we console you by a holy life and so come to share the eternal life Christ gained by His Cross. Amen.

20 September: Our Lady of Csíksomlyó

HE WEEPING MADONNA is a larger-than-life statue, thought to have originated in a Hungarian workshop of the 1500s, on the high altar of the Franciscan Monastery in Sumuleu Ciuc, Transylvania, Romania (Csíksomlyó in Hungarian): a standing late Gothic Madonna and Child with gilded drapery, set against an aureole of solar rays. On Pentecost in 1567, Hungarian Zsigmond Janos, King of Trasylvania and a Protestant, set his army against a Catholic gathering here. With prayers to Our Lady, the Catholics rallied and drove Janos out. Ever since, in commemoration, pilgrims flock to Csíksomlyó on Pentecost Sunday. The Virgin of Csíksomlyó is especially dear to the Székely and Csango ethnic groups, who bring to her pilgrimage a rich heritage of music, dancing, costume, and cuisine.

> The wandering swallows rest
> again in Mother's nest;
> so once again we go
> home to Csíksomlyó.

In 1661, Tatars burned the church, but the image remained. Tradition holds that one of the Tatar leaders tried to steal the precious statue, but it became so heavy that even with eight oxen he could not move it. The angry commander struck the Virgin's face and neck with his sword, leaving marks still visible today. After the attack, the statue was seen to weep. On 20 September

1798 the Church confirmed the miracles of Csíksomlyó and crowned the statue.

21 September: The Smiling Madonna of Mariastein

N THE EARLY FIFTEENTH CENTURY, a shepherd boy was grazing the cows with his mother on the field of the top of a rocky outcrop, where today the abbey of Mariastein in Switzerland now stands. While his mother looked for a spot to take a nap, in the heat of the afternoon, the little boy played on the precipice and fell down the steep rock face. When the mother woke up, she did not see his son and realized that he might well have fallen into the abyss: she then hurried to the valley, and found the child unharmed. He told her he had been saved by a Lady as he fell. The child's father was sure that, from the description offered by the child, it had been Our Lady. In gratitude for saving he had a chapel built in honour of the Mother of God on the rock in the cave, where his wife had dozed off: the site soon attracted many pilgrims.

The first chapel was destroyed by fire in 1466 but four years later it had already been rebuilt. In 1530, in the full swing of the Reformation, this second chapel was plundered and destroyed. The Swabian Jakob Augsburger rebuilt it once again.. A second miracle occurred which revitalized the pilgrimages, after the Reformation, when a Swiss nobleman of the Reichenstein family, Hans Thüring, survived a fall from the very same precipice. The Reichenstein family have considered ever since that the sanctuary was a family chapel, which was called the Reichensteiner Kapelle.

The main focus of the pilgrimage is an underground cave—now a chapel—containing a miraculous image of the smiling Madonna. In 1648 Mariastein Abbey was established here with the relocation of the remnants of the failing community at Beinwil, and the foundation of the Benedictine abbey to house them. The abbey was extremely successful both as a revived Benedictine community and as promoters and custodians of the pilgrimage site, which assumed at that period its present importance.

The abbey was secularised twice, in 1792, because of the French Revolution, and in 1874, as a result of a conflict between the state and the Roman Catholic Church known as Kulturkampf, after which the monks were obliged to seek refuge first in France, at Delle, and then, when in 1902 they were expelled as a result of legal changes in France, for a short time at Dürrnberg near Hallein in Austria, and finally in Bregenz, also in Austria. In 1926, the image of Our Lady was solemnly crowned on the orders of Pope St Pius X by the papal nuncio in Switzerland. When the monastery at Bregenz was closed down by the Gestapo, the monks returned to Mariastein, where they were granted asylum in 1941. In 1971 the abbey was officially re-established. The abbey has been a member of the Swiss Congregation, now a part of the Benedictine Confederation, since 1647.

22 September: Our Lady of Ranton

ANTON IS A commune in the Vienne department in the Nouvelle-Aquitaine region in western France. The surrounding countryside was dangerous for travellers because of the many marshes. In pagan times people used to invoke the protection of Jupiter when going through this district, a fact which is still commemorated in the name of a small town called Pas-de-Jeu. When Christianity was introduced, the altar of Jupiter became Our Lady's altar. The cult of Our Lady of Compassion, better known as the good Lady of Ranton, dates back to the beginnings of Christianity.

A legend that is common to the stories of many early shrines is also told about this one. A labourer found a statue in the marshes, one that had been hidden during the Norman invasions. A chapel was built to house the statue and was increased in size according to the needs of the pilgrims. Although the chapel was rather poor, at the time of the Revolution, the Revolutionaries pillaged and profaned it then sold it. The person who bought it only to save the statue. At the beginning of the nineteenth century this shrine was again opened to public worship and was later given over to the diocese in which Ranton lay.

Around 1864 the old chapel was threatened with ruin; the parish of Ranton was unable to take upon itself the work of reconstructing it. A zealous and energetic priest, Father Briant, who had been cured by Our Lady of Ranton when a boy of 17, set himself to the task of architect, contractor and mason. The first stone was blessed in 1867. It was only in 1871 after the Franco-Prussian War ended, Father Briant returned from captivity and the work was finished. It is now once again a place of pilgrimage and miracles.[7]

23 September: Our Lady, Mirror of Justice

MIRROR IS A shining surface which reflects an object placed before it. What image was reflected in Mary? Why is she called a mirror? We need hardly ask, for we know that it was God in His glorious perfections, Jesus Christ, Who was reflected in Mary. The more perfect, the more smooth and spotless the mirror, the more perfect will be the likeness of the object reflected. To her are applied the words of Sacred Scripture: "For she is a reflection of the eternal light, untarnished mirror of God's active power, and image of his goodness" (Ws 7:26). Her soul was clear, calm, unruffled, spotless, and in Her the perfect image of Jesus is always seen. She is, as it were, His echo.

Then, to be adequately reflected, the object must be placed close to the mirror. No one was ever so close to Jesus as His Mother, no one ever had such opportunities of studying Him, of modelling herself on His virtues, on His character. Why is She called "Mirror of Justice" and not—"Mirror of Jesus?" Justice, in the language of Scripture, means not only that great moral or cardinal virtue which gives everyone his due, but it represents a perfect state of soul, the perfection, the completion of all virtues.

Mary was a perfect copy of the virtues of Jesus, of His humility, His love, His patience, His charity, His mercy. She lived with Him in the closest intimacy for thirty years. For all that time she had Him all to herself. When one lives with a person, without even reflecting upon it, views, ideas, and ways are adopted unconsciously, until the two who love one another seem almost one, so alike are they in everything. They love the same things, their dislikes are identical, they desire and work for the same ends. Mary, loving Jesus so uniquely, so intensely, so completely, grew hourly, daily, more and more like Him.

How much do the members of a family, generally speaking, resemble one another! As the proverb runs, "Love either finds or makes its like." A mirror, again, is used to view ourselves in, to see if there is anything disorderly or out of place in our attire or appearance, so that we may put it right. Sometimes we may put our looking-glass to a wrong use, by looking in it out of sheer vanity, in order to admire ourselves and take pleasure in our supposed good looks. This danger will never be ours when we look into our "Mirror of Justice"—Mary. We may admire her beauty our whole life long, and never come close to realizing all there is in her that is lovely and worthy of our praise and admiration. Again, we may compare ourselves in that mirror, and see what is wrong and faulty in ourselves, in our spiritual attire; how unlike we are to Mary, our model, and what we have to do to better reflect her virtues.

Our fallen human nature is constantly tempted to fix its gaze upon ourselves, to admire our own good qualities, our achievements, just as vanity tempts us to admire ourselves in a mirror. Spiritually, there are two dangers in looking at ourselves. If we keep our eyes fixed on our own good points, we become proud, vain, and self-satisfied. There is also the opposite danger, for if we look only at our own faults, constantly dwelling on our miseries and shortcomings, we may grow faint-hearted, discouraged, and fall into despondency and despair.

It is always better to aim at a positive good than a negative one. To aim at doing what is good will keep us from evil far more effectively than merely turning away from evil. For example, it is good and necessary to avoid the occasions of sin, but it is better and more effective to strive to always be mindful of the presence of God. It is good to fear God, but better to love Him. So Our Lord has given us this lovely, spotless Mirror of Our Mother's life and virtues to contemplate, to gaze lovingly and thoughtfully upon. How much easier it is to do a thing well if we have a perfect and beautiful model of what we have to do before us! We keep looking at the beautiful ideal or example, and the very act of looking impresses the image on our soul; and insensibly, without consciously reflecting on the process, we begin to love the beauty held up to us, until it almost seems to pass into us and become part of our being.[8]

24 September: Our Lady of Ransom

HE STORY OF Our Lady of Ransom begins with Saint Peter Nolasco, born in Languedoc about 1189. At the age of twenty-five he took a vow of chastity and made over his vast estates to the Church. After making a pilgrimage to Our Lady of Montserrat, he went to Barcelona where he began to practice various works of charity. He conceived the idea of establishing an Order for the redemption of captives seized by the Moors on the seas and in Spain itself; they were being cruelly tormented in their African prisons to make them deny their faith. He spoke of it to the king of Aragon, James I, who knew him well and already respected him as a Saint; for the king had already asked for his prayers when he sent out his armies to combat the Moors, and he attributed his victories to those prayers.

In effect all the Christians of Europe, and above all of Spain, were praying intensely to obtain from God the remedy for the great evil that had befallen them. The divine Will was soon manifested. On the same night, 1 August 1218, the Blessed Virgin appeared to Saint Peter, to his confessor, Raymund of Peñafort, and to the king, and through these three servants of God established a work of the most perfect charity, the redemption of captives. On that night, while the Church was celebrating the feast of Saint Peter in Chains, the Virgin Mary came from heaven and appeared first to Saint Peter, saying that She indeed desired the establishment of a religious Order, later known as the Mercedarians, bearing the name of Her mercy. Its members would undertake to deliver Christian captives and offer themselves, if necessary, as a guarantee.

The Order, thus solemnly established in Spain, was approved by Pope Gregory IX under the name of Our Lady of Mercy. By the grace of God and under the protection of His Virgin Mother, the Order spread rapidly. Its growth was increased as the charity and piety of its members was observed; they very often followed Her directive to give themselves up to voluntary slavery when necessary, to aid the good work. It was to return thanks to God and the Blessed Virgin that a feast day was instituted and observed on 24 September, first in this Order of Our Lady, then everywhere in Spain and France. It was finally extended to the entire Church by Pope Innocent XII. Pope Leo XIII encouraged the devotion by making this feast proper to all the dioceses of England, with a focus on how Our Lady ransoms us from the slavery of our sins, and brings us the grace of conversion.

25 September: Our Lady of Walsingham

N THE YEAR 1061 in a small village in North Norfolk, in England, in the reign of Edward the Confessor there lived a devout young widow, Richeldis de Faverches, Lady of the Manor of Walsingham. Our Lady appeared to that young widow three times in a vision and each time showed her the house in which the Holy Family had dwelt in Nazareth. Mary requested that Richeldis build a replica of this house in Walsingham. Some have identified Richeldis with Edith the Fair, the wife of future King Harold (the last Anglo-Saxon king of England) and daughter of Wulfhilda, sister of Edward the Confessor.[9] To Richeldis, Our Lady said:

> Do all this unto my special praise and honour. And all who are in any way distressed or in need, let them seek me here in that little house you have made at Walsingham. To all that seek me there shall be given succour. And there at Walsingham in this little house shall be held in remembrance the great joy of my salutation when Saint Gabriel told me I should through humility become the Mother of God's Son.

By the Middle Ages, Walsingham had become one of the greatest pilgrimage sites in all of Europe. A church was constructed around the house to protect it from the elements. From Britain, Ireland, and the continent of Europe, people came to the shrine, from all walks of life: peasant, king, rich and poor. At the Holy House, all were equal. From the time of Henry III in 1226, almost every king and queen of England as well as Queen Isabella of France, and King Robert Bruce of Scotland visited the shrine. In the early 1500s, Henry VIII visited the Holy House of Walsingham more than once as a pilgrim. On one such occasion he walked barefoot twice the usual distance traversed by penitents. But Henry's ways changed as the years passed. In his effort to be rid of his wife, Queen Catherine, and marry another, the king broke with Rome and had himself declared by his parliament to be the head of the English Church. Then, in 1538, Henry, about to move against all religious orders in his domains, confiscated and burned the Holy House of Our Lady of Walsingham. The magnificent priory church adjacent to it fell into ruin so that only a portion of the massive east wall is visible today. Of the Holy House itself, archaeologists have found remnants of its foundation beneath a thin layer of ash on a rectangular knoll near the ruins of the priory church.

A wealthy Anglican woman, Charlotte Boyd, in the nineteenth century commenced the restoration of the shrine, just as another wealthy woman had initially endowed it in the eleventh century. For pilgrims travelling from London to Walsingham, the last stopping place had been a chapel about a mile away known as the Slipper

Chapel, because they left their shoes there before walking barefoot the last mile to the shrine. The small fourteenth century building was used as a barn to house animals prior to Charlotte Boyd's desire to restore it. Before her plan materialized, she became a Catholic, and in the 1890's bought the chapel and donated it to Downside Abbey. The Guild of Our Lady of Ransom took care of the restorations, and carved the statue of a standing Virgin and Child was given the place of honour. That statue is now in King's Lynn.

In 1897 Pope Leo XIII re-founded the ancient shrine of Our Lady of Walsingham and on 20 August 1897, a procession of pilgrims from King's Lynn to the Slipper Chapel marked the renewal of public devotion to Our Lady of Walsingham. In 1922, the parish priest at the church of St Mary the Virgin in Walsingham, Fr Hope Patten, made a statue of Our Lady of Walsingham. He had discovered in the British Museum a medieval seal of the old monastery, and at its centre was an image of our Lady—presumably a representation of the image that had been destroyed at the Reformation. This statue was placed in the parish church, and at once pilgrims returned once more seeking the blessings of pre-Reformation Walsingham. By 1931 the numbers had become too many for the parish church to cope with and a new shrine church was built, with the Holy House at its centre and the image above its altar. So the Shrine of our Lady of Walsingham was reborn, and in our own time it continues to draw thousands each year who, like the medieval predecessors come to discover the reality of "God with us," and the effects of God's loving and healing Grace and Love. In August 1934 Cardinal Bourne led the Catholic bishops of England and Wales and ten thousand pilgrims to the Slipper Chapel, and from this date it became the official Catholic National Shrine.

Prayer

O blessed Virgin Mary, Our Lady of Walsingham, Mother of God and our most gentle Queen and Mother, look down in mercy upon us, our parish, our country, our homes, and our families, and upon all who greatly hope and trust in your prayers. By you it was that

Jesus, our Savior and Hope, was given to the world; and He has given you to us that we may hope still more. Plead for us your children, whom you did receive and accept at the foot of the Cross, O sorrowful Mother. Intercede for our separated brethren, that with us in the one true fold they may be united to the Chief Shepherd, the Vicar of your Son. Pray for us all, dear Mother, that by faith fruitful in good works we all may be made worthy to see and praise God, together with you in our heavenly home. Amen.

26 September: Santa Maria in Via

HE ORIGINS OF this Roman church are entirely unknown. However a bull of Pope John XII in 962, apparently confirming a lost earlier one of 955 by Pope Agapetus II listing the assets of the monastery of San Silvestro in Capite, has this to say: "Two churches, one big and one little, called St Mary and situated in front of the gate of the abovementioned monastery."[10] It is thought that one of these is the present Santa Maria in Trivio, and the other Santa Maria in Via.

On the night of 26 September 1256 the waters of the well, which was originally placed in the stables attached to the house of Cardinal Pietro Capocci, began to overflow threatening to flood the stable. It caused the horses to panic and wakened the grooms who were anxious to see what had happened. The water was several inches higher than the rim of the well and natural curiosity led them to investigate further. An image of Mary on a tile or slate fragment had floated to the surface disappearing when they tried to retrieve it.

Cardinal Capocci was alerted and descended in his robes into the stable along with his full noble court. He said a brief and fervent prayer to Our Lady and without hesitation waded into the water. He was able to recover the blessed picture of Mary without difficulty and the water of the well receded to its natural level. His servants and family then carried the miraculous image to the Cardinal's rooms and remained the whole night long in prayer before the picture. The following morning the Cardinal went to the Pontiff to tell him what had happened in his house. He asked the Pope to approve his plan of converting the stable into a shrine dedicated to Our Lady. The Holy Father Pope Alexander IV ordered that first a judicial investigation should take place. All those who witnessed the miracle were subjected to a rigorous interrogation. Once satisfied with the truth of the account the Pope not only approved the Cardinal's project but ordered that there should be a solemn procession of all the clergy and that he himself would take part, and that the miraculous image should be solemnly installed in a shrine not far from the well where the miracle had taken place.

The church was rebuilt "from the foundations" between 1491 and 1513, on the orders of Pope Innocent VIII. When it was finished, in 1513, it was granted to the Servite Order by Pope Leo X (1513-1521), and they still serve the church and parish. The feast of Our Lady of the Holy Well is kept on 8 September, which is Our Lady's Birthday, and a night vigil is held on 26 September, the anniversary of the miracle of the well.

27 September: Our Lady, Star of the Sea

ARY'S TITLE "STAR OF THE SEA" is thought to derive from the account in 1 Kings 18:41–45 which refers to a little cloud appearing above the sea as a sign of hope that rain would soon come to water the parched earth. This little cloud, seen by the prophet Elijah on Mount Carmel, is believed to be the "Star of the Sea", and is why the Carmelites named the church they would later build on the site, *Stella Maris*. The star as a symbol of Mary is rich in meaning. It is used to articulate several characteristics of Mary: her privileges, in particular her mission as Mother of the Redeemer or her holiness; her anticipatory role (forerunner, announcer) with regard to Christ; and her role as luminous and enlightening. St Ephraim calls Mary "the safe harbour of all sailing on the sea of the world".

One of the earliest references we have to Mary as *Stella Maris* is found in the writings of Paschasius Radbertus (d. 865): "Mary, Star of the Sea, must be followed in faith and morals lest we capsize amidst the storm-tossed waves of the sea. She will illumine us to believe in Christ, born of her for the salvation of the world." This beautiful quote reminds us that just as this title of Our Lady speaks in a special way to her patronage for those who travel or work on the seas, as the spiritual Mother of all God's children, she guides us and intercedes for us throughout the sea of our life until we finally arrive at heaven's safe harbour. In the twelfth century, Saint Bernard of Clairvaux interpreted Miriam (Hebrew for "Mary") as meaning Star of the Sea, and outlined how Mary protects us:

> You who feel yourself tossed by the tempests in the midst of the shoals of this world, do not turn away your eyes from the Star of the Sea, if you want avoid shipwreck. If the winds of temptation blow, if tribulations rise up like rocks before you—look at the Star, send a sigh towards Mary! If the waves of pride, ambition, calumny, or jealousy seek to swallow up your soul—look at the Star, send a prayer to Mary! If anger, avarice, or love of pleasure toss your fragile boat—seek the eyes of Mary. If horror of your sins, trouble of conscience, or dread of the judgments of God begin to plunge you into the gulf of sadness, the abyss of despair— attach your heart to Mary. In dangers, in sufferings, in doubt—think of Mary and invoke her aid. Let Mary be always in your heart and often upon your lips. To obtain her help in death, follow her example in life. In following her, you will not go astray; by praying to her, you will not despair; if you cling to her, you will not go wrong. With her support, you will not fall; under Her protection you will have no fear; under her guidance you shall not grow weary; if she is gracious to you, you will reach the port.[11]

Almost all the figures of speech in Scripture about the sea refer to its power and its dangers. All dreaded the unknown sea. Having no compass in those days, many ships were lost in the great traffic on the Mediterranean. The sea has always had its dangers. St

Bonaventure compares life to a tempestuous sea into which sinners have fallen from the ship of Divine Grace. "O poor lost sinners," he makes Our Lady say, "despair not; raise up your eyes and cast them on this beautiful star; breathe again with confidence, for it will save you from this tempest and will guide you into the port of salvation." The Apostleship of the Sea has, for many years now, been commemorating the Feast of Our Lady, Star of the Sea, with Mass each year in September for seafarers.

Hymn

Deep night hath come down on us, Mother, deep night,
And we need more than ever the guide of Thy light;
For the darker the night is, the brighter should be
Thy beautiful shining, sweet Star of the Sea.

28 September: Our Lady, Undoer of Knots

ARY UNDOER OF KNOTS (also Untier of Knots) is a title of Mary derived from a 1700 painting by Johann Schmittdner. The image, called Maria Knotenlöserin in German, is located in St Peter am Perlach church in Augsburg, Germany. Earliest reference to Mary using the image of untying knots is in an ancient text of St Irenaeus in the late second century. He wrote "the knot of Eve's disobedience was loosed by Mary's obedience." "For what the virgin Eve had bound fast through unbelief, this did the virgin Mary set free through faith."[12] This is one of the earliest examples of Mary portrayed as the New Eve, and there lie the beginnings of devotion to Our Lady, Undoer of Knots.

The painting depicting Our Lady untying the knots of a white wedding ribbon was commissioned in the year 1700 by Fr Hieronymus Ambrosius Langenmantel in thanksgiving for her intervention in his family. Earlier in the 17th century, Fr Hieronymus' relatives, the noble Wolfgang Langenmantel and his wife, Sofia, began having trouble in their marriage. Having reached the point of considering divorce, they approached Fr Jakob Rem, a Jesuit, who lived 70 kilometres north of Augsburg. Fr Rem was known for his strong Marian devotion and his wise counsel. The couple made four visits to this priest to pray with him and receive his advice over a 28 day period. During the final visit, Fr Rem was praying before an image of Our Lady and in a symbolic act raised the white wedding ribbon and presented it to Our Lady untying knots in the ribbon one by one as he did so. (At that time, it was common in the wedding ceremony for the couple to be draped and joined by a single white ribbon symbolizing their union. This is still done today in various forms in some cultures.) As the ribbon was presented to Our Lady, it became brilliant white. After this time spent in prayer and the intervention of Our Lady, the noble couple persevered in their marriage and was no longer in danger of divorce.

The painting that Fr Hieronymus commissioned in thanksgiving for Our Lady's intervention in his family still hangs over the family altar in the church of St Peter am Perlach in Augsburg, Germany. The painting itself, realized by Johann Melchior Georg Schmittdner, depicts Our Lady untying knots in a wedding ribbon, but in the lower portion of the painting, Wolfgang Langenmantel can be seen being guided by the Archangel St Raphael in his journey to resolve the crisis in his marriage. The advocation of Mary, Untier of Knots, has become widespread and efficacious particularly in the resolution of marital and family conflicts. The devotion has spread worldwide, finding particular popularity in Argentina and Brazil.

28 September is listed as a day to commemorate her under this title—sources indicate that is the date of the intervention in the Langenmantel family. It also seems symbolic that there is a connection to St Raphael and the archangels whose feast is the day following. With St Raphael being pictured and the image associated with healing of marriage struggles it is that Raphael/marriage connection. This prayer to Our Lady Undoer of Knots, was written by our Holy Father Pope Francis, when he was a bishop in Argentina.

Prayer

Holy Mary, full of God's presence during the days of your life, you accepted with full humility the Father's will, and the Devil was never capable to tie you around with his confusion. Once with your Son you interceded for our difficulties, and, full of kindness and patience you gave us example of how to untie the knots of our life. And by remaining forever Our Mother, you put in order, and make more clear the ties that link us to the Lord. Holy Mother, Mother of God, and our Mother, to you, who untie with motherly heart the knots of our life, we pray to you to receive in your hands (the name of person), and to free him/her of the knots and confusion with which our enemy attacks. Through your grace, your intercession, and your example, deliver us from all evil, Our Lady, and untie the knots that prevent us from being united with God, so that we, free from sin and error, may find Him in all things, may have our hearts placed in Him, and may serve Him always in our brothers and sisters. Amen.

29 September: Our Lady of Tirano

T THE FIRST SIGN of dawn on Sunday 29 September 1504, on the feast day of Saint Michael the Archangel, a young nobleman, Mario Omodei, was going towards the vineyard to collect some fruit when suddenly he felt himself being lifted from the ground and transported with sweetness to a little orchard not too far from home. The little orchard was right outside the village of Tirano, protected then by walls, erected by Ludwig the Moor, near the Folla Bridge of the Poschiavino River. Terrorized by what was happening, Mario found himself in front of a young Lady, of about fourteen or fifteen years, of extraordinary beauty and clothed with soft perfume. She started to speak to him in an affectionate tone: "Mario, Mario!" He responded: "Well, Our Lady" with great fear. The Virgin replied: "Goodness you shall have. Know that I am the Glorious Virgin Mary, do not be afraid". "Know that during this year, there came a great illness of man and beast" and the Virgin continued "there will be more and it will be worse, if a church in my honour is not constructed on this site; and everyone that visits this holy and blessed place, giving a good and holy offering, according to their personal means, will be freed and saved from this plague". Thus Our Lady promised to end the plague, which at that time was raging in the Valtellina in northern Italy. Dazed by what was happening, the boy fell to his knees. Mary ordered him: "Go everywhere you can to publicize this apparition and miracle." Mario obeyed immediately. He rushed back to the city to recount the event to Knight Luigi Quadrio, one of the highest authorities of the valley, the man that six years earlier had attempted to defend the land from invaders. He was also the owner of the orchard where Our Lady appeared. The rich knight immediately donated a strip of land for the construction of the church.

The privileged life that nobleman Mario Omodei had lived so far, radically changed: the young man left Tirano in order to fulfil the wish of the Virgin Mary, in which she asked him to go from place to place, as far as his strength could take him, to ask for money to build a shrine. He finally died in Trento, while he was collecting donations. Our Lady rewarded him: in addition to saving his brother, who was struck by the plague, she saved his son from a very grave illness. His son then also received the gift of the priesthood which he exercised in the Shrine of Tirano. The residents of Tirano began the construction on 25 March 1505, and during a solemn ceremony that day, the first stone of the building was placed at the foot of the medieval church of Santa Perpetua, which is located on a rocky spur overlooking the piazza. In 1528, the basilica was officially consecrated. Because of its crossroads location, it has always drawn pilgrims from throughout Europe. Many people have knelt before the statue: simple people and pilgrims of high rank: kings and queens, emperors and ambassadors, princes of the Church and saints. In 1946 Pope Pius XII proclaimed the Blessed Virgin of Tirano "special heavenly patron of all Europe".

The people of the Valtellina region to this day are very devoted to Our Lady who always has favoured them with healings, resurrections of still-born babies, protection during plague and famine. Every day the red Bernina Express train departs from Tirano, crosses the city, and stops at a district called "Madonna", taking hundreds of devotees to their destination; then it continues to Switzerland. Cardinal Angelo Roncalli, who later became Pope John XXIII and Cardinal Giovanni Battista Montini, who later became Pope Paul VI, often made stops there during their summer vacations.

30 September: Our Lady of Zlaté Hory

EAR THE TOWN of Zlaté Hory in Czechia (the Czech Republic) near the Polish border, the pilgrimage centre Maria Hilf started as a simple forest shrine. During the 30 Years' War, a woman named Anna Tannheiserová gave birth there while hiding from Swedish Lutheran soldiers. Her son became a city councillor, and in 1718 his daughter hung a painting of Our Lady at her father's birthplace in the woods. Based on Lucas Cranach the Elder's widely-copied altarpiece in Innsbruck Cathedral, this painting by Simon Schwarzer was moved to the parish church in 1729 and a copy was placed in the forest, where a small chapel now hosted pilgrims and miraculous healings.

A larger church was consecrated on 8 September 1841, gradually flanked by a Way of the Cross, chapels to Saints Anne and Martha, a Lourdes grotto, and a holy well. Before World War II, up to 100,000 people visited annually, including many Germans and Poles. The war embittered the Czech people toward the Germans and led to the Communist takeover in 1948. Because of the strong German presence at the shrine to Our Lady of Help, as well as the religious intolerance of the period, the sanctuary was already in decline by 1973, when the Communist regime demolished it. Since the 1989 Velvet Revolution, the shrine has been rebuilt as a Centre for Spiritual Revival, dedicated to Our Lady, Help of Christians, Guardian of Life. Pope St John Paul II blessed the foundation stone on 22 April 1990. The Pilgrimage of Three Nations—Czech, German, and Polish—takes place the day before the local pilgrimage on the fourth Sunday in September.

Notes

1   See M. Lamberty, *The Woman in Orbit: Mary's feasts every day everywhere* (Chicago: Lamberty Co, 1966), 4 September.
2   See *ibid.*, 5 September.
3   See *ibid.*, 11 September.
4   St. Alphonsus de Liguori, *The Glories of Mary*, Chapter X, "O Dulcis Virgo Maria".
5   St. Alphonsus de Liguori, *The Glories of Mary*, Reflection on the First Dolour.
6   See *ibid.*, Discourse IX, "On the Dolours of Mary".
7   See Lamberty, *The Woman in Orbit*, 22 September.
8   See *Salve Maria Regina*, Volume 49, No. 157 (Summer 2009).
9   See B. Flint, *Edith the Fair: Visionary of Walsingham* (Leominster: Gracewing, 2015).
10 Duae ecclesiae, una maiore at alia minore, que dicitur S. Maria namque site ante portam suprascripti monasterii.
11 St Bernard of Clairvaux, *Sermon on the Feast of the Holy Name of Mary*.
12 St Irenaeus, *Adversus haereses*, 3, 22.

OCTOBER

1 October: Our Lady, Mother of priests

OHN, THE DISCIPLE whom Jesus loved, is the model of the priests in their love and devotion to Mary. John took Mary into his home: "and from that hour the disciple took her to his own home" (Jn 19:27). Priests, following the example of the disciple John, also take Mary into the interior home of their priesthood and welcome the Mother of Christ as their mother. Priests take Mary as Mother into the interior "home" of their priesthood, for they belong to the faithful in whose rebirth and development the Mother of God cooperates with maternal love. Mary deserves the offering of the full rights in the home of their priestly lives, of their faith, of their affections, and of their commitments.

Mary is the Mother and model of priests in their spiritual battle against the forces of evil. Priests turn their eyes to the Mother of God, the "Woman clothed with the sun", for she is the one who continues to take part in the spiritual battle for the victory of good over evil. Mary is an example to priests in their thanksgiving to God for the gift of the priesthood which they have received, and this is best expressed in her *Magnificat*: "The Almighty has done great things for me, and holy is His name"(Lk 1:49). Blessed Columba Marmion (1858–1922) observed:

> Mary is in a special manner Queen and Mother of priests. Because of their resemblance to her divine Son, Our Lady sees Jesus in each one of them. She loves them not only as members of the mystical body, but on account of the priestly character imprinted on their souls, and for the sacred mysteries which they celebrate in persona Christi.[1]

Pope Pius XII (1876 –1958) remarked that inasmuch as "priests can be called, by a very special title, sons of the Virgin Mary, they will never cease to love her with an ardent piety, invoke her with perfect confidence, and frequently implore her strong protection." Mary is the "loving Mother of all Catholic priests", he added.[2]

The priest needs the love of Mary' feminine heart to bring him to the fulfilment of the masculine ideal: to protect humanity from all that is detrimental to salvation. Jesus, the New Adam, is the Redeemer and protector of the human family. The priest is the protector of all that belongs to Christ: men, women, and children, heaven and earth. The priest is at his best when, like Christ, he guards the dignity and vocation of every man, woman, and child. God chose Mary to be a guardian of the priest' dignity and vocation. The Mother gently moves the priest to be transfigured into Christ. Through the maternal mediation of Mary, the priest becomes the sacrifice that offers the perfect Sacrifice; the priest becomes the love that offers Love.[3]

Pope Francis has also indicated how Our Lady is the Mother of priests, referring to the manifestation at Cana:

> A first icon of the good news would be the stone water jars at the wedding feast of Cana (cf. Jn 2:6). In one way, they clearly reflect that perfect vessel which is Our Lady herself, the Virgin Mary. The Gospel tells us that the servants "filled them up to the brim" (Jn 2:7). I can imagine one of those servants looking to Mary to see if that was enough, and Mary signalling to add one more bucketful. Mary is the new wineskin brimming with contagious joy. Without her, dear priests, we cannot move forward in our priesthood![4]

Prayer

O Mary,
Mother of Jesus Christ and Mother of priests,
accept this title which we bestow on you
to celebrate your motherhood
and to contemplate with you the priesthood.[5]

2 October: Our Lady, Spiritual Vessel

 VESSEL IS MADE to contain something. A "Spiritual Vessel," then, means one made to contain something which does not appear outwardly to the senses, but is of the spirit, of the soul. "All the glory and beauty of the King's daughter is within." This title, then, describes the beauty of Mary's soul. We should all like to have a detailed description of Our Lady's personal appearance, but this is not given to us. She is a "Spiritual Vessel." She hides her virtues even from her own eyes, like some lovely flower, folding in upon itself, lest the precious fragrance should escape. No, every portion of the precious gift is to be kept all alone for her Beloved. It is strange how little mention there is of Our Lady in the Gospels, although before she came, Prophets and the Scriptures had described her perfections by many wonderful types, such as the great women of the Old Testament— Esther, Judith, and others—and by beautiful images, such as the cedar of Lebanon, the cypress tree, the palm tree, the rose of Jericho, the fair olive tree in the plains, and all the others which we read of in Ecclesiasticus chapter 24, and in many other passages from the Books of Wisdom in the Bible.

This silence of the Gospels about Mary is her own doing. She it was who must have instructed St Luke in the details of the Sacred Infancy and the Hidden Life of Jesus, for no one but Holy Mary and St Joseph had been eye-witnesses of them. Yet how little mention there is of Mary; nothing but the barest narration of facts, and then only what is needful for the history of her Son. But we have one little phrase which tells us something of what was within that Spiritual Vessel. Mary treasured all these things and pondered them in her heart (Lk 2:19). Her thoughts were always full of Jesus, of the words He spoke, of the things which happened to Him. This was the constant occupation of her mind, the food of her thoughts. How different are the ordinary subjects of our thoughts when we are left to ourselves. If we find we are brooding over slights and injuries, and considering reprisals on the first opportunity, or gloating over some word of praise, some little success which has flattered our vanity, dreaming of future conquests and successes, and perhaps despising others less fortunate, or harbouring harsh and uncharitable judgments of others. Then our hearts are very far indeed from being spiritual vessels! Here we may learn a precious lesson from Our Blessed Mother. We can all ponder, turn over in our minds, the deeds and sayings and events of the life of Jesus, and make them our chosen mental occupation. Thus our minds will become a little more spiritual, a little more like that of Our Mother, the Spiritual Vessel. If we persevere in this practice of making Jesus, His Life and His Mysteries, the sovereign preoccupation of our minds and hearts, we shall have found a treasure which will be to us a priceless blessing. We shall learn gradually to be quiet, contented, and happy within our own minds, and lose that restless craving after outside excitement—which is the source of so much unhappiness—because we have found within an unfailing source of joy and contentment.

Even with the great tragedy of her Son's Passion so clearly foreseen, and its black shadow ever looming in front, and the deep surges of sorrow welling in undercurrents beneath, Mary could still say: "My soul proclaims the greatness of the Lord" (Lk 1:46). Deep peace, calm, and contentment in God were always Hers. And they will be ours, too, if we, like her, always "keep all these words"— the happenings of the Life of Jesus, pondering them in our hearts.

Beautiful Spiritual Vessel! It is the beauty of Mary's soul which it concerns us most to know. Her whole thought is of her blessedness in being the Mother of God. See how many centuries passed before her own great glory, her Immaculate Conception, was brought out and proclaimed before men! It is as though that vase of beautiful and costly fragrance, her soul and its perfections, were kept sealed up, and only gradually let its perfume escape. She had no desire to attract praise and notice. Never in her whole life was there one thought, word or deed aimed at her own honour, glory or advantage; She was always and only "all for Jesus".[6]

3 October: Our Lady of Willesden

 HE CHURCH OF St Mary dates back to a foundation of King Athelstan, 10th-century King of England and grand-son of King Alfred the Great, and was built above the holy well that gives Willesden (well's 'down') its name. The church possesses many hallmarks of its age: an 11th-century oak door, a square stone font of equal age, and the water from the holy well is now piped up into a little fountain in the chancel. The great treasure of Willesden was its statue of the Blessed Virgin Mary with the Child Jesus, blackened with age—the Black Virgin of Willesden. It was a great mediaeval pilgrimage site, and the statue and well were the source of many a healing miracle.

In the summer of 1538, King Henry VIII's chief minister Thomas Cromwell ordered England's venerated images of Our Lady to be removed from their shrines—along with any treasures found with them. Among them was the ancient black Virgin of Willesden, burned at Chelsea that autumn. In 1892, Catholics had a new statue made from the wood of an oak tree growing in the cemetery of the Anglican Church of St Mary. Since 1903, the Catholic statue goes through the streets in an annual procession on the second Sunday in May. There is also a torchlight procession the second Sunday in October. In 1931, the Catholic Church of Our Lady of Willesden opened in the area, northwest of Charing Cross in outer London. On 3 October 1954, Cardinal Bernard Griffin crowned the Black Madonna at a Marian Pageant in Wembley Stadium. Eventually, the Anglicans of St Mary's commissioned their own Black Virgin, dedicated in 1972. In 1998 they dedicated a new Holy Well on the grounds, renewing a tradition long associated with the Willesden pilgrimage. The Anglican procession takes place the first weekend of July.

4 October: Our Lady of the Plaza

HAT BEGAN OVER 200 years ago as a small pueblo populated by eleven homesick families from Mexico, stands today as Los Angeles, the world's largest city named in honour of Our Lady. The only major United States city bearing a title of the Blessed Virgin, Los Angeles today, with its population of nearly 4 million persons, is a far cry from the tiny farm town that was founded 4 September 1781, merely as La Plaza "The Square". And the church which bears the city's name, Our Lady of the Pure Angels, is a far cry from the hut built so rudely in 1784, where Franciscan Friars were forbidden to celebrate Holy Mass.

The site of the city lay originally near the Junction of the Los Angeles River and the Arreye Sece, was chosen on 2 August 1769, the day after the great Franciscan feast of Our Lady of the Angels of Portiuncula, and so was named in honour of that feast.

The eleven original families included some of Spanish, Indian and Negro extraction. The city's first real church was dedicated 8 December 1822. It was as original, great and beautiful as the town it served. Still standing today and commonly known as the Plaza; the Church on the Square, the first structure was built by Joseph Chapman, a shipbuilder—symbolic, since the church is the "barque" or the ship of St Peter; and Joseph constructed the church named after St Joseph's Spouse, Mary, the Mother of God and our Mother, who reigns as Queen in every place. Los Angeles' first church has grown with the city itself. While all around it, the steel and concrete giant has risen that make up a modern city, the Square (Plaza) Church has remained a centre of Latin American religious and social culture; mixing the lives of peoples of many Places into one common blend of devotion to their Heavenly Mother, Mary.

Thy lovely features, Virgin sweet,
I see in pictures thousand-fold,
But none to match the vision bright
I in my inmost soul behold;

The world and all its panoply
Have vanished in it brilliant light,
In place a heavenly serenity
Now fills my heart with chaste delight.[7]

5 October: Our Lady of la Gomera

 HE SECOND-SMALLEST OF the seven Canary Islands—near-circular and with a diameter of only 25 kilometres—La Gomera feels like the island that time forgot. You can drive through soaring ravines and sleepy mountain villages down to deserted rocky beaches without encountering a single traffic light.[8]

In the 1500s, a ship bound for America passed near the island of La Gomera, where the crew observed brilliant lights coming from a cave on land. Attracted, they disembarked and found in the cave a small image of the Virgin Mary holding her child. They took it aboard, but then couldn't sail no matter how they tried. After returning the image to the cave, they ship was able to proceed into port on the island, near San Sebastián. When the crew told the authorities about what had happened, everyone went to the cave on Punta Llana (Level Point). The islanders named the 25 cm brown sculpture Our Lady of Guadalupe, after the famous dark Virgin of Guadalupe in central Spain (much as the Mexican miracle image was named around the same time).

The statue of Our Lady of Guadalupe, patron of La Gomera, was canonically crowned 12 October 1973. Her *Bajada*, or Descent among the people, is the island's biggest festival, held every five years (2008, 2013). Over a period of weeks, the miraculous statue processes down decorated streets to every community on the island. The Monday after the first Saturday in October is the high point in the celebrations. Accompanied by singing and dancing, the statue processes from the Puntallana sanctuary to the church in San Sebastián, where the bishop celebrates mass. There follow concerts and dancing into the night.

6 October: Our Lady of Eternal Aid

N 574 ST COLUMBANUS and twelve of his companions landed on the northern coast of France in the region now known as Brittany. They founded many hermitages and monasteries. Other missionaries followed, among them St Gall, who in 610 founded the chapel in Montrel Langast. In Querrien, a small village Brittany, St Gall built a chapel and sculpted a statue of the Virgin and Child. Over time the chapel collapsed and the statue was lost.

On 15 August 1652, Jeanne Courtel, a poor shepherdess age 12, was tending her father's flock of sheep. She had been both deaf and mute ever since her birth. She was reciting her prayers when she was surprised by the sudden appearance of the Blessed Virgin Mary. Our Lady was holding the Child Jesus on one arm and holding a stalk of lilies in the other.

Blessed Mary had only spoken a few words when Jeanne suddenly realized that she could actually hear her! The twelve-year old had been miraculously healed. Our Lady spoke in a sweet voice, "I choose this place to be honoured. Build for me a chapel in the middle of this village and many people will come." Then a dialogue began between the Holy Virgin and the shepherdess.

Mary continued, "Charming shepherdess, give me one of your lambs." Jeanne would have willingly given one to the Lady, but she replied,

"These sheep are not mine; they are my father's."

Then Mary replied with these directions,

"Return to your parents and tell them that I require a lamb."

Jeanne turned to leave, but then turned back and asked Our Lady,

"But who will keep my herd?"

Blessed Mary replied,

"Myself. I will keep your sheep!"

The little girl returned to her parents quickly—and they were astonished to hear her speak! Jeanne excitedly told them,

"A Lady came to see me, and she asked me for one of your lambs."

The father was overjoyed at his daughter's miraculous recovery and replied,

"Ah, my daughter. Because this Lady has made you speak, we will give her all the flock."

Jeanne also related that her father should dig in the nearby pond to find a statue of this Lady that had been buried there for centuries – according to Our Lady. The father asked his daughter if the Lady had stated who she was?

"She said that she was the Virgin Mary, and we need to build a chapel in the village so many pilgrims will go there to honour her."

The father responded,

"If this is true, we will ask the bishop to allow us to build a shrine to the Virgin Mary."

In the days that followed, the Virgin appeared again and repeated her request for a chapel. On 20 August, having been divinely directed by Our Lady to search the pond for the statue, her statue lost since the time of St Gall was duly found and proved to be in excellent condition—despite having been buried in water for centuries.

During that same year 1652, Mgr Denis de La Barde, bishop of that region, made an appearance on 11 September and was informed about all that had taken place. Several days later on 20 September, after conducting his investigations, he formally recognized the validity of the apparitions and blessed the first stone of the future chapel. The chapel was begun that year in 1652 and was completed four years later. It was enlarged in 1779 because of the large crowds that visited the shrine. The body of visionary Jeanne Courtel was entombed within the shrine after her death in 1703 at the age of 63. On 14 August 1950, some 20,000 pilgrims visited Querrien for the coronation of the miraculous statue by the local bishop—who did so in the presence of many ecclesiastics. One of the most splendid ceremonies to take place at the shrine was celebrated by Cardinal Lustiger, Archbishop of Paris, who paid homage to Our Lady and then blessed the new buildings on 10 September 2000. The shrine of Our Lady of Eternal Aid is proud to be the only one in Brittany that has been authenticated by the Catholic Church.

7 October: Our Lady of the Rosary

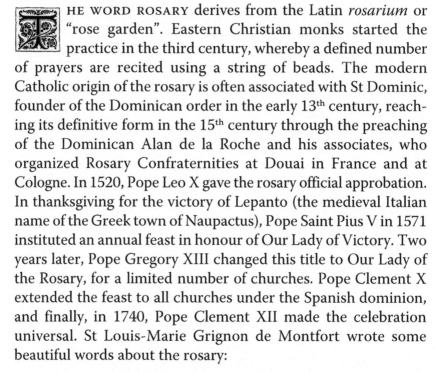 HE WORD ROSARY derives from the Latin *rosarium* or "rose garden". Eastern Christian monks started the practice in the third century, whereby a defined number of prayers are recited using a string of beads. The modern Catholic origin of the rosary is often associated with St Dominic, founder of the Dominican order in the early 13th century, reaching its definitive form in the 15th century through the preaching of the Dominican Alan de la Roche and his associates, who organized Rosary Confraternities at Douai in France and at Cologne. In 1520, Pope Leo X gave the rosary official approbation. In thanksgiving for the victory of Lepanto (the medieval Italian name of the Greek town of Naupactus), Pope Saint Pius V in 1571 instituted an annual feast in honour of Our Lady of Victory. Two years later, Pope Gregory XIII changed this title to Our Lady of the Rosary, for a limited number of churches. Pope Clement X extended the feast to all churches under the Spanish dominion, and finally, in 1740, Pope Clement XII made the celebration universal. St Louis-Marie Grignon de Montfort wrote some beautiful words about the rosary:

> Good and devout souls, who walk in the light of the Holy Spirit, I do not think you will mind my giving you this little mystical rose tree which comes straight from heaven and which is to be planted in the garden of your soul. It cannot possibly harm the sweet-smelling flowers of your contemplations; for it is a heavenly tree and its scent is very pleasant. It will not in the least interfere with your carefully planned flower-beds; for, being itself all pure and well-

ordered, it inclines all to order and purity. If it is carefully watered and properly attended to every day, it will grow to such a marvellous height, and its branches will have such a wide span that, far from hindering your other devotions, it will maintain and perfect them. Of course, you understand what I mean, since you are spiritually minded; this mystical rose tree is Jesus and Mary in life, death and eternity.

Its green leaves are the Joyful Mysteries, the thorns the Sorrowful ones, and the flowers the Glorious Mysteries of Jesus and Mary. The buds are the childhood of Jesus and Mary, and the open blooms show us both of them in their sufferings, and the full-blown roses symbolize Jesus and Mary in their triumph and glory.

A rose delights us because of its beauty: so here we have Jesus and Mary in the Joyful Mysteries. Its thorns are sharp, and they prick, which makes us think of them in the Sorrowful Mysteries, and last of all, its perfume is so sweet that everyone loves it, and this fragrance symbolizes their Glorious Mysteries.

So please do not scorn this beautiful and heavenly tree, but plant it with your own hands in the garden of your soul, by making the resolution to say your Rosary every day. By saying it daily and by doing good works you will be tending your tree, watering it, hoeing the earth around it. Eventually you will see that this little seed which I have given you, and which seems so small now, will grow into a tree so great that the birds of heaven, that is, predestined and contemplative souls, will dwell in it and make their nests there. Its shade will shelter them from the scorching heat of the sun and its height will keep them safe from the wild beasts on the ground. And best of all, they will feed upon the tree's fruit, which is none other than our adorable Jesus, to whom be honour and glory forever and ever. Amen.[9]

8 October: Our Lady of Hardships

RIGINATING IN SPAIN, veneration of Our Lady of Hardships (Nuestra Senora de las Peñas) was carried to the New World by Spanish explorers and missionaries. About fifty miles from Arica, a northern coastal city of Chile in the region of Arica and Parinacota, lies the sanctuary of Las Peñas of Livilcar and the site of the annual celebration of the Virgin of the Rosary of Las Peñas; but the celebration did not originate in Chile, it originated next door in Bolivia. Tradition tells of the celebration of the Virgin of the Rosary of Las Peñas in the small village of Carangas (Oruro), Bolivia, adjacent to the province of Arica in Chile. As the story goes a young second lieutenant was in charge of the feast, but he was poor, and the celebration was modest. A rich man from the village, contemptuous at what he believed to be a lack of reverence, took the banner of Mary for the next year, saying he would keep the celebration and the holyday as it should be kept. When the next year came, the church was festooned with flowers and candles, more than anyone had ever seen before. But the church burned to the ground, and the image of Our Lady disappeared. As it happened, some shepherds were approaching the village to join in the celebration when they met an unknown Lady. They asked her why she was not at the celebration, and she answered that she was going to another place where they adored her more. As she made her reply, a white dove was seen to fly to the West. Thus the celebration arrived in Arica.

Another legend of Our Lady of las Peñas recounts the events that occurred in the town of Humagata in Chile, now deserted, a short distance from Las Peñas sanctuary. It seems that his wife of the governor of the town fell gravely ill and that the governor called on the healer to treat her. His wife died, and the governor condemned the poor man to death by fire. Not only that, but he ordered him to go out and collect the wood for the fire. The healer, a good man, wept much and went to find firewood. With tears in his eyes, he came to the Livilcar rocks and saw a White

Dove that landed and rested against the rock. It was the dove who came had come from Carangas, Bolivia. The healer thought to bring the dove to the governor and to ask for compassion. As he moved forward, the dove disappeared and where it lighted again there appeared an image of Our Lady in the rock. The frightened ran to the governor to tell him what had happened.

The governor threatened the healer with a fate worse than death if he was lying to him, and then went into the wood, found that the healer was telling the truth and summoned the Franciscan fathers of Codpa. Since the rock was much too large to move, the fathers thought they could chisel away the part of the rock with the image and place it in their chapel. The rock was very hard, and the fathers were still working when darkness came. That night the parish priest suffered a severe headache and heard a voice of a lady who told him that she too was suffering from the striking of the hammer. When he awoke, the parish priest ordered the work on the rock be stopped and declared that it was there on that miraculous spot that the people were to venerate the Virgen de las Peñas.

The present church dates back to 1910. Some claim the sanctuary dates back to 1700; others put the year only some time before 1840. The image carved in the rock depicts a beautiful young woman about two feet in height. It is said that the image grows a centimetre each year and that originally it had been the size of a dove. Celebrations are held annually on the first Sunday in October.[10]

9 October: Our Lady of Champion

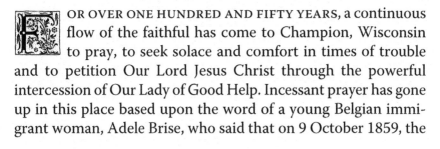

OR OVER ONE HUNDRED AND FIFTY YEARS, a continuous flow of the faithful has come to Champion, Wisconsin to pray, to seek solace and comfort in times of trouble and to petition Our Lord Jesus Christ through the powerful intercession of Our Lady of Good Help. Incessant prayer has gone up in this place based upon the word of a young Belgian immigrant woman, Adele Brise, who said that on 9 October 1859, the

Blessed Mother, a Lady clothed in dazzling white, had appeared to her. The Lady was elevated slightly in a bright light and gave words of solace and comfort and a bold and challenging mission for the young immigrant woman. The Lady gave her a two-fold mission of prayer for the conversion of sinners and catechesis:

> I am the Queen of Heaven who prays for the conversion of sinners, and I wish you to do the same. You received Holy Communion this morning and that is well. But you must do more. Make a general confession and offer Communion for the conversion of sinners... Gather the children in this wild country and teach them what they should know for salvation... Teach them their catechism, how to sign themselves with the sign of the Cross, and how to approach the sacraments; that is what I wish you to do. Go and fear nothing, I will help you.

Adele Brise began immediately to fulfil the mission entrusted to her by the Lady and often at great personal sacrifice went to the homes of the children to instruct them in the largely unsettled and forested area in Wisconsin. Adele was always obedient to the authorities of the Church and steadfast in the mission entrusted to her by Our Lady, no matter what difficulty she encountered. The mission given her became such a commitment that she set up a Catholic school of instruction for children and even began a community of Third Order Franciscan women, who assisted her in her obedience to the mandate of Our Lady to pray for the conversion of sinners and to instruct the children. A long tradition of oral and some documented sources recounting answered prayers at the Shrine of Our Lady of Good Help include conversions and many physical healings attributed to the Blessed Mother's intercession. Many physical healings are immortalized by the multitude of crutches and other mementoes of thanksgiving for answered prayers left at the Shrine. Prayers for physical healing are answered even to this day through the intercession of Our Lady of Good Help. Though none of these favours have been officially declared a miracle by the Church, they are clear evidence of spiritual fruitfulness and the history of devotion to the Blessed Virgin Mary at the Shrine.

Graces have been poured out through the sacraments celebrated in this place especially through the celebration of the Mass and the Sacrament of Reconciliation, as well as through the recitation of public devotions and private prayers. Our Lady has lessened or relieved the burdens of the People of God, whether about financial, familial, relationship or employment matters or even through diminishing inclement and tempestuous weather. This holy place was preserved from the infamous Peshtigo fire of 1871, when many of the faithful gathered here with Adele and prayed through the intercession of Our Lady of Good Help, with the result that the fire that devastated everything in its wake in this entire area stopped when it reached the parameters of the Shrine. There is clear testimony to the upright character of Adele Brise, her devotion to Jesus Christ and the Blessed Virgin Mary, and her unwavering commitment to the mission Mary entrusted to her. Moreover, the uninterrupted history of faith and devotion testifies to the spiritual fruits bestowed upon the pilgrims to the Shrine.

On 8 December 2010, the solemnity of the Immaculate Conception of Our Lady, Rt Rev Mgr David Ricken, the twelfth bishop of Green Bay decreed:

> I declare with moral certainty and in accord with the norms of the Church that the events, apparitions and locutions given to Adele Brise in October of 1859 do exhibit the substance of supernatural character, and I do hereby approve these apparitions as worthy of belief (although not obligatory) by the Christian faithful.

10 October: Our Lady of the Cloister

 CERTAIN YOUNG MAN entered the Cistercian Monastery at Cîteaux. He had been gracefully brought up, and found the religious life very hard, especially the coarse fare that was served in the refectory. He almost died of hunger, for he could not force himself to eat of it. He therefore prayed with great fervour to Our Blessed Lady to help him to overcome this weakness of the flesh. One night, when he had prayed even more earnestly than usual, he fell asleep with the piece of bread that had been given him for his supper in his hand; it was so hard and sour that he could not eat it.

Our Lady, who is full of tenderness for those young souls who seek to follow her Son in the narrow way of religion, had compassion on him and came to him where he lay, and said "Come, little Son, rise up and follow me, and I will give you that food of which you stand in need. Now shall you eat and be satisfied, for the bread I will give you is the banquet which my Son had spread for his friends." He rose up, full of joy at her kind words. She took him to the place where the great Crucifix was hung, whereon Our Lord and Savior shows His Five Sacred Wounds. "Look," she said, "here is your feast made ready, for My Son died to make all things sweet to you. Take this crust of bread, which you so much dread, and dip it into His Wounded Side, which was pierced for you; thereby you shall know the savour of that food wherewith poverty is nourished for His sake."

When with great awe and reverence he had dipped his crust in the Wound of Our Savior's Side, Our Lady said to him: "Behold the Bread of Angels", and when the novice ate of that crust, an exceeding great peace entered his soul, his hunger was stilled, and he was refreshed in body and mind. It seemed to him the sweetest food he had ever tasted. Kneeling down, he gave thanks to Our Lord and His Blessed Mother, and was filled with love to endure the hardships of holy poverty, for He knew Our Lord would strengthen him through the virtue of His Most Sacred Passion. This legend shows the prudence of Our Blessed Mother in a true manner. She chose this gentle and persuasive way to help the monk in his weakness, when all other means might have failed.[11]

11 October: Our Lady, Mother of the Church

 HE DOCTRINE WAS already contained in a statement made in 1748, more than two centuries ago, by Pope Benedict XIV. Before the Second Vatican Council, this expression was found in the teaching of Pope Leo XIII, in which it is affirmed that Mary is in all truth mother of the Church. The title was later used many times in the teachings of Pope St John XXIII and Pope Bl Paul VI. The liturgical memorial of Our Lady, Mother of the Church is kept in the Vatican on 11 October. It was Pope Paul VI, who during an address of at the close of the Third Session of the Second Vatican Council on 22 November 1964, solemnly proclaimed this title of Our Lady:

And so, for the glory of the Blessed Virgin and our own consolation, We declare Mary Most Holy to be the Mother of the Church, that is of the whole Christian people, both the faithful and the bishops, who call her a most loving Mother. We decree that from now on the whole of the Christian people should use this sweetest of names to pay more honour to the Mother of God and to pour out their prayers to her.

It is a name that is not unusual as far as Christian devotion is concerned, Venerable Brethren. As a matter of fact, it is under this name of Mother in particular that the faithful and the whole Church prefers to call upon Mary. This name goes with a genuine understanding of devotion to Mary, since it is firmly based on the dignity Mary has as Mother of the Incarnate Word of God.

In this mortal life, she showed herself the perfect image of what it means to be a disciple of Christ. She was the mirror of all virtues and she took the beatitudes that were preached by Christ Jesus and reproduced them to the full in her own life. As a result, the universal Church, in developing the many sides of its life and activity, finds the definitive model for perfect imitation of Christ in the Virgin Mother of God.

And so after due promulgation of the Constitution on the
Church, upon which We have set a kind of crown by
declaring Mary to be Mother of all the faithful and of the
bishops, that is, of the Church, We trust that the Christian
people will be sure to call upon the Most Blessed Virgin
with greater confidence and more fervent devotion, and
will show her the honour and devotion that is due her.[12]

12 October: Our Lady of El Pilar

HE SPECIAL FEATURE of this apparition of Our Lady is
that it dates back before Our Lady's Assumption. While
Our Lady was in Ephesus before her Assumption, Jesus
appeared to her and asked her to go with the angels to see St
James who was in Zaragoza at the time. She was to tell James that
Jesus wished him to return to Jerusalem to be martyred. The
tradition of the shrine of El Pilar, as the Spaniards call it, is that
Our Lady was carried on a cloud by the angels to Zaragoza during
the night. While they were travelling, the angels built a pillar of
marble, and a miniature image of Our Lady. Our Lady gave the
message to St James and added that a church was to be built on
the site where the apparition took place. The pillar and the image
were to be part of the main altar. Special graces and protection
would be granted to the people of Zaragoza in exchange for a
pure devotion to Our Lord and Our Lady. Mass began to be
celebrated at the little church and people began to venerate Our
Lady through the image left there by her and the angels. For
twelve years before Our Lady's Assumption into heaven the
people of Spain were venerating Our Lady as Our Lady of the
Pillar. This is the only apparition of Our Lady we have heard of
taking place prior to her Assumption. The year when this
apparition occurred was around 40 or 41 AD. The pillar, now
presently enshrined by the larger Basilica of Our Lady of the
Pillar, is believed to be the same one given and promised by Mary,
in spite of numerous disasters that beset the church. Our Lady
of the Pillar is also celebrated on 2 January (the day on which the

apparition is supposed to have occurred) and is the patroness saint of the country of Spain, the Hispanic peoples, and the Spanish Civil Guard.

A multitude of miracles have been wrought at the Shrine of Our Lady of El Pilar, but the following stands out both for splendour and authenticity. Through this devotion to Our Blessed Lady it stands on record that a man recovered, at this Church in Zaragoza, one of his legs which had been amputated. His name was Miguel Juan Pellicer, aged at that time 19 years, and born at Calanda, a town of Aragon and the home of his parents. One day the young man, being in the service of his uncle, Diego (James) Blasco, at Castellon de la Plena, in Valencia, fell out of a wagon and broke his leg. He was taken to the hospital at Valencia, and after many remedies had been tried in vain, he was taken to the great hospital at Zaragoza, where he was placed under the care of Juan d'Estanga, a celebrated surgeon. The young man had a great devotion to Our Lady of El Pilar, and when he was taken to Zaragoza, he first received the Sacraments at Her Church. When the surgeon was obliged to amputate his leg—a finger's breadth below the knee—Miguel invoked the Blessed Virgin with great fervour.

When the wound had begun to heal, he dragged himself to Her image to offer up thanks and place his whole life in Her hands; and when, afterwards, he suffered intense pain in the sore limb, he used to go to the Church of El Pilar and anoint the stump with the oil from one of the lamps which burned before Her. He did this consistently, and for two years was known by everybody to frequent the Church of Our Blessed Lady, sometimes imploring Her aid, sometimes begging the charity of the passers-by. In 1640 he returned to Calanda, and used to beg for alms. On 29 March 1641, after having exhausted himself cutting grass, he hung up his wooden leg, and went to bed. Later that night his mother entered his room, and was amazed to see two feet in her son's bed. At first she thought one of the soldiers quartered in the town had got into the house, and ran to tell her husband. But when Miguel's father arrived, he saw it was his son, and awoke him. The son cried out on awakening, "I dreamt that I was in the chapel of Our Lady of El Pilar, where I was anointing my stump with the oil of the lamp!" The father instantly answered, "Give thanks to God, my son. His Holy Mother has restored you your leg." Miguel did not know it till then.

News of the event immediately spread all over the town, and the same night all the inhabitants came to witness the miracle. The next day a large crowd accompanied him to the church to render thanks, and all beheld him with two legs, who, the day before, was known to have but one. The young man was conducted to Zaragoza, and judicially examined. An advocate was named, witnesses were questioned, the question was debated, and at length, on April 27, 1641, the most illustrious Lord Pedro Apaolara, Archbishop of Zaragoza, pronounced that the fact was true, and that it surpassed all natural powers. The verdict was also signed by the Prior of St Cristina, the Vicar-General, the Archdeacon, the senior professor of canon law, and several other professors and provincials of Religious Orders. Pope St John Paul II recalled his visit to the shrine on 6 November 1982 and also on 10 October 1984:

> In my spiritual Pilgrimage of today, I wish to direct my thoughts to the Virgin of the Pilar in Zaragoza, Spain, whose basilica I had the pleasure of visiting, fulfilling my wish of kneeling as a devout son of Mary before Her sacred Column. This venerable Shrine, built on the banks of the Ebro River, is a great symbol of the presence of Mary since the beginning of the preaching of the Good News in the Iberian Peninsula. According to an ancient local tradition, the Virgin appeared to James the Apostle in Zaragoza to console him, and she promised him her help and maternal assistance in his works of Apostolic preaching. Furthermore, as a signal of protection she left him a marble Column that, through the centuries has given the Shrine its name. Since then, the Pilar of Zaragoza, as it is commonly called in Spain, is considered as the symbol of the firmness, the constancy of the faith of the Spanish people

and moreover, it is also an indication of the road that leads to the knowledge of Christ through the Apostolic teaching. The Spanish Christians have seen in the Pilar a clear analogy with the column that guided the people of Israel in their pilgrimage to the Promised Land. Therefore, through the centuries, they have been able to sing "*Columnam ducem habemus*", we have as a guide a Column that accompanies us to the new Israel.[13]

Traditional Prayer to Our Lady of Pilar

O Virgin Mother of El Pilar, deigning to appear to your beloved disciple, St James, promising him the victory over paganism, and blessing so abundantly his labours for the spread of the True Catholic Faith, secure for us also, who are the children of that same Faith, the victory over our many foes and the paganism that is laying waste the harvest of souls in our day. Through the intercession of Your Apostle, St James, the "Son of Thunder", may we as clouds flying through the air at the least breath of the Holy Spirit, establish everywhere the true devotion to Your Immaculate Heart that Jesus wills for the conversion of all sinners. Amen.

13 October: Our Lady of Gifts

HE STORY OF Our Lady of Gifts, also known as Our Lady of Thanks and Our Lady of Grace, is intertwined with many legends. Like all the Pre-Reformation statues in Ireland, the actual records have been lost and one must depend on the memory of the faithful. According to the legends, an Italian youth of good family, who had been shipwrecked off the coast of Ireland, was admitted to the Dominican priory of the Holy Cross at Youghal, probably at some time during the early sixteenth century.[14] The youth had had some training in sculpture; he had a fine piece of marble which by some miracle had been saved from shipwreck. This he planned to carve into a Madonna, but the prior insisted that he use it for a pedestal for a statue of the Prior's favourite saint. The boy obeyed, though reluctantly. Some time later, a small piece of ivory drifted in with the tide. It was badly stained and had several bad flaws, but the prior told him to use it for a statue of Our Lady, as long as he was anxious to carve one. The young man decided to complete the statue for the Prior's feast day, but the work was slow and by the eve of the feast it was still unfinished. He stayed up most of the night working on it, but still could not finish it satisfactorily, so finally he went to bed. In the morning he resolved to throw the piece away and ask for a new one, he was dissatisfied with it; but when he went to look at it, he realized that someone else had been working on it. It was beautiful, and it had some strange power to make his heart content. The statue was set up in the cloister hall, and soon the brothers began reporting miracles through the intercession of Our Lady. Eventually the statue was placed in the chapel, where visitors could pray before it. The miracles continued yielding the title for the little statue of Our Lady of Gifts.

In 1581, the soldiers of Elizabeth I raided the countryside, burning and looting monasteries. The brother who had carved the little statue was old by that time, too old to go to the rescue of the statue when the soldiers came. He gave it into the care of a novice and told him to hide it. The novice fled into the forest but was seen by a soldier and shot down. Dying he thrust the statue into the niche of a layer of trees. No one knew where it had gone and for many years the Dominicans like other religious were banished from Ireland. Many years later, the Irish Dominicans reorganized on the coast of Brittany. They were very poor. One day a great log floated in and lodged on the beach. After splitting it, they found, wrapped in a blood stained Dominican scapular, the tiny statue. With great rejoicing Our Lady was once more enthroned. In 1756 the Dominicans were back in Youghal, where they re-established their old ruined priory and set up the little ivory statue. Many further miracles occurred at the shrine on the return of the Dominicans to Ireland. The priory was built up and enriched by several benefactors who had received help through the intercession of Mary, Our Lady of Gifts. The statue is now in the Dominican church at Cork, set into a magnificent shrine of Our Lady of Gifts and Graces. In thanksgiving, too, somebody named her the Lady of Thanks. The statue is very tiny, hardly three inches tall, carved of a very simple piece of ivory. Our Lady is seated, and has the Holy Infant on her lap.[15]

14 October: Our Lady of La Rochelle

 HEN LOUIS XIII of France moved against the rebellious Huguenots who had entrenched themselves in the fortress of La Rochelle, he had recourse to Our Lady of the Rosary. Before beginning the siege, he went on foot to visit the altar of Our Lady of Victories in Paris. The Duke of Buckingham had been preparing a formidable invasion to help the French Huguenots. He appeared off the coast of France with a large fleet, landed in the isle of Ré, occupied it and laid siege to the citadel of St Martin. King Louis XIII, reigning monarch, placed all his trust in Mary— the Isle of Ré was recaptured.

The King then ordered the public recitation of the Rosary. On 20 May 1627, the Archbishop of Paris publicly recited the Rosary in the presence of the clergy, the Queen Regent, many of the nobility, and an immense congregation of people. The petition was renewed every Saturday for the triumph of the King's army against his enemies. Meanwhile the Rosary was zealously preached in the soldiers' camp. More than fifteen thousand Rosaries were distributed among the soldiers, and at the appointed hours of the day and night the whole camp resounded with Mary's praises. Finally, they stormed the fortress. Once again the Rosary triumphed over the enemies of the Blessed Virgin, and once again France was saved for the Catholic faith.

The victory was accepted, in an official declaration, by the University of Paris as a miracle of the Holy Rosary. At the formal request of the King, of Anne of Austria and of Marie de Medici a rosary crusade in thanksgiving was organized. Father Louvet from the Dominican convent of Paris was called to preach the crusade. To commemorate the event, the King dedicated the church of Our Lady of Victories in Paris in honour of the rosary triumph of La Rochelle.

15 October: Virgin Most Prudent

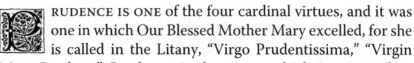 RUDENCE IS ONE of the four cardinal virtues, and it was one in which Our Blessed Mother Mary excelled, for she is called in the Litany, "Virgo Prudentissima," "Virgin Most Prudent." Prudence is the virtue which is opposed to rashness, heedlessness, inconsiderateness. Our Lady was most perfect in prudence; She was careful, guarded, circumspect in all she said or did. She reflected, and was silent and asked God's help before she spoke or acted. When the Angel announced to her that she was to become the Mother of God, She thought over his words and asked, "How shall this be done?" remembering that she had consecrated herself to God, and could agree to nothing that might interfere with her vow. There are on record only seven occasions on which she spoke at all, and how wise, how guarded, how prudent, were her words on all those occasions!

It is a very good idea to take the Gospel and study these words of Our Blessed Lady. Notice to whom she speaks, what she says, what is her motive for speaking, as, for instance, her kindness and charity at the marriage feast of Cana. It may be that when we are among strangers, we are less careful than we would be among friends. We are carried away by the novelty and excitement of our surroundings and experiences, and perhaps say things that we afterwards find to have been very foolish, or even wrong. We may be amongst worldly people, who gossip uncharitably, and we join in and add to the mischief by our unconsidered words. All this comes from want of prudence. We are, again, not careful to keep things secret that were told us in confidence. Love of excitement is likely to lead us into much imprudence. We will join in anything that promises amusement, regardless of consequences. If this is our disposition, we should watch over ourselves very carefully, that we may not be led astray.

We may, for instance, be led into extravagance and debt, if we are with people who gamble for high stakes, and we join in without reflection. We may, in the same way, be led into temptation by rashly reading some book or magazine which is dangerous or unsuitable for us, or by watching some film which is harmful. We should ask advice about these things, and heed the warnings of the wise. It is a positive habit to be thoughtful and circumspect in all our doings. If it is our way to act on the spur of the moment, to give way to every passing impulse, we shall certainly sin against prudence before long, and against every other virtue when the occasion presents itself. Let us fix our eyes on Mary, the Most Prudent Virgin, and ask Her help and guidance in everyday matters. Act, like her, always on principle, that is, according to rule and law, in all the small things of life, and you will gain a habit of carefulness and prudence which will guide you in all your ways.[16]

16 October: Mother Most Pure

HE WHOLE PHILOSOPHY of Our Lady's life is described when she went to the Temple for the rite of purification, bearing her God-child and two turtle doves. It never occurred to Our Lady to "put on airs" or to look down upon the common mass of humanity as beneath her dignity. So pure and humble, she kept her crown as Heaven's Queen yet invisible.

Through Mary's most pure heart we learn the lesson of mercy for those who have made failures of their lives and have pock-marked the beauty of their souls by sin and lust. From her, too, we learn the great lesson of charity that teaches us not only to pity those who have fallen but by prayer and kindness to bend down and help them up.

We need Mary in this fallen world, we need all the graces she can obtain for us. We know her great compassion for all of us; we know that in calling her Mother Most Pure, we are not placing her beyond the reach of the weakest and frailest of mankind; in fact, the opposite is true, because so pure, she can understand the need of all of us—weak and faltering as we are.

For the Virgin Mother of Purity, given to us as a model, her place in history is as secure as her place in Heaven. We cannot add anything to her purity nor take anything away from it no matter what we do. In imitating her we can only help ourselves and the age in which we live. There is a place beside her at the foot of the cross for all of us; the place where St Mary Magdalen knelt. We pray that all may find her, Mother Most Pure, and find all that is required to be pure and the contribution of our age will be a life dedicated to purity, and reparation for all who are too blind to see that her way is the only way that leads to peace and happiness.[17]

17 October: Our Lady of El Pueblito

N 1632 THE MIRACULOUS IMAGE of Our Lady of El Pueblito was carved by the humble priest and religious Franciscan Friar Sebastian Gallegos, who lived in the convent of San Francisco el Grande city of Queretaro, and the statue depicts the Blessed Virgin Mary in the mystery of her Immaculate Conception. Father Gallegos gave the small image to his confrère Fr Nicholas Zamora, then parish priest of Queretaro, who was trying to help the citizens of El Pueblito turn away from paganism. It appeared that native Otomies were congregating at the nearby pre-Hispanic temple mound, known as Cerro Pelon, and allegedly offering gifts of flowers and incense to their idols, crying for the protection and aid of their pagan gods, and dancing at the foot of the man-made shrine. Once Gallegos crafted the sculpture of the Immaculate Conception, the Franciscan guardian installed it at the offensive site.[18] The natives, seeing the image, were enchanted by its beauty, and then convinced by the miracles that God began to work and so led them to abandon idolatry, and embrace the Christian faith:

They began to view her for long periods of time, gazing in suspense... at that portrait of the Queen of Heaven and Earth... Admiring her overwhelming beauty, love entered them through the eyes, seeing and admiring so much loveliness and majesty in that marvellous image that it won't be the first or last time that the eyes are the instruments by which the heart surrenders.[19]

The statue of the Virgin of El Pueblito became famous for showing signs of life as early as 1648, repeatedly perspiring, weeping, flashing its eyes, and working miracles of healing and protection. The most sustained growth of the Pueblito devotion took place during the eighteenth century, thanks especially to this association with the city and regular visits by the image for novenas in times of drought, epidemic, and other calamities after the visits were formalized by the crown in 1735 with written rules. Two years later a larger and more substantial chapel for the Virgin at the El Pueblito site was completed with the help of the city council, local Indians, and a bequest from a leading citizen of the city, Captain Don Pedro de Urtiaga.

Popular interest was also fuelled by reports in the 1730s and 1740s that the statue was showing signs of life and that a star had appeared on the Virgin's forehead. Meanwhile, the Franciscans naming her patron of their province in 1745. The 1760s were perhaps the apogee of the Pueblito Virgin's popularity in the city during the colonial period, with news of scores of miracles including cures, narrow escapes, mining bonanzas, and relief from drought and disease, culminating in the widely publicized miracle of a Franciscan friar, Andrés Picazo, surviving certain death at the hands of an assassin when he invoked the Virgin of El Pueblito. The image continued to be taken to the city often for novenas in times of trouble to the end of the colonial period and was regarded as the great protectress of the city during the Independence period.[20]

On the orders of Pope Pius XII, the statue was solemnly crowned by the local bishop Don Marciano Tinajero on 17 October 1946. On 17 October 1982 350 years of devotion to Our

Lady were celebrated under the her venerable title of El Pueblito. The solemn celebration of the fiftieth anniversary of the papal coronation of the statue occurred on 17 October 1996.

18 October Our Lady of Rheims

OMINATING THE CITY, the Cathedral of Our Lady of Rheims (Notre-Dame de Reims) stands on the site of the basilica where Clovis was baptized by Saint Rémy, bishop of Rheims, in 496 AD. The shrine to Our Lady of Rheims was built by St Nicasius, Archbishop of Rheims in the year 605. The church, having fallen into decay, was rebuilt by Ebo and Hincmar. It was finished in the year 645 and still remains a place of pilgrimage to the Mother of God.

At one time, enemies of the cathedral chapter set fire to a monastery of Rheims. Among the relics which the sacristan tried to save was an ivory statue of the Virgin Mary. The sacristan prayed fervently to the Virgin that she would preserve this relic. The abbot entering the ruins of the church found the statue upright and unharmed as if placed there reverently. From thence forward, the image was believed to be miraculous. The present edifice was started around 1211 and completed by the end of the century, with the exception of the west front, that dates from the 14th century. The treasury contains the Sainte Ampoule, a holy flask containing the oil with which French kings were anointed. The original one was shattered during the French Revolution, but a fragment of it was incorporated to the replica.

19 October: Our Lady of the Forsaken

HE ORIGINS OF THE DEVOTION to the Patroness of Valencia go back to a sermon by Friar Juan Gilabert Jofré (a friend of Saint Vincent Ferrer), delivered in the cathedral on 24 February 1409. While walking to the church he noticed that some boys were making fun at a parishioner suffering from mental illness. In his sermon, the friar called on all the faithful to help the abandoned, the poor and the sick. Among the congregation was Lorenzo Salmon, a tradesman who began a project to build a hospice for the mentally ill—an institution that is considered to be the first psychiatric hospital in the world.

Even more interesting is the origin of the image that is venerated today. It is said that in 1414, three young men, dressed as pilgrims came to the brotherhood that looked after the hospital. The brother that lived there had a wife that was blind. The young men said that if they were given food and lodging for four days they would build an image of Our Lady. Four days went by and nothing had been heard from the room where the young men were working. On the fourth day the monks then forced opened the door. To their complete astonishment they found a beautiful statue of Our Blessed Lady. The food was still there; the block of marble intact; but the young men had disappeared. they knew then that the young men were angels sent from heaven. The statue was later copied and the authors of the copies said they recognised 'something supernatural' about the original image.

Moreover, before opening the room, brothers of the monastery had asked an elderly blind lady, who had a reputation for sanctity, what they should do. She told them she would pray, and in a short time give them an answer. When they returned to find her answer, she had told them to break open the door and they would find the statue but no young men. They were from heaven she said. It was very fitting indeed, that the first of many miracles wrought through the intercession of Our Lady of Valencia or Our Lady of the Forsaken should be the return of her sight to that pious, old blind lady.

20 October: The Golden Virgin of Lausanne

 ONSTRUCTION ON THE cathedral of Lausanne, Switzerland, began in 1175 and it was consecrated on 20 October 1275 by Pope Gregory X in the presence of the emperor

Rudolf von Hapsburg. It was never completed—it still remains unfinished today. Throughout the Middle Ages, pilgrims flocked to the cathedral to pray before the Golden Virgin, a miraculous statue of the Virgin Mary, to whom the cathedral is dedicated.

Lausanne was one of many medieval cities to institute a night watch to prevent the all-too-common threat of devastating fires. Although it is mostly stone stone, the city was once made mostly of wood and burned down several times. Every night, watchmen stationed on the wall surrounding the town would call out to each other, ensuring that there were no fires and that no enemy was approaching. The cathedral night watch was the most important. Every night, the watchman walks up the 153 stairs to the top of the tower. Every hour on the hour from 10pm to 2am, he calls out to the four directions: "C'est le guet; il a sonné l'heure!" ("This is the nightwatch; the hour has struck"). Lausanne is the only city in Europe to continue this tradition to this day. Nowadays, the reassuring sound of the nightwatchman's voice startles lovers on park benches and revelling students stumbling home.

In 1536, the combined forces of the Reformation and Bernese army stripped Lausanne Cathedral of virtually all its decoration, including altars, statues and paintings. The beloved Golden Virgin was melted down to make coins. Its treasury, a unique collection of liturgical vestments and tapestries, was taken over to Bern, where it is now preserved in a museum. The architect-restorer Eugène Viollet-le-Duc began a restoration of the cathedral in the 19th century—and it is still going on today.

21 October: Our Lady, House of Gold

E CAN SEE at once why Our Lady is called a House. In Holy Scripture the human soul is often spoken of as "God's house." In the liturgies for the Dedication of a Church, the descriptions of God's House can all be applied to the soul, like "Holiness is fitting to Your house," "My house shall be called a house of prayer". "Wisdom has built herself a house."

Wisdom, as we have seen, is a Scriptural name for Our Lord, Who is the Wisdom of the Father, as the Holy Spirit is Love. The house that Eternal Wisdom built for Himself is, of course, Our Blessed Lady, though the text is also applied to the Church. The title "God's House" perfectly befits Our Lady. For nine months Our Lord dwelt really and truly within Her; She was His dwelling in the literal sense of the word. In Holy Communion each one of us also becomes literally God's house.

Why is Our Lady called "House of Gold?" Gold is the most beautiful, the most prized, the most durable of metals; it is the union of these three qualities that makes it so precious. When you want to give the highest praise to anything, you say it is "of gold," as for instance, "a heart of gold." How elegant is the appearance of anything made with gold—a monstrance, a chalice, for instance, or a beautifully illuminated painting. Gold glitters and sparkles as nothing else does, and at once gives an appearance of splendour and value to anything. It is traditionally the richest of all material objects. Gold is thus a worthy image of Our Lady's spiritual qualities.

We can only imagine what a splendid, rich, dazzling thing would be a church or a house all made of gold—for one does not see such a building. But we can picture it to our mind's eye as a thing of surpassing magnificence and resplendent beauty. How it would flash and glitter and sparkle in the sunlight, and how we should love to stand and gaze upon it! Just as if we could see Our Lady's soul, we should be rapt and enthralled by its spiritual splendour and brilliance. Precious, solid, true, beautiful, and durable as gold were all Our Lady's virtues. However, there is one virtue which is most specially signified by gold. It is the highest and greatest virtue, just as gold is the most precious of metals. namely love, charity. You can buy anything on earth, in the material order, with gold. In the sphere of heavenly things, you can buy everything with charity. To say, then, that Our Lady is a House of Gold, means that her soul was resplendent and glowing with charity, with love of God and Her neighbour—that is what made it so precious to God, that it was a House of Gold.

When Our Lord comes into our souls in Holy Communion, He longs to find them like Our Lady's—all "houses of gold," all full of love for Him and for our neighbour, for that is what will make them golden in His sight. He comes to make them so for us. Be full of love and kindness to others; that is one of the best ways to prepare for Holy Communion. We must beg of Our Lady, the "House of Gold," to give us more and more of this heavenly charity, which makes us rich and precious in God's sight. The poorest in this world's goods may thus be the richest before God. On the Day of Judgment, Our Lord will say: "Come you blessed of My Father," to those who have been kind and charitable. Charity is, then, the gold which will buy for us the Kingdom of Heaven. If we have not this charity—if we are cold, selfish, and unloving and the house of our soul is not of solid gold, but poor and full of holes like a mud-hovel—we must ask Our Lady, the "House of Gold," to make it golden, to fill it with love for God and man. She only waits for us to ask Her for this favour, for She does not want to be the only "House of Gold." No, She wants every one of us to be a beautiful House of Gold in which to receive Jesus Christ, Her Divine Son.[21]

22 October: Our Lady of Victories

 OPE ST PIUS V established the Feast of Our Lady of Victory in 1571 in thanksgiving after the defeat of Moslem forces during the naval battle off Lepanto, Italy. Two years later, Gregory XIII changed the name of the feast to Our Lady of the Rosary, and set the date for its celebration as the first Sunday in October. Pope Clement XI extended the feast to the Universal Church in 1716, and later the date for the feast was set as 7 October.

However there is also a celebration for the Feast of Our Lady of Victories. In 1620, King Louis XIII made a vow in 1620 that if his troops were successful in ousting the Protestants (Huguenots) from their fortress in La Rochelle, he would build a church in honour of the Blessed Virgin Mary. After the victory in 1628, a site for the church was chosen on the property of the Discalced Hermits of St Augustine in Paris. Louis laid the first stone himself, one that was inscribed with a dedication to Our Lady of Victories, on 9 September 1629. The church building was completed only in 1740. In 1630, a poor labourer entered the Augustinian order and took the name Brother Fiacre. He took up residence at the shrine and lived there until his death in 1684. Brother Fiacre was renowned as a mystic. He had a vision of the Virgin Mary in 1637, when Mary asked him to tell the King that he would soon be blessed with a son who would inherit his throne. Louis XIV was born on 10 February 1638 and, in thanksgiving, his father consecrated France and the royal family to the Blessed Virgin. Blessed John Henry Newman went there to give thanks for his conversion, which had been the subject of prayer there. Later, the young St Thérèse of Lisieux prayed before the statue of Our Lady of Victories for Mary's help in realizing her vocation.

Litany of Our Lady of Victories

Lord, have mercy on us,
Christ, have mercy on us,
Christ, hear us,
Christ, graciously hear us.
God, the Father of Heaven, Have mercy on us.
God, the Son, Redeemer of the world, Have mercy on us.
God, the Holy Spirit, Have mercy on us.
Holy Trinity, One God, Have mercy on us.
The response for the following invocations is Pray for us.
Our Lady of Victory,
Victorious daughter of the Father,
Victorious Mother of the Son,
Victorious Spouse of the Holy Spirit,

Victorious servant of the Holy Trinity
Victorious in your Immaculate Conception,
Victorious in crushing the serpent's head,
Victorious over all the children of Adam,
Victorious over all enemies,
Victorious in your response to the Angel Gabriel,
Victorious in your wedding to St Joseph,
Victorious in the birth of Christ,
Victorious in the flight to Egypt,
Victorious in your exile,
Victorious in your home at Nazareth,
Victorious in finding Christ in the temple,
Victorious in the mission of your Son,
Victorious in His passion and death,
Victorious in His Resurrection and Ascension,
Victorious in the Coming of the Holy Spirit,
Victorious in your sorrows and joys,
Victorious in your glorious Assumption,
Victorious in the angels who remained faithful,
Victorious in the happiness of the saints,
Victorious in the message of the prophets,
Victorious in the testimony of the patriarchs,
Victorious in the zeal of the apostles,
Victorious in the witness of the evangelists,
Victorious in the wisdom of the doctors,
Victorious in the deeds of the confessors,
Victorious in the triumph of all holy women,
Victorious in the faithfulness of the martyrs,
Victorious in your powerful intercession,
Victorious under your many titles,
Victorious at the moment of death,
Lamb of God, who takes away the sins of the world, Spare us, Lord.
Lamb of God, who takes away the sins of the world, Hear us, Lord.
Lamb of God, who takes away the sins of the world, Have mercy,

Lord.

V. Pray for us, blessed Lady of Victory.

R. That we may be made worthy of the promises of Christ.

Let us pray: Our Lady of Victories, we have unshaken confidence in your influence with your Son, our Lord, Jesus Christ. Humbly we ask your intercession for all of us associated under your title, Our Lady of Victories. We beg your powerful assistance also for our own personal needs. In your maternal kindness please ask Jesus to forgive all our sins and failings, and to secure His blessings for us and for all the works of charity dedicated to your name. We implore you to obtain for us the grace of sharing Christ's victory and yours forever in the life that knows no ending. May we join you there to praise forever the Father, His Son, Jesus Christ, and the Holy Spirit, one God, for all the ages to come. Amen.

23 October: Our Lady of Comfort

N THE MONASTIC calendar today this feast is kept as the feast of Our Lady of Consolation. It became a popular devotion in the Low Countries in the sixteenth and seventeenth centuries, when it was adopted by the English Benedictine nuns of Cambrai. English sailors took the devotion to Galicia in Spain where you can still find the occasional statue dedicated to Our Lady under this title.

Consolation is a beautiful word, so is comfort in its former sense of giving strength. Consolamini, consolamini, Comfort, comfort ye my people... Every Christian must be, in some measure, a giver of strength and consolation to others, but it is not something we can do through our own efforts. Mary, the Mother of God, was a *mulier fortis*, a strong woman, a valiant woman, one who allowed grace to flower in her, an excellent teacher of what it means to be a giver of comfort to others. I like the way in which Mary is always and everywhere leading us to her Son. As she said to the servants at the wedding feast of Cana,

'Do whatever He tells you.' With that advice she solved the problem of the wine running out, taking nothing to herself but giving the glory to God, to whom alone it belongs.

24 October: Our Lady of the Enclosed Garden

HE CATHOLIC HERMITAGE of Our Lady of the Enclosed Garden is situated in the former reformed church of Warfhuizen, a village in the extreme north of the Netherlands. It is the only Dutch hermitage currently inhabited by a hermit. The name draws upon the traditional epithet for Our Lady of *hortus conclusus* or enclosed garden, a reference to the Song of Songs (Sg 4:12) that indicates the Mary's "perpetual virginity and at the same time her fruitful maternity".[22] The hermitage was founded in 2001 as the dwelling of a Catholic consecrated hermit. As is typical of Dutch hermitages, it includes a public chapel that has a distinct role in popular devotions, here to the Our Lady. It is the northernmost Marian shrine in the Netherlands.

The Confraternity of Our Lady of the Garden Enclosed is a so-called 'devotional fraternity'. It is popularly known as the 'Marian Confraternity of Warfhuizen'. A devotional fraternity is a company of faithful who share a certain preference for a specific devotion. There are many such fraternities in the Catholic Church. The Confraternity of Warfhuizen was founded when the statue of Mary in the chapel of Warfhuizen suddenly triggered a pilgrimage. It is in the first place a community of prayer, but a number of members also help with the reception of pilgrims and the organisation of processions, in part to relieve the hermit.

Warfhuizen is known worldwide for the devotion of the handkerchief. Our Lady holds a large white handkerchief to dry her tears with. When coming to Warfhuizen, pilgrims bring a new one for her, often on behalf of someone who is ill or who is facing a difficult task. They give this handkerchief to the brother or the sacristan of the confraternity, who places the new handkerchief in the hands of Mary. The pilgrim is given the old one to take home, to give to the person concerned.

25 October: Our Lady of Philermos

 HIS ICON OF OUR BLESSED LADY was discovered in Rhodes by the Knights of St John known as the Knights of Rhodes and then of Malta, while withdrawing from Palestine in 1306. This ancient image had been preserved in a sanctuary on Mount Philermos in the midst of thick woods after having been brought from Jerusalem around 1000 AD, where, tradition has it, the painting had been executed by the Evangelist Luke, together with the *Salus Populi Romani*, now in the Basilica of St Mary Major in Rome. Strongly believed to bear a very close resemblance to the Virgin Mary, this accounts for the outstanding veneration which has accompanied the icon throughout the centuries.

The Knights of Malta adopted Our Lady of Philermos as their patron and took the image with them when the Turks drove them out of Rhodes in 1522. For many years, the Knights and the icon resided in Malta. After Napoleon conquered Malta in 1798, the Knights dispersed. The Philermos icon moved to Russia, where on 12 October (in the Julian calendar), 1799, it was presented to Emperor Paul I, then Grand Master of the Order, at his residence in Gatchina, 30 miles from St. Petersburg. From then on, Russian Orthodoxy has honoured the Mother of God of Philermos on this date (25 October in the modern calendar). The icon survived the Russian Revolution of October 1917 because it was in a church at Gatchina, together with the other relies of the Knights, for a celebration on 12 October. In 1920, dowager Empress Maria Fyodorovna took it with her when she fled to Denmark. After her death the Orthodox clergy moved the sacred image to Belgrade, then, in 1941, to a Montenegran monastery to hide it from the Nazis. In fact, it hid so well that it was believed lost until its rediscovery there in 1997, with even most of its jewels surprisingly intact. The Mother of God of Philermos icon now has a place of honour in the National Museum of Montenegro, where it hangs in the Blue Chapel.

26 October: Our Lady, Mother of Fairest Love

 HE EXPRESSION "MOTHER OF FAIREST LOVE" is revealed in the Book of Ecclesiasticus in the Latin Vulgate text:

> I am the mother of fairest love, of fear, of knowledge, and of holy hope; being eternal, I am therefore given to all my children, to those who are named by him. I will again make instruction shine forth like the dawn, and I will make it shine afar; I will again pour out teaching like prophecy, and leave it all to future generations. Observe that I have not laboured for myself alone, but for all who seek instruction. (Si 24:18, 32-34)

Over the centuries the phrase has been applied to the Mother of God. Devotion to the Blessed Virgin Mary as the "Mother of fairest love" is found in the liturgies dedicated to the Mother of God in the tenth century. In the 1962 Missal,there is a specific Mass dedicated to Blessed Mary, Queen of Saints and Mother of Fairest Love. It was not a universal feast for the whole church, but was only celebrated for certain places. The day of the feast was May 8. In the collection of Masses of Our Lady, there is one specifically dedicated to Our Lady, Mother of fairest love.[23]

In his Letter to Families, *Gratissimam Sane,* Pope St John Paul II adopts the phrase, "mother of fairest love" when describing the love between the Blessed Virgin Mary and Saint Joseph and love of Jesus Christ.

> The history of "fairest love" begins at the Annunciation, in those wondrous words which the angel spoke to Mary, called to become the Mother of the Son of God. With Mary's "yes", the One who is "God from God and Light from Light" becomes a son of man. Mary is his Mother, while continuing to be the Virgin who "knows not man"

(cf. Lk 1:34). As Mother and Virgin, Mary becomes the Mother of Fairest Love. This truth is already revealed in the words of the Archangel Gabriel, but its full significance will gradually become clearer and more evident as Mary follows her Son in the pilgrimage of faith.

...This mutual spousal love, to be completely "fairest love", requires that he should take Mary and her Son into his own house in Nazareth. Joseph obeys the divine message and does all that he had been commanded (cf. Mt 1:24). And so, thanks also to Joseph, the mystery of the Incarnation and, together with it, the mystery of the Holy Family, come to be profoundly inscribed in the spousal love of husband and wife and, in an indirect way, in the genealogy of every human family. What Saint Paul will call the "great mystery" found its most lofty expression in the Holy Family. Thus the family truly takes its place at the very heart of the New Covenant.

"Fairest love" always begins with the self-revelation of the person. At creation Eve reveals herself to Adam, just as Adam reveals himself to Eve. In the course of history newly-married couples tell each other: "We shall walk the path of life together". The family thus begins as a union of the two and, through the Sacrament, as a new community in Christ. For love to be truly "fairest", it must be a gift of God, grafted by the Holy Spirit on to human hearts and continually nourished in them (cf. Rm 5:5). Fully conscious of this, the Church in the Sacrament of Marriage asks the Holy Spirit to visit human hearts. If love is truly to be "fairest love", a gift of one person to another, it must come from the One who is himself a gift and the source of every gift.

Mary was the first to enter this realm [great mystery], and she introduced her husband Joseph into it. Thus they became the first models of that "fairest love" which the Church continually implores for young people, husbands and wives and families. Young people, spouses and families themselves should never cease to pray for this. How can we not think about the crowds of pilgrims, old and young,

who visit Marian shrines and gaze upon the face of the
Mother of God, on the faces of the Holy Family, where
they find reflected the full beauty of the love which God
has given to mankind?[24]

Prayer

O God, through the intercession of the Holy Family—Jesus, Mary,
and Joseph, we ask that the our families today embrace the "great
mystery" which will lead us to "fairest love." May our modern
families embrace the cross of Jesus Christ and walk with each
other leading each human person in the family directly to the
Heavenly Banquet. Amen.[25]

27 October: Our Lady of the Door

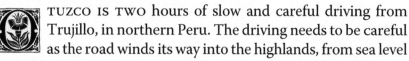 TUZCO IS TWO hours of slow and careful driving from
Trujillo, in northern Peru. The driving needs to be careful
as the road winds its way into the highlands, from sea level
up to over 2600 metres, through steep-sided river gorges and
dramatic mountain scenery. Its main claim to fame is Our Lady of
the Door, and people come from all over Peru to present her with
offerings in the hope of getting favours. The cult of the Virgin
began in 1674 when a statue of Our Lady of the Immaculate
Conception helped to defend the town against the threat of pirates.

The Augustinian Fathers had founded the highland city of
Otuzco in 1560, dedicating both town and church to the Immaculate Conception. On the main altar of the church was a statue
of Our Lady from Spain, carried in procession once annually on
the feast of the Immaculate Conception, 8 December. Gradually,
the octave of the feast assumed public importance, and since it
was not considered proper for the altar statue to leave its post
more than once, parishioners ordered a second processional
statue for use on 15 December and other occasions, from a
workshop in Venezuela, and installed it in a side altar.

In 1670, word came that freebooters had plundered towns to the north and were on their way to Otuzco. Townspeople took the processional statue of Our Lady Immaculate out to the road where the attackers would come, and remained there three days in prayer. When the freebooters failed to appear, the thankful people joyfully returned to the town. Unwilling to return the statue of the saving Virgin to the side altar, they enshrined it above the church door. Devotion to the Virgin of the Door continued through the centuries. Soon after the statue was crowned on 27 October 1943, a Brotherhood of the Virgin of the Door was established, which began planning a new sanctuary for their patron. The coronation anniversary has been celebrated ever since with a procession recalling the statue's trip to the city of Trujillo for the occasion. On 27 October 1983, the Virgin of the Door moved to a shrine above the door of the new church. Our Lady of the Door is now patron of northern Peru, and her celebration on 15 December always draws crowds from near and far.

28 October: Our Lady of the Palm

 HE CHURCH OF Our Lady of the Palm preceded by some time the miracle which made it famous. There is no exact record of why it was named that way. The miracle for which it is best known took place during an earthquake and a tidal wave on the first of November, 1755. Cadiz is a seaport of Spain exposed to the Atlantic Ocean and was directly in the path of the tidal wave said to be more than 30 metres high. The townspeople were in terror and were on the point of abandoning the town when two unidentified men—thought later to be the patron saints of the city—closed the water gates and urged the people to go to the Capuchin Church of Our Lady of the Palms. Here a Mass was in progress. The priest finished the Mass, seized a banner with a picture of Our Lady on it, and went out into the street where the wall of water was already advancing upon them. He planted the banner in the street and called out, "Thus far, my Mother".

The water advanced as far as the banner, and stopped. Then, as he walked into it with the banner, the wall of water receded and returned to the ocean. An anniversary procession was established, along with a confraternity of Our Lady of the Palm. With the exception of 1837, when there was a Civil War, the procession was held annually. The rosary was recited along the route of the tidal wave, and prayers of thanksgiving said.

Many years after the first miracle, another storm caused the people to remember Our Lady of the Palm. Ships were wrecked in the harbour of Cadiz, and the ocean was impassable. The people demanded a procession of Our Lady of the Palm, though it was out of season, and when the procession was finished, the storm abated.

29 October: Our Lady of Oropa

HE SANCTUARY OF the black Virgin of Oropa, high in the Alps north of Biella, is traditionally associated with St Eusebius of Vercelli, who was martyred in 371. According to tradition Luke the Evangelist carved this statue and St Eusebius brought it to Italy. He had spent some time in exile in the Holy Land, because he openly opposed the Arian heresy. During his days in Jerusalem divine inspiration led him to three statues buried under ancient ruins. He gave two of the statues away and he installed the statue in a cave that was a pre-Christian site, in order to end the local pagan practices. Soon, the villagers of Fontanamora began to organize annual pilgrimages to Our Lady, making this one of the oldest pilgrimages continuing to this day.

Our Lady became quite attached to this sacred place. When, more than a thousand years later, a group of monks tried to move her to a new location, she refused to go. She allowed herself to be moved half a mile, but then the three foot tall wooden statue became so heavy that no one could move her until it was decided to return her to her cave. On the night of 26 July 1620, the feast day of St Anne (the mother of the Blessed Virgin Mary) Anne appeared to a nun and told her that it would be pleasing to Heaven if the statue was crowned. Since the Madonna of Oropa has worked so many miracles and has become so important to the Italians, she was crowned not only by the Pope of that year, but by three other Popes, once every hundred years, in 1620, 1720, 1820, and 1920. Like many Black Madonnas, Our Lady of Oropa was invoked against the Black Death, the bubonic plague. The statue captures a scene described in Luke 2:22–24 as the ceremony of the presentation and dedication of Baby Jesus to the Father. These were performed in accordance with Mosaic law forty days after the birth of Jesus. Mary holds in her right hand the coins for the temple offering and Jesus in his left holds the sacrificial dove.

Popular belief affirms that the wooden statue has some peculiar characteristics: despite the age of the statue it has no woodworm; despite the ancient tradition of touching the foot, is not worn out; dust does not settle on the faces of the Virgin and of the Child. Guglielmo Marconi invented the radio and sent his first radio message to the Vatican from Oropa, under Our Lady's patronage. The area was a favourite of two well-known hikers: Blessed Pier Giorgio Frassati (whose tomb is in Turin) as well as Pope Saint John Paul II. In fact, Pope St John Paul II paused to pray at a spot on the path dedicated to Blessed Pier Giorgio. Pope St John Paul II declared in an Angelus message at Oropa:

> To those who are devoted to her, especially young people—like Pier Giorgio Frassati, who used to come up here to give himself to prayer—the Blessed Virgin proposed to be a shelter and a refuge, the heavenly Mother who opens her house to give everyone the invigorating experience of a more profound contact with God. Dear young people who are listening to me! Like Pier Giorgio, may you also discover the way of the Shrine, in order to undertake a spiritual journey which, under Mary's guidance, brings you closer to Christ. You can then become His witnesses with the conviction and keenness which characterized Pier

Giorgio's apostolic activity. You will bear witness to Christ, as he did, especially in the university world, in which there are boys and girls who perhaps have not yet resolved the question of the meaning of their life. By word and example you can show that Christ has the really satisfactory solution for the crucial problems of life.[26]

30 October: Our Lady, Morning Star

N HER LITANY, a most descriptive title of Our Lady's loving service to humanity is that of Morning Star. Every star, indeed, is an image of her. Her most popular figure is "Star of the Sea", due no doubt to the loveliest of her hymns— the *Ave Maris Stella*, which goes back at least to the ninth century, and to the *Alma Redemptoris Mater*, of the eleventh century. Mary had much to do with stars. The Star of Bethlehem was the only lamp for the cave. "We have seen His star in the East," said the Magi, and they found it again reflected in the eyes of Mary. A lovely legend about an old well in the Holy Land, called "Mary's well", recounts that once when the Holy Family was going from Bethlehem to Jerusalem they rested by that well and drank of its waters. When the Wise Men were on their way to Bethlehem, they lost the star for a while, but they found it again shining in the waters of Mary's well.

The "Morning Star" has always had a special application to Mary. The Church interprets the verse in the Song of Songs (6:10) as descriptive of Her. "Who is this arising like the dawn, fair as the moon, resplendent as the sun, formidable as an army?" St John in the Apocalypse tells of the Woman Clothed with the Sun: "Now a great sign appeared in heaven: a woman, robed with the sun, standing on the moon, and on her head a crown of twelve stars" (Rev 12:1). Every church today, as in ages past, has its altar of the Blessed Virgin. In the old Cathedrals, the Lady Chapel was situated behind the choir and the high altar, and to the extreme east, as the symbol of Mary as the Morning Star. We read in an ancient 16th century text: "Like the morning coming before the rising sun, dividing the night from the day, so the Virgin Mary rose as the morning before the Sun of Justice, and divided the state of grace from the state of sin, the children of God from the children of darkness. The Church sings praise to her that her glorious Life gave light to the world and illumined all the Church and congregations of faithful people." St Bridget of Sweden calls Our Lady "the star preceding the sun".

31 October: Our Lady, Queen of the World

 ARY LOVINGLY GUIDES humanity towards God. The relation between God and Our Lady is something like the connection between rain and the earth. Rain falls from heaven but the earth produces flowers and fruit from it. God comes from Heaven, but the human nature of God the Son comes from Mary. Again, earth gives life through Heaven's gift of the sun, but Our Lady, Queen of the World gives us the Eternal Light, Christ the Lord.

Mary, Queen of the World, exists where Christ is not yet fully present, where His Mystical Body is not yet visible. For the people who suffer from fear —the fear of the slavery of paganism and for modern man who lives in dread, the dread that comes from loss of faith, the answer must ever be, "Look at the Woman"; look at the Woman who will lead you to God. There are millions of people to whom the Gospel of Jesus Christ is forbidden to be preached; no missionaries are allowed in their lands. Many people in the world are still under the tyranny of Communism. These people along with the Buddhists and pagans in general cannot say: "Our Father", because God is not a Father unless He has a Son. However they may be able to say "Hail Mary", because they believe in an ideal woman. Jesus may not yet be given a manger in Bethlehem but Mary is among them preparing them for grace. She is grace where there is no grace. She is the Advent where there is no Christmas. In all lands where virgins are venerated, or where one lady is set above all other ladies, the ground is fertile for accepting the Woman as the prelude for embracing Christ. Where there is the presence of Jesus, there is also the presence of His Mother, as there is among us who have faith; but where there is the absence of Jesus, either through ignorance or wickedness, there is still the presence of Mary. As she filled up the gap between the Ascension and Pentecost, so she is filling up the gap between the ethical systems of the East and their incorporation into the Mystical Body of her Divine Son. Mary is the fertile soil from which, in God's appointed time, the faith will flourish and bloom in the East, and all over the world.

Though, compared to the total population, there are few tabernacle lamps in certain lands, nevertheless, Our Lady is there. Mary is also present among millions in our own land, and to all who are fearful, sad and frustrated. We beg that all may have to courage to approach her in prayer: Never was it known that anyone, who fled to her protection or sought her intercession, was left unaided. Our Lady, Queen of the World! Pray for us![27]

Notes

[1]   Blessed C. Marmion, *Christ, the Ideal of the Priest* (Leominster: Gracewing, 2005), chapter 18.

[2]   Pope Pius XII, *Menti nostrae* (1950), 49, 141.

[3]   K. Beckman, "What Mary Does for Priests"in *Catholic Exchange* (26 May 2016).

[4]   Pope Francis, *Homily at Chrism Mass* (13 April 2017).

[5]   Pope St John Paul II, *Pastores dabo vobis*, 82.14.

[6]   See *Salve Maria Regina*, Volume 50, No. 160 (Spring 2010).

[7]   See M. Lamberty, *The Woman in Orbit: Mary's feasts every day everywhere* (Chicago: Lamberty Co, 1966), 3 October.

[8]   "La Gomera: the Canary island that time forgot" in *The Daily Telegraph* (14 January 2016).

[9]   St Louis-Marie Grignon de Montfort, *The Secret of the Rosary*, 5–6.

[10]   See N. J. Santoro, *Mary In Our Life: Atlas of the Names and Titles of Mary, The Mother of Jesus, and Their Place in Marian Devotion* (Kansas City, MI: iUniverse, Inc, 2011), pp. 335–336.

[11]   See Lamberty, *The Woman in Orbit*, 10 October.

[12] Pope Bl Paul VI, *Discourse at the close of the Third Session of the Second Vatican Council* (22 November 1964).

[13] Pope St John Paul II, *Angelus Message* (15 November 1987).

[14] Youghal (Irish: Eochaill, meaning "yew wood") is now a seaside resort town in County Cork.

[15] See Lamberty, *The Woman in Orbit*, 8 October.

[16] See *Salve Maria Regina*, Volume 48, No. 151 (Winter 2008).

[17] See Lamberty, *The Woman in Orbit*, 16 October.

[18] C. Cruz Gonzalez, "Our Lady of El Pueblito: A Marian Devotion on the Northern Frontier" in *Catholic Southwest* 23 (2012), p. 10.

[19] Hermenegildo de Vilaplana, *Histórico y sagrado novenario de la milagrosa imagen de Nuestra Señora del Pueblito de la santa provincia de religiosos observantes San Pedro y San Pablo de Michoacán* (Mexico: Bibliotheca Mexicana, 1765), pp. 15–16, as translated in Cruz Gonzalez, "Our Lady of El Pueblito", p. 10.

[20] W. B. Taylor, *Theater of a Thousand Wonders: A History of Miraculous Images and Shrines in New Spain* (New York: Cambridge University Press, 2016), p. 195.

[21] See *Salve Maria Regina*, Volume 51, No. 166 (Autumn 2011).

[22] See P. Haffner, *The Mystery of Mary*, Hillenbrand Books studies series (Leominster, Herefordshire, Mundelein, IL: Gracewing; Hillenbrand Books, 2004), p. 15.

[23] See *Collection of Masses of the Blessed Virgin Mary*, volume I, *Missal* (Collegeville, MI: Liturgical Press, 2012), n. 36, pp. 232–234.

[24] See Pope St John Paul II, Letter to Families, *Gratissimam Sane* (1994), 20.

[25] See T. Perna, "Mother of Fairest Love" on *Mondays with Mary* (30 December 2013)

[26] Pope St John Paul II, *Angelus Discourse* (16 July 1989).

[27] See Lamberty, *The Woman in Orbit*, 31 October.

NOVEMBER

1 November: Our Lady, Queen of All Saints

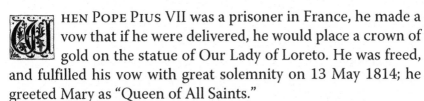HEN POPE PIUS VII was a prisoner in France, he made a vow that if he were delivered, he would place a crown of gold on the statue of Our Lady of Loreto. He was freed, and fulfilled his vow with great solemnity on 13 May 1814; he greeted Mary as "Queen of All Saints."

St Aelred of Rielvaulx has a tribute to Our Lady that reads like a poem: "The Spouse of Our Lord is surely Our Lady; the Spouse of Our King is surely Our Queen." The title "Queen of All Saints" ought to have a special appeal to us all, for it is by this title that She is, in anticipation, our very own Queen, since, by the grace of God, we hope to be numbered among the saints in Heaven one day. Hidden saints, hidden to the world, but known to God and Mary. We shall probably not be canonized martyrs, or confessors, or virgins—but we hope to be of that "great multitude, which no man could number, of all nations, and tribes, and peoples, and tongues, standing before the throne, and in sight of the Lamb, clothed with white robes, and palms in their hands" (Ap 7:9).

The first in that throng of created beings, angels or men, is Mary, so immeasurably above them all that she is, as it were, a distinct creation. St. Anselm says: "O Lady, nothing equals You: for all is either above You, and this is God alone, or beneath You, and this is all that is not God." It is that holiness, given to her because she is the Mother of God, which makes her Queen of All Saints, the immeasurably greatest of all the saints. That is the prime meaning of the title, the proclamation of her personal holiness. The secondary meaning has a very special interest for us. It is that the saints in Heaven regard her and venerate her as their Queen, not only because of her dignity as Mother of God and her personal sanctity, but because, as saints they owe it, after

God, to her intercession. Since Mary is our Mediatrix, all graces given to people are dispersed by God through her hands. Even those who do not know her, those who ignore Her, belittle Her in their ignorance, receive whatever actual graces they get come through her hands. More so because she is not a mere instrument, but our Intercessor, "our Life, our Sweetness, and our Hope". The saints know that well enough. They did not have to reach Heaven to discover that. They realized it on earth, and that is why they are in Heaven today. The saints have been Mary's greatest glorifiers. Their sanctity began when they recognized her supreme sanctity. St Teresa of Avila, for example, set out on the high road to sanctity the day she chose Mary for her Mother after her own earthly mother had died. The Little Flower abandoned herself to sanctity that day when as a child, thought to be dying, she begged Our Lady to have pity on her, and Our Lady answered her by smiling upon her. "The expression of Our Lady's face was ineffably sweet, tender and compassionate; but what touched me to the very depths of my soul was her glorious smile."

St. Catherine of Siena was a saint, when as a child of seven she climbed the stairs in the Benincasa house and stopped on every step to say an Ave. But why go on? In the life of every saint there is a solid devotion to the Mother of God. This is no superficial sentimentality in the writings of the saints. They are too level-headed for that. Their feet are firmly set upon the ground, even though their heads are above the clouds and their souls swimming in ecstasy. The greater the saint, the greater their love for Mary. The greater the saint, the more they recognizes her sanctity; and, conversely, the more they recognize her sanctity, the more inspiration they gets to pursue sanctity.

And if the saints while on earth loved Mary so much, what must their love and gratitude be to her now when they are beholding her in Heaven. We have little idea of what blessedness it is to see God face to face. "Eye has not seen, ear has not heard." Nor can we appreciate the blessedness of seeing the glorified Mother of God. Our Lady has appeared many times on earth since her Assumption, but "beautiful Lady" that she was to St Bernadette and others, the vision was necessarily tempered to their earthly eyes. They could not have seen her as she is and lived. On the authority of many saints, we could not gaze upon the beauty of a soul in the state of grace and live. Now the saints see her in Heaven. When we say that, we can say no more, for it is beyond us to visualize what they see. It is all summed up by St Albert the Great, when he says: "Mary could not be more closely united to God without becoming God." It is an inspiration to us, who hope to be joined to that host of saints one day.

Meanwhile we are on our way. We are, please God, saints in the making. "Your sons shall come from afar, and your daughters shall rise up at your side" (Is 60). We all want to save our souls, and thus be saints finally. We all want to go home, and the beauty of it is that we know how to get there. Not only does our Mother keep a light in the window to show the way, but she comes to get us, to take us by the hand and lead us—rather she carries us. She hears us when we sing, in the *Ave Maris Stella*, "Show Thyself a Mother;" in the *Memorare*, "O Virgin of virgins, our Mother;" in the *Salve Regina*, "Mother of Mercy." The more we love Her, the more we pray to Her; the more She loves us, the more She prays for us.

Our sorrow is that we do not love Her more. In this regard, Fr Faber said: "There can be no repentance in Heaven, else when we see Mary we shall wish we had known Her better, prayed to Her more often, and loved Her more; for we shall see brighter places than our own, further forward in the glory of Heaven, where we might have been had we loved Her more!" So our souls are filled with new zeal, new determination to win at last the place that is prepared for us at the foot of the throne of the Queen of All Saints.[1]

2 November: Our Lady, Mother of the Faithful Departed

 HE VIRGIN MARY is also Mother of the Faithful Departed. In fact, with regard to the supernatural life of every man, Mary's role is comparable to that of a mother with regard to her children during their earthly life. After death, Mary never abandons her children, especially those who are not very far from joining God. Mary contributes, then, to their "purification" by making them capable of being welcomed into the heavenly City. She does this all the more willingly when we ask her trustfully. By standing at the foot of the Cross, and uniting herself with the sacrifice of her Son, Mary acquired the capacity to intercede for all people whose mother she has become.

Standing permanently near the heart of the glorified Christ, she desires to see the souls still in Purgatory introduced as soon as possible into intimacy with God: "The Blessed Virgin Mary has the power of delivering souls from purgatory by her prayers, and by applying her merits for them. This is especially true for souls that were devoted to her on earth."[2] The intercessory power of Our Lady for the souls in purgatory has also been expressed in poetic form by Frederick Faber:

> O turn to Jesus, Mother! Turn,
> And call Him by His tenderest names;
> Pray for the Holy Souls that burn
> This hour amid the cleansing flames.
>
> They are the children of thy tears;
> Then hasten, Mother ! To their aid;
> In pity think each hour appears
> An age while glory is delayed.
>
> O Mary, let thy Son no more
> His lingering Spouses thus expect;
> God's children to their God restore,
> And to the Spirit His elect.
>
> Pray then, as thou hast ever prayed;
> Angels and Souls, all look to thee;
> God waits thy prayers, for He hath made
> Those prayers His law of charity.[3]

3 November: All-Holy Comforter

 HE ALL-HOLY COMFORTER or Mother of Consolation, in Greek *Panagia Paramythia*, is an eighth century miraculous icon of the Virgin Mary from the holy and great Monastery of Vatopedi, on Mount Athos, Greece. Near the monastery, the son of Emperor Theodosius the Great fell off a ship and into the sea. By miraculous intercession of the Mother of God, he was carried safely to shore unharmed and found sleeping in a bush, not far from the Vatopedi monastery. This is the event that defined the name of the monastery (*Vato* and *paidi*, derived from "Batos paidion", the bush of the child).

Tradition describes how the original expression on the faces of the figures and the position of the bodies of Christ and the Blessed Virgin changed when the following miracle occurred on 21 January 807. Algerian pirates had secretly landed on the shore of the monastery and were hiding, waiting for the gates to open in the morning in order to launch an attack on the monastery of Vatopedi. The Abbot, who had remained behind after the end of Matins in order to continue his prayer, heard these words from the icon of the Blessed Virgin: "Do not open the gates of the Monastery today, but go up on the walls and drive away the pirates." As he turned to look, he saw the Theotokos turned towards her right shoulder and looking at him, while the Holy child was stretching out His hand to cover the mouth of His mother saying: "No, Mother, do not watch over this sinful flock, let them fall under the sword of the pirates and be punished as they deserve." But the Blessed Virgin, taking Her Son's hand in Hers and turning Her head a little to free her mouth, repeated the same words. This last arrangement of the figures has remained permanently on the icon. The monks, miraculously saved from the pirates, gave thanks to the Theotokos and named the icon *Paramythia*, which means "calming down" or "restraining" words which convey the content of the miracle. The icon is a wall-painting and is on the right choir of the chapel named after it. In memory of this miraculous event a perpetual lamp burns in front of the wonderworking icon. Every day a Canon of Supplication is chanted in honour of the icon and on Fridays the Divine Liturgy is celebrated.

4 November: Our Lady of Máriapócs

APTURED BY TURKS and held as a prisoner of war, Laszlo Csigri celebrated his release in 1696 by commissioning a wooden icon of the Virgin and Child for the Greek Catholic church in his home town of Pócs (pronounced Poach) in eastern Hungary. The artist was the pastor's brother, Istvan Papp; although he had studied in Italy, the work has a primitive immediacy more typical of Coptic art than of the Italian baroque. In a variation of the classic *hodigetria* or way-pointing pose, the Virgin not only gestures toward the Child, who wears a cross and holds a three-petaled flower; he points back toward her.

That same year, on 4 November, toward the end of Mass, a farmer named Mihaly Eory noticed the icon was shedding tears. During the two weeks of this first weeping, word spread throughout the area. A dying child recovered when held up to the tears by a Catholic priest from a town ten miles away. In gratitude, the mother gave the icon a jewelled necklace, the first of many such offerings, which eventually covered the image almost completely. In December, it wept for another two weeks, starting on the 8th. Pócs then became known as Máriapócs. Hungary was then part of the Austrian empire, and in February 1697, Emperor Leopold II had the miraculous image moved to St Stephen's Cathedral in Vienna, where it has remained ever since, in a chapel to the right of the entrance. It never wept again. However, a copy of the image given by the Emperor to the church in Máriapócs wept three more times, in 1715, 1750, and 1905. Máriapócs is now the most important Marian shrine in Hungary, with daughter shrines wherever Hungarians have settled around the world.

5 November: Our Lady of Scherpenheuvel

 HE MARIAN DEVOTION on the hill of Scherpenheuvel, Belgium centred on a small statue of the Virgin Mary that hung in an oak tree on top of the hill. According to legend, around the year 1500 a shepherd boy noticed that the image had fallen to the ground and decided to take it home. After he had lifted it, he discovered he was unable to move. As the herd did not return in the evening, his master got worried and went to look for the shepherd. Only by restoring the statue to its original place in the oak tree could the master release the shepherd, thereby discovering the spiritual importance of the site. The inhabitants of the nearby town of Zichem frequented the site in the second half of the sixteenth century whenever a member of the family suffered from illness, especially fevers. They would traditionally walk round the tree three times while praying.

Zichem was part of the barony of Diest, a possession of the House of Orange-Nassau. In the course of the Dutch Revolt the barony changed hands several times. While occupied by Protestant forces of the United Provinces between 1580 and 1583, the statue was removed in an act of iconoclasm. After the town was retaken by Alexander Farnese, the parishioners of Zichem restored the devotion in 1587. It was later claimed that they did so after discovering the original statue and returning it to the tree. From then on the cult of Our Lady of Scherpenheuvel began to expand. Soldiers and almoners of the Army of Flanders that were stationed in nearby Diest or Zichem helped to spread its reputation. After an official enquiry, Mathias Hovius, Archbishop of Mechelen, approved the cult of Scherpenheuvel in 1604. The approval was accompanied by the publication of a accounts of miracles ascribed to the intercession of the Virgin of Scherpenheuvel in Dutch, French and Spanish. An English translation followed in 1606.

The statue of the Our Lady of Scherpenheuvel was solemnly crowned by Cardinal Deschamps on behalf of Pope Bl Pius IX on 25 August 1872. Fifty years later, Pope Pius XI accorded the church the status of a minor basilica on 2 May 1922. On 2 February 2011, Pope Benedict XVI dedicated that year's Golden Rose to the basilica. It was ceremonially presented by the papal nuncio on 15 May 2011.

6 *November: Our Lady of Good Remedies*

N 1519 CORTEZ brought with him a famous little statue to participate in the Conquest of Mexico. The statue was first set up in a temporary chapel in one of the rooms of Montezuma's palace where the Spanish officers made their devotions. On the terrible night when the Indians rose against the Spanish invaders, one of the officers rescued the statue before fighting his way out of the palace. He did not get far out when he was cut down by Aztec arrows and died at the foot of a Maguey tree.[4] The tiny statue was either pushed or it fell into the roots of the tree where it was overlooked by the Indians.

Some twenty years later, an Aztec convert prince, John the Eagle, was walking near the tree when he heard a sweet voice calling him; puzzled, he went to the nearby mission of the Franciscan Fathers and told them about it. They thought it was his imagination. Some days later John met with an accident, a large pillar of a church under construction, fell on him; badly crushed, he was given the Last Sacraments. During the night when he was thought to be dying, the memory of the sweet voice kept returning to him. He prayed to Our Lady to help him; very early in the morning she gave him a sash to wear and cured him. A few days later he passed the tree again, and heard the sweet voice; curiously he looked carefully around the roots of the tree; half buried in the sand, he found the tiny statue of Our Lady. The Aztec convert thought he should do something about it. "Come home with me, gracious Lady", he said, "I will see that you have a good home and are cared for." He brought the little statue home wrapped in his cape and placed it on a simple altar.

Here Our Lady reigned as Queen in his humble home for ten or twelve years; John kept the little shrine supplied with flowers, and occasionally with fruit and pretty stones. Gradually people came to pray at the shrine, their number increasing so that had to walk there day and night. John took up the local schoolmaster's suggestion to build a little chapel. He set about building a shrine and enthroned Mary there. The next day to his horror, she was gone. Lonely and sorrowful, John went to the Maguey tree where he had first found her—and there she was! He returned the statue to the new shrine and decorated it carefully but she disappeared again—just when John became ill with a type of fever which was often fatal in Mexico. John's relatives hurried to carry him to Our Lady's feet in Guadalupe; as he lay gasping before the shrine he heard the same sweet voice say: "Why do you come to my house when you put me out of yours?" John apologized and she continued: "If you did not want me in your house, why not take me back to the Maguey tree and build me a chapel there?" "If you cure me, I most certainly will," promised the sick man.

He was as good as his word. He built a chapel into a hermitage and spent the rest of his life there. After John's death it fell into ruins. In 1574 the Spanish governor happened to see the ruins and was told the story. He ordered the building of a beautiful church to house the statue. At one time during an Indian uprising the Indians determined to exile Mary as dangerous to their tribe. After the danger was passed, Our Lady was reinstated in the church. She was called Our Lady of Good Remedies and also "The Little Lady of the Rain", because she brought relief to the dry areas there. Other cities sometimes borrowed her for a procession around their parched fields, begging her to help them—which they say she always does.[5]

7 November: Our Lady of Suffrage

 ARY LOVES THE POOR SOULS in Purgatory because she has also gone through a kind of Purgatory, a fire of tribulation—not indeed, in punishment for her sins, for she had none—but that she might have more compassion on us, and be more fully entitled to the name by which she is so well known; "Comforter of the Afflicted." For this reason she descended into a sea of sorrow, into the depths of tribulation, into the furnace of poverty, exile, persecution. For this reason she suffered those pains of mind and soul, which were caused by the loss of her Son, and by His absence during the years she lived after His death. All those sufferings were a real Purgatory to her. Its flames simply increased her love for the poor souls, and made her more truly the Mother of the Poor Souls in Purgatory.

While we still sojourn in this valley of tears, let us beg Mary to increase daily our ardour, and give us perseverance in good works, to obtain for us a happy death and assure us of her advocacy at the judgment-seat of God. St Alphonsus de Liguori tells us that if we truly venerate Mary and faithfully serve her during life, we can certainly hope, when we die, to be led by her at once into Heaven without having to undergo the pains of Purgatory. The best means to obtain this is to imitate Mary's love for the Poor Souls. Pray often to the Mother of Mercy for these suffering souls; those of parents, relatives, friends, acquaintances gone before. Above all, say the Rosary for these holy souls. Our compassion will be most pleasing to the Mother of Mercy, and when our hour shall come, she will remember us and show herself a true mother.

That which was but vain conceit among the ancients, is truth and reality among Christians; for the spiritual roses of the Rosary can and do help the souls of the departed.

In the Revelations of St Brigit of Sweden we read that Mary said, "I am the Mother of all those who are in the place of expiation... My prayers wipe away the punishments inflicted on them for their faults." St Peter Damian recounts that each year, on the day of the Assumption, Mary delivers several thousand souls from Purgatory. The more we place ourselves in Mary's care, the more quickly will she lead us to God. Let us call on Mary constantly for our suffering ones; we can feel confident that her tender, loving heart will reach out to those poor, afflicted, helpless ones, free them from their place of exile and lead them to their eternal destiny, the face to face vision of Heaven.[6]

8 November: Our Lady of Fair Mountain

EOPLE CALLED THEM the "shining hills". Their white tops glistened against the western sky like some lovely mirage that beckoned to the land beyond. Fr Pierre-Jean De Smet (30 January 1801–23 May 1873), a Belgian Jesuit, active in missionary work among the Native Americans of western North America, had put into words the exhilaration that others felt in beholding these tremendous rocky hills: "You think you have before you the ruins of a whole world, covered with the eternal snows as with a shroud..." Other people later named them the Rockies.

By these barriers the tribes west of the mountains were isolated from the certain corruption that followed the white man's coming. The Indians here had somehow got a bare inkling of the Truth and sent three delegations to Saint Louis begging for priests. Their hearts were ready. So, on Christmas Eve of 1841, Father De Smet was jubilant. On the coming feast he would baptize 150 neophytes; he had regularized 32 marriages in the past weeks. Here in the wilderness was another Bethlehem, where the congregation of St Mary's of the Bitterroot would sing hymns in honour of Christ's nativity and join in the Rosary. It was fitting that Our Lady should come to Bitterroot to smile approval; and she did come that Christmas night to a little Indian boy named Paul.

Paul was an orphan and trying to learn his prayers, which he did not know. A few hours before midnight Mass he had gone to the hut of an aged woman, and in his own words, he saw someone very beautiful:

> Her feet did not touch the earth; her garments were white as snow; she had a star over her head, a serpent under her feet and a fruit which I could not recognize. I could see her heart from which rays of light burnt forth and shone upon me. When I first beheld all this, I was frightened, afterward

> my fear left me, my heart was warmed, my mind was clear,
> and—I do not know how it happened—but all at once, I
> knew my prayers.

He ended by saying that she had appeared several times in his
dream and told him she was pleased that the first village of the
Flatheads should be called St Mary's.

Father De Smet wrote his accounts in French which were then
translated. Father De Smet began his work at Bitterroot by
consecrating the Indians to the Immaculate Heart. He adds in his
records that he did not doubt the child's words, since he was
good. The following year, 1842, the month of Mary was kept. At
the end a statue of the Virgin was borne in triumph to the place
of the apparition, since that day he wrote: "A sort of pilgrimage
was established under the name of Our Lady of Prayer."

Little Paul died from eating some poisonous herbs. His death
occurred on the eve of disaster for the Indians, when the white men
moved into the valley. For a land so blessed by Our Lady we have
been strangely unresponsive to her. How badly we today need Our
Lady of Prayer—if she came to us now, would she smile on America?"

9 November: Our Lady of Almudena

NE STORY RELATES that Calocerus, a follower of St James
the Greater who came with him to Spain, brought the
statue of the Virgin to Madrid in the year 38. Others
claim that Nicodemus, who helped bury Jesus, carved the statue;
that St. Luke the Evangelist painted it; and that S. James himself
brought it from Jerusalem. St Calocerus built a small chapel on
the height of Cuesta de la Vega, which lies in present day Madrid.
This sanctuary was spared profanation during the persecutions
suffered by the Christians in Gothic Spain. It became a large
church during the fourth century under the Emperor Constantine.

During the Arab invasion of the eighth century, the Christians
of old Madrid hid the image of Mary to avoid its being profaned
or destroyed. It was sealed in a niche formed in one of the dados

of the ramparts in a section close to the shrine.[8] Once the statue was placed there in the year 714, they covered the place over so that it looked like a plain mending of the ramparts.

For three centuries and a half the Muslims were in Madrid. The shrine was turned into a Mosque. In 1083 Alfonso VI conquered Madrid and after the old shrine was purified and converted into a church dedicated to Mary, he ordered that on the wall of the major chapel a picture of the Blessed Virgin be painted to take the place of the lost image. In the course of centuries knowledge of the whereabouts of the statue had been hidden and lost.

After many efforts, the king determined to celebrate a novena of prayers, fasts, and penances as well as almsgiving, asking Heaven to grant that it be found. At the end of the novena, a procession took place on 9 November 1085. It was supposed to leave the church of Our Lady and march around the walls of the city. When the procession (in which the king himself and many other notables marched) arrived opposite to where the statue was hidden, the stones of the wall fell away and the statue appeared in the niche. The next day the statue was taken to the church. All Madrid celebrated a festival of great jubilation. The statue was borne by four prelates and carried to the church of Our Lady. It was given the name of Nuestra Senora de la Almudena.

Alfonso VI ordered the building of the larger church which was given over to the Augustinians. In 1664 the municipal government of Madrid decided to participate in the feast and the procession celebrated in honour of the Holy Patroness. When the church was torn down in 1868, the statue was taken to the church in the Calle del Sacramento.[9]

10 November: Our Lady of our Last Agony

ARY, TO WHOM WE OWE, next to God, our restoration in the spiritual life, who gave us new birth so to say on Calvary, while her Divine Son agonized on the Cross, deserves the above title in full measure. Her title is an application of her mission as Corredemptrix of the Human Race, since the work of Salvation has for all of us its full consummation only in the decisive moment of death. Besides, the Church invites us to ask God for the grace of a happy death through the merits and the intercession of the Queen of Martyrs.

How gratefully, therefore, ought we to thank God for having secured for us, by the assistance of His Mother, at the moment of our death, the palm of victory! Where did Mary obtain the extraordinary privilege of procuring for those who are faithful in invoking her, the grace of a happy death and the assurance of eternal salvation? Without doubt, devotion to the Mother of God faithfully practiced during life, is a sign of predestination and, as such, assures for us at the hour of death the assistance of this divine Mother. How could Mary abandon at this supreme moment anyone who has faithfully called upon her during life?

Because Mary has merited by her own death the power of succouring her faithful servants at the moment of the great passage from life to eternity; having assisted her Divine Son during His agony and death on the Cross, she received from Him the mission of assisting us equally during our agony and at the hour of our death. It is through Mary that Jesus was given to us, when He came a tiny Baby in the frailty of human flesh, wrapped up in swaddling clothes, in order to save us; it is equally through Mary that on the last day we hope to see face to face this same Jesus surrounded by the glory of the Father—the source of eternal happiness for us: "And after this our exile, show unto us the Blessed fruit of thy womb, Jesus."

A true servant of Mary cannot perish because devotion to this divine Mother, in keeping us virtuous, gives us a certain pledge that Heaven will be ours. Death is the crown of life: a good life cannot end in eternal loss. If we prove ourselves worthy of Mary's assistance, she is bound to procure for us the special grace of a holy death.[10]

11 November: Our Lady of the Portuguese

HE PORTUGUESE BEGAN building the stronghold of Diu, their symbol of Portuguese influence and authority in the region protecting their lucrative trade with India, on 20 November 1535, and finished the work a short time later on 29 February of the following year. The fort was circular in shape, having thick walls made of solid stone and lime. There was a deep ditch immediately before these stout walls, and the fort had three triangular shaped bastions. Manned with a garrison of three hundred and fifty men, it was further supported by a fleet of eleven ships. Manuel De Souza was named the fort's first Captain.

It was not long before the Portuguese came under siege, as an Ottoman fleet made up of 72 ships laid siege to the stronghold in September of 1538. There were many pitched battles, but as time wore on the Portuguese suffered from a shortage of men and ammunition, and a lack of adequate nutrition brought scurvy and great suffering to the defenders. The fort had less than 40 men left alive when the siege ended after a strong Portuguese relief force arrived on scene, but in actually the victory was the result of the gallantry of the men and women defending the fort and the grim determination with which the Portuguese held the bastions against every manner of assault. In 1546 there was a second assault on Diu that began on the eve of Easter, and this time the Portuguese thwarted the efforts of the Turks to capture the fort in a pitched battle recorded as one of the greatest ever fought by the Portuguese troops in India. The siege had continued uninterrupted from 20 April until 7 November 1546, when a Portuguese fleet finally arrived on scene under Viceroy Juan de Castro.

The Portuguese success in Diu confirmed their dominion and hold over the region. Contemporary accounts, of course, do not mention the miraculous intervention of the Blessed Virgin Mary during the siege, even though it was recorded that she appeared on the ramparts holding a lance in her hand to defend the fort from the enemy.

12 November: Our Lady of the Secret Tower

 T JOHN BOSCO, the amiable saint of the nineteenth century built a major shrine in Turin to Our Lady Help of Christians, linking it with the past and with the future. The church was begun in 1863 with the sum of 8 soldi.[11] Don Bosco never revealed all that Our Lady had told him in the various visions that preceded this, but he did reveal that she asked him to build a great shrine and that it would be a source of grace to all who came there to pray. The saints do not ask as many questions as other people do; he simply got the permission, hunted up an architect who was willing, in the coldly realistic nineteenth century, to begin a church on 8 soldi, and said when the work was finished that he had been paid every cent owing to him; but, that he had been confronted in the beginning by a man who many people said was completely mad. The architect must have had real faith even to listen to Don Bosco.

Like everything else accomplished by this great saint of Turin, the building was beset with difficulties. No one could understand why he insisted on naming it in honour of Our Lady; even his own fellow priests. The money to pay for the project did not come in by the thousands of dollars, or even by the hundreds, but by the penny. Every stone in the building, every item of decorations, was a gift of love, and sacrifice from some grateful person who had benefited from Our Lady's help. The completed building is a testimonial of miracles and a shrine of beauty fit to stand with the world's finest.

The curious thing about Don Bosco's shrine to Our Lady, and the one that should cause us thought, is the story of the right-hand tower. There is a large central dome, and on each side of it, a smaller one. On top of the left-hand one is an angel holding a banner. The right-hand dome is built in the same way, but its decoration is an angel offering a crown to Our Lady. One who saw the original sketches of the Church, drawn out of Don Bosco's own hand, saw on the right-hand tower, a date 19..., indicating that at some time in that warring century there would be a victory over evil to correspond with Lepanto. Our Lady often tells her secrets to the saints, and apparently Don Bosco knew the name and the place, and thought it better not to reveal what he knew. Our Lady of the Tower would see to it in time; and the left-hand angel bearing a banner labelled Lepanto would have a counterpart, if mankind proves worthy. Don Bosco's church with Our Lady of the Tower was raised to the rank of a basilica by Pope Saint Pius X.[12]

13 November: Our Lady of the Seven Joys

 N 1422, DURING AN APPARITION of Our Lady, Italian Franciscan St James of the Marches (1391–1476) learned a new devotion.[13] The "Franciscan Crown" is a rosary of seven decades, one for each of the Joys of Mary: the Annunciation, Visitation, Birth of Jesus, Adoration of the Magi, Finding in the Temple, Resurrection, and Ascension of the Lord. The Franciscan Order spread this devotion rapidly through Europe. A chapel of Our Lady of the Seven Joys was founded in 1445 in the Swiss village of Sembrancher. The Virgin of Seven Joys was especially loved in this area of southern Switzerland after the Battle on the Planta, 13 November 1475.[14] A Savoyan army of 10,000 invaded the region, destroyed the church and villages of Savièse, and massacred those who were unable to escape. They threatened to attack the regional capital of Sion, but at the sound of the warning bell, the local militia arose en masse to defend the city. Quickly exhausted, they were about to surrender when a reinforcement of 4,000 poured through the mountain pass from Berne and Soleure, and soon helped defeat the Savoyards.

It is likely that the defenders had prayed to Our Lady for such relief, for that evening, after the enemy's horses and arms paraded through Sion, Bishop Walter Supersaxo ordered "that in the future the anniversary of this triumph will be a holiday, that the feast of the seven joys of the Holy Virgin will be celebrated throughout the diocese, and on that day the penitential psalms

and collects for the dead will be read, after having read the names
of those who took part in combat." The Diocese of Sion celebrated the feast of Our Lady of the Seven Joys on November 13
until its removal from the diocesan calendar in 1915.[15]

14 November: Our Lady, Defender of the Faithful

 HE Blessed Virgin Mary is the defence of the Church,
more terrible to her enemies than "an army set in battle
array". She is invoked in her Litany under the titles:
"Tower of David, Tower of Ivory" (Jl 2:5). Just as, together with
St Joseph, she saved the life of the Divine Infant from the wicked
king Herod, many times also, has she saved from harm the
Mystical Body of Christ, the Church, when threatened by powerful enemies. As Our Divine Lord was a sign of contradiction in
life—greatly loved or greatly hated—until He was crucified, the
same is true of His Spotless Bride, the Church. From century to
century, new Herods and new Pilates have continually attacked
her, laying snares for her children. Yet the Blessed Virgin Mary,
Mother of the Church, has always rendered her victorious. In
fact, Jesus did not promise the Church perpetual peace, but
perpetual victory. Our Lady will always crush the head of the
enemy: "The gates of Hell shall not prevail against it" (Mt 16:18).

This battle is renewed in every century. In fact, it was one such
conflict that became the occasion for Our Lady's gift to us of her
Holy Rosary. The impious Albigensians, a revolutionary and
sacrilegious sect, were blaspheming the truths of our Holy Faith,
and militantly opposing the Church. Their obstinate violence was
devastating beautiful regions of France, Spain, and Italy. St
Dominic, founder of the Order of Preachers, devoted himself
wholeheartedly to the task of eradicating this error throughout
the Province of Toulouse. In order to be certain of victory, he
constantly implored the help of the Blessed Virgin, whose dignity
the heretics had impudently attacked, for he knew that to her is
given the office of destroying heresies throughout the world. At

first, he tried to oppose and convert them with his zealous words of persuasion, but to no avail, and the heresy became more deeply rooted with each passing day. He then had even more fervent recourse to Our Lady, putting the matter entirely and confidently in her capable hands. St Dominic then received from her the admonition to preach the Rosary as a singularly effective weapon against heresy and vice, and the fervour and success with which he carried out the task entrusted to him was truly amazing. Wherever he established the devotion to the Most Holy Rosary with meditation on the mysteries, he witnessed the most astounding conversions. The Albigensians were subdued through the power of Divine grace, and peace returned. But an even greater need for the power of the Rosary was threatening Christendom.

In the early centuries of Islam, from about 700 to 1000 AD, Christians often fared quite well. They were, of course, required to pay the traditional taxes laid down for subject peoples and were not allowed to bear arms, but in return they enjoyed protected status. There were Christian secretaries who were so influential upon the caliph that they were able to turn imperial policy to their own ends, Christian physicians whom the caliphs preferred to Muslims, and financiers and jewellers who were patronised by the nobles and courtiers of the time. In addition, Christians provided an important service to Islam and future generations by transmitting the thought of the ancient world. The House of Wisdom set up in Baghdad under the early 'Abbasid caliphs was entirely staffed by Christians translating philosophical and other texts from Greek and Syriac.[16] Later on came times of conflict. As the Muslims seized innumerable Christians of Spain, Africa, and other countries on the Mediterranean coast and sold them as slaves, the Blessed Virgin Mary intervened on behalf of her faithful children. In 1218, she appeared to St Peter Nolasco, St Raymond of Peñafort, and to James I, King of Aragon. To these three holy men Our Lady manifested her desire that they institute an Order for the redemption of Christian slaves from the cruel slavery of Islam. Thus the Order of Our Lady of Ransom, whose noble purpose was to ransom and free Christian slaves, was instituted. The Battles of Belgrade (1546), Lepanto (1571), Vienna (1683), Zenta (1697), Belgrade (1717) testify to the protection of Our Lady against the various enemies of Christendom.

In the latter part of the nineteenth century, when the Church was enduring vicious attacks from her enemies, including the violent seizure of the Papal States by the Freemasons, and when for a long time a veritable fury of pressing evils was raging, Pope Leo XIII, in a series of encyclical letters (one for every year of his Pontificate) earnestly besought the faithful all over the world to recite the Rosary frequently, especially during the month of October, as an antidote to the assaults of the legions of Hell. In the words of the Holy Father:

> The heavenly Patroness of the human race will receive with joy these prayers and supplications, and will easily obtain that the good shall grow in virtue, and that the erring should return to salvation and repent; and that God who is the avenger of crime, moved to mercy and pity may deliver Christendom and civil society from all dangers, and restore to them peace so much desired.[17]

The earnest pleas of the Roman Pontiffs are particularly relevant today, for the powers of Hell never rest. The second World War is now recorded history. Yet, unfortunately, people still did not "cease offending God" as Our Lady of Fatima pleaded, and the close of the twentieth century was awash in the blood of literally millions of its victims, in Israel, Lebanon, Sudan, Indonesia, Ethiopia, Rwanda, the Philippines, Cyprus, Malaysia, Tunisia, Algeria, and dozens of other countries throughout the world.

At the dawn of a new millennium, we have awakened to the terrible horror of fundamentalist Islam, a terror which threatens to plunge our world into chaos and anarchy, and also to the equally dreaded horror of a one-world socialist police state. However, in such a time of uncertainty and crisis, we must be careful to maintain a truly Catholic perspective and motivation. The legions of Hell must again be resisted as of old, but not for the purpose of preserving the insidious materialism and hedonism of our world, which is gravely offensive to God; nor yet for purposes of revenge: "Never try to get revenge: leave that, my dear friends, to the Retribution. As Scripture says: Vengeance is mine—I will pay them back, the Lord promises" (Rm 12:19); but rather to preserve the freedom to practice our holy Catholic Faith in relative peace and security, and to continue to labour for the reign of Christ the King, for the salvation of humankind, and the ultimate triumph of Mary's Immaculate Heart.[18]

Prayer

Defend us, O Lord, from all dangers of soul and of body; and through the intercession of the blessed and glorious ever-Virgin Mary, Mother of God, together with that of all the Saints, grant us, we beseech You, health and peace, that all adversities and errors being overcome, Your Church may serve You with tranquil liberty; through Our Lord Jesus Christ, Your Son, Who lives and reigns with You in the unity of the Holy Spirit, God, forever, unto ages of ages. Amen.

15 November: Our Lady of the Dew

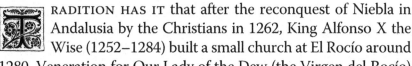 RADITION HAS IT that after the reconquest of Niebla in Andalusia by the Christians in 1262, King Alfonso X the Wise (1252–1284) built a small church at El Rocío around 1280. Veneration for Our Lady of the Dew (the Virgen del Rocío) began in Spain in the thirteenth century and later spread to the Americas and throughout the Spanish-speaking world. In the 1600s, in Brazil, an African or native fisherman named Pai Berê found in his net a statue which settlers identified as Our Lady of the Dew, the beloved Virgin of Andalucia in southern Spain. Over the years many miracles and healings were attributed to the intercession of Our Lady of the Dew in this area along the south coast of Brazil. People called on her successfully for help during storms at sea, the plague of 1901, and the influenza of 1918. In 1977 the Catholic

bishops and Pope declared her patron of the state of Paraná, where her feast day is celebrated annually on November 15.

The history of Our Lady of the Dew had begun in the 15th century, when a hunter approached the great woods near the village of Almonte, in the province of Huelva in south-western Spain. His interest and curiosity were stirred when he heard something like the bark of a dog and saw a mysterious movement among a tangle of thorn bushes. With great difficulty, he guided his horse through the high grass, while small animals scurried away and birds fluttered overhead. His interest was no longer in hunting, but in following an inner prompting to travel deeper into the forest. Presently he saw a large bush with a lily nestled on top among a cluster of thorns. Then, looking aside, he saw a vision of the Queen of Heaven. Standing close beside a tree was a Woman of heavenly beauty and elegant bearing. Dressed in a linen tunic of pale green, she said nothing. She mysteriously disappeared, leaving behind a statue of remarkable beauty. Whether the statue itself had become animated or whether the vision was separate from the statue is unclear. What is known is that the hunter dismounted and stood in awe before the apparition. Filled with unbounded happiness at seeing the vision and then discovering the statue, the hunter wanted to share his happy experience and decided to carry the statue on his shoulders to the open road. After walking three leagues to the town, he was extremely tired. The excitement of the apparition likewise added to his fatigue so that when he arrived home, he decided to rest before telling about his experience. In a few moments, he fell fast asleep. Upon awakening he found the statue missing. Greatly troubled, he reported the happening to the city clerk, who journeyed with him to the woods accompanied by some others who had overheard the story. There in the forest beside the tree of the apparition and covered with dew was the statue exactly as the hunter had found it. The beauty of the statue was immediately appreciated by all. Despite the dampness of the weather, the people were amazed that it had remained in excellent condition.

With all devotion and respect, the statue was carried to the local church and a temporary shrine was erected. In the woods, at the place of the apparition, a small chapel was soon built with the trunk of the tree serving as a pedestal for the miraculous statue.[19]

In time, the image of the Blessed Mother was preserved in the gleaming white sanctuary of Our Lady in the village of El Rocío within the municipality of Almonte. An annual pilgrimage is held in her honour in June when pilgrims come from throughout Spain. In 1532. the village of Almonte acquired the area known as the Mother of the Wetlands adjacent to the church and the village of El Rocío itself. The popularity and devotion to Our Lady of El Rocío and the little stone church quickly spread. The church received a significant endowment in 1587 that provided for a resident priest and restoration of the church itself. In 1653, the village of Almonte proclaimed Our Lady of El Rocío as the patroness of the town for having saved the inhabitants from the plague. In 1755. an earthquake damaged the church. and the image of Our Lady was transferred from El Rocío to Almonte while repairs were made and then was returned to El Rocío in 1760. The church was once again restored in 1915. The present sanctuary Our Lady of Rocío was completed in 1969. The image of Our Lady of Rocío was canonically crowned 3 June 1919. in accordance with the Papal Bull of 8 September 1918. His Holiness Pope St John Paul ll visited the Sanctuary of Rocío 14 June 1993.[20] Saint Germanus I (634–733), Patriarch of Constantinople had already formed a theology around Our Lady of the Dew in one of his prayers.

Prayer

O my Lady, my comfort
divine dew, balm to my thirst,
rain falling from God upon the hardness of my heart,
shining light in the darkness of my soul,
guide in my journey,
support in my weakness,
clothing for my nakedness,

richness in my poverty,
healing for my wounds,
terms for my tears and sighs,
freedom from my misfortunes,
relief from my sorrows,
freedom from my servitude
hope of my salvation.
So be it, O My Lady
So be it, my refuge,
my life and my help,
my protection and my glory,
my hope and my strength. Amen

16 November: Our Lady of Montligeon

DMINISTERED BY THE COMMUNITY of Saint Martin since 2001, the sanctuary of Our Lady of Montligeon in France, situated 160 kms from Paris is the sanctuary of prayer for the dead. Pilgrims have been coming here for over a century from all over the world. Father Joseph Buguet (1843–1918) made known the basilica of Our Lady of Monligeon. In August 1878, he settled into the little village of Chapelle-Montligeon where he was named parish priest. After the sudden death of his brother in 1876, he asked himself often the same question: "What becomes of the soul of the dead? Actually, the destiny of the souls of the dead lived constantly within him. In 1884 he decided to found "the expiatory Work for the deliverance of the forgotten souls in Purgatory".

So as to promote his work, Father Buguet made several trips within France and abroad, obtaining international acclaim and drawing pilgrims from around the world. The first pilgrimages were held in 1885. In 1892, Father Buguet envisaged building a larger building so as to receive more people. Work began in 1894 and the first stone was blessed in 1896 by Mgr Trégaro in the presence of 200 priests and 6000 people. On 28 August 1928, 50 years after the arrival of Father Buguet, the church was consecrated and placed under the protection of Our Lady Liberator. The following day it was honoured as a Minor Basilica by Pope Pius XI. Each year there is a Catholic pilgrimage to Our Lady of Montligeon to pray to the Blessed Virgin Mary for the deliverance of souls from Purgatory and for the dead of families of the pilgrims.

The statue of Our Lady of Montligeon, Our Lady the Liberator, which overlooks the main altar depicts the Virgin Mary presenting the Child Jesus, symbolizing eternal life. At His feet, there are two female characters: one, pleading, sitting in the purifying flames of Purgatory, exchanges a look of trust in the Virgin Mary, who extends her hand in a gesture of intercession. The other, with her hands on her chest, in an expression of thanksgiving, is in heaven and receives the crown of the elect from the Child Jesus. Both women are in fact one soul in different stages of life after death.

17 November: Our Lady of Sion

HEODORE RATISBONNE WAS born in Strasbourg in 1802 into a Jewish family and while he grew up in an atmosphere of learning and affection, religion did not play a significant part. One day this prayer arose out of his confusion: "Oh God, if you really exist, let me know the truth, and I swear to consecrate my life to it." The teaching of a young philosophy professor, Louis Bautain, who drew on the Scriptures in his studies, gradually set Theodore on the path of discovery of the God of the Old and New Testaments. He was baptized at the age of 24 on Holy Saturday, 14 April 1827. Throughout his life as a Christian, and later as a priest, the Word of God inspired him and called him to an apostolic life, a call that was to be fulfilled only 15 years later. On 20 January 1842, his younger brother Alphonse also decided to become a Christian after Our Lady appeared to him in a vision in Rome.[21] In the light of the Word of God, Theodore was able to interpret this sign from Mary and, encouraged by his brother, founded the congregation of Our Lady of Sion in 1843.

Our Lady fulfils the glory of a long line of Hebrew heroines. After Eve, Mary's prototype, came Sara, "the princess", whose ravishing beauty saved Abraham, who is the great-great grandfather of Jacob (Israel); even as Mary later shielded the Head of the Mystical Body. The daughters of Laban, Lia the lovely, and Rachel the renowned were "foundresses" of the House of Israel as Mary "mothered" the Infant Church. Then Miriam, the virgin, was a dim foreshadowing of her virgin namesake as she protected her baby brother on the banks of the Nile. Deborah followed, "a mother in Israel"—the Jewish Maid of Orleans, whose song like Mary's Magnificat, was Israel's battle song of freedom. However the sweetheart of ancient Judaism was Ruth whose loyalty lead to royalty and who, through David fulfilled a Marian role. Then beauty and bravery joined wisdom and wit to make Judith "the Jewess" a national heroine from whom we borrow the antiphon to Mary: "You are the glory of Jerusalem; you are the joy of Israel." Fair and feminine, came Esther, the shining star, whose trust in God redeemed her people and made her a type of our Corredemptrix. Susanna means lily of innocence. From the days of Daniel to Mary Goretti many lilies have grown, but none bloomed fairer than the Virgin most chaste. Salome, heroic mother of the Machabees, watching her offspring go to a cruel death, prefigured Mary at the foot of the Cross.

Standing between two covenants, Mary fulfilled the hopes of the one and inflamed the hearts of the other. More beautiful than Sara, more chaste than Susanna, stronger than Judith, more loyal than Ruth and more popular than Rachel, Mary was the chosen one of all the chosen many. She was and is truly Our Lady of Sion, the Queen of the Jews.[22]

18 November: Our Lady of Chiquinquira

 IGH UP ON THE ANDEAN PLATEAU, 150 kilometers to the north of Bogota, Colombia, is the city of Chiquinquira, founded in 1856; here at the country house of the

Spaniard Don Antonio de Santana, a wondrous miracle occurred. Don Antonio, in 1555, being a devout Christian had an oratory built in his home and requested the Dominican Brother, Fray Andrews Jadraque, to have the image of the Holy Virgin painted. The silversmith and painter, Alonzo de Narvaez did the work. The brother demanded that the Virgin bear a rosary, the official emblem of his order. The cloth had room for two other images at the side, and it was decided to put St Anthony of Padua at the right and St Andrew the Apostle at the left. The painting was done in tempera, but since the chapel was of straw, the paint faded under the action of the sun, the air and the rain.

The damage was such that the local priest had it removed from the altar as unworthy for the celebration of Holy Mass. The canvas was taken to Chiquinquira and was used for a rag to dry the wheat under the sun. Seven years later Doña Maria Ramos arrived from Spain and grieved to find the chapel used for animals. Day after day she prayed there that Our Lady comfort her soul, hopeful that her prayers would be heard. On Friday, 26 December 1586, at 9 o'clock in the morning, the canvas was suddenly brightened by the Holy Virgin. Maria was in pious astonishment, almost in a trance and soon the miracle drew crowds of people.

This wonderful happening was followed by miraculous cures. The Church authorities ordered an investigation to be made to verify the truth of the miracle and in the year 1630, the Dominican Brotherhood authorized by the archbishop of Bogota, took charge of the sanctuary, and built a church which was replaced by the present Basilica in 1801. The Holy See, after discussion of the wonderful miracle, granted a liturgical feast day that is celebrated with special services also in some sections of Venezuela and Ecuador as well. In 1919, by order of the Holy See, the Holy Image was crowned with splendour in Bogota, and in 1944 it was granted the gold sceptre and precious jewels as the mother queen of Colombia. The Virgin of Chiquinquira is the comforting heart of Colombia, Venezuela and Ecuador; prelates, magistrates, and other leaders of the nation have knelt down at Mary's feet and throngs of people, rich and poor, continuously flow to this place to pray for consolation and guidance through this earthly life.[23]

19 November: Our Lady of Divine Providence

 HE TITLE OF MARY, Mother of Divine Providence is often traced to her intervention at the wedding in Cana. Christ's first public miracle was occasioned in part by the intercession of his mother. She helped through her foresight and concern to avoid an embarrassing situation for the newlywed couple. Our Lady of Providence is sometimes also identified as Queen of the Home. Devotion to Our Lady of Divine Providence originated in Italy, and spread to France and Spain. Around 1580, the Italian painter Scipione Pulzone created a work titled "Mater Divinae Providentiae," which depicted the Blessed Mother cradling the Infant Jesus.

Devotion to Mary, Mother of Divine Providence in the first house of the Congregation of the Clerics Regular of St Paul (Barnabites) in Rome at San Carlo ai Catinari church began around year 1611, when one of the clerics travelled to Loreto to pray for assistance in finding the financial resources to complete the Church of San Carlo. Upon his return, they received the necessary assistance, and the Barnabites began to promote devotion to Our Lady of Providence. Pulzone's painting was given to the Barnabites in 1663. It was placed on the altar of a chapel on the first floor of the Saint Charles rectory behind the main altar. In 1732, a copy of the painting was placed in a location adjacent to the main altar of the church of San Carlo ai Catinari in Rome, where it drew many faithful visitors.

In 1774, Pope Benedict XIV authorized the Confraternity of Our Lady of Providence, a lay organization created for the purpose of promoting special works of Christian charity or piety. Pope Gregory XVI elevated it to an Archconfraternity in 1839. In 1888, Pope Leo XIII ordered the solemn crowning of the "Miraculous Lady" and approved the Mass and Office of Mary, Mother of

Divine Providence. On 5 August 1896, Superior General of the Barnabites Father Benedict Nisser decreed that every Barnabite have a copy of the painting in their home. The devotion was brought to Puerto Rico in the early 1850s by the Servite Fathers. According tradition, Philip Benizi (1233–1285) prayed to Mary for help in providing food for his friars, and subsequently found several baskets of provisions left at the door of the convent. Our Lady of Providence was declared the patroness of Puerto Rico by Pope Paul VI on 19 November 1969. Her feast day is celebrated in many immigrant Puerto Rican communities.

Hymn to Mary, Mother of Divine Providence

O Provident Mother, sweet Mother of Jesus,
Oh, what a concern for your Son you expressed!
When lost in the Temple, in worry but trustful,
You sought Him and joyful You found Him in there.

At Cana you pleaded for us, too, your children:
"They're wanting, my Jesus, the wine of sheer gladness."
Oh, give them the wine of pure grace and pure bounty.
They will, then, your Kingdom of justice e' er seek.

At Cana, persuasive, you called on us saying:
"Whatever He tells you, in earnest, perform it."
Assurance you won't have of greater fulfillment.
Oh. help us to listen, whenever He speaks.

This Feast our Forefathers a legacy left us;
Delighted we make it our duty and glory.
In joyful thanksgiving your glories, Dear Mother,
In chorus confessing, God Triune we praise.

Prayer

Virgin Mary, Immaculate Mother of Divine Providence, protect our life and sanctify us with the gift of grace. Obtain for us from the Father of mercy and the God of consolation pardon for our sins, reconciliation with our brothers and sisters, and comfort in the midst of afflictions. Renew our hearts that they may become worthy dwelling places of your Divine Son, Jesus. Help us in our struggles against mediocrity, self-seeking, and pride so we can generously serve our neighbour. We entrust ourselves to you, O Mary, in our pilgrimage in this world. We invoke you as our guide and our defence against dangers. In the present tribulations, give us secure refuge. O sweet Mother of Divine Providence, turn your eyes toward us, you who are our hope on earth. Grant that we may have you as our Mother in the glory of heaven. Amen.

20 November: Our Lady of Guard

ATHER AEGEDIUS SMULDERS, a newly-ordained priest had come from Holland to give missions in the wild-wooded northlands of Michigan before Detroit was a city. The young men crowded around his horse and led the priest to the little log cabin about 100 yards from the lake. The women had a blazing fire ready, as the wind whisked and rustled through the young Redemptorist's black habit, and he was glad to step indoors.

He enquired whether all the families were on this side of the lake. "Sixteen on the other side", was the answer. "Tell them to come, too". The men informed him that it would not be safe to do so, since the ice might thaw, and the people would not get back to their side of the lake safely. After being informed that the priest would not be back for another year, word was sent to the other side of the lake. The mission started, baptism was administered, confessions heard, Holy Communion given, and marriages performed. One night during the services in the crowded cabin, a burly, unshaven man burst in with the news that the lake had begun to thaw and the lives of the people would be in danger trying to get home. They would have to remain in the cabin-chapel all night. "How could 30 families be cared for here?" was the priest's worried thought, of the freezing children and distraught mothers.

Facing the picture of Our Lady on the wall, Father Smulders said, "We're going to pray to Our Holy Mother of Guard, and she will freeze the lake over for us." He whispered frantically under his breath: "Mary, you must... you will! I know you will!" Then he began in a strong confident voice: "Hail Mary, full of grace..." The urgent voices of the people answered, "Holy Mary, Mother of God..." Again and again; after the third Hail Mary, the priest turned to the people and smiled. His lips were filled with a dry tremor and his eyes with cold sweat which looked like tears. "All right, home with you now. Mass at 8:00 tomorrow." They were motionless. "I said go! Our Lady has frozen the lake."

Slowly one or two edged out of the door; then ten, twenty...he could hear them walking on the sand; now trotting, now racing for the shore. He held his breath, and prayed to Mary. No, he couldn't pray. He just thought of Mary, and said nothing. Minutes passed—surely, they reached the shoreline. Not a sound! Another minute. The priest clutched his rosary. "O Mary", he prayed, "guard the people safely across; make the lake freeze again. Then it came! A wild gusty shout: "It's frozen! It's frozen!"

The mission went on for two more weeks. Every day the 16 families crossed and re-crossed the lake. On the tenth day the thaw came again—the people quietly this time mentioned it to the priest. He turned to the picture of Our Lady, and led them in another three Aves to Our Lady of Guard. Once again the lake was frozen, and remained so until the two weeks of the mission were happily and blessedly ended. The young priest and the thirty families recounted over and over again how Our Lady had guarded the families safely to and fro so they could make a complete mission in those early days of Detroit, then known as Otter Creek.[24]

21 November: Presentation of Our Lady

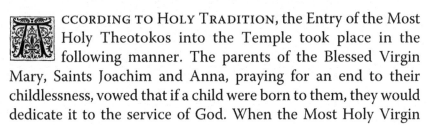

CCORDING TO HOLY TRADITION, the Entry of the Most Holy Theotokos into the Temple took place in the following manner. The parents of the Blessed Virgin Mary, Saints Joachim and Anna, praying for an end to their childlessness, vowed that if a child were born to them, they would dedicate it to the service of God. When the Most Holy Virgin reached the age of three, the holy parents decided to fulfill their vow. They gathered together their relatives and acquaintances, and dressed the All-Pure Virgin in her finest clothes. Singing sacred songs and with lighted candles in their hands, virgins escorted Her to the Temple (see Psalm 45:14–15). There the High Priest and several priests met the handmaiden of God. In the Temple, fifteen high steps led to the sanctuary, which only the priests and High Priest could enter. The child Mary, so it seemed, could not make it up this stairway. But just as they placed her on the first step, strengthened by the power of God, she quickly went up the remaining steps and ascended to the highest one. Then the High Priest, through inspiration from above, led the Most Holy Virgin into the Holy of Holies, where only the High Priest entered once a year to offer a purifying sacrifice of blood. Therefore, all those present in the Temple were astonished at this most unusual occurrence. According to tradition, on this occasion Our Lady made her vow of perpetual virginity.

From the East, the Church received the feast of the Presentation of Our Lady, where it was celebrated from the end of the seventh century. For example, St Germanus of Constantinople (+730) composed this prayer:

> Hail, holy throne of God, divine sanctuary, house of glory, jewel most fair, chosen treasure house, and mercy seat for the whole world, heaven showing forth the glory of God. Purest Virgin, worthy of all praise, sanctuary dedicated to God and raised above all human condition, virgin soil, unplowed field, flourishing vine, fountain pouring out waters, virgin bearing a child, mother without knowing man, hidden treasure of innocence, ornament of sanctity, by your most acceptable prayers, strong with the authority of motherhood, to our Lord and God, Creator of all, your Son who was born of you without a father, steer the ship of the Church and bring it to a quiet harbour.

By the ninth century, the feast was celebrated in the monasteries of southern Italy which had been influenced by the traditions of the Byzantine churches. By the fourteenth century, it had spread to England. Pope Gregory XI adopted the feast day in 1372 at the pontifical court of Avignon. A year later, King Charles V introduced the feast of the Presentation at the Royal Chapel in Paris. It was introduced in 1418 at Metz, and in 1420 at Cologne. In 1460, Pope Pius II granted the feast with a vigil to the Duke of Saxony. Finally, in the year 1472, Pope Sixtus IV extended its celebration to the universal church.

Meditation

If a tree is known by its fruit, and a good tree bears good fruit (Matthew 7:17; Luke 6:44), then is not the Mother of Goodness Itself, she who bore the Eternal Beauty, incomparably more excellent than every good, whether in this world or the world above? Therefore, the coeternal and identical Image of goodness, Preeternal, transcending all being, He Who is the preexisting and good Word of the Father, moved by His unutterable love for mankind and compassion for us, put on our image, that He might reclaim for Himself our nature which had been dragged down to uttermost Hades, so as to renew this corrupted nature and raise it to the heights of Heaven. For this purpose, He had to assume a flesh that was both new and ours, that He might refashion us from out of ourselves. Now He finds a Handmaiden perfectly suited to these needs, the supplier of her own unsullied nature, the Ever-Virgin now hymned by us, and whose miraculous Entrance into the Temple, into the Holy of Holies, we now celebrate. God predestined her before the ages for the salvation and reclaiming of our kind. She was chosen, not just from the crowd, but from the ranks of the chosen of all ages, renowned for piety and understanding, and for their God-pleasing words and deeds.

God is born of the spotless and Holy Virgin, or better to say, of the Most Pure and All-Holy Virgin. She is above every fleshly defilement, and even above every impure thought. Her conceiving resulted not from fleshly lust, but by the overshadowing of the Most Holy Spirit. Such desire being utterly alien to Her, it is through prayer and spiritual readiness that She declared to the angel: "Behold the handmaid of the Lord; be it unto me according to thy word" (Luke 1:38), and that she conceived and gave birth. So, in order to render the Virgin worthy of this sublime purpose, God marked this ever-virgin Daughter now praised by us, from before the ages, and from eternity, choosing her from out of His elect.[25]

22 November: Our Lady of LaVang

 HE FIRST CATHOLIC missionaries arrived in Vietnam in 1533. A scant hundred years later, there were over a hundred thousand Catholics. Seminaries were established and by 1668, two native priests were ordained. A group of women religious was formed in 1670, which is still active today.

Throughout history, Catholics have been persecuted for their faith. Vietnam was no exception. Severe persecutions broke out in 1698. In the eighteenth century, there were three more persecutions. And again in the nineteenth century there were persecutions. The sturdy Vietnamese Catholics stood firm, in spite of the danger. Over one hundred thousand Catholics were martyred in the mid 1800's alone. Today, under the communist regime, the bishops and priests are still harassed. Fragmentary reports on the status of the church since the war are not encouraging. In spite of this, pilgrims flock annually to the shrine of Our Lady of LaVang. This shrine was established in 1800 at Hue, near the centre of the country. At the end of the 17th century, the persecution of Catholics in central Vietnam was so severe that many of the people fled to a remote jungle area in the mountains near LaVang. They wished to be free to practice their religion, as well as to save their lives.

One evening as the community was reciting the rosary together, there was an apparition of a beautiful Lady holding a little child in her arms, and with angels surrounding her. The lady was dressed simply, but wearing a crown. The people recognized the beautiful Lady as the Queen of Heaven. She spoke to the people in the loving tones of a mother. She encouraged and comforted them. Displaying a tender concern for her children, she taught the people how to make medicines from the plants and herbs that grew in the area. She also promised her protection to any who would come to that particular site to pray. Unlike her messages at Fatima and Lourdes, the Lady of LaVang brought only messages of comfort, not warnings. She simply expressed her tender mother's care for her persecuted children. The apparition appeared again a number of times.

The people of LaVang built a simple church of leaves and rice straw, and dedicated it to their mother Mary. Devotion to her grew, and a number of miraculous cures and favours were reported. Through other persecutions, the LaVang area continued to be a sanctuary for oppressed Catholics.

In 1805, officers of the Vietnamese emperor began an anticolonial movement. They were determined to rid the country of all Catholics. No longer was LaVang safe. Thirty Catholics were put to death by the emperor's soldiers right at the door to their little church. The church was burned, although not by one of the soldiers. The soldiers had heard of the miraculous deeds at LaVang and were frightened to destroy the chapel. Amazingly, the altar and the chandeliers, both made of wood, survived the fire. The people then rebuilt their beloved shrine. On the site where the original apparitions took place, a new brick church was begun in 1885. It was completed in 1900, and in 1901 the first annual celebration of the Shrine of Our Lady of LaVang took place. Over 130,000 Catholics from all over the country participated. Devotion to Our Lady of LaVang grew rapidly, and by 1925 it was necessary to enlarge the complex because of the throngs of worshippers. This church was completed in 1928. Many non-Christians acknowledged that there was something special about this place. In the early 1920's, the emperor of Vietnam fell ill. A non-Christian, he sent one of his Christian ministers to pray for him at the shrine. He recovered speedily.

During World War II, Vietnam was a battleground for the Japanese and the French. After this, the French and the communists, known as the Vietcong, battled until 1954 when they split the country into two governments. Almost a million people fled from the communists in the North. At this time, LaVang became a center of pilgrimage. In 1961, the conference of the Vietnamese bishops made the church the national shrine of the country. In August of 1961, Pope Bl Paul VI conferred on the church the title of Basilica of Our Lady of LaVang.

By April of 1975 when South Vietnam fell under the control of the communists, the LaVang complex had enlarged to include a retreat centre, a hospitality centre, an outdoor amphitheatre and a beautiful statue of Mary commemorating her apparitions. The Vietnamese people have always had a special devotion to the Blessed Mother. They carry this love for her with them, wherever they go. They trust their mother to keep them in her loving care, just as she cared for those who were privileged to see her at the apparitions at LaVang.

Prayer

Blessed Lady of LaVang be my mother and comfort me, especially in times of trial and unhappiness. Enter my heart and stay with me wherever I may go. Grant that one day, through you, I may find rest and peace in my Father's house.

23 November: Our Lady of America

N THE EVE of the feast of the North American martyrs, 25 September 1956, Our Lady appeared to Sister Mary Ephrem. Beginning in 1938, Sister had begun to have mystical spiritual experiences. She thought little of them, presuming all religious have them. As these visits took on the nature of a specific program of devotion to Mary which she was asked to propagate, she then turned to Monsignor Paul F. Leibold. Monsignor Leibold, later Archbishop of the Cincinnati, Ohio Archdiocese, would be her spiritual director for many years until 1972, when he suddenly died of an aneurysm. Archbishop Leibold had become so convinced of the authenticity of this message that he approved Sister's writings and placed his imprimatur on the design of the medal. Our Lady had asked Sister Mary Ephrem to have struck a medal that would bear the image of Our Lady of America on the front and the symbol of the Christian Family and the Blessed Trinity on the back.

Our Lady promised that greater miracles than those granted at Lourdes and Fatima would be granted in the United States in particular, if her requests were followed. Sister Mary Ephrem stated that Our Lady called herself Our Lady of America in response to the love and desire that reached out for this special title in the hearts of her children in America. For example, Our Lady repeatedly spoke approvingly about the National Shrine of the Immaculate Conception in Washington DC.

Sister Mary Ephrem quoted Our Lady as saying:

> It is the United States that is to lead the world to peace, the peace of Christ, the peace that He brought with Him from heaven. Dear children, unless the United States accepts and carries out faithfully the mandate given to it by heaven to lead the world to peace, there will come upon it and all nations a great havoc of war and incredible suffering. If, however, the United States is faithful to this mandate from heaven and yet fails in the pursuit of peace because the rest of the world will not accept or cooperate, then the United States will not be burdened with the punishment about to fall.
>
> Weep, then, dear children, weep with your mother over the sins of men. Intercede with me before the throne of mercy, for sin is overwhelming the world and punishment is not far away.

It is the darkest hour, but if men will come to me, my Immaculate Heart will make it bright again with the mercy which my Son will rain down through my hands. Help me save those who will not save themselves. Help me bring once again the sunshine of God's peace upon the world.

If my desires are not fulfilled much suffering will come to this land. My faithful one, if my warnings are taken seriously and enough of my children strive constantly and faithfully to renew and reform themselves in their inward and outward lives, then there will be no nuclear war. What happens to the world depends upon those who live in it. There must be much more good than evil prevailing in order to prevent the holocaust that is so near approaching. Yet I tell you, my daughter, even should such a destruction happen because there were not enough souls who took my warning seriously, there will remain a remnant, untouched by the chaos who, having been faithful in following me and spreading my warnings, will gradually inhabit the earth again with their dedicated and holy lives.

On 13 October 1956, Our Lady again appeared as Our Lady of America, but instead of a lily in her hand, she held, with both hands, a small replica of the finished Shrine of the Immaculate Conception:

This is my shrine, my daughter. I am very pleased with it. Tell my children I thank them. Let them finish it quickly and make it a place of pilgrimage. It will be a place of wonders. I promise this. I will bless all those who, either by prayers, labour, or material aid, help to erect this shrine.

According to Sister Mary Ephrem, Our Lady often emphasized her desire that the Shrine of the Immaculate Conception in Washington, DC, be made a place of special pilgrimage and that she be honored there under this image and the title "Our Lady of America, the Immaculate Virgin."

Strong warnings were repeated by Our Lady throughout 1957 and 1958, and thereafter, indicating that the hour grows late and Sister must tell the Bishops of the United States of Our Lady's desires and how she wishes them to be carried out. In August 1957 the Blessed Virgin warned:

> What am I to do, child of my heart, when my children turn from me? The false peace of this world lures them and in the end will destroy them. They think they have done enough in consecrating themselves to my Immaculate Heart. It is not enough. That which I ask for and is most important many have not given me. What I ask, have asked, and will continue to ask is reformation of life. There must be sanctification from within. I will work my miracles of grace only in those who ask for them and empty their souls of the love and attachment to sin and all that is displeasing to my Son. Souls who cling to sin cannot have their hands free to receive the treasures of grace that I hold out to them.

The Blessed Virgin Mary has promised that her statue as Our Lady of America once placed in the National Shrine of the Immaculate Conception would be a safeguard for our country, and her picture or statue honored in all homes, a safeguard for the family. She also promised that the medal would be a safeguard against evil for those who wear it with great faith and devotion.

On 22 and 23 November 1957, Our Lady was revealed as she really and truly was, the Immaculate Tabernacle of the Indwelling God. In 2007, Archbishop Raymond Burke affirmed: "What can be concluded canonically is that the devotion was both approved by Archbishop Leibold and, what is more, was actively promoted by him. In addition, over the years, other Bishops have approved the devotion and have participated in public devotion to the Mother of God, under the title of Our Lady of America."[26]

24 November: Our Lady of Myans

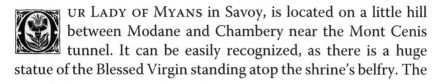 UR LADY OF MYANS in Savoy, is located on a little hill between Modane and Chambery near the Mont Cenis tunnel. It can be easily recognized, as there is a huge statue of the Blessed Virgin standing atop the shrine's belfry. The

shrine has been a pilgrimage centre since at least the thirteenth century, and its small Black Virgin was an object of the devotion of Saint Francis de Sales. The church became famous for a miracle that occurred there on 24 November 1248. A tremendous earthquake shook the region causing Mont Granier, the tallest mountain of the Chartreuse Massif, to disintegrate into huge boulders which came crashing down into the valley. Some of these boulders were the size of a house, and 16 villages were crushed and 5,000 lives lost. The church of Myans, however, was spared, and gigantic boulders were stopped abruptly at the very door of the church. Some of these boulders can still be seen around the church grounds.

A marvellous answer to prayer occurred in 1534 in favour of Jean Grandis of Savoy, who was on a vessel bound from Genoa to Livorno. When the ship was threatened during a tempest and seemed likely to sink, Jean Grandis called upon Our Lady of Myans, Queen of Savoy. Battered by the waves, the ship foundered and sank. Jean Grandis was the only survivor. As a gesture of thanksgiving, he travelled barefoot to the shrine and there placed his ex-voto. It is said to be one of the oldest to survive. Another miracle attributed to Our Lady of Myans favoured the brother of St Francis de Sales, Count Louis de Sales, who in 1603 was travelling to the Chateau of Cusy to marry Claudine Philiberte de Pingon. Since there was no bridge in sight, the Count attempted to cross the River Cheran at a place that he thought was shallow and safe. However, the Count was swept away by flood water. Invoking the name of Our Lady of Myans and promising to make a pilgrimage, he was suddenly thrust onto an object that saved his life. The wedding ceremony was conducted on 2 April. The next day St Francis de Sales offered a Mass of thanksgiving in the little crypt chapel before the miraculous image of Our Lady of Myans.[27]

The church was half destroyed during the French Revolution, but the statue was saved and later enshrined again in the restored building, where it was crowned in 1905 by order of Pope St Pius

X. The sanctuary is particularly resorted to by pilgrimages of men, and the image was taken to Rome by a Savoyard pilgrimage for the definition of the dogma of the Assumption in the year 1950.

25 November: Our Lady of Thanksgiving

OWADAYS IN THE UNITED STATES, Thanksgiving Day is kept of the fourth Thursday of November. The first American Thanksgiving was actually celebrated on 8 September (feast of Our Lady's birthday) in 1565 in St Augustine, Florida. The Native Americans and Spanish settlers held a feast and the Holy Mass was offered. Don Pedro Menendez came ashore amid the sounding of trumpets, artillery salutes and the firing of cannons to claim the land for King Philip II and Spain. The ship chaplain Fr Francisco Lopez de Mendoza Grajales chanted the Te Deum and presented a crucifix that Menendez kissed. Then the 500 soldiers, 200 sailors and 100 families and artisans, along with the Timucuan Indians celebrated the Holy Sacrifice of the Mass in gratitude to God. Even today Our Lady can help us give the thanks to God for all His blessings in the spirit of her Magnificat: "The Almighty has done great things for me: Holy is His Name" (Lk 1:49).

> To be able to offer thanks, to be able to praise the Lord for what he has done for us: this is important! So we can ask ourselves: Are we capable of saying "Thank you"? How many times do we say "Thank you" in our family, our community, and in the Church? How many times do we say "Thank you" to those who help us, to those close to us, to those who accompany us through life? Often we take everything for granted! This also happens with God. It is easy to approach the Lord to ask for something, but to return and give thanks... That is why Jesus so emphasizes the failure of the nine ungrateful lepers: "Were not ten made clean? But the other nine, where are they? Was no one found to return and give praise to God except this foreigner?" (Lk 17:17–18).

We are given a model, indeed the model, to whom we can look: Mary, our Mother. After hearing the message of the Angel, she lifted up her heart in a song of praise and thanksgiving to God: "My soul magnifies the Lord…" Let us ask our Lady to help us recognize that everything is God's gift, and to be able to say "Thank you". Then, I assure you, our joy will be complete. Only those who know how to say "Thank you", will experience the fullness of joy… The heart of Mary, more than any other, is a humble heart, capable of accepting God's gifts. In order to become man, God chose precisely her, a simple young woman of Nazareth, who did not dwell in the palaces of power and wealth, who did not do extraordinary things. Let us ask ourselves— it will do us good—if we are prepared to accept God's gifts, or prefer instead to shut ourselves up within our forms of material security, intellectual security, the security of our plans. Let us cling to this simple faith of the Holy Mother of God; let us ask her that we may always come back to Jesus and express our thanks for the many benefits we have received from his mercy.[28]

26 November: Our Lady of Soufanieh

 N 22 NOVEMBER 1982, three women of different faiths— Catholicism, Orthodoxy, Islam—stood in prayer around a sickbed in the Soufanieh neighbourhood of Damascus. Thus began the spiritual career of Myrna (Maria) Al Akharas, a member of the Melkite Greek Catholic Church, then only 18 and recently married to Nicolas Nazzour, of the Antiochan Greek Orthodox Church. In November of that year her sister-in-law, Layla, had become quite ill. Seeing light, then oil, coming from the Myrna's hands, the Muslim woman urged her to put them on Layla, who was instantly healed. Five days later, oil began oozing from a small picture of Our Lady of Kazan in Myrna and Nicolas' home— an icon both Catholics and Orthodox Christians revere, known for miracles and healings. With a year's break in 1985–86, oil flowed from the image until 26 November 1990. The clergy and civil authorities all investigated for any evidence of a fraud or trick; they could only conclude that oil was indeed coming from the picture.

On 15 December 1982, Myrna saw Our Lady coming from a globe of light in a eucalyptus tree; from her right hand hung a long Rosary. Then Mary spoke:

> My children, be mindful of God because God is with us. You know much, but you really know nothing. Your knowledge is incomplete. One day you will know everything as God knows me. Do good to evil-doers. Do not mistreat anyone. I have given you oil, more than you have asked for. I give you something stronger than oil. Repent and believe! Be mindful of me in your joy. Announce my Son Emmanuel. He who announces Him is saved. He who does not ... his faith is in vain. Love one another.
>
> I do not ask you to give money to churches. I ask you to love. Those who give money to the poor and to the churches but yet have not love, have lives of no value. I will visit the homes of my children more frequently, because those who go to church do not always go there to pray. I do not ask you to build a church for me but rather a shrine. Give. Do not deprive anyone who asks for help. Be humble, my children. Do not insult the proud. Forgive them. Then you will be forgiven.

From then on she repeatedly saw and received messages from both Mary and Jesus, until 26 November 1990, when she reported the Virgin's farewell: "... you are seeing Me for the last time until the feast is unified". Consistent with the seer's personal location in a nexus of faiths, the messages of Soufanieh call for Christian unity, including agreement on the date of Easter, historically different in the Western and Eastern Churches. Often Myrna heard the Virgin repeat the Biblical sayings of Jesus: "Love one another... Forbear and forgive... Do not fear, I am with you." In an early message from Mary, Myrna learned the affirmation, "God saves me, Jesus enlightens me, the Holy Spirit is my life, thus I fear nothing."

Since 1983, Myrna has occasionally suffered intense stigmatic wounds during ecstasy, visible to others during the day and completely gone by midnight. Many miracles have been attributed to the oil from her icon and hands. On 31 December 1982, an official declaration was made by Patriarch Ignatius IV Hazim, who had studied the supernatural events carefully. Recognition was spread throughout the Greek Orthodox churches in Damascus. On 18 June 1990, the Catholic archbishop of Damascus attested to being an eyewitness on several occasions to oil exuding from Myrna and her little icon. Priests and bishops, both Catholic and Orthodox, have celebrated Masses in connection with the devotions. Annual anniversary celebrations begin 26 November with Mass in a church, followed by evening prayers and festivities at the Nazzours' home, with Myrna, Nicolas, their two children, relatives, friends, and followers.[29]

27 November: Our Lady of the Miraculous Medal

ZOË LABOURÉ WAS the daughter of a farmer at Fain-les-Moutiers in France, where she was born in 1806. She was the only one of a large family who did not to go to school and did not learn to read and write. Her mother died when she was eight, and when her elder sister, Louisa, left home to become a Sister of Charity, the duties of housekeeper and helper to her father fell upon her. When her mother died she chose the Blessed Virgin for her mother, and when she was about 14 she heard a call to the religious life. After some opposition from her father, she was allowed to join the Sisters of Charity of St Vincent de Paul at Châtillon-sur-Seine in 1830. She took the name Catherine, and after her postulancy was sent to the convent in the Rue du Bac in Paris, where she arrived four days before the removal of the relics of St Vincent de Paul from Notre Dame to the Lazarist Church in Rue de Sèvres. On the day of those festivities, a series of visions began which were to make the name of Catherine Labouré famous. On many occasions during Mass, Catherine beheld Our Lord in front of the Blessed Sacrament and on other occasions she saw symbolic visions of St Vincent above the reliquary containing his incorrupt heart.

The first of the three principal visions took place three months later. On the night of 18 July, at about 11:30 pm she was woken up suddenly by the appearance of a "shining child", who led her down to the chapel. There Our Lady appeared and talked with her for over two hours, telling her that she would have to undertake a difficult task. Our Lady continued:

> The times are evil. Sorrows will come upon France; the throne will be overthrown. The Cross will be thrown down and trampled. The Archbishop will be stripped of his clothes. Blood will flow in the streets. The side of Our Lord will be pierced anew. The whole world will be afflicted with tribulations.

But as if giving a remedy, she pointed toward the foot of the altar and said, "Come to the foot of the altar. Here graces will be shed on all who ask for them. Graces will be shed especially on those who ask for them." On 27 November in the same year, Our Lady appeared to Sister Catherine in the same chapel, in the form of a picture and as it were standing on a globe with shafts of light streaming from Our Lady's hands. Catherine described the event:

> I saw the Blessed Virgin standing on a globe, Her face was beautiful beyond words. Rays of dazzling light were streaming from gems on Her fingers, down to the globe. And I heard a voice say: "Behold the symbol of graces which I will shower down on all who ask Me for them!" Then, an oval frame surrounded Our Lady on which I read the prayer, in letters of gold: "O Mary, conceived without sin, pray for us who have recourse to Thee!" The oval frame turned and I could see, on the reverse side, enclosed in a frame of twelve stars, the letter M surmounted by a cross with a bar beneath. Below these symbols were the Hearts of Jesus and Mary, one surrounded by a crown of thorns, the other pierced by a sword. I heard a voice, which said to me: "Have a medal

struck according to this model. Those who wear it, when it
is blessed, will receive great graces, especially if they wear it
around their necks. There will be graces in abundance for
all who wear it with confidence."

Sister Catherine confided in her confessor, Père Aladel, and after
making very careful investigations, he was given permission by
the Archbishop of Paris, Mgr de Quelen, to have the medal struck.
In June 1832, the first 1,500 were issued. The Faith was encountering difficulties in France at this time and its revival has been
attributed to this medal. So many conversions and physical cures
were attributed to the medal that the name *Miraculous Medal*
was given it by popular acclaim.

The Archbishop of Paris undertook a canonical inquiry into
the alleged visions in 1836, before which, however, Sister Catherine could not be induced to appear. Further inquiries took place
and eventually the tribunal decided in favour of the authenticity
of the visions, taking into consideration the circumstances, the
character of the sister concerned, and the prudence and level-
headedness of Père Aladel. Until her death on 31 December 1876,
Catherine lived unobtrusively among the community at Enghien-
Reuilly caring for the sick, the aged and the infirm. Although the
other sisters were aware that the one in their midst was the
celebrated visionary of the Miraculous Medal, the identity was
not made known until Catherine was on her death bed. Her
funeral was the occasion of an outburst of popular veneration,
and a child of twelve, crippled from birth, was instantaneously
cured at her grave soon after. Sister Catherine's body had been
placed in a triple coffin and buried in a crypt in the chapel at 77,
rue de Reuilly where it remained for over 50 years.

Following the announcement of her beatification the coffin
was opened and the customary recognition of the relics took
place, and it was then discovered that the remains were found to
be perfectly intact and incorrupt. The hands and the face were
of a pinkish colour slightly tinged, but intact. The following day
the face had slightly darkened on account of its first contact with

the air. After a cursory examination, the body was borne in solemn procession to the mother house. The body was later placed in the mother house chapel under the side altar of Our Lady of the Sun, where it still reposes behind a covering of glass, allowing it to be viewed by the many visitors to the chapel.

On 23 July, 1894, Pope Leo XIII, after a careful examination of all the facts by the Sacred Congregation of Rites, instituted a feast, with a special Office and Mass, of the Manifestation of the Immaculate Virgin under the title of the Miraculous Medal, to be celebrated yearly on 27 November by the Priests of the Congregation of the Mission. Saint Catherine was canonized on 27 July 1947 and her feast day is observed on 28 November, the day after the feast of the Miraculous Medal. Pope St John Paul II adopted a slight variation of the reverse image of the Miraculous Medal as his coat of arms, the Marian Cross, a plain cross with an M underneath the right-hand bar (which signifies the Blessed Virgin at the foot of the Cross when Jesus was being crucified).

Prayer

O Virgin Mother of God, Mary Immaculate,
We dedicate and consecrate ourselves to you
under the title of Our Lady of the Miraculous Medal.
May this Medal be for each one of us a sure sign
of your affection for us
and a constant reminder of our duties toward you.
Ever while wearing it,
may we be blessed by your loving protection
and preserved in the grace of your Son.
O Most Powerful Virgin, Mother of Our Savior,
keep us close to you every moment of our lives.
Obtain for us, your children,
the grace of a happy death;
so that in union with you,
we may enjoy the bliss of Heaven forever. Amen.

28 November: Our Lady of Kibeho

UR LADY OF Kibeho is the name given to Marian apparitions involving several adolescents, in the 1980s in Kibeho, south-western Rwanda. The apparitions communicated various messages to the schoolchildren, including an apocalyptic vision of Rwanda descending into violence and hatred, very probably foretelling the 1994 Rwandan genocide.

The Kibeho apparitions began on 28 November 1981, at a time of increasing tension between the Tutsis and the Hutus. They occurred at Kibeho College, a secondary school for girls, and included an apocalyptic vision of Rwanda descending into violence and hatred. The Virgin Mary appeared to the group with the name "Nyina wa Jambo" (Mother of the Word) synonymous with "Umubyeyi W'Imana" (Mother of God).The teenage visionaries reported that the Virgin Mary asked everyone to pray to prevent a terrible war. In the vision of 19 August 1982, they all reported seeing violence, dismembered corpses and destruction.

The longest series of visions were attributed to Alphonsine Mumureke who received the first vision on 28 November 1981 and the last on 28 November 1989. Anathalie Mukamazimpaka's visions began in January 1982 and ended on 3 December 1983. Marie Claire Mukangango had visions for six months, lasting from 2 March 1982 until 15 September 1982. She was later killed in the massacre of 1995 at the same location. During his 1990 visit to Rwanda, Pope St John Paul II exhorted the faithful to turn to the Virgin as a "simple and sure guide" and to pray for greater commitment against local divisions, both political and ethnic.

In the 100 days that followed the April 1994 assassination of dictator Juvénal Habyarimana, by most accounts, 800,000 Rwandans, by some accounts, over one million, were slaughtered by their countrymen and, in some cases, their next-door-neighbours. The violence was the culmination of intensifying animosity between the two ethnic groups—the Hutus and Tutsis—and the civil war that had preceded it. Twice, Kibeho was the site of a large massacre, first at the parish church in April 1994, and then a year later in April 1995 where more than 5,000 refugees who had taken shelter at Kibeho were shot by soldiers.

Only the visions of the first three seers (Alphonsine, Nathalie, and Marie Claire aged 17, 20 and 21) received local Bishop Augustin Misago's solemn approval. The others claiming visions were Stephanie Mukamurenzi, Agnes Kamagaju, Vestine Salima and Emmanuel Segastashya, the last of whom was previously a pagan and became a Christian evangelist. Emmanuel's alleged visions included meeting Jesus Christ in a bean field.

The visions may be regarded as an ominous foreshadowing of the Rwandan genocide of 1994, and particularly the 1995 Kibeho Massacre. The school where the visions occurred became a place of slaughter during the genocide as dozens of children were hacked to death by Hutu terrorists. Some of the visionaries were among the victims. Catholic Bishop Augustin Misago of Gikongoro, Rwanda approved public devotion linked to the apparitions on 15 August 1988 (the Solemnity of the Assumption of Mary) and declared their authenticity on 29 June 2001. He was accused in 1999 and acquitted on 24 June 2000 of involvement in the Rwandan genocide. The feast day of Our Lady of Kibeho is November 28.

The Marian sanctuary at Kibeho was named "Shrine of Our Lady of Sorrows" in 1992. The first stone was laid on 28 November 1992. In a 2003 agreement between the local ordinary and the Society of the Catholic Apostolate (Pallotines), the rectorate of the Shrine of Our Lady of Kibeho is entrusted to the Pallotine Fathers. The rector is appointed by the local bishop and the Regional Pallottine Rector.

29 November: Our Lady of Beauraing

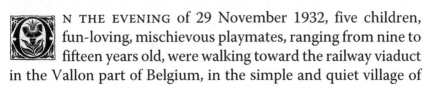 N THE EVENING of 29 November 1932, five children, fun-loving, mischievous playmates, ranging from nine to fifteen years old, were walking toward the railway viaduct in the Vallon part of Belgium, in the simple and quiet village of

Beauraing. Suddenly one of them exclaimed that there was a bright light moving at the viaduct. First they thought these the lights of a moving car. Very soon, however, they discovered the figure of a lady, and they instantly recognized that this could be nothing less than the Blessed Virgin Mary.

Our Lady of Beauraing, also known as the Virgin of the Golden Heart, appeared to Fernande Voisin (15), Andree Degeimbre (14), Gilberte Voisin (13) Albert Voisin (11) and Gilberte Degeimbre (9) between 29 November 1932 and 3 January 1933. The children were from two different families—three from a railway clerk and his wife, and two girls from a farmer's widow.

Nobody wished to believe what the children related. But the next evening they came home with the same story. The village laughed at them and their parents were angry. The next time the children related with more details that they had seen a lady who was more beautiful than her statues, dressed in pure white, with a crown of golden rays on her head. On 2 December the children asked the Lady some questions; she confirmed with a smile that she was the Immaculate Virgin and demanded that they "always be good". As the vision continues, more people came to Beauraing, including police officials, doctors and psychologists.

There were thirty-three apparitions in all. On 29 December the children related, the Blessed Virgin revealed a heart of gold on her breast. The next evening she asked for more prayers. On 1 January 1933, she reiterated this request and told Fernande, the fifteen year old girl: "If you love my Son and love me, then sacrifice yourself for me." In 1933, two million pilgrims arrived in the small town. The Belgian bishops at first forbade any processions or cults and started an investigation that was to last for ten years, during which serious objections were brought against the children. Finally, in 1943, a decree was issued by the Bishop of Namur authorizing the cult of Our Lady of Beauraing. On 18 July 1947, Mgr Charue personally received papal blessings for the Sanctuary dedicated to Our Lady of Beauraing—the Virgin of the Golden Heart. This devotion has since taken on new and ever increasing proportions.

The final approbation was issued on 2 July 1949. The cures of Miss Van Laer and Mrs Acar were declared miraculous by a decree given by Mgr Charue. Many conversions and graces have been obtained through the intercession of Our Lady of Beauraing. Among these, the editor of the Belgian Communist paper *Le Drapeau Rouge* (The Red Flag), was one of the first to become a Catholic at the shrine of Our Lady of Beauraing.[30] The last visionary of the Beauraing apparitions, Gilberte Degeimbre, born in Wancennes on 13 August 1923, passed away 10 February 2015; she died in Mont-Godinne at the age of 91.

Prayer

Our Lady of Beauraing, Immaculate Virgin, carry to Jesus, your Son, all the intentions which we confide to you this day. (Here mention your intentions) Mother with the Golden Heart, mirror of the tenderness of the Father, look with love upon the men and women of our time and fill them with the joy of your presence.

You who promised to convert sinners, help us discover the infinite mercy of our God. Awaken in us the grace of conversion so that all our life becomes the reflection of this mercy. Holy Mother of God, look down upon our miseries, console us in our sorrows, give strength to all those who are suffering. Queen of Heaven, crowned with light, help us grow in faith, hope and love, and we shall be able to give thanks without end.

You brought Jesus into the world, may we by prayer, by sharing His Word and by the testimony of our life filled with love and joy make Him be born in all hearts. May every instant of our life be a YES to the question, which you are asking us today: Do you love my son? Do you love me? Then the reign of Jesus will come into the world. Amen.

30 November: Our Lady of the Conception

RAY MIGUEL DE BOLONIA, of the Spanish Netherlands, was one of the first Franciscans to enter Mexico in 1524. A saintly missionary who learned the native languages and stood up for natives when Spanish rulers threatened them, he travelled through Mexico, teaching and building until his death in 1580. In 1542, he founded the village of San Juan Bautista de Mezquititlán (land of mesquite trees), where he built a hospital and chapel, in which he placed a statue of Mary Immaculate.[31]

In 1623, some trapeze artists brought the the body of their daughter to the San Juan chapel for burial. The young acrobat had fallen during practice onto some upright blades sticking up from the ground to make the show more thrilling. The chapel caretaker, an old woman named Ana Lucia, put the Our Lady's statue on the girl's breast, and the child revived. The grateful father took the fragile statue, made of cornstalks and glue, to Guadalajara for restoration. From then on the shrine's fame and miracles multiplied. Meanwhile, the town grew, changing its name to San Juan de los Lagos (St John of the Lakes). A new church was built, and then another—each larger, more splendid, more worthy of the Immaculate Virgin. On 30 November 1769, the statue was installed in the third church.

San Juan de los Lagos began holding a market fair in commemoration, annually around 30 November, with festivities extending to the Feast of the Immaculate Conception, 8 December. The celebration eventually became so rowdy that the hierarchy decided to move the feast of the Virgen de San Juan de los Lagos to 2 February (Candlemas). The Candlemas fiesta has evolved into a month-long, mass pilgrimage to the shrine from all over Mexico, but 8 December is still observed, as well as 15 August. The statue was canonically crowned 15 August 1904.

Notes

[1]   See *Salve Maria Regina* 55/181 (Summer 2015).
[2]   St Bernardine of Siena, *Sermo 3 de glorioso nomine Mariae*, art 2, cap. 3.
[3]   F. Faber, "The Queen of Purgatory".
[4]   The Maguey is *Agave americana*, or American aloe; it is a species of flowering plant in the family Agavaceae, native to Mexico, and the United States in New Mexico, Arizona and Texas. Today, it is cultivated world-wide as an ornamental plant.
[5]   See M. Lamberty, *The Woman in Orbit: Mary's feasts every day everywhere* (Chicago: Lamberty Co, 1966), 6 November.
[6]   See *ibid.*, 7 November.
[7]   See *ibid.*, 8 November.
[8]   In architectural parlance, the dado is a slot or trench cut into the surface of a piece of material.
[9]   Lamberty, *The Woman in Orbit*, 9 November.
[10] See *ibid.*, 10 November.
[11] The *soldo* was the name of an Italian medieval silver coin, issued for the first time in the late 12th century at Milan by Emperor Henry VI. The name derives from the late Roman coin *solidus*. As time passed, the *soldo* started to be coined from the 18th century, in copper. The Napoleonic reformation of Italian coinage (early 19th century) made it worth 5 cents, while 20 *soldi* were needed to form a *lira*.
[12] See Lamberty, *The Woman in Orbit*, 12 November.
[13] He was known in Italian as San Giovanni della Marca.
[14] The Battle on the Planta, fought in November 1475, was part of the Burgundian Wars, a conflict between the Dukes of Burgundy and the Old Swiss Confederacy and its allies.
[15] See www.abbaye-saint-benoit.ch/pelerinagessuisses.
[16] See D. Thomas, "Early Muslim Relations with Christianity"in *The Anvil* 6/1 (1989), p. 24.
[17] Pope Leo XIII, Encyclical *Supremi Apostolatus Officio* (1883), 10.
[18] See *Salve Maria Regina* Vol. 41, No. 116.
[19] See J. C. Cruz, *Miraculous Images of Our Lady: 100 famous Catholic statues and portraits* (Charlotte, NC: TAN Books, 2012), chapter 98 "Our Lady of the Dew".
[20] See N. J. Santoro, *Mary In Our Life: Atlas of the Names and Titles of Mary, The Mother of Jesus, and Their Place in Marian Devotion* (Kansas City, MI: iUniverse, Inc, 2011), pp. 669–670.
[21] This is described in detail above under 20 January: Our Lady of the Miracle.

[22] See Lamberty, *The Woman in Orbit*, 17 November.

[23] See *ibid.*, 18 November.

[24] See *ibid.*, 20 November.

[25] Gregory Palamas, *Discourse on the Feast of the Entry of our Most Pure Lady Theotokos into the Holy of Holies.*

[26] Archbishop R. L. Burke, *Letter to the United States Conference of Catholic Bishops* (31 May 2007).

[27] See Cruz, *Miraculous Images of Our Lady*, chapter 25 "Our Lady of Myans".

[28] Pope Francis, *Homily at Marian Jubilee* (9 October 2016).

[29] See R. J. Fox, *Light from the East Miracles of Our Lady of Soufanieh* (Hanceville, AL: Fatima Family Apostolate, 2002).

[30] See D. Sharkey, *"I will convert sinners." Our Lady's Apparitions at Beauraing, 1932–1933* (Techny, IL: Divine Word Publications, 1957).

[31] The mesquite is the common name for the genus *Prosopis*, containing over 40 species of small leguminous trees. They are native to the south-western United States and Mexico. The mesquite originates from the Tamaulipan mezquital ecoregion, in the deserts and xeric shrublands biome, located in the southern United States and northeastern Mexico.

DECEMBER

1 December: Our Lady of Mettenbuch

EAR METTENBUCH, a small hamlet on the edge of the Bavarian forest, in the vicinity of the monastery of Metten, not far from Deggendorf, lights had been seen by various children from the middle of September 1877 onwards, hovering about a damp spot in a ravine, where a blackberry bramble was growing over the stump of a tree. These were considered to be "lights of the souls in purgatory", and prayers for the dead were offered up on the spot. Mettenbuch subsequently became famous during the period of the Kulturkampf (conflict between the Germanic Empire and the Catholic Church) as a result of the supernatural events recorded there, including a miraculous deliverance from possession: that of Barbara Eder. The apparitions were manifested in the period between 1 and 21 December 1876 and again, one last time, Mary appeared in 1878. The main visionaries, Mathilde Sack, Catherine and Joseph Kändler, Caroline and Francis Xavier Kraus, Theresa and Anna Liebl, were all aged between eight and fourteen years, and some adults also witnessed some aspects of the apparitions. The boys had the privilege of receiving the apparitions of the Virgin, the Child Jesus, and sometimes also of St Joseph and several rows of angels and saints, as well as to see light phenomena.

Our Lady appeared as the Comforter of the Afflicted and the Mother of God of Advent. Our Lady also asked for the construction of a simple chapel and invited everyone to confess their sins. The mothers of the boys talked with the parish priest, and tried to convince him to build a chapel in honour of Our Lady Comforter of the Afflicted. In the summer of 1877, duchess von Thurn und Taxis brought a large pilgrimage to Mettenbuch. These events were recorded in detail by the parish priest and examined by the local bishop of Regensburg, Mgr Ignatius von Senestrey. The latter, however, immediately distanced himself from the apparitions and was hostile to the apparition from the beginning. The bishop deprived the seers of their liberty, and were subjected to inquisitorial methods of interrogation conducted by Bishop von Senestrey personally; nowadays he would have been accused of "unlawful detention, isolation, torture and child abuse". After months of solitary confinement almost all the children broke down and signed a statement saying that they had lied about the phenomena.

On 23 January 1879, Bishop von Senestrey issued a pastoral letter in which he decreed that he deemed the phenomena of Mettenbuch to be false, and forbade Catholics to make the pilgrimage or adopt the devotion. Despite Church opposition Mettenbuch became a place of pilgrimage. Opposing the bishop's decision, several professors, priests and monks of the monastery of Metten protested in Rome. It was hoped to obtain ecclesiastical recognition when twenty-year-old Barbara Eder, who suffered from severe forms of possession, was miraculously cured by bathing in the spring of the forest, where they had manifested the phenomena considered supernatural. Despite this alleged extraordinary healing, the bishop refused any further investigation. Furthermore in what rather seems an abuse of power, the heavy-handed bishop suspended the two Benedictine monks who supported the apparitions. After the death of Fr Francis Nock and Fr Ugo Dieringer, both monks of the monastery of Metten (who were both in favour of opening an ecclesiastical investigation) any hope of a possible recognition seemed lost.

Senestrey's successor, Bishop Rudolf Graber reopened the investigation, saying that the question should not be forgotten and was still to be proven. On 7 June 1887, 10 years after the apparitions, the children, now young people and teenagers, publicly recanted their earlier statements. The explanation opens with the words: "The time seems to have come when we can overturn the evil we have committed against Our Lady in 1878,

... we retract our earlier statement. We made it at the time in a moment of fear and confusion, which we regret." In the following years more than 100,000 believers came in pilgrimage to Metten-buch. Even today people still come to this place of grace to seek the help of "Mary, comforter of the afflicted", and then go to the spring to collect water. With the passage of time a small chapel was built, the image of the Virgin was incorporated, as well as a crucifix, some pictures of angels, a tap to draw water from the fountain, and benches where pilgrims sit to pray, especially at during the great Marian feasts and in Advent.[1]

2 December: Our Lady of the Apocalypse

HE WOMAN OF THE APOCALYPSE (or the Woman clothed with the Sun, *Mulier amicta sole*) is a figure from Chapter 12 of the Book of Revelation. In this narrative the woman gives birth to a male child that is attacked by the Dragon identified as the Devil and Satan. When the child is taken to heaven, the woman flees into the wilderness leading to War in Heaven in which the angels cast out the Dragon. The Dragon attacks the woman, who is given wings to escape, and then attacks her again with a flood of water from his mouth, which is subsequently swallowed by the earth. Frustrated, the dragon initiates war on "the remnant of her seed" identified as the righteous followers of Christ.

The image is very appropriate for reflection in the liturgical season of Advent, and represents the Church and Our Lady at the same time; above all, the Woman of the apocalypse is Mary herself. Though not named, this woman is described as the Mother of the Messiah. In poetic language akin to the Bible's other prophetic books, Saint John says she faced the threat of "a huge red dragon, with seven heads and ten horns," and "fled into the desert where she had a place prepared by God". The sun-clad woman appears "clothed in sunlight", that is, clothed in God. The Virgin Mary is in fact completely surrounded by the light of God and lives in God ... The "Immaculate One" reflects with all of her person the light of God.

Besides representing Our Lady, this sign personifies the Church, the Christian community of all times. The Church is pregnant, in the sense that she carries Christ and must give birth to Him to the world. This is the labour of the pilgrim Church on earth, that in the midst of the consolations of God and the persecutions of the world, she must bring Christ to men. Because the Church continues to bring Jesus into the world, it finds opposition in a ferocious adversary, symbolized in scripture by the "dragon" that has tried in vain to devour Jesus, and now directs his attacks against the woman—the Church—in the desert of the world. However, in every age the Church is supported by the light and the strength of God; she is nurtured in the desert with the bread of his word and the Holy Eucharist. In this way, in every tribulation, through all of the trials that she finds in the course of the ages and in the different parts of the world, the Church suffers persecution, but comes out the victor.

The only pitfall of which the Church can and must be afraid is the sin of her members, which is the key difference between the Church and the Woman who is its prototype. While in fact Mary is immaculate—free from every stain of sin—the Church is holy, but at the same time marked by our sins. While sinless herself, Mary remains in solidarity with the Church struggling against sin. That is why the people of God, pilgrims in time, turn to their heavenly mother and ask for her help. May Mary help us to see that there is a light beyond the veil of fog that appears to envelop reality.[2]

3 December: Our Lady of Montesanto

ANTA MARIA IN MONTESANTO, erected over a church with the same name that lay at the beginning of Via del Babuino, was served by Carmelite monks. The name Montesanto (Holy Mountain) refers to Mount Carmel in Israel. The construction of the present church was begun on 15 July

1662, under the patronage of Cardinal Girolamo Gastaldi, and finished in 1675, with other additions by 1679. Originally designed by Carlo Rainaldi, the plans were revised by Gian Lorenzo Bernini, and ultimately completed by Carlo Fontana. A belfry was added in the 18th century. The statues of saints on the exterior have been attributed to Bernini's design. The interior has an elliptical plan, with a dodecagonal cupola. In 1825, the church was made a minor basilica.

The altarpiece is a 16th century copy of the icon of Our Lady of Montesanto (actually Our Lady of Mount Carmel), allegedly preserved from the former convent chapel that the church replaced. A pair of floating *putti* in stucco embellish it. The picture shows Our Lady holding a globe and the Brown Scapular in her right hand, and a label reads: *In Monte Sancto suo Carmelo steterunt pedes eius* ("On his holy mountain Carmel stood his feet"). This is a reference to the prophet Elijah, whom the Carmelites used to claim as their original founder. The original painting, a miraculous Madonna and Child, was believed to have been painted by an 11-year-old girl with supernatural help. After the painting was canonically crowned on 3 December 1659, Cardinal Gerolamo Gastaldi decided to build Our Lady a more splendid sanctuary.

On 10 August 1904, Angelo Giuseppe Roncalli, the future Pope John XXIII was ordained to the priesthood, by Patriarch Giuseppe Ceppetelli in this church. In 1953, Mgr Ennio Francia established the tradition of the Mass of the Artists. On the last Sunday of October till June 29, a Mass is held every Sunday with reading by an artist, and animated by music. At the end of the Mass, a prayer for the artists is recited. For these reasons the Montesanto church is also called the Church of the Artists.

4 December: Our Lady of Crowns

 ROM THE BEGINNING of history, we know of kings and princes who were marked above all others with the royal sign of their dignity—a crown. But much more fittingly this applies to Jesus, our King, and Mary, our Queen-Mother. The crowns of old were set with precious gems and sparkling pearls. Crowns were a sign of the possession of a country and of a people. The crowns of history were a mark of authority. The crowns of ancient times were a mark and an omen of justice for the enemies of the king and the offenders of morality. Crowns were always an indication of honour and majesty.

We all know of the custom of crowning the May Queen with a garland of roses. Often we hear tell of the Rosary as the Crown of Mary, and an appropriate title it is. It has the richness of antiquity, and the tradition of many ages. The Rosary is a string of precious pearls, precious stones, depicting our faith which is a sign of Mary's ownership of the hearts of her Christians; it is a sign of authority over the faithful flock of Christ's church. The Rosary shows clearly that Mary is singularly honoured and revered as Queen of all others.

The Rosary is like a bouquet of sweet smelling flowers of every size and colour, depicting the virtues we practice every time we say it with devotion. But above all gems, pearls and flowers, the Rosary is the instrument of intercession calling down God's vengeance upon the enemies of God and blessings upon his children; with the Rosary we can win Mary's love: with it we can acquire peace for individuals, families and nations; through her whom it honours, we can wend our way to the heart of God. We have everything to hope for and all to gain, if we place this rich crown upon the head of Mary each day. Through the Rosary we have as our Queen, Mother and Intercessor, her to whom God can refuse nothing, but nothing.[3]

5 December: Our Lady of Clos Evrard

 HE SHRINE OF OUR LADY OF CLOS EVRARD is in the city of Trier, which is the oldest city in Germany, founded before the time of Christ on the bank of the Moselle

River. Trier boasted of having Christian citizens as early as the second century, and had a bishop in the third.

An image of the Blessed Virgin was fastened to an oak tree by a wine-dresser, who wished to honour Mary; but Our Lady ordered him to build a small hut in her honour. In fact the expression *clos* is a French word, meaning and enclosed space, referring to a walled vineyard as used in France and Germany. The miracles which were wrought there caused this hut first to be changed into a little chapel, and finally into a church which was dedicated to Our Lady of Clos Evrard in the year 1449 by James de Siruq, Archbishop of Trier, who strove to restore order to the confused finances of the diocese at that time.[4]

6 December: Our Lady of Séez

T LATUIN (LATUINUS) built the first cathedral to Our Lady in the diocese of Séez around the middle of the fifth century. A later church replaced it; one dedicated under the title of Notre Dame du Vivier. The Normans destroyed this structure at the beginning of the ninth century. A third church was built, a hundred meters away also under the titles of the martyrs Saints Gervase and Protase, whose relics were enshrined in it. A special chapel in the cathedral recalled the memory of the first cathedral dedicated to Our Lady of Séez, for Mary remained the principal patroness of the diocese.

Many famous people made pilgrimages to Our Lady of Seez; among them were St Germain, Bishop of Paris; St Evroult, founder of the Abbey of Ouche; St Osmond, Count of Séez, who became Bishop of Salisbury; St Thierry, Abbot of St Evroult; St Louis arrived there in 1259; and about the same time Blessed Giles, one of the early companions of St Francis came to recommend to Mary's protection the first French convent of Franciscans, which he was going to found at Séez. The Augustinians served the sanctuary from 1127.

In the latter half of the 18th century, the Bishop of Séez, in response to the wishes of the entire diocese, repaired and embellished the chapel of Our Lady at considerable expense. Later the work of redoing the entire cathedral was undertaken. In June of 1784, the cathedral chapter asked the Bishop to consecrate the new altar and the entire cathedral under the patronage of Our Lady; this was completed in 1786. Mary rewarded the prelates for their zeal in promoting her honour by granting all of them the grace of martyrdom in the violent persecution that broke out in 1792, in the wake of the French Revolution. The beautiful façade of the cathedral was destroyed in 1795. A revolutionary bought the debris with the intent of building a house from it. Two attempts proved failures and he finally gave up the attempt.

7 December: Our Lady of Wigratzbad

IGRATZBAD IS A HAMLET in the Lindau district of Bavaria, Germany. Antonie Radler (20) from this village contracted the Spanish influenza in 1919 and was gravely ill. Her mother prayed desperately to the Blessed Virgin for help. Suddenly, Blessed Mary appeared at her bedside and laid her hands upon the young victim. Antonie was instantly healed. Fully recovered, Antonie was working one day in her father's butcher shop when the Gestapo arrived and ordered her to replace the painting of the Virgin on the wall with that of the Fuhrer, Adolf Hitler. She was also ordered to salute him in the Nazi fashion, saying, "Heil Hitler". Antonie refused and barely escaped several attempts upon her life. She always maintained that her Guardian Angel—in the form of a mysterious cyclist—protected her.

Her parents were so delighted with her escape from harm that they erected a small Lourdes grotto in their garden. It was blessed by Father Basch on 11 October 1936, the feast day of the Maternity of Mary at that time. A month later, while praying before the statue, Antonie saw Our Lady smile sweetly and then heard the words: "O Beloved Lady of Victory, conceived without sin, pray for us." Then, on 15 December 1936, while praying at the Lourdes grotto in their garden (during the octave of the Immaculate Conception), and while reciting the third sorrowful mystery of the Rosary, Antonie heard an "angelic chorus" singing these words: "O Mary! Immaculate, conceived without sin. Beloved Lady of Victory, pray for us."

A second appearance of the Blessed Virgin happened to a young girl named Cecilia Geyer on 22 February 1938. It was about 6:30 am when Cecilia heard a "murmur" and then saw Our Lady appear in a bright cloud:

> Suddenly, I found myself in the little grotto of Antonie and heard this message: "Build a chapel here for me. I shall trample underfoot the serpent's head. People will come here in large numbers, and I will pour upon them a flood of graces. St Joseph, St Anthony, and the souls in Purgatory will help you. Go now and worship my Son in the Blessed Sacrament."

Realizing that all the churches were closed at that hour, Cecilia asked Mary where she should go? Before her astonished eyes there appeared a chapel in the place designated by Our Lady. Inside, on the altar, was Jesus in a monstrance, surrounded by beautiful rays of light.

Work began on the chapel on 2 July 1938. All went well until the night of 21 November when Antonie was arrested by the Nazis and jailed in the local prison. She underwent numerous interrogations. On the night of 7–8 December, Antonie witnessed a large bright cloud forming and rising in her jail cell. Suddenly, the Virgin Mary appeared to her and announced her impending release. She would spend Christmas with her family; Antonie was indeed released on 18 December, the Feast of the Expectation of Our Lady. Today, the chapel built at the site of the apparitions is host to an estimated 500,000 pilgrims each year. Although no official statement was made by Bishop Stimpfle, he was frequently known to say: "I know that Wigratzbad is authentic!"

8 December: The Immaculate Conception of Our Lady

HE DOGMA OF THE IMMACULATE CONCEPTION teaches that Mary was conceived without original sin and thus exempted from the consequences of the fault of our first parents. In the 12ᵗʰ century this doctrine was formally affirmed by the Eastern Church, which had long celebrated a liturgical feast in honour of the "Conception of the Virgin." In the 10th century, when this feast began to be adopted in the West, questions arose regarding its doctrinal significance. Great doctors like St Bernard, St Bonaventure, and St Thomas Aquinas refused to admit that Mary had been conceived without sin. The first to teach the doctrine of the Immaculate Conception were Eadmer of Canterbury and Osbert of Clare; it was Blessed John Duns Scotus to whom its triumph is due. The Sorbonne rallied to its support and remained constant to the doctrine. In 1432, Pope Sixtus IV forbade the partisans of the contrary opinion to censure their adversaries; Gregory XV in 1622 and Alexander VII in 1661 forbade that this contrary opinion be taught. In 1854, one hundred and fifty years ago, Pope Blessed Pius IX proclaimed *ex catbedra* that the Immaculate Conception is an article of faith. We cite here from his Bull *Ineffabilis Deus*:

> The Fathers proclaimed with particular and definite statements that when one treats of sin, the holy Virgin Mary is not even to be mentioned; for to her more grace was given than was necessary to conquer sin completely. They also declared that the most glorious Virgin was Reparatrix of the first parents, the giver of life to posterity; that she was chosen before the ages, prepared for Himself by the Most High, foretold by God when He said to the serpent, "I will put enmity between you and the woman" (Gn 3:15), unmistakable evidence that she crushed the poisonous head of the serpent. Hence they affirmed that the Blessed Virgin was, through grace, entirely free from every stain of sin, and from all corruption of body, soul and mind; that she was always united with God and joined

to Him by an eternal covenant; that she was never in darkness but always in light; and that, therefore, she was an entirely fit habitation for Christ, not because of the state of her body, but because of her original grace.

They affirmed that the same Virgin is, and is deservedly, the first and especial work of God, escaping the fiery arrows of the evil one; that she is beautiful by nature and entirely free from all stain; that at her Immaculate Conception she came into the world all radiant like the dawn. For it was certainly not fitting that this vessel of election should be wounded by the common injuries, since she, differing so much from the others, had only nature in common with them, not sin. In fact, it was quite fitting that, as the Only-Begotten has a Father in heaven, whom the Seraphim extol as thrice holy, so He should have a Mother on earth who would never be without the splendour of holiness.

This doctrine so filled the minds and souls of our ancestors in the faith that a singular and truly marvellous style of speech came into vogue among them. They have frequently addressed the Mother of God as immaculate, as immaculate in every respect; innocent, and truly most innocent; spotless, and entirely spotless; holy and removed from every stain of sin; all pure, all stainless, the very model of purity and innocence; more beautiful than beauty, more lovely than loveliness; more holy than holiness, singularly holy and most pure in soul and body; the one who surpassed all integrity and virginity; the only one who has become the dwelling place of all the graces of the most Holy Spirit. God alone excepted, Mary is more excellent than all, and by nature fair and beautiful, and more holy than the Cherubim and Seraphim. To praise her all the tongues of heaven and earth do not suffice.

We declare, pronounce, and define: the doctrine which holds that the most Blessed Virgin Mary was, from the first moment of her conception, by a singular grace and privilege granted by Almighty God and in view of the merits of

Jesus Christ, the Savior of the human race, preserved immune from all stain of original sin, is a doctrine revealed by God and therefore to be believed firmly and constantly by all the faithful.[5]

9 December: Our Lady of Penrhys

HE SHRINE OF Our Lady of Penrhys lies deep within the valleys of Wales, yet it is only a mere 20 minutes or so by road from Cardiff. The beginning of devotion to Mary at Penrhys is shrouded in legend but it is certain that from Medieval times there was a shrine to Our Lady on that spot that flourished for many years.

In 1179, the Cistercian monks founded an abbey at Llantarnam, and in 1205, Llantarnam Abbey and Margam Abbey agreed on a boundary between the two monasteries, which meant that Penrhys was within the boundary of Llantarnam, some 25 miles away. The monks built a grange there, enabling them to care for their land and sheep in the outer regions of their property. The original complex of buildings also included a hostelry maintained by the monks for the pilgrims, and possibly a grange farmhouse. Tradition has it that an image of Mary was discovered in an oak tree and, as news spread, crowds of ordinary men and women flocked from far and wide. The statue was thought to have been immovable from the oak tree until a shrine chapel had been erected on top of Penrhys Mountain, just above the Holy Well. Over the well stands a small stone hut-like structure.

During the Reformation in 1538, the shrine was destroyed and the image seized under cover of darkness. Thomas Cromwell instructed his emissaries to act "with quietness and secret manner as might be" but were confronted by an "audience" who we can assume had to be overawed before the image could be taken away to Chelsea and burned in the same fire as the images of Our Lady of Walsingham and Our Lady of Ipswich. Although the shrine was destroyed, it is recorded by William Llewellyn, writing in

1862, that in the previous 20 years, there were accounts of people making pilgrimages to the top of Penrhys Mountain. Archbishop Michael McGrath in the 1950s furthered the modern popularity of the shrine. He was anxious to purchase the land on the top of Penrhys Mountain for the Catholic Church in Wales. A statue of Our Lady of Penrhys was erected in 1953, which stands on the foundations of the former chapel. In 1977, 2000 people came to Penrhys for the first official pilgrimage of the sick, with Mass celebrated by Bishop Mullins.

10 December: Our Lady of Loreto

OWARDS THE END of the thirteenth century, the terrible news reached Europe that the Holy Land was lost to the Christians, who during two centuries had been able to maintain the Latin kingdom there by virtue of their repeated Crusades. However, at the time the Church was deploring this painful loss, a new joy was given: the holy house of Nazareth—site of the birth of the Mother of God, of Her early education and of the Annunciation by the Angel Gabriel of the wondrous news of the Incarnation of the Son of God—had been found, transported miraculously, near Tersatz in Dalmatia on 10 May 1291. Between Tersatz and nearby Fiume, the residents of the region beheld one morning an edifice, in a location where never had any been seen before. After the residents of the region talked among themselves of the remarkable little house surmounted by a bell tower, and which stood without foundations on the bare ground, describing its altar, an ancient statue of Our Lady, and other religious objects which their wondering eyes had seen within it, another surprise came to astound them once more.

Their bishop suddenly appeared in their midst, cured from a lingering illness which had kept him bedridden for several months. He had prayed to be able to go see the prodigy for himself, and the Mother of God had appeared to him, saying, in substance:

> My son, you called me; I am here to give you powerful
> assistance and reveal to you the secret you desire to know.
> The holy dwelling is the very house where I was born... It
> is there that when the announcement was brought by the
> Archangel Gabriel, I conceived the divine Child by the
> operation of the Holy Spirit. It is there that the Word was
> made flesh! After my passing from this world, the Apostles
> consecrated this dwelling, illustrated by such elevated
> mysteries, and sought the honour of celebrating the
> August Sacrifice there. The altar is the very one which the
> Apostle Saint Peter placed there. The crucifix was intro-
> duced by the Apostles, and the cedar statue is my faithful
> image, made by the hand of the Evangelist Saint Luke...
> Your sudden return to health from so long an illness will
> bear witness to this prodigy.

Nicolas Frangipane, governor of the territory of Ancona, was
absent, but when the news was carried to him, he returned from
a war in order to verify its authenticity. He sent to Nazareth, at
the eastern limits of the Mediterranean Sea, the bishop and three
other persons, to examine the original site of the house. Indeed
the house was no longer there, but its foundations remained and
were found conformable in every detail of dimension and substance, to the stones at the base of the house now in Dalmatia.
The testimony of the delegates was drafted according to legal
formalities, and confirmed by a solemn oath.

Next, after three years spent in Dalmatia, the house disappeared. Paul Della Selva, a holy hermit of that period of the region
of Ancona, wrote:

> During the night of 10 December, a light from heaven
> became visible to several inhabitants of the shores of the
> Adriatic Sea, and a divine harmony woke them that they
> might contemplate a marvel exceeding all the forces of
> nature. They saw and contemplated a house, surrounded
> by heavenly splendour, transported through the air.

The angelic burden was brought to rest in a forest, where again the local residents were able to contemplate the signal relics which it contained. The antique Greek crucifix mentioned by Our Lady was made of wood, and attached to it was a canvas on which the words *Jesus of Nazareth, King of the Jews*, were painted. The cedar statue of the Virgin had been painted also; she wore a red robe and a blue cloak and held the Infant Jesus in Her arms. His right hand was raised in blessing; His left hand held a globe, symbol of His sovereign power.

The story was far from ended. The house moved again, after robbers began to intercept pilgrims coming through the forest to visit the marvel. Twice more it rose from its place, the first time coming to rest on a private terrain, which became then a source of dispute between two brothers; and finally on a hilltop where a dusty and uneven public road became its permanent site. For centuries the people of Dalmatia came across the sea on pilgrimage, often crying out to Our Lady and Her House to come back to them! Finally in 1559, after one such visit by 300 pilgrims, the Sovereign Pontiff had a hospice built at Loreto for families who preferred to remain near the house, rather than return to a land deprived of its sacred presence.

The reddish-black stones of the house are a sort entirely foreign to Italy; the mortar cementing them is again entirely different from the volcanic-ash-based substance used in that country. The residents of the region put up a heavy brick wall to support the house, which was exposed to the torrential rains and winds of the hilltop and was completely without foundation. But no sooner was that wall completed, than they came back one morning to find it had moved away from the house, as if to express its reverence, to a distance which permitted a small child to walk around it with a torch in hand. The Author of the miracle wanted it to be well understood that He who had brought it without human assistance, was capable also of maintaining it there where He had placed it, without human concourse.

The episodes concerning the Translation of the Holy House, all duly verified, were consigned in documents borne to Rome to the Popes at various epochs. Pope Sixtus IV declared that the house was the property of the Holy See, and assigned duties to a specified personnel named to be its custodians. By Pope Leo X the indulgence applicable to the visit of several churches of Rome was accorded also to a pilgrimage to Loreto. Eventually a magnificent basilica was built around the house, which within the basilica was itself enhanced by a white marble edicule. Pope Clement IX in 1667, placed the story of the House in the Roman Martyrology for the 10 December under the title: *At Loreto, in the territory of Ancona, translation of the Holy House of Mary, Mother of God, in which the Word was made flesh.* Pope Benedict XIV, a prodigious scholar before he became Pope, established the identity of the house with that of Nazareth, against its detractors, and later worked for the embellishment of the August sanctuary. The feast of Our Lady of Loreto is observed in many provinces of the Church, inscribed in the Proper of their dioceses by their bishops.

Pope Benedict XVI, pronounced this prayer at Loreto on the occasion of his visit on 1 September 2007.

Prayer

Mary, Mother of the "Yes", you listened to Jesus,
and know the tone of His voice and the beating of His heart.
Morning Star, speak to us of Him,
and tell us about your journey of following Him on the path of faith.

Mary, who dwelt with Jesus in Nazareth,
impress on our lives your sentiments,
your docility, your attentive silence,
and make the Word flourish in genuinely free choices.

Mary, speak to us of Jesus, so that the freshness of our faith
shines in our eyes and warms the heart of those we meet,
as you did when visiting Elizabeth,
who in her old age rejoiced with you for the gift of life.

Mary, Virgin of the *Magnificat*
help us to bring joy to the world and, as at Cana,
lead every young person involved in service of others
to do only what Jesus will tell them.

Mary, look upon the *Agora* of youth,
so that the soil of the Italian Church will be fertile.
Pray that Jesus, dead and Risen, is reborn in us,
and transforms us into a night full of light, full of him.

Mary, Our Lady of Loreto, Gate of Heaven,
help us to lift our eyes on high.
We want to see Jesus, to speak with Him,
to proclaim His love to all.

11 December: Our Lady of Warraq

ARRAQ EL-HADAR IS a small island in greater Cairo's Nile river (Giza governorate, part of Greater Cairo). It is a poor district. More than 200,000 people (Christians and Muslims) witnessed the apparitions between 10 and 22 December 2009 on the domes of Virgin Mary and Archangel Michael Coptic Orthodox Church in El-Warraq. Apparition lights in the night sky could also be seen several kilometres away from the church. People used their mobile phones to make videos of the apparitions and share them via Bluetooth and on YouTube. The full silhouette of the Blessed Holy Virgin Mary dressed in a light blue gown could be clearly seen over the domes of the church between the church crosses. The apparitions also received wide media coverage in Egyptian newspapers and Arabic TV channels. An article of *Agence France-Presse* (AFP), dated 24 December 2009, recounted nightly gatherings bringing crowds of up to 10,000 people to watch the tower in anticipation of the "mysterious light over the church tower", which upon its appearance each night "jolted the gathering into a frenzy of cries".[6] The apparitions started in the Coptic month of Kiahk (December 2009), the Marian month and Nativity Fast in the Coptic Calendar. During this month the Coptic Church celebrates a special Midnight Praise dedicated to the Holy Virgin and the Incarnation.

The Giza Coptic Orthodox Bishopric expressed provisional approval in these terms:

> The Bishopric of Giza announces that the Holy Virgin has appeared in a transfiguration at the Church named after her in Warraq al-Hadar, Giza, in the early hours of Friday 11 December 2009 at 1:00am. The Holy Virgin appeared in her full height in luminous robes, above the middle dome of the church, in pure white dress and a royal blue belt. She had a crown on her head, above which appeared the cross on top of the dome. The crosses on top of the church's domes and towers glowed brightly with light. The Holy Virgin moved between the domes and on to the top of the church gate between its two twin towers. The local residents all saw her. The apparition lasted from 1:00am till 4:00am on Friday, and was registered by cameras and cell phones. Some 3,000 people from the neighbourhood, surrounding areas, and passers-by gathered in the street in front of the church to see the apparition.
>
> Since Friday, the huge crowds gathered in the vicinity of the church have been seeing luminous white pigeons soaring above the church during various times of the night, as well as a star which emerges suddenly in the heaven, travels some 200 metres across, then disappears. The huge crowds gathered around the church do not cease singing hymns and praises for the Holy Virgin. This is a great blessing for the Church and for all the people of Egypt. May her blessing and intercession benefit us all.[7]

12 December: Our Lady of Guadalupe

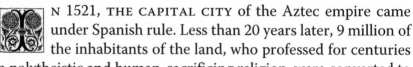 N 1521, THE CAPITAL CITY of the Aztec empire came under Spanish rule. Less than 20 years later, 9 million of the inhabitants of the land, who professed for centuries a polytheistic and human-sacrificing religion, were converted to

Christianity. What happened in those times that produced such an incredible and historically unprecedented conversion?

In 1531, a "Lady from Heaven" appeared to a humble Native American at Tepeyac, a hill northwest of what is now Mexico City. His native name was Cuauhtlatoatzin, which could be translated as "One who talks like an eagle" or "eagle that talks". Between 1524 and 1525 he was converted and baptized, as well as his wife, receiving the Christian name of Juan Diego and her wife the name of Maria Lucia. In April of 1990 Juan Diego was beatified by Pope John Paul II. On July 2002 he was canonized by the Church, during a ceremony celebrated by John Paul II, again in the Basilica of Guadalupe.

In the apparition, Our Lady identified herself as the ever virgin Holy Mary, Mother of the True God for whom we live, of the Creator of all things, Lord of heaven and the earth. She made a request for a church to be built on the site, and submitted her wish to the local Bishop. When the Bishop hesitated, and requested her for a sign, the Mother of God sent Her native messenger to the top of the hill in mid-December to gather an assortment of roses for the Bishop. After complying to the request for a sign, She left for us an image of herself imprinted miraculously on the native's *tilma*, a poor quality cactus-cloth, which should have deteriorated in 20 years but shows no sign of decay nearly 500 years later and still defies all scientific explanations of its origin. It apparently even reflects in her eyes what was in front of her in 1531.

Her message of love and compassion, and her universal promise of help and protection to all mankind, as well as the story of the apparitions, are described in the "Nican Mopohua", a 16th century document written in the native Nahuatl language. There is reason to believe that at Tepeyac, Mary came in her glorified body, and her actual physical hands rearranged the roses in Juan Diego's tilma, which makes this apparition very special. An incredible list of miracles, cures and interventions are attributed to Her. Yearly, an estimated 10 million visit her Basilica, making her Mexico City home the most popular Marian shrine in the

world, and the most visited Catholic church in the world next to
the Vatican. Altogether 25 popes have officially honored Our
Lady of Guadalupe. His Holiness John Paul II visited her Sanctuary four times: on his first apostolic trip outside Rome as Pope in
1979, and again in 1990, 1999 and 2002. In 1999, Pope St John
Paul II, in his homily from the Solemn Mass at the Basilica of Our
Lady of Guadalupe, during his third visit to the sanctuary,
declared the date of 12 December as a Liturgical Holy Day for the
whole continent. During the same visit Pope John Paul II
entrusted the cause of life to her loving protection, and placed
under her motherly care the innocent lives of children, especially
those who stand in danger of not being born.

> In consenting to the Divine Word, Mary, the daughter of
> Adam, became the Mother of Jesus and, while embracing
> the salvific will of God with a full heart and unburdened
> by any sin, she devoted herself completely as the handmaid
> of the Lord to the person and works of her Son, serving
> the mystery of redemption under Him and through Him
> by the grace of God. She poured Life itself into the world,
> renewing all things, and appearing for us as a Mother in
> the order of grace as well. Finally, raised to the glory of
> heaven, she accompanies the pilgrim Church always and
> everywhere with motherly love, so that the Church,
> contemplating the image of her own perfection and
> mission in the holy God-bearer (*Theotokos*), may instruct
> all nations with the praise of the Gospel's salvation, and,
> by the working of the Holy Spirit, fill the whole world with
> children of a new people. For this reason, the Christian
> people greatly revere this Mother and Queen, and invoke
> her aid in the difficulties and trials of life, so that she may
> obtain grace for them by the mercy of God.

> The close relationship between this Tender Mother and
> the Christian faithful in America was manifested in a
> wonderful way on the hill known as Tepeyac, where the
> Mother of God under the title of the Blessed Virgin Mary
> of Guadalupe was already fervently honored for four

centuries as the Empress of all the Americas, signifying by her own appearance the necessity of a perfect union of the Word of God with the humanity of native peoples in evangelizing this Continent. Hence, from the beginning of the modern age, she offered an extraordinary example of care particularly for the poor and the indigenous. This cult of the Virgin has been spread by continual observance even to the present, so that, in approaching the Third Millennium of the Savior's Incarnation, the members of the Special Synod of Bishops of America, at the close of their meeting in Rome in 1997, fervently invoked blessed Mary, Virgin of Guadalupe, as Patroness of all America and as the Star of both the first and now of the new evangelization of this same Continent.

Likewise, the Supreme Pontiff, John Paul II, acceding to the requests of the synod Fathers, and joyfully receiving their recommendation, recalled on the first anniversary of the Plenary Council for Latin American, assembled in Rome, through his Apostolic Exhortation *Eccelsia in America* (The Church in America), promulgated on 22 January, 1999 in Mexico City, and then graciously approved in his homily on the following day, delivered in the Basilica of Our Lady of Guadalupe, that in all America the celebration of Blessed Mary, the Virgin of Guadalupe, is to be observed henceforth with the rank of feast, thereby earnestly desiring that this same Virgin, through whose intercession the faith of the first disciples was strengthened, would lead the Church of this Continent with her maternal love and that she would obtain an outpouring of the Holy Spirit upon the Church so that a new evangelization might flourish by the witness of Christian life.[8]

13 December: Our Lady of Baños de Agua Santa

 FEW YEARS BEFORE the founding of Quito in Ecuador, Dominican missionaries travelled throughout the Ecuadorian province of Tungurahua bringing the Faith to the people. A bamboo chapel was erected at Baños de Agua Santa, where the Blessed Virgin of Montserrat was venerated. One night the sacristan of the church saw a small statue of the Virgin accompanied by two beautiful angels hovering in the air then coming down to the foot of a waterfall that flowed from the mountain. This event was repeated several times, so the people gathered in the chapel to beseech the Blessed Virgin to clearly manifest her intentions. The following night the Virgin appeared asking for the erection of a chapel at the spring, promising to heal the sick who bathe with faith in those waters.

A new church was built as Our Lady asked, but the statue of the Virgin of Montserrat had disappeared before it could be transferred to the new church. A mule came to the town square with a box containing a beautiful statue of Our Lady of the Rosary. When this was unclaimed by anyone, it was seen as a gift from Our Lady and the image of "La Reina del Rosario de Agua Santa" was lovingly placed in the church. The present basilica was completed in 1929. A brief of Pope Pius XII in 1957 declared the Virgin of Banos de Agua Santa the principal patroness of the missions of eastern Ecuador. On 13 December 1959, the Archbishop of Quito, H. E. Cardinal Carlos M. de la Torre, solemnly crowned the statue of the Virgin in the presence of the President of the Republic, Dr Camilo Ponce, who offered to the Mother of God the Presidential baton invoking her as the Patron of Ecuador.

Many miracles of healing were granted by Our Lady of the Rosary of Agua Santa, and numerous times the church has provided a sanctuary when the volcano Tungurahua erupted. On one occasion, a horrendous eruption began while many were gathered to honour Our Lady. Lava was flowing toward the church so the people lifted up the statue of Our Lady of Agua Santa and processed to the town square. There, Our Lady lifted her hand silencing the roaring volcano and and diverting the flow of lava. In 1916, a nearby farmhouse was burned completely to the ground, except for a picture of Our Lady of the Rosary of Agua Santa.

14 December: Our Lady of Alba Regis

UR LADY OF ALBA REGIS is a shrine in Hungary, built by St Stephen, King of Hungary, who gave his kingdom to the Blessed Virgin; and so erected this shrine to commemorate the event and remind himself and his whole kingdom that she was royalty there, not he. As the saintly King Stephen came to his coronation, he begged that the crown be placed on the head of the statue of Mary, and not on his own head. The stately church built in honour of the Mother of God is at Szekesfehervar (Latin: Alba Regia, German: Stuhlweißenburg) the medieval capital of Hungary, and was the place where the Kings of Hungary were both crowned and, in 1038, was also the place where Saint Stephen was buried.[9] King Stephen was so devoted to Our Lady that throughout his kingdom, all bent the knee at the very mention of her holy name.[10]

Szekesfehervar, was established at the convergence of several important trade routes, as traders and craftsmen began to settle there. It was Saint Stephen who replaced the tribal districts with regular counties. Later, the town was also one of the most important stations on the Crusader route to the Holy Land. The vast majority of the Hungarian kings were crowned at Szekesfehervar, and fifteen kings of Hungary are buried there. Work on the basilica continued for centuries, including towers reaching 70 meters in height, so that it could be said that the cathedral of Saint Stephen was a marvel of its time. The Hungarian throne was kept inside, and there were many royal weddings and funerals that took place within its walls.

Little now remains of the basilica but ruins, as it was captured by the Turks in 1543, who ransacked the church, and in 1601 finally destroyed the basilica with gunpowder and fire. At one time the basilica had held the crown jewels and the Holy Crown of Hungary. The Turks were finally driven from the town in 1688, and Szekesfehervar is currently said to be the eighth largest city in Hungary.

15 December: Perpetual Virginity of Our Lady

 HE VIRGINITY OF OUR LADY, so intimately united with her Motherhood, and with Christ's Incarnation, has ben expressed as virginity of the mind or of the spirit (*virginitas mentis*), virginity of the senses (*virginitas sensus*) and virginity of the body (*virginitas corporis*). While making these distinctions, we should remember that in theology it is helpful to distinguish in order to unite, to analyse in order to synthesise. The distinction is made in order to shed light on the mystery of Mary's virginity as a whole, remembering that each aspect is important in the realist perspective which this work proposes. In particular, recent attempts to exaggerate the spiritual aspect of Mary's virginity at the expense of the physical aspect could endanger the true doctrine concerning Mary's great privilege. Virginity of the mind is the determination of Our Lady to refrain from any thought word or action contrary to perfect chastity. Consideration of a vow of chastity made by Our Lady would come under this heading. Virginity of the senses describes Our Lady's complete freedom from disordered movements of the flesh, and is included in her freedom from concupiscence. Virginity of the body refers to the virginal state of Our Lady's body, which excludes all damage to or violation of the generative organs, and all experience of venereal pleasure.[11]

The bodily virginity of Our Lady is further elaborated as virginity before the Birth of Christ, during his Birth and after His Birth (*virginitas ante partum, in partu,* and *post partum*). The doctrine of *virginitas ante partum* teaches the absence of marital relations between Our Lady and St Joseph up to the time of Christ's birth, and therefore the virginal conception. The *virginitas in partu* includes the non-rupture of the hymen at the moment of birth, which takes place without any opening of the membranes or damage to Our Lady's body, and without pain. This description of the *virginitas in partu* involves a miraculous Birth, during which Christ passed from His Mother's womb, as

He later passed from the closed sepulchre. At the same time, it was a true Birth. The teaching concerning *virginitas post partum* excludes marital relations, and thus the generation of other children, after the Birth of Christ. Taken together these truths constitute the perpetual virginity of the Blessed Virgin Mary. Often Western Patristic theology tended to focus on Mary's virginity in terms of its exemplary value, as is found in an affirmation of St Ambrose: "Mary's life should be for you a pictorial image of virginity. Her life is like a mirror reflecting the face of chastity and the form of virtue. Therein you may find a model for your own life, showing what to improve, what to imitate, what to hold fast to."[12] In Eastern Christendom, the Christological significance of this truth was emphasised, as St Gregory of Nyssa illustrates: "It was fitting that He who became man to give all men incorruption should begin human life of an incorrupt Mother; for men are accustomed to call her incorrupt who is unwed."[13]

Various statements of the Magisterium indicated that the perpetual virginity of Mary was part and parcel of the faith. The Council of the Lateran in the year 649 defined:

> If anyone does not, according to the Holy Fathers, confess truly and properly that the holy and ever virgin and immaculate Mary is really and truly the Mother of God, inasmuch as she, in the fullness of time, and without human seed, conceived by the Holy Spirit, God the Word Himself, who before all time was born of God the Father, and without loss of integrity brought Him forth, and after His birth preserved her virginity inviolate, let him be condemned.[14]

In his discourse in Capua, Pope St John Paul II noted a highly significant correlation with regard to patristic teaching on the *virginitas in partu* and the Resurrection:

> It is a well-known fact that some Church Fathers set up a significant parallel between the begetting of Christ *ex intacta Virgine* (from the untouched Virgin) and his

Resurrection *ex intacto sepulcro* (from the intact sepulchre). In the parallelism relative to the begetting of Christ, some Fathers put the emphasis on the virginal conception, others on the virgin birth, others on the subsequent perpetual virginity of the Mother, but they all testify to the conviction that between the two saving events—the generation-birth of Christ and his Resurrection from the dead—there exists an intrinsic connection which corresponds to a precise plan of God: a connection which the Church, led by the Spirit, has discovered, not created.[15]

The consequences of a renewed affirmation of and a devotion to Our Lady's perpetual virginity would be an antidote to the errors and abuses concerning sexuality in the world today, a renewal of Holy Church and the restoration of the Catholic religion. Therefore, in order that this doctrine of the Faith be more fully appreciated, it is opportune that there should be instituted in the Universal Church a Feast of the Perpetual Virginity of Our Lady, to be celebrated each year on 15 December, the Octave of the Solemnity of the Immaculate Conception.

16 December: Our Lady of the New Advent

 DVENT IS THE PERIOD of preparation for Christmas, from the Latin *adventus*, coming—a time of longing and waiting for the Saviour's birth as well as for his second coming at the end of time. For Christ's disciples, the nine-day period between his ascension and Pentecost was a similar interval, as they waited in prayer until the coming of the Holy Spirit. That nine-day prayer period is the basis of the Catholic novena, in which people petition God or a saint for a particular purpose for nine days, often starting on the tenth day before the relevant feast—so the Christmas Novena begins on December 16.

As the Archdiocese of Denver began preparing for the Jubilee Year 2000, Archbishop Francis Stafford decided to hold a nine-year novena to Mary leading up to the new millennium. In 1991 he commissioned Jesuit iconographer Fr William Hart McNichols to create an image representing Our Lady of the New Advent. Fr McNichols chose to use the icon type known as the Sign, showing the infant superimposed on his mother rather than in her arms, which are lifted in prayer. This became the official icon of the Archdiocese (although its patron saint is Francis). In 1992, in response to Archbishop Stafford's request for a liturgical feast day with a Mass in honour of Our Lady of the New Advent, the Vatican designated 16 December. On 12 August 1993, at the opening of World Youth Day in Denver, Pope St John Paul II prayed, "O Mary, Our Lady of the new Advent, who kept all these things, pondering them in your heart, teach these young people to be good listeners to your Son, the Word of Life." The archbishop presented him with a second version of the image painted by Fr McNichols. In 1999, Stafford's successor, Archbishop Charles Chaput, dedicated Our Lady of the New Advent Theological Institute, an educational complex for the training of priests, missionaries, deacons, lay ministers, and catechists, located in Denver.

17 December: Our Lady of the Armed Forces

E OFTEN READ in the news about the sacrifices and sufferings of the armed forces personnel in the service of their countries, far away from home. Days and nights—nights and days of anxiety, tension and violence; and so many a mother prays to Mary for her child, as we can imagine in these or similar words:

> My boy, whom I zealously guarded from the little hurts and pains of life, lies down tonight in the dirty straw of some deserted barn, or even under the icy stars without even that much shelter, crouches on the rough floor of a moving truck, or plods wearily through the endless snow. Mary, my soul longs for peace for him—he is so young!

Comfortingly, Mary whispers into the mother's heart:

The night was cold at Bethlehem, the stable rough and dirty, the town filled with strangers and hostility. There, in the cold He lay that night long ago. I had good things planned for my Son—a tiny bed prepared at Nazareth, a warm safe home, little garments made during the long days of waiting. But it was at Bethlehem that he was born; the night was cold; the straw rough. And, He was just a Babe.

Prayerfully the soldier's mother continues:

He's so young to be away from me—from home and family—just a boy, really, with the dreams and hopes of a boy. A tow-headed, bright-eyed football captain last year— a serious, sombre soldier now. My arms are empty, my heart is so heavy, and he is so young!

Our Lady replies:

My Son was young once, too, playing on the streets of Nazareth at twelve, the dusty hills—helping Joseph in the carpenter shop... brightening the small home with His boyish ways. My heart was so heavy during the long search through the unfamiliar streets of Jerusalem; and how my empty arms ached when I found Him among the doctors in the Temple—a boy no longer but a Man about His Father's business.

The soldier's mother then adds:

My son fights among an alien land far from all he knows and loves. He is whipped into near submission—my son who was so tall and straight and proud. He lies in the dust trampled by an enemy's boot—my son who never hated anyone, who loved life and living. His wounds are deep and painful and he is so young!

And Mary responds:

My Son walked among a hostile people in Jerusalem and along the Jordan. He was scourged at the pillar—He Who was also tall and straight and noble. He fell in the dust on the road to Calvary—He Who ministered to all and rejected none. His Hands and His Feet were pierced through with nails and His side was opened by the spear of the soldier. And—He is God!"

The mother insists: "My heart is heavy for my son who walks alone and suffers this night—for he is so young!" And Our Lady offers her final words of comfort:

My Son Who knew a soldier's life, and fears, and pains, shall walk with you son tonight and heal his wounds of body—and heart—for He is God. Your dear, good son carries with him all the time the sign of victory—the Rosary—and he prays my favourite prayer daily and even oftener when he can; the scent of his prayers delights me; I shall never forsake your son as long as he asks me to help him. Do you now know, I am Our Lady of the Armed Forces all over the world?[16]

18 December: Expectation of Our Lady

 HIS LOVELY FEAST, which was kept not only throughout the whole of Spain, but also in many other parts of the Catholic world, owes its origin to the bishops of the 10th Council of Toledo, in 656. These prelates thought that there was an incongruity in the ancient practice of celebrating the Feast of the Annunciation on 25 March, inasmuch as this joyful solemnity frequently occurs at the time when the Church is intent upon the Passion of Our Lord, so that it is sometimes obliged to be transferred into Easter time, with which it is out of harmony for another reason. They therefore decreed that, henceforth, in the Church of Spain there should be kept, eight days before Christmas, a solemn Feast with an octave, in honour of the Annunciation, and as a preparation for the great solemnity of Our Lord's Nativity. In the course of time, however, the Church of Spain saw the necessity of returning to the practice of the Church of Rome and of the whole world, which keeps 25 March as the day of Our Lady's Annunciation and the Incarnation of the Son of God.

However, such had long been the devotion of the people for the Feast of 18 December, that it was considered requisite to maintain some vestige of it. They discontinued, therefore, to celebrate the Annunciation on this day; but the faithful were requested to consider, with devotion, what must have been the sentiments of the Holy Mother of God during the days immediately preceding Her giving Him birth. A new Feast was instituted, under the name of the Expectation of the Delivery of the Blessed Virgin Mary.

In Spain, this celebration sometimes went under the name of Our Lady of O, or the Feast of O, on account of the great antiphons which are sung during these days, and, in a special manner, of that which begins *O Virgo virginum*, which is still used in the Vespers of the Expectation. A High Mass was sung at a very early hour each morning during the octave, at which all who were with child, whether rich or poor, considered it a duty to assist, that they might thus honour Our Lady's Maternity, and beg her blessing upon themselves. It is no wonder that the Holy See approved of this pious practice being introduced into almost every other country. Each mother offers an echo of this in her own time of expectancy. As the body of her baby develops over the months of waiting, so does her longing develop, her eagerness to meet this gift of a child, uniquely intended for her particular family. The feast of Our Lady's Expectation gives us the occasion for reflecting on her generous service to God, and on her humility and joy. Our own preparation for Christmas will be purified and enhanced as we unite ourselves with her time of waiting, with her intense longing for the Redeemer of mankind.

Poem

By the seven stars of her halo
By her seven swords of woe
Oh Holy Spirit anneal my pen
To utter sweet words for the ears of men
In praise of Our Lady of O.

O Woman, the Word in Thy keeping
Thy secret from God most High,
Shall soon be whispered over the earth
And men shall listen and leap for mirth
Like stars in the Christmas sky.

O Stalk on the brink of blossom,
Shooting green through the frosty mire;
The peoples pray for thy Spring to come
And the mighty ones of the earth go dumb
For the Flower of the World's Desire.

O Tower of Grace untrespassed
Since Eden by God's decree;
At thine ivory spire and jasper gate
The pining kindred of Adam wait
For the turning of Christ the Key.

O milk-and-honey-run Mountain
Whence the crystal Cornerstone
Shall issue unsullied by tool or hand
The Stone that shall fasten each race and land
Together like flesh and bone.

O City ashine on the hill-tops
The nations uplift their eyes
From rainy island and sunken sea
And the ends of the earth they throng to Thee
To dwell in thy Christ-lit skies.

By the seven stars of Thy halo
By Thy seven swords of woe
Forgive us, O Lady, these phrases worn
In praise of Thy season with God unborn
O ineffable Lady of O.[17]

19 December: Our Lady of Hope

HE MAJESTIC CHURCH of Candolim is situated at the foot of the hills of Candolim and facing the Nerul river, in Goa, India. The primitive church of Candolim was built in 1560 by Fr Pedro de Belem and was repaired and refurbished in 1661. Despite this, the Franciscans were not satisfied with the result. The Provincial, Fr Antonio de Assumpcaô then ordered the old church to be demolished and a new one to be constructed. Fr Jeronymo de Natividade who had some knowledge of architecture, revised the original plans and considerably cut down the cost. The entire cost for all this construction was borne by the village community.

The church is unique as it was built using the Mannerist Neo-Roman style. Its large twin towers have special pagoda-like roofs. The finials are of spear type; something which makes the church of Our Lady of Hope (*Nossa Senhora de Esperança*) rare is the bell towers which rise high above the central gable. In 1948 the left side tower of the church collapsed and had to be rebuilt.

The feast of the patroness was celebrated in ancient times on 16 December, later the date of the feast was shifted to 27 December but from 1997 onwards the feast has been kept on 19 December. The main altar of the church is dedicated to Our Lady of Hope. On the left of the main altar there is the richly carved altar of wood. It has a huge cross with Jesus crucified on it, and below are two big statues of Jesus and Our Lady. On 13 November 2013 Archbishop Filipe Neri Ferrao blessed and installed the statue and relic of St Teresa of Calcutta.

20 December: Our Lady of the Fir Tree

ARIA IN DER TANNE ("Mary in the Fir") is a small baroque church in Triberg in the Black Forest, Germany, which has been a destination for pilgrims since the 17th Century. In 1644 a 7-year-old girl named Barbara Franz was walking with her mother. They came to a stately fir tree near a spring. Someone had, at an earlier time, attached a picture of Mary in her Immaculate Conception to the tree, but it had fallen to the ground. Barbara picked up the picture and took it home. There she placed it on the home altar, where the whole family venerated it. Three days later Barbara became very ill, with an affliction in her eyes. No remedy seemed to help, so her afflicted parents begged for God's help through Our Lady. In a dream, Barbara was told she would be cured when she returned the picture to the fir tree by the spring. She did so and, together with her parents, prayed fervently. When Barbara washed her eyes in the spring, she was instantly cured.

The next year, a master tailor aged 68, Friedrich Schwab became very ill with leprosy. Having heard of the miraculous cure, he made a pilgrimage to the tree-shrine and promised to make a wood carving of Our Lady if he was cured. He, too, washed in the waters of the spring and was instantly cured. He kept his promise and replaced the ageing picture with his lovely carving. Unfortunately the statue was almost forgotten as the years passed. On the evening of 20 December 1692, three Tyrolean soldiers heard beautiful angelic singing near the area. They made inquiries and discovered that others had also heard the singing. Then they were told that there had formerly been a shrine of Our Lady in a fir tree in that place. They diligently searched the area and at last located the little statue, almost grown over in the fir tree. The soldiers uncovered, cleaned and decorated the statue, naming it, "Mary, Patroness of Soldiers". Then a fourth soldier, Gabriel Maurer, fell ill in 1694 and promised Our Lady of the Fir that he would join the Franciscans if she were to heal him. Maurer was indeed healed For 35 years he helped in the building of the pilgrimage church. This time the shrine was not forgotten. As more cures took place, more and more pilgrims came. The first small chapel was soon replaced by a magnificent baroque church, where the little wood carving was enshrined. In 1805 St Clement

Mary Hofbauer arrived with four Redemptorist companions in Triberg and encouraged the pilgrimage that still continues today.[18]

21 December: Our Lady of Peace

ROUND 1570, THE STORY GOES, a woman with distinctive features and a youthful glow began coming from the mountains in the afternoon to buy candles at a market in the Carmona district of Trujillo in western Venezuela. When some curious men asked her why she walked alone, she answered, "Not alone, but with God, the sun, and the stars." "Where are you from?" "From nearby." "How do you cross the full ravine, and who helps you?" "My sons, don't forget that I go with God, my Protector." One day some townsfolk followed her and saw her disappear into a cleft in the rock. Then people noticed the rock sparkling and shining, and decided that the mysterious maiden was not someone from the community, but the Virgin Mary.

The Virgin's Rock became a place of legend and devotion. Some said that Our Lady held back the source of three rivers—one of water, one of blood, and one of milk—from sweeping away the town. To this day, large numbers of pilgrims gather at the *cueva*, cave, to place votive offerings, recite rosaries, and sing hymns in thanks for favours granted, especially around the feast of Our Lady of Peace on 24 January 24. On 21 December 1983, the President of Venezuela, Luis Herrera Campins, dedicated a monumental statue of the Virgin of Peace on the rock above the cave. Designed by architect Manuel de la Fuente, constructed of concrete on a steel frame, the monument weighs 1,323 tons and stands 154 feet high. Our Lady extends one hand and holds a dove in the other. Visitors can go inside and ascend to five lookouts that survey nearly the entire state of Trujillo. In Trujillo Cathedral there is a much older devotional statue of Our Lady of Peace, patron of Trujillo city and state.

22 December: Our Lady of Milk

 N 1478, PLAGUE STRUCK San Giovanni Valdarno, a village near Arezzo in Tuscany. A destitute elderly lady, Mona Tancia, 75, was left to care for a 3-month-old grandson, Lorenzo, whose parents Francesco and Santa had both died. On 22 December, she searched the city for a wet nurse but found no one willing to come to her house. Stopping at a fresco of the Virgin Mary on the old city gate of San Lorenzo, she begged Our Lady in tears for help: "Please provide for this innocent creature!" She immediately experienced a great sense of comfort and consolation and returned home. The old grandmother went home and went to bed, tired and with the baby at her side. Instinctively the baby look to feed from his grandmother, and miraculously at her age she was able to breastfeed him for several months.

News of the miracle spread quickly and a shrine, now a basilica, grew up around the image, sometimes called the *Madonna del Latte* (Our Lady of Milk), although it depicts the child Jesus admiring a bird, not nursing. It is a typical Tuscan work of the 1300s, painted by an unknown artist. The bird appears to be a swallow, symbolic of the Resurrection in that period, because of a belief that swallows spent the winter buried in pond mud, like frogs. Little Lorenzo grew up healthy and well, and most devoted to Our Lady. He became a Franciscan friar taking Giles as his name in religion, and died in the odour of sanctity, and was buried in Madrid. The image of Our Lady was crowned on her feast day, 8 September 1704.

23 December: Our Lady of Good News

EAN DE MONTFORT founded the Dominican convent of Our Lady of Good News (Notre-Dame-de-Bonne-Nou-velle) in Rennes in 1368 to fulfil a vow made during the battle of Auray in 1364, where his victory over the Blois settled him as Duke of Brittany. In the following century, a panel painting in the convent cloister gained a reputation for miracles, so a separate chapel was built for it. Another vow was fulfilled after the plague of 1632, which hit Rennes less hard than the surrounding areas. In thanksgiving, the city gave Our Lady of Good News a solid silver model of the town and, from 1634, observed a votive celebration every year on 8 September, the Feast of Mary's Birth.

A further miracle occurred during the great fire of 23 December 1720, when, as their wooden houses burned, the people of Rennes saw Our Lady of Good News look down in compassion from the sky. During the French Revolution, the city sold its silver model, which was melted down. The chapel was destroyed and the convent used to store fodder. A gardener saved the holy image, which he gave to the neighbouring Church of St Aubin in 1803. In 1849, a cholera epidemic inspired a new vow. A new silver-plated model city was commissioned from Napoleon III's goldsmith and the September votive feast reinstated. When St Aubin's became too small for all the pilgrims, a new church was built, dedicated in 1904 to St Aubin and Notre-Dame de Bonne Nouvelle. The painting was canonically crowned in 1908. In recent years the votive feast has been held on the first Sunday in October rather than 8 September.

24 December: Our Lady the New Eve

ROM THE EARLIEST CENTURIES of the Church, Christians have believed that as the first Adam had a female helper named Eve, so Jesus the New Adam (1 Corinthians 15:45) had a New Eve associated with Him: His Mother Mary. The New Eve is a theme which runs through the entire Scriptures, from Genesis to Revelation. God first foretold the coming of the second Adam and Eve in the same prophesy: "I shall put enmity between you and the woman, and between your offspring and hers; it will bruise your head, and you shall strike its heel" (Gn 3:15). Now the "seed" is the Messiah, Jesus Christ, the New Adam. Since God calls Jesus the "seed (or offspring) of the woman", this woman must be the mother of the Messiah—the Blessed Virgin Mary. Christ is truly the Seed of the Woman because He was born of a virgin (without the seed of a man), and Mary is that Virgin Mother.

Early Christians taught that the Annunciation marks the reversal of the temptation of the first Eve. For example, in 150, St Justin Martyr wrote:

> Christ became man by the Virgin that the disobedience which issued from the serpent might be destroyed in the same way it originated. Eve was still an undefiled virgin when she conceived the word of the serpent and brought forth disobedience and death. But the Virgin received faith and joy at the announcement of the angel Gabriel... and she replied, "Be it done to me according to your word." So through the mediation of the Virgin He came into the world, through whom God would crush the serpent.[19]

Later that same century, St Irenaeus of Lyons wrote:

> The seduction of a fallen angel drew Eve, a virgin espoused to a man, while the glad tidings of the holy angel drew Mary, a Virgin already espoused, to begin the plan which would dissolve the bonds of that first snare... For as the former was lead astray by the word of an angel, so that she fled from God when she had disobeyed his word, so did the latter, by an angelic communication, receive the glad tidings that she should bear God, and obeyed his word. If the former disobeyed God, the latter obeyed, so that the Virgin Mary might become the advocate of the virgin Eve. Thus, as the human race fell into bondage to death by means of a virgin, so it is rescued by a virgin; virginal disobedience is balanced in the opposite scale by virginal obedience.[20]

In the Garden, Eve believed the lies of a fallen angel, disobeyed God and so became the cause of Adam's Fall (Gn 3:1–7). At the Annunciation, Mary believed the words spoken by a holy angel, obeyed God and so became the Mother of the One who would save us from Adam's Fall. Mary's obedience reversed Eve's disobedience; thus Mary is the New Eve for the New Creation in

Christ. St John's depiction of Calvary (John 19:25–27) clearly parallels the Garden of Eden: there is a tree (the Cross—see Galatians 3:13), a Man (Jesus) and a woman (Mary). The New Adam again calls the New Eve "Woman" and declares her to be the Mother of his beloved disciple (and, by extension, of all Christians). As Eve was the "mother of the living" (Gn 3:21), so Mary is the Mother of all who have eternal life in Christ.

Hymn

A very great cause it was for lamenting and mourning,
That through the counsel of the serpent, sorrow and guilt
flowed into woman.
For that woman, whom God had set to be the mother of us all,
she destroyed her own womb with the wounds of ignorance
and gave birth to all pain for her children.
But, O dawn, from your womb
a new Sun rises,
which has cleansed all Eve's sins,
and through you a blessing flows
greater than the harm Eve did to men.
And thus you have saved us, you who bore the New Light for humankind.
Gather then the members of your Son into celestial harmony.[21]

25 December: Our Lady at Christmas

 AIL, HOLY MOTHER! The Child to whom you gave birth is the King of Heaven and earth forever. Christmas celebrates Our Lady's unique role in the Mystery of the Incarnation and also sheds light on our own efforts to live the Mystery of Christ along the path of Christian discipleship; the path of devout humility. Devotion to our Lady has always had a privileged place in popular piety in the Christmas season.

Christmas focuses us more intently on Mary's undeniable and essential role in that incredible, unrepeatable action: the Logos (Word)—the Second Person of the Most Blessed Trinity—becoming flesh and pitching His tent among us. Mary accepted that Word, embraced that Word, loved that Word, and learned from that Word. This Real Presence of Christ enjoyed by His sinless Mother and chaste foster-father Saint Joseph is effected and continued today—and will be until Jesus comes again—by the Holy Sacrifice of the Mass, which would not exist without the Incarnation. So, along with Jesus Christ our Lord and Saviour, Mary, His Mother and ours, is largely responsible for our long-awaited reconciliation to the Godhead. She gave her consent to the Almighty by way of her Fiat uttered in the presence of the Archangel Gabriel. History was changed dramatically at that significant event known as the Annunciation, which promptly prepared the groundwork for the glorious Death and Resurrection of the Messiah thirty-three years later when the members of sinful mankind would be granted, through no merit of their own, the golden opportunity to enter one day into Paradise in order to be united to God for all eternity, thanks to the selfless suffering and death of Christ and the wholehearted, free cooperation of His Ever-Virgin Mother.

We can imagine Mary's astonishing humility on that Christmas night. She participated uniquely in that universe-changing event and she trusted in her benevolent Creator, knowing that He would supply the needed graces for her to do what was required. The many days and years after Jesus' Birth showed Our Lady to be a real and solicitous mother. Our Blessed Lady nourished Jesus with her milk, bathed Him and instructed Him in the Jewish laws and rituals. She formed Him spiritually and emotionally, contributing to the development of His human nature that was joined to His divine nature. As unique as the Virgin is in salvation history, the joy of intimacy with her Divine Son is not hers alone. All persons are able to know the Lord Jesus and surrender to Him and His all-wise plan, thereby ensuring a profound level of closeness with Him. How can this happen? We must learn from Mary.

The Sacrament of the Most Holy Eucharist shapes us in the way of Christ. To eat the Flesh and drink the Blood of the

God-Man, which were known, adored and loved with so much fervour by the Maiden of Nazareth, is to increase in union with Christ. We experience more forcefully the connection to Christ that the obedient Mary enjoyed—a valuable and life-giving bond that is evident for all to see, like the one shining in that rustic stable over two millennia ago.[22]

26 December: Our Lady of Andacollo

UR LADY OF ANDACOLLO is a celebrated statue of the Virgin Mary located in the town of Andacollo, in the Coquimbo Region in the north of Chile. This small wooden statue of the Virgin Mary is said to have been found by a local indigenous person near the mines of Andacollo at the beginning of the conquest period, in the year of the founding of the city of La Serena by Don Juan Bohon. In the year 1549 that city, which was the second most important in Chile, was devastated and destroyed by a fire caused by a rebellion of the natives of Copiapó. That same year, the city was rebuilt by the conqueror Pedro de Valdivia. Following the destruction of the city, the Spaniards fled south in search of shelter, and they climbed to the top of the mountain and there came upon a small native settlement of Molle origin, with Inca influence. They were so amazed to see the ravines filled with unrefined gold that they decided to hide the small image there and continue south. Thus a native man of that area, named Collo, found the image of Our Lady. Initially Collo heard a heavenly voice saying to him: "Take courage, Collo! Make me and the true God known to your people." Then he realized that the mine where he had gone had suddenly lit up and that the light was increasing in intensity. Then he heard again, in a clear and distinct manner, a distant but understandable voice telling him: "At a few steps from you there is an enormous wealth; search on the highest mountains of the plateau extending over your head. Go, Collo!"

The following day the native Collo departed together with some of his relatives, and found a small roughly-carved wooden statue, with a graceful face and olive complexion; it had been partly hidden because of the landslide of a large unstable rock, and appeared surrounded by light. The native took the image and brought it to his house to venerate it. From that moment, the inhabitants of the place started to perform dances in honour of Our Lady, very similar to the ones of the natives of Peru and Bolivia. Attracted by the gold of Andacollo, the Spaniards returned and built there the first Marian chapel of Chile at the request of Don Juan Gaytán de Mendoza. The building was simple at first, with stockade walls and a straw roof.

Four churches have been built for Our Lady over the years. The first was constructed in the 16th century and the second in the 17th century, but this only lasted until 1776. The third church, constructed in the 18th century after undergoing numerous repairs for earthquake damage, is where the image of the Virgin now resides for most of the year. Finally, between 1873 and 1893, a new church was constructed. After four centuries of veneration in Andacollo and devotion coming from beyond Chilean borders, Cardinal Mariano Rampolla del Tindaro decreed on 15 June 1899, at the command of Pope Leo XIII, that the statue be given a canonical coronation. The decree was implemented by the Claretians, who took on stewardship of the sanctuary in 1900, and the crown and jewels were paid for in large part by local fundraising. The statue of Our Lady of Andacollo was crowned on 26 December 1901. The church was declared a minor basilica by Pope St John Paul II in 1998.

27 December: Our Lady of Kevelaer

ROUND 1640 THE SMALL VILLAGE of Kevelaer, Germany, had suffered greatly from a tragic fire and the ravages of the Thirty Years War. It was considered a vast moorland and a place where few ventured. Hendrik Busman, a pious travelling salesman, was on his journey from Weeze to Geldern when he stopped at a cross on the heath of Kevelaer to pray for a few minutes. As he later recounted:

> At Christmas in 1641, I was making my way when I came to the region around Kevelaer. There was a cross by the roadside, and I heard a voice coming from that direction say to me, "Here you shall build me a chapel." I looked around me—but saw no one. I resolved to press on and put all thoughts of the phenomenon out of my head. About a week later, I passed the place again and there heard the same voice speaking the same words as before. Then I heard it again a third time. I was sad because I was poor, and I had no means by which I might build a shrine. Nevertheless, I saved regularly from my petty cash in the distant hope that one day I should have a fund to fit the purpose.
>
> Then, four weeks before Whitsunday, my wife, Mechel Schouse, received a vision by night. She saw a great light, and in the midst of it a shrine. And in that shrine was a picture of Our Lady of Luxembourg—like one she had been shown some time earlier by two soldiers passing through our village. The soldiers had offered to sell Mechel the picture, but, upon asking the price, she realized that she could not afford it. (A night watchman, making his usual rounds, saw a strange light in the home of the Busmans, confirming their supernatural visitation that night.) When Mechel told me of her vision, I connected it with my own experience near Kevelaer. I urged her to find the soldiers and the picture. She discovered that the picture was now in the possession of a lieutenant presently in prison in Kemen. Mechel obtained the picture from him.

Convinced that the vision experienced by his wife was a confirmation of his heavenly assignment, Hendrick used the little money that he had saved and began to construct a shrine according to Mechel's description. This project was supported by the parish priest of Kevelaer, Fr Johannes Schink. The portrait was a copper-printed picture measuring only twelve centimetres tall and eight centimetres wide. "Our Lady of Luxembourg" was known as the "Comforter of the Sad and Depressed" whom everyone had venerated during the Plague Epidemic of 1623.[23] The text on the picture said, "A faithful portrayal of the Mother of Jesus, the Comforter of the Sad and Depressed renowned for miracles and venerated by many people." At first, the Carmelite nuns of Geldern offered to keep it safe during the construction. After that, during a temporary period of caring for the image in his own home, Hendrick appealed to the Capuchin priests to house it safely in their chapel because so many pilgrims were already travelling to venerate the image. The crowds became so great that monks soon asked for him to please take it back as soon as he could for placement in the shrine.

On 1 June 1642, Rev. Schink officially brought the image in great ceremony to the new shrine where large crowds awaited. Miracles were soon reported. On 8 September, feast of the birthday of Our Lady, Reinier and Margaretha van Volbroek travelled with their invalid son, Peter, who had been paralysed for five years—unable to walk or stand. Although his case had been declared hopeless by physicians, just two days after their visit to Our Lady of Luxembourg, Peter was totally cured and able to walk again without any difficulty. A woman suffering open wounds on her legs that no treatments had helped for years was healed miraculously after just two visits. Her healing was so dramatic and profound that it was reported by the Mayor of Huissen, Holland for official documentation on 13 August 1643. Many other miraculous cures were documented at the shrine.

Five years after Hendrick's death, the old chapel was replaced by a new one in 1654. A basilica was built between 1858 and 1864. Today it is a huge and beautiful complex with multiple buildings, bubbling fountains, and an outdoor Stations of the Cross. The little picture of Our Lady, Comforter of the Afflicted, has been decorated through the years with golden angels, golden roses, golden medals, and jewelled ornaments—donated by grateful pilgrims.

In 1892, the 250ᵗʰ anniversary of the shrine's inauguration was celebrated with a papal coronation—a crown studded with diamonds and jewels, placed above the picture. In 1923 the church was raised by Pope Pius XI to the rank of Minor Basilica. Kevelaer was in the front line of the Second World War. At one point the population was ordered to evacuate. In their need the people fled to Our Lady. Some women began a Novena at the Gnadenkapelle. Their numbers increased each evening up to about one thousand. Still, the forced evacuation seemed inevitable. The imprisonment of the caretaker of the basilica and the bombing of the town only made the trust and prayers stronger and more zealous. Before the German soldiers retreated, the diabolical order was given to blow up the basilica. The inevitable result would have been the destruction of the basilica, the *Gnakenkapelle*, and the *Kerzenkapelle*—but the explosion failed and all three buildings were saved. The prayers had been heard; the trust rewarded. On 2 May 1987, Pope St John Paul II visited Kevelaer and venerated the miraculous image.

28 December: Our Lady of Elche

According to tradition, on 28 December 1370, a sentinel named Francesc Cantó, watching the coast off Elche, discovered a chest floating in the sea. In it was a statue of Our Lady of the Assumption and the libretto of a mystery play enacting her death and translation to heaven. After Francesc Cantó found the chest on the shore, in the morning he went on horseback to relate the event to the town council. Our Lady went with him, waiting at Garden of the Red Gates until the Council issued a proclamation and sent a committee to fetch her. That play, the *Misterio de Elche*, is presented annually at the Feast of the Assumption in August. The *Venida de la Virgen*, the Coming of the Virgin, is enacted yearly on 28 December. On odd-numbered years, an abbreviated reenactment begins in the afternoon at the Garden. An elaborate procession takes the image to the Basilica of Santa

María. On 29 December, solemn Mass in the Basilica follows a citywide procession. The old statue burned with the church during the Civil War in 1936. In 1940, Valencian sculptor José Capuz made the replacement statue, which was canonically crowned 29 December 1970.

29 December: Our Lady of Flowers

N THE EVENING of 29 December 1336, on the outskirts of the small town of Bra, in the province of Cuneo of the diocese of Turin, Egidia Mathis, a young expectant mother was passing by a votive column consecrated to the Blessed Virgin Mary, with a Byzantine image of Our Lady. Two rough soldiers, from a band of mercenaries, were lying in wait. Seeing that she was going to be attacked by men who intended to violate her despite her condition, clung on desperately to the image of the Our Lady painted on the column, calling for her help. Suddenly, a beam of light flashed from the image, blinding the two mercenaries who fled in a panic. Then, Mary herself appeared to Egidia comforted her for several minutes and assured her that the danger was now passed; afterwards Our Lady vanished. As a result of extreme feelings of fear and emotion, Egidia gave birth then and there at the foot of the column. With her new-born child wrapped in her shawl, the young mother managed to reach the nearest house.

The news of this incident spread like wildfire all around town: although it was late, crowds flocked to the place where the attempted attack and the apparition of the Virgin had taken place. There, an extraordinary sight greeted them: the column was surrounded with thick blackthorn bushes which were unexpectedly covered in white flowers despite the harsh late December weather. Popular devotion developed rapidly and finally, in 1626, the old sanctuary of Our Lady of Flowers was constructed. Then in 1933 a new sanctuary was built.

Since the time of the miracle, the bushes flower yearly over the same period of days, except at particular times of crisis. For example in 1914 and 1939, the years in which the two World Wars began, the bushes did not flower. Sometimes also there have been extraordinary flowerings of the bushes, such as on 20 February 1878, marking the election of Pope Leo XIII, and in November 1989, marking the fall of Communism.

30 December: Our Lady of the Cloud

HEN MGR SANCHO de Andrade y Figueroa, Bishop of Quito in Ecuador, was gravely ill, his flock decided to carry the image of Our Lady from the Guápulo district to the Cathedral in procession to ask the Lord for his restoration to health. On 30 December 1696, at 4:45 pm, when the procession reached St Francis's Church, its bell sounded the signal for praying the *Gloria Patri*. Suddenly Don José de Ulloa y la Cadena, chaplain of the Nuns of the Immaculate Conception, was pointing east, exclaiming, "The Virgin! The Virgin!"

According to official documents in the archdiocesan archives, in the sky between the sanctuaries of Guálupo and Quito, the Blessed Virgin appeared standing on a cloud somewhat darker and denser than the others, which served as her pedestal. She wore a crown on her head and carried a bunch of lilies in her right hand like a sceptre. In her left hand she carried her Divine Son. She was dressed in a white silk tunic that draped to her feet in soft pleats, half hidden by a majestic mantle. On her head was a long white veil. This apparition, which was viewed by the close to 500 persons in the procession as well as many others in the environs of Quito, lasted for the length of a Glory be and the praying of one Our Father and one Hail Mary. Testimonies of the miracle include those of the President of the Royal Chamber Don Mateo de Mata Ponce de León and other respected town officials. Then the vision faded and the cloud covered the image. As confirmation of the miracle, the bishop was immediately healed. Soon afterward, he authorized the devotion to Our Lady under the invocation *The Virgin of the Cloud*, and erected an altar to her in the Cathedral of Quito. The bishop, who remained very devoted to the Blessed Virgin and the Rosary, lived some years more, dying in May of 1702.. Our Lady of the Cloud is honoured with an annual *fiesta* and procession on January 1.

Prayer

O Miraculous Virgin of the Cloud! Mother of Jesus and our Mother, we greet you with all the affection of our hearts. We desire that on this day we should do nothing to displease you. We want to honour you as the Angels in Heaven honour you, praise you with all the just, and serve you with the faith and devotion of thy true children. Mother of mercy, supply for our poverty and misery. We are not worthy that the Mother of God come to our house. Our Lord and our God, we repent the sins and wrongdoings of our past with our whole heart.

Pardon us, O Lord, and makes us worthy of the mercies and blessings of Mary, Your Holy Mother. Blessed Virgin of the Cloud, supply the remedies for our needs. Keep us away from evil, impurity, coldness in your service, and the appeal of the world. Give us success in our enterprises. Bless us in our work. Cure us in our sicknesses. Free us from our enemies and give us peace of heart. Help us in our poverty and console us in our suffering. To you we consecrate our whole house with all that we have—our parents, our children, our spouses, and all our goods belong to you today and always.

Receive us, O most sweet Virgin, under your protection and care, so that having conquered the world, the devil and the flesh, we can love and serve you in this life, and afterward sing your praises in your heavenly homeland. Amen.

31 December: Our Lady of the Closing Year

 E FACE A closing year with mixed emotions and strange nostalgia; happy at the thought that the unpleasant, the sad, the painful is at an end. We look forward hopefully to a better and brighter year; yet we experience a deep dread of what might cloud our horizon.

How blindly foolish we mortals can be! We so easily lose sight of the loving Providence of Our Father, Who has counted the very hairs of our heads, and lets not a sparrow fall to the ground without His Holy Will. How childishly independent of both Father and Mother we appear, on our own, instead of clasping tightly our Mother Mary's hand, and placing confidently the other into the mighty, but loving Hand of our dear Father, God.

Mary will close for us the doors of the "might-have-been"; and open the "yet-to-be". Drawing across the first the all-forgiving, the all-forgetting curtain of God's infinite Love, she will open the bright doors of the coming year, and lead for us the way to Her Son's Sacred Heart. Mary, Mediatrix of all Graces, will also mediate with us in balancing our accounts; she will burn up the dross, and make clear the path for a new beginning of the future year. Strength, help, grace, all are ours for the asking. Could we wish for greater or hope for more?[24]

Notes

[1]   See G. Hierzenberger and O. Nedomansky, *Erscheinungen und Botschaften der Gottesmutter Maria: Vollständige Dokumentation durch zwei Jahrtausende* (Augsburg: Weltbild, 2005). pp. 231–237.

[2]   See Pope Benedict XVI, *Reflection at Rome's Spanish Steps*, 8 December 2011.

[3]   See M. Lamberty, *The Woman in Orbit: Mary's feasts every day everywhere* (Chicago: Lamberty Co, 1966), 7 December.

[4]   See *ibid.*, 24 June.

[5]   Pope Bl Pius IX, Bull *Ineffabilis Deus*.

[6]   M. Salem, "Virgin Mary sighting a glimpse of hope for Egypt Christians" on *Agence France-Press* (24 December 2009).

[7]   H. E. Bishop Anba Theodosius, *Statement concerning the Apparitions at El-Warraq*.

[8]   Congregation for Divine Worship and the Discipline of the Sacraments, *Decree declaring the celebration of the Blessed Virgin Mary of Guadalupe on 12 December as a feast in all the countries of America* (25 March 1999).

9   The name Székesfehérvár means "white castle of the royal seat".

10 N. J. Santoro, *Mary In Our Life: Atlas of the Names and Titles of Mary, The Mother of Jesus, and Their Place in Marian Devotion* (Kansas City, MI: iUniverse, Inc, 2011), p. 374.

11 P. Haffner, *The Mystery of Mary*, Hillenbrand Books studies series (Leominster, Herefordshire, Mundelein, IL: Gracewing; Hillenbrand Books, 2004), p. 135.

12 St Ambrose, *The Virgins* 2, 2, 6 in PL *16*, 208.

13 St Gregory of Nyssa, *In diem natalem Christi* in *PG* 46, 1135–1136.

14 Lateran Council (649), *Condemnatio errorum de Trinitate et de Christo*, canon 3 in DS 503.

15 Pope St John Paul II, *Discourse in Capua* (24 May 1992).

16 Lamberty (ed.), *The Woman in Orbit*, 15 December.

17 J. J. Galvin, "Lady of O" as found in Sr M. Therese, *I Sing of a Maiden—The Mary Book of Verse* (London: Macmillan, 1947).

18 J. Läufer, *Wallfahrtskirche "Maria in der Tanne"*, Triberg im Schwarzwald, Kunstführer. Nr. 403 (Regensburg: Schnell & Steiner, 2016⁸).

19 St Justin Martyr, *Apologia*, ch. 100.

20 St Irenaeus of Lyons, *Against the heresies*, Book 3, 22, 4.

21 St Hildegard of Bingen, Sequence *O virga ac diadema purpurae Regis*, translation by Kate Brown.

22 See Mgr C. M. Mangan, "Our Blessed Mother and the Christmas Mystery" on *Mother of All Peoples* (25 December 2004).

23 See above 20 June: Our Lady of Luxembourg.

24 Lamberty (ed.), *The Woman in Orbit*, 31 December.

FURTHER READING

Christian, W. A., *Apparitions in late Medieval and Renaissance Spain.* Princeton, NJ: Princeton University Press, 1981.

Connell, J. T., *Meetings with Mary: Visions of the Blessed Mother.* New York: Ballantine Books, 2015.

Connolly, D., *One Message One Truth: The Prophecies of the Blessed Virgin at Fatima, Lourdes, Akita and Other Approved Apparitions*: CreateSpace Independent Publishing Platform, 2012.

Cruz, J. C., *Miraculous Images of Our Lady: 100 famous Catholic statues and portraits.* Charlotte, NC: TAN Books, 2012.

Driscoll, M. T., *Origin and development of Marian feasts in the Roman and Carmelite rites.* Washington, DC: Catholic University of America, 1977.

Duetao, M. P., *Marian feasts: Their history and themes.* Manila, 1996.

Edmisten, K., *Through the Year with Mary: 365 meditations.* Cincinnati, OH: Servant Books, 2010.

Foley, D. A., *Marian Apparitions, the Bible, and the Modern World.* Leominster, Herefordshire: Gracewing, 2002.

Fox, R. J., *Light from the East Miracles of Our Lady of Soufanieh.* Hanceville, AL: Fatima Family Apostolate, 2002.

Haffner, P., *The Mystery of Mary.* Leominster, Herefordshire, Mundelein, IL: Gracewing; Hillenbrand Books, 2004.

Harris, M., *Sacred folly: A new history of the Feast of Fools.* Ithaca, NY: Cornell University Press, 2011.

Heintz, P., *A Guide to Apparitions of Our Blessed Virgin Mary.* Sacramento, CA: Gabriel Press, 1995.

Hierzenberger, G., & Nedomansky, O., *Tutte le apparizioni della Madonna in 2000 anni di storia* 6th ed.). Casale Monferrato: Piemme, 1998.

Hierzenberger, G., & Nedomansky, O., *Erscheinungen und Botschaften der Gottesmutter Maria: Vollständige Dokumentation durch zwei Jahrtausende.* Augsburg: Weltbild, 2005.

Ilardi, M. M., *More Mary-minded: Favorite Marian feasts*. Buffalo: Society of St. Paul, 1952.

Ilibagiza, I., & Erwin, S., *Our Lady of Kibeho: Mary speaks to the world from the heart of Africa* 9th ed.). Carlsbad, CA: Hay House, 2012.

Kalvelage, F. M., Manelli, S. M., & Fehlner, P., *Marian shrines of Italy. Saints and Marian shrine series*. New Bedford, MA: Faith Factory, 2000.

Koenig-Bricker, W., *365 Mary: A daily guide to Mary's wisdom and comfort* 1st ed.). San Francisco, CA: HarperSanFrancisco, 1997.

Lamberty, M., *The Woman in Orbit: Mary's feasts every day everywhere*. Chicago: Lamberty Co, 1966.

Läufer, J., *Wallfahrtskirche "Maria in der Tanne", Triberg im Schwarzwald* (8th ed.). *Kunstführer: Nr. 403*. Regensburg: Schnell & Steiner, 2016.

Laurentin, R., Sbalchiero, P., & Etchegaray, R., *Dictionnaire des "apparitions" de la Vierge Marie: Inventaire des origines à nos jours : méthodologie, bilan interdisciplinaire, prospective*. Paris: Fayard, 2012.

Manelli, S. M., *Devotion to Our Lady: The Marian Life as Taught by the Saints*. New Bedford, MA: Academy of the Immaculate, 2001.

Mora, M. E. C. G., *Life of the Venerable Elizabeth Canori Mora*. Translated from the Italian, with a preface by Lady Herbert. London: R. Washbourne, 1878.

Obbard, E. R., *A Year with Mary: Prayers and readings for Marian feasts and festivals*. Mystic, CT: Twenty-Third Publications, 1999.

Odell, C., *Those who saw her: Apparitions of Mary*. Huntington, IN: Our Sunday Visitor, 2010.

O'Neill, M., *365 Days with Mary*. USA: Salt Media, 2016.

Orsini, M., *La Vierge. Histoire de la Mère de Dieu, complétée par les traditions d'Orient, les écrits des Saints Pères et les moeurs des Hébreux*: Publiée par la Société des Beaux-Arts, 1842.

Orsini, M., *The history of the devotion to the Blessed Virgin Mary, Mother of God*. New York, Boston, Montreal: D. & J. Sadlier, 1864.

Santoro, N. J., *Mary In Our Life: Atlas of the Names and Titles of Mary, The Mother of Jesus, and Their Place in Marian Devotion*. Kansas City, MI: iUniverse, Inc, 2011.

Sharkey, D., *"I will convert sinners": Our Lady's Apparitions at Beauraing, 1932–1933*. Techny, IL: Divine Word Publications, 1957.

Taylor, W. B., *Theater of a Thousand Wonders: A History of Miraculous Images and Shrines in New Spain*. New York: Cambridge University Press, 2016.

Thavis, J., *The Vatican prophecies: Investigating supernatural signs, apparitions, and miracles in the modern age*. New York: Viking, 2015.

Lightning Source UK Ltd.
Milton Keynes UK
UKOW04f0708191217
314747UK00001B/133/P